AppleScript Bourne shell

<FORM> *gateway* encoding

Mnemonic

regex chown java

D1219862

Web Programming
SECRETS ®
with HTML, CGI, and Perl

crawlers *OpenLook*

POSIX remsh

AUTH_TYPE *archie* **bandwidth**

PATH_INFO

daemon

Shockwave *CSU/DS*

charset BIND

HTTP EVIPS <EMBED

Web Programming SECRETS®
with HTML, CGI, and Perl

ED TITTEL, MARK GAITHER,
SEBASTIAN HASSINGER,
AND MIKE ERWIN

Web Programming SECRETS, with HTML, CGI, and Perl

Published by
IDG Books Worldwide, Inc.
An International Data Group Company
919 E. Hillsdale Blvd.
Suite 400
Foster City, CA 94404

Library of Congress Catalog Card No.: 95-81954

ISBN: 1-56884-848-X

Printed in the United States of America

10 9 8 7 6 5 4 3 2 1

1B/QS/SQ/ZW/BR

First Printing, March 1996

Distributed in the United States by IDG Books Worldwide, Inc.

Distributed by Macmillan Canada for Canada; by Computer and Technical Books for the Caribbean Basin; by Contemporanea de Ediciones for Venezuela; by Distribuidora Cuspide for Argentina; by CITEC for Brazil; by Ediciones ZETA S.C.R. Ltda. for Peru; by Editorial Limusa SA for Mexico; by Transworld Publishers Limited in the United Kingdom and Europe; by Al-Maiman Publishers & Distributors for Saudi Arabia; by Simron Pty. Ltd. for South Africa; by IDG Communications (HK) Ltd. for Hong Kong; by Toppan Company Ltd. for Japan; by Addison Wesley Publishing Company for Korea; by Longman Singapore Publishers Ltd. for Singapore, Malaysia, Thailand, and Indonesia; by Unalis Corporation for Taiwan; by WS Computer Publishing Company, Inc. for the Philippines; by WoodsLane Pty. Ltd. for Australia; by WoodsLane Enterprises Ltd. for New Zealand.

For general information on IDG Books Worldwide's books in the U.S., please call our Consumer Customer Service department at 800-762-2974. For reseller information, including discounts and premium sales, please call our Reseller Customer Service department at 800-434-3422.

For information on where to purchase IDG Books Worldwide's books outside the U.S., contact IDG Books Worldwide at 415-655-3021 or fax 415-655-3295.

For information on translations, contact Marc Jeffrey Mikulich, Director, Foreign & Subsidiary Rights, at IDG Books Worldwide, 415-655-3018 or fax 415-655-3295.

For sales inquiries and special prices for bulk quantities, write to the address above or call IDG Books Worldwide at 415-655-3200.

For information on using IDG Books Worldwide's books in the classroom, or ordering examination copies, contact the Education Office at 800-434-2086 or fax 817-251-8174.

For authorization to photocopy items for corporate, personal, or educational use, please contact Copyright Clearance Center, 222 Rosewood Drive, Danvers, MA 01923, or fax 508-750-4470.

is a trademark under exclusive license to IDG Books Worldwide, Inc., from International Data Group, Inc.

IDG Books Worldwide, Inc., is a subsidiary of International Data Group, the world's largest publisher of computer-related information and the leading global provider of information services on information technology. IDG was founded more than 25 years ago and now employs more than 7,700 people worldwide. IDG publishes more than 250 computer publications in 67 countries (see listing below). More than 70 million people read one or more IDG publications each month.

Launched in 1990, IDG Books Worldwide is today the #1 publisher of best-selling computer books in the United States. We are proud to have received 8 awards from the Computer Press Association in recognition of editorial excellence and three from Computer Currents' First Annual Readers' Choice Awards, and our best-selling *...For Dummies®* series has more than 19 million copies in print with translations in 28 languages. IDG Books Worldwide, through a joint venture with IDG's Hi-Tech Beijing, became the first U.S. publisher to publish a computer book in the People's Republic of China. In record time, IDG Books Worldwide has become the first choice for millions of readers around the world who want to learn how to better manage their businesses.

Our mission is simple: Every one of our books is designed to bring extra value and skill-building instructions to the reader. Our books are written by experts who understand and care about our readers. The knowledge base of our editorial staff comes from years of experience in publishing, education, and journalism — experience which we use to produce books for the '90s. In short, we care about books, so we attract the best people. We devote special attention to details such as audience, interior design, use of icons, and illustrations. And because we use an efficient process of authoring, editing, and desktop publishing our books electronically, we can spend more time ensuring superior content and spend less time on the technicalities of making books.

You can count on our commitment to deliver high-quality books at competitive prices on topics you want to read about. At IDG Books Worldwide, we continue in the IDG tradition of delivering quality for more than 25 years. You'll find no better book on a subject than one from IDG Books Worldwide.

John J. Kilcullen

John Kilcullen
President and CEO
IDG Books Worldwide, Inc.

IDG Books Worldwide, Inc., is a subsidiary of International Data Group, the world's largest publisher of computer-related information and the leading global provider of information services on information technology. International Data Group publishes over 250 computer publications in 67 countries. Seventy million people read one or more International Data Group publications each month. International Data Group's publications include: **ARGENTINA:** Computerworld Argentina, GamePro, Infoworld, PC World Argentina; **AUSTRALIA:** Australian Macworld, Client/Server Journal, Computer Living, Computerworld, Digital News, Network World, PC World, Publishing Essentials, Reseller; **AUSTRIA:** Computerwelt, PC TEST; **BELARUS:** PC World Belarus; **BELGIUM:** Data News; **BRAZIL:** Annuário de Informática, Computerworld Brazil, Connections, Super Game Power, Macworld, PC World Brazil, Publish Brazil, SUPERGAME; **BULGARIA:** Computerworld Bulgaria, Networkworld/Bulgaria, PC & MacWorld Bulgaria; **CANADA:** CIO Canada, ComputerWorld Canada, InfoCanada, Network World Canada, Reseller World; **CHILE:** Computerworld Chile, GamePro, PC World Chile; **COLUMBIA:** Computerworld Colombia, GamePro, PC World Colombia; **COSTA RICA:** PC World Costa Rica/Nicaragua; **THE CZECH AND SLOVAK REPUBLICS:** Computerworld Czechoslovakia, Elektronika Czechoslovakia, PC World Czechoslovakia; **DENMARK:** Communications World, Computerworld Danmark, Macworld Danmark, PC World Danmark, PC World Danmark Supplements, TECH World; **DOMINICAN REPUBLIC:** PC World Republica Dominicana; **ECUADOR:** PC World Ecuador, GamePro; **EGYPT:** Computerworld Middle East, PC World Middle East; **EL SALVADOR:** PC World Centro America; **FINLAND:** MikroPC, Tietoverkko, Tietoviikko; **FRANCE:** Distributique, Golden, Info PC, Le Guide du Monde Informatique, Le Monde Informatique, Reseaux & Telecoms; **GERMANY:** Computer Business, Computerwoche, Computerwoche Extra, Computerwoche Focus, Electronic Entertainment, GamePro, I/M Information Management, Macwelt, PC Welt; **GREECE:** GamePro, Macworld & Publish; **GUATEMALA:** PC World Centro America; **HONDURAS:** PC World Centro America; **HONG KONG:** Computerworld Hong Kong, PCWorld Hong Kong, Publish in Asia; **HUNGARY:** ABCD CD-ROM, Computerworld Szamitastechnika, PC & Mac World Hungary, PC-X Magazine; **INDIA:** Computerworld India, PC World India, Publish in Asia; **INDONESIA:** InfoKomputer PC World, Komputek Computerworld, Publish in Asia; **IRELAND:** ComputerScope, PC Live!; **ISRAEL:** PC World 32 BIT, People & Computers; **ITALY:** Computerworld Italia, Computerworld Italia Special Editions, Lotus Italia, Macworld Italia, Networking Italia, PC Shopping, PC World Italia, PC World/Walt Disney; **JAPAN:** Macworld Japan, Nikkei Personal Computing, SunWorld Japan, Windows World Japan; **KENYA:** East African Computer News; **KOREA:** Hi-Tech Information/Computerworld, Macworld Korea, PC World Korea; **MACEDONIA:** PC World Macedonia; **MALAYSIA:** Computerworld Malaysia, PC World Malaysia, Publish in Asia; **MEXICO:** Computerworld Mexico, GamePro, Macworld, PC World Mexico; **MYANMAR:** PC World Myanmar; **NETHERLANDS:** Computable, Computer! Totaal, LAN Magazine, Macworld, Net Magazine; **NEW ZEALAND:** Computer Buyer, Computerworld New Zealand, MTB, Network World, PC World New Zealand; **NICARAGUA:** PC World Costa Rica/Nicaragua; **NIGERIA:** PC World Africa; **NORWAY:** Computerworld Norge, Computerworld Privat, CW Rapport Klient/Tjener, CW Rapport Nettverk & Telecom, CW Rapport Offentlig Sektor, IDG's KURSGUIDE, Macworld Norge, Multimedia World, PC World Ekspress, PC World Nettverk, PC World Norge, PC World's Produktguide, Windows Spesial; **PAKISTAN:** Computerworld Pakistan, PC World Pakistan; **PANAMA:** GamePro, PC World Panama; **PARAGUAY:** PC World Paraguay; **P. R. OF CHINA:** China Computerworld, China Infoworld, Computer & Communication, Electronic Product World, Electronics Today, Game Camp, PC World China, Popular Computer Week, Software World, Telecom Product World; **PERU:** Computerworld Peru, GamePro, PC World Profesional Peru, PC World Peru; **POLAND:** Computerworld Poland, Computerworld Special Report, Macworld, Networld, PC World Komputer; **PHILIPPINES:** Computerworld Philippines, PC Digest, Publish in Asia; **PORTUGAL:** Cerebro/PC World, Correio Informático/Computerworld, Mac•In/PC•In Portugal; **PUERTO RICO:** PC World Puerto Rico; **ROMANIA:** Computerworld Romania, PC World Romania, Telecom Romania; **RUSSIA:** Computerworld Rossiya, Network World Russia, PC World Russia; **SINGAPORE:** Computerworld Singapore, PC World Singapore, Publish in Asia; **SLOVENIA:** MONITOR; **SOUTH AFRICA:** Computing S.A., Network World S.A., Software World; **SPAIN:** Computerworld España, COMUNICACIONES WORLD, Dealer World, Macworld España, PC World España; **SWEDEN:** CAP&Design, Computer Sweden, Corporate Computing, MacWorld, Maxi Data, MikroDatorn, Nätverk & Kommunikation, PC/Aktiv, PC World, Windows World; **SWITZERLAND:** Computerworld Schweiz, Macworld Schweiz, PCtip; **TAIWAN:** Computerworld Taiwan, Macworld Taiwan, PC World Taiwan, Publish Taiwan, Windows World; **THAILAND:** Thai Computerworld, Publish in Asia; **TURKEY:** Computerworld Monitör, MACWORLD Turkiye, PC WORLD Turkiye; **UKRAINE:** Computerworld Kiev, Computers & Software Magazine, PC World Ukraine; **UNITED KINGDOM:** Acorn User, Amiga Action, Amiga Computing, Amiga, Appletalk, CD Powerplay, CD-ROM Now, Computing, Connexion, GamePro, Lotus Magazine, Macaction, Macworld, Open Computing, Parents and Computers, PC Home, PC Works, The WEB; **UNITED STATES:** Cable in the Classroom, CD Review, CIO Magazine, Computerworld, Computerworld Client/Server Journal, Digital Video Magazine, DOS World, Electronic, InfoWorld, I-Way, Macworld, Maximize, MULTIMEDIA WORLD, Network World, PC World, PUBLISH, SWATPro Magazine, Video Event, WebMaster; **URUGUAY:** PC World Uruguay; **VENEZUELA:** Computerworld Venezuela, GamePro, PC World Venezuela; and **VIETNAM:** PC World Vietnam
10/17/95

CREDITS

Vice President and Publisher
Christopher J. Williams

Publishing Director
John Osborn

Senior Acquisitions Manager
Amorette Pedersen

Managing Editor
Kim Field

Editorial Director
Anne Marie Walker

Creative Services
Julia Stasio

Project Editor
Ralph E. Moore

Manuscript Editor
Eileen Kramer

Technical Editor
Karen Goeller

Composition and Layout
Beth A. Roberts

Proofreader
Nancy Kruse-Hannigan

Indexer
Elizabeth Cunningham

Cover Design
Liew Design, Inc.

Acknowledgments

We have too many people to thank for this book to fit everyone in, so we'd like to start out by thanking everybody who helped us. Actually, we couldn't have done it without you, even if we don't mention you here!

Ed Tittel

To my family: Suzy, Austin, Chelsea, and Dusty—thanks for putting up with me over the Christmas that almost wasn't! Extra-special thanks go to Charlie Scott, who wrote the text for Chapters 3, 8, 10, 11, 16, 17, and 19 (the only reason he's not on the cover of this book was that we stupidly started this project without him). Charlie's the main reason we finished this project anywhere close to on time.

Special thanks also to Michael Stewart and Dawn Rader, who did most of the really hard running around and fact-checking. It's a pleasure working with you, as always. To my co-authors, Mark, Mike, Charlie, and Sebastian: From a tight schedule on the preceding book, to a book made up almost entirely of original code, it's been a wild ride all the way. It's been a privilege to work with each of you; I hope our next book is even more fun!

Mark Gaither

Thanks to Conleth O'Connell for his expert SGML advice and input into the PUML DTD. Also thanks to Roy Fielding at the University of California, Irvine for creating MOMspider. Thanks to Pam Hanes, a very patient system adminstrator at HaLSoft in Austin. Finally, unmeasurable thanks to Sherry Moe and Steve Williams, formerly of HALSoft in Austin, for putting up with my moonlighting and odd hours.

Sebastian Hassinger

I'd especially like to give thanks and much love to Nina, Eyre, and Haefen for their patience, support, and love. Without them I'm nothing.

Thanks are also due to Ed Tittel, for pulling the writing team together, both at the onset of the project and at various points during the process when it looked like we might all come apart. Thanks also to Mike Erwin, Charlie Scott, and Mark Gaither for all their hard work.

Mike Erwin

I want to personally thank a few individuals, without whose assistance and guidance this book wouldn't have happened. A very rich thank you to Ed Tittel, who held the reins close when managing the overall direction of this book. He was able to aggregate the writing of four unique contributors into a single flow. Finally, my heartfelt thanks to the folks at OuterNet (especially Paul Wolfe and Charlie Scott), who were happy to help with providing test systems and top-notch service to go along with them.

Charlie Scott

My contribution to this book wouldn't have been possible without the support of my wife Mary. I would also like to thank the happy corporation of OuterNet for its time, facilities, and the corporate slogan—"We never sleep!"—that I needed to complete this book (not to mention for giving me the best job I've ever had). Very special thanks go to Ed Tittel for getting me involved in the first place, and to Sebastian Hassinger, Mike Erwin, and Mark Gaither for the inspiration and code at the core of this project.

From All of Us

There's a whole crowd of other folks whose information has helped us over the years, especially the originators of the Web—most notably, Tim Berners-Lee and the rest of the CERN team, as well as Earl Hood, Brigitte Jellinek, and Tom Boutell. We'd also like to thank the geniuses at NCSA, MIT, Netscape Communications, Stanford, HaL, and anyplace else whose Web collections we visited, for helping to pull the many strands of this book together. Our extra-special thanks to Amy Pedersen and Ralph Moore, our partners in grime from IDG, who made this project not only possible, but stuck with us until it was actually finished! And finally, neither the team nor the book would have been complete without the technical assistance of Karen Goeller, our Technical Editor, and the mighty pen of Eileen Kramer, our devoted Manuscript Editor.

The publisher would like to give special thanks to Pat McGovern, without whom this book would not have been possible.

ABOUT THE AUTHORS

This group of authors has collaborated on numerous other projects for IDG Books. As a group, their credits also include *Foundations of World Wide Web Programming with HTML and CGI*. Ed, Sebastian, and Mike teamed up to produce both *HTML for Dummies* and *Mecklermedia's Official Internet World 60 Minute Guide to VRML*. Additionally, Mark and Ed co-authored *Mecklermedia's Official Internet World 60 Minute Guide to Java*.

ED TITTEL is the author of numerous books about computing and a columnist for MAXIMIZE! magazine and a columnist for *Windows NT* magazine. He's the co-author (with Bob LeVitus) of three best-selling books *Stupid* books for Dos & Windows. These days, Ed's turning his focus to Internet-related topics and activities, both as a writer and as a member of the NetWorld + Interop program committee.

Ed has been a regular contributor to the computer trade press since 1987 and has written more than 100 articles for a variety of publications, with a decided emphasis on networking technology. These publications include *Computerworld, InfoWorld, LAN Times, LAN Magazine, BYTE, Macworld, MacUser, MAXIMIZE!, NetGuide,* and *IWAY*.

Contact Ed at:

```
etittel@zilker.net
```

MARK GAITHER is currently a freelance consultant and writer, and the principal at WebTechs, Inc., his Austin-based software development and research company. Prior to going it alone, Mark was a Software Engineer at HaL Software Systems in Austin, TX, where he was part of a five-person team in charge of maintaining and extending an SGML filtering gateway.

Mark's experience with SGML started by chance when he was volunteered to aid Steven DeRose, who was delivering an introduction to SGML and Hypertext at Hypertext 92 in San Antonio, TX. As a result, Mark's SGML experience has blossomed in the Web world. He righteously evangelizes the need to validate HTML, sometimes to his own detriment. He maintains the HaL HTML Validation Service and the HaL HTML Check Toolkit available at:

```
http://www.hal.com/~markg/WebTechs/
```

Finally, Mark is a co-founder and the current Director of the Austin WWW Users Group whose membership is nearing 200, and a member of the Board of Directors on the Austin Area Multimedia Alliance.

Mark was graduated by Texas A&M University in Computer Science in 1990 (Bachelors) and is nearing completion of his MA from the same institution. Mark has attended conferences like AIIM 92, SGML 92 and 93, and CALS 92 and 93. Mark can be found on the weekends laying waste to rust and grime on his nearly-complete, frame-off restoration of a 1970 Chevelle SS 454 LS-5 (grunt, grunt!) while reciting quotes from favorite movies like *Fletch*, *Raising Arizona*, *Tombstone*, *Stripes*, and the *Blues Brothers*.

Contact Mark at:

`markg@webtechs.com`

SEBASTIAN HASSINGER is an independent consultant and programmer who concentrates on all things Internet, with a special affinity for CGI programming and World Wide Web wackiness. Currently, clones of Sebastian can be seen working part-time at Apple Computer, Inc. and at OuterNet Connection Strategies. He is occasionally sighted around his supposed home, in beautiful south Austin, Texas.

Sebastian is a graduate of Concordia Unversity, Montreal, Canada, with a BA in English received in 1989. Before his tenure at Apple Computer, he worked for Simon Fraser University in Vancouver, BC, Canada, in the Macintosh Multimedia Laboratories (EXCITE) as a jack-of-all-programming-trades and disciplines. He has also written manuals and technical white papers for a number of high-tech organizations in Canada.

Contact Sebastian at:

`singe@outer.net`

MIKE ERWIN is an independent consultant and programmer who is frankly obsessed with the Internet, with a focus on CGI programming and Internet connectivity at any speed (the faster, the better). Mike also works part-time at Apple Computer, Inc. and is the President and CEO of OuterNet Connection Strategies, an Austin-based Internet service provider.

Mike is a graduate of UT Austin, with a BBA in Finance received in 1989, and a BS in Computer Science in 1991, also from UT Austin. Before his tenure at Apple Computer, he worked as a contract programmer for companies like IBM, Microsoft, the State of Texas, and other industry heavyweights. He has also written science fiction and fantasy for publications like *TSR* in the mid-1980s.

Contact Mike at:

`mikee@outer.net`

Contents Summary

The Tool is used to create a sample project, there is a discussion of the reasoning behind the project and its feature set, and there is an examination of how tasks are accomplished using Perl code.

This chapter examines how to add options and capabilities to the Form Generation Tool. This discussion includes how to decide if a feature is needed, what's involved in adding an additional element, as well as some of the issues involved in adding a new feature to the Tool.

A discussion of how to install a form and the accompanying CGI generated with the Form Generation Tool, this chapter outlines how to troubleshoot installation and execution problems and explores the options for extending forms to be part of a working application.

The first half of this chapter discusses the authors' development environment and tools of choice, as well as why the environment and tools were chosen. The second half points to some resources and Web sites that make useful information and code available to the public.

PART II PUTTING CGI PROGRAMMING TO WORK

This chapter provides a set of forms and utilities to handle requests for domain names from users and organizations and to track the status of those requests at the InterNIC.

This chapter includes all of the software tools and techniques you'll need to deliver faxes to their intended recipients over the WWW.

CHAPTER 12: BUILDING A BETTER INTERFACE: MAJORDOMO ADMINISTRATION VIA THE WEB 357

This chapter provides a simple, friendly Web-based user interface for the notoriously picky mailserver known as *Majordomo*. It also includes tips to extend the tool's coverage to other common mail servers like *LISTSERVE* and *listproc*.

CHAPTER 13: WEB-BASED CALENDARING AND SCHEDULING 409

This chapter provides a suite of programs for a shared Web-based scheduling tool, including end user viewing and event request capabilities, and administrative tools to manage a shared calendar and events database.

CHAPTER 14: THE ONLINE HTML EDITOR............................467

This chapter supplies a simple way for users to download and edit their home pages through a simple Web-based interface. It also explains how to generalize this tool for more sophisticated editing capabilities.

CHAPTER 15: WEB COMMERCE OPTIONS............................489

This chapter provides a brief overview of the most common Web commerce encryption and secure data delivery techniques. It also includes an example order form for the First Virtual commerce environment.

CHAPTER 16: A WEB-BASED UNIX ACCOUNT MANAGER 527

In this chapter, you'll find a set of Web-based utilities to evaluate the most common UNIX user/account management tasks, including account creation, password management, and file system access controls.

CHAPTER 17: FROM A PROGRAM USAGE STATEMENT TO AN HTML FORM 567

This chapter supplies a tool that can parse a UNIX command's program usage statement to create an equivalent HTML <FORM>. It also covers the general programming techniques required to create the underlying CGI program that must accompany such a form.

Contents

INTRODUCTION

Welcome to *Web Programming SECRETS with HTML, CGI, and Perl* (*WPS, Web Programming Secrets*)! This book is shamelessly devoted to informing and educating programmers who seek to extend the capabilities of their Web server. Our primary goal is to provide you with tools, tips, tricks, and approaches to enable you to grapple with any Web-related programming task.

WPS will arm you with techniques for analyzing, understanding, and solving programming problems, so that you can tackle just about any kind of Common Gateway Interface (CGI) programming project. *WPS* includes a disk that contains all the code included in the book, as well as a few public domain and shareware tools, libraries, and ready-to-run CGI programs. For more information on the companion disk, please consult the section entitled "About the Disk."

DON'T BUY THIS BOOK UNLESS...

Don't buy this book unless you understand and agree to some of its fundamental assumptions and premises. Here's a list of things you shouldn't differ with too violently (if you do, perhaps you should move down the shelf at your bookstore and try a different tome):

1. *Our programming language of choice is Perl.* Most of the code in this book is written in Perl 4 or a fairly vanilla version of Perl 5. If you're an anti-Perl enthusiast, you won't find the programs in this book very interesting, because that's the only language we use here (except for a few short chunks of Bourne or C shell).

2. *Our operating system of choice is UNIX.* If you're developing CGIs or other Web-related programs for Windows NT or the Macintosh, you'll have to do some work on these programs to make them run on your target system. This is not as much a "make-or-break" factor as our choice of language, but it's still worth considering that moving the code in this book from UNIX to other operating systems will take some effort on your part. For some programs, this will be trivial; for others, it will involve major rewrites.

3. *This is not a beginner's book.* We assume that you understand the basics of what the Web is and how it operates. We provide a pretty technical overview of the basics in Chapter 1, but after that we assume you know the basics of CGI, how it operates, and how to install and use programs on a Web server. If you're not pretty comfortable with these concepts, you might want to read our other book—*Foundations of World Wide Web Programming with HTML & CGI* (IDG Books, 1995)—first, because it will lead you through a lot of introductory or elementary material that we just breeze right past in this book.

These few fundamental sticking points aside, we think there's a lot of valuable material in this book. For one thing, we provide an automatic (Perl) code generator that can build HTML forms at the same time it builds the back-end CGI code to handle the data they accept. On top of that, we provide tools that range from a Web-based calendaring and scheduling program, to a program that can automatically generate price quotes for Internet services.

If you're willing to spend the time to learn how the programs in this book were built, you should be able to use these programs yourself with ease. Even better, you should be able to take the principles and practices they demonstrate and use them in your own Web-related programming efforts.

PARTS IS PARTS

This *SECRETS* book is divided into two parts. Part I covers some terminology and background on CGI programming but is primarily devoted to exploring the motivation for, and the design and implementation of, a code generation tool that supports the interactive design of HTML forms. The Form Generator Tool is built with CGI "skeleton programs" that already contain the input-handling logic necessary to actually *do something* with the data delivered.

Part II includes a compendium of Web-based tools, most of which were built using the Tool from Part I, and all of which should add immediate value to your Web site, while you study them to further your own Web-related programming skills.

Part I: The Form Generation Tool

We begin Part I with a concentrated overview of the basic concepts, standards, and technologies needed to handle Web programming tasks. We proceed to examine the options available for such activities, including suitable programming languages, development tools, and approaches. Next, we move on to analyze the current state of the art in HTML authoring and programming, to help set the stage for why a form generation tool is useful.

Then we tackle the Form Generator Tool in-depth, beginning with a detailed discussion of the factors and features that went into its design. From there, we dive into the code for this Tool, with discussions of its setup, initialization, and interactivity, interface, and runtime behavior. Next, we tackle how this initial version might be extended and enhanced, while weighing the pros and cons of the effort involved. Finally, we discuss the details of installing and using the Form Generator, with a detour to fully document our own development environment, and the tools and approaches we used to construct all of the code for this book.

Part II: Putting CGI Programming to Work

Part I describes a tool for building other tools; Part II demonstrates how to build a variety of functional tools that most Web sites will find interesting, if not of immediate use.

In Chapters 10 through 20, we'll walk you through the design, implementation, installation, and use of Web-based tools for the following kinds of topics and areas:

- DNS administration
- Fax delivery and routing
- Mail server administration and use
- Interactive calendaring and scheduling
- Web-based HTML online editing
- Web commerce issues, technologies, and techniques
- UNIX user management
- Web-based UNIX system command access
- A price quote generator
- A Web site search-and-reporting tool

Our goal is not just to provide software you can use, but also to explain why that software was built in the first place, how it was designed and implemented, and how to install and use it effectively. Our goal is to illuminate not just the "how" of the programming part, but also the "hows" and "whys" of Web server administration, configuration, and management. The real "secret" behind this book is that is was written by people who manage Web servers for a living, and that it shares our efforts to make our own lives easier. We hope you'll gain some of the same benefit from this book!

How to Use This Book

If you're a relative novice to Web programming and CGI, we strongly recommend that you read this book in its entirety, even if you just skim the parts that don't currently interest you. You'll probably also want to read other references, both online and offline, as you work through the book. Once you've made an initial pass, you can dip in again from time to time as other topics catch your eye.

If you're a seasoned Web hand, you'll probably want to skim the first two chapters. After that, we think you'll find the discussion of the Form

Generation Tool downright fascinating. In the same vein, Part II covers topics such as Web commerce and Program Usage Statements that might not be of immediate interest. Nevertheless, you'll find gems of wisdom and pearls of experience throughout this book, even in areas that you might not think are that compelling. That's why we recommend you skim the chapters you don't think are too germane, as well as reading chapters you find more attractive.

In general, we'd recommend reading a chapter or two any time the mood strikes you, or using the book's index and table of contents to search for information on specific topics.

CONVENTIONS USED IN THIS BOOK

We've tried to be clear and consistent about what's what in this book. This can get tricky, so we used the following typographical conventions to distinguish among a variety of elements that you're likely to encounter while programming:

- When we include fragments of code, or whole programs, we'll often set them off from the rest of the text, like this:

  ```
  # Because these lines start with a '#' they're valid comments in a
  # variety of programming languages (like Perl and the UNIX shells).
  ```

- When we quote an element of code in running text, you'll see a different typeface used to set them off; for example, "The `chop` command in Perl provides a tool for extracting and manipulating substrings, based on the definition of a specific delimiter character."

- When we name UNIX or other programs, system commands, or special terms, they'll be italicized; for example, "The *grep* command provides a way to manipulate data based on pattern-matching and regular expressions."

- When we name an environment or program variable, we surround it with straight-up single quotes; for example, "The variable 'DocumentRoot' is important to define for an NCSA *httpd* server, because it controls access to the Web server's document tree." (Note: Because *httpd* is the name of a UNIX program, we set it in italics.)

- Filenames, including full filenames, stem names, and extensions are bracketed in straight-up double quotes; for example, "The file named "home.html" has a stem name of "home" and an extension of ".html"." Notice that the final period in this sentence falls between the two double quotes, because there's no period in the extension of the filename (whatever's inside is a literal representation of the name).

- URLs and directory names are italicized; for example, "From the URL, *http://www.outer.net/cgi-bin/formgen.pl*, we know that our scripts live in the directory called */cgi-bin*."

- Owing to the margins in this book, some long lines of code, or designations of World Wide Web sites (called URLs, for Uniform Resource Locators), may wrap to the next line. On your computer though, these wrapped lines will appear as a single line of code, or as a single URL, so don't insert a hard return when you see one of these wrapped lines. Each instance of wrapped code is noted as follows:

```
{ http://www.infomagic.austin.com/nexus/plexus/lexus/sexus/this_is_a_
          deliberately_long.html
```

If you can follow—and master—these simple rules, you'll be well equipped to keep up with the content of this book. It's not too much harder than mastering the details of any programming language we know of, so we're pretty sure you can handle the job!

In addition, we've employed a couple of margin icons that merit explanation. Whenever you see the following icons lurking in the margin, here's what you should expect:

The *Inside Scoop* icon flags a particularly useful tip, trick, or technique that will do the job it's built to do, but that can also be creatively reapplied for lots of other neat uses. When you see this icon, ask yourself "How can I use this stuff?"

The *High Risk Programming* icon indicates that you can actually build code using the approach flagged, but by doing so you're taking your life into your own hands. The only reason we recommend this approach from time to time is because we couldn't think of a better way to do it. Just remember that if you follow the advice flagged by this icon and something goes awry, don't say we didn't warn you.

BUT WAIT, THERE'S MORE!

In addition to the materials you'll find in this book, we've established a Web server that includes the materials on the disk, with an interactive search engine, an online registration form, and the opportunity for you to give us some feedback (and suggestions, we hope) about the book or related topics and activities.

On the "live" Web pages, you'll find pointers to the most current versions of the tools, libraries, and code. (We're still waiting for somebody to figure out how to update a CD-ROM after it's shipped!) You'll also be able to share your code, ideas, or suggestions for additional online materials or resources, using an electronic suggestion box. Please visit our pages, and share your comments and experiences with us—we can't promise you fame or fortune, but you might very well get a plug in the next edition of this book, or in one of the others we'll be working on soon!

To visit the *WPS* Web server, point your browser at this URL:

```
http://www.outer.net/wps/
```

While you're there, don't forget to register your purchase and tell us what you liked and didn't like about the book. If you've located any cool resources, mailing lists, libraries, or other information that we didn't include, please let us know about those, too. We'll be adding some of your suggestions to our "official" Web pages (after we check them out, too) and your suggestions will be visible to the whole world as soon as you offer them.

BON VOYAGE!

We hope you find the materials, code, pointers, and information in this book useful. Please share your thoughts and ideas with us, pro or con (our e-mail addresses are listed in the "About the Authors" section). At this point, we're finished with the introduction, so we'd like to close with: Thanks for buying our book—enjoy your reading!

THE FORM GENERATION TOOL

*T*he nine chapters in Part I introduce and explain the
fundamental Tool introduced in this book, a Form
Generator that enables its users to simultaneously compose the
front-end HTML for an on-screen form while, in the
background, the Tool generates the necessary Perl code to
name and accommodate that form's input data.

In Chapter 1, we begin with a look at the philosophical and
technical underpinnings for the Common Gateway Interface
(CGI), the most broadly used interface for adding functionality
to any Web server. In Chapter 2, we explore the variety of
programming languages suitable for CGI implementation.
Then, in Chapter 3, we make the case for a Form Generation
Tool, in part by examining what kinds of tools are already
available for HTML and CGI development today.

In Chapter 4, we tackle a formal design specification for
the Form Generator, including an evaluation of the pros and
cons of a plethora of features and a discussion of why some
were ultimately implemented while others were not. Chapters 5
and 6 finally open the hood on the code for the Form
Generator, as we take you on a top-to-bottom tour of the
program and its many capabilities.

Then, in Chapter 7, we look beyond the program's current capabilities to discuss how it might be extended and enhanced in future revisions. Chapter 8 describes how to deal with the CGI development process in general, and with installing, configuring, and using the Form Generator in particular. Part I concludes with Chapter 9, a brief overview of our own development environment, as we discuss the operating system, tools, and approaches we used in building all the programs discussed in this book.

The Common Gateway Interface and the Basics of CGI Programming

1

World Wide Web (*WWW*, or *Web*) documents lead a completely different life from their conventional, print-bound counterparts. They can change with a single keystroke, and the effects are immediately visible to the whole world. Also, server programs can generate custom-built Web documents on-the-fly in response to interaction with end users. This makes online WWW publishing much more responsive and open-ended than traditional publishing.

Quick response to change and dynamic behavior are the underpinnings of the power behind the WWW. But unless you implement the right approach to building and maintaining Web documents, your information can just lie stagnant and be virtually "dead to the world."

Dynamic behavior is a vital aspect of the Web that is sometimes hard to identify or appreciate. This is particularly true when documents are created on-the-fly, usually in response to some event on the Web. Although what appears to a user in response to a query may look like "just another Web page," it might actually be an evanescent document created for one-time use in direct response to that query.

The same is often true for the results of a Web search, or even when clicking a link or a button on a particular page. The result is a custom-built response, tailored around previous interaction with the user (or from information provided by users, even if they're unaware of the underlying communications involved).

THE HIDDEN LIFE OF HTML

What makes all this possible is a special mechanism that supports the dynamic creation of HTML documents. This mechanism is based on the invocation of external applications, usually referred to as CGI scripts, that run under the auspices of a WWW server, and that are called by the browser in the form of an ordinary-looking URL from the Web document currently in use. Each of these external applications can be tailor-made to deliver customized, on-demand HTML documents.

The WWW provides the infrastructure and mechanisms for seamless integration of many types of information, including customer and product databases; sales documents such as spec sheets, brochures, testimonials, and whatnot (which we'll refer to rather loosely as *collaterals*); and other types of information products such as technical documents and training modules. A key technology underlying the WWW permits static information to be queried and imported on demand, and also supports custom construction of Web documents on-the-fly. This technology is called the Common Gateway Interface (CGI) and is the primary focus of this chapter (and a powerful subtext for the rest of this book).

WHAT IS THE COMMON GATEWAY INTERFACE?

The Common Gateway Interface supplies the middleware between WWW servers and external databases and information sources. CGI scripts or programs may be considered extensions to the core functionality of a WWW server, like that supplied in the CERN or NCSA *httpd* packages. CGI applications perform specific information-processing, retrieval, and formatting tasks on behalf of their WWW servers. The CGI interface defines a method for the Web server to accommodate additional programs and services that may be used to access external applications from within the context of any active Web document.

The term *gateway* describes the relationship between the WWW server and the external applications that handle data access and manipulation chores on its behalf. This gateway incorporates enough built-in intelligence to guarantee successful communication between the server and the external application. Normally, a gateway handles information requests in some orderly fashion, and then returns an appropriate response—for example, an HTML document generated on-the-fly that includes the results of a query applied against an external database.

In other words, CGI allows a WWW server to provide information to WWW clients that would not otherwise be available to those clients in a readable form. This could, for example, allow a WWW client to issue a query to an Informix database and receive an appropriate response in the form of a custom-built Web document. That's why we believe that CGI's main purpose is to support communications with information and services outside the normal purview of WWW, ultimately to produce HTTP objects from non-HTTP objects that a WWW client can render. In short, CGI is what enables the Web to be truly World Wide—it enables the Web to encompass virtually any type of data, rather that being restricted to native HTTP objects and HTML documents.

Gateways can be designed and deployed for a variety of purposes, but the most common is the handling of <ISINDEX> and <FORM> HTTP requests. Some common uses of CGI include:

- gathering user feedback about your product line or your WWW server through an HTML form
- dynamic conversion of your system's documentation (for example, *man* pages) into HTML, for easy Web-based access
- querying Archie or WAIS databases and rendering results as HTML documents

Working in tandem with the HTTP server application *(httpd)*, CGI applications service requests made by WWW clients by accepting requests for services at the server's behest, handling those requests, and then sending appropriate responses back to the client. A client HTTP request consists of the following elements:

- a Universal Resource Identifier (URI)
- a request method
- other important information about the request provided by the transport mechanism of the HTTP

In the sections that follow, you'll have a chance to understand all of these elements in detail, as you become familiar with the structure and function of a client HTTP request.

THE CGI SPECIFICATION: EXTENDING HTTP

The CGI specification was created and documented by the main HTTP server authors: Tony Sanders, Ari Luotonen, George Phillips, and John Franks. These folks discovered that they didn't want to keep adding functionality to their HTTP servers every day, in keeping with the needs of one particular Web activity or another. They decided to build a clearly defined core of WWW server functionality and to provide a way to extend services and capabilities from there.

They needed an application programming interface (API) available to any Perl, C, or shell hacker willing to learn the appropriate interface details. Hence, the creation of CGI as a formal, rigorous specification that includes some nasty notation and grammar.

For more information about the CGI specification, please consult the following URL:

```
http://hoohoo.ncsa.uiuc.edu/cgi/interface.html
```

In the subsections that follow, you'll have a chance to cover the elements of the specification, as we prepare you to build CGI programs of your own.

A Cast of Environment Variables

Environment variables are entities that exist within a particular user's computer environment. Many of these variables attain their values whenever a user logs onto a computer, or when the computer is booted for a single-tasking operating system like DOS. Environment variables are pervasive within UNIX, where they are used to pass information to applications from the runtime environment.

Because the environment persists even as execution threads come and go, environment variables sometimes function as placeholders, to pass data from one application to another within the same user session. In the case of CGI, environment variables known to the server and CGI are used to pass data about an HTTP request from a server to the CGI application. These variables are accessible to both the server and any CGI application it may invoke.

The WWW server may also use command-line arguments, STDIN, and environment variables to pass data about an information request from a WWW client. This allows specific control over program parameters or execution to originate with the server, as well as providing a mechanism for clients to pass short input sequences to the CGI program involved. Likewise, these variables may also be set (or assigned their values) when the server actually executes a CGI application.

Accessing CGI Variables

The requirements of a specific WWW server control how CGI applications access variables. If a variable does not have a value, this indicates a zero-length value (NULL in the UNIX realm). If the variable is not defined in the server's system (omitted or missing), it is assumed to have a zero-length value and hence, is also assumed to be NULL. As with variable access, the system requirements for the specific WWW server dictate the means of value representation for CGI variables.

Likewise, the names for environment variables are system-specific. For historic reasons, we will discuss UNIX environment variables in detail. Please notice that these names are case sensitive, so they must be reproduced exactly in order to reference the correct information. Table 1-1 is a quick reference to the standard environment variables that are specific to each request handled by a CGI application. For most HTTP implementations, these variables will apply; for some flavors of UNIX, you may find small differences in variable names, or in the kind of data associated with them. By and large, though, we've found them to be consistent across SunOS, Solaris, Linux, and BSDI.

Table 1-1
Standard environment variables quick reference

Environment Variable	Description
AUTH_TYPE	access authentication type
CONTENT_LENGTH	size in decimal number of octets of any attached entity
CONTENT_TYPE	the MIME type of an attached entity
GATEWAY_INTERFACE *	server's CGI spec version
HTTP_(string)	client header data
PATH_INFO	path to be interpreted by CGI app
PATH_TRANSLATED	virtual to physical mapping of file in system
QUERY_STRING	URL-encoded search string
REMOTE_ADDR	IP address of agent making request
REMOTE_HOST	fully qualified domain name of requesting agent
REMOTE_IDENT	identity data reported about agent connection to server
REMOTE_USER	user ID sent by client
REQUEST_METHOD	request method by client
SCRIPT_NAME	URI path identifying a CGI app
SERVER_NAME *	server name; host part of URI; DNS alias
SERVER_PORT	server port where request was received
SERVER_PROTOCOL	name and revision of request protocol
SERVER_SOFTWARE *	name and version of server software

*Not request-specific (set for all requests).

AUTH_TYPE

This variable is used to provide various levels of server access security. If your server supports user authentication, this environment variable value indicates the protocol-specific authentication method used to validate a user.

HTTP provides a simple challenge–response authorization mechanism. This mechanism can be used by a server to challenge a client's request or by a client to provide authentication information to a server. The variable's value is deciphered from the HTTP *auth-scheme* token in the client's request HTTP header. If no access authorization is required, the value is set to NULL.

For example, a server may require a client to provide a user-id and password to access a specific part of its Web. In order to make this happen, the client must set the AUTH_TYPE environment variable to a value that matches the supported protocol of the server. For HTTP applications, the most common value is:

```
AUTH_TYPE = Basic
```

This provides a basic authentication scheme where the client must authenticate itself with a user-id/password pair. For more information on this (and other) environment variables, please consult section 10.1 of the HTTP 1.0 specification at the following URL:

```
http://www.w3.org/hypertext/WWW/Protocols/HTTP1.0/HTTP1.0-ID_40.html
```

CONTENT_LENGTH

This variable's value equals the decimal number of octets for the attached entity, if any. If there is no attached entity, it is set to NULL. For example:

```
CONTENT_LENGTH = 9
```

CONTENT_TYPE

The value of this variable indicates the media type of the attached entity, if any. If there is no attached entity, it is also set to NULL. HTTP 1.0 uses MIME Content-Types, which provide an extensible and open mechanism for data typing and for data-type negotiation.

With HTTP, you can represent different media, such as text, images, audio, and video. Within such media, there often exist various encoding methods. For instance, images can be encoded as jpeg, gif, or tiff. The value of the CONTENT_TYPE variable for an attached gif image file could therefore be:

```
CONTENT_TYPE = image/gif
```

For HTTP requests, a client may provide a list of acceptable media types as part of its request header. This allows the client more autonomy in its use of unregistered media types. Although data providers are strongly encouraged to register their unique media types and subtypes with the

Internet Assigned Numbers Authority (IANA), this does provide additional flexibility. But since both client and server must be able to handle unregistered items, media types registered with the IANA are preferred over unregistered extensions.

Subtype Specifications

Whenever an environment variable supports subtyping, note that some subtype specification is *mandatory* for that variable. That is, there are no default subtypes.

All type, subtype, and parameter names are case *in*sensitive. For example, 'IMAGE', 'Image', and 'image' are all equivalent. The only constraint on subtype names is that their uses must not conflict. It would be undesirable to have two different uses of 'Content-Type: application/grunge'. The name provides a simple mechanism for publicizing its uses, not constraining them.

See Table 1-2 for the seven standard predefined MIME Content-Types. (The primary subtype is presented in italics.)

Table 1-2
MIME registered Content-Types used by HTTP

Type	Subtypes	Description
application	octet-stream	transmit application data
text	plain	textual information
multipart	mixed, alternative, digest, parallel	multiple parts of independent data types
message	rfc822, partial, External-body	an encapsulated message
image	gif, jpeg	image data
audio	basic	sound data
video	mpeg	video data

application

This MIME Content-Type describes transmitted application data. This is typically uninterpreted binary data. The primary subtype is 'octet-stream' intended to be used in the case of uninterpreted binary data. An additional subtype, 'PostScript', is defined for transporting PostScript documents within MIME bodies.

The simplest and most common action when a client requests 'application' MIME Content-Type data is to offer to write the information to a file. For example, in many browser setups, encountering the environment variable:

```
CONTENT_TYPE = application/octet-stream
```

would result in the client asking the user if he or she would like to save the binary data to a local file on his or her hard drive.

Other expected uses for 'application' could include such content as spreadsheet data, data for mail-based scheduling systems, compressed binary data such as *gzip*, and languages for "active" e-mail.

text

This MIME Content-Type describes textual data. The primary subtype is 'plain', but the subtype most commonly associated with the Web is 'html'. This is unformatted text and it requires no special software to render the text although the indicated character set must be supported by the client. Text subtypes are forms of enriched text where software may enhance the presentation of the text. This software must not be required in order to grasp the general idea of the text's content. One such possible subtype is 'richtext' which was introduced by RFC 1341 and enhanced in RFC 1521.

An example of this environment variable is:

```
CONTENT_TYPE = text/plain; charset=us-ascii
```

For more information about 'richtext', RFC 1341, and RFC 1521, as well as current implementation details, please consult the most current version of these RFCs. The full collection, which includes pointers from obsolete to current versions, can be accessed through the following URL:

```
http://www.cis.ohio-state.edu/hypertext/information/rfc.html
```

multipart

This MIME Content-Type describes data consisting of multiple parts of independent data types. There are four common subtypes.

1. 'mixed' is the primary subtype.
2. 'alternative' represents the same data type in multiple formats.
3. 'parallel' for parts intended to be viewed at the same time.
4. 'digest' for parts of type 'message'.

message

This MIME Content-Type subtype is an encapsulated message. A MIME body of Content-Type 'message' is itself all or part of a fully formatted message. This message must comply with the Internet Mail Header protocol described in RFC 822. This RFC 822-compliant message may contain its own completely different MIME Content-Type header field.

There are three subtypes:

1. 'rfc822' is the primary subtype.
2. 'partial' is defined for partial messages, which allows fragmented transmission of MIME bodies deemed too large for normal mail transport facilities.
3. 'external-body' is for specifying large MIME bodies by reference to an external data source such as an image repository.

Here's an example of a standard e-mail text message header:

```
CONTENT_TYPE = message/rfc822
```

image

This MIME Content-Type describes image data. The MIME Content-Type 'image' requires a display device such as a graphical display, a FAX machine, or a printer to view the image data. There are two subtypes that are defined for two widely used image formats, JPEG and GIF.

For example, data of a `gif` encoded image would be:

```
CONTENT_TYPE = image/gif
```

audio

This MIME Content-Type describes audio or sound data. The primary subtype is 'basic'. Audio requires an audio output device such as a speaker to display the contents.

An example of a MIDI attached MIME body would be:

```
CONTENT_TYPE = audio/x-midi
```

Note that the `x` prefix declares this MIME Content-Type subtype to be an extended data type.

video

This MIME Content-Type describes video data. Video requires the capability to display moving images. This is typically accomplished with specialized hardware and software. The primary subtype is 'mpeg', but you'll also see 'quicktime' as a fairly common subtype as well.

An example of a video data entity would be:

```
CONTENT_TYPE = video/mpeg
```

For more information about the IANA, see this URL:

```
http://ds.internic.net/rfc/rfc1590.txt
```

GATEWAY_INTERFACE

This environment variable represents the version of the CGI specification to which the server that supplies this value complies. This variable is not request-specific and is set for all HTTP requests. An example value would be:

```
GATEWAY_INTERFACE = CGI/1.1
```

HTTP_*

CGI environment variables beginning with the string 'HTTP_' contain HTTP header information supplied by the client. These are the MIME Content-Types that the client will accept, as supplied in HTTP request headers. Each data type in this list should be separated by a comma, as required in the HTTP 1.0 specification.

The HTTP header name is converted to all uppercase characters. All - (hyphen) characters are replaced with _ (underscore). Finally, the 'HTTP_' string is prepended, resulting in the set of HTTP_* environment variables (in this case, * (asterisk) is a wildcard indicator and stands for any legal string of characters).

The HTTP request header data sent by the client may be preserved, or it may be transformed, but it will not change its meaning. An example of this behavior occurs when a server may strip comment data from an HTTP request header. If necessary, the receiving server must transform the HTTP request header data to be consistent with the legal syntax for a CGI environment variable.

In the course of its operation, the WWW server handles many HTTP request headers. It is not required to create CGI environment variables for all received header data. In particular, the server should remove any headers containing authentication data such as 'Authorization'. This is valuable information that should not be available to other CGI applications. The following example identifies the MIME Content-Types that a particular server supports and services:

```
HTTP_ACCEPT = application/zip, audio/basic, audio/x-midi, application/x-rtf,
video/msvideo, video/quicktime, video/mpeg, image/targa, image/x-win-bmp,
image/jpeg, image/gif, application/postscript, audio/wav, text/plain, text/html,
audio/x-aiff, audio/basic, application/x-airmosaic-patch, application/binary,
application/http, www/mime
```

PATH_INFO

This variable represents extra path information, provided by a requesting client. It describes a resource to be returned by a CGI application once it completes successfully. Clients can access CGI applications using virtual pathnames, followed by extra information appended to this path. Because URLs use a special encoding method for character data, this path information will be decoded by the server if it comes from a URL before it is passed to a CGI application.

The value of the PATH_INFO variable can be one of the following:

1. It may be contained in some trailing part of the requesting client's URI.

2. It may be some string provided by the client to the server.

3. It may be the entire client's URI.

A CGI application cannot decipher how PATH_INFO was chosen or constructed based solely on its value. As a CGI programmer, you must determine the context in which this variable is to be used in your CGI application. An example of a valid PATH_INFO variable is:

```
PATH_INFO = /raising/arizona/
```

PATH_INFO is relative to server-root; it's not usually an explicit path on the machine, but rather a path relative to the directory set as server_root in the Web server's setup. It's important to understand this distinction if you want to create and manage CGI programs.

PATH_TRANSLATED

This variable represents the operating system path to a file on the system that a server would attempt to access for a client requesting an absolute URI containing the PATH_INFO data. The server provides a translated version of PATH_INFO, which takes the path data and does any virtual-to-physical file system mapping.

For security reasons, some servers do not support this variable and will set it to NULL. This variable need not be supported by a server. The algorithm a server uses to decode PATH_TRANSLATED is invariably operating-system dependent. Therefore, CGI applications utilizing PATH_TRANSLATED may have limited portability. Here's an example of an NCSA server's 'DocumentRoot' equal to /u/Web that builds on the preceding example:

```
PATH_TRANSLATED = /u/Web/raising/arizona/
```

QUERY_STRING

This variable represents a URL-encoded search string. The value of this variable follows the ? character in the URL that referenced a CGI search application. The value of this variable is not decoded by the server, but is passed on to the CGI application untouched.

The information after the ? in a URL can be added by one of the following:

- an HTML <ISINDEX> document
- an HTML <FORM> CGI application (only using the GET method)
- manually appended by the HTML document's author in which the reference occurs, in an <A> (anchor statement)

The value of QUERY_STRING is encoded in the standard URL format of replacing a space with a + and encoding nonprintable characters with the hexadecimal encoding scheme of %dd where d is a digit. You will need to decode this hexadecimal information before you use it. You will learn how to do this in Chapter 8.

This variable is always set when there is query information requested by a client, regardless of any command-line decoding by the CGI application.

An example of a client's query URL for a CGI search application (places.pl) to locate a place named Sunset Crater could look like this:

```
http://www.flagstaff.az.us/cgi-bin/places.pl?Sunset_Crater
```

The resulting QUERY_STRING value for this URL would be:

```
QUERY_STRING = Sunset_Crater
```

REMOTE_ADDR

This CGI environment variable represents the Internet Protocol (IP) address for a requesting agent. This is not necessarily the address of the client, but could be the address of the host for that client, depending on the type of connection and operating system the client is using. Here's an example:

```
REMOTE_ADDR = 199.1.78.25
```

REMOTE_HOST

This variable represents the fully qualified domain name for a requesting agent. If the server cannot decipher this information, REMOTE_ADDR is set to NULL. Domain names are case insensitive. Here's an example:

```
REMOTE_HOST = ppp1.aus.sig.net
```

This is the address of the machine of one of the author's Internet service providers, where the client actually resides on his machine at home. It communicates to the Internet through the host via the Point to Point Protocol (PPP)—in this case, using connection 1 (which is why the first term in the domain name is ppp1). Thus, the agent is not necessarily the client.

REMOTE_IDENT

This variable represents the remote user's name retrieved from the server. This RFC 931 (Authentication Server) identification must be supported by the HTTP server. It is highly recommended that use of this CGI environment variable be limited to logging actions. The current RFC 931 documentation implies that the HTTP server must attempt to retrieve the identification data from the requesting agent if it supports this feature. Finally, the value of this variable is not appropriate for user authentication purposes. An example would be:

```
REMOTE_IDENT = inmate.state.prison.az.us
```

REMOTE_USER

The value of this environment variable is the authenticated user's name. Two conditions must apply for this variable's value to be set:

1. The client and the server must both support user authentication.
2. The CGI application must be protected from unauthorized access.

If the AUTH_TYPE variable's value is 'Basic', then the value for REMOTE_USER will be the user's identification sent by the requesting client:

```
REMOTE_USER = gail_snokes
```

REQUEST_METHOD

The value of this CGI environment variable represents the method with which the client request was made. For HTTP 1.0, this is 'GET', 'HEAD', 'POST', 'PUT', 'DELETE', 'LINK', and 'UNLINK'. The method name is case sensitive. An example for a client posting HTML form data to a server is:

```
REQUEST_METHOD = POST
```

SCRIPT_NAME

This variable's value is the URI path that identifies a CGI application. It is the virtual path to a CGI application being executed by a server. In this example, the client's query URL of a CGI application that calculates an engine's maximum horsepower is:

```
http://www.muscle.cars.org/cgi-bin/calc_max_hp.pl
```

and the corresponding SCRIPT_NAME variable's value is:

```
SCRIPT_NAME = /cgi-bin/calc_max_hp.pl
```

SERVER_NAME

This variable represents the server's hostname, DNS alias, or IP address as it would appear in URLs. This variable is not request-specific and is set for all requests. An example is:

```
SERVER_NAME = www.hal.com
```

SERVER_PORT

This variable is the port on which a client request is received. This is deciphered from the appropriate part of a URL. Most HTTP server implementations use port 80 as the default port number. URLs that do not explicitly specify a port can be accessed via port 80. For example, the following URL specifies that port 8119 is the designated HTTP server port:

```
http://www.chevelle.org:8119/index.html
```

SERVER_PROTOCOL

This variable's value represents the name and revision of the information protocol that the requesting client utilizes. The protocol is similar to the URL scheme used by a requesting client and it is case insensitive. An example is:

```
SERVER_PROTOCOL = HTTP/1.0
```

SERVER_SOFTWARE

This variable represents the name and version of the information server software. This variable is not request-specific and is set for all requests:

```
SERVER_SOFTWARE = NCSA/1.4
```

The CGI Command Line

Some operating systems support methods for providing data to CGI applications via the command line. This technique should now be used only in the case of an HTML <ISINDEX> query.

POST Versus GET: What's the Deal?

The only real difference between the GET and POST methods is the way the information is passed to the CGI application. In the GET method, it's passed on the command line, which means that it needs to be short (some systems restrict command-line length, which causes long command lines to be truncated; on most UNIX systems, for instance, this restriction is either 128 or 256 characters). Using the POST method, which is now strongly recommended for all applications other than simple <ISINDEX> queries, the input information is encoded into a block of data that is passed through STDIN to the CGI application. This method avoids all restriction on command-line length, and offers a more reliable data delivery mechanism between forms and their underlying CGI programs.

A server identifies this type of request by the GET method, accompanied by a URI search string that does not contain any *unencoded* = characters. This method trusts the clients to encode the = character in an <ISINDEX> query. This practice was considered safe at the time of the design of the CGI specification and requires that you, as a CGI programmer, be careful to observe this restriction.

A server parses this string into words using the rules in the CGI specification, as follows:

1. The server decodes the query information by first splitting the string on the + characters in the URL (which map to spaces, following URL encoding techniques).

2. The server then performs any additional decoding before placing each split string into an array named 'argv'.

   a. Typically, this consists of separating out individual variable strings by splitting the input stream at each ampersand (&).

   b. Then, the resulting substrings must be split again at the equal sign (=) character to establish name/value pairs, where the left-hand side value provides the name of the variable, and the right-hand side value supplies its corresponding value.

This approach follows the UNIX method for passing command-line information to applications. 'argv' is an array of pointers to strings, where the length of the 'argv' array is stored in the environment variable 'argc'. (Love that UNIX!)

Inside HTML's ISINDEX Mechanism

The ISINDEX mechanism is a special data-passing technique in HTML, originally developed to allow short queries to be passed to a search engine (or other index-retrieval mechanism) from user input. The command line and URL that are passed to the Web server differ from FORM input, primarily in the use of different characters as field delimiters, and because no field names are passed along with field values.

In a form, the data passed with the GET method would look like this (assuming the name of the CGI is **query.pl**):

`query.pl?state=arizona`

Using the ISINDEX data-passing technique, the data looks like this:

`query.pl?arizona`

In its latest incarnation, ISINDEX has been changed somewhat. It's now handled as a preloaded fill-out form rather than as a browser dialog box or a simple text field on the screen. In keeping with this new definition, Mosaic has implemented an undocumented feature—if you have only one text field in a form, and if you name the field **isindex**, and if you submit it using the GET method, the command line behaves as though it were <ISINDEX> (i.e., **url?query** rather than **url?isindex=query**).

If the server finds that it cannot send the 'argv' array to the CGI application, it will include *no* command-line information. Instead, it will provide the non-decoded query information within the environment variable QUERY_STRING. This failure may be attributed to internal limitations of the server like those imposed by *exec()* or */bin/sh* command-line restrictions. Another example of such a failure occurs when the number of arguments sent by the server to the CGI application may exceed the operating system's or server's limitations. It may also occur when a string in the 'argv' array is not a valid argument for the CGI application that it enters.

For demonstrated examples of command-line usage see this URL:

`http://hoohoo.ncsa.uiuc.edu/cgi/examples.html`

INSIDE SCOOP! Make sure when you run these examples, that you pay close attention to the values for the command-line variables 'argc' and 'argv'. We'd argue strongly that the first integrity check on accepting CGI input in a program is to make sure that 'argv' is non-zero, and that the number matches the expected number of arguments to your program! ▲

It's also noteworthy that this command-line data-passing is seldom used for handling HTML forms, which can contain arbitrarily large amounts of data. HTML forms normally utilize environment variables to pass data using the POST method, because this method bypasses command-line length restrictions, and the occasional data-passing problem that context-switching can sometimes cause in the UNIX runtime environment.

CGI Data Input

For requests with data attached following the HTTP request header, like HTTP POST or PUT, the data is delivered to the CGI application using a standard input file descriptor. All CGI applications follow this method of reading data. For UNIX operating systems, this uses the so-called standard input device, commonly referred to as *stdin*.

The server will send a number of bytes of information, at least as long as the value specified by the variable CONTENT_LENGTH, using the *stdin* file descriptor to pass the data to the CGI application. The CGI application is not required to read all of this data, but neither must it attempt to read more than CONTENT_LENGTH bytes. If it does, the data may be totally irrelevant to the application and could easily foul up any ongoing input-handling routines!

The server also provides the CONTENT_TYPE for data passed to the CGI application. This enables the application to decide how to handle the data it receives. At the end of the data stream, the server is not required to transmit an end-of-file marker; both server and application assume that reading will cease immediately after the CGI application reads the number of bytes specified by the value of CONTENT_LENGTH.

For example, let's assume you are working with an HTML form that provides its data using the <FORM METHOD="POST">. Let's say this form's results are 15 bytes encoded and look like one=bob&two=cat (in decoded form).

In this example, the server will set CONTENT_LENGTH to 15 and CONTENT_TYPE to application/x-www-form-urlencoded. The first byte on the script's standard input file descriptor will be the character a, followed by the rest of the encoded string.

CGI Data Output

A CGI application always returns *something* to the client that invokes it or to the Web server that invokes it. The CGI application sends its output to a standard output file descriptor. UNIX calls this *stdout*. The CGI application output might be a document generated by the application (typically HTML, destined for delivery to the client), or it might be data retrieval instructions to the server (e.g., to transfer a file to the client).

Output is usually returned in one of two ways. The first form is non-parsed header output. Using this form, a CGI application must return a complete HTTP response message.

The second form of returned data is parsed header output. Only a server is required to support this form. In this case, the CGI application returns a CGI response message. This response consists of headers and a body, separated by a blank line. These headers are either CGI headers that will be interpreted by a server or they are HTTP headers to be included within the response message. Here, the body is optional; but if it is supplied, the body must be prefaced by a MIME Content-Type header.

If the body is excluded, the CGI application must transmit either a Location or Status header. The Location header is used to indicate to the server that the CGI application is returning a reference to a document rather than the document's bits and pieces. The Status header is utilized to provide information to the server about the status code the server should use in its response message to the client. For information about the syntax of these CGI headers, please consult the CGI specification. For now, we'll assume you're ready to tackle working with CGI input and output, in the sections that follow.

CGI INPUT AND OUTPUT

To programmers, it sometimes appears that if only they could get the right handle on their data, it would solve all their problems and answer all their prayers. We think this might be a bit overstated, but we're more than willing to concede that graceful handling of CGI input and output can be tedious and difficult. But hey, that's why they pay CGI programmers the big bucks, right?

Even so, it's become obvious to everybody that where CGI programming is concerned, the world is just one wide web of opportunity. CGI-savvy programmers are in high demand, and it looks like it's going to stay that way for some time. That's why it's time to sharpen your CGI skills, clean up your keyboard, and mash the pedal to your CGI metal. That's why we'll start off with where the real CGI action begins (and ends), with accepting input from clients and returning nicely formatted results for them to "ooh" and "aah" over.

In this chapter you'll learn the ins and outs of CGI input and output. We'll cover the two HTTP methods, POST and GET. For GET, we'll look at <ISINDEX> and <FORM> examples. For POST, we'll look at a more complex and interesting <FORM> example.

A DIFFERENT SORT OF INPUT METHOD

The CGI specification supports two HTTP methods for handling CGI input: GET and POST. The METHOD field in HTTP indicates the method applied on an object identified by a URL. GET is always supported by CGI (it's the default method, in fact), and POST by nine out of ten implementations. While it's true that GET is the default, to quote NCSA, the developers of the NCSA *httpd* server, one of the most common Web servers on the entire planet, "POST is *strongly*, STRONGLY recommended" for use with all fill-out forms except ISINDEX.

A list of other methods accepted by your HTTP server will be returned in response to either an HTTP SimpleRequest or FullRequest statement. Method names are case sensitive—so write 'em as you see 'em. For more information about these requests, please consult the HTTP 1.0 specification:

```
http://www.w3.org/hypertext/WWW/Protocols/HTTP/Request.html
```

GET It While You Can

The GET method instructs a server to retrieve the data referenced by a URL, where the URL specifies a CGI application. For instance, a simple CGI application that echoes the CGI environment variables back to the client is coded in HTML as:

```
<A HREF="http://www.hal.com/hal-bin/test-cgi">
```

The value of the attribute, HREF, is a URL that refers to a CGI application residing on the referenced server—in the example just shown, the server is www.hal.com and the CGI script is /hal-bin/test-cgi.pl.

The following is the `test-cgi` Bourne shell script that will be used throughout this chapter:

```
#!/bin/sh
echo Content-Type: text/plain
echo
echo CGI/1.0 test-cgi script results:
echo
echo argc = $#   argv = "$*"
echo
echo SERVER_SOFTWARE    = $SERVER_SOFTWARE
echo SERVER_NAME        = $SERVER_NAME
echo GATEWAY_INTERFACE  = $GATEWAY_INTERFACE
echo SERVER_PROTOCOL    = $SERVER_PROTOCOL
echo SERVER_PORT        = $SERVER_PORT
echo REQUEST_METHOD     = $REQUEST_METHOD
echo HTTP_ACCEPT        = "$HTTP_ACCEPT"
echo PATH_INFO          = $PATH_INFO
echo PATH_TRANSLATED    = $PATH_TRANSLATED
echo SCRIPT_NAME        = $SCRIPT_NAME
echo QUERY_STRING       = $QUERY_STRING
echo REMOTE_HOST        = $REMOTE_HOST
echo REMOTE_ADDR        = $REMOTE_ADDR
echo REMOTE_USER        = $REMOTE_USER
echo CONTENT_TYPE       = $CONTENT_TYPE
echo CONTENT_LENGTH     = $CONTENT_LENGTH
```

As well as being educational, this script is a handy testing tool to examine the values assigned to the most common environmental variables used in CGI programs. We find it quite useful for testing and debugging our environment, and we think you will, too!

Using the GET Method

The main use for the GET method is to perform searches or to address queries to a database.

<ISINDEX> Query

In HTML 3.0, all you need to do is add the <ISINDEX> tag to your document's head using an HREF attribute to the CGI program that will perform the search or query on your behalf. The necessary HTML looks like this:

```
<HEAD>
<ISINDEX HREF="http://www.hal.com/hal-bin/query">
</HEAD>
```

The HREF supplies a URL for the CGI application that will service any <ISINDEX> queries elsewhere in your HTML document. The browser is responsible for assembling the query string; the CGI program referenced in the <ISINDEX> tag needs to be able to take it from there when it's delivered by the server.

The resulting query URL includes the URL defined in the <ISINDEX> statement and a set of arguments for use in the CGI program. These arguments are preceded by a ? (question mark). For instance, the browser would build a URL from the text entered by the user into the search text widget. For a search on the two keywords blues and brothers the resulting string passed to the server (and on to the CGI program) will be:

```
http://www.hal.com/hal-bin/query?blues+brothers
```

In such URLs, a special form of encoding called URL-encoding is used. That is, keywords are separated with a +. Spaces, plus signs, and other illegal characters are encoded as hexadecimal ASCII escape sequences. Remember, these numeric entities take the form: %## where # is a hexadecimal number—for example, space = %20, plus = %2B.

A finer level of content control that is invisible to users is sometimes supplied by more advanced browsers. These clients may allow multiple keywords as input and require the use of the numeric entity %20 to get a space (" "). If you are building applications targeted specifically for such browsers, you'll need to consider this possibility in your input-handling routines.

The <ISINDEX> query is built by appending a ? to a URL and following it by keywords separated by a + sign. For instance,

```
<A HREF="http://www.hal.com/hal-bin/test-cgi?one+two+three+four">
```

would send four keywords—namely, one, two, three, and four—to the CGI application *test-cgi* via the standard input device (*stdin*). For this kind of HTTP request, the default method is GET. Here's the result of this query:

```
CGI/1.0 test results:

argc = 4 argv is one two three four

PATH = /bin:/usr/bin:/usr/etc:/usr/ucb
SERVER_SOFTWARE = NCSA/1.3
SERVER_NAME = www.hal.com
GATEWAY_INTERFACE = CGI/1.1
```

```
SERVER_PROTOCOL = HTTP/1.0
SERVER_PORT = 80
REQUEST_METHOD = GET
HTTP_ACCEPT = */*
PATH_INFO =
PATH_TRANSLATED =
SCRIPT_NAME = /bin/test-cgi
QUERY_STRING = one+two+three+four
REMOTE_HOST = ppp2.aus.sig.net
REMOTE_ADDR = 199.1.78.26
...remaining elements empty and omitted for that reason...
```

Notice the value of the environment variable REQUEST_METHOD = GET. This is expected because GET is the default HTTP method. Also notice the value of the array 'argv'. It is the string of keywords separated by blanks one two three four. This information in another form is the value of the QUERY_STRING variable, which is one+two+three+four.

How would you parse the QUERY_STRING variable to get at the data and do something with it? You basically split the QUERY_STRING environment variable up into pieces by using the + as the separator between keywords. The following bit of Perl code deciphers this variable for the GET method:

```
# Determine the request method, make sure data is defined in
# ARGV, and determine if query string is defined.
if ($#ARGV != -1  &&  $ENV{REQUEST_METHOD} eq 'GET' &&
                 $ENV{QUERY_STRING} ne ''){
    # Split the query string into an array of keywords.
    @keywords = split("+", $ENV{QUERY_STRING}); }
```

The array of keywords, @keywords, has the value of:

```
@keywords = ( "one", "two", "three", "four")
```

You can now query an external database of indexes for the occurrence of each of these keywords and return the hit list in the form of an HTML document to the client via the server.

<FORM>

HIGH RISK PROGRAMMING

Form data may be sent to CGI applications for processing by using the GET method as well as the POST method, but it's not recommended that you do this. It's especially inappropriate for any kind of form that might generate more than 30 or 40 characters' worth of data! ▲

For example, this chunk of HTML code:

```
<FORM METHOD="GET" ACTION="http://www.hal.com/hal-bin/test-cgi">
<INPUT TYPE="submit" VALUE="Submit Query">
</FORM>
```

results in the following output from our *test-cgi* program:

```
CGI/1.0 test results:

argc = 0 argv is

PATH = /bin:/usr/bin:/usr/etc:/usr/ucb
SERVER_SOFTWARE = NCSA/1.3
SERVER_NAME = www.hal.com
GATEWAY_INTERFACE = CGI/1.1
SERVER_PROTOCOL = HTTP/1.0
SERVER_PORT = 80
REQUEST_METHOD = GET
HTTP_ACCEPT = */*
PATH_INFO =
PATH_TRANSLATED =
SCRIPT_NAME = /bin/test-cgi
QUERY_STRING =
REMOTE_HOST = ppp2.aus.sig.net
REMOTE_ADDR = 199.1.78.26
...remaining elements empty and omitted for that reason...
```

Notice that here again the value of REQUEST_METHOD is GET. This matches the METHOD attribute of <FORM>. QUERY_STRING is empty because we didn't send it any arguments.

This simple form will now give QUERY_STRING a value:

```
<FORM METHOD="GET" ACTION="http://www.hal.com/hal-bin/test-cgi">
Enter text: <INPUT NAME="widget">
<INPUT TYPE="submit" VALUE="Submit Query">
</FORM>
```

and produces these results:

```
CGI/1.0 test results:

argc = 0 argv is
```

```
PATH = /bin:/usr/bin:/usr/etc:/usr/ucb
SERVER_SOFTWARE = NCSA/1.3
SERVER_NAME = www.hal.com
GATEWAY_INTERFACE = CGI/1.1
SERVER_PROTOCOL = HTTP/1.0
SERVER_PORT = 80
REQUEST_METHOD = GET
HTTP_ACCEPT = */*
PATH_INFO =
PATH_TRANSLATED =
SCRIPT_NAME = /bin/test-cgi
QUERY_STRING =
    widget2=I%27d%20rather%20be%20sailing.&widget1=Gone%20fishin%27
REMOTE_HOST = ppp2.aus.sig.net
REMOTE_ADDR = 199.1.78.26
...remaining elements empty and omitted for that reason...
```

Look at the value of QUERY_STRING. Look funny? Its value is a series of text input widget name/value pairs; in this case, two widgets. Each variable/value pair in QUERY_STRING is separated by an ampersand (&).

The funny-looking characters are ASCII hexadecimal representations for two different characters. In this example, apostrophe = %27, and space = %20. Notice the . after sailing is *not* encoded. Why? The HTTP specification determines which characters to represent as hexadecimal and which to leave as written.

How should you decipher this version of QUERY_STRING? Extending our previous Perl code example, we now have to build an array of widgets, each having a name and an associated value, to match the name/value pairs returned by the form. Here's the extended Perl code:

```perl
# Determine the request method, make sure data is defined
# in ARGV, and determine if query string is defined.
if ($#ARGV != -1  && $ENV{REQUEST_METHOD} eq 'GET' &&
                 $ENV{QUERY_STRING} ne '') {
    # Split the query string into an array of keywords.
    foreach $widget (split("&", $ENV{QUERY_STRING})) {
      # Get the keyword and value pair from the widget string.
      if ($widget =~ /(.*)=(.*)/)  {
         ($key, $value) = ($1, $2);
          $value =~ s/\+/ /g ; # replace "+" with " "
          # Unescape ASCII hexadecimal characters.
          $value =~ s/%(..)/pack('c',hex($1))/eg;
          $inputs{$key} = $value; # add keyword/value pair to a list
      }
    }
```

The associative array, %inputs, has the value of:

```
%inputs = {
   widget1 = Gone fishin' ,
   widget2 = I'd rather be sailing.
}
```

Having acquired the associative array that lets you inquire about the value of forms elements by their names, you can proceed from here to write more code to handle these name/value pairs in any way you like. But remember to unescape those nasty ASCII hexadecimal characters before you use them (that is, to convert them from their hexadecimal representations to their ASCII equivalents).

That's all the coverage we plan to give the GET method. In fact, it's not recommended for most serious CGI programming because it's limited in the number of characters it can safely accommodate for transfer between the browser and the host to an effective maximum of 255 characters (including the plus and equal signs used for URL encoding). That may sound like a lot, but for a complex form, it's nowhere near enough!

They're at the POST!

In the sections that follow, we'll take a gander at the POST HTTP method, preferred by most CGI programmers for serious data-passing because it is not subject to the limitations that restrict GET's abilities to transfer data from the browser to the server (and on to your CGI programs).

The POST method is used to make a request to a server. This request is to accept the entity enclosed within the HTTP request as a new object for the server that is subordinate to the object specified in the URL field in the Request line of the HTTP request that carries it. The contents of this new object (the data that we're trying to transfer to the server and on to a CGI program) is enclosed in the MIME body of the request. For instance, this full HTTP request:

```
POST /hal-bin/test-cgi HTTP/1.0
```

asks the server to create a new object subordinate to the /hal-bin/test-cgi object. A URL will be allocated for the new object by the server and returned to the client. The new object is the data part of the request. For more detailed information about HTTP requests (and other methods and terminology), please consult the HTTP 1.0 specification at:

```
http://www.w3.org/hypertext/WWW/Protocols/HTTP/Request.html
```

POST allows a ubiquitous method for providing the following functions to a WWW client:

- posting a message to a bulletin board, mailing list, or newsgroup
- obtaining information about existing server resources
- providing form data to a CGI application

What does a POST query to a CGI application look like? You can make a connection to a WWW server with Telnet if you know the server's name and port number. The following example is a simple POST query of the www.hal.com server that is accepting WWW access requests on port 80:

```
austin 11: telnet www.hal.com 80
Trying...
Connected to hal-alt.hal.COM.
Escape character is '^]'.
POST /hal-bin/test-cgi HTTP/1.0
**** blank line here  ****
```

Once Telnet has connected, it sits and waits for your input. You can then enter an HTTP request. In the above example, we made a POST request by entering:

```
POST /hal-bin/test-cgi HTTP/1.0
```

After the POST request, the HTTP 1.0 Request specification requires a carriage return/line feed (CrLf). You must enter a blank line after the POST query—this is critical. So after typing in the POST query, hit the carriage return twice! Here's what is returned by the server in response to this request:

```
HTTP/1.0 200 OK
Date: Friday, 02-Jun-95 21:11:13 GMT
Server: NCSA/1.3
MIME-version: 1.0
Content-type: text/plain
```

This header information precedes the new object created by the server and returned to the requesting client. Here's what *test-cgi* has to tell us about the object that's returned:

```
CGI/1.0 test results:

argc = 0 argv is

PATH = /bin:/usr/bin:/usr/etc:/usr/ucb
SERVER_SOFTWARE = NCSA/1.3
SERVER_NAME = www.hal.com
GATEWAY_INTERFACE = CGI/1.1
SERVER_PROTOCOL = HTTP/1.0
SERVER_PORT = 80
REQUEST_METHOD = POST
HTTP_ACCEPT =
PATH_INFO =
PATH_TRANSLATED =
SCRIPT_NAME = /bin/test-cgi
QUERY_STRING =
REMOTE_HOST = austin.aus.sig.net
REMOTE_ADDR = 199.1.78.2
REMOTE_USER =
AUTH_TYPE =
CONTENT_TYPE =
CONTENT_LENGTH = -1
Connection closed by foreign host.
```

You can try some simple example POST queries of your own. Telnet to *www.hal.com* and use port 80 (`telnet www.hal.com 80`). Try it and check the results:

```
POST /hal-bin/test-cgi?query HTTP/1.0
POST /hal-bin/test-cgi?simple+query HTTP/1.0
POST /hal-bin/test-cgi?widget1=Big+Block&widget2=Bow+Tie HTTP/1.0
```

These POST examples indicate how a WWW client sends information to a server. It creates an HTTP request and fires it off to the specified server. The server recognizes that a CGI application is referenced and it passes the data downstream to that application.

The CGI application then creates a new object on the server. Once the CGI application terminates, it sends the server its output, which in turn sends that output back to the client. Later in this chapter, we'll look at CGI output. First, let's look at a <FORM> example that uses the POST method.

THE INS AND OUTS OF <FORM> DATA

HTML allows users to build extensive forms using <FORM> and its associated tags. Forms look good on most graphical WWW clients and are popular because they are incredibly useful and have commercial potential.

With a form, your WWW site's visitor can do some of the following:

- Provide you with feedback about your WWW site or your product line.

- Ask technical questions.

- Query a database of information.

- Leave his or her name in a guest book.

- Order a product or information about a product.

- Enter a travel request with your company's secretary.

A set of <FORM> tags lets clients render a small set of input widgets. The form's user can enter text or choose options in the form; when it's complete, he or she submits the data to a targeted server where the data is processed. (These tags are discussed in more detail later in this chapter.)

The targeted server passes the form data as named variables with associated values to a CGI application specified in the initial <FORM> tag that sets up the form. This CGI application parses the data, performs whatever processing is required, and prepares a response—typically another HTML document that it constructs on the spot. Then, the application returns the output to the server, which in turn hands it back to the client. Figure 1-1 shows this interaction between the client, the server, and the CGI application, with the associated data flows.

In Figure 1-1, the client requests a form from a remote WWW server. It then renders that form on the user's display. Such a form can contain input widgets like:

- one-line text fields

- multiple-line text widgets

- checkboxes

- radio buttons

- scrollable menus of options

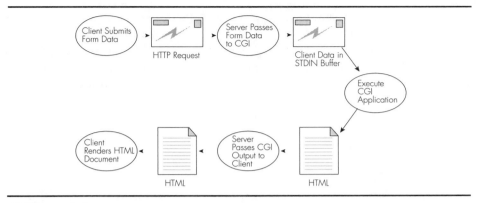

Figure 1-1
Data flows from the Client to the Server, and on to the Application for an HTML <FORM>, before reversing the journey to deliver its results.

Users see a form and respond by entering data into its various input widgets. Once a user has completed all the input fields, or selected all the necessary input boxes and buttons, he or she typically chooses a "Submit" button on the form with an input device—a mouse or pointer, for example—to tell the browser to pack up the form's contents and deliver it to the server.

Once the form data has been received, the server determines that the client has requested services from a CGI application. Next, the server hands the form data to the customized CGI application named in the HTTP request.

The receiving CGI application deciphers the input data, does the right thing, and then returns its customized output back to the server. The server accepts the CGI output and finally pumps it back across the Internet to the requesting client where the output is rendered. Typically the output is an HTML document that was created on-the-fly. It can also be a reference to a document, like another URL, that will then be delivered to the client. Either way, the client gets an answer of some kind (which is all that clients typically care about).

<FORM> Tags and Attributes

The IETF HTML working group considered many ways to implement forms handling, but they decided to extend the 1.0 HTML DTD and develop a forms language. These extensions are included in the IETF level 2 HTML DTD. This forms language makes it possible for a browser to retrieve a form, render it on the user's display, accept user input, and finally, send the form data to a specified server for further handling.

The <FORM> HTML tag allows an HTML author to create a small set of nice input widgets without writing any GUI application code. Therefore, you can rapidly build a useful graphical interface, for example, for your travel request form. Table 1-3 presents the HTML <FORM> tags and their attributes for the IETF level 2 HTML DTD.

Table 1-3

HTML 2.0 <FORM> tags and attributes

Tag	Description	Attributes
<FORM> </FORM>	input form	*ACTION*, METHOD*, ENCTYPE**
<INPUT>	input field	ALIGN, NAME, TYPE***, VALUE, CHECKED, SIZE, MAXLENGTH, SRC
<SELECT> </SELECT>	selection list	*NAME*, MULTIPLE, SIZE
<OPTION>	selection of a selection list; item of <SELECT>	SELECTED, VALUE
<TEXTAREA> </TEXTAREA>	multiple line text input	*NAME*, ROWS, COLS

Required ATTRIBUTES are in *italics*.
*default value = GET
**value = 'application/x-www-form-urlencoded', only valid with method POST.
***values: TEXT (default), PASSWORD, CHECKBOX, RADIO, SUBMIT, RESET, IMAGE, HIDDEN

Let's look at an in-depth example to examine the ins and outs of CGI data. Our example is based on the simple "Travel Request Form" shown in Figure 1-2.

An Example Form

To utilize the power of forms on the WWW, Alternative Software Solutions, Inc. builds a request form that their employees must fill out two weeks prior to traveling. On this form, all information is required—that is, all input widgets must be completed by the employee—after which it gets submitted to the company secretary via e-mail.

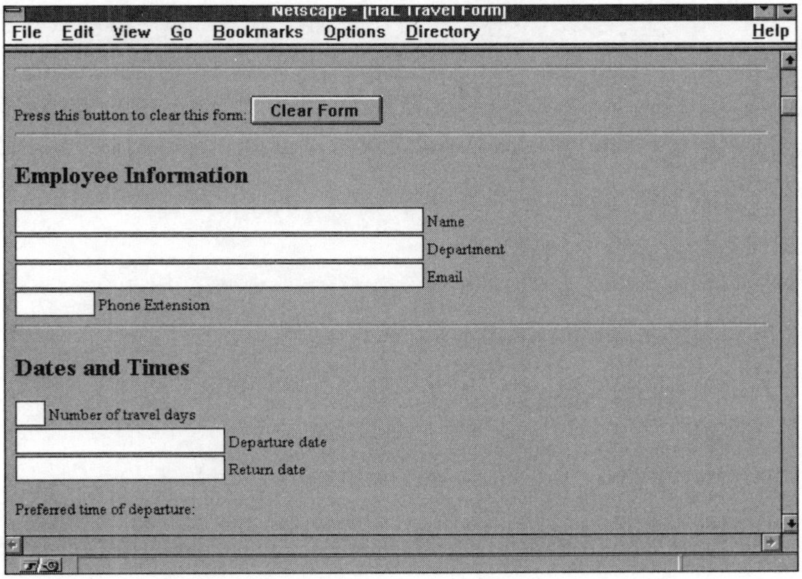

Figure 1-2
The HTML <FORM> tag permits easy construction of a simple travel request form.

The secretary receives travel requests via e-mail, which are then booked with the company's travel agency, based on the information provided by the traveler. Here are the typical kinds of information required from traveling employees:

- first and last name
- department/billing code
- e-mail address
- acceptable departure and return dates
- preferred departure and return times
- preferred hotel accommodations
- purpose of trip

Here's the HTML for this form:

```
<!DOCTYPE HTML PUBLIC "-//IETF//DTD HTML 2.0//EN">
<HTML>
<HEAD>
<TITLE>Altenative Software Solutions, Inc. Travel Form</TITLE>
</HEAD>
```

```
<BODY>
<H1>Alternative Software Solutions, Inc. Travel Form</H1>
<P> Please try to give Biff (biff@ass.com) this information at least
two weeks in advance.
<HR>
<FORM METHOD="POST" ACTION="http://www.ass.com/cgi-bin/travel_request.pl">
<INPUT TYPE="reset" VALUE="Clear Form">
<HR>
<H2>Employee Information</H2>
<HR>
<INPUT SIZE=40 NAME="fname"> First Name<BR>
<INPUT SIZE=40 NAME="lname"> Last Name<BR>
<INPUT SIZE=40 NAME="email"> E-mail<BR>
<INPUT SIZE=25 NAME="billto"> Department Billing Code<BR>
<HR>
<H2>Dates and Times</H2>
<INPUT NAME="ddate"> Departure date
<P>Preferred time of departure:<BR>
<INPUT TYPE="radio" NAME="dtime" VALUE="5AM-9AM"> <I>5AM-9AM</I>
<INPUT TYPE="radio" NAME="dtime" VALUE="9AM-12PM"> <I>9AM-12PM</I>
<INPUT TYPE="radio" NAME="dtime" VALUE="12PM-4PM"> <I>12PM-4PM</I>
<INPUT TYPE="radio" NAME="dtime" VALUE="4PM-8PM"> <I>4PM-8PM</I>
<INPUT TYPE="radio" NAME="dtime" VALUE="8PM-12AM"> <I>8PM-12AM</I>
<P><INPUT NAME="rdate"> Return date
<P>Preferred time of return:<BR>
<INPUT TYPE="radio" NAME="rtime" VALUE="5AM-9AM"> <I>5AM-9AM</I>
<INPUT TYPE="radio" NAME="rtime" VALUE="9AM-12PM"> <I>9AM-12PM</I>
<INPUT TYPE="radio" NAME="rtime" VALUE="12PM-4PM"> <I>12PM-4PM</I>
<INPUT TYPE="radio" NAME="rtime" VALUE="4PM-8PM"> <I>4PM-8PM</I>
<INPUT TYPE="radio" NAME="rtime" VALUE="8PM-12AM"> <I>8PM-12AM</I>
<HR>
<H2>Airlines</H2>
<INPUT TYPE="checkbox" VALUE="indifferent" NAME="airline-ind"> Don't
care which airline<BR>
<INPUT TYPE="checkbox" VALUE="profile" NAME="airline-prof"> Use my
profile<BR>
<INPUT SIZE=40 NAME="airline1"> First choice <BR>
<INPUT SIZE=40 NAME="airline2"> Second choice <P>
<H3>Airline Seating Preference</H3>
<DL>
<DD><INPUT TYPE="radio" VALUE="indifferent" NAME="seating"> Don't
care about seating
<DD><INPUT TYPE="radio" VALUE="profile" NAME="seating"> Use my
profile
<DD><INPUT TYPE="radio" VALUE="window" NAME="seating"> Window
<DD><INPUT TYPE="radio" VALUE="aisle" NAME="seating"> Aisle
<DD><INPUT TYPE="radio" VALUE="emergency" NAME="seating"> Emergency
row
</DL>
```

```
<HR>
<H2>Destination</H2>
<INPUT SIZE=45 NAME="city"> City<BR>
    <SELECT NAME="state" SIZE="3">
      <OPTION> Alabama
      <OPTION> Alaska
      <OPTION> Arizona
      <OPTION> Arkansas
      <OPTION> California
      <OPTION> Wyoming
</SELECT>State<BR>
<HR>
<P> Smoking preference:<BR>
<INPUT TYPE="radio" NAME="smoking" VALUE="no"> <i>Non-smoking</I>
<INPUT TYPE="radio" NAME="smoking" VALUE="yes"> <i>Smoking</I>
<HR>
<H2>Reasons for Trip</H2>
<TEXTAREA NAME="reasons" ROWS="5" COLS="55"></TEXTAREA><BR>
<HR>
<P>
<INPUT TYPE="submit" VALUE="Submit Travel Plans to Biff">
</FORM>
<HR>
<ADDRESS> Last updated Mon 11 Jul 94 by elvis@ass.com</ADDRESS>
</BODY>
</HTML>
```

Reading the specification for <FORM> tag, it's easy to see that the HTTP method specified is POST—the value of the METHOD attribute. This tells the browser what kind of request to make to the server at the URL in the ACTION attribute—in our example, this is:

```
http://www.ass.com/cgi-bin/travel_request.pl
```

This URL is actually a request for a CGI application on the www.ass.com server. The CGI application must read and parse the input differently from the GET method. Let's take a closer look.

This bit of Perl handles CGI input using the POST method:

```perl
# flush stdout buffer
$| = 1;
# Print this MIME data no matter what.
print "Content-type: text/html\n\n";
# Check for the POST method.
if ($ENV{'REQUEST_METHOD'} eq 'POST')
{
    # How many bytes are we supposed to receive?
```

```
read(STDIN, $buffer, $ENV{'CONTENT_LENGTH'});
# Make a list of keyword/value pairs.
@pairs = split(/&/, $buffer);
# Cycle through each pair and decipher the values.
foreach $pair (@pairs)
{
    # Get the name/value pair strings.
    ($name, $value) = split(/=/, $pair);
    # Translate "+" to a space.
    $value =~ tr/+/ /;
    # Decipher ASCI hexidecimal escaped characters, if any.
    $value =~ s/%([a-fA-F0-9][a-fA-F0-9])/pack("C", hex($1))/eg;
    # Add the pair to a list keyed on the name of the variable.
    $contents{$name} = $value;
}
}
```

So, how do we get the data from the client? Remember, for the POST method, the standard input device (*stdin*) is the mechanism used. This bit of Perl code reads the STDIN buffer:

```
# How many bytes are we supposed to receive?
read(STDIN, $buffer, $ENV{'CONTENT_LENGTH'});
```

The environment variable CONTENT_LENGTH determines the number of bytes of information to read from the *stdin* buffer. This buffer contains the data stream sent by the client to the server.

The server then passes this information via *stdin* to the CGI application. That is where we extract the input data. Once the buffer has been split into keyword/value pairs, we decipher each pair and store it in an associative array. This array allows us to instantly access a variable's value.

For instance, this bit of Perl code references the '%contents' associative array and its contents:

```
print <<"HTML";
<HTML>
<HEAD>
<TITLE>Travel Request for $contents{'name'}</TITLE>
</HEAD>
<BODY>
<H1>Travel Request from $contents{'name'}</H1>
</BODY>
</HTML>
HTML
```

As you can see from this example, the CGI application used the name of the user—$contents{'name'}—to create an HTML document. Voila! You have just dynamically created a custom HTML document. This document will be sent back to the traveler and rendered on his or her display.

THE INSIDE SCOOP ON CGI OUTPUT

CGI output—the data returned to the requesting client—is also sent in the body of a MIME message. The standard output device, *stdout*, is the pipe that CGI uses to push data back to the requesting client. But before purging loads of data, the first thing a CGI application must write to *stdout* is a MIME Content-Type header.

In the previous Perl examples, you might have noticed this declaration:

```
print "Content-type: text/html\n\n";
```

Look familiar? The CGI application is indicating that the type of MIME body it is returning to the requesting client is text/html. Remember, 'text' is the type and 'html' is a subtype. This instructs the client to render the attached MIME body as an HTML document.

Later in this chapter, we'll look at a more complicated Content-Type declaration. For now, let's look at a more complicated Perl script to handle the complete sample Travel Request form. In this example, notice how the input is parsed and put into an associated array. In this example we also begin to look at CGI output:

```perl
#!/usr/tools/bin/perl—-*-perl-*-
# You'll want to customize the preceding line to match Perl's
# location on your system.
# Print this out no matter what.
print "Content-type: text/html\n\n";
# flush stdout buffer
$| = 1;
if ($ENV{'REQUEST_METHOD'} eq 'POST')
{
    # How many bytes are we supposed to receive?
    read(STDIN, $buffer, $ENV{'CONTENT_LENGTH'});
    @pairs = split(/&/, $buffer);
    foreach $pair (@pairs)
    {
      ($name, $value) = split(/=/, $pair);
```

```perl
            $value =~ tr/+/ /;
            $value =~ s/%([a-fA-F0-9][a-fA-F0-9])/pack("C", hex($1))/eg;
            $contents{$name} = $value;
        }
    }
    chop($date = `date`);
    ###############################################
    # CGI Output: As HTML and as an e-mail message.
    ###############################################
    # Create an HTML document on-the-fly. Yee-haw!
    print <<"HTML";
    <HTML>
    <HEAD><TITLE>A.S.S. Travel Form Entries</TITLE></HEAD>
    <BODY>
    <H1>Travel Request from $contents{'name'}</H1>
    <P><HR><P>
    <I>$date</I>
    <UL>
    <LI> Name = $contents{'name'}
    <LI> Email = $contents{'email'}
    <LI> Departure date = $contents{'ddate'}
    <LI> Departure time range = $contents{'dtime'}
    <LI> Return date = $contents{'rdate'}
    <LI> Return time range = $contents{'rtime'}
    HTML

    # Check the airline section of the form data.
    if($contents{'airline-ind'} eq 'indiffernt') { ; }
    else {
        print "<LI> Airline (first choice) = $contents{'airline1'}\n";
        if($contents{'airline2'} ne '') {
      print "<LI> Airline (second choice) = $contents{'airline2'}\n";
        }
    }
    print <<"HTML";
    <LI> Destination City = $contents{'city'}
    <LI> Destination State = $contents{'state'}
    <LI> Smoking preference = $contents{'smoking'}
    <LI> Reason for trip = $contents{'reasons'}
    HTML

    if($contents{'reasons'} ne '') {
        print "<LI> Reasons = $contents{'reasons'}\n";
    }
    print <<"HTML";
    </UL>
    </BODY></HTML>
    HTML
    # Now create an e-mail message and mail it.
```

```
$subject = "Travel Plans for " . $contents{'name'};
$sendto = "biff@ass.com";
# Open a named UNIX pipe to send the mail.
open (MAIL, "| /usr/lib/sendmail $sendto") || die "Can't send mail:
$!\n";
# This selects the open pipe handle.
select(MAIL);
print <<"EMAIL";
Date: $date
From: $contents{'email'}
To: $sendto
Subject: $subject

Name = $contents{'name'}
Email = $contents{'email'}
Bill-to = $contents{'billto'}
Departure date = $contents{'ddate'}
Departure time range = $contents{'dtime'}
Return date = $contents{'rdate'}
Return time range = $contents{'rtime'}
EMAIL

if($contents{'airline-ind'} eq 'indiffernt') { ; }
else {
    print "Airline (first choice) = $contents{'airline1'}\n";
    if($contents{'airline2'} ne '') {
      print "Airline (second choice) = $contents{'airline2'}\n";
    }
}
print <<"EMAIL";
Destination City = $contents{'city'}
Destination State = $contents{'state'}
Smoking preference = $contents{'smoking'}
Reason for trip = $contents{'reasons'}
EMAIL

if($contents{'reasons'} ne '') {
    print "Reasons = $contents{'special'}\n";
}
close(MAIL);
exit;
```

This CGI Perl script echoes the data back to the user as an HTML document and the same information is mailed to Biff, the secretary who will make the travel arrangements. This information could also have been saved to a log file for future reference.

So far so good. As these things go, this is a fairly simple CGI application. Now, let's look at a piece of a CGI application that has a complex MIME Content-Type. What do you expect the requesting client to do with this MIME Content-Type?

```
Content-type: application/octet-stream;type=tar;conversions=gzip
```

The primary subtype of `application` is `octet-stream`. This indicates that the MIME body contains binary data. The two parameters in this example are:

- `type`—the general type of binary data
- `conversions`—the set of operations that are performed on the data before writing it to *stdout*

The MIME specification recommends that the proper action for an implementation that receives 'application/octet-stream' information is to offer to put the binary data in a local file.

The `application/octet-stream` parameters used here are two members of a larger set. You can find more information about MIME (RFC 1521) in section 7.4.1 at:

```
http://www.cis.ohio-state.edu/htbin/rfc/rfc1521.html
```

SUMMARY

In the first half of this chapter, we presented the middleware needed to bridge the abyss between Web and non-Web information repositories. The second half then covered the primary methods for CGI input/output, including the GET and POST methods for passing input from a browser to a Web server.

On the input side, GET is used for <ISINDEX> queries and is discouraged for form data, while POST is the method of choice for forms because it is not limited by a system's command-line length limit. Output from a CGI application is in two parts, an HTTP header with an attached MIME body of Content-Type. Once you've grabbed that data, though, the rest is up to you (and is the topic for much of the rest of this book).

In the next chapter, we introduce you to some old and proven programming languages along with some new and exciting programming languages that you can use to implement CGI applications.

CGI PROGRAMMING LANGUAGES AND RESOURCES

2

*P*rogramming languages come in many different flavors: procedural (e.g., C, Basic, and FORTRAN), object-oriented (e.g., C++, Smalltalk, and Java), logic languages like Prolog, and functional languages like Lisp. There are more programming languages out there than most of us could ever learn, even in several lifetimes!

Because each programming language best solves specific types of problems, an application's design is influenced by the philosophy and solution domain of the language it's written in. For example, Lisp isn't practical for number crunching, nor is FORTRAN the best choice for heavy-duty string manipulation.

Languages taken from the same paradigm, like C and Pascal, have different syntaxes but you can translate between them with relative ease. Both are procedural languages with similar constructs and design principles.

Across the board, though, computer language philosophies can differ substantially, as can the expressive style in the resulting programs. The four computer language paradigms that we're concerned with in this book are:

- Procedural—describes the steps of an algorithm.
- Object-oriented—describes interactions among objects.
- Logical—deduces solutions from predicates.
- Functional—describes transformation functions.

Remember, programming language philosophy influences program design. What does all this hooey have to do with CGI applications? Lots!

In this chapter we will look at some considerations involved in choosing a CGI programming language. We will then peek under the hood of two compiled programming languages, C and C++. Then we'll delve into interpreted languages such as Perl, the C and Bourne shells, Python, and Tcl (pronounced "tickle"). Finally, we'll look at Java, which is a compiled and interpreted programming language. While there are numerous other choices possible for writing CGI programs, we decided that confining ourselves to accepted practice still left plenty of options open!

Choosing a CGI Programming Language

Choosing the right programming language should be the result of a thorough and painstaking problem analysis. In some cases, a language might be selected simply because the programmer knows the language well and can use its constructs and syntax to their best advantage.

In other cases, languages are chosen because they are considered more understandable, reliable, efficient, or extensible than others. Where all these things are true, there will usually also be a huge amount of public domain source code available.

When it comes to writing code, there is seldom much sense in reinventing the wheel. Working from public domain, freeware, or shareware source code is usually a great way to learn a new language because of the variety of algorithms implemented and examples available. In any case, once a language is chosen, there's no going back without considerable work.

The Five Primary Considerations

There are five primary considerations when choosing a language for CGI programming:

1. the amount of public source code in easily-accessible repositories

2. the availability of support and infrastructure tools like debuggers, compilers, interpreters, tutorials, books, classes, and "language-aware" editors

3. your own knowledge of a particular language or class of languages

4. the desired throughput for data, compared to support for special operations

5. the "ilities" in the language: extensibility, modularity, usability, and reusability

All of these characteristics play an important role in your selection, but typically the first two or three outweigh the rest.

Public Source Code Repositories

This consideration for choosing a particular CGI programming language is probably the most popular. Many CGI programmers want to hit the road running—they want to code up a form-handling CGI application as fast as they can type, aided only by fermented beverages and pizza. Right from the get-go, you can visit many different Internet sites with public CGI source code libraries.

These sites contain wonderful nuggets of code that any CGI applications programmer could slap together with very little effort. Voila! A near-instant CGI application. "Instant code" has great appeal, and many CGI programmers rely heavily on mining the Internet to fill their coffers with prefabricated code.

There is, however, some slight danger in reusing such code: A malicious programmer might donate a tainted piece of CGI software to a public source code repository. This code could have a bomb wedged deep inside, ready to go off and wipe out your entire hard drive.

Do yourself a favor: When reusing public CGI source code, check it for lines such as *cd /; /bin/rm -rf **. These two nasty little commands can ruin your weekend, if not your life. And get in the good habit of using virus-checking software (easily updated via bulletin-board patches) and, of course, make frequent backups, especially before executing downloaded files.

Also, be careful when downloading binary executables. You have no idea what has been rolled into these "black boxes" built from somebody else's code. A good example is a recently advertised DOS program that claimed to turn your read-only CD-ROM into a writeable CD-ROM. Instead of delivering the promised functionality, this program fired off a low-level disk format and went on to wipe out the whole hard disk.

When it comes to using other people's code: *caveat emptor* (use at your own risk). Try it on a test system before letting it loose on your production system.

Language Support

Your system administrator can be helpful in determining the level of support you'll receive when using any potential CGI programming language. This will require asking some detailed questions and possibly helping your administrator figure out the answers.

First, determine the availability of programming languages at your site. On most UNIX systems you can look in either */usr/local/bin*, */usr/local/pkg*, or */usr/share/bin* for languages like Perl, C, C++, or Tcl. For example, if you want to determine if your UNIX site has Perl installed, look for the Perl interpreter */usr/local/bin/perl* that you need to execute a Perl program. You can also use the UNIX commands *which* and *whereis* or the K shell command *whence* to find these compilers and interpreters:

```
% which perl
/usr/local/bin/perl
% whereis perl
perl: /usr/local/bin/perl /usr/local/perl5.000
% whence perl
/usr/local/bin/perl
% whence -v perl
perl is a tracked alias for /usr/local/bin/perl
```

Ask if you have source-level debuggers like *xdbx* for C. If your site currently does not have source-level debuggers, ask your system administrator what it takes to get one installed (bribing them with lunch usually works). C shell, Bourne shell, and Perl include built-in shell debuggers, so this may not be much of an issue.

Finally, you'll need to determine the availability and the quality of programming language reference material. Your company library may contain the invaluable O'Reilly *Nutshell Handbooks* on Perl, the C and Bourne shells, or an extensive tutorial on Tcl.

You can also find out if your site has any online documentation *man* pages or *help*. For example, typing *man perl* at the command prompt on a UNIX machine will quickly let you know if you have access to a readable set of reference pages. If you get a "not found" message, don't give up quite yet: Maybe this *man* page is not in your path. See your system administrator if you don't know how to alter your *man* path.

Your Level of Knowledge and Understanding

This consideration is by no means purely quantitative. You are the only one who knows your level of understanding of a particular language or class of languages. You are also the one who best knows your strengths and weaknesses.

When considering a CGI language, take a good hard look at your past experiences with programming languages. You should have a good feel for how long it would take you to master a "how to" book on a new language that is a member of a familiar class of languages. If you're a hot-shot Bourne shell programmer, then learning another shell scripting language— like Perl—typically involves simply learning the new syntax and how to apply it. The intellectual overhead needed to switch to a new language within the same class should be small for the experienced programmer.

Desirable Data Throughput

Since the WWW was developed on UNIX, many of the repositories of public CGI source code contain UNIX-based languages like Perl, C shell, Tcl, Bourne shell, and C/C++. Each of these languages is found on nearly every UNIX box.

There are two distinctions to be made among these six languages. Perl, the C and Bourne shells, and Tcl are interpreted languages. This means that their source objects are not compiled into a binary format, loaded, and then executed. Each has an interpreter that reads every line of the source code each time it is run, which slows down the interpreted application. It also slows down the throughput of the data.

By comparison, C and C++ are compiled into a binary executable, loaded into RAM, and executed at faster speeds, resulting in faster throughput. If you have a mission-critical or a real-time embedded application, an interpreted language usually won't cut it. In those cases an executable binary object is just what the doctor ordered.

Finally, there is a language like Java that is a combination of compiled and interpreted. Java requires a runtime system—including a Java interpreter—native to a platform and an "architecture-neutral" compiled binary object. The execution speed of a Java "application" is not notably different from the same type of program written in C or C++.

Desirable "Ilities"

Considering a few of the more important "ilities" is another popular way to decide on a CGI application programming language:

- **extensibility**: A measure of how easy it is to write applications that build upon core mechanisms while adding functionality, new methods, or subclasses (depending on the paradigm).

- **modularity**: A measure of how easy and efficient it is to package each object into a self-contained unit.

- **reusability**: A measure of how easily and efficiently you can leverage prior work (both design and code) and art in your programs.

- **understandability**: A measure of the complexity of the language's concepts and constructs.

All of these elements are important, but how important they are depends on your circumstances. For instance, if you want to leverage existing code and public domain materials in your work, reusability will be most important. If you need to work with an unfamiliar language, understandability may be all-important.

Compiled CGI Programming Languages

Compiled languages create binary objects that are loaded and executed in the computer's main memory. These objects are the result of a compiler assembling ASCII source code into binary information (zeros and ones).

A compiler is typically native to a particular computer architecture and you can assume that binary objects from one architecture will not execute on another architecture. For example, don't expect Pascal code compiled into a binary object and run on a PC to execute successfully on a UNIX machine. Instead, the original Pascal source code must be compiled with a native UNIX Pascal compiler into a UNIX compatible binary object.

In the sections that follow, we'll discuss some of the more popular compiled languages you can use to develop CGI applications.

C

The C language was first implemented in 1972 on a DEC PDP-8 that lay dormant in a hallway at Bell Labs. Brian Kernighan and Dennis Ritchie created C for their own use and amusement. Over 20 years later, it's still one of the most popular languages in use.

C is a procedural language that describes the steps of an algorithm, like a procedure on how to install a water pump on a Chevy. You complete each successive step until you have a new and functional water pump installed, or your sorting algorithm assembles a list in ascending alphabetical order.

There are two primary advantages in choosing C as a CGI programming language. First, it can be compiled into a very tight binary object that takes up minimal space compared to interpreted languages. Some C compilers include command-line options that instruct it to create an optimized binary object. This results in an even smaller binary object. Second, binary objects typically execute faster than interpreted languages. If speed of execution is a major concern, you should definitely pick a compiled programming language. The primary disadvantage to using C for CGI programming is it that it is difficult to manipulate strings with C language constructs. Nearly 90% of all CGI applications involve heavy string manipulation. This means that character and string data must be massaged, transformed, converted, or translated from one form to another.

By contrast, integer and floating-point math CGI applications are few and far between. Most CGI applications take string and character data such as <FORM> data or query data and return other string and character data based on some embedded heuristics. For example, a typical CGI application gathers <FORM> data from a "Comments and Suggestions Form" interface. The CGI application then assembles the <FORM> data into a MIME mail message and mails it to the designated address. It can also record <FORM> data to a log file. "Heavy string manipulation" describes a day in the life of a typical CGI applications engineer.

C++

C++, a successor to C, is a member of the object-oriented (OO) paradigm of programming languages.

Objected-oriented languages like C++ offer many advantages. They provide superior reusability of classes, which reduces the cost of development for similar applications. They also allow extensibility of core classes by allowing programmers to add functionality.

The Incremental Paradigm

One historical note: The "++" signifies that C++ is an increment of one paradigm from the procedural paradigm of its parent, the C language. In the C language, the unary operation "++" increments the value of a variable by one unit. Bjarne Stroustrup, who created C++ at AT&T, claims that C++ is "much better" than plain vanilla C.

For example, a core class such as "Automobile" could have functions like "transport" or "stop." A programmer could add an "accelerate" function to the class without disrupting other already deployed instances of the "Automobile" class. They also support modularity, which is the methodology of breaking a problem down into its smallest understandable units, where each module acts as a separate functional unit.

Finally, OO languages stress the reusability of classes across many different problem domains. Reusability of source code is a popular research topic because it reduces the cost of development, testing, deployment, and, ultimately, training. It can also increase the quality of source code, but this depends heavily on the quality of the software engineering of the component classes in use. As yet, reusability is talked about far more than it's practiced, so its benefits remain more theoretical than actual.

The main disadvantage of using C++ is that it belongs to the OO paradigm. OO development of source code is a completely different beast, requiring substantial training and street smarts. Designing classes for reusability, understanding the polymorphism of functions within a class, and providing effective management of classes within and across applications are new concepts for many applications engineers. OO programming is not a recommended adventure for amateurs or for those who simply need a little forms processing.

Shifting to a new programming paradigm is usually preceded by an act of nature—like an earthquake. Or more likely, you're a laid-off COBOL programmer, and the classifieds are full of "OO Developers Desperately Needed" ads. Need we say more?

Another disadvantage to using C++ is that there is only limited public domain CGI source code available. This is probably because CGI is a relatively new area, and few OO CGI applications have been released for public consumption. But this should begin to change once software engineers begin to develop OO Web solutions (which we're expecting to see on the market any day now).

Interpreted CGI Programming Languages

In this section we look at some of the common interpreted languages you can use to create CGI applications—namely Perl, the C and Bourne shells, Python, and Tcl.

Perl

Perl (Practical Extraction and Report Language) is an interpreted language optimized for easy manipulation of files, text, and processes. Perl is typically used when scanning text files, extracting text strings, and printing reports based on the information that's extracted. Perl was created by Larry Wall in the early 1980s.

Perl provides a lucid and succinct way to solve many programming problems typical in the CGI realm. Before Perl, these tasks were accomplished only with difficulty by C or shell applications which, unlike Perl, were not designed for heavy string, text, and file manipulation.

Although Perl is not yet a standard part of UNIX, it is widespread and likely to be available at your site. Consult your system administrator for more details. If Perl isn't on your system, it is available via anonymous ftp from various Internet sites. For more information about Perl, see this URL:

```
http://www.cis.ufl.edu/perl/
```

Perl is intended to be easy to use, but to be complete and efficient, rather than tiny, elegant, and minimal. Perl combines some of the best features of C, *sed*, *awk*, and *sh*. Programmers familiar with these languages should have little difficulty learning and applying Perl.

Perl's syntax and structure is very similar to C. Many of the constructs in Perl like *if*, *for*, and *while* correspond to their counterparts in C. With Perl, you can manipulate and match regular expressions much more easily than with *sed*, *awk*, or *lex*.

Unlike *sed* and *awk*, Perl does not arbitrarily limit the size of your data. Perl can incorporate your entire text file into a single string. Recursion has no depth restrictions. The only real restriction on these operations and data structures is your machine's memory size. Finally, hash tables used by associative arrays are gracefully built and handled to prevent wicked performance reductions.

Perl is the gem of the interpreted languages because of its ability to do heavy string manipulation. It uses sophisticated pattern-matching techniques to scan vast amounts of text quickly and efficiently. Although optimized for scanning text, Perl can also manipulate binary data with the same ease as text.

Perl can also prevent security breaches through *setuid* applications. Such applications can be exploited in malicious ways in order to wreak havoc in a computer system, but Perl applications are safer than *setuid* C programs. A data flow-tracing mechanism is implemented in Perl to avoid many foolish security holes.

Perl can make up for the limits of UNIX utilities you would otherwise use, like *sed*, *awk*, or *sh*. Some of these utilities have line-length limitations that do not exist for Perl. The translators that are usually part of the Perl distribution will turn existing *sed* and *awk* scripts into Perl scripts. Also, Perl will typically run a little faster than these utilities because of its design. Finally, if the prospect of writing a text file-manipulation application in C drives you to distraction, pick up a Perl book and use it instead.

Today, most CGI applications use Perl because of its many positive characteristics. You will notice that in many of the public CGI source code repositories, more than half the code is written in Perl. You will find out later in this book where to find these sites and what to retrieve, so you can hit the road running when building your first CGI applications.

UNIX Shell Scripting Languages

There are two main flavors of UNIX: Berkeley (BSD 4.3) and AT&T System V. There is a push to combine the best of both of these, but that is yet another book (its topic, in case you're interested, would be "POSIX"). Then, too, there are other "completely different" implementations, like those from SGI and Hewlett-Packard (HPUX), that are starting to play a role in the Web world as well. Within these UNIX environments you will find three common shells: Bourne, Korn (frequently referred to as *ksh*), and C shell. All of them support processes, pipes, directories, filters, and other standard UNIX functions.

The shell is the most important user interface on a UNIX computer. The shell is just another program; it has no special status. It can be updated and modified with little effort, resulting in different flavors of shells. These alternative shells can also live on a UNIX box that has a native shell. Each shell operates as a separate program, and the user can choose which shell (user interface) to use when working on a UNIX machine.

Here we'll look at two shells: the C shell and the Bourne shell. (The Korn shell has the same functionality as the Bourne shell and combines many of the features of the C shell.) The C and Bourne shells are not syntactically compatible. Each shell's interactive commands and script languages differ somewhat, and each has unique behaviors and characteristics, atop a core of common functionality. Finally, each shell has its own scripting language that can be the foundation for writing CGI programs. Since that's why you're here, let's look at each one in turn.

The Bourne Shell

UNIX machines typically have one native command interpreter or shell. On many machines this is the Bourne shell, named after S.R. Bourne in 1975. The Bourne shell is part of the standard configuration for every flavor of UNIX. Because it is smaller than the C and Korn shells, it is the most efficient for shell processing.

The Bourne shell is compact, executes quickly, and requires minimal resources. Developed at AT&T, it has become the most widely used shell. Major advantages of the Bourne shell include:

- It allows exception handling via the *trap* command that is unique to the Bourne shell.

- It supports both local and global variables.

- It takes advantage of System V's named pipes.

The scripting language is somewhat C-like but works more like a conventional command language. While it is excellent for small, throwaway activities, the Bourne shell does not have the kind of flexibility and extensibility you'd look for in a "real" programming language.

The C Shell

The shell that executes under most UNIX operating systems is the C shell, developed by Bill Joy while at the University of California at Berkeley. It is a command interpreter and provides an important user interface to the UNIX operating system.

The advantages of the C shell include its:

- history function, which keeps track of the commands as you input them and permits you to go back and execute them without retyping the command in the shell

- direct evaluation of built-in (native UNIX) commands

- aliasing mechanisms, which allow you to create mnemonic names for commands, files, paths, or other system objects

- control of foreground and background tasks
- syntax that is similar to the C programming language

Even though the C shell's scripting language is C-like, it works more like a conventional command language than a complete programming language. While it is useful for small, throwaway activities and applications, the C shell (like the Bourne shell) doesn't have the power and extensibility you'd look for in a "real" programming language.

Tcl

The Tool Command Language (Tcl, pronounced "tickle"), is a simple scripting language for extending and controlling applications. Tcl can be embedded into C applications because its interpreter is implemented as a C library of procedures. Each application can extend the basic Tcl functions by creating new Tcl commands that are specific to a particular programming task.

Accompanying Tcl is a very popular Tcl extension called Tk (pronounced "tee-kay"). It is a toolkit for the X Window System found on most UNIX machines. Tk extends the basic Tcl functionality with commands to rapidly build Motif or X Window user interfaces. Tk is also implemented as a C library of procedures, allowing it to be used in many disparate applications. Like Tcl, Tk can be extended, typically by constructing new interface widgets and geometry managers in C.

The combination of Tcl and Tk (Tcl/Tk) is a programming system developed by John Ousterhout at the University of California at Berkeley. The Tcl/Tk system is easy to use and possesses powerful graphical interface capabilities. Tcl provides the scripting language, while Tk is a toolkit for creating and maintaining user interface widgets (widgets are graphical objects used in a user interface). These are similar to widgets found in other GUI toolkits, like OpenLook, Motif, and XView.

With Tcl/Tk, manipulation of GUI widgets does not require writing a C or C++ application. This differs from many of the other GUI toolkits. One of the true beauties of Tcl/Tk is that you can rapidly build a user interface, as compared to the challenge of writing a Motif application. Many C and C++ programmers want to use the Tk widgets in their own applications, so they should be pleased to learn that Tcl/Tk can work cooperatively with C and C++.

Since Tcl is interpreted, Tcl applications typically will not execute as fast as their C counterparts. For a small class of applications this may become a disadvantage, but with the blinding speed of today's computer systems, Tcl/Tk represents an adequate applications system. If the speed of execution is critical in your application, don't fret. Tcl can be compiled, or heavy-duty processing can be written in a compiled language such as C and C++, and the user interface programmed in Tcl/Tk.

If this is unacceptable, create a throwaway prototype of the user interface using Tcl/Tk and get feedback from your target users to build a faster final implementation. We've been informed that there are numerous conversion utilities to take Tcl/Tk into C/C++, which may be a boon for those who want to prototype in Tcl/Tk and leave their scripts interpreted until they've stabilized, and then translate them to create a more permanent version.

There are Tcl versions for different platforms and operating systems that make Tcl fairly portable. The one feature of Tcl that affects portability is its support for native operating system calls. If these facilities are used, portability will be sacrificed for convenience.

Tcl/Tk provides five benefits to applications developers:

- It allows any application to have a powerful scripting language (Tcl) by linking in the Tcl interpreter.

- It supports rapid development of applications; you can create GUI applications faster than using C and C++ applications.

- It can execute interpreted scripts on-the-fly without recompiling or restarting applications.

- It provides an embeddable "glue" language that allows developers to combine features from different programs into a single application.

- It is amazingly easy to learn.

Because of its extensibility and depth, Tcl/Tk is adequate for all but the most processor-intensive applications. It is particularly well suited for those that require complex graphical displays or sophisticated user interfaces.

More information about Tcl/Tk can be found at:

```
http://www.sco.com/Technology/tcl/Tcl.html
```

Python

Python is an interpreted, interactive, object-oriented programming language. It combines an understandable and readable syntax with note-worthy power compared to other interpreted languages. It has modules, classes, exceptions, and dynamic data types and typing. Python also provides interfaces to many system calls and libraries, and to various win-dowing systems like X11, Motif, Tk, and Mac. Python can even be used as an "extension language" for applications that require a programmable interface. Finally, new built-in Python modules can be implemented in either C or C++.

Python executes on many platforms, including UNIX, Mac, OS/2, MS-DOS, Windows 3.1, and NT. Python is copyrighted but freely usable and distributable to individuals as well as commercial institutions.

Python has been used to implement a few WWW modules. Currently these modules include a CGI module, a library of URL modules, and a few modules dealing with electronic commerce. For information about these WWW applications of Python, see the URL:

```
http://www.eeel.nist.gov/python/
```

General information about Python is available at:

```
http://www.cwi.nl/~guido/Python.html
```

The Virtual Reality Modeling Language (VRML)

Today, there's a surge of activity to make the Internet and the WWW an easier and more productive place to use. The Virtual Reality Modeling Language (VRML) is emerging as one the most promising candidates from a variety of three-dimensional rendering contenders, as a tool to make the presentation of realistic-looking spaces and places part of the Web's capabilities. VRML is a generic text-based language that describes how to construct 3-D images on-the-fly.

From our study of VRML's capabilities, we believe that the VRML specification could possibly represent the Internet's next big step in interface design. In much the same way that the delivery of a common, powerful hypertext language—namely, HTML—led to the explosion of the World Wide Web, we expect a paradigm shift to an online world to follow.

From the VRML Specification 1.0 Document

The Virtual Reality Modeling Language (VRML) is a language for describing multi-participant interactive simulations—virtual worlds networked via the global Internet and hyperlinked with the World Wide Web. All aspects of virtual world display, interaction and internetworking can be specified using VRML. It is the intention of its designers that VRML become the standard language for interactive simulation within the World Wide Web.

The first version of VRML allows for the creation of virtual worlds with limited interactive behavior. These worlds can contain objects which have hyperlinks to other worlds, HTML documents or other valid MIME types. When the user selects an object with a hyperlink, the appropriate MIME viewer is launched. When the user selects a link to a VRML document from within a correctly configured WWW browser, a VRML viewer is launched. Thus VRML viewers are the perfect companion applications to standard WWW browsers for navigating and visualizing the Web. Future versions of VRML will allow for richer behaviors, including animations, motion physics and real-time multi-user interaction.

The full text of this document can be found at the following URL:

`http://vrml.wired.com/vrml.tech/vrml10-3.html`

This world will be filled with fully rendered 3-D offices, storefronts, and conference areas. No more *point and click* with the mouse; rather, it will be *grab and twist* or *pull and manipulate* with a gloved hand. And instead of your limited view on a flat screen monitor, you'll be using a set of goggles, or some other, more panoramic viewing device. This new paradigm should result in a more human-oriented interface, scoped in real-space, and rendered completely on-the-fly.

From its very inception, VRML's developers intended this language to be a separate but parallel markup language, similar to HTML, but a *distinct* and *different* language nonetheless. VRML is not meant to augment HTML, nor even to be an extension to HTML. HTML supplies a common text-and-graphics delivery mechanism for the Web, whereas VRML is meant to handle all forms of interactive graphic and visual presentation.

Just as a Web page is comprised of different elements of different classes, such as two-dimensional images, sounds, and formatted text, a VRML "document" (or *scene*, as it is normally called) represents a three-dimensional backdrop against which humans can interact with information. Following this approach, polygonal objects would be coded in VRML and would be rendered when a user retrieves a scene across the network, in much the same way the HTML is rendered to display 2-D text and graphical images today.

VRML also supports a hyperlinking feature that resembles the Uniform Resource Locator (URL) system used on the Web today. By selecting hyperlinked objects, VRML browsers can "transport" users to another site, with other images and scenes, that are constructed as they arrive. In fact, VRML's not-too-distant future should have a wealth of enhancements in store. While real-time interaction is probably the biggest change involved, we can easily predict the development of a system of gateways—comparable to the Web's CGI—that allows different scenes to be erected every time a page is retrieved, making each visit a unique and rewarding experience.

We must point out that in order to access VRML objects from Web-space, you'll need a viewer that supports the language. Consider this example: You connect to the *outer.net* WWW site and select a scene that contains a VRML walk-through for a new office building that the site's owners plan to build next year. Since VRML (like HTML) is a text-based document that has been marked up on-the-fly, you would be able to download the scene to your browser, but would need a helper application to fully realize its three-dimensional aspects. Otherwise, it would just appear as a long, obtuse collection of text elements. The exchange of information between the Web browser and the proper helper application needed to render the scene is handled by a set of predefined MIME definitions, which select and launch the right VRML viewer application. This, in a nutshell, is how VRML can extend today's 2-D Web into 3-D space.

VRML was designed as an ASCII text language for a variety of reasons. One reason is to permit it to be easily read by human beings and to be easily written with a variety of tools. ASCII format means that no special file formats or word processing applications are required. Likewise, platform independence is an absolute must for a networking language because there is such a large variety of systems on the Internet running a multitude of operating systems.

Performance was another consideration driving VRML's design. As we mentioned earlier, it could be terribly time-consuming if rendering an object took place on a server, and then the image was sent to the requesting system. Instead, a VRML server sends the basic raw text data for creating a virtual world, which is then translated and rendered by a VRML-aware browser on the requesting machine. This saves significant amounts of time and makes transformations and perspective shifts much smoother.

The VRML language itself is essentially a way to create objects, where each object defines a *tool* that can be used to help create a 3-D virtual world. In VRML-speak, these objects are called *nodes*. A node may be a specific geometric shape (e.g., a sphere or a cube), a texture, or even a movement. Each node has characteristics, or *fields*, that set it apart from other nodes, including its size, the image it uses for a texture, or its angle of rotation.

A node can also be given a unique *name* so that you may call it somewhere else in a virtual world. This greatly increases the flexibility of your objects. Some nodes are allowed to have *child* nodes, which means that they can contain other nodes. A node that has a child is called a *group* node, and has the potential to be a very elaborate object. Suffice it to say that VRML supports a rich and varied representational structure.

Compiled/Interpreted CGI Programming Languages

A class of languages that are both compiled and interpreted ("a breath mint AND a candy mint!") is starting to emerge in the computer industry. These languages create binary code for everything in a script except for local references or system calls, both of which will later be bound at run-time. This creates the potential for terrific portability, as the inventors of Java are wont to exclaim.

Java

Java is a new object-oriented programming language and environment from Sun Microsystems. Along with C and C++, Java is compiled into an architecture-neutral binary object and then interpreted like Perl or Tcl for a specific architecture. A "friendly" version, called JavaScript, is currently under joint development by Netscape Communications and Sun Microsystems, which promises to bring easy access to Java's interactivity to normal mortals. So, in more ways than one, Java is both a dessert topping and a floor wax!

With Java, you can create either standalone applications or applets to be used within CGI applications. Sun characterizes Java using a standard, but formidable, set of industry buzzwords:

> Java: A simple, object-oriented, distributed, interpreted, robust, secure, architecture-neutral, portable, high-performance, multithreaded, dynamic language.

Whew! Our take is that Java is a strictly-typed object-oriented language, similar to C++ *sans* many of that language's shortcomings. For instance, Java will not let you cast an integer type to a pointer.

Java applications can execute anywhere on a network, making it highly suitable for CGI applications. Another really interesting aspect of the language is that the Java compiler creates an architecture-neutral binary object. This object is executable on any platform that has a Java runtime system installed. You can write *one* Java program that can execute on all other supported platforms including Mac, UNIX, NT, and Windows.

Netscape has licensed Java to implement within their Netscape Navigator browser. Their main motivation is to increase the extensibility of Navigator and to enable the creation of a new class of client/server networked applications.

Java and HotJava—the WWW browser from Sun written in Java—are freely available in binary form to individuals. Java can also be licensed to commercial institutions. Currently the supported platforms for HotJava include Solaris, SunOS, Windows NT, and Windows 95. The Macintosh version has not been completed as of this writing but will probably be ready before you read this paragraph.

For online information about Java, see this URL:

```
http://java.sun.com/
```

Java Is Object-Oriented

Java is a member of the object-oriented (OO) paradigm for programming languages. Languages that adhere to this paradigm, such as Java and C++, have the same underlying philosophy but differ in syntax and the style in which the language is expressed. In a nutshell, OO languages describe the interactions among objects.

Every language paradigm heavily influences application design. Therefore, most systems implemented in Java are OO systems. This is not an absolute requirement, but it is typical, because OO design is well understood and supports many new tools and environments.

In any OO system, you may have many active objects. Each individual object retains its own internal states and interfaces. This implies that any object has a strong sense of autonomy. During execution of an OO system, an object may invoke one or more procedures to accomplish some task. This is initiated by a message sent to an object, where the invocations supply instructions on how to behave, governed by the content of the message. Java uses a simple single inheritance mechanism—no multiple inheritance—to build a hierarchy of system objects.

One of Java's primary advantages is that each Java object is a self-contained module. Therefore, every module is inherently reusable. Each module is also extensible, meaning that programmers can add new procedures and new subclasses to any object. With Java, you can also decompose any problem into logical, intuitive, and salient objects. For instance, an "OO" hot rod engine builder would focus mainly on the engine being built and, secondarily, on the tools used to build it. This system could be described from a data standpoint and the defined interfaces, rather than from the point of view imposed by the tools in use.

Java's difficulties are shared with other languages that adhere to the OO paradigm. Although they're well documented in OO theoretical literature, they bear repeating here:

- Substantial message passing can cause high system overhead.

- An OO language may require dynamic method bindings because polymorphism demands multiple definitions of a single operation.

- OO languages have their own design methodology and philosophy—they support multiple active objects rather than sequentially active objects.

Java has the same basic capabilities as C++ but adds the dynamic method resolution features of Objective C to its arsenal.

Java Is Distributed

This characteristic is essential for client/server applications. In fact, it describes the relationship among system objects that may be on local or remote systems. Distribution of information for sharing and collaboration, along with distribution of the processing workload, is typical of client/server applications. In the case of the WWW, it takes advantage of both information sharing and workload distribution. Therefore, Java is designed to facilitate distributed information as well as client/server applications.

Fortunately for Java programmers, a library of TCP/IP procedures has already been developed and is included in the Java source and binary distribution. This makes it easy for programmers to access remote information using protocols like HTTP and FTP.

The characteristic of distributed behavior solves the problems of collaboration and system workload. It's also an integral part of client/server architectures that are distributed by nature.

Java Is Interpreted

"It's a dessert topping and a floor wax!"—first uttered on "Saturday Night Live"—described a consumer product that has a dual purpose. Well, Java is no exception, which is why we introduced Java using these words. Here's why: You compile a Java program into a binary form that is then interpreted by a platform-specific Java runtime environment. Therefore, it's both compiled and interpreted.

What does this buy a developer? Only one source of Java code must be maintained, but the compiled binary will run in all platform-specific Java runtime environments. For example, you could develop and compile a Java program on UNIX and then run the same program on a Mac or PC, as long as each one has a platform-specific Java runtime environment installed. One source, multiple platforms! This allows you to develop applications for the Web faster while pushing the envelopes of functionality and technology. Other developers (like Sun and similar companies) do the hard work of building the runtime environments; you simply write the code that runs in them.

What does an interpreted computer language buy you? It relieves developers from having to worry about the version mismatch problems common to most development environments. By employing the UNIX *make* tool and resolving inconsistent definitions for module interfaces, this approach enables developers to maintain a single source collection of Java code that can easily move to multiple targets!

Java Is Architecture-Neutral

This characteristic of Java is fascinating but not a new concept. Deriving from the nature of the Web—distributed information in a client/server architecture—one important design feature in the Java language is support for clients and servers in heterogeneous network configurations. To make sense of the absolute insanity (or random variability) of the Internet's network configurations, a Java bytecode binary object must execute on many different platforms. The method chosen to realize this aim is an architecture-neutral binary representation for Java programs. Such compiled binary objects can now be executed in any platform-specific Java runtime environments. Here again, Java requires only one source but can reach many target platforms using its architecture-neutral binary executable objects.

Today, WWW software developers usually develop UNIX, then PC, and finally Mac versions of their products. This is not the most productive marketing strategy and imposes an exhausting development lifecycle for such applications. Also, the programming staff must be expert in each platform, resulting in a specialized work force. Many resources must be spent to support each platform, just in the maintenance phase of the software lifecycle. An architecture-neutral format removes this economic drag and allows developers to concentrate on other aspects of development—like functionality and reusability. For an interesting discussion of strategies surrounding multiple-platform development, see Alan Cooper's *About Face: Essentials of User Interface Design* (IDG Books, 1995).

Java Is Portable

Java's architecture-neutral characteristic is a big reason why a Java program is portable. Another aspect of portability deals with the inherent data structures or types in the language, like integer, string, and floating-point data types.

Java takes advantage of the IEEE's standards for many common data types found on many types of computers. For instance, in Java, a "float" type of data structure will always comply with the IEEE 754 standard for floating-point numbers, while an "int" data type is always a signed two's complement 32-bit integer. These aspects of Java differ from other languages such as C++ because the Java bytecode binary has no implementation dependence; hence, it's portable to many different platforms.

Following in the portable footsteps of the Java language, the Java runtime environment is also portable. The Java compiler is written in Java itself, while the runtime environment is written in ANSI C and sports a well-defined and succinct portability interface. The Java language specification indicates that the POSIX standardization effort was a huge influence on its portability interface.

What does portability buy you? Implementing an abstract Java Window class object with its associated methods that will run on a Mac, PC, and UNIX computer goes straight to the bottom line because it completely eliminates redundant implementation, testing, and maintenance efforts.

Java Is Multithreaded

If you have ever participated regularly in a mailing list dedicated to a particular subject, you've probably interjected your two cents' worth in several streams of conversation. Each conversation can be considered a "thread" of discussion. A "multithreaded" discussion describes your simultaneous participation in two or more discussions.

Similarly, the execution of Java bytecode binary objects can consist of multiple threads of execution. These are known as either "execution contexts" or "lightweight processes." C and C++ languages are members of a typical single-threaded execution paradigm, but Java represents a more multifaceted, and therefore more powerful, approach to programming.

It's a fact of life that many things around us happen simultaneously, and may not be represented in a strictly sequential fashion. Multithreading, though sometimes difficult to implement, is a method for implementing the simultaneous execution of multiple threads in parallel.

Java utilizes a complex set of synchronization primitives that were first introduced in 1974 by Anthony C. Hoare in the monitor/condition paradigm within operating system theory. Because of the integration of these primitives, the implementation of multithreading in Java programs is straightforward and considered to be quite robust. According to the Java language specification, much of the multithreading capability may be attributed to the Xerox Cedar/Mesa system.

What else does multithreading buy you? Users realize real-time behavior and superior interactive responsiveness. But the Java language specification is quick to point out that these benefits are limited by the runtime computer platform and by reliance on other platform-specific characteristics. A standalone Java application that has no platform-specific dependencies can exhibit tremendous real-time responsiveness.

Java Is Dynamic

This design characteristic allows Java programs to adapt to changing computing environments. For example, most typical C++ development relies heavily on class libraries that may be owned and developed by other parties. When a class library gets updated, all C++ applications that use that class library must be recompiled, redistributed, and redeployed to all licensed sites. This adds yet another cost to the maintenance phase of a software application's lifecycle.

Java avoids this overhead by delaying the binding of modules. This allows programmers to take complete advantage of OO paradigm concepts. New methods and instance variables for an existing class in a library can be added without the risk of breaking a current program, application, or client. "Plug-and-play" modules are completely realized in Java.

How is this done? In a nutshell, a Java interface specifies inter-object interaction while excluding any instance variables or implementations of methods. A Java class has a runtime representation that allows programmers to query the type of class—this isn't possible in C++—and to dynamically link the class according to the result of the query. These runtime representations also allow the runtime environment to check data structure casts at compile-time as well as at runtime.

What does dynamic execution buy you? In short, it buys you real plug-and-play software modules.

Java Is Robust

The more robust an application, the more reliable it is. This is as desirable to software developers as it is to software consumers. Most OO languages like Java and C++ are strongly typed—this means that most of the data type checking is performed at compile-time rather than at runtime. This avoids and eliminates many errors and errant conditions in applications. Java, unlike C++, requires method procedure declarations that increase the reliability of its resulting applications. Finally, the Java linker repeats all compiler-type check operations to avoid interface and method version inconsistencies.

According to the Java language specification, the most significant difference between C++ and Java is that Java's pointer paradigm does not support pointer arithmetic. Java implements true arrays rather than linked lists of pointers. With true arrays, boundary or subscripting checks can be performed and can guarantee that memory boundaries cannot be violated (which can result in suspect or invalid data). By the same token, memory leaks are completely avoided. This means that Java denies you a mechanism to cast an integer (value) to an integer pointer.

Dynamic languages such as Tcl, Smalltalk, and Lisp are typically considered to be quite robust because programmers need not worry about memory management and memory corruption. Likewise, Java programmers can also deal fearlessly with memory. Plus, many of these languages include garbage collection facilities—another feature that Java has. These capabilities relieve programmers from the sometimes bewildering and awesome responsibilities inherent in memory management.

Such dynamic languages—including Java—are also suitable for rapid application prototyping. Why is this so? For one thing, they don't require developers to make all implementation decisions up-front. Even though Java requires developers to define all interface definitions prior to implementation, the compiler can catch mistakes. This guarantees proper method invocation.

What does robustness buy you? It buys your application increased reliability, a no-memory-leak guarantee, and an assurance of proper method invocations in your Java program. All of these things help to ensure speedy, correct program operation.

Java Is Secure

Since Java is designed to work in networked environments, the design of security features has received lots of attention. Java applications are guaranteed to be tamper-resistant and virus-free because they cannot access system heaps, stacks, or memory. The Java language specification points out that user authentication is implemented with a public-key encryption methodology. This effectively prevents hackers and crackers from examining protected pieces of information, like account names, passwords, and other important identification and access control information.

What does security buy you? Peace of mind and a good night's sleep!

Java Is Simple

One of the main design goals driving Java was the desire to create a language as close to C++ as possible. This has helped ensure Java's rapid acceptance in the OO development world. Another design goal was to eliminate obscure and maligned features of C++ that detract from the language's comprehension and add to the confusion that can sometimes occur during the development, implementation, and maintenance phases of the software lifecycle. These features include overloading operators—that is, operators that have more than one semantic interpretation—support for multiple class inheritance, and automatic coercion of data types. All of these have caused much grief for OO programmers.

When the designers of Java included garbage collection capabilities they were forced to make a tradeoff. They relieved programmers of the burden of memory management but increased the complexity of the Java runtime system. Java's garbage collection facility eases the burden of OO programming and contributes heavily to the reduction of inherent source code bugs.

Finally, Java is simple because it is small. According to the Java language specification, the size of the basic Java interpreter is approximately 40K, excluding the multithread support and standard libraries, which themselves take up another 175K of memory. Even the combination of all these elements—215K of memory—is insignificant when compared to other programming languages and environments.

Here's the infamous "Hello world!" program in Java:

```
class HelloWorld
  static public void main (Strings args[]) {
    System.out.println("Hello world!");
  }
}
```

What does simplicity buy you? Less time in coding and tracking bugs, and more time spent solving problems and satisfying customers. Simplicity also allows Java programs to run on computers that offer only small or primitive memory models (like embedded systems or older computers).

Java Offers High Performance

There are many situations where interpretation of bytecode objects provides acceptable performance. But other sets of circumstances demand higher performance—Java can accommodate these by providing runtime translation of bytecodes into native machine codes.

The design of the bytecode format takes this fact into consideration. The generation of native machine code, according to the Java language specification, is relatively simple so that good machine code is produced. The Java specification claims that the performance that results from translating bytecode to native machine code is comparable to that of C and C++.

What does high performance buy you? It lets you implement your Web applications in Java, resulting in small, fast programs that can significantly extend both client and server capabilities.

LOCATING CGI RESOURCES

For the remainder of this chapter, we'll change focus to discuss what kinds of programming resources are available on the Internet and how to find them.

Given the ever-changing nature of the WWW, it should come as no surprise that the Web is also the right place to look for CGI information, programs, and other related resources. In fact, the Internet contains a plethora of information on CGI and other topics that can add capabilities to your own Web pages. All you need to do is establish the habit of monitoring what's new and interesting in order to keep up with the latest and greatest CGI ideas, tools, and techniques.

Here are a few suggestions for information trolling on the Internet:

- Follow ongoing debates and information exchanges about CGI programming to keep abreast of the hot topics and burning issues. You'll develop a sense of who the real players are, what they're keen on, and the cutting-edge capabilities they discuss, as well as the more mundane—and practical—topics that others may be researching.

- Watch the regular online Question & Answer (Q&A) exchanges for essential clues to the kinds of problems or stumbling blocks that you may eventually encounter in your own CGI programming. Often you'll also gain access to the solutions or workarounds necessary to fix or avoid these potential gotchas without learning about them the hard way!

- Peruse the collections of code, tools, and information available online. You may find ready-to-use versions of programs or routines that you would otherwise have to build from scratch. Why reinvent the wheel when wheels of all kinds and sizes are there for the (re)using?

- Observe the traffic devoted to particular CGI widgets, algorithms, and data-handling problems. You'll be exposed to new programming ideas and approaches to enrich your abilities and the code you write. It'll force you to think about aspects of data structures, parameter passing, and variable manipulations that you might never have considered on your own. In short, exposure to new, innovative methods and ideas will help you to grow as a programmer.

We could go on and on about the joys and beauties of online information mining, but we hope you've gotten the idea by now. Suffice it to say that there's tons of interesting CGI stuff out there, a surprising amount of which can be educational, enlightening, and labor-saving to boot!

Then, too, there are other sources of CGI information besides those that are online. We'll try to make sure you hear about the best of these and that you know where to find current information about the more conventional forms of these sources.

Going Straight to the Internet Sources

The Internet is truly an infinite information resource, so locating the "right stuff" requires a certain amount of savvy. It also requires a tight focus (to avoid the Web's many distractions), a sense of direction (to avoid looking for CGI in all the wrong places), and enough knowledge of how the Internet works to know what kinds of resources are worth investigating further.

In the following sections, we'll lay out a set of Internet resource types. Then we'll discuss each type in detail to get you comfortable enough to do your own investigating after that. Along the way, we'll try to equip you with information on related tools, locations, and techniques for using each type of resource to the max!

Internet Resource Types

In a search for CGI information, specifications, and examples, here's what you're most likely to find:

Focused Newsgroups

Focused newsgroups are groups of interested individuals who congregate around a specific topic on USENET, BITNET, or one of the other regular message exchange areas on the Internet.

Where CGI is concerned, this involves a handful of primarily USENET newsgroups with varying levels of interest in (and coverage of) CGI-specific or related topics, like CGI itself, programming languages used for CGI, Web authoring and programming, and other related areas.

When we cover these newsgroups, we'll also briefly explain the USENET hierarchy and how to go looking for CGI topics.

Focused Mailing Lists

Focused mailing lists originate from targeted mail servers that collect message traffic from active correspondents and then broadcast the accumulated traffic via e-mail to anyone who signs up for the mailing list.

Entering and leaving a mailing list takes a little more effort than subscribing to or leaving a USENET newsgroup, but otherwise these two categories provide the same kind of information: daily message traffic—sometimes quite voluminous—focused on CGI or related topics.

Locating mailing lists can sometimes be tricky. We'll try to give you some pointers to help locate them when we discuss what's available for CGI-related topics.

Information Collections from "Interested Parties"

Sometimes individuals with special interests in a particular area—like CGI—will collect information about their area of concern and publish it in a variety of forms ranging from Web pages to file archives on private or public servers.

While such collections can often be eclectic and idiosyncratic, the best of them can offer outstanding jumping-off points for investigating any particular topic. This is as true for CGI as it is for other topics.

Information from Special Interest Groups

Special interest groups cover a multitude of approaches to their topics: they can be trade or industry organizations, research or standards groups, or even companies involved in particular activities.

Often the groups with vested interests in a technology will provide information on that technology, along with pointers to other sources. This is as true for CGI as it is for other topics, but because these groups are nonpareils of Web and Internet presence, they are often among the best places to start looking.

It's often been said that "It's not *what* you know, it's *who* you know, that counts." When it comes to locating Internet resources, this may sometimes seem more like "*where* you know," but the principle remains pretty much the same. By the time you finish this chapter, our goal is to make sure you've gotten some familiarity with all five W's regarding Internet resources, including *who*, *what*, and *where*, but also *when* and *why*!

Other Sources Worth Investigating

Even though they may not be as dynamic and interactive as online resources, don't overlook the information you can glean from conventional print-based publications. (We know you've got to be somewhat open-minded in this regard because you're reading this book!) We'll do our best to acquaint you with some books, magazines, and publishers to check out in your quest for the latest and greatest CGI information.

In the final analysis of information resources, whether online or otherwise, it all comes back to people. To conclude our review of important CGI resources, we'll also identify some key individuals and groups as sources of further enlightenment when all other avenues dry up.

Please, please, *please*, be humble and courteous when you deal with CGI gurus: Since these people are ultimately the source of all CGI wisdom, it's a good idea to approach them respectfully and circumspectly, and not to demand too much from them. As with successful and knowledgeable people in any niche, they're all very busy and might not be able to drop whatever they're doing just to talk to you. E-mail is a great interactive technique when approaching the great ones because it lets them choose if and when to consider your requests, and how to reply.

For Every Resource Type, There's a Search Method

As we investigate the various sources for CGI information on the Internet (and elsewhere), we'll also try to tell you how to best explore and exploit each resource. For some types this can mean simple searching techniques or access to *pro forma* documents; for other types, you may actually use specialized tools or ask some questions in the right places to help you find where to look for CGI enlightenment.

We hope you'll agree that simply knowing that these types of resources exist is a good thing. We also hope that you'll be able to appreciate the value of the questions and answers, the code fragments and programs, and the other goodies you'll find as you begin to explore them. In the sections that follow we'll treat each type of resource in more detail and provide examples for each one. Once you've finished our coverage, though, we can only suggest that you take the I-way to the destinations of your choice because only you know what you *really* need to know!

CGI-Related Newsgroups

When it comes to dealing with USENET and related collections of newsgroups (like BITNET, IMSI, MAIL, etc.), there's plenty of raw material to be found that sometimes relates to CGI. The secret to locating the right resources is knowing how to cast your net.

To begin with, you'll want to obtain a list of the newsgroups that your Internet Service Provider (ISP) carries. You probably already have access to this list through whatever newsreader you're using, but you can usually get a plain-text version of this list just by asking for it.

The names for USENET and other newsgroups consist of strings of lowercase names separated by periods. For example,

```
comp.infosystems.www.authoring.cgi
```

is a part of the computing infosystems hierarchy on USENET, in the area devoted to WWW topics that are related to authoring. As its name suggests, this newsgroup focuses entirely on CGI-related matters and technologies and is a prime source for CGI-related information.

As it also happens, *comp.infosystems.www.authoring.cgi* is the only newsgroup we found with "cgi" anywhere in its name. But it's not the only newsgroup that covers relevant information, so we'd like to suggest some additional terms to search on when perusing the list of available newsgroups from your ISP:

- "www" will help you locate all the Web-related newsgroups that are available. Our search turned up 24 of them. Not all of these are necessarily focused on, or even related to CGI, but most of them are worth checking out. This is the list we came up with from our own ISP:

```
bit.listserv.www-vm
cern.www.announce
cern.www.talk
comp.infosystems.www
comp.infosystems.www.advocacy
comp.infosystems.www.announce
comp.infosystems.www.authoring.cgi
comp.infosystems.www.authoring.html
comp.infosystems.www.authoring.images
comp.infosystems.www.authoring.misc
comp.infosystems.www.browsers.mac
comp.infosystems.www.browsers.misc
comp.infosystems.www.browsers.ms-windows
comp.infosystems.www.misc
comp.infosystems.www.providers
comp.infosystems.www.providers
comp.infosystems.www.servers.mac
comp.infosystems.www.servers.misc
comp.infosystems.www.servers.unix
comp.infosystems.www.users
comp.os.os2.networking.www
imsi.mail.www-talk
list.www-de
mail.www
```

From experience we know that the groups most worth following belong to the *comp.infosystems.www.authoring* hierarchy, since that's the collection of newsgroups devoted to constructing Web pages, programs, and more. For those of you with interests in particular platforms—like Macintosh, Windows, or UNIX—the newsgroups that cover the intersection of the Web and these platforms will be helpful, if only as a source of pointers to where the real stuff is. As for the rest, the only way to find out if they're worthwhile to you is to drop in and see!

- Another USENET hierarchy worth watching falls within the *comp.lang* newsgroups, which are devoted to particular computer languages. We've found useful CGI scripts in the following newsgroups:

```
comp.lang.c
comp.lang.c++
comp.lang.perl
comp.lang.perl.misc
comp.lang.python
```

but you should consider following whatever languages you use to build your CGI programs, as a source of inspiration, information, and code fragments galore!

One last recommendation for the USENET newsgroup hierarchy is to keep tabs on *news.announce.newusers*; that's the group where new newsgroups are announced, and it's worth polling at least once a month to see if any new CGI groups have popped up.

CGI-Related Mailing Lists

The thing about Internet mailing lists is that you'll hear about them only in the most off-handed ways. Even our favorite search engines (see the section entitled "Searching for Satisfaction" at the end of this chapter) turned up very little information on CGI-related mailing lists.

Yet when we started reading the USENET and other newsgroups and following particular conversations, we quickly learned about a handful of such lists. Keeping an ear to the groundswell of information about CGI appears to offer your best hope for locating a CGI-related list that's right for your needs.

Here's what we came up with:

- *cgi-pm@webstorm.com*
  type: Majordomo
  This list covers lots of interesting CGI issues and regularly features interesting code samples and example programs. Old threads are archived at the following URL:

```
http://www.webstorm.com/local/cgi-perl/
```

To subscribe to this mailing list, send an e-mail to the address on the first line, with the word "subscribe" as the message body. If your mailing insists on attaching a ".sig" (signature) file at the end of your messages, follow the word "subscribe" with the word "end" on the next line. Thus, the body of your message would look like this:

```
subscribe
end
```

■ *webedge-talk@webedge.com*
type: Majordomo
This list springs from the WebEdge Technology Conference, hosted twice a year, that brings Apple-focused Web developers together. This particular list covers many CGI-related topics, but primarily those focused on AppleScript, Apple's scripting language for use on the MacHTTPd software. The URL for Webedge is:

```
http://www.webedge.com/
```

To subscribe to this mailing list, send an e-mail to the address on the first line, with the words "subscribe webedge-talk" as the message body. If your mailing insists on attaching a ".sig" (signature) file at the end of your messages, follow the word "subscribe" with the word "end" on the next line. Thus, the body of your message would look like this:

```
subscribe webedge-talk
end
```

If you're a budding or current Mac WebMaster, you'll find this list fascinating.

When reading mailing lists, as with USENET newsgroups, you have to be willing to overcome what's called the "signal to noise" ratio: that is, the ratio of helpful, interesting, or informative messages to irrelevant and useless ones. Only you can decide if it's worth the effort, but be aware that for some of these lists or groups the noise can sometimes be deafening!

Parties Interested in CGI

As you read through the newsgroups and mailing lists, you'll begin to notice that certain people are very active in these areas. You'll also come to appreciate that some of them are witty and knowledgeable, and that a few will offer gems of wisdom or programming expertise that leave you thoroughly bedazzled.

When you find somebody who proves him- or herself to be worth listening to about CGI, try to see if they've got a personal Web page or hotlist that you might be able to use. You can look for URLs in their ".sig" files (often a dead giveaway), or use the UNIX *finger* command to see if they've published any URLs in their personal profiles. These individual resources can often be very useful, especially if the person's interests or expertise overlaps substantially with your own.

If you see that someone is conversant on a particular topic that catches your fancy or might help you solve a problem but they don't publish a URL, send them an e-mail asking for more information. Be sure to ask them if they know of any good Web resources, mailing lists, or file archives with information on the subject. This kind of direct inquiry can also turn up resources that you might never have known existed.

Just remember that while it never hurts to ask for help or information, it's always a good idea to ask politely. E-mail is a very good way to get (and give) information, but don't expect instant or incredibly detailed responses. It's an unwritten but powerful rule on the Internet that you shouldn't demand any more from others than you are willing to give in return (a digital version of the Golden Rule, as it were). Be nice, be terse, and be patient, and you'll probably get all the help you can stand!

Here's another point worth mentioning, "Try it before you ask about it." You're much more likely to get a helpful response if you say, "I've tried the following strategies to do X, but none seem to work properly. Can you suggest where I might look to develop an alternate strategy?"

CGI-Focused Groups and Organizations

When it comes to dealing with CGI, there are certain groups that naturally spring to mind. All of these organizations have a more than casual interest in the technology; some have an interest in CGI that could accurately be called proprietary. Who do we mean?

This list includes organizations responsible for the CGI specification, who actually implement CGI for their HTTP servers, or who use CGI as routine elements of their professional activities. To be more specific, Table 2-1 lists some of these organizations, with their URLs.

Table 2-1
CGI-focused organizations

Organization	Who are these guys?	URL
World Wide Web Consortium (W3C)	Joint venture between CERN, MIT, and others to manage the WWW.	http://www.w3.org/ hypertext/WWW/Daemon/ User_3.0/CGI/ Overview.html
National Center for Supercomputing Applications (NCSA)	Developer of MOSAIC Web browser and another key *httpd* implementation.	http://hoohoo.ncsa. uiuc.edu/cgi/ Overview.html
WWW Virtual Library (a W3C project); be SURE to use their built-in search engine on "CGI"	Comprehensive catalog of online info; URL is for the Web Developer's Library.	http://www.stars.com/
Enterprise Integration Technologies (EIT); be sure to check out their "WebMaster's Starter Kit"	A Stanford spin-off; tools for installing and maintaining Web services.	http://wsk.eit.com/wsk /doc/

Each of these URLs is a treasure-trove of CGI information that can lead you to other sources as well. The only way to find out what they have to offer is to spend some time surfing—not such a bad assignment!

This is by no means an exhaustive list of possible organizations either: we'd also recommend that you check out the home pages for browser vendors like Netscape Communications Corporation.

CGI-Related Publications and Off-Line Resources

At present, we're not aware of any books that specifically target CGI programming (but since we're writing one, we figure others are working in the same area). However, there are lots of good resources worth checking out.

For one thing, most Web- and HTML-focused books cover CGI at some level of detail. For another, most of them point to a variety of useful resources.

We've found the following books to be particularly useful:

- Mary E. Morris: *HTML for Fun and Profit*; Prentice-Hall, Upper Saddle River, NJ, 1995. (List Price $35.95; ISBN 0-13-359290-1.) Some of the best coverage on CGI tools and techniques we've seen anywhere.

- Ed Tittel, Mark Gaither, Sebastian Hassinger, and Mike Erwin: *Foundations of WWW Programming, with HTML and CGI*; IDG Books Worldwide, Indianapolis, IN, 1995. (List Price: $39.99; ISBN 1-56884-703-3.) Includes detailed coverage of CGI fundamentals with tools and techniques for a broad range of CGI programs.

- Laura LeMay: *MORE Teach Yourself Web Publishing with HTML in a Week*; SAMS Publishing, Indianapolis, IN, 1995. (List Price: $25.00; ISBN1-57521-005-3.) Includes coverage of CGI and related terminology, with several interesting sample programs.

- Randall Schwartz (foreword by Larry Wall): *Learning Perl*; O'Reilly & Associates, Inc., Sebastopol, CA, First Edition, 1993. (List Price: $24.95; ISBN: 1-56592-042-2.) *A Nutshell Handbook*, this step-by-step, hands-on tutorial is designed to get you writing useful Perl scripts as quickly as possible.

Don't forget that there are also plenty of magazines that cover the Internet (some, more or less exclusively). We've found the following ones to be particularly informative:

- *Internet World*
  A monthly publication aimed specifically at Internet topics and technology, so new Web-related announcements proliferate here. Send inquiries via e-mail to info@mecklermedia.com or call 203-226-6967. Address: 20 Ketchum Street, Westport, CT, 06880.

- *IWAY*
  A bimonthly, hands-on publication aimed at the Internet, with coverage for beginning to intermediate users trying to master related tools and technologies. Send your queries via e-mail to editors@iway.mv.com or call 603-924-9334. Address: 80 Elm Street, Peterborough, NH, 03458.

- *NetGuide*
  An online services magazine that covers all of the major online information services by category and includes occasional coverage of programming topics. Submit queries via e-mail to netmail@netguide.cmp.com or call 526-562-5000. Address: 600 Community Drive, Manhasset, NY, 11030.

- *WebWEEK*
  Subtitled "The Newspaper of Web Technology and Business Strategy," this magazine is published monthly despite its name. It provides the most detailed coverage of the companies doing Web-related business and, consequently, provides excellent coverage on the burgeoning crop of commercial Website, CGI, and related applications development and management utilities. Free to qualified subscribers, send queries to customer-service@webweek.com, or call 708-564-1385 (Western Hemisphere only). Address: Mecklermedia Corporation, 20 Ketchum Street, Westport, CT, 06880.

- *Wired*
  This is the trendiest and most fashionable of the online coverage magazines. Chances are that CGI-related information will only appear if it's something catchy or outrageous. Submit queries via e-mail to editor@wired.com or fax to 415-222-6249. Address: 520 Third Street, San Francisco, CA, 94107.

We can't say that you'll walk away from any of these sources completely enlightened about CGI, but we've found all of them to contain occasional nuggets of useful information. When it comes to the magazines, maybe you could borrow someone else's copies or buy single issues from a newsstand, before plunking down your hard-earned cash for a subscription!

Searching for Satisfaction

Using the right tools makes researching the Web much simpler. There is a class of software tools called *search engines* that can examine huge amounts of information to help you locate Web sites of potential interest. Here's how most of them work:

- Somewhere in the background, laboring in patient anonymity, you'll find automated Web-traversing programs, often called *robots* or *spiders*, that do nothing but follow link after link around the Web *ad infinitum*. Each time they get to a new Web document, they peruse and catalog its contents, storing the information for transmission to a database elsewhere on the Web.

- At regular intervals these automated information gatherers transmit their recent acquisitions to a parent database, where the information is sifted, categorized, and stored.

- When you run a search engine, you're actually searching the database that's been compiled and managed through the initial efforts of the robots and spiders, but which is handled by a fully functional database management system that communicates with the CGI program for your search form.

- Using the keywords or search terms you provide to the form, the database locates "hits" (exact matches) and also "near-hits" (matches with less than the full set of terms supplied, or based on educated guesses about what you're really trying to locate).

- The hits are returned to the CGI program by the database, where they are transformed into a Web document to return the results of the search for your perusal.

If you're lucky, all this activity will produce references to some materials that you can actually use!

We'd like to share some pointers to our favorite search engines with you, which you'll find in Table 2-2. This is not an exhaustive catalog of such tools, but all of them will produce interesting results if you use "CGI" or "CGI scripts" as search input.

Table 2-2

Web search engines

Search engine name & info	URL:
Excite Corporation's Excite search engine	http://www.excite.com
Infoseek Available through Netscape Navigator	http://www.infoseek.com
Lycos Carnegie-Mellon engine	http://lycos.cs.cmu.edu

(Continued)

Table 2-2

W3 Consortium Virtual Library W3 Consortium outsourced project	http://www.stars.com
Wandex MIT spinoff's engine	http://www.netgen.com/cgi/wandex
WebCrawler University of Washington engine	http://webcrawler.cs.washington.edu/ WebCrawler/WebQuery.html
World Wide Web Worm (WWWW) University of Colorado engine	http://www.cs.colorado.edu:80/ home/mcbryan/WWWW.html
Yahoo	http://www.yahoo.com

When you're using these search tools, the most important thing to remember is that the more specific you can make your search request, the more relevant the results. Thus, if you're looking for CGI program listings, you might try using "CGI program listings" or "CGI scripts" as your search terms instead of simply "CGI." While you may get plenty of nothing when using search terms that are too specific, that's better than looking through a plenitude of irrelevant materials when nothing is all that's in there!

SUMMARY

Choosing a programming language for your CGI applications should not be done lightly. You'll want to carefully consider the amount of available public source code, the support available for the language, your level of knowledge of its programming paradigm, its data-handling abilities, and its extensibility, modularity, usability, and the reusability of its software components. You'll also want to consider its special facilities for data representation (like VRML and 3-D objects) or for Web-based interactivity (like Java or JavaScript). Once you've considered these factors, as we discussed in the first half of this chapter, selecting a language should be simple.

When it comes to finding information about Web-related stuff, whether to help you select a language or to find tools for the language you've chosen, the Web's a good place to look! But there are other valuable sources of information available, too, both on and off the Internet. In the second half of this chapter, you've learned where to look for Web and CGI programming information and how to make an effective information search. Hopefully this will stand you in good stead when you go out looking for the "ultimate widget." In the next chapter, we'll help you get a leg up on building HTML documents within your CGI programs, as you take a look at some snazzy CGI return-page templates.

WHAT'S THE PROBLEM?
(THE CASE FOR AN HTML AND CGI FORM GENERATOR)

3

When talking to people who are creating their own HTML pages, we often hear the same thing: "I was surprised at how easy it is!" They're correct. HTML is, after all, a *markup* language for plain text, with a few simple syntax rules and markup commands. Contrast this to C, with its many logical and syntactical rules and huge number of functions, and it's easy to see why someone would say HTML is easy. While a first-timer can learn basic HTML merely by looking at someone else's page, you can't do the same with C code without prior programming experience.

It's not HTML itself that's hard—it's doing something creative with it that's challenging. HTML is like a set of colored pencils. In an artist's hand, these simple tools can be used to create beautiful, useful illustrations. In unskilled hands, however, they can be used only to write grocery lists or to create ugly-but-colorful designs.

None of us likes to hear that our job is easy, but for many Web developers, this statement brings smiles to their faces. The tools (e.g., books and HTML authoring programs) that assist users with HTML and CGIs are written by Web developers such as ourselves. We're always glad to know that we can help make Web development smoother, so that others can join in the fun!

The Monotony of HTML Forms Programming

Programming HTML forms by hand is certainly simple enough when you're dealing with only a half-dozen pages or so. But when you're programming for a site with lots of pages, or several different sites, it can get tedious. How many times do you want to have to fill in the values for your checkboxes? How many pages do you want to break by forgetting to close your angle brackets?

You Have Your Form, Now What?

Forms are becoming more and more popular on the Web. They provide an interface for user feedback, database queries, and online commerce. At the back-end of these forms you'll find the CGI programs that actually do the work of mailing the feedback, interfacing to the database, or processing the order.

Creating a CGI script usually requires some preparatory work, such as a routine to parse the form data, to place the input values into variables your program can work with later on. Even these basic tasks can be intimidating to neophytes, and boring for advanced programmers.

Alleviating the monotony of HTML forms programming and the difficulty of creating a CGI application that uses the form is what this book is all about. In fact, we want to give you a tool to help automate the task of handling forms data, either to ease newbies into CGI programming or to alleviate the boredom for the old-timers. To make a case for our Tool, we'll explore current HTML and CGI programming options to see what they're lacking.

HTML Programming Methods

HTML editing ranges from a painful manual process to drag-and-drop creation. We'll go over each of these approaches and discuss their limitations.

HTML Editing by Hand

Editing HTML by hand means that you use a word processing application or text editor to create pages from scratch. The benefit of editing HTML by hand is that it can be done anywhere, without the benefit of a special tool that you have to learn to use. However, there are some problems with editing by hand:

1. It requires that you know (or learn) the syntax of the HTML commands.

2. If you're not editing directly on the system you're publishing on, you need to somehow get the file to that site.

3. It does nothing to alleviate tedium.

4. If you're working for other people on their system, you might get stuck with an editor you don't like.

5. When using a text editor, you have to remember to save the document in plain text format. There's no built-in interface between the editor and an HTML browser. (Though it's quite simple to keep a browser going in another window.)

6. No automatic error checking is available.

If you're working with a small site (your personal home page, for instance), editing by hand may be fine for you. For anything larger, however, you'll probably want to explore other options, and that's what we'll do next.

Text Editor Converters, Templates, and Extensions

Many computer users already have a favorite text editor and find it easy to use. It's only natural that some of these applications would be extended to HTML creation. We'll discuss a few of these options here, but you can probably find something for your preferred editor in Yahoo's list of HTML editors:

```
http://www.yahoo.com/Computers_and_Internet/Internet/
World_Wide_Web/HTML_Editors/
```

Before we look at some of the possibilities, we'd like to share a caveat regarding word processor extensions for HTML. That is, most word processors are "page oriented," which leads them to be quite unsuited for authoring output for a page*less* environment like the Web. This includes serious text-handling tools like Framemaker, which we love for page layout and word processing for paper-based output, but which can't handle online authoring very well. Likewise, even MS Word is so page-oriented that using it for online authoring almost inevitably results in placing artificial restrictions on your output. Such tools are OK as a starting place, or as a way to get your initial text content online, but not as an overall, integrated authoring tool for the Web.

Internet Assistant for Microsoft Word 6.0 for Windows

As part of its Internet offerings, Microsoft introduced its *Internet Assistant* for Microsoft Word 6.0 for Windows. It's much more than just a template offering a few HTML commands; Internet Assistant is actually a Word tool (like the Spelling Checker or Thesaurus) that extends the program's core functionality. There's a version 1.0 for Windows 3.1, and version 2.0 for Windows NT and Windows 95.

The Internet Assistant gives users shortcuts for programming in HTML. Unfortunately it's only HTML 2.0 compliant at this time, so you're limited in the tags you can use. Another feature is that it lets you use Word as an HTML browser, even over the Internet. So now you can create Web documents and browse them with the same application. Again, however, the HTML 2.0 limitation applies, so there are scores of documents out there that aren't going to look very good through this particular window onto the Web.

The Internet Assistant is freely distributed by Microsoft at the following URL:

```
http://www.microsoft.com/msoffice/freestuf/msword/download/ia/
default.htm
```

WordPerfect 6.1 Internet Publisher for Windows

Novell has also entered Web publishing with the WordPerfect 6.1 *Internet Publisher* for Windows. Like Microsoft's offering, Internet Publisher extends WordPerfect with a variety of tools and templates for HTML document design. It even guides you through the process of creating your first HTML document.

Internet Publisher is HTML 2.0 compatible but also includes some of the Netscape extensions. Rather than attempting to make WordPerfect into a browser, as Microsoft has with Word, Novell includes Netscape Navigator as part of the Internet Publisher package.

As with the Internet Assistant, the Internet Publisher is freely distributed on Novell's Web site:

```
http://wp.novell.com/elecpub/inttoc.htm
```

The Ant HTML Tools for Word 6.0

You may have noticed that both of the preceding tools are available only for the Windows versions of their respective applications and that neither tool's creator has announced plans to extend them to other platforms. The *Ant HTML Tools* for Word 6.0 is a Word document template that works on all versions of Windows *or* Mac versions of Word 6.0 or higher.

The Ant has toolbars that you use to apply the various HTML styles to your document. The entire document (with the exception of forms) is in a quasi-WYSIWYG format. To check your work, though, you'll still need to use an external browser.

Ant Tools include modules to help you with forms, tables, and practically any other HTML 2.0 or 3.0 feature. Figure 3-1 shows you the layout of the toolbars, as well as the form creation tool.

The Ant Tools are the independent creation of Jim Swift. A free demo version is available on the Internet but to keep it, the registration fee is $39. For more information see:

```
http://mcia.com/ant/
```

Limitations and Benefits of Extensions, Templates, and Converters

The nice thing about tools that work with your word processing application or text editor is that you're already familiar with the operation of the application, and these tools just increase its functionality. Here's a summary of the benefits:

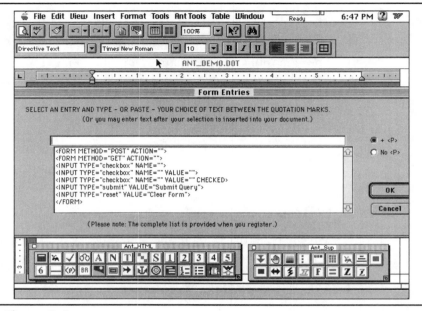

Figure 3-1
The Ant tools for Word 6.0, focusing on the toolbars and Form Generation tool.

1. They run as an add-on to your preferred word processing or text editing application, so you're already familiar with the operation.

2. They make the conversion of existing documents into HTML easier.

3. They reduce the number of applications needed for Web development.

However, there are several things that these tools don't provide, and many are features we would want in a form generator:

1. They are specific to the application and sometimes machine specific, which decreases their portability.

2. They are limited to a certain HTML specification and often cannot be changed by the user.

3. You still need to upload or copy the final document to your Web server when you're finished.

4. Their WYSIWYG capabilities don't always provide a good example of what the document will actually look like on a browser when being accessed on a server.

Despite their power and usability, such tools are much better for creating the textual portions of HTML documents, rather than dealing well with forms, image maps, or other more complex elements.

HTML Editing Applications

While text editor tools are handy, there are also several applications specifically designed for HTML editing. These tools either provide a quasi-WYSIWYG interface that hides or beautifies some of the tags for you, or full WYSIWYG, with drag-and-drop capabilities that continuously display your page as it would look through an HTML browser.

HoTMetaL Pro

HoTMetaL is one of the oldest HTML editors. It has been around for quite some time as shareware on UNIX and Windows systems. It's now available on Windows, Mac, and UNIX and comes in both an unsupported freeware version as HoTMetaL Free and a supported commercial version as HoTMetaL Pro.

Version 2.0 of HoTMetaL is compatible with HTML 3.0 and most Netscape extensions. It has a multitude of toolbars and menus to assist in HTML programming (see Figure 3-2). It displays the document in quasi-WYSIWYG form that uses its own, cleaner tag style rather than the standard HTML angle-bracket delimiters. For viewing the pages in final form, however, this means you'll need an external browser.

One annoying thing about HoTMetaL is that it insists on strict "rules" checking and enforces those restrictions even with "rules checking" turned off. This means that it will refuse to even load a file that it doesn't consider valid HTML.

HoTMetaL Free is available from SoftQuad at:

```
http://www.sq.com/products/hotmetal/hmp-org.htm
```

The commercial version costs $59 and can be ordered through the same URL.

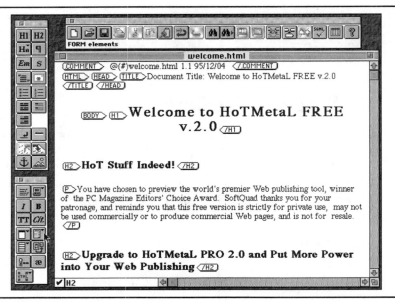

■ **Figure 3-2**
■ *HoTMetaL Free has a multitude of toolbars to assist with HTML programming.*

Adobe PageMill

Adobe *PageMill* is the first true WYSIWYG and drag-and-drop HTML development tool. It allows you to edit an HTML document inline, exactly as it would appear on a browser—you'll never need to see the HTML code. To add a style to text, use a toolbar, as you would in a word processor. To add a graphic, simply drag it from your hard drive onto the page.

The same applies to HTML forms: You can drag radio buttons, checkboxes, text input fields, and other form elements directly onto the page and edit them there. This makes form creation even simpler than with a dialog box as with HoTMetaL. Figure 3-3 shows you an example of the page previewer for PageMill.

As with anything else that's made easier for you, you give up some control with PageMill. You're limited to working with the program's built-in set of HTML commands because it performs error checking as you enter data. If you're ready to support some browser-specific extension that PageMill doesn't support, then you'll have to work that material in outside this program.

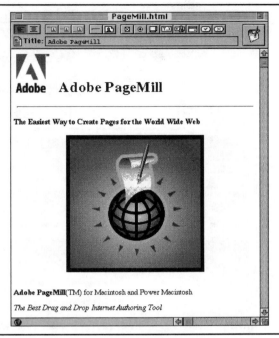

Figure 3-3
Adobe PageMill's page previewer makes page creation easy with drag and drop.

PageMill is currently available only for the Mac, but a Windows version is coming soon (and may already be available by the time you read this). Both versions are commercial software from Adobe, and there's no demo or free, unsupported version available. The cost is $99. For more information on PageMill, visit Adobe at:

```
http://www.adobe.com/Apps/PageMill/
```

BIprotocol Page EDitor (BIPED)

BIPED is a CGI-based HTML editor that lets you see your page while you work on it exactly as it will appear on the Web. To accomplish this, it uses HTML 3.0 tables to format a "split screen" view of both the editable HTML window and the HTTP output. You can see this in Figure 3-4.

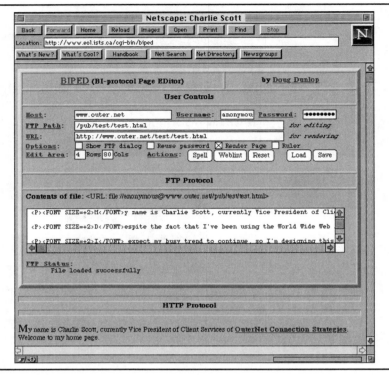

Figure 3-4
A view of BIPED's "split screen" HTML editing.

To create or edit an HTML document on a server, you run the BIPED CGI and tell it the server, path, and filename for the document you want to create (the document doesn't necessarily have to be on the server BIPED is running on). You must also enter your username and password for the server the document will be housed on.

BIPED then opens up an FTP session to that server and looks for the file you want to edit. If it doesn't see it, then it assumes that you want to create it. If the document is available, it will also display the HTTP output of the page, so you can see what it actually looks like on the Web. You then create or edit your HTML document in the editing window. When you're ready to upload it, tell BIPED to save the document. It will open up another FTP session to the server and save the new document, showing you what the new version looks like on the Web in the HTTP window.

BIPED will NOT work with many firewall systems if you're doing your work outside the firewall boundary. As consultants, we work at home a lot, which means that to do something like this, we must dial through or *telnet* through the client's corporate firewall (the only two permitted methods of access for most firewalls). Sadly, this means we can't use this tool because it can't handle the firewall login through which we must access corporate systems. ▲

The fact that you can see the results of your editing immediately in the HTTP window, and that the output is true to what it will look like to other Web users, makes BIPED truly WYSIWYG. The problem with BIPED is that all the editing is done within an HTML form <TEXTAREA> space, and there are no easy tools provided for generating HTML, so use this HTML editor with caution. But BIPED also includes links to a spelling checker and an HTML validation service, to make sure what you've entered is correct.

BIPED is a Perl 5 CGI written by Doug Dunlop. Its current incarnation is UNIX-specific, though it can probably be ported to other systems. Plus, even though you may need a UNIX system to run it, your server can be any type of Web server that's running FTP and HTTP services. BIPED is also freely distributed and is available from Doug Dunlop at:

```
http://www.eol.ists.ca/~dunlop/biped/
```

HotDog and HotDog Pro

HotDog, from Sausage Software in Australia, has an MS Word-like interface, so it's extremely easy to learn. Using toolbars, you select for example, that you want to insert an image in your document. You get a dialog box that talks you through all the information you need to provide about the image, giving you the option of specifying a remote URL for it or browsing through your hard drive to find the right one.

Tables are created by simply telling HotDog that you want 2 cols, 3 rows, with 1 header row and 1 header column, borders on, etc., by checking options in a dialog box—as you check options, a preview shows you what that selection will do to the table you're designing. When you've got it the way you want it, you click OK, then type the contents of each cell.

There are two ways to enable WYSIWYG in HotDog. It has a built-in "real-time HTML previewer" that splits the screen vertically—as you type or edit in the top window, your changes are displayed in a standard Web browser interface in the bottom window. (Standard HTML up through 3.0 there.) You can also simply tell HotDog where to find the browser or browsers of your choice on your system, and then be able to click on the

Preview button at any time, and have the file displayed in the browser of your choice (you don't have to be on a server to do this, as it uses the local file option). You needn't save the file to do this, so it's great for what-if experimentation.

HotDog currently actively supports all the HTML tags, through 3.0, plus the Netscape extensions and the Microsoft Network extensions. However, if you want to use extensions that aren't actively supported, you can simply use them— you'll see them in the preview browser if it supports those extensions, or they'll be saved in the final file. When you use HotDog's HTML checker, it will highlight them as non-standard but won't force you to do anything with them. You can also add your own tags through a Create New Tag menu, which lets you extend it for whatever tags you want.

Another great benefit is that it lets you create templates simply and easily. If you have an HTML file that reflects a design you want to use repeatedly, you can click on the option "make template from file" and it will prompt you for a name. The next time you choose File—>New, that template is on the list for your use.

When saving files, you can choose from a wide variety of formats, including plain ASCII, HTML 2, HTML 3, UNIX HTML, etc.

HotDog is currently available for Windows, with a Mac and UNIX version soon to follow. Visit the Sausage site for a free 30-day evaluation and pricing information on the Pro version:

```
http://www.sausage.com
```

Benefits and Limitations of HTML Editing Applications

Of course, the main benefits of HTML editing applications is the user interface. These programs were designed to make HTML programming easier and do this in a variety of ways:

1. The GUI, with toolbars and pull-down menus for HTML styles, makes programming easier. BIPED is the only exception.

2. Syntax check keeps you from making mistakes.

Many of the problems with HTML editing applications are the same as for word processing and text editing tools. Many of these will be overcome in our form generator (albeit only for special-purpose use):

1. Some of these tools are machine-specific, and the formats they use are not portable between each other. This makes it more difficult to work on a variety of machines.
2. They may be limited to a certain HTML feature set, and users cannot add their own browser-specific tags.
3. With the exception of BIPED, you'll need to upload or copy your final document to the server. This adds an extra step.
4. With the exception of BIPED and HotDog, the internal browser view, the WYSIWYG view, or the external browser view that most of these apps include will not give you a good idea of what the final document will look like being viewed from a server with a Web browser.

WHAT ABOUT CGIs?

What all of these HTML programming methods lack are easy ways to integrate your forms with CGI programs. This is a subject that many do not want to tackle yet, mostly because there are several possible languages that CGIs can be written in, such as Perl, C, and Visual BASIC. Since we've already settled on Perl as our CGI language because of its portability, we'll focus on that particular language to the exclusion of the others (for more information on our development environment, please read Chapter 9).

Lack of Third-Party CGI Development Tools

There is only a smattering of third-party CGI development tools, and most of these can't really be called "tools" at all. What you'll usually see are libraries that can assist you in getting through the more complex CGI functions, but nothing that actually implements and improves your development environment. The one exception to this that we're aware of comes from Spider Technologies.

Spider Technologies

Spider Technologies has created a CGI development system specifically for SQL database systems. Their product is called *Spider 1.5* and makes HTML and CGI database programming into a drag-and-drop process. Here is the process as Spider describes it:

1. Open an HTML file in the HTML viewer. This file can be created ahead of time in an HTML editor, or can be a file that is dynamically generated from the database by another application file.

2. Select the action on the database: Query, Insert, Update, Delete, Stored Procedure.

3. Define the SQL statement in the SQL editor. The SQL editor supports multiple clauses and table joins.

4. Define output, by dragging columns or tables from the output fields list.

5. Customize output, error handling, and security restrictions.

6. Save the file. In deployment, the Spider deployment module will dynamically generate the SQL as input to the database and HTML as output to the browser.

Of course, Spider is *only* usable with SQL database systems and cannot be used to generate other types of CGIs.

Spider can be run on UNIX systems such as Solaris, IRIX, and HP-UX (an NT version is under development and should be ready by mid-1996) and can be used with any Web server that can use CGIs. It does, however, have several features that integrate nicely with the Netscape server APIs. Spider is also compatible with the more popular UNIX database systems, including Informix, Sybase, and Oracle.

You can download a free 30-day evaluation copy of Spider. To purchase it, you need to contact Spider Technologies to get a price quote. More information about Spider and Spider Technologies can be found at:

```
http://www.w3spider.com/website/product.html
```

What's in Store?

CGI development tools are probably just around the bend. As CGI programming becomes more object-oriented, so will the development applications. In the near future, we'll probably see CGI development aids from Microsoft for Visual BASIC. Sun, of course, will continue with its Java efforts, now with the assistance of Netscape.

In addition, IBM has already announced that it wants its *VisualAge* object-oriented development environment to be the Web programming platform of the future. We'll no doubt see many more exciting Web development and CGI integration utilities for every imaginable programming language, Computer Added Software Engineering (CASE) tool, and code editor by the end of this decade.

Our HTML and CGI Form Generation Tool

We've learned that Web development isn't always easy. We've also seen that current development applications don't assuage the more cumbersome and confusing aspects of Web development, such as CGIs. Based on our survey of HTML and CGI development tools, we've come up with a wish-list of abilities for inclusion in our Form Generation Tool.

It Creates HTML Forms and CGIs to Serve Them

This is what none of the other development tools can do. We can either make a standalone HTML form or embed that form in a Perl CGI that can also be extended as the back-end to the form. The CGI in which we place the form already has the HTML and form-parsing code in place, which ends up saving us considerable time when programming a CGI to handle the form. Having both the form and the code that handles it in one script is also very convenient for moving or changing the form.

Programmatic Creation

That is, our HTML and CGI code is created by our Tool. This gives it a consistent look-and-feel and helps us avoid coding errors. It also saves us a considerable amount of time in coding the essentials and niceties of the form or CGI, such as comments or HTML tag values.

Quick Programming of Popular Tags

Our Tool includes "dialog pages" that assist the user in setting up tags. Tags for HTML elements will include: Bold, Line Breaks, Italics, Horizontal Rules, Title, Comments, Anchors, and Headers. Form elements will include: Text Input, Password Input, Text Area, Radio Buttons, Checkboxes, and Submit Buttons.

Easy to Get Forms or Scripts onto the Server

We've seen that only BIPED truly makes uploading and downloading a form seamless to the user. With our Tool, we'll use a similar technique. We'll allow the user to copy the form or script *directly* into its final destination directory. Alternatively, they can download the script via FTP, or send it to themselves using Internet mail. We can also extend it to use practically any Internet communication channel available, including FTPing it to other servers, like BIPED. However, unlike BIPED, our Tool works through firewalls.

View the Form from a Server with a Standard Browser

As with BIPED, we'll want to be able to see our HTML form as it would appear from a server, using an HTML 3.0 compliant browser. As we've seen, most WYSIWYG HTML editors don't truly preview a form—they perform their own special decoding of the HTML styles. Even when using a browser to preview, the form is read locally, not served off a server, which means that the back-end processing of the form is not functional.

Our Tool's preview presents a more realistic view of the form on a server. This shortens development time because less jumping around among applications is required when creating the form or when tweaking it to make it look "just right."

Highly and Easily Extensible Feature Set

We've chosen to write our Tool in Perl to make it simple to update and enhance. As you'll see, the Tool's HTML and CGI generation structure is modular, so it's easy to add features. If you want to support a new Netscape extension, just edit the Tool's code and add a routine for that tag. This makes it much more open-ended than most of the word processing tools or HTML editing applications, which are limited to the HTML specification(s) that their developers support.

Provides for HTML Validation

Like many HTML development tools, we provide a way to validate our HTML by making our Tool parse the code it has written. This prevents mistakes such as nesting a form within a form.

Being on the Web Makes the Tool Portable

Since the Tool itself is a Web CGI that uses an HTML form, it can be operated from any Web browser from any machine with access to the server over a local network or the greater Internet. "Wherever you are, there it is." But if the server on which the Tool resides is within a firewall, you could have problems. You should make sure your setup enables SLIP/PPP access through the firewall, which often requires some specialized setup of the firewall itself, as well as (usually) some specialized WinSock or other communications setup to tell the browser what's happening.

Web-Based Access Means It Can Be Centralized

Many companies allow their employees to put up home pages on their servers. They do, of course, want to make it easy for them to do this, while also making sure everything is kept secure and that resources can still be effectively managed.

Our Tool lends itself to this kind of outlook: Because it's centralized, you can limit access to who uses it and set parameters on what they're allowed to create. You can also set it up to prevent users from placing their pages anywhere except in a specified, managed location. This prevents them from putting information in a potentially dangerous area, or from using up valuable disk space on your server.

SUMMARY

As we've seen, Web development isn't necessarily as easy as it seems. We've also seen that there are very few comprehensive tools out there. Many perform HTML development, but they're limited in their feature set and have no facilities to ease integration with CGIs. Tools that perform CGI development are slow in coming and right now are highly application-specific. Thus we can see the need for a tool that can generate both HTML forms and the basic CGI applications needed to handle those forms.

Here, we've also covered a list of features that can make our Tool user friendly, highly extensible, and accessible from any platform. Now that we see the need for such a tool, and know what we want, let's get on with its development!

DESIGNING AN HTML FORM GENERATOR

*I*n Chapter 3, we introduced the concept of an HTML Form Generator—an interface that enables users who lack an in-depth knowledge of HTML and CGI to quickly and easily create workable forms. Here, we'll move to the next step in turning that concept into a reality as we now turn to the design phase of the project. We examine the entire process of taking an idea for an application from a "wish list" to an algorithm from which we can begin coding. We start with a brainstorming session that expands the initial concepts into a list of desirable functions. From this list we'll winnow out the less feasible ideas and consider the criteria used to make our decisions. Finally, we'll begin the initial stages of conceptualizing the logical path our code needs to take to implement the required feature set.

THE DESIGN PROCESS

Until now, our Form Generation Tool has been rather loosely defined. The idea of a Web-based HTML form generator is a good one, but it remains to be decided what exactly it will and won't do. In addition, the creation of a design includes not only the identification of the desired features, but also the user interface.

Our main challenge is to create a script or collection of scripts that works within the confines of the CGI specification, HTML, and HTTP to create a meta-form/CGI combination that allows users to create fully functional HTML forms to use on any HTTP server.

In the first phase of this project we walk through the HTML form creation process in the abstract, identifying the distinct steps we must take. These steps define the logical path or set of rules our script must follow to fulfill its functions. Each step must be analyzed in order to identify its components and to determine its necessity. If a component is mandatory, we must find a way to embody it in our code. If it's optional, we may choose to file it away, returning to it only after our core functionality is firmly in place, and add it to our script only if it's feasible to translate into working code.

Once we've designated a core suite of critical features, we can define how to implement them. This is the first stage where it is necessary to bring the ideal features conceived in our imaginations into the realm of reality. For each feature, therefore, we must ask the question, "How do we present this to the user so that its function is self-evident?" The answer must be balanced between an optimal solution from the user's perspective and what's possible within the defining boundaries of HTML and Perl (not to mention budget and schedule).

On Limitations

Of the two limiting technical factors, it's far more important to consider HTML and its delivery mechanism, HTTP, than it is to ruminate much about Perl. As a scripting language designed specifically for string manipulation and general-purpose computation, with most of the functionality of the C language, Perl possesses more than enough flexibility and power to outstrip the capabilities of its environment. In addition, the ease with which any particular function can be prototyped and put into action with Perl lowers significantly any concerns about biting off more than we can chew during the design stage.

Still, the latter concern is a factor in deciding whether a feature should be included in the *initial* version of the Form Generation Tool. All features contain the potential for over-complicating the design of a project like this and can bog down the development of a prototype. You should always balance the productivity gains represented by a feature against the development time required to make the feature work.

In general, the initial brainstorming and design phases should attempt to craft an elegant solution to the problem posed by the project's goals. It should be as full-featured as possible and should include everything the designers can dream up that the users might possibly want (there'll be plenty of time later in the design process to decide what's feasible and what's not).

To return briefly to our discussion of the limitations that confront a CGI-development project, we stated that HTML, HTTP, and the CGI specification itself define the boundaries of the possible. Specifically, the most obvious limitation is the stateless nature of HTTP. Each request a browser makes to a server presupposes nothing of its previous communications. This poses a challenge to any CGI application that attempts to provide a tool for creating a single document of arbitrary size in an arbitrary number of steps. This will have to be in our minds as we proceed through the various design phases.

We mention this concern about statelessness partly as a general pointer to larger issues in CGI design, but also to demonstrate a discontinuity between the way we are describing the design process and the way it actually works. In actuality, you can't separate the purely imaginative, abstract thought processes from the more concrete, analytical ones. Not only do these two streams of thought overlap, they complement each other as well. A practical concern for workability and completeness begins to manifest a logical path that should be taken to deliver a solution. This logical path may suggest other capabilities hitherto undiscovered in the project. Conversely, a creative burst that produces a desirable feature may also spark the analytical thought that turns the idea into actual code.

This is not to say that we're merely describing the entire process as a formal structured exercise for the reader and that in "real life" we leave these proceedings to chance. Instead, we always attempt to use this approach as an orienteering map of sorts, as a device that can verify that we've covered all our bases and can get us back on track when we get lost in pipedreams or obfuscated code.

With all this in mind, we shall now outline how the design process unfolds for the specific case of our Form Generation Tool.

Brainstorming

Our first step was to select a codename for the developmental stages of this project. We'll spare you those all-too-often silly details. Eventually, we settled on a release name, "Form Generation Tool" and in this book we'll refer to it simply as "the Form Generator" or "the Tool."

With nomenclature out of the way, we set the stage for the first real work on the Tool with a few assumptions:

- The Tool would be a CGI or set of CGIs written in Perl.
- We would develop on a UNIX server, running NCSA HTTPD, to maintain the closest thing to a standard that exists on the Web.
- The Form Generation Tool's main purpose would be to enable users equipped with Web browsers to create HTML forms using the Web itself.

Given these assumptions as a starting point, we began discussing the features that we wanted the Tool to have. We've imposed a somewhat artificial dividing line between the formulation of ideas for features and UI design. Logically these two are distinct tasks, but in practice they, like creative and technical design, cross-pollinate in the design process as a whole.

The Feature Set

Once the brainstorming's over, it's time to start getting a little more real. Here's where we try to take the "wish list" compiled during the previous phase of design, and match it up with features and functions that we'll need to build to make the Form Generator work. In the sections that follow, we cover some of the major issues and topics we debated at this point in the design process.

How Much HTML?

The first important decision to make was to choose the subset of HTML that we wanted the Tool to support. Basic 2.0 functionality was mandatory for form support, but the real questions were: Would we support *all* of the specification's elements? Would we include next generation features like tables? What about the other Netscape extensions? Probably the best answer would be the usual one—that is, to include as many features as were feasible, beginning with the critical ones and working down the list, adding the highly useful but not critical next, and so on. In this case, it means starting with form elements such as the various <INPUT> types, <SELECT>, and <TEXTAREA>; then moving on to the most common HTML tags, such as <HR>, the headings, font usage (like <B>, <I>, <STRONG>), etc.

With this 80/20 kind of approach, you're bound to disappoint the people who desperately want, for example, blinking text in their forms. However, this is the only realistic strategy for projects you want to actually complete. Hopefully, when building the support for all these elements, we'll be able to structure our code so that adding support for other elements later will be relatively easy.

Flexibility/Extensibility

Ease of maintenance and extensibility are especially important factors to consider because they make the difference between success and failure for many projects. When creating a utility or application for the Web or the Internet-at-large, you want a project that adapts to changing standards, protocols, hardware, and bandwidth and that can evolve over time.

We built our Form Generation Tool to adhere to this principle. If it isn't designed for flexibility and adaptability, it will quickly become stagnant and obsolete as users incorporate Java applets or Shockwave components into their forms.

The key to achieving flexibility, especially when you're creating a program or script intended for use on other people's systems, is to make it as portable as possible. This is a recurring theme, especially in the UNIX world, where even minor differences among "flavors" of UNIX can make a program useless. We have two factors on our side in this area, however; the first of which is our choice of scripting language.

Perl's Portability

Larry Wall, Perl's author, has taken great pains to make Perl scripts as portable as possible. Perl has been compiled to run on almost every flavor of UNIX on the planet, as well as DOS and Mac platforms, and each port of Perl maintains a consistent environment in which scripts can run. This is not to say that every Perl script is, by default, portable from one platform to

another. It's easy to write a script that is dependent on its initial platform—
as easy, in fact, as:

```
system ("/usr/bin/mailx singe@outer.net < /usr/lib/aliases");
```

This one line, if present in a Perl script, makes that script depend upon
that particular UNIX mail agent residing in that particular directory and the
"aliases" file residing at that path. Our point is this: To take maximum
advantage of Perl's strengths in the area of portability means careful
programming that doesn't make explicit references to elements or services
that may not be present in other environments. And don't forget to
comment everything that may not be portable "as is"—this can be the
greatest of all possible boons to developers who want to move the code to
other systems (especially non-UNIX platforms).

There are several ways to do this: First, rely on Perl's internal functions
and structures, even when a shortcut exists by going outside the Perl
environment. Second, when a shortcut eliminates a substantial amount of
work, use a variable if that shortcut relies on elements you can assume are
present on most platforms targeted by your project.

A good example of this is the use of *mailx*, in our earlier example.
Writing your own mail client is too much work for the average Perl script,
and a mail client exists on every Internet-aware UNIX server on the planet.
Therefore, define a variable, say '$mail_command', at the beginning of the
script and use it in any instance where the mail program is needed. Then,
when someone is localizing it for use on their own server, they need only
change the value of that variable in one place to adapt the script for use on
their system (and be sure to comment the variable call).

The HTTP Advantage

Our second advantage is HTTP in general and the CGI specification in
particular. As a part of the hand-off from the HTTP server to the CGI script
or program, a set of environment variables is created and initialized with
information from both the server and the client. These variables are defined
in Table 4-1.

Table 4-1

Standard environment variables quick reference

Environment Variable	Description
AUTH_TYPE	access authentication type
CONTENT_LENGTH	size in decimal number of octets of any attached entity
CONTENT_TYPE	the MIME type of an attached entity
GATEWAY_INTERFACE *	server's CGI spec. version
HTTP_(string)	client header data
PATH_INFO	path to be interpreted by CGI app.
PATH_TRANSLATED	virtual to physical mapping of file in system
QUERY_STRING	URL-encoded search string
REMOTE_ADDR	IP address of agent making request
REMOTE_HOST	fully qualified domain name of requesting agent
REMOTE_IDENT	identity data reported about agent connection to server
REMOTE_USER	user ID sent by client
REQUEST_METHOD	request method by client
SCRIPT_NAME	URI path identifying a CGI app.
SERVER_NAME *	server name; host part of URI; DNS alias
SERVER_PORT	server port that received the request
SERVER_PROTOCOL	name and revision of request protocol
SERVER_SOFTWARE *	name and version of server software

* Not request-specific (set for all requests).

From these variables, our script can discern information about its external environment, most notably the name of the server on which it is installed, its own name, and the path that appears in its own URL. By parsing 'SERVER_NAME' and 'SCRIPT_NAME', these pieces of data can be obtained and preserved in variables for use throughout the script. With a user-supplied path to the local CGI directory, we can also build an absolute path to ourselves on this server, and by patching the information together, we can create a URL for the script.

All this text manipulation requires less work from the user who's attempting to make the script run on a local server.

Words into Reality, or Feet in Our Collective Mouths?

The preceding digression into the portability issue illustrates our earlier point about the overlap between the phases of brainstorming and technical design. While coming up with raw ideas for what a script should or shouldn't do, we launched into a discussion of the technical aspects of Perl and CGI portability.

However, it's natural that an abstract idea should spark a cascade of analytical thought and technical details. It's a good way to solve a problem: The "what if" is posed, followed by a torrent of possible solutions.

Basic Functionality: The Cycle of Creation

To return to the task at hand—identifying desirable features for the Form Generation Tool—we'll look at the basic features that will allow users to create forms on the Web. Creating HTML in a general text or HTML-specific editor involves the following steps:

- First, create an HTML framework (<HTML><HEAD><TITLE> </TITLE></HEAD><BODY></BODY></-HTML>) as the minimum basic elements required in a valid HTML file.

- The next element type for insertion in the document is identified. This can be an HTML element such as a text style or line break, or a form element such as an <INPUT> or <TEXTAREA>.

- The values for that element are configured. This could be as simple as the text to be styled or the name of the form element, or as complex as a multiple option like <SELECT>.

- The element is inserted in place and users see the resulting HTML source, or a browser display of the form's current state. Editing functions are active to some degree to correct errors and tweak output.

- When feedback is complete, the user identifies the next element to be created.

From this algorithm, it's obvious that we need the ability to choose the next element, specify its particular options or values, and then commit it to the working document. The exact selection method and interface, as well as the precise set of selections available, will be specified later, when we begin the technical design phase.

To this most basic of abilities we should definitely add as many avenues for user feedback as possible. Previewing the form in progress would be most helpful, so that the user won't get lost in a tangle of HTML tags. This should be easy to accomplish because the application that delivers the Tool to our users is a Web browser.

The ability to view HTML source is essential, so that the user can validate those portions of the document that are invisible when HTML is parsed by a browser.

After receiving feedback, the user should be able to choose one or more actions to correct any possible mistakes. The most crucial control mechanism is an Undo capability.

The Tool should support at least a single level of Undo, and preferably many levels, even infinite levels all the way back to the beginning of the document. Depending on how the Tool stores the interim steps that make up the document, this may be fairly simple to implement.

A more advanced and subtle method for allowing the user to correct any mistakes would be to provide a way to edit the HTML source directly. Placing the disabled HTML into a text area should accomplish that. However, this feature has pros and cons because a large portion of our intended audience may be HTML novices.

Besides fixing mistakes, being able to edit source would increase the Tool's flexibility by allowing users to manually add a tag the Tool does not currently support, or to cut and paste large sections of other documents into the working one.

Beginning the Begin

Now that we've established this cycle, we need to take a step back and look at how the user begins creating a form. First, the user establishes the HTML form's purpose, name, and title.

Our Tool can collect the document's name and title. In addition, if we want the Tool to track usage, we may want to capture the user's e-mail address as well. In fact, we need this last piece of information if we want to deliver the finished form via e-mail.

Two other initial options are the ability to edit an existing HTML form and to resume work on a form started and abandoned at an earlier date. The first option is beyond the scope of the initial project because it means creating an HTML form parser instead of a generator. It's an idea with quite a bit of merit and shouldn't be dismissed out of hand. Perhaps it's the type of idea that, while not immediately doable, may prove useful later, if you decide to extend the original Tool's capabilities.

The second option is also quite useful, but it raises questions of privacy and validating ownership. Additionally, because it would entail the creation of a different path through the script, and picking up where the form was left rather than starting a form from scratch, it has the potential to clutter up the design of the Tool's core functionality.

Again, our feeling is that this idea should be back-burnered, perhaps to emerge later on, when more of the core of the project exists and is operational. It's good practice to maintain a farm league of ideas like this, so that in the unlikely event that some part of the project proves to be easier than expected, you'll have additional work lest your code mill run idle. More often than not, coding and debugging CGIs tends to take longer than your longest estimates, and these features don't surface until you've forgotten the pain of initial development and you're drawn into the pitfalls of revising existing code.

It is critically important to maintain a laser-sharp focus on the project's immediate goal and always seek to simplify that goal to its most basic elements. This sometimes leads to more elegant solutions because the definition of elegance is simplicity of design. Convolution is the enemy and can cause you to produce nearly unusable code and projects, or even kill a project by sending it into a decaying orbit around its own navel.

A final consideration for the "welcome" page would be a linked help document. Because we're making assumptions about the users' needs, preferred work habits, and information in hand, we owe them the courtesy of explaining these assumptions. More important, it provides a venue to prepare users for the Tool's interface and features, so that we can minimize the difficulties they'll encounter when using the Tool. Obviously, the help document will be created once the Tool is finalized and running smoothly.

Once all this data is collected, it can be applied in the following ways:

- Use the supplied name as the working title and as the final name for the HTML document the Tool creates.

- Initialize certain information in the first section of the document, including the document's <TITLE> and all the standard tags that comprise HTML files.

- Create a comment that includes the program's name, the user's e-mail address, and the form's creation date.

- Set up the HTML document so that it's ready to accept the first form element.

With all that out of the way, we can proceed to the next logical phase of form creation. This will be the repetitive cycle of selecting an element and supplying its parameters until the form is complete.

The Meat of the Matter: Creating the Body of the Form

Now that we've established the basic guidelines for the Tool's feature set, we can begin pushing ahead. We know that we want to present a good subset of HTML to the user and that this subset should include the most useful tags. One way to begin extending this feature set is to start thinking of ways we could enhance support for certain tags to bring them beyond the level of bare usability.

An obvious example is the way we could enrich support for radio buttons. A subset of the <INPUT> tag, radio buttons typically exist in groups of two or more that share the same name, each with its own value. If we can support creation of an arbitrary number of button/value pairs in one operation, this would be a real timesaver. The same basic feature could also be applied to checkboxes and selects. From a single good idea we can make three of the most commonly used form elements easier to use and more powerful.

Another necessity is to prepend input fields with text that explains what information the user is expected to provide. We can incorporate this into our Tool by providing an input field when the user sets the options for the element. This shortens a process that may have otherwise required two steps.

Also, since we're providing a way for users to insert text before each element in their forms, we can implement another feature: We can ensure that the label field is handled in our code so that any HTML tags input in it are preserved. Then, users can create stylized text for labels and enhance the look of their forms. In actual fact, this is incredibly easy to include because it requires only that we do not strip or otherwise process any HTML tags in the input text.

This type of synergy is a good illustration of the kinds of opportunities to watch for while brainstorming. Never underestimate the accidental feature or the feature that can be implemented almost as an afterthought. Keep an objective eye on the project at all times, and always look at your programming from the user's perspective.

Continually quiz yourself about how users might respond if you explained what your program is designed to do. Often, one capability suggests, or even demands, another feature to make it truly useful. Sometimes aspects of a program that don't particularly interest programmers will excite users, and vice versa. That's why you want to stay as openminded as possible and solicit feedback all along the way.

The same technique can not be used only to add or discover hidden features; it can also axe features that appeal to programmers but not to users. This aspect of programming most resembles creative writing, where the audience and its needs must always be first in the writer's mind. This dialectic must especially be present when designing your project's user interface.

There's Form and There's Format

HTML's purpose is online presentation, but this is often left to uninspired afterthought. Someone may produce pages of beautifully structured HTML-formatted materials that, when loaded into a Web browser, look awful. Forms are especially prone to this failing. The addition of a number of rectilinear shapes that are fairly firmly anchored to their positions on the page makes layout even more of a challenge. If we could lend aids to the user that will assure at least a modicum of style in the resulting form design, we'd be doing the Web audience a big favor!

One approach is to simplify the addition of tags or formatting to be included with almost every added form element. The first value we could add to form creation would be a simple ability to group form elements on a single line. Most elements exist one to a line, so it makes sense for the default behavior of the Tool to include a line break at the end of each addition to the form. However, we'll design this to toggle on and off, in case the user wants to group several buttons or other small elements on a single line.

This last feature may seem overly simplistic, but we find that one of the most common ailments that afflicts Web forms is the uniform grouping of one element to a line. It not only makes for longer document pages and increased scrolling, it's an eyesore.

The advent of HTML <TABLE> support on high-end browsers represents a major advance for controlling page layout with some degree of precision. Careful use of data cells and rows can result in clean, economical designs. Tables are typically used to organize and present text and graphical data, but there's no reason why they can't be used for forms as well. However, while tables are supported on many browsers nowadays, they're still not supported by all of them, so you may want to consider providing a text-only alternative for <TABLE> data or eschewing their use to reach the broadest possible audience. In our case, we decided that tables were essential, and therefore built our design around them.

If we add this twist to our form creation, our default behavior can become one element to a table row, with the field label in one data cell and the data entry field in another cell. With no additional modifications, we'll end up with an interesting and clean design. Once the form is done, the user can alter the look of the document with just a few tweaks to the table options.

From the basic implementation, a border could be added, and individual cells' options such as padding, spacing, alignment, and width can be adjusted. As with the carriage return's default behavior, we need to ensure that the table mode is easily toggled off and on within the form and that its current state is preserved from the creation of one element to the next.

With the last two features we've mentioned explicitly that we want to preserve the feature's state across multiple HTTP transactions. Yet one of HTTP's selling points is its stateless transactions. How can we reconcile this? This question is critical for the Tool as a whole. If we're unable to preserve the working document name and possibly the number for the current step, we can't make the Tool work. We'll file this concern away for the time being and return to it when we begin translating our abstract vision of the Tool into actual code.

Pie in the Sky: Super Features

With all the features that have emerged from our brainstorming session, one familiar to all programmers is, "This is a great idea but far beyond the scope of the initial project." The best example we've encountered so far is the capability to read in an existing form and modify it. This could be a real boon because it would allow you to maintain pages from anywhere, without having to download files to your client machine for editing. It would also, by its very nature, become a way to check the syntax of forms, since a feature like this would almost have to employ some type of syntax validator.

Perhaps if a read-in form could be coerced into our table-assisted layout, this would also become a quick spruce-up tool for older documents. However, it is simply too much to expect to be able to write an HTML generator and a parser at the same time.

Sometimes, however, ideas are just too good to lie fallow for long, and when that is the case, you can rest assured that somewhere down the road they'll appear as code. Another example of a good feature is data validation.

It would be useful indeed to allow the user to specify the valid data for a specific field and then to generate the code that allows the CGI to check the input when the form is submitted. However, creating a uniform interface to specify the data range is troublesome. If the input is numeric, it would be simple enough to ask the user for maximum and minimum values, but for text, it isn't that simple. How do you specify a check for a proper name? A valid phone number? A zip code?

The programming necessary for any one of these validation routines is simple enough: It's merely a problem of allowing the user to communicate the desired data type and values. Nevertheless, this feature could be so useful that we might keep it back-burnered, perhaps for future development.

Another idea involves allowing the user to provide a file that contains a plain text form, with some predictable format, such as:

```
name:
address:
phone number:
e-mail:
age:
```

And so on. But even this tiny fragment demonstrates that it would be nearly impossible with this amount of information for a script to determine whether age: was a text or numeric input. To require users to specify the data type or an allowable data range is unacceptable for two reasons. First, it requires users to manually create the kind of data that the Tool is meant to automate, and second, it pushes us toward the parsing territory that we so fastidiously avoided previously. This idea qualified for the "close, but no cigar" category and was back-burnered into oblivion.

Tying Up Loose Ends

Once the user is finished, we'll need to perform whatever activities are necessary to tie up the HTML document. For example, if any <TABLE> tags are left open, the Tool should close them. The completed form could then be delivered by the user's chosen method.

Several methods can be implemented. The simplest way to get the form to the user is to view the source in its entirety in the Web browser's window. At that point, the user can save the window as text and store the complete form on the local hard drive. Another way, since we had the foresight to collect the user's e-mail address at the very beginning, is to e-mail the source to that address. This is trivial to program in Perl but, as mentioned earlier, is a potential pitfall for portability. We'll need to make sure we set a variable for the value of the desired mailer, so it can be modified for the proper local idiom.

Another alternative would be to prepare the form as a *zip*ped or *gzip*ped downloadable via a simple HTTP link to the document on the server.

A final alternative, since we are creating the user's form on an actual Web server, is to actually install it on the server so that it's instantly ready-to-run. This is undoubtedly the kind of idea that delights users and terrifies administrators because of the inconvenience and security risks involved. If we permit a reasonable level of security while preserving the functionality, we may actually be able to please both parties. Thus, the best protection is to use HTTP's authentication and access controls to require a login name and password for installation. That way, the administrator can dole out this privilege only to specified users rather than to the whole world.

Beyond security, server installation also requires properly setting the file's owner, group, and permissions. Luckily, Perl supports internal functions to perform these tasks, so we don't have to compromise the program's portability.

Speaking of administrators, another feature that may appeal to this particular segment of our Tool's audience would be to maintain a log of the people who use it. Here again, the e-mail address will do admirably for a log file entry. The e-mail address can be captured either when a user successfully completes a form or initially, when it's first entered in the e-mail address field.

Validated HTML Is Good HTML

Every Web page designer understands the importance of adhering strictly to specified tag syntax for universal readability across various Web browsers. Each browser has its own idiosyncratic interpretation and is more or less tolerant of one syntactical mistake or another. Netscape, for example, ignores runs of more than one <P> tag, whereas Mosaic and its offspring tend to ignore multiple <BR> tags.

While there is little you can do about browser interpretation, you can ensure that your source complies as strictly as possible with the specification for the version of HTML you're using. Using the Tool is a good first step in this direction because you're guaranteed consistent output, rather than relying on your own typing skills. To allow users to double-check that something wasn't omitted or broken in the process of creating the form, we can also build in formal HTML validation capability.

Thanks to some hard work by one of the co-authors of this book, Mark Gaither, there is a public HTML validation service currently run out of HALsoft, Inc., in Austin, TX. In addition to running the validation service from its Web site, Mark has provided HTML source to link your pages to his validation tool.

By integrating a button from the HTML validation site, we can give the user the option to run the source through the Tool and view the response returned. The Tool's output consists of any portions of the HTML that do not comply with the specification chosen by the user. HTML 1.0, 2.0, 3.0, and Netscape extensions can all be validated. Here again we are implementing a feature that is more a matter of leveraging resources already available to us, rather than conjuring something out of thin air. If you're behind a firewall or are using some of the newer extensions (e.g., <FRAME>) there will be problems, but you should be able to work out the kinks without too much effort, as long as you can figure out how to customize our code for your particular environment.

Going a Step Further: Creating a CGI to Serve the Form

With our form complete and validated, the next step is to create a CGI script to serve as a back-end processing tool. An interesting concept at this point would be to build at least a running skeleton of a CGI that would do just that, without the user having to lift a finger. This is actually simple to do, since all forms are serviced in essentially the same way. The environment-variable values are examined to verify that the CGI is being called in the proper way, and then the form input is extracted and URL-decoded. Typically the next step is to parse the input fields' names and values into an associative array.

In fact, without any way to actually make the CGI do anything for the user but extract data, this feature would probably not be worth much. Obviously, the range of possibilities for what a CGI does is far too wide for us to even consider attempting to supply code for the user's needs. Creating a CGI would also mean ending up with two separate files and complicating the entire delivery phase of the Tool. The danger in this would be to confuse the user and thereby nullify the Tool's original benefits.

However, what if the CGI we produced was actually the final product, complete with the form? This would simplify things even further, and our CGI would perform a valuable service instead of merely extracting variables. This may be accomplished by a CGI that detects which METHOD is used to call the script. When called by a GET, it simply spits back the user's form, complete with a <FORM ACTION> tag that posts the form back at itself, this time with the POST method. Because the calling method is different, we can cause the script to execute different code, extracting the variables from the form input and perhaps echoing them back to the user.

The end result is a useable, extensible script that, coupled with the ability to install it and make it run on the host server, could chop considerable time off the normal form/CGI development cycle.

Wrap It Up, I'll Take It

We've brainstormed about as much as we need to at this point. From the basic concept, we've defined the core functionality of the Tool and identified a rich suite of additional features. Some will be implemented in the Tool's first incarnation, and some will have to wait, but all have merit from the user's perspective. The next task is to design a good user interface for the feature set.

Interface

Designing a reasonable UI can make or break any programming project. If the program's look and feel communicates well with the user, clarifying what the program does and how to use it, you'll have won some key battles. You'll have ensured that people will give your program a try—many interfaces intimidate or confuse users and keep them from getting past the first screen.

Once you've drawn the user in, each subsequent step must suggest how to proceed. By looking at the program's working environment, the user should be able to intuit something about the program's functions. Each feature should be readily accessible, easily navigated, and finally should deposit the user in an expected and logical place. Above all, nothing about the use of the program should surprise the user. Like a well-crafted story, each progression may or may not be obvious beforehand, but it must seem like a foregone conclusion when it's done.

None of this is news to anyone who has worked on user interfaces. The same goals and difficulties exist, no matter what programming language or platform you use. However, each environment brings its own unique idiosyncrasies and shortcomings, and HTML and CGIs are no exception.

As a vehicle for delivering an interface to a user, HTML is actually quite limited. A handful of text styles, a few layout elements, and a small set of tightly defined input widgets is pretty much the extent of what you have to work with. With these kinds of constraints, it's a challenge to deliver an interface design with any kind of flair. As we stated before, the general level of HTML form layout is limited, but that probably doesn't reflect on the aesthetic sensibilities of those who create them.

With these kinds of obstacles standing in the way of good form design, how should we approach designing forms? This may have been the most difficult question we had to ask before embarking on this project. We looked at many different approaches to the Tool's basic interface but discarded all but the final two.

Toolbar Approach

The first approach we considered was to present a toolbar for selecting the next element to be inserted in the form. Once the element was inserted, the user would be presented with the toolbar once again, with the last element added. In other words, the toolbar would "float" down the window as elements were added, and the user would see the form emerge in true WYSIWYG fashion.

This idea has many merits, not the least of which is the ability to continually see what the form looks like. However, it has a few weak points as well, and careful weighing of the pros and cons eventually led us to discard this approach. Some of the most troubling problems with this approach included:

- While the toolbar could be laid out fairly elegantly on its own, when added to the bottom of a complex form the overall effect could be confusing.

- If the form being created was longer than the length of the browser's window, the toolbar would not be initially visible. This would be annoying and confusing.

- As we began tallying up the "universal options" and commands that needed to be on the initial form where the user selected the next element, it became apparent that it would soon become too large to be manageable.

- There were many potential problems with tacking one form's source to the bottom of another form. Depending on what the user was inserting into the form, the toolbar's behavior may have been adversely affected. There were ways we could see to defend the integrity of the toolbar, but that would mean lots of extra programming and debugging.

- Implementing our Undo feature would be more difficult in this paradigm than in some of the others we considered. The simplest way to allow for Undos is to keep each element in a separate area all to itself. Undoing simply becomes a matter of removing a specific segment of the document. In the case of the toolbar, however, we'd need to see the form as one big entity every time the user returned to the main page of the Tool. That would mean either stitching the many parts of the working document together every time or doing away with the separate parts entirely. The former would mean a performance degradation, and the latter would mean Undo would be much, much, more difficult to implement.

In the end, we realized that the toolbar concept was probably born from minds that have spent most of their time using real GUIs that can pull this sort of thing off with some style. HTML, at least in its present state, is not capable of this level of sophistication. However, while investigating the toolbar both speculatively and practically with scripted prototypes, we did identify a number of important considerations for the Tool's interface.

Now Entering the Winner's Circle...

These considerations persisted from our failed toolbar experiments into our final candidate and eventual winner in the interface sweepstakes. One key point is the importance of previewing in as close to real time as possible, but not to let the preview interfere with creating the form. On another platform that would simply mean separating the preview and the toolbar into two separate windows, but in HTML that kind of capability still eludes us. (This may not be the case for much longer. Our brief look at Netscape 2.0's frames in the latter stages of the Tool's development made us think about the next version of the Tool's interface in a whole new way.)

The best part of the toolbar was the idea of grouping options that applied universally to the form elements on the page where the user selected those elements. In HTML's current single window environment, separating interface elements for clarity means placing those elements on separate pages. In the same way, our new interface presents the user with a simple form that allows the selection of the next element and setting the options to be applied to that element (no matter what selection is made).

Another important feature that we liked about the toolbar was its access to all commands, in the form of multiple Submit buttons with custom labels. All major features should be represented in this central area of the Tool—central because it will be designed to serve as the "top" of the form creation cycle described earlier—that is, the point to which the user returns again and again as each segment of the form is created and the next step is planned.

Therefore, this staging ground should have a button to create the next element, as well as buttons to preview the form, view the source, undo the last step, and end the document. It should also have toggle mechanisms for the table on/off and carriage return features we discussed earlier.

Most important, it should set the tone for the rest of the interface design the user is going to encounter and for the type of layout we're attempting to make the Tool create. At the same time, since the Tool will be a little simple-minded in its first incarnation, we shouldn't constrain ourselves strictly to an interface that someone could create with our own code. Making the interface clear to our users is the most important design consideration.

All that said, after some wrestling with HTML in an editor, we arrived at our initial staging ground form, which embodies some of the principles and ideals we've discussed in this chapter.

You'll notice in Figure 4-1 that we've separated the available options into two categories: HTML elements and form elements. This is a somewhat arbitrary division, obviously, because form elements are a subset of HTML. But our reasoning was to force the user to think of each element as either an input element or a layout element, in the hopes that this would improve the general design of the HTML document.

Beneath this staging area are the two layout options that apply to all elements: the table mode and the carriage return option, with their default values clearly marked. Beneath this, you'll find the four buttons that represent the major actions that users can perform during the first stage of form creation. This includes previewing the form, viewing the document's source, creating the currently selected element, and ending the document. Once the first element has been added to the document, the Undo button is then added to the interface.

We also made the decision to make all major commands accessible through named Submit buttons rather than links. From a look-and-feel standpoint, buttons are more intuitively associated with tasks than highlighted text. In addition, making users submit data to the script permits a much cleaner URL because all our data can be passed internally rather than on the command line.

Finally, please notice that we use a standard footer that contains information about the script and its author, the time the page was created, and a link to allow you to start over. This persists from one form to the next throughout the Tool, to provide a consistent interface.

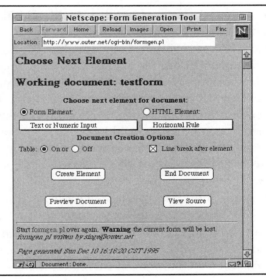

Figure 4-1
The Form Generation tool's central user interface.

How Did I Get Here?

Of course, we can't just drop our users straight into this central clearinghouse form. Before we begin, we'll need to collect some data from the user so that we can initialize the form. Usually you'd use a static HTML form document to do this, but that's a problem because it requires a separate document to be installed in a different directory from the script itself. (This isn't a big problem, really, but it makes the Tool less portable by making it harder to install and maintain on the server.)

There's an alternative to a static page that involves a slightly more creative use of the CGI specification. Every script that's called as a CGI by an HTTP server is run in a shell with a set of environment variables. The

METHOD variable is what we're particularly interested in at the moment. When it's called using a URL in an <A> tag or typed by the user directly, the METHOD variable is set to GET. But when it's called by a user clicking on a Submit button in a document with the script in its <FORM> tag, it's set to POST. By watching the value of the variable, we can vary the behavior of the Tool according to how it's called.

Thus, when the Tool script is called by a GET, either by clicking on a link to it or typing in its URL, we instruct it to output the entry form. The <FORM> tag specifies the same script as its ACTION, except with the POST method. Upon noticing that the METHOD is set to POST, the Tool extracts the form data and gets to work. The most tangible benefit from this approach is that the Tool can remain a single, integrated piece, with corresponding gains in the ease of installation and maintenance.

This same model also provided an efficient way to roll the finished form and its supporting CGI code into a single entity. The same portability and maintenance gains could then be passed on to the Tool's end users. When the form was finished, we could give users an option to roll the form into a self-contained CGI and then generate the necessary code. But now we're back to brainstorming features when we're supposed to be creating an interface!

If we recall the data we needed when we discussed the steps to take before entering the form creation cycle, we must capture the document's working name, its HTML title, and the user's e-mail address. This was a fairly straightforward form to design (see Figure 4-2). As with the central form, we attempted to remain true to our tenets of simplicity. This was particularly easy to do because we had so few elements to present.

From this welcome screen, in addition to entering the pertinent information, the user can access a help document that explains how to use the Tool. Once the user enters the document's filename, title, and an e-mail address, the Submit button is clicked and the data is fed back into the script to initialize the document.

The next page that is presented to the user is the staging ground form we saw in Figure 4-1. From there, the user can decide on the next element to include in the form and submit the form's data, after being satisfied that it's complete. Since we decided on an integrated approach to the first stages of the Tool, it makes sense to continue that approach. Therefore, whatever next step the user wants to take, every path leads back to the Tool script. Instead of spreading the process out over several scripts, we've designed a single all-in-one script to do the work.

Figure 4-2
The Form Generator's Welcome screen requests key information needed before creating a form.

When this script receives the user's choice of element data, it returns a form to enable the user to set options for the selected element (see Figure 4-3). In other words, each available form or HTML element has a form designed to let the user specify the element's characteristics.

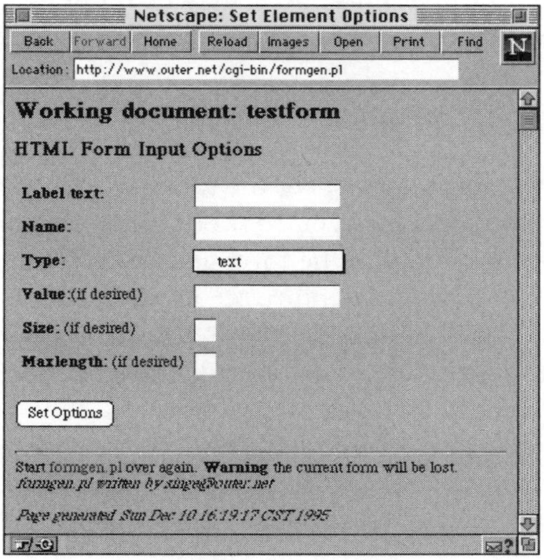

Figure 4-3
An Option Form interface for a text or numeric input field.

Each of these interfaces also needs to be designed for simplicity, clarity, and completeness. As much as possible interface code from one element should be adapted and reused for other, related elements. By doing this we not only save ourselves time but also lay the groundwork for a consistent interface. If we get enough of the core code running for the Tool, we can then use it to create the interface for as many elements as possible.

One interface grouping results naturally from our planned design of the radio buttons, checkboxes, and selects. Earlier, we identified a common core for these three form widgets, and we wanted to find a way to allow the user to easily create an arbitrary number of buttons, boxes, or options. Such a feature needs a good interface, but that same interface will work, with minor alterations, for all three of these elements.

Setting its options and submitting this form brings the user back to the staging ground form, and the new element will be written to the working file.

We believe this segmented approach is more workable than the toolbar approach. We've preserved the toolbar's most valuable characteristics while avoiding its pitfalls. Thus, the task of form creation has been distilled into a two-step process:

1. Choose the next element.
2. Set the options specific to that element.

WYSIWYG previewing is always just a button click away from the staging ground form, as is viewing the HTML source for the working document. Universal options may be set in this page, too, leaving only the decisions specific to the selected element for the second form.

Exit Stage Right

When the form is finished, the user exits the form creation loop by clicking on the End Document button. Because we have quite a large number of options that wrap up the form and deliver it to the user, we'll need to create another interface to capture the user's wishes in this regard.

As you can see in Figure 4-4, the form is divided logically into two sections. The mode of delivery defines the first section, with radio buttons grouped together to allow selection of a delivery technique. Second, the two post-processing options let users either encapsulate their forms into a Perl CGI script, validate the form's HTML, or do both.

Each direction represented by this form's decision tree has it own feedback and results page that displays the results of the user's input. The user collects the form and/or CGI, and our job is done!

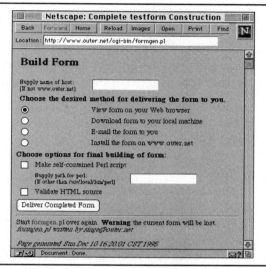

■ **Figure 4-4**
The Document Delivery Form lcaptures the user's wishes regarding form delivery.

Implementing Design

We may have belabored the point regarding cross-pollination of the technical and imaginative aspects of this design. If we did, it's only because we feel strongly that this is a crucial part of project planning. We believe that understanding how a programming language affects your project (and vice versa) is important to its outcome.

While this synergy is important to the creative side of this process, it becomes even more crucial when it's time to implement our design. If our design decisions fail to be informed by our technical understanding of the language, we may find ourselves in serious trouble. Every language has its weaknesses; there may be certain jobs that it just can't do, and the end of the planning phase and beginning of the coding phase is not the right time to find that out.

On the other hand, a project design driven by technical input throughout will not only be entirely feasible, but may also benefit from headstarts to various portions of the programming. Since some of the features we chose were born from some technical aspect of the language or environment, we already knew how to implement them.

Overall, the more time you spend in the design phase, the less time you'll spend coding, and the closer your end results will be to your goals. Never underestimate the value of thinking about a project, rather than plugging away when you may not be mentally prepared.

SUMMARY

In this chapter, we've run through the design process behind the Form Generation Tool. We took the basic concept of a CGI that made forms and explored what that actually meant, on a finer scale. We decided on a basic feature set and discussed the factors that must be weighed when including or discarding features.

Next we planned the Tool's user interface. We looked at several different possible approaches and explained why one approach was discarded and another developed. Throughout, we espoused some highly personal ideas about interface design.

Finally, we must emphasize again that this written account of our process has been artificially compartmentalized for readability. The actual process is more organic, with features-brainstorming and interface design intermingling, and a continual dialog between imaginative and technical aspects. If there is one message we wish to impart, it would be to stress the importance of a balanced approach to program design and programming. Keep both creative and analytical minds open, active, and talking to each other, and you're sure to end up with the best scripts and programs you can make!

In the next chapter, we'll start to explore the issues related to installing and using the *formgen* script on your server (or someone else's), before we dive into the source code in Chapter 6, "The Form Generator's Behavior and Internal Workings."

SETUP, INITIALIZATION, AND INTERACTIVITY IN THE FORM GENERATOR

5

*A*fter our focus on the abstract in the previous chapter, we now turn to the concrete. We've taken our Form Generation Tool from the design phase to completion and are now ready for assembly. We'll begin by taking you through the steps necessary to install and run the Tool on your server. Don't worry, you can run it off our server if you don't have access to one!

Once the script is installed, we'll run a test drive, exploring and explaining the Tool's many features. After that, we'll create a form to examine some of the Tool's more important aspects. Finally, we'll delve into some tips and tricks regarding the Form Generator. We'll also discuss how to push the envelope of what this Tool can do and how to achieve some advanced effects.

INSTALLING ON YOUR WEB SERVER

First, let's look at the steps necessary to install the Tool on a Web server. This discussion may seem basic at times, depending on your skill level, but we intend to cover the basic tasks required for a CGI installation on most Web servers. To do this, we need to make sure that we cover all pertinent steps and potential issues.

Uploading the Distribution Archive

The Form Generation Tool included on this books's companion disk is supplied for use with UNIX, in a *tar* archive called "formgen.tar". We built this tool on a Linux system, but we've successfully used it on BSDI and SunOS as well (with minor modifications).

The first step is to upload this file from your local machine to your server.

The *tar* file should be placed in the directory where CGIs are run. This is often */usr/local/www/cgi-bin* or *www/htbin*, but it could be a different directory. If you're not sure, there are several ways to find out. If you know a URL for a script that runs on your server, examine that URL's path and extrapolate it. Here's an example:

```
http://www.outer.net/cgi-bin/formgen.pl
```

From this, you can see that scripts live in the directory called *cgi-bin*, which is beneath the server's root directory. If you're not sure about the server's root directory, ask your system administrator. If you are the administrator and you're still not sure where to put CGIs, we come to our final method for finding out.

The server's configuration file will identify the CGI directory. For example, in an NCSA-derived HTTP server, the configuration file is called "server.conf" and lives in the *conf* directory, which is a subdirectory of the directory where your Web server itself is installed. On many machines, this is */usr/local/etc/httpd*. On a machine running Korn shell, you can find out by typing *whence -v httpd*.

Extracting the Archive

Once you've correctly placed the archive, you can move on to extracting the files. The *tar* utility is standard on nearly every UNIX machine, and there are *tar* utilities for Macintosh and DOS as well. The easiest, one-step method to *untar* the file is the following command:

```
tar xvf formgen.tar
```

However, because the script and its support files are owned by the Web server user, there's a shortcut you can include. If you are able (i.e., you have superuser privileges), you can *su* to the user ID that runs the Web server. This is often *www* but can potentially be any user name. Once you are that user, you can extract the files as follows:

```
tar xvfo formgen.tar
```

The 'o' flag tells *tar* to change the ownership to your user ID as it extracts the files and directories.

Should this last step not work, you'll need to change the ownership manually. *Untarring* should produce the following output:

```
x ./formgen/form_install.pl, 2035 bytes, 4 tape blocks
x ./formgen/formgen.end, 31 bytes, 1 tape blocks
x ./formgen/formgen.perl, 1085 bytes, 3 tape blocks
x ./formgen/validate.html, 446 bytes, 1 tape blocks
x ./formgen.pl, 31425 bytes, 62 tape blocks
x ./formlib.pl, 3813 bytes, 8 tape blocks
x ./debugforms.pl, 1954 bytes, 4 tape blocks
```

As you can see, the *formgen.pl*, *debugforms.pl*, and *formlib.pl* scripts are extracted into a current directory. The directory *formgen* is created and is populated by the files "formgen.end", "formgen.perl", "validate.html", and the script *form_install.pl*. All of these need to be changed to reflect the ownership of the HTTP server. In UNIX, you'd use the *chown* utility.

Localization

Localization refers to the changes that need to be made to a script or a program so it will run in your environment. The localization for *formgen.pl* is minimal.

First and foremost, because the Tool is entirely coded in Perl, you must ensure that the script can find Perl on your server. The first line of the script uses the standard path to Perl:

```
#!/usr/local/bin/perl5.001
```

The script expects Perl version 5.001 to be available. If this is not the path to your version of Perl, or if your version is named differently, then you'll need to edit this line to reflect those differences. If you don't have version 5.001 of Perl, we suggest getting it and compiling it for your platform: That will be less work than retrofitting this code to run with a 4.x Perl implementation.

Whatever you end up doing to get *formgen.pl* to run, do the same to *form_install.pl*, as it may face the same issues.

Further down the *formgen.pl* listing is a cluster of variable initializations. It is here that the remaining localization efforts are needed. The first group of variables are self-initializing and do not require any adjustments. They are sufficiently interesting, however, for us to take a closer look:

```
$debug = 0;
$host = $ENV{SERVER_NAME};
$ENV{SCRIPT_NAME} =~ s/([a-zA-Z0-9\.\-_]+)$//;
$program = $1;
$scriptpath = $ENV{SCRIPT_NAME};
```

The first variable, $debug, is a simple Boolean flag that can be defined as zero or one. We'll use this flag to control when the program produces debug output (when you would want to enable such output, and what that will accomplish, will be discussed in the near future).

The hostname for the local Web server is plucked at runtime from the CGI's environment variables, specifically the 'SERVER_NAME' variable. Therefore, there's no need for the user to manually set this in the script. We could also have derived the hostname from the UNIX command *hostname*, but that creates a potential platform dependency. We're not directly aware of any UNIX flavor that doesn't support the *hostname* utility, but our rule of thumb with UNIX is, "Never assume anything."

It's not unlikely that on some UNIX flavor somewhere the same utility has a name that would break our script. Additionally, the 'SERVER_NAME' variable is set from the URL used to call the script, so it properly reflects what you call your Web server. In contrast, *hostname* would return the machine's true name, which isn't necessarily the same thing.

The next environment variable we'll play with is 'SCRIPT_PATH', which is set to the URL path to call the script. If the URL reads:

```
http://www.outer.net/cgi-bin/formgen.pl
```

then 'SCRIPT_PATH' would be set to */cgi-bin/formgen.pl*. This information will prove to be useful, but not all in one lump. Therefore, we match against the variable to trap everything after the last directory slash in $1 and then set $program equal to $1. This lets us determine the name of the script, even if a user changes it on a local server.

Since, in the process of determining the script's name, we sliced it off the environment variable, we can use the remainder of the value to determine the URL path to the script, so we'll preserve this value in $scriptpath:

```
$readablepath = "/www/httpdocs/";
$datapath = "formgen/";
$compress = "/usr/local/bin/gzip";
$mail = "/usr/bin/mailx -s 'Wondertwin Form Delivery' ";
```

These four variables are the only ones that you may have to change for your installation. The first, $readable_path, is set to the root document directory of your Web server. This will be used to construct absolute paths to files on your server.

The directory under your CGI directory where the Tool's data files are kept should be assigned to the $datapath variable. By default, this variable is set to *formgen/* because this is what the distribution *tar* file will create. However, if you move or rename this directory, this variable will need to be changed.

The last two variables reflect the Tool's only real dependencies on the UNIX OS. The first is the path to a compression utility. You can use any program that will take as an argument the name of the file to be compressed. In this case, we're making use of the excellent GNU utility, *gzip*. The standard UNIX *compress* would also do just fine.

The *mail* command is used for SMTP delivery of the final form/CGI to the user. The default uses the *mailx* program, which takes an '-s' flag with an argument to set the message's subject line. The path to this program may need editing, or the program may not be available. In the latter event, you may choose any other mail program that sends the message to the address on the command line and takes standard input for the body of the message.

Security

The final step involves the secure operation of the Tool. The script *form_install.pl* in the data directory has the ability to write HTML and CGI files and scripts to any directory to which the Web server's user ID has access. This can be a security risk, especially when you consider the potential scope of what an unhindered Perl script can accomplish.

But even though *form_install.pl* may be able to write CGI files and scripts anywhere, the way the server itself is configured governs whether or not those scripts can be run from those places. If the server's administrator has set up script boundaries appropriately, the security risks will be greatly lessened. This helps to explain why the ../cgi-bin/.. subtree is sacrosanct on so many Web servers and why administrators are loathe to grant CGI developers carte blanche to that area. Our best advice is to work things out with your administrator and be convincing that these (and the other programs in this book) are well-behaved and won't wreak havoc on his or her Web server.

In addition the Tool has some internal security precautions, but to be even safer, you'll want to restrict user access to the scripts. The easiest way to do this is by using the access controls that are built into almost all Web servers, possibly combined with judicious use of UNIX permissions settings (particularly the useful *group* setting).

The way server access control is configured and implemented differs from one vendor's Web server to another. Because we tend to run the NCSA server, or variations thereof, we'll use it to demonstrate. Essentially, access control is meant to place password protection on a given directory and to limit access to users who can provide valid passwords.

Only two files are required to make this work on the NCSA family of Web servers: a password file, whose placement is arbitrary, but which usually resides in the server's *auth* directory, and a file named ".htaccess", placed in the directory to be protected; in this case, the directory is *formgen*. The password file entries should take the form:

```
username:encrypted password
```

This file can be created manually, provided you have a way to set the encrypted passwords. More typically, its entries will be exports from the "/etc/passwd" file, leaving out the entries that aren't needed, such as real name and shell. In this way, a user can have the same Web password as their login password (this may cause less incidents where a user forgets one or the other). This approach works well to protect single directories, especially where a group of developers may share access to a common collection of materials, but we'd like to point out that ".htaccess" is by no means the be-all and end-all of Web security tools!

The ".htaccess" file is quite flexible and powerful, but for our limited purposes it need only look something like the following:

```
AuthUserFile /www/auth/.htpasswd
AuthGroupFile /dev/null
AuthName "Form Generation Tool Installation"
AuthType Basic
```

```
<Limit POST>
require user biffo
</Limit>
```

The first line provides the absolute path, below the Web server's root (not the absolute path on the machine), to the password file you created. The AuthName field is used to identify the directory being accessed in the login dialog box displayed by the browser. The <Limit POST> tag is the meat of the file because it stipulates that the server should perform authentication before allowing users to access files in the directory using the CGI POST method.

Because this is the only way our script will run, returning an error message if it is run with the GET method, this is safe enough. Finally, the line require user specifies one of the people allowed to access this directory. If a user doesn't appear in this file, he or she will not be allowed to access the directory.

Of course, in the example file above, you would replace biffo with your user name, as well as those of other users you grant access to. Make sure there are entries in the password file for each user in the ".htaccess" file. We strongly suggest you follow these steps or the variations specific to your server that will accomplish the same end. Leaving the *form_install.pl* script unprotected could lead to disaster!

Once these changes are made, you're ready to test the script to see if it's installed properly.

Testing the Form Generator

With so little to adapt to make the script run on any typical UNIX Web server, there are considerably fewer opportunities for the script to break. However, Murphy's Law is especially active in the computer world, as anyone who works with the technology will attest. There are several things that could potentially go wrong, so we'll run down some tests you can use to make sure everything is in order and what to do if something goes wrong. Again, this may seem basic, depending on your experience and abilities. However, these chapters are meant to serve double-duty: to act as a guide for this installation as well as a primer for any CGI installation.

Once you've localized the script source, you should perform a basic integrity test on the script by running it from the UNIX command line. If you've introduced any syntax errors, or if there's a mismatch between the Perl on your system and the version the script is written for, you should expect error messages.

Perl is generally good about providing intelligible error feedback. It will specify the line of the script that caused the error and quote code from around where the error occurred. Sorting through these errors shouldn't be too difficult. A note on Perl debugging: A missing semicolon (;) somewhere in the body of the script generates errors that appear to be totally unrelated to the missing semicolon and on lines far afield from where it is missing. So if everything appears to be OK on the lines cited, look for the last and next semicolon and check that there aren't any missing!

There are several error messages that indicate problems with the way the script is installed. If you see a message that says something like "command not found," chances are better than average that the path to Perl on the first line of the script is wrong.

If, however, you see anything that mentions permissions, check the way you set the ownership and permissions for the script. In a long listing, the script should look something like this:

```
-rwxr-x---   1 www      httpd     31425 Dec 10 15:42 formgen.pl*
```

The script's mode should be 755 or 750, and it should be owned by the user ID under which the Web server runs.

If everything works as it should, you'll see a torrent of HTML-formatted text printed out to your terminal screen. This is the welcome form that will end up going to your browser when we hit the script from the Web, which is our next step. Fire up a Web browser, preferably Netscape, and open the URL that points to your server and the *formgen.pl* script. For our installation that URL would be:

```
http://www.outer.net/cgi-bin/formgen.pl
```

Provided everything is set up correctly, you should see the Form Generation Tool's welcome screen, which looks like the one shown in Figure 5-2.

There are only two results that indicate the script is still not installed properly. If you receive the familiar "404 File not found" error from your server, you typed the URL's path or the script name wrong, or the script isn't where you're expecting it to be. If, instead, you get a "500 Server Error" message, there is something wrong with the script itself. This may be an indication that Perl can't run it due to errors, or that the user who runs the Web server can't run the script or can't get to the directory where the script resides.

Debugging Mode

If you're getting some output from the Tool, but things aren't going the way you thought they should, the Tool has an internal mechanism that can make troubleshooting somewhat easier. The $debug variable that we glossed over previously can be set to 1 to enable additional, verbose output that would otherwise drive you nuts (see Figure 5-1). But when things aren't working, it can be a real godsend!

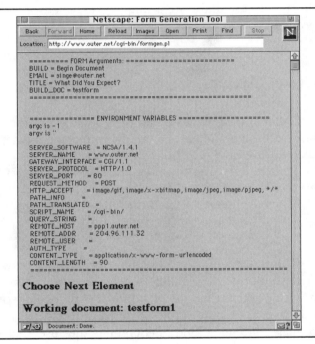

■ **Figure 5-1**
The Tool's Debugging output can save much frustration when things aren't working.

This output can be useful for analyzing exactly what data is being passed from the form to the CGI. It displays the environment variables, their values, and the fields and values the script is extracting from the browser's input.

In addition, the $debug flag is used at various points in the script as a trigger to output information regarding what is being done at that moment. If you decide to extend the script by adding code, you can use this feature to test your additions. The standard implementation of $debug is as follows:

```
if ($debug) {
  print "table status has changed<P>";
}
```

Of course, normally you will want to leave debugging off. Otherwise, it produces about a screenful of information every time the script is called from a form.

In the same vein, the ever-helpful *post-query.pl* can be called by the form to echo back exactly what is being passed to the script from the form. This is very useful during debugging, especially if you're getting unexpected results in your data.

BEHIND THE WHEEL

Now that you've made certain the Tool is operational, let's embark on a short tutorial that creates a sample form, step-by-step. We'll test all the basic features and see exactly how they work.

First, call the Tool from its initial URL. This can be done on your own server, if you have installed it locally, or on the server that hosts this book's CGIs, *www.outer.net*. Here's the URL to access the Tool on this server:

```
http://www.outer.net/cgi-bin/formgen.pl
```

This will bring up the welcome form that we saw in Figure 4-2. For the purposes of this tutorial, let's assume we want to create a form for capturing registration information for a particular software package. We'll want to get the users' names, contact information, where they bought the software, and what kind of computers they use. Our first step is to fill out the form with our sample form information.

Enter the data as shown in Figure 5-2, substituting your own e-mail address in the appropriate field. Once completed, click the Begin Document button.

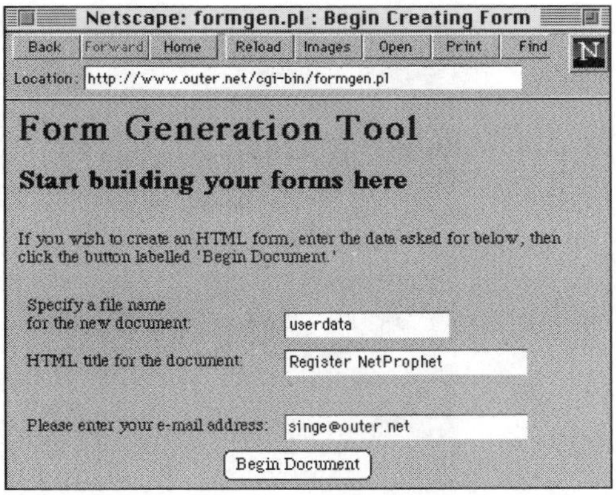

Figure 5-2

For the tutorial, the Welcome Form should contain this information.

If someone has, your file's name will have a number appended to it. This number will be incremented until the name is unique. In other words, if there was already a file in the data directory called "userdata", the Tool would check to see if there was also a "userdata1". If not, this will become the name for your document. If such a file does exist, the number will be increased by one, creating "userdata2", and so on.

To get our form off to a quick start, let's create a header that identifies the form's function. First, click on the HTML Element radio button, then pull down the selection beneath it until it shows Header. Since we have not begun the form entry portion of the document, we will also turn off the table option by clicking the Off radio button. We keep the Line break after element option on, however. When the form looks like the one in Figure 5-3, click the Create Element button.

When the next form page loads, you'll see options for the heading element. Notice that the name of the working document, "userdata", is preserved from one form to the next. This ensures that you are adding elements to the proper file. This is a very simple form, so we'll tell you how to fill it out without the benefit of a figure. For the "level," select 2, for the "alignment," select Center, and type the following for the heading text:

```
Please take the time to register your copy of NetProphet
```

Once you're ready, click on the Set Options button. After a brief wait, you're back at—surprise!—the element selection form again. If you look closely, you'll notice one difference on this page. The top line should read Added Heading element. This is a bit of feedback to assure you that your data was received and you're not going in circles.

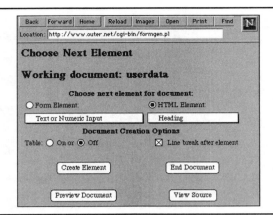

Figure 5-3
The Header will be the first element we create in our sample document.

If you wish, before we add the next element, you can view the source you created, or preview the way the parsed HTML will look by clicking the View Source or Preview Document buttons. Feel free to take a look at how the form is coming along any time we return to this page. That's what the buttons are there for.

Looking at the element selection form before continuing, you'll notice the addition of the Remove Last Element button. Since we now have elements to remove, this button appears on this page from now on. If you make a mistake in data entry, click this button and the element will be removed. Be careful, though, because if it's clicked again, it will keep removing elements until you have nothing left. Still, a little risk is worth having a powerful feature like this available.

Next, we'll start into the input fields. Click on the Table On button to make sure we get the benefit of the Tool's formatting abilities. The rest of the form should actually be filled out for you, since Form Element and Text or Numeric Input are the defaults for the page, but verify that these two fields are indeed filled out. The form should look like the fragment shown in Figure 5-4.

After verifying your input, click on the Create Element button again and wait for the text/numeric input option form to appear. This form is the prototype for most of the form element option forms left. It was the first we created and soon thereafter was used to create the interfaces for many of the remaining elements. It consists of the fields defined in Table 5-1.

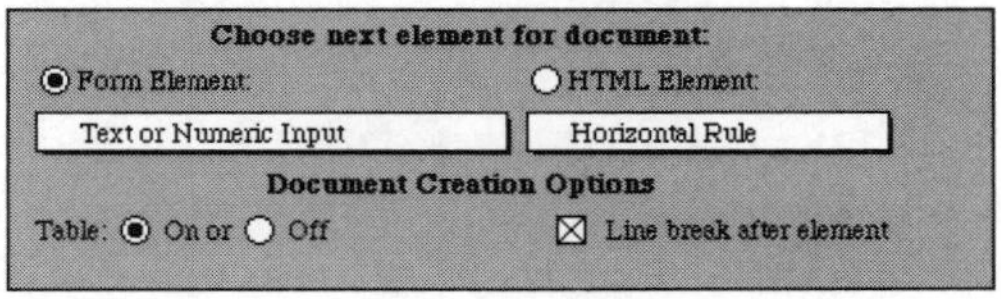

Choose next element for document:

⦿ Form Element: ○ HTML Element:

| Text or Numeric Input | | Horizontal Rule |

Document Creation Options

Table: ⦿ On or ○ Off   ☒ Line break after element

Figure 5-4
The next element will include input fields.

Table 5-1

Text/numeric form element option fields

Field	Description
Label text	The text that will precede the field on the form used to identify what data you expect the user to enter in the field.
Name	Used to identify the field to the CGI that will serve the form. If planning a Perl CGI, it is recommended to make field names all uppercase.
Type	Options are text, number, or password. Password is also text, but the value typed into the field is echoed back masked off.
Value	Optional default value for the field. It will appear in the field when the user sees the form, and the user can add to it or delete it at will.
Size	An optional parameter, with default value 20 (monospaced) characters wide.
Maxlength	Another optional field, the default is not to limit length. Can serve as a rudimentary data validation tool.

We'll configure this text field to capture the user's name. Enter your data so that it matches what's shown in Figure 5-5; then click the Set Options button.

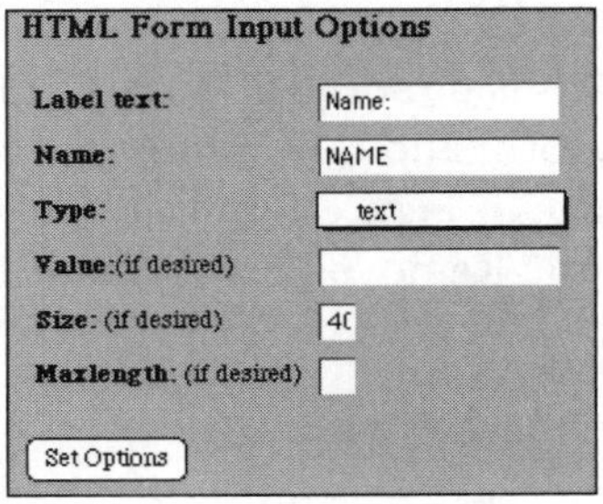

HTML Form Input Options

Label text: | Name: |

Name: | NAME |

Type: | text |

Value: (if desired) | |

Size: (if desired) | 40 |

Maxlength: (if desired) | |

| Set Options |

Figure 5-5
The configuration for the Text Input field.

We'll pick up the pace now and add five more text fields to our form. For all five fields you can leave the table and line break options as they are. None will have default values defined. The label text and the names for all five are shown in Table 5-2. Of the five, ADDRESS, CITY, and EMAIL will keep the same length as our previous field, namely 40.

Table 5-2
Label text and names for five text input fields

Label Text	Name
Street Address:	ADDRESS
City:	CITY
State:	STATE
Zipcode:	ZIP
E-mail Address:	EMAIL

Only STATE and ZIP will be handled differently. Before creating STATE, click in the Line Break After Element checkbox. Then click the Create Element button. STATE will have a size of 2 and a maxlength of 2, so the user is forced to use the two-letter state abbreviation.

Once STATE's options are set and you're back at the element selection form, you will notice that the line break option is checked again. That's because it's assumed that most of the time you'll want this on, so it gets reset each time. This is in contrast to the Table option that "remembers" its state from one step to another. It toggles on or off until you change it.

Now we'll create the ZIP field. This will be a numeric input, so make sure the select is on the proper option, i.e., number. Also, the size will be 5 and the maxlength will be 10 so the field is the size of a standard zip code, with enough space to take a full zip code with a form of "12345-6789." Set these options for the ZIP field and then create the EMAIL field with the standard type of text and a size of 40.

Once all this is done, click on the Preview Document button from the element select form and take a look at your handiwork. It should look very close to the form in Figure 5-6. If it does not, go back as many steps as needed, using the Remove Last Element button, and redo the steps until you have a match.

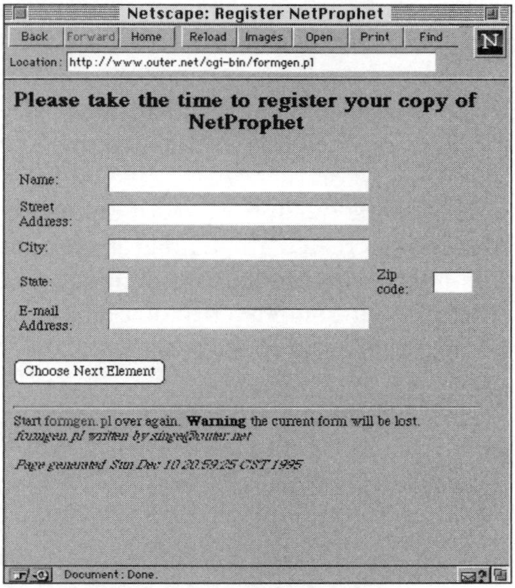

Figure 5-6
Preview Document lets you see the Registration Form in progress.

From this form fragment you can see the effect of the Tool's table formatting option. Instead of a ragged line along the right-hand side of the browser window, the table rows and cells line everything up according to the longest piece of data in each row.

In addition, you can see the result of turning the line break off between fields. The STATE and ZIP fields are grouped on the same row. It would be more pleasing if we could tuck the ZIP label and field under the overhang created by the CITY field above, but the heuristic logic Netscape uses to calculate table layout does not allow for it easily. One workaround would be to edit the form source once finished, placing the label and field for STATE and ZIP in one data cell each, making a two-cell row like the rest of them.

Creating the Second Half of the Form

With the first half of the form complete, let's proceed with the second half. This will consist of a divider, a short thank-you message, and some optional data. We'll use some of the elements we have not yet seen and continue to work with the universal formatting options to achieve the desired effect.

Each step of the way, as you set the options for an element, the Form Generator wrote the results to a small HTML file. That file is identified with the working name of your document, and the element's number is appended to it to make a unique filename. This way, the infinite Undo can work, and the Tool can keep track of all the pieces of the form you are creating.

First, let's divide the upper part of the registration form from the lower. The first fields we created are mandatory for the user's registration to be processed; the ones that follow are optional. Click on the first line of the HTML Element button and verify that Horizontal Rule is selected. Turn off the Table option, and click the Create Element button.

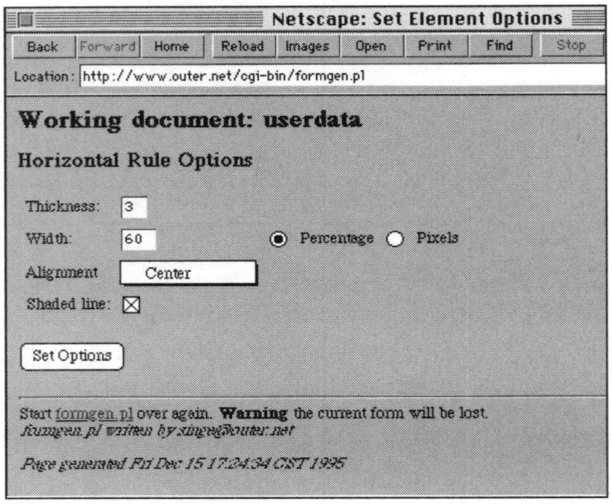

Figure 5-7
The configuration for the Horizontal Rule options.

The options for the horizontal rule element reflect the Netscape extensions available for this HTML tag. Once you've set the options the way they appear in Figure 5-7, you may proceed.

Now we will add a small piece of text to explain the rest of the form to the user. With the table option still turned off, we will click the HTML Element button and select Text. Type the following to the supplied <TEXTAREA>:

```
     Thank you for supplying your registration information above. Now if you
will please take the time to answer the following question, we can enter you
into our drawing for a free t-shirt!
```

Select the text style Bold and set the options.

The next element we'll create is a group of radio buttons that allows users to specify where they bought the product. You create the label for this set of buttons the same way you entered the text above, but first add some space between the text and the label. With the table still off, click HTML Element again and select `Line Break`. The selection on the options form allows you three choices for the type of break you want: a line break, paragraph break, or word break, which produce <BR>, <P>, and <WBR> tags, respectively. Select `Paragraph Break` and set the options.

Back at the element selection form, you create the label for the buttons. Click HTML Element and select `Heading`. The table option should still be off, and you can turn off the line break option as well. Set the heading size to 3 and type `Where did you purchase NetProphet?`

Now, for the buttons. Select `Radio Button`, turn the table option on, and click Create Element. The next form should look slightly different from the options forms we've encountered thus far. First, the `Label text` field is missing, which makes sense, because each individual radio button usually has its own label. Second, after the usual `Name` field there's a numeric field used to specify the number of buttons to be created. This can be as large as you want, which makes it easy to create arbitrarily large groups of radio buttons.

The next deviation from the norm is the TEXTAREA provided for the labels and values of the buttons to be created. As the form's instructions state, buttons are created by typing each button's label/value pair on a line by itself with the label and value separated by a comma. If no value is provided, the label for the button will also be its value.

The last field enables you to specify which button should be checked as the default. Buttons are specified by their line numbers, where the first is 1, second 2, etc. You can also input 0 (zero) if no default is desired.

To continue the tutorial, fill out the form so that it matches Figure 5-8; then click Set Options.

The next element is a Select that specifies the user's version of the software. At the element selection form, click Select and proceed. The option form for a Select bears a striking resemblance to the radio button interface. The `Label text` field has reappeared, but the `Number of options` field, the TEXTAREA, and the selected option field are taken directly from radio buttons. In addition, there is a checkbox that allows for multiple selections and another field to specify the size of the selection window.

For our purposes, you can make the Select's label `Which version of the program did you buy?` and the name read `PLATFORM`. The following four options will then appear:

```
Macintosh
Windows
DOS
BeBox
```

The rest of the fields can be left with their default values intact. Once this element is created, you're finished with the body of the form.

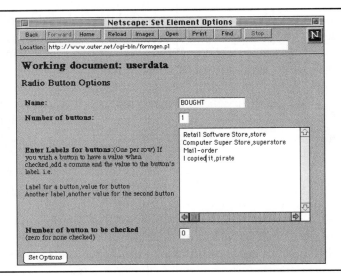

Figure 5-8
A completed Button Option form.

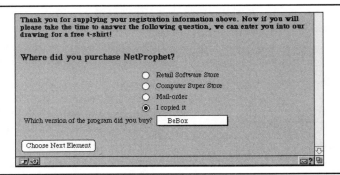

Figure 5-9
The second half of the form is completed.

Just by way of comparison, let's look at Figure 5-9 and see how the bottom of the form turned out. You can see that our <HR> really did turn out to be three pixels thick, centered, and 60% of the window wide. Our <B> text is bold and our inserted whitespace and <H3> text are there. The radio buttons are embedded in a table with the buttons right-aligned in one cell and the label left-aligned in the next cell, each on one row. Finally, the Select looks as we would expect.

The last step is to add a Submit button and then turn to the myriad ways in which the Tool will let us complete the project.

Finishing Your Sample Form

The last element to set is the Submit button. You can also turn the table option off because we don't need it for formatting anymore.

On the options form you'll see both `Name` and `Value` text input fields, and radio buttons allowing you to specify a Submit or a Reset button. The name field is optional and won't be needed unless you are building a form with multiple Submit buttons. The value field will be displayed on the button itself, so we'll make it `Register NetProphet`. We leave the radio button set to its default value, so we create a Submit button.

When we return to the element selection page, we've finished creating the form. All we need to do after previewing it is to somehow get our hands on the HTML document.

The first step is to click on the End Document button, which brings you to the form we saw in Chapter 4. The first field you see is the `hostname` field, which needs to be filled out if the form is not destined for the server that the Tool is running on. Below that are the four available delivery options.

View Source Online

The simplest option is to view the entire document's HTML source in your browser's window (see Figure 5-10). This looks exactly like the View Source button's output, except that it presents a completed document. The "source" effect is achieved by filtering out the < and > characters and replacing them with `&lt;` and `&gt;`. This way, the source is not parsed as HTML, but passed raw to the browser window just as text would be. From your window you can easily save the text using the Save option from your File menu and have a completed form on your local machine.

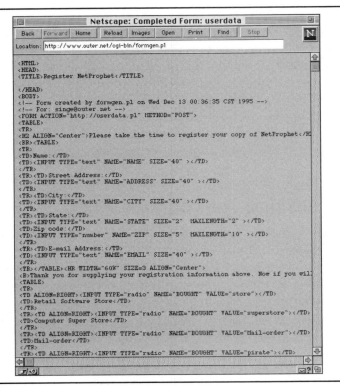

Figure 5-10
Our sample form as viewed in a browser.

Downloading the Form Document

A more direct approach is to have the Tool complete the form, compress it, and present you with a link for downloading. That is what the next option does. Your completed document is copied to the Web server's document root directory, compressed, and you are presented a simple page with a link to download the form, as shown in Figure 5-11. This link will perform an HTTP file transfer to your machine. If your browser is properly set up for file extensions and helper applications, the file should be passed off to your *gzip* decompression utility.

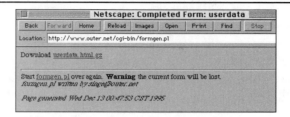

Figure 5-11
The Download Link performs an GTTP file transfer to your machine.

If, for some reason, your browser is not set up properly, you'll probably see a message that mentions not knowing what to do with a file of this type, which will give you the choice to pick an application or save the file for post-processing. Consult your browser application's documentation for setting this up properly.

Once on your local machine and decompressed, you are free to edit your form. We'll cover the entire question of customizing the Form Generator's output in Chapter 8.

What if you don't want to get the file immediately? If you're busy on your computer and can't fiddle with getting the form to your machine, the next option is for you!

Receiving the Form in E-mail

If you want to receive the form asynchronously, that is, without an immediate investment of time on your part, you may want to choose e-mail delivery. The form is completed as before, but instead of requiring extra steps to get it to your local machine, it's sent via e-mail. When the message comes, you can save it to disk and edit out whatever remains of its SMTP headers.

The Tool doesn't prompt you for an e-mail address where it should send the form because it knows yours from when you first started building the document. In other words, the form is sent to the e-mail address supplied in the welcome and initialization form, using the *mail* command defined at the beginning of the script. The default is *mailx*, which sends the mail with the subject Form Generation Delivery.

If, on the other hand, you have been building this form so you could use it on the same machine the Tool is running on, none of these options is particularly convenient. For example, if you've toiled to install the Tool on your Web server with the intention of creating documents for that server, you probably don't want to get the form at your local machine. In this instance, what was a convenience turns into an annoyance as you go through the steps to upload and install the form on the server. The irony here, of course, is that the form was built and resides on the server before the Tool ever got it to your machine. Well, have no fear, we saw this coming, too.

Installing Your Form Online

Remember the *form_install.pl* script we took great pains to make secure in the early sections of this chapter? Now's the time to put its considerable functionality to use. If you click the radio button labeled `Install the form on...<the name of the server on which you are running the Tool>`, you'll be asked to provide a path where you wish to place the form. Once you type the absolute path to this target directory, click the Submit button, and the script will attempt to place your completed form there. It maintains a backup copy at its own server, so you'll be able to retrieve it if your transfer fails.

Not only does the script install the document in a directory of your choice, it also sets permissions so that it will be accessible from the Internet. The ability to place your script in the target directory is dependent on the permissions set for that directory. If the Web server ID is able to write to the file, it will succeed. If this user ID doesn't have permission to write, the installation will fail.

This method is the most convenient that the Tool offers because it requires no action on the user's part to make the form functional on the local Web server. By contrast, the other methods require the user to get the file on a local machine, upload it to the server, then, possibly, to set the ownership and permissions for access.

However, for all its functionality, *form_install.pl* does present a security risk, as we discussed earlier.

Integrating the Form into a CGI

When we were considering the feature set for the Form Generator, we thought about the process of creating forms on the Web. What we realized was that creating HTML-formatted text represents less than half of the work involved in getting a form up and running. In most instances, the more difficult part of the job usually occurs when creating the CGI to service that form.

Sometimes, there's an existing CGI—a simple e-mail script, for example, for which you are writing the form—but most of the time this is not the case. In most instances, you will be faced with the challenge of writing a custom script, or hiring someone else to write it. Either option can be costly, both in time and money.

When considering what we could do to reduce this investment for our readers, we considered generating part or all of the necessary CGI code along with the Perl script. In fact, the idea of generating all the code or a finished CGI was quickly discarded because there was no way for us to anticipate all the potential uses for the form and its associated CGI. Generating partial code is an entirely different story.

All CGIs share a core functionality. They all must have the ability to verify that they are being called by the expected method and then must extract the data submitted by the client. After that point, they deviate, doing whatever their designers wished them to do. This commonality, however, presents us with an opportunity to provide the user with a kind of boilerplate CGI script to use with the newly authored form.

By itself, this idea doesn't hold enormous appeal for the user. If the CGI shell isn't doing anything specifically for the form, then it would have been easier to download the shell separately. Additionally, attempting to give the user two separate files during the delivery process would complicate our fairly elegant process.

The answer lies in the way the Tool's primary script, *formgen.pl*, behaves. If you recall, when it's called from a simple URL, whether supplied by a link or manually typed into the browser, the Tool responds with the welcome form. The FORM tag on the welcome form names *formgen.pl* in the ACTION HREF, effectively pointing back at itself, with the POST method. When the Submit button is clicked, *formgen.pl* tests the calling method, recognizes it as POST, and begins creating the form.

If we built the user's new form into a Perl CGI that returned the form when called by a GET and then posted back to itself, we'd be offering some real value. We'd be providing the shell CGI code along with their form, in one easy-to-deliver package. Not wanting to pass up a chance to skip some drudgery, that's exactly what we did!

On the delivery form, below the delivery mode radio buttons, there's an option to incorporate your form into a Perl script and a field to supply the path to Perl, if it is not the same as the one found on the Web server. If this button is checked, your form will be rolled into a Perl script that resembles the Tool script—it's what we like to call a self-referential CGI. When you click on a link containing its URL or type it manually into the browser, it runs and spits out the HTML source for the form, along with a button. This button, when clicked, calls the same CGI using a different method, and this time, the CGI extracts the form data and spits it back at the browser for debugging purposes.

What you do with this shell after the Tool delivers it to you is your business, but we'll discuss some possibilities in Chapter 8, "Making Things Work: Installing and Testing Your Forms and CGIs." All in all, it's an open-ended solution that eliminates a decent amount of the work you would otherwise have to do.

There are a few instances where you would not want to have an integrated form/CGI of this type. It does take more system resources to run a CGI than it does to open and read a simple text file. However, the difference is not so great that a form, subject to an average amount of use, is going to take down your server when rolled into a CGI. However, if you're expecting heavy traffic on a particular form, you may want to monitor the server load or ask your administrator if the CGI is harming the system.

Last Step: Validating Your HTML

In the previous chapter we mentioned HaL's HTML validation service that was designed and implemented, for the most part by Mark Gaither, one of this book's co-authors. This service is quite valuable for debugging HTML code and making sure it works consistently with all HTML browsers. The validation service home page is at:

```
http://www.halsoft.com/html-val-svc/
```

These HTML validation pages also include an HTML form fragment that adds a URL that links its validating capability to any page. We'll use this to add the capability of checking for any errors that may have crept into our user's form, either from our code or from the combination of elements that the user has added since it was generated.

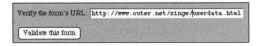

Figure 5-12
The HTML Validation Form interface.

The validation service works on either a plain form or a form rolled into a CGI. Therefore, the form fragment can be added to the user's end product, regardless of what other options are chosen. When installed, the form looks like the one in Figure 5-12. The field is used to enter the form's URL, and its default value is set to what the Tool guesses is going to be the final URL. If it is incorrect, however, the user can edit it to reflect the correct value.

When it's submitted, the URL is passed to the *html_check.pl* CGI on HAL's Web server, and the results are passed back to the browser. If there are errors, the line numbers where these errors occur are identified and the type of error explained. This proves to be an excellent debugging tool, especially if the user uses the error messages to edit the form and then resubmits the URL for validation.

The checkbox for this feature is located just beneath the Make CGI checkbox. Selecting it causes the HTML fragment to be added to whatever final form and mode of delivery you have chosen.

SUMMARY

We have now completed our tutorial overview of the Form Generation Tool. After discussing its installation and localization, we explored how to use the Tool and all its features. A sample form was created, using a good subset of the elements that the Tool currently supports. Finally, we discussed the various delivery methods provided by the Tool, including the options to roll the form into a CGI and to validate the HTML source.

Next, we'll delve deeper into the Tool, taking a look at the source code that makes it tick.

The Form Generator's Behavior and Internal Workings

*N*ow that we've discussed the Tool's external behaviors, features, and functionality, we'll examine the code that makes it work. We'll move through the source listing of the main script, *formgen.pl,* in a mostly linear fashion, highlighting the portions of code that perform the most crucial functions. Wherever possible, we'll parallel our discussion of the code with the actual use of the script, mirroring the sequence we mapped out in the Chapter 5 tutorial. Finally, we'll take apart the CGI shell for the program.

INITIALIZATION: THE SCRIPT WAKES UP

When the *formgen.pl* script is called initially, it is from a link or a manually typed URL. When a CGI is called in this manner, the default method used is called a GET, as opposed to POST, the usual method from a submit button within a form. A simple point, perhaps, and certainly one we have harped upon enough in these pages. However, the Tool's functions hinge upon the fact that we can ascertain which method called the script from within the running script itself.

In either case, this initial block of code runs every time *formgen.pl* is called:

```
$| = 1;                    # output NOT buffered
print "Content-Type:\ttext/html\n\n\n";
```

These two lines are familiar to anyone who has looked at Perl CGI scripts before. The $| variable turns off data buffering to avoid data loss, which can occur when the browser/CGI connection is broken before Perl dumps the remainder of the output from its buffers.

The print statement is used to "prime" the HTML browser. It takes the place of the header that the server would normally send to the browser when an HTML file is requested. The browser is informed by the header to expect the response to be HTML-formatted. It is useful to get this feedback to the client as soon as the script starts, so that the browser's connection does not time out while the script is at work.

The *date* command in our script is a hidden dependency on UNIX:

```
chop($date = `/bin/date`);
# For the 'this page created' line at the bottom.
```

However, *date* is prevalent among flavors of UNIX so the risk is minimal. We primarily use this to stamp the pages with the time the script is run. This is a useful way to inform the user that the page is being generated on-the-fly. The date is also used to log the script's use.

The debugging flag variable was discussed in an earlier chapter. It is used to activate various commands that create debugging output as the script runs:

```
$debug = 0;
```

The following lines extract information from our environment variables regarding the machine we are running on, the path to the script, and the script's name itself:

```
$host = $ENV{SERVER_NAME};
$ENV{SCRIPT_NAME} =~ s/([a-zA-Z0-9\.\-_]+)$//;
$program = $1;
$scriptpath = $ENV{SCRIPT_NAME};
```

The SCRIPT_NAME variable holds the path part of the URL that was used to call the script. This would look something like */cgi-bin/formgen.pl*. Using regular expression matching, we chop off all the characters that follow the last / in the path and store the results in $1. Any text inside parentheses that matches in a Perl script is automatically placed in these numbered variables: $1 for the first match, $2 for the second, and so on.

Finally, the modified environment variable, now just containing the path, is assigned to its own variable.

This last group of initializations handles localization:

```
$readablepath = "/www/httpdocs/";
$datapath = "formgen/";
$compress = "/usr/local/bin/gzip";
$mail = "/usr/bin/mailx -s 'Form Generation Delivery' ";
```

$readablepath is the document directory of your Web server and is used to download the finished product to the user. The variable $datapath specifies the relative path from the directory where the Tool's main script resides, to the directory where support and data files are installed. The path to your favorite compression utility is stored in the $compress variable, and the $mail variable stores the name of the mail agent that is available on your system. We use an agent that is capable of setting the Subject line with a -s flag on the command line, but this is not mandatory.

Now that its runtime environment is properly configured, the script turns its attention to the user who awakened it. In particular, it looks at the way in which it was invoked and tailors its behavior accordingly.

POST or GET, the Eternal Question

As we mentioned, CGIs are called by either GET or POST. Since all our form parts of the Generation Tool used the POST method, we can assume that if the GET method is being used, the script was called externally. Any POST method request can safely be assumed to be a request that originated from the script itself and so will be handled in an entirely different way.

The following line of Perl code is the critical point at which the path through the script branches out into two disparate paths:

```
if ($ENV{REQUEST_METHOD} eq "POST") {
```

Since this statement will be false the first time the script is accessed, we'll jump over the block of code that executes if it is evaluated as true. This will actually bring us to the very end of the script, where the welcome form is generated and returned to the waiting browser.

The Welcome Form

When the if statement evaluates as false, the script jumps to the following block of code:

```
} else {
  print "<HTML>\n",
   "<HEAD>\n",
   "<TITLE>",
   "$program : Begin Creating Form",
   "</TITLE>\n",
   "</HEAD>\n",
   "<BODY>\n",
   "<FORM ACTION=\"http://$host$scriptpath$program\"",
   " METHOD=\"POST\" >\n",
   "<H1>Form Generation Tool</H1>\n",
   "<H2>Start building your forms here</H2>\n",
   "<BR>\n",
   "If you wish to create an HTML form, enter the data ",
   "asked for below, then click the button labeled ",
   "'Begin Document.'<P>",
   "<TABLE>\n",
   "<TR><TD>Specify a filename<BR>\n",
   "for the new document: </TD>\n",
   "<TD><BR>\n",
   "<INPUT TYPE=\"text\" NAME=\"BUILD_DOC\" SIZE=\"20\"",
   " MAXLENGTH=\"80\"></TD></TR>\n",
   "<TR><TD>\n",
   "HTML title for the document:</TD><TD>\n",
   "<INPUT TYPE=\"text\" NAME=\"TITLE\" SIZE=\"30\" ",
   "MAXLENGTH=\"80\">",
   "</TD></TR>\n",
   "<TR><TH><BR></TH></TR>\n",
   "<TR><TD>Please enter your e-mail address: </TD><TD>\n",
   "<INPUT TYPE=\"text\" NAME=\"EMAIL\"",
   " SIZE=\"30\" MAXLENGTH=\"80\"></TD></TR>\n</TABLE>\n",
   "<CENTER><INPUT TYPE=\"submit\" NAME=\"BUILD\" VALUE=\"Begin",
   " Document\"></CENTER>\n",
   "</FORM>\n",
   "</BODY>\n";
   "</HTML>\n";
  &footer;
}
```

Since this is our first look at a form embedded in Perl code, we include this block *in toto*, so that you can get a good idea of the general behavior involved. As you can see, getting the form's HTML source back to the browser from within a CGI script is a simple matter of printing it to STDOUT. The connection between the browser, the server, and the CGI script passes the output all the way back to the user, where it is parsed and displayed.

The only special considerations you must keep in mind when embedding HTML Perl code are the handling of quotes and formatting for readability.

Quote marks are easily dealt with by escaping them with a backslash, as you see in the previous code sample. When Perl encounters a \ (backslash) in front of a quote mark, it ignores any meaning the quote has other than its ASCII value. There is another way to deal with this — by using *here* documents. This would look something like:

```
print <<"EOF";
<HTML>
<HEAD>
<TITLE>Right Here!</TITLE>
</HEAD><BODY>
<A HREF="http://$host/singe">This is my home page.</A> <P>
I call it a "work in progress," tell me what you would call it!<BR>
</BODY>
</HTML>
EOF
```

Please note the following about a *here* document: Quote marks don't have to be escaped and variables are substituted by their values. This may seem like a cleaner way to embed HTML in a script, but there is a catch that keeps this method from being the ideal it may at first appear to be. Any whitespace at the beginning of a line inside a *here* document is output with the print.

In other words, unless you want to produce HTML that has massive amounts of whitespace at the beginning of each line, you must format the *here* document with its lines flush against the left margin. This may seem minor, but when producing readable, maintainable Perl code, large chunks of unindented text don't produce the desired effect.

Even with their drawbacks, *here* documents can be a useful way to produce HTML from within Perl. The authors of this book use several approaches, depending upon the script's context and intended use.

The second consideration when using regular print statements to output HTML is source readability. The code may look readable, and the parsed HTML will look fine regardless of whitespace, but, if left to its own devices, the HTML source will be all on one line. This can be remedied by inserting a newline character, \n, wherever it seems appropriate. This may seem like a small point but when debugging, it can be critical.

To that end, there's a third alternative that may be more palatable to programmers' aesthetics — namely, to place the contents of the *here* document in a separate file, one that is called explicitly with a Perl print << statement. If you scrupulously use variables when calling the document, you can create a "template" script that calls in different files from different directories, that pertain to the specific entries created.

For example, you could create a response-generation script that returns different *here* documents based on the options chosen in the form — if a variable named "doulike" has its script-passed value set to "like.html," return file "like.html"; if the variable is set to "dislike.html," return file "dislike.html", but do it without if/else statements by defining the pathname of the file to be returned as $doulike.

Then, simply create files "like.html" and "dislike.html". This form of modularizing is especially useful if you want people to be able to get to the same page several different ways: Using this approach, they can access the files directly, or the script can do it for them.

This technique eliminates the problem of whitespace interfering with your Perl code's readability.

Now that our general discussion is out of the way, what exactly does this portion of the script do? Quite simply, it returns the welcome form that you saw in the tutorial in Chapter 5, "Setup, Initialization, and Interactivity in the Form Generator." The entire document, the title, explanatory labels, input fields, and Submit button, are created when the HTML is returned to the browser. The important points to note are that the FORM tag cites the same script, *formgen.pl,* as its ACTION HREF. Therefore, when the user inputs data, the Submit button calls the script again, this time using the POST method.

They're at the POST!

So, what other than terrible puns, does the POST method produce? The script is run by the Web server again, as it was before, but this time the METHOD environment variable is explicitly set to POST, and all the submitted form's field names and values are passed via STDIN. The script steps through the initialization and setup lines detailed earlier, and then comes again to this statement:

```
if ($ENV{REQUEST_METHOD} eq "POST") {
```

which of course this time evaluates as true. The script now takes the other major branch in the code. This time, before returning anything to the browser, it extracts the form data. This is accomplished using Brigitte Jellinek's *formlib.pl*:

```
require "./formlib.pl" || print "<H1>Can't find formlib:$</H1>!";
&GetFormArgs();
# Parse arguments passed from FORM (now in %in).
$ENV{PATH_INFO} ne '' && &GetPathArgs($ENV{PATH_INFO});
```

The `require` loads the library into our script and makes Jellinek's subroutines accessible. If it fails, it will return error messages to the browser before dying. If it succeeds, it will go on to call the `GetFormArgs` subroutine, which thoroughly checks the browser's input and then extracts the form data, putting the field name/value pairs into the `%in` associative array.

Next we check the status of the `$debug` variable. If it is set to any non-zero value, an additional library will be called, *debugforms.pl*, which makes a debug subroutine available to the script:

```
if ($debug) {

    require "./debugforms.pl";
    &debug;
}
```

When this subroutine is called, as it is on the line after the `require`, it produces a response to the browser that resembles the output in Figure 6-1. Finally, a last piece of initialization code is executed before we really start to look at our data:

```
$build_doc = $in{BUILD_DOC};
```

Whenever a form is submitted to *formgen.pl* the working document's name is included in the data, either hidden or, in the case of the welcome screen, supplied by the user. This statement stores it in an easier-to-type variable, because our code is going to use it frequently.

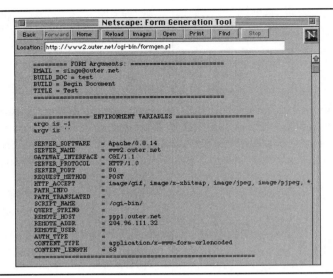

```
                Netscape: Form Generation Tool

 Back  Forward  Home   Reload  Images  Open  Print  Find   Stop        N

 Location: http://www2.outer.net/cgi-bin/formgen.pl

 ========== FORM Arguments: ========================
 EMAIL = singe@outer.net
 BUILD_DOC = test
 BUILD = Begin Document
 TITLE = Test
 =================================================


 =============== ENVIRONMENT VARIABLES =================
 argc is -1
 argv is ''

 SERVER_SOFTWARE   = Apache/0.8.14
 SERVER_NAME       = www2.outer.net
 GATEWAY_INTERFACE = CGI/1.1
 SERVER_PROTOCOL   = HTTP/1.0
 SERVER_PORT       = 80
 REQUEST_METHOD    = POST
 HTTP_ACCEPT       = image/gif, image/x-xbitmap, image/jpeg, image/pjpeg, *
 PATH_INFO         =
 PATH_TRANSLATED   =
 SCRIPT_NAME       = /cgi-bin/
 QUERY_STRING      =
 REMOTE_HOST       = ppp1.outer.net
 REMOTE_ADDR       = 204.96.111.32
 REMOTE_USER       =
 AUTH_TYPE         =
 CONTENT_TYPE      = application/x-www-form-urlencoded
 CONTENT_LENGTH    = 68
 =================================================
```

Figure 6-1
The debugging output produced when $debug is set to a non-zero value.

The BUILD Variable

Once we've extracted the form data, the largest deciding factor that controls the script's actions is the button that was clicked to call the CGI script. Buttons throughout the Tool's forms are consistently named BUILD and given different values according to their purpose. The value of a given button is visible on the button itself, and it is also included in the form input to the CGI. Therefore, by testing the extracted variable $in{BUILD}, we know what the user expected when the button was clicked.

In this way, the remainder of the script can be seen as a large if/elsif/elsif tree, where the value of the BUILD variable is tested over and over, until the proper command is found. When it is found, the appropriate code block is executed and the script can end.

The First Step in Creating a New Form

When starting a new document, the BUILD value is Begin Document. For readability's sake, this is also the first value tested for by the if decision tree:

```
if ($in{BUILD} eq "Begin Document") {
```

This conditional is the exact format for any test of the `BUILD` variable's value:

```
$build_doc =~ s/( |&|\+|\/|\\|,|'|"|!|\$|\*|\(|\))/_/g;
```

Next we translate into underlines any characters that might cause difficulties with the shell. We can thereby ensure that we aren't going to create a UNIX file that is a headache to try to copy and move, breaks the script, or is a security risk.

We are going to supply the correct suffix according to whether the user ends up with a form or a CGI, so if there are any common suffixes on the working document name, we chop them off. Note the use of the trailing `i` on the regular expression. It tells Perl to ignore case when matching and can be a real timesaver:

```
$build_doc =~ s/\.(html|htm|pl)$//i;
```

Now we initialize a counter variable to nothing; then test to see if a working document with the user's desired name exists already:

```
$counter = "";

while (-e "$datapath$build_doc$counter.HEAD") {
  $counter++;
}

$build_doc .= $counter;
```

If it does exist, we increment the counter and try again. Once we find a name that doesn't exist, we modify the `$build_doc` variable by appending the counter number that makes it unique.

In other words, if the user typed "test" for the name of the working document, but two people chose this name before and are either still working on their documents or have abandoned them unfinished, the following will happen: First, the script checks to see if "test" exists. It does, so it increments `$counter` to 1. It then checks to see if "test1" exists. It does because the second person to use the name "test" would have actually gotten "test1". The counter is incremented, and the existence of "test2" is checked. It doesn't already exist, so we permanently append "2" to the document's name. It's a crude kind of lock file, but it works fine in this context.

Once we have determined that our filename is unique in this directory, we can open the first file fragment for our form:

```
open (DOC, ">$datapath$build_doc.HEAD") || &liedowndie;
    print DOC "<!DOCTYPE HTML PUBLIC \"-//IETF//DTD HTML",
        " 2.0//EN\">\n<HTML>\n<HEAD>\n",
        "<TITLE>$in{TITLE}</TITLE>\n\n",
        "</HEAD>\n<BODY>\n<!- Form created by",
        " $program on $date ->\n",
        "<!- For: $in{EMAIL} ->\n";
    close DOC;
```

This fragment contains the form's first bits, so we give it the suffix ".HEAD", and write the standard HTML stuff to it. We'll specify the document's HTML title as well and wrap the user-supplied title in the <TITLE> tag. Finally, we write a comment to the file that describes when and how the form was created and for whom, and we're done.

A quick entry in a log file enables us to keep tabs on the Tool's level of usage:

```
open (LOG, ">>${datapath}${program}.log");
    print LOG "$date : $in{EMAIL}\n";
    close LOG;
```

These variables play an important role in the standard element selection form, as we'll soon see:

```
$step = 0;
    $table[1] = " CHECKED";
    $table = 0;
```

This subroutine is the real meat for most of the Tool:

```
&toolbar;
```

Even though we said we'd traverse the script linearly, it's important to look at this subroutine so we'll jump beyond the end of the script, where our subroutines are defined.

Toolbar Equals Element Selection Form

The toolbar subroutine, somewhat of a holdover from our planned "floating toolbar" interface, is called toolbar, though it is almost an entire page of form interface.

The following lines merely set up the page for the user — identifying the working document's name and prompting the user with the action this form requires — choosing the next element for inclusion in the form:

```
sub toolbar {
  print "<HTML>\n",
    "<HEAD><TITLE>Form Generation Tool</TITLE>\n",
    "</HEAD>\n",
    "<BODY>\n",
    "<FONT SIZE=5><B>Choose Next Element</B></FONT><BR>",
    "<H2>Working document: $build_doc</H2>\n",
```

Here is the now famous FORM tag that points back to the script that generated it. Using the variables set up from the environment variables, the ACTION names the script's URL. Note also that the POST method is explicitly specified:

```
"<FORM METHOD=\"POST\" ",
  "ACTION=\"http://$host$scriptpath$program\">\n",
```

In a sense, the hidden form fields are the real meat of the script. They maintain the user's state from one stateless connection to another. These are the variables we saw initialized before the subroutine was called:

```
"<INPUT TYPE=\"hidden\" NAME=\"TABLE_STATUS\"",
  "VALUE=\"$table\">\n",
  "<INPUT TYPE=\"hidden\" NAME=\"BUILD_DOC\" ",
  "VALUE=\"$build_doc\">\n",
  "<INPUT TYPE=\"hidden\" NAME=\"STEP\" VALUE=\"$step\">\n",
```

In general, these variables will be extracted from our previous form's input, so that the continuity is maintained from form to form. The three fields describe three different aspects of the current form. The first is the TABLE_STATUS, which keeps track of whether the user has the Table formatting option turned on or off. When we begin creating a form, the option button for "on" is clicked, so the default is to initialize the table formatting.

The second is the working document's name, as initially supplied by the user, and the third is a counter that keeps track of which STEP we're on. This is important because every step of the form creation is saved to a separate file with the step number as a suffix, and the final value of this variable will be used to gather all these pieces together. In other words, from this one counter we enable the infinite undo feature and the final build process.

There's a profound difference between the program's Undo command and using your browser's "Back" button or its bookmarks to return to an earlier screen. The Undo button actually backs out each change one at a time, and rolls back to an earlier version of your form. If you try to "go back in time" using your browser, however, you'll quickly discover that its abilities to display on-screen HTML greatly exceed its time-travel capabilities. The bottom line is: Use the Undo button to reverse changes in the Form Generator, not the Back button! ▲

After the invisible fields come the visible, formatted input fields, selects, and buttons. In the following `print` statement you can probably identify the form elements that make up the top half of the element selection form that we saw in the tutorial:

```
print "<TABLE>\n",
    "<TR>\n",
    "<TH COLSPAN=2>Choose next element for ",
    "document:</TH></TR>\n",
    "<TR><TD><INPUT TYPE=\"radio\" NAME=\"ELEMENT_TYPE\" ",
    "VALUE=\"FORM\" CHECKED>Form Element:\n",
    "</TD>\n",
    "<TD><INPUT TYPE=\"radio\" NAME=\"ELEMENT_TYPE\" ",
    "VALUE=\"HTML\" >HTML Element:</TD></TR>\n",
    "<TR><TD><SELECT NAME=\"FORM_ELEMENT\" SIZE=\"1\">\n",
    "<OPTION>Text or Numeric Input\n",
    "<OPTION>Large Text Area\n",
    "<OPTION>Hidden Field\n",
    "<OPTION>Radio Button\n",
    "<OPTION>Checkbox\n",
    "<OPTION>Select\n",
    "<OPTION>Submit\n",
    "</SELECT></TD>\n",
    "<TD><SELECT NAME=\"HTML_ELEMENT\" SIZE=\"1\">\n",
    "<OPTION>Horizontal Rule\n",
    "<OPTION>Line Break\n",
    "<OPTION>Heading\n",
    "<OPTION>Comment\n",
    "<OPTION>Image\n",
    "<OPTION>Link\n",
    "<OPTION>Text\n",
    "</SELECT></TD></TR>\n",
```

The table frames the entire form, and the layout of the input fields should look very familiar if you have looked over the form we built in Chapter 5. Here again we have the label in the left-hand cell and the field in the right-hand cell.

This next section sets up the options for form creation in the form and is most notable for how it handles the Table option radio buttons:

```
"<TR><TH COLSPAN=2>Document Creation Options</TH></TR>\n",
    "<TD>Table: <INPUT TYPE=\"radio\" NAME=\"TABLE\" ",
    "VALUE=\"1\"",
    " $table[1]> On or <INPUT TYPE=\"radio\" NAME=\"TABLE\" ",
    "VALUE=\"0\" $table[0]> Off </TD>\n",
    "<TD ALIGN=\"right\"><INPUT TYPE=\"checkbox\" ",
    "NAME=\"LINE_BREAK\" CHECKED> Line break after ",
    "element</TD></TR>\n",
    "<TR><TH><BR></TH></TR>\n";
```

As you recall, we initialized the table variables but said that after the first step they would be set according to the state of the table option on the previous step. That's how the table option state is preserved from one form element to the next.

To translate the state of the variable into the pair of radio buttons, we take the value of the previous state, either 1 or 0, stored in $in{TABLE}, and use it as an index for the statement:

```
$table[$in{TABLE}] = " CHECKED ";
```

Then, when the radio buttons are created, the variables $table[0] and $table[1] are embedded within the tags for the Off button and the On button, respectively. When the print statement is interpreted, one variable will be replaced with a NULL and the other with the value CHECKED. This will cause the correct button to be selected out of the pair when the user sees the form.

It's a small effect, but it serves to demonstrate the possibilities open to the programmer when dealing with a programming language specifically geared to manipulating text and a formatting language designed to create sophisticated graphical interfaces entirely out of the same raw material. Truly boundless.

We find it interesting that Netscape is proposing a "magic cookie" extension to HTML, when the resourceful programmer can use hidden elements and this type of tag and option manipulation to achieve many, if not all, of the same effects right now. Of course, by storing a "cookie" file on the user's machine, the user can come back to a site months after the initial visit and complete a transaction as though it were started minutes ago. Plus, cookies can remember other things about the user that customize the way the user interacts with the site. This could make our job easier, if only it were universally available!

The next portion of the element selection form consists of the various buttons: Create Element, View Source, Preview Document, End Document, and Remove Last Element.

This next chunk displays the Undo button if there was a last element to remove:

```
if ($in{STEP} > 0) {
    print "<TR><TD COLSPAN=2 ALIGN=\"center\"><INPUT ",
    "TYPE=\"submit\" NAME=\"BUILD\" VALUE=\"Remove last ",
    "element\"</TD></TR>";
}
```

On the first visit to the element selection form $in{STEP} will be undefined, and the button will therefore not appear. Finally, the four buttons are displayed by the following statement:

```
    print "<TR><TD ALIGN=\"center\"><INPUT TYPE=\"submit\" ",
    "NAME=\"BUILD\" VALUE=\"Create Element\"></TD>\n",
    "<TD ALIGN=\"center\"><INPUT TYPE=\"submit\" ",
    "NAME=\"BUILD\" ",
    "VALUE=\"End Document\"></TD></TR>\n",
    "<TR><TH><BR></TH></TR>\n",
    "<TR><TD ALIGN=\"center\"><INPUT TYPE=\"submit\" NAME=",
    "\"BUILD\" VALUE=\"Preview Document\"></TD>",
    "<TD ALIGN=\"center\"><INPUT TYPE=\"submit\" ",
    "NAME=\"BUILD\" ",
    "VALUE=\"View Source\"></TD></TR>\n",
    "</TABLE>\n",
    "</FORM>\n";

  &footer;
}
```

And on the last line of the subroutine, the `footer` subroutine is called again to create the recognizable signature at the bottom of the page.

The Undo Command

To jump back into our main `elsif` tree, we'll look at what happens if the user clicks the Remove Last Element button. Of course, the *formgen.pl* script is called again, the POST method is detected, and the value of the Submit button is tested.

The Begin Document block of code is skipped over, and this next conditional evaluates as true:

```
} elsif ($in{BUILD} eq "Remove last element") {
# Undo last document element created.
```

The first task the code performs is to roll back the counter variable. Because the counter is incremented before the form for selecting the next element is sent back to the user, the value of $in{STEP} needs to be decremented so that it points to the previous element:

```
$in{STEP} -= 1;
    open (TARGET, "$datapath$build_doc.$in{STEP}");
    print "<B>Removed the following source:</B><P>\n";
    while (<TARGET>) {
      s/</&lt;/g;
      s/>/&gt;/g;
      s/\n$/<BR>/;
      print
    }
    unlink ("$datapath$build_doc.$in{STEP}");
```

Once that is done, we will open the file where the element has been stored and show the user exactly what is being removed. Finally, the file itself is deleted.

Another small point to note: The tag begin and end characters, < and >, are replaced with the HTML character entities < and >. This allows the user to see source and not parsed HTML. It's the same technique used to view the document's source while it is being built and also during the script's delivery phase.

Now we're faced with a bit of a technical problem. The table option's state may or may not have been changed when the form was submitted, so we don't have a reliable way to determine if the table was on or off in the step prior to the one we just deleted. (Actually, this is only partially true. There is no reliable way to tell from the submitted form data.) There is, however, a way to access the final authority on this question: the actual file that contains the previous form fragment. That's what we'll do next:

```
open (LAST, "$datapath$build_doc".$in{STEP}-1);
while (<LAST>) {
  $element = $_
}
close LAST;
if ($element =~ /<TR>/) {
```

```
  $in{TABLE_STATUS} = 1
} else {
  $in{TABLE_STATUS} = 0
}
```

The previous file is accessed by opening a filename with the STEP variable decremented once again. The lines of the file are run straight through, so that the last line of the file is stored in the $element variable. This variable's value is then tested for the presence of the <TR> tag, which would indicate that the table option was on. If this is the case, the TABLE_STATUS variable is set accordingly. Conversely, if it doesn't, TABLE_STATUS is set to 0.

The last line of the Undo block of code will become familiar as we look at other blocks. It's a subroutine that creates a small form with a button that will properly call the toolbar subroutine, to bring the user back to the element selection form. It reads, simply:

```
&next_element;
```

Create Element

The button that's clicked most often by the user creating a form is the one that "stays on" for the next element. Its value is Create Element and, like the Remove Last Element button, it drops into another block of code in the elsif tree:

```
} elsif ($in{BUILD} eq "Create Element") {
```

This is the actual condition that evaluates as true after the "Begin" and "Remove" conditional statements fail. This block is actually one of the two largest logical chunks of the script. It sets up the universal elements of the form that will allow the user to set the options for the form element before actually creating it. Within this block of code is nested another if/elsif tree that mirrors the structure of the top-level tree. This conditional tree finds out which element was chosen and then outputs the form elements that allow the options for this specific element to be set.

First, though, it deals with niceties like the beginning structure of the page and the hidden fields that store the values selected on the previous form, like this:

```
print "<HTML>\n",
"<HEAD><TITLE>Set Element Options</TITLE>\n",
"</HEAD>\n",
"<BODY>\n",
```

```
"<H2>Working document: $in{BUILD_DOC}</H2>\n",
"<FORM METHOD=\"POST\" ",
"ACTION=\"http://$host$scriptpath$program\">\n",
"<INPUT TYPE=\"hidden\" NAME=\"TABLE_STATUS\" ",
"VALUE=\"$in{TABLE_STATUS}\">\n",
"<INPUT TYPE=\"hidden\" NAME=\"BUILD_DOC\" ",
"VALUE=\"$in{BUILD_DOC}\">\n",
"<INPUT TYPE=\"hidden\" NAME=\"TABLE\" ",
"VALUE=\"$in{TABLE}\">\n",
"<INPUT TYPE=\"hidden\" NAME=\"LINE_BREAK\" VALUE=\"",
"$in{LINE_BREAK}\">\n",
"<INPUT TYPE=\"hidden\" NAME=\"STEP\" ",
"VALUE=\"$in{STEP}\">\n";
```

Because we've added two more hidden fields to the complement, it's obvious that we're big fans of this technique. The ability to preserve client state from one connection to another really opens doors to other worlds of possible applications using HTTP. Have a time-sensitive application? Embed a timestamp in a form and have data expire based on the differential between the time the form was generated and when its data was submitted. User preferences? Embed them in the form. But we've evangelized enough for the time being.

It's important to remember two things: The user can always see the hidden input through a View Source, so don't include anything sensitive; hidden input can always be overridden by a knowledgable user, so don't rely on it totally for important data.

Now we move on to the top level of the tree. The structure of the entire tree is not a simple, flat string of conditionals like the top level is. Instead, as with the element selection form, the entire tree is split between FORM and HTML elements. This is mostly to maintain consistency with the program's external structure, but also for general organization and readability.

The Form Tree

The pair of radio buttons that indicates the user's choice of HTML or FORM element set a FORM variable called ELEMENT_TYPE:

```
if ($in{ELEMENT_TYPE} eq "FORM") {
```

If the radio button for a FORM element was highlighted when the form was submitted, the if statement evaluates as true. This brings the flow of the script down into the next level of the tree, where the specific type of FORM element will be identified. First, we'll test to see if the user selected a text or numeric input type:

```
if ($in{FORM_ELEMENT} eq "Text or Numeric Input") {
```

This is the form of the actual conditional that will test all the possibilities until the user's selection is found. Because we know in this part of the tree that $in{FORM} was defined, we're testing the contents of the select named FORM_ELEMENT to find the user's choice.

We probably don't have to quote any more "make a form" sections of code in their entirety, because you're familiar with the format by now. What you should notice about this block is that it is merely a fragment of a form that supplies the fields for the options for this specific element:

```
print "<H3>HTML Form Input Options</H3>\n",
        "<TABLE>\n<TR><TD><B>Label",
        " text:</B></TD>\n",
        "<TD><INPUT TYPE=\"text\" ",
        "NAME=\"LABEL\" SIZE=",
        "\"20\" ></TD></TR>\n",
        "<TR><TD><B>Name:</B></TD>\n",
        "<TD><INPUT TYPE=\"text\" ",
        "NAME=\"NAME\" SIZE=",
        "\"20\" MAXLENGTH=\"40\"></TD></TR>\n",
        "<TR><TD><B>Type:</B></TD>\n",
        "<TD><SELECT NAME=\"TYPE\" SIZE",
        " =\"1\">\n",
        "<OPTION>text\n<OPTION>number\n",
        "<OPTION>password\n</SELECT></TD></TR>\n",
        "<TR><TD><B>Value:</B>(if ",
        "desired)</TD>\n",
        "<TD><INPUT TYPE=\"text\" ",
        "NAME=\"VALUE\" SIZE=",
        "\"20\" MAXLENGTH=\"40\"></TD></TR>\n",
        "<TR><TD><B>Size:</B> (if ",
        "desired)</TD>\n",
        "<TD><INPUT TYPE=\"text\" ",
        "NAME=\"SIZE\" SIZE=",
        "\"2\" MAXLENGTH=\"4\"></TD></TR>\n",
        "<TR><TD><B>Maxlength:</B> (if ",
        "desired)</TD>\n",
        "<TD><INPUT TYPE=\"text\" ",
        "NAME=\"MAXLENGTH\" SIZE=",
        "\"2\" MAXLENGTH=\"4\"></TD></TR>\n";
```

The higher-level code that this section is nested within provides the common start and finish sections for the overall form.

If we look at the rest of the branch of the tree we're on right now, omitting the details of the actual code, the structure looks like this:

```
} elsif ($in{FORM_ELEMENT} eq "Large Text Area") {

} elsif ($in{FORM_ELEMENT} eq "Hidden Field") {

} elsif ($in{FORM_ELEMENT} eq "Radio Button") {

} elsif ($in{FORM_ELEMENT} eq "Checkbox") {

} elsif ($in{FORM_ELEMENT} eq "Select") {

} elsif ($in{FORM_ELEMENT} eq "Submit") {
```

As we've stated, whenever a conditional evaluates as true, the block of code it contains is entered and executed, producing the input fields and user prompts necessary for the current form element.

Finally, once out of the inner branches of the tree, the code quickly inserts a hidden field that identifies the form element to the script when these options are submitted:

```
print "<INPUT TYPE=\"hidden\" ",
  "NAME=\"ELEMENT\" VALUE=",
  "\"$in{FORM_ELEMENT}\">";
```

HTML Elements

A similar structure awaits us if our higher-level conditional fails. That is, if ELEMENT_TYPE is not equal to "FORM," the interpreter drops to the following statement:

```
} elsif ($in{ELEMENT_TYPE} eq "HTML") {
```

This evaluates as true if the other radio button is clicked. Since one of the two will always be "on," we're guaranteed to enter one of these two major branches of code. From here it's on to another sub-tree, with a conditional for every possible HTML element and blocks of code to provide the form for each. For the exercise, let's take a look at the first of these blocks:

```
if ($in{HTML_ELEMENT} eq "Horizontal Rule") {
```

The conditional is straightforward enough; it simply tests the contents of the other select to see if the Horizontal Rule element was chosen. If true, the code goes on to create a form interface for the user to specify the element's options:

```
print "<H3>Horizontal Rule Options</H3>",
"<TABLE><TR>",
"<TD>Thickness:</TD>",
"<TD><INPUT TYPE=\"number\" SIZE=\"2\" ",
"NAME=\"THICK\" MAXLENGTH=\"3\" ",
"VALUE=\"1\" ></TD>",
"</TR>",
"<TR><TD>Width:</TD>",
"<TD><INPUT TYPE=\"number\" SIZE=\"3\" ",
"NAME=\"WIDTH\" MAXLENGTH=\"4\" ",
"VALUE=\"100\" ></TD>",
"<TD><INPUT TYPE=\"radio\" NAME=\"UNITS\"",
"VALUE=\"PERCENT\"",
"CHECKED></TD>",
"<TD>Percentage</TD>",
"<TD><INPUT TYPE=\"radio\" NAME=\"UNITS\"",
"VALUE=\"PIXELS\"></TD>",
"<TD>Pixels</TD></TR><TR>",
"<TD>Alignment</TD>",
"<TD><SELECT NAME=\"ALIGN\">",
"<OPTION>Default",
"<OPTION>Center",
"<OPTION>Left",
"<OPTION>Right",
"</SELECT></TD></TR>",
"<TR><TD>Shaded line:</TD><TD><INPUT",
" TYPE=\"checkbox\" ",
"NAME=\"SHADE\" CHECKED></TD>",
"</TR>";
```

This block of code is easy to follow, but it's worth noting that we have the ability, in this context, to set normal values for all the options. This is done with the VALUE= option inside various tags or by making the appropriate button CHECKED.

This is a boon because the user has complete control over the appearance and function of this element without having to set each option every time. Instead, only one option may be changed or none at all, creating a default element with reasonable values. It is also important that the user is allowed to see those reasonable values, instead of filling them in on the back end, sight unseen. Therefore, even without supplying values, the user can see how the form is going to be created.

After the remainder of the conditional tree and its associated blocks of code are behind us, the last statement in the HTML element-block resembles the one we saw in the form element section. It inserts a hidden field that identifies the name of the element to preserve state information when the form is submitted.

Bipartisan End Note

Once we've produced the options form interface for the current element, there are a couple of finishing touches we need to put on the page.

Specifically, the table needs to be closed, a Submit button is needed, and other housekeeping tasks taken care of. The following chunk of code is placed after the two separate branches of the code complete, and the flow of the script has once again converged:

```
print "</TABLE><BR>\n",
    "<INPUT TYPE=\"submit\" NAME=\"BUILD\" VALUE=",
    "\"Set Options\">\n</FORM>\n</BODY>\n";

&footer;
```

With the form in the user's hands, the script's next job is to wait for a reply, looking for the BUILD value in the Set Options line.

Committing the Form Element to Disk

The user sets the options, hits the button, and the script is run yet again, this time with the BUILD variable set to Set Options:

```
} elsif ($in{BUILD} eq "Set Options") {
    # Create actual HTML object in working doc.
```

This causes the script to fall through all the conditional statements we've examined thus far, until it gets to the correct one. The block of code that this conditional encompasses handles the actual work of translating option settings and element choice into HTML tags in a file.

The structure in the code nested in this conditional statement is similar to the block we looked at earlier. Universal tasks are accomplished, then we enter another tree where the specific element is found, and the steps are taken to create it.

Open the File

First we create a file to hold the current element:

```
open (DOC, "> $datapath$build_doc.$in{STEP}");
$step = $in{STEP} + 1;
```

Our filehandle is opened to write to a file fragment with the working document's name as the prefix and the step number as a suffix. The step number is then incremented. In actual fact this isn't necessary until we're ready to give the user the element selection form again, but conceptually it makes sense to do it here.

The Table Option

Next we'll handle the table option. This is no simple matter of testing to see which radio button is clicked and creating the associated table tags. Tables require formatting to begin and end and to define rows and data cells. Therefore, with the table option now turned off, we must insert the proper formatting tags. Conversely, if the table option were now turned on, different tags would be required.

To keep track of this, we have created another hidden field, called TABLE_STATUS. This remembers the state of the table option one step before the current step. In this way, we can test to see if the status of the table option has changed and take the appropriate action:

```
if ($in{TABLE_STATUS} != $in{TABLE}) {
  if ($debug) {
    print "<P>Table status has changed</P>";
  }
```

If we enter this block of code, we know that the current state of the table option, embodied by the variable $in{TABLE}, is not the same as it was on the previous element. Next we can add the correct tags according to whether it is now on or off:

```
if ($in{TABLE}) {
  print DOC "<TABLE>\n<TR>\n";
} else {
  print DOC "</TABLE>";
}

}
```

Now that we have dealt with changes in the table status, we can prepare any tags necessary for the current element. Because we are attempting to do this in the universal portion of the code, we need to find a way to do this once for all elements. This is tricky, without using a test to see if the table option is turned on in each of the element creation blocks of code.

The solution lies in using a variable that is embedded in the element's output regardless of whether the table option is on, and only defining that variable if we need it. In other words, if table is turned off, the variable is set to null and will produce no change in the element's final product. If table is on, we set the variable (actually, variables) to the appropriate tags and they get inserted into the element. The following code demonstrates:

```
if ($in{TABLE}) {
  $td="<TD>";
  $endtd="</TD>";
}
```

Now we can prepend and append $td and $endtd to the final output of each element, knowing that it will produce any necessary formatting tags.

Element-Specific Tags and Option Translation

Our shared code out of the way, we can proceed with a decision tree very much like the ones we saw for FORM and HTML elements in the option setting section. This chain of if/elsif statements zeros in on the specific element type and then interprets the option settings to produce the proper HTML end product:

```
if ($in{ELEMENT} eq "Text or Numeric Input") {
```

The old familiar Text or Numeric Input is easily spotted and serves as an admirable guinea pig for our experimentation. Now that we know what element we're dealing with, we know what variables to look for and what to do with their values to end up with correct HTML form elements. It is here that your programming skills may be required. The more elegant the back-end programming at this exact point, the more effective the tool will appear from the user's perspective. The text input example does not require any particularly clever code, however:

```
if ($in{LABEL}) {
  print DOC "$td$in{LABEL}$endtd\n";
}
print DOC "$td<INPUT TYPE=\"$in{TYPE}\" ",
      "NAME=\"$in{NAME}\" ";
```

Here you have a good example of the basic methodology at work in the majority of the code blocks in this portion of the script. First, the presence of a defined label is tested, and if one exists, the label is output to the working document. Note the use of $td and $endtd. If the table option is on, the label forms the content of the left-hand data cell in the row. Second, the form widget itself is started, with as much as possible of the element written out at once. The rest of the options were not required of the user, so we will test for the existence of a defined value for each and create the necessary elements from any values we find:

```
if ($in{SIZE}) {
  print DOC "SIZE=\"$in{SIZE}\" ";
}
if ($in{MAXLENGTH}) {
  print DOC " MAXLENGTH=\"$in{MAXLENGTH}\" ";
}
if ($in{VALUE}) {
  print DOC " VALUE=\"$in{VALUE}\" ";
}
print DOC ">$endtd\n";
```

Finally, we invoke a subroutine to deal with the end of the line:

```
&line_break;
```

This subroutine is required because there are several permutations and combinations of the line break and table options that need to be sorted out many times before we are through.

Line Breaking

This is a relatively simple subroutine. Its basic role is to test the states of the line break and table options and then write out the correct code to the working file. It could have been broken out of the individual blocks of code for each element and placed in the common area at the end of entire section. However, the way that the code for buttons and boxes works means that a variable number of line breaks may be needed, depending on what the current element is and how it is configured.

Therefore, we placed it in a separate subroutine that is called at least once from inside the code for each individual element:

```
sub line_break {

  if ($in{LINE_BREAK}) {
```

If the user wanted a line break for this element, we need to create the right kind of line break. If not, we have nothing to do but return:

```
    if ($in{TABLE}) {
      print DOC "</TR>\n<TR>";
    } else {
      print DOC "<BR>";
    }
  }
}
```

As you can see, there are two types of line break. If the table option is on, the current row is ended and a new one begun. If the table option is not on, a simple <BR> is used.

More Complex Element Handling

In the Chapter 5 tutorial, you saw how we extended the basic interface concept for elements that could have multiple components. The result was a simple way to create any number of grouped radio buttons or checkboxes at one stroke. Beyond the simple interface design necessary to make this a possibility, we needed to change the basic approach to the back-end coding to make it really work.

If you recall, the user is presented with a <TEXTAREA> for typing the label text and values to as many buttons as desired. The separator is the newline character, since the user has been instructed to keep each label/value pair on its own line. Therefore, our first step in the supporting code is to separate the label/value pairs into separate elements of an array, using the Perl *split* function. Before we can safely do that, however, we filter out any stray carriage returns inadvertently introduced into the submitted text:

```
} elsif ($in{ELEMENT} eq "Radio Button") {

    $in{LABELS} =~ s/\r//g;
    # Strip any possible carriage returns.
    @buttons = split(/\n/, $in{LABELS});
```

As you can see in the next fragment, using radio buttons, we'll be fiddling somewhat with the normal course of events regarding table formatting:

```
if ($td eq "<TD>") {
        $td1 = "<TD ALIGN=RIGHT>"
    }
```

Here, if the $td variable is defined as <TD> we will assign a slightly customized data cell definition to the variable $td1. The reason for this is that we want our button, the left-hand data cell on each row, to butt up against the label text in the right-hand cell. The ALIGN=RIGHT option is what makes this happen.

Now that our button definitions are safely split into an array variable, we can get to work actually creating them. We'll use a for loop and take advantage of the automatically defined $#<arrayname> variable:

```
for ($i = 0; $i <= $#buttons; $i++) {
        if ($debug) {
          print "Loop index $i<P>";
        }
```

Whenever an array is defined, this variable is set to the number of items in the array minus one, in other words the maximum index number defined. Our first job with our current button definition is to split the label from the button's value. Here again, we'll call on the split function, this time using the comma as the delimiter:

```
@butt = split (',', $buttons[$i]);
print DOC "$td1<INPUT TYPE=\"radio\" NAME=\"",
  "$in{NAME}\"";
```

Our next task is to apply the parameters of this button to the actual creation of the HTML entity. The $td1 variable is inserted so that if the table option is on, we will get the formatting right. The button element tag is set up, again putting in all the options we know will be defined. Next we'll deal with the voluntary options.

If there is a value defined for the current button, we'll insert it into the button tag:

```
if ($butt[1]) {
        # There is a value for the button.
        print DOC " VALUE=\"$butt[1]\"";
```

```
      } else {
        print DOC " VALUE=\"$butt[0]\"";
      }
```

If there is no defined element, we'll use the actual label text for the value. In other words, if the user defined two buttons like this:

```
On,1
Off
```

the resulting HTML, assuming the buttons' names were defined as test, would be:

```
<INPUT TYPE="radio" NAME="test" VALUE="1"> On
<INPUT TYPE="radio" NAME="test" VALUE="Off"> Off
```

Of course this ignores any line breaks or table formatting.

The last option we'll examine is the number the user supplied for the button to check. Since the user will probably be counting from one rather than from zero as our array does, we'll check to see if the number they supplied minus one is equal to our current button's number. If it is, we'll add the CHECKED option to the button's tag:

```
      if ($i == ($in{CHECKED} - 1)) {
          print DOC " CHECKED";
      }

      print DOC ">$endtd\n";
```

Finally, we close the button element with the greater than character and the $endtd variable. The newline character \n is added to produce readable source.

With the button itself out of the way, we can move on to the button's label. This is simple enough, accomplished by simply writing out the first element of our button's array, @butt. This is, as always, wrapped in the $td and $endtd variables:

```
      print DOC "$td$butt[0]$endtd\n";
```

To finish up this button, we need to handle the line break issue again. This is exactly the situation that forced us to call the linebreak subroutine from inside each element's block of code. Since the user could have made any number of buttons with one submission of the form, we need to perform the appropriate action at the end of each pass through the for loop:

```
      if ($in{LINE_BREAK}) {
        if ($in{TABLE}) {
```

```
                  print DOC "</TR>\n<TR>";
            } else {
              print DOC "<BR>";
            }
          }
        }
```

And with that, our group of buttons is completed. The code that handles checkboxes and selects is very much like the radio button code. This is no surprise because the three different elements are similar both conceptually and in interface design.

In fact, between the text input example and the button example, we have seen almost all of the techniques used to create the available elements. Instead of repeating ourselves with other elements that exhibit similar techniques, let's look at one element that needs special handling.

The Horizontal Rule

The handling of this element shares many aspects with the blocks of code we've looked at thus far, with one major exception: The <HR> tag does not work well inside a table. While you can define a horizontal rule inside a data cell, it limits you in terms of the scope of the options you may exercise. The <HR> tag was really meant to operate across the full width of the browser window, not within the confines of a variable-width data cell.

Before we create the <HR> element, we'll check to see if the table option is on. If it is, we'll turn it off temporarily, then insert the tag in the same way we do any other tag, and then turn the table on again. Please be aware of this limitation when using the Form Generator Tool. ▲

Also, because the <HR> tag forces a paragraph break, we won't worry about calling the subroutine to do the work. Now, here's the source:

```
        } elsif ($in{ELEMENT} eq "Horizontal Rule") {
          if ($in{TABLE}) {
            print DOC "</TR>\n</TABLE>\n";
          }

          print DOC "<HR";

          if ($in{SHADE} ne "on") {
            print DOC " NOSHADE";
          }
```

```
if (!(($in{WIDTH}==100)&&($in{UNITS} eq "PERCENT"))) {
  print DOC " WIDTH=\"$in{WIDTH}";

  if ($in{UNITS} eq "PERCENT") {
    print DOC "%"
  }
  print DOC "\"";
}

if ($in{THICK} != 1) {
  print DOC " SIZE=$in{THICK}";
}

if ($in{ALIGN} ne "Default") {
  print DOC " ALIGN=\"$in{ALIGN}\"";
}

print DOC ">\n";

if ($in{TABLE}) {
  print DOC "<TABLE>\n<TR>\n";
}
```

Between the special handling of the table formatting at the beginning and end of the block, you can see more of the programming techniques we first saw with text input and radio buttons.

Finding Closure

Once the entire tree is traversed, the element is found, and its block of code executed, we're ready to put the finishing touches on this phase of the script's execution. We'll close the working document, give the user some feedback about what's been done, set up a couple of variables, and then shoot out the element selection form again:

```
close DOC;
print "Added $in{ELEMENT}\n<P>";
$table[$in{TABLE}] = " CHECKED";
$table = $in{TABLE};
```

The first two lines are counterparts to the table initialization we did when first starting the form. Here, we assign the CHECKED option to the proper table option array element, so that either the On button or the Off button is checked. Also, we set the $table variable to the current state of the table option, as discerned from the form input.

The toolbar subroutine is called and the user sees its output, the element selection form:

```
&toolbar;
```

We've now completed our tour of the most common paths through the *formgen.pl* script. Most of the time it will be moving through the code to allow the user to select an element to add, to set that element's options and parameters, and then to commit that element to disk.

Now let's turn to what happens when the other buttons on the toolbar form are clicked, specifically the View Source, Preview, and End Document buttons.

View Source

Viewing text in a Web browser is easy. Generally, a file on a server that contains plain text will have a suffix that the server maps to the MIME type 'text/plain'. In turn, when the browser requests such a file, the server informs the browser of its MIME type, and the browser interprets the resulting stream of data accordingly.

However, because we want to allow the user to view text that is HTML source in the middle of a stream of parsed HTML, our circumstances aren't so simple. If the user wishes to look at the raw HTML file that is being built with the Tool, we'll somehow need to convince the browser not to parse our text for HTML tags.

Second, because our work-in-progress is in the form of an arbitrary number of separate files, we'll need to stitch the parts together to present the user with a uniform whole. Luckily we have the STEP field to tell us how many files to expect to find.

You will recognize the form of the following conditional statement that directs the flow of the script into its block of code:

```
} elsif ($in{BUILD} eq "View Source") {

    print "<HTML><HEAD><TITLE>View $in{BUILD_DOC}",
        " Source</TITLE></HEAD><BODY>\n";

    print "<PRE>\n";
```

It is looking for the case in which the value of the BUILD submit button is View Source. When it evaluates as true, the first thing that is done is to "prime" the return page with the tags shown. Next, we will begin to collect the parts of the form and send them back to the user. We began the source listing with the <PRE> tag to format the text in monospaced type.

The first portion of the form to be output is the HEAD document, the file we used to start the form:

```
open (HEAD, "$datapath$in{BUILD_DOC}.HEAD");

    while (<HEAD>) {
      s/</&lt;/g;
      s/>/&gt;/g;
      print
    }

    close HEAD;
```

You'll notice that we use a regular expression substitute statement to filter the text, replacing the beginning and ending characters of the HTML tags with the HTML entities that represent the actual characters. That is, we change < to < and > to >. This will prevent the HTML from being parsed but retain its content for display.

Here we do the same for each individual piece of the form, using the STEP field value as the top of our for loop and filtering each file's content as we send them out to the browser:

```
for ($loop = 0; $loop <= $in{STEP}; $loop++) {
    open (PART, "$datapath$in{BUILD_DOC}.$loop");
    while (<PART>) {
      s/</&lt;/g;
      s/>/&gt;/g;
      print
    }
    close PART;
}
```

This block ends very simply, with the closing of the block of <PRE> formatted text and then by calling the next_element subroutine:

```
print "</PRE>\n";

    &next_element;
```

This subroutine provides the mini-form that presents the user with the button to lead to the element selection form, as we explored earlier.

WYSIWYG Preview

The preview feature of *formgen.pl* is much easier to deal with than viewing source. We aren't concerned with the browser interpreting the HTML; in fact, we want it to do that very thing. Therefore, we don't need to worry about filtering or special tags. The only special piece we need to provide is the <FORM> tag, since it isn't defined yet for this document.

The opening lines look almost exactly like those seen for the view source segment. The only differences are ones of simplification because this block doesn't need the extra complexity:

```
} elsif ($in{BUILD} eq "Preview Document") {


    open (HEAD, "$datapath$in{BUILD_DOC}.HEAD");
    print while <HEAD>;
    close HEAD;
```

The following statement injects the dummy <FORM> tag into the document, which ensures that the browser renders all the input fields as they should look:

```
print "<FORM ACTION=\"http://$host$scriptpath$program\"",
      " METHOD=\"POST\">\n";
```

Here again we step through all the document's component parts, reading and outputting each one as we go; no filtering is necessary here either:

```
for ($loop = 0; $loop < $in{STEP}; $loop++) {
    open (PART, "$datapath$in{BUILD_DOC}.$loop");
    print while <PART>;
    close PART;
}
```

Finally, the form-in-progress is closed out with the </TABLE> and </FORM> tags, to preserve the integrity of the rest of the page. Calling the `next_element` subroutine completes the page:

```
print "</TABLE>\n</FORM>\n";

    &next_element;
```

Completing the User Experience

The next sections of code are run when the user is done and clicks the End Document button. The sequence of events for finishing a *formgen.pl* project is as follows: The script returns to the user a form for capturing precisely how the user wants to have the end product delivered, and what options the user wants.

When that form is submitted, the options and preferences are deciphered and the appropriate action is taken. There are four different end pages that may be returned, and each can be the last output the user sees from the script. After the options are set, the script invisibly stitches together all the disparate pieces of the document and puts finishing touches on them to complete the form.

The first option the user must decide on is the name of the host where the form will be installed (the name of the local host is supplied as a convenient default). The supplied hostname is used in the <FORM> tag for the completed document:

```
} elsif ($in{BUILD} eq "End Document") {

        print "<HTML><HEAD><TITLE>Complete $in{BUILD_DOC} ",
        "Construction</TITLE></HEAD>\n<BODY>\n",
        "<FORM ACTION=\"http://$host$scriptpath$program\"",
        " METHOD=\"POST\">\n",
        "<TABLE><TR><TD COLSPAN=2><H2>Build Form",
        "</H2></TD></TR>",
        "<TR><TD><FONT SIZE=-1>Supply name of host where ",
        "form will be installed: <BR></TD>",
        "<TD VALIGN=top><INPUT TYPE=\"text\" NAME=\"HOST\" ",
        "SIZE=\"20\" VALUE=\"$host\"></TD></TR>",
```

The last method presented as an option to the user also makes use of the $host variable, since the Tool has the ability to install the end product on the local server only:

```
    "<TR><TD COLSPAN=2><B>Choose the desired method for",
        " delivering the form to you.</B></TD></TR>",
        "<TR><TD><INPUT TYPE=\"radio\" NAME=\"METHOD\"",
        "VALUE=\"view\" CHECKED></TD>",
        "<TD>View form on your Web browser</TD>",
        "</TR>",
        "<TR><TD><INPUT TYPE=\"radio\" NAME=\"METHOD\"",
        "VALUE=\"download\"></TD>",
        "<TD>Download form to your local machine</TD>",
        "</TR>",
        "<TR><TD><INPUT TYPE=\"radio\" NAME=\"METHOD\"",
```

```
"VALUE=\"email\"></TD>",
"<TD>E-mail the form to you</TD>",
"</TR>",
"<TR><TD><INPUT TYPE=\"radio\" NAME=\"METHOD\"",
"VALUE=\"install\"></TD>",
"<TD>Install the form on $host</TD>",
"</TR>",
```

Here, another option is presented to the user, to make the form a self-contained, self-serving Perl CGI script. If this is desired, the user also has the opportunity to supply the path to Perl on the machine where they'll install the end product:

```
"<TR></TABLE><B>Choose options for final building of",
    " form:</B><BR><TABLE>",
    "<TD><INPUT TYPE=\"checkbox\" NAME=\"OPTIONS\"",
    "VALUE=\"perl\"></TD>",
    "<TD>Make self-contained Perl script</TD>",
    "</TR>\n",
    "<TR><TD></TD>",
    "<TD><FONT SIZE=-1>Supply path for perl<BR>",
    "(If other than /usr/local/bin/perl):</FONT></TD>\n",
    "<TD><INPUT TYPE=\"text\" NAME=\"PERL\" SIZE=",
    "\"20\"></TD></TR>\n",
```

The default is presented as a static string rather than a "best guess" derived from the local system. This is because */usr/local/bin/perl* is the path to Perl on a large majority of machines, and it didn't seem worth the effort to figure it out on-the-fly at this point.

After the option to include HTML validation as a part of the form, we embed two hidden fields to preserve the vital data regarding the form. The first is the document's working name so that we can find its data files, and the second is the STEP value, so we know how many pieces to expect:

```
"<TR><TD><INPUT TYPE=\"checkbox\" NAME=\"OPTIONS\"",
    "VALUE=\"validate\"></TD>",
    "<TD>Validate HTML source</TD>",
    "</TR></TABLE>",
    "<INPUT TYPE=\"hidden\" NAME=\"BUILD_DOC\" ",
    "VALUE=\"$in{BUILD_DOC}\">\n",
    "<INPUT TYPE=\"hidden\" NAME=\"STEP\" VALUE=\"",
    "$in{STEP}\">\n",
    "<INPUT TYPE=\"submit\" NAME=\"BUILD\" VALUE=\"",
    "Deliver Completed Form\">";

    &footer;
```

Beginning to End:
The Preparatory Steps to Finish the Form

When this form is submitted, the value of BUILD causes the script to drop down into the block of code below. This is a comparatively complicated section of the script because the four delivery methods require different handling and the options to make a CGI and to validate the HTML must be woven into all these methods.

The variable $progname is derived from the program's name minus the ".pl" suffix and is used to find the support files:

```
} elsif ($in{BUILD} eq "Deliver Completed Form") {

    $program =~ /(.*)\.pl/;
    $progname = $1;
```

After briefly setting up the return page, we will dive right into the preparations necessary if the user has decided to make the form a self-contained CGI:

```
print "<HTML>\n<HEAD>\n<TITLE>Completed Form: $build_doc",
    "</TITLE>\n</HEAD>\n<BODY>\n";
```

Cash or Perl?

The decision to roll the form into a CGI is signaled by the OPTIONS field containing the value perl. If the form is to be a CGI, the way we process the form for delivery will change dramatically at several points.

The end product's name is finally set, by adding the suffix ".pl" to the working name:

```
if ($in{OPTIONS} =~ /perl/){

    $build_final = $build_doc . ".pl";
```

Of course, if the user has chosen to simply end the document as just a form, the suffix ".html" will be added, as defined in the else statement that's shown toward the end of this section.

The following block of code handles the two options presented to the user in two slightly different ways:

```
if ($in{PERL} eq "") {
    chop ($in{PERL} = `which perl`);
```

```
    }

    if ($in{HOST} eq "") {
      $in{HOST} = "$host/$scriptpath";
    }
```

If the user has left the path to the Perl field empty, the path is derived by using the *which* command. This is a built-in UNIX command and therefore does not jeopardize the script's portability. It searches the directories in the current path for the program named on the command line. Because Perl almost always resides in a directory that is on a standard path, this should work in nearly every case.

The hostname, on the other hand, if left blank, is set to the name of the host as divined from the environment variables, with the path portion of the script's URL appended. Our thinking here is that the script is being run from the CGI directory on this server, so this would be a good guess as to the final destination for a CGI under construction.

Our method for building the final version of the document from its component parts and in the state desired by the user is to store each line in a separate element of the array called @doc:

```
$doc[0] = "#!$in{PERL}\n";
$doc[1] = "# perl script to both supply and support" .
          " the $build_doc HTML form\n";
$doc[2] = "# generated by http://$host/$scriptpath/" .
          "$program on $date\n";
$doc[3] = "\n\n";
$count = 4;
```

Thus, we can build it up piece by piece, with some assigned directly using a static string or a string with embedded, interpreted variables (as we do here), and others assigned by reading values in from text files.

An example of what we were just mentioning, the "$progname.perl" file, in our distribution version called "formgen.perl" contains the boilerplate CGI code for handling POST requests from the form back to the script. We read each line of the file into a separate element of the array and keep a running account of how many lines we have assigned, by incrementing $count:

```
open (PERL, "${datapath}$progname.perl") ||
      print "<B>ERROR</B> Can't open ${datapath}",
            "$progname.perl : $!";
```

```
while (<PERL>) {
  $doc[$count] = $_;
  $count++
}

close PERL;
```

If the user has not chosen the CGI option, all that needs to be done is to assign the final name by appending ".html" and to initialize the $count variable to zero:

```
} else {

    $build_final = $build_doc . ".html";
    $count = 0

}
```

Stitching It Together

Our next steps are common to either the plain form or the form encapsulated in a Perl script. We'll go through the familiar routine of opening and reading the HEAD document and then all the rest of the fragments of the form, one by one. One item of note when we read the HEAD document: This is where the user's e-mail address is stored, so we will capture this data in case the user wants to receive the end product via e-mail.

Here, if the form is not being rolled into a Perl script, each line of the HEAD file and all the files to come can be assigned directly to the @doc array:

```
open (HEAD, "$datapath$build_doc.HEAD");
while (<HEAD>) {
    /For:\s*(.*\@.*)\-\-/;
    $email = $1
    if ($in{OPTIONS} =~ /perl/){
        chop;
$_ =~ s/"/\\"/g;
        $doc[$count] = "\tprint \"" . $_ . "\";\n";

    } else {
$doc[$count] = $_;
    }
```

If, however, the perl option is on, each line of each file must be encapsulated in a Perl print command, much as the HTML inside our own *formgen.pl* did.

The encapsulation is achieved by prepending a tab and `print ""` and appending `\n;` to each line. Before this occurs, a regular expression match and substitution is run to escape quote marks. Finally, the counter variable is incremented, the HEAD document is closed, and then unlinked, its function fulfilled:

```
$count++;

}

close HEAD;
unlink ("$datapath$build_doc.HEAD");
```

We want to insert our <FORM> tag between the HEAD and the rest of the numbered fragments. If we are building a CGI, we'll make the ACTION option point at the final product script if it were to reside on the local server, using the variables we extracted from the environment variables:

```
if ($in{OPTIONS} =~ /perl/) {
    $doc[$count] = "\tprint \"<FORM ACTION=\\\"http://" .
    "$in{HOST}$build_doc.pl\\\" METHOD=\\\"POST\\\">\";\n";
    } else {
    $doc[$count] = "<FORM ACTION=\"http://$in{HOST}" .
      "$scriptpath$build_doc.pl\" METHOD=\"POST\">\n";
    }
    $count++;
```

You'll note what looks like triple escaped quote marks. In actual fact the first escape affects the next escape, so that the actual slash gets into the HTML source, and then next escapes the quote mark. This is necessary because we're encapsulating HTML in Perl.

If our end product is just good old HTML, however, we make our best guess again, by pointing at a hypothetical Perl script with the same name as the form on the desired server. We know this application in all likelihood doesn't exist, but it is necessary to have a <FORM> tag in the document at this point. Thus, if the chance exists that we might actually point at the correct CGI, we might as well take it. Finally, as always, when we add a form element to the array, we increment the counter.

Now we'll repeat the same routine we went through with the HEAD file with the rest of the fragments:

```
for ($loop = 0; $loop <= $in{STEP}; $loop++) {
  open (PIECE, "$datapath$build_doc.$loop");
  while (<PIECE>) {
```

```
        if ($in{OPTIONS} =~ /perl/){
          chop;
          $_ =~ s/"/\\"/g;
          $_ =~ s/;/:/g;
        $doc[$count] = "\tprint \"" . $_ . "\";\\n\n";
        } else {
          $doc[$count] = $_;
        }
        $count++;
      }
      unlink ("$datapath$build_doc.$loop");
    }
```

At the end of this for loop we have gathered together all the materials that the user created for the form. Next we'll have to close the form properly and then deliver it.

Ending the Ending

We've lost the table state variable, but even if we hadn't, we'd want to do the following test, to avoid leaving anything to chance:

```
if ($_ =~ /<TR>/) {
    # very last line of form contains open row tag
    $doc[$count] = "</TR></TABLE>\\n\n";
    $count++
  }
```

The test looks for a table element in the final line of the final fragment of the file. If it finds it, we'll insert the closing tags for the last row and for the table itself.

Next we'll open another support file, this one named "formgen.end", which contains all the tags we want to append at the end of the final form's HTML. The current version simply contains a </FORM> tag, but it's good to have this as an extensible file:

```
    open (END, "${datapath}$progname.end") ||
      print "<B>ERROR</B> Can't open ${datapath}",
          "$progname.end : $!";

  while (<END>) {
    if ($in{OPTIONS} =~ /perl/) {
      chop;
```

As before, if the `perl` option is turned on, we need to filter for quotes and wrap every line in Perl print statements:

```
$_ =~ s/"/\\"/g;
      $doc[$count] = "\tprint \"" . $_ . "\";\n";
   } else {
      $doc[$count] = $_;
   }
   $count++;
}
close END;
```

Last, we can deal with the HTML validation option. Should a user want the validation form at the bottom of the form they create, we'll append the contents of another support file to the end of the working form. We use a support file in this case because we want the flexibility to edit the source should a URL or the syntax for the HTML validation tool change:

```
if ($in{OPTIONS} =~ /validate/) {

   open (VAL, "${datapath}validate.html");
   while (<VAL>) {
      if ($in{OPTIONS} =~ /perl/) {
         chop;
         $_ =~ s/"/\\"/g;
         $doc[$count] = "\tprint \"" .
               $_ . "\";\n";
      } else {
         $doc[$count] = $_;
      }
      $count++;
   }
   close VAL;
}
$doc[$count] = "</BODY></HTML>\n";
$count++;
```

With all the possible <BODY> elements taken care of, the preceding statement closes the working form once and for all.

If we have a Perl script in the works, we can now close the block of code that outputs the form. This is done by closing the curly bracket that we opened so long ago:

```
if ($in{OPTIONS} =~ /perl/) {
   $doc[$count] = "}\n";
   $count++;
}
```

The form, whether it is a form or a form inside a CGI, is now complete. Now all that remains is yet another conditional tree, this time to ascertain the user's desired delivery method.

The View Method

This is the simplest of methods, which is probably why it comes first in the program structure. It is a veritable steal off the View Source command we looked at earlier, except that we are spooling the source in its entirety out of the @doc array:

```
if ($in{METHOD} eq "view") {
  print "<PRE>\n";
  for ($loop = 0; $loop < $count; $loop++) {
    $doc[$loop] =~ s/</&lt;/g;
    $doc[$loop] =~ s/>/&gt;/g;
    print $doc[$loop];
  }
  print "</PRE>\n";
  &footer;
```

The Download Method

Only marginally more complex than the View method, carrying out the download entails writing the form to a file before going any further:

```
} elsif ($in{METHOD} eq "download") {
  open (FINAL, ">$readablepath" .
        "$in{BUILD_DOC}.html");
  for ($loop = 0; $loop < $count; $loop++) {
    print FINAL $doc[$loop]
  }
  close FINAL;
```

With the document all in one piece on the local file system, it's now possible to compress it and then present the user with a link for downloading the final product:

```
system ("$compress " .
"$readablepath$in{BUILD_DOC}.html");
print "Download <A HREF=\"http://$host/",
    "$in{BUILD_DOC}.html.gz\">",
    "$in{BUILD_DOC}.html.gz</A><P>";
&footer;
```

Mail Delivery

It's easy to e-mail the final product from within Perl. Because we captured the user's e-mail address when we read in the HEAD of the document, we may simply use the command defined in the $mail variable to send the contents of the array to that address:

```perl
} elsif ($in{METHOD} eq "email") {
  if (open (MAIL, "|$mail $email")){
    for ($loop = 0; $loop < $count; $loop++) {
      print MAIL $doc[$loop]
    }
    close MAIL;
    print "<H2>Mail sent successfully to $email",
        "</H2>\n";
  } else {
    print "<H2>Error</H2><P><B>Could not send mail to",
        " $email.</B><BR>";
  }
  &footer;
```

The error checking performed on the open function is merely there to verify that the installed form has a valid e-mail command defined and that no problems were encountered when attempting to use it.

Install It Here

The last method is the most complex, by a small measure. It requires the construction of a small form that calls the *form_install.pl* form, from the secure data directory. This functionality could be handled internally by *formgen.pl*, but at a cost of the access control flexibility. One would have to either restrict access to *formgen.pl* entirely or leave the script, and the ability to install executable code on the server, open to anyone. With the two scripts separated, *formgen.pl* can be made publicly accessible, and its one security risk more closely controlled:

```perl
} elsif ($in{METHOD} eq "install") {
  open (FINAL, ">$datapath$build_final");
  for ($loop = 0; $loop < $count; $loop++) {
    print FINAL $doc[$loop]
  }
  close FINAL;
```

With the contents of the array dumped into the final filename in the data directory, we can now build the form that will pass the crucial data to *form_install.pl*:

```
print "<FORM ACTION=\"http://$host$scriptpath",
  "${datapath}form_install.pl\" METHOD=",
  "\"POST\">\n<",
  "INPUT TYPE=\"hidden\" NAME=\"FORM\" ",
  "VALUE=\"$build_final\">\n",
  "<TABLE>\n<TR>\n<TD><B>Specified desired target ",
  "directory:</B></TD>",
  "<TD><INPUT TYPE=\"text\" NAME=\"TARGET\" SIZE",
  "=\"20\"></TD></TR>\n",
  "<TR><TD COLSPAN=2 ALIGN=center><INPUT TYPE",
  "=\"submit\" VALUE=\"Install Form\"></TD></TR>\n",
  "</TABLE>";
  &footer;
  }
}
```

The one user-supplied piece of data is the desired target directory. This can be any valid UNIX path, but if the HTTP server's *uid* cannot write to the target, the installation will fail.

When the submit is clicked, the name of the final product and the target directory will be passed to *form_install.pl*, which will attempt to install the file where the user wants it. It is an exceedingly simple script consisting of a very few lines of code. It's also self-explanatory so we won't go through it here.

SUMMARY

We've used the Tool to create a sample project, discussed the reasoning behind the project and its feature set, and explored the way it accomplishes all its tasks in actual working Perl code. From here we'll look at the two ways in which you may want to extend the script or its output. In Chapter 7 we'll look at ways in which you can enhance or expand the capabilities of the Tool itself. Then in Chapter 8 we'll talk about validating, testing, and installing the resulting CGIs on your Web server.

EXTENDING THE GENERATOR'S OUTPUT

We recognize that our Form Generation Tool doesn't produce perfect HTML forms. This is version 1.0 and is meant to contain as much core functionality as possible. Time constraints and the desire to design "clean" code necessitated shelving several features for future investigation. In addition, the Web is anything but a stationary target. Our fairly complete subset of the most often-used elements may seem hopelessly meager in just a few short months. Today's "killer app" may be tomorrow's old hat, no matter how good the program appears initially.

To our credit, we considered the effects of aging when designing the Tool. As a result, we've come up with a number of ways to extend its functionality. Now that the Form Generator is in your hands, you may need a feature not included in its feature set. Or while taking the tour through the Tool's feature set and code, you may have had the urge to get your hands into it just for fun, for your own education, or to solve a specific problem.

CUSTOMIZING THE TOOL'S FEATURES

Whatever the case, there are several avenues open to those who want to extend this Tool. The end product of the user's interaction with the Tool, whether a simple form or a standalone CGI, is the easiest thing to customize and extend. Because it is in your hands and performs only a limited function, it should be easy to customize.

The scripts that make up the Tool itself are also extensible. New HTML and form elements could be added, or whole new features programmed in.

In Chapter 8, "Making Things Work: Installing and Testing Your Forms and CGIs," we'll look at the details of customizing the Tool's end products. In this chapter, we'll explore what's involved in extending *formgen.pl*. Specifically we'll examine what it takes to enhance existing elements or to add support for new ones and examine ways in which entirely new features could be introduced into the Tool.

ENHANCEMENTS TO THE TOOL WITHIN THE EXISTING FRAMEWORK

Extending the functionality of the Tool within the existing feature set is quite simple. If you simply wish to add choices to the element selection form—for example, to add support for the new Netscape <EMBED> tag or the file upload widget—you shouldn't have too much difficulty.

This is a direct result of the modular design we used when creating the script in the first place. The separate functions required to present an element as a choice, to set its options, and to write that information to disk are a well-defined set of simple tasks. Any or all of these software components will be easy to change or extend.

It's even easier to modify or enhance the options available for an element already included in the Tool. Here, instead of adding choices to the script and increasing the user's options, you are merely extending the capabilities of existing blocks of code. To dip into the script's environment and get you acclimated, we'll take a look at adding support for a WRAP option for large TEXTAREA widgets.

Minor Surgery

The latest spate of new HTML features added to the Web's mix has come with the release of beta versions of Netscape Navigator 2.0, Microsoft Internet Explorer, and other advanced browsers. In addition to brand-new HTML and FORM elements, Netscape has added options to some existing tags. One that comes as a particular boon to form designers is the ability to control the text wrapping behavior in a <TEXTAREA>.

Previously, text typed into such an input never wrapped, so it was possible that a user could keep typing on one line forever, or that he or she would have to hit the Return key when the text reached the right side of the window. Neither was desirable; the former was an annoyance and a waste of the form real estate dedicated to the <TEXTAREA>, and the latter introduced extra characters into the user's input that could complicate back-end processing.

The new WRAP option goes inside the <TEXTAREA> tag and can be set to OFF, SOFT, or HARD. The OFF setting keeps the <TEXTAREA> exactly as it has always behaved, while the SOFT and HARD options wrap words at the end of each line in the window. SOFT and HARD wraps differ in their handling of newline characters. HARD transmits the text exactly as it appears in the window, with newlines at the end of each visible line, while SOFT strips newlines and sends the text as the user typed it.

That explanation out of the way, let us pose this problem: We have <TEXTAREA> available in the Tool but it doesn't currently support the WRAP option. The next sections of this chapter will therefore focus on the steps we'd take to add support for this option to the Tool and, more specifically, to add this functionality to *formgen.pl*.

Step One: Examine Existing Options

The first step is to examine the existing options form for <TEXTAREA>. You can see that we supply fields for the standard label text and field name, and optional fields for a default value and the number of rows and columns of text. Since the WRAP option has three possible values, we can use a SELECT or a group of RADIO buttons. In keeping with the rest of the element options pages, we'll use a SELECT. This is an arbitrary choice; feel free to design your interfaces however you see fit.

Step Two: Create the Extra Field

Because we want to insert HTML code into the portion of the Perl script that generates the form in Figure 7-1, the most efficient approach is to use the Tool itself to create a single input—our SELECT—and then to roll it into a CGI and view the source. When we do so, we end up with something like what's shown in Figure 7-2. If we cut just the portion that specifically creates the new field and set it aside for a moment or two, we can quickly find the portion of *formgen.pl* that creates the <TEXTAREA> option form. Once it's been located, you'll see that the existing code reads as follows:

```
} elsif ($in{FORM_ELEMENT} eq "Large Text Area") {
    print "<H3>HTML Form Textarea Options</H3>\n",
        "<TABLE>\n<TR><TD><B>Label ",
        "text:</B></TD>\n",
        "<TD><INPUT TYPE=\"text\" ",
        "NAME=\"LABEL\" SIZE=",
        "\"20\" ></TD></TR>\n",
        "<TR><TD><B>Name:</B></TD>\n",
        "<TD><INPUT TYPE=\"text\" ",
        "NAME=\"NAME\" SIZE=",
        "\"20\" MAXLENGTH=\"40\"></TD></TR>\n",
        "<TR><TD><B>Value:</B>(if ",
        "desired)</TD>\n",
        "<TD><INPUT TYPE=\"text\" ",
        "NAME=\"VALUE\" SIZE=",
        "\"20\" MAXLENGTH=\"40\"></TD></TR>\n",
        "<TR><TD><B>Rows:</B> (if ",
        "desired)</TD>\n",
        "<TD><INPUT TYPE=\"text\" ",
        "NAME=\"ROWS\" SIZE=",
        "\"2\" MAXLENGTH=\"4\"></TD></TR>\n",
        "<TR><TD><B>Columns:</B> (if ",
        "desired)</TD>\n",
        "<TD><INPUT TYPE=\"text\" ",
        "NAME=\"COLUMNS\" SIZE=",
        "\"2\" MAXLENGTH=\"4\"></TD></TR>\n";
```

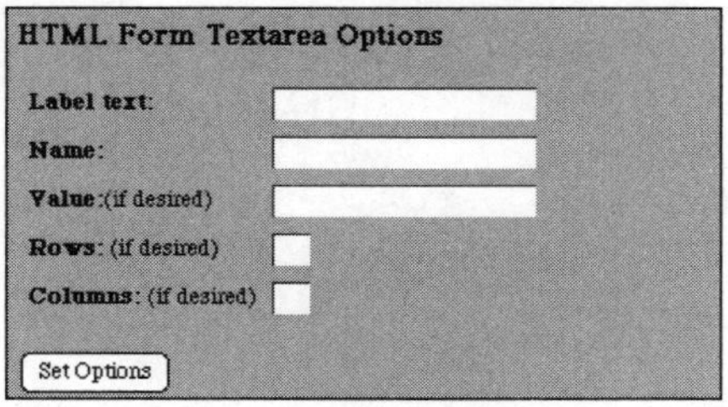

HTML Form Textarea Options

Label text:

Name:

Value :(if desired)

Rows: (if desired)

Columns: (if desired)

[Set Options]

■ **Figure 7-1**
■ *The Form Generator's existing options page for the TEXTAREA tag.*

Having decided for aesthetic reasons that the best placement for the SELECT would be under the optional default value field, we merely locate that portion of the code and insert the following:

```
"<TR>\n",
"<TD><B>Text wrap mode:</B></TD>\n",
"<TD><SELECT NAME=\"WRAP\">\n",
"<OPTION>No Wrap\n",
"<OPTION>Soft Wrap\n",
"<OPTION>Hard Wrap\n",
"</SELECT></TD></TR>\n",
```

Notice that we converted the individual `print` statements that the Tool creates, into the extended `print` used in the script. This was done mostly for readability but isn't necessary, as long as you end and begin the `print` statement you are inserting into the inserted code.

Not Just a Pretty Face

Once inserted, the options form for the <TEXTAREA> looks like Figure 7-2. However, having built the interface, we're still only halfway toward a functioning option. At this point, if the user selects any wrap mode, the input will go off into space, because our supporting code has not been written to convert this option's setting into HTML.

If we find the support code for the existing <TEXTAREA> tag and options, we can see that it mostly consists of testing each option in the following `elseif/if` statement to see if it is defined and, if so, writing it in the proper format to the working file:

```
} elsif ($in{ELEMENT} eq "Large Text Area") {
    if ($in{LABEL}) {
        print DOC "$td$in{LABEL}$endtd\n";
    }
```

```
print DOC "$td<TEXTAREA NAME=\"$in{NAME}\" ";

if ($in{ROWS}) {
    print DOC "ROWS=\"$in{ROWS}\" ";
}
if ($in{COLUMNS}) {
    print DOC "COLS=\"$in{COLUMNS}\" ";
}
print DOC ">";
   if ($in{VALUE}) {
    print DOC " in{VALUE}";
}
print DOC "</TEXTAREA>$endtd\n";

&line_break;
```

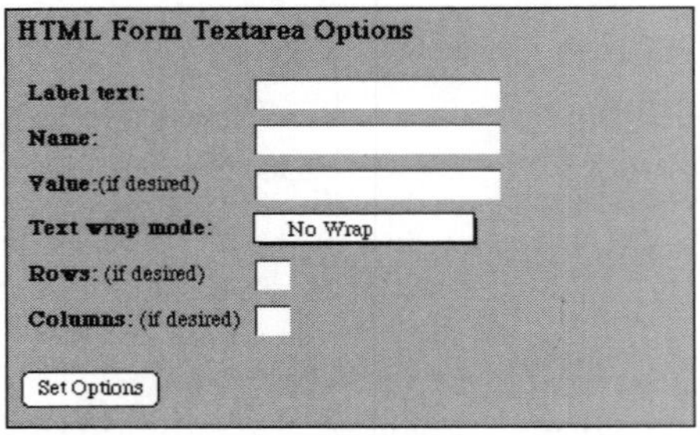

HTML Form Textarea Options

Label text:	
Name:	
Value:(if desired)	
Text wrap mode:	No Wrap
Rows: (if desired)	
Columns: (if desired)	

Set Options

Figure 7-2
The modified <TEXTAREA> options form interface.

To support our new option, we'll need to add a few lines that test the value of the WRAP select field and add the appropriate option to the tag. Because it's a SELECT, there will always be a defined value. Even if the user doesn't touch the pop-up menu, the default option defined for the SELECT will be passed with the rest of the form data to the CGI.

Since the WRAP option must be inside the 〈 and 〉 brackets around the TEXTAREA tag, we'll want to put our code before the line that reads:

```
print DOC ">";
```

Because the value No wrap requires no action on our part, we only have to make a conditional statement that senses the other two possible states of the select field and acts appropriately on them. Its default behavior is to add nothing to the tag, and this behavior is overridden only by values of SOFT or HARD wrap. A casual stab at the required code yields the following:

```
if ($in{WRAP} eq "Soft wrap") {
    print DOC " WRAP=SOFT";
} elsif ($in{WRAP} eq "Hard wrap") {
    print DOC " WRAP=HARD"
}
```

This code will produce the desired effect. The leading space in each of the potential insertions to the tag separates the WRAP option from whatever goes before it. This may be a value for the ROW or COLS options, or it may be the TEXTAREA tag itself, but whatever it is, a space is required between options or options and their values.

This is potentially one of the most tricky bugaboos when generating HTML from within Perl. If you are overly hasty, as some of us are, then the difference between:

```
print DOC "WRAP=HARD";
```

and:

```
print DOC " WRAP=HARD";
```

may be difficult to discern. The difference in the resulting output, when inserted into the middle of an HTML tag, is plain to see. The instance that inserts a space works and the other does not. The broken HTML tag won't be recognizable to the browser, and the field will simply not show up. Talk about making something simple mysterious, its failure to appear is harder to explain than doing it right the first time!

Taking the Bandages Off

With these steps and precautions in mind, you can add support for new tag options quite simply. The entire process is a matter of following the path an element takes on its way through the script, and carefully choosing the appropriate points to customize by inserting your own code. It's even less complicated to modify the way an element handles an existing tag because you need merely edit code that's already there.

Next, we'll look at a slightly more complicated way to extend the capabilities of the Tool: adding a brand new HTML element to the user's choices.

Teaching an Old Tool New Tricks

With a little know-how, you can add new HTML elements to the Tool as easily as you can add words to your own vocabulary. Like the knowledge of your native language that you carry in your head, the Form Generator has established rules and well-worn paths for new information to follow. If you define your problem in those terms and follow the paths other elements take, your task will be easily accomplished.

If you remember from our investigation of *formgen.pl's* internal structure, a series of multibranching decision trees defined the core of how the Tool supports any given element. To add an element, all you do is add another branch on the various decision trees that the script traverses in collecting data from the user and creating the final element on disk.

In essence, you're following a well-beaten track down the middle of the script, rather than trying to chart an entirely new course. We'll look at the more complex task of adding a whole new feature later in this chapter, but for now, let's look at what's involved in extending existing features.

We'll take a closer look now at the steps to add a new element to the Tool. As an example, we'll use the new tag introduced by the Netscape 2.0 beta: the file upload form element. Here's an example of this element:

```
<FORM ENCTYPE="multipart/form-data" ACTION="_URL_" METHOD=POST>
<INPUT TYPE="file" NAME="uploaded.file">
<INPUT TYPE="submit" VALUE="Upload File">
</FORM>
```

where _URL_ is replaced with the actual URL for the file in question. This form widget is new to the Netscape 2.0 betas, as we've stated, and we haven't had much experience using it. Therefore, our implementation of this element in the Tool may not be the most elegant or efficient way to accomplish this task. Please bear with us and treat our example as an illustration of a principle, rather than an exact recipe to follow.

There are three steps to adding this element to the Tool:

1. Modify the element selection form.
2. Supply the option selection interface.
3. Supply the code that turns option choices into finalized HTML.

The order of these steps applies only if you're not working "live" on a site that's in use. In that case, you're going to want to change the order to 3-1-2. That way, people aren't trying to use an interface option before the supporting code is in place.

These steps mirror those taken by any already defined element in the Tool. In fact, they also mirror the steps we took to add the WRAP option to TEXTAREA; this time we'll need to delve a little deeper.

Adding a New Element

The element selection form is where the user is presented with two radio buttons used to indicate the choice of FORM or HTML element. A SELECT is used to specify the exact element the user wishes to add. To make another element available to the user, you must insert the name of that element into the appropriate SELECT.

Since we'll be adding another FORM element, it makes sense that we would add it to the SELECT with the rest of the FORM elements. The code fragment that contains the HTML for the SELECT is in the `toolbar` subroutine in *formgen.pl*:

```
"<TH COLSPAN=2>Choose next element for ",
"document:</TH></TR>\n",
"<TR><TD><INPUT TYPE=\"radio\" NAME=\"ELEMENT_TYPE\" ",
"VALUE=\"FORM\" CHECKED>Form Element:\n",
"</TD>\n",
"<TD><INPUT TYPE=\"radio\" NAME=\"ELEMENT_TYPE\" ",
"VALUE=\"HTML\" >HTML Element:</TD></TR>\n",
"<TR><TD><SELECT NAME=\"FORM_ELEMENT\" SIZE=\"1\">\n",
"<OPTION>Text or Numeric Input\n",
"<OPTION>Large Text Area\n",
"<OPTION>Hidden Field\n",
"<OPTION>Radio Button\n",
"<OPTION>Checkbox\n",
"<OPTION>Select\n",
"<OPTION>Submit\n",
"</SELECT></TD>\n",
```

To add `File Upload` as a choice, we'd simply insert a line that reads:

```
"<OPTION>File Upload\n",
```

before the line that contains `</SELECT>` (which ends the SELECT statement) or wherever in the list of options we feel it is appropriate.

When the user chooses `File Upload`, the field named `FORM_ELEMENT` is set to this value. This field and value trigger the next behavior we create.

The Option Selection Form

Our next task is to create a form interface that allows the user to specify the parameters for this particular element. Since we're working with a form generator, this shouldn't be too hard.

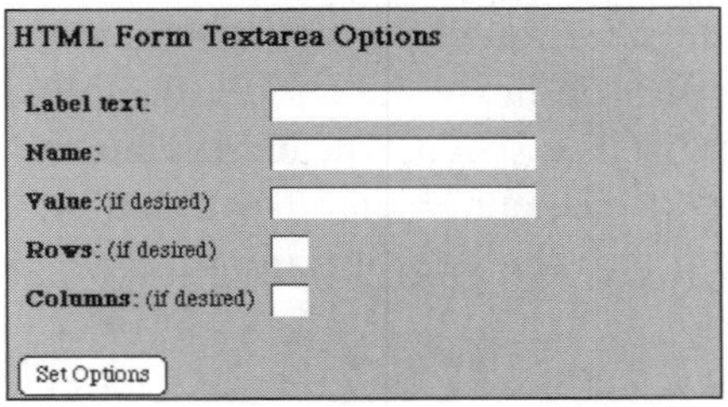

Figure 7-3

The form interface for File Upload.

After taking a quick look at the options we needed to set in the element, we created the form in Figure 7-3. It consists of three text inputs, one for the MIME encoding type, one for the target URL, and one for the label on the Submit button. We've supplied defaults for two of the three, first for the encoding type because it seems to work only if its value is `multipart/form`, and second for the button label.

As with the addition to the TEXTAREA tag in the previous section, we'll ask the Form Generator to end the document, roll the form into a CGI, and display the results on our browser window. A quick cut-and-paste garners the chunk of code we're particularly interested in, namely:

```
print "<TR>\n",
"<TD><B>Encoding type:</B> <BR><FONT SIZE=-1>don't change ",
"this unless you really know what you're doing.</FONT></TD>\n",
"<TD><INPUT TYPE=\"text\" NAME=\"ENCTYPE\" SIZE=\"35\"  ",
"VALUE=\"multipart/form-data\" ></TD>\n",
"</TR>\n",
"<TR><TD><B>URL where the file will go:</B></TD>\n",
"<TD><INPUT TYPE=\"text\" NAME=\"URL\" SIZE=\"35\" ></TD>\n",
"</TR>\n",
"<TR><TD><B>Upload button label:</B></TD>\n",
"<TD><INPUT TYPE=\"text\" NAME=\"LABEL\" SIZE=\"35\"  ",
"VALUE=\"Send File\" ></TD>\n",
"</TR>\n";
```

Again, as with the previous example, we've changed the multiple print statements into a single multiline print by chopping the word `print` off the beginning of each line (except the first line), and changing the trailing semicolons into commas.

Insert Tab A into Slot B

Our next task is to fit this portion of code into the tree of conditional statements that controls which element option form the user sees. The corresponding button is labeled `Create Element`, which drops the script into the block of code contained by the following conditional statement:

```
} elsif ($in{BUILD} eq "Create Element") {
```

The next level of the tree separates the two SELECTs `HTML` and `Form Element` on the element selection form. Since our new element is most definitely a form element, our insertion point must occur in this block of code. You can identify this section by the conditional that marks its entry point:

```
if ($in{ELEMENT_TYPE} eq "FORM") {
```

From there, the script walks a series of conditionals that zero in on the specific element. Looking at one of the existing elements tells us how to add another one:

```
} elsif ($in{FORM_ELEMENT} eq "Hidden Field") {
    print "<H3>HTML Form Hidden Field ",
          "Options</H3>\n",
          "<TABLE>\n<TR><TD><B>Name:",
          "</B></TD>\n</TR>",
          "<TD><INPUT TYPE=\"text\" ",
          "NAME=\"NAME\" SIZE=",
          "\"20\" MAXLENGTH=\"40\"></TD></TR>\n",
          "<TR><TD><B>Value:</B></TD>\n",
          "<TD><INPUT TYPE=\"text\" ",
          "NAME=\"VALUE\" SIZE=",
          "\"20\" MAXLENGTH=\"40\"></TD></TR>\n";
```

Using the preceding block of code as a model, we can see exactly what we need to write for our new conditional and its associated block of code. What's nice about the design of *formgen.pl* is that, since the conditional tree doesn't force processing in a specific order, we can insert our new block after any existing `elseif` at the same level.

In other words, if we insert the test for the value `Upload File` directly after the first `if` statement, it won't interfere with the following elements' blocks of code. Conversely, if we place the new chunk at the very end, after the last `elsif` is closed, none of the preceding conditionals will interfere with its operation.

In the name of logic and maintainability, we'd suggest you add any new elements at the bottom of the pop-up select menu on the element selection form and then follow up with the inserted code at the bottom of the tree. If there is some compelling reason to insert the new element higher on the pop-up, try to match the placement of the code in the tree. If, for example, you insert a new element after `Text or Numeric Input` and before `Large Text Input`, your block of code should be sandwiched between the conditionals that test for these same two element choices.

Because we're dealing with the hypothetical in this situation, we'll return now to the heart of this exercise: actual code examples. We'll start with the conditional that evaluates as true when our new element is selected:

```
} elsif ($in{FORM_ELEMENT} eq "Upload File") {
            print "<H3>Upload File  ",
                  "Options</H3>\n",
                  "<TABLE>\n",
```

Next we'll set up the interface form document, then hit the user with the actual interface that captures options and their associated values.

This fragment would be followed by the fields and labels we created earlier. The Tool is now equipped to respond to the user's choice of `File Upload` with the proper interface.

Batteries Not Included

Our new element, like the additional option in our TEXTAREA example, is only half complete. In its present state, the Tool will present the user with an interface to set the options for a file upload widget, but it won't do anything more with the user's selections.

To complete the additions to the Tool, we need to write code that translates the user's option settings into actual working HTML code. Here again, the structure of the script lends a hand. The BUILD field's value when an options form is submitted is `Set Options`, and the following conditional supports all these elements:

```
} elsif ($in{BUILD} eq "Set Options") {
```

Inside this statement's block we find yet another conditional tree that isolates the specific element chosen by the user. Similar considerations determine the placement of our code here as they did with our option selection form code in the preceding section.

If you chose what we consider to be the default position at the bottom of the SELECT, then your code should be located at the bottom of the tree. Once again, though, there is no "wrong" answer here, since every conditional is treated equally in Perl.

The next code we must write is like a tiny program, or a sort of function or subroutine. Its operating environment is pre-initialized, the file handle is opened, the variables initialized, and the set of data is handed to it in an easily digestible form. It has a simple, well-defined task that's reducible to a small handful of basic components. Given the data for the element's options, it must write a viable piece of HTML out to the working document.

The first step is the conditional statement that causes the script to drop into our block of code. Modeled after the other conditionals in the tree, it would be written as:

```
} elsif ($in{ELEMENT} eq "Upload File") {
```

Because our previous block of code, contained within the Set Options tree, preserved the user's original choice within the ELEMENT field, this conditional evaluates as true.

Our next step is to create the actual supporting code. Using our sample of a correct file upload form as a template, the code must interpret the user's input and insert the desired values at the appropriate points. The three pertinent fields to examine will be assigned to these variables: $in{ENCTYPE}, $in{URL}, and $in{LABEL}, which represent values for the MIME encoding type, destination URL, and value for the Submit button. Writing code that inserts them into the HTML template is fairly trivial:

```
print DOC "<FORM ENCTYPE=\"$in{ENCTYPE}\" ACTION=\"$in{URL}\"",
    " METHOD=POST>\n",
    "<INPUT TYPE=\"file\" NAME=\"uploaded.file\">\n",
    "<INPUT TYPE=\"submit\" VALUE=\"$in{LABEL}\">\n",
    "</FORM>n\";
```

The only critical point to note here is that we must print to the DOC filehandle so this new element can be included within the user's current file-in-progress.

While this code fragment works as written, there are some additional considerations you may want to work into it for this or any other new element you create. First, there is the matter of data validation. HTML forms have very little built-in validation, checking only if the input is numeric or text and the length of the field if a MAXLENGTH is defined. Beyond that, the content of the field is unknown to the form, which has no built-in way to judge whether or not the data is valid.

With this in mind, you may want to include some of your own validation, and this code fragment would be exactly the place to do it. Before writing out the HTML, for example, you might want to verify that the ENCTYPE field contains a valid MIME type. This could be done by defining an array of the applicable MIME types on the spot and testing the contents of the field to make sure it matches with one of the elements of the array.

Or if you wanted a more open-ended test and didn't mind introducing a dependency on an external file, you could store a list of MIME types outside the script. When it's time to test the data, it could be accomplished as follows:

```
open (MIME, "${datapath}valid.mime.types");
# Note: the above presupposes that a file containing the valid mime
# types is located in the Tool's data directory and is named
# "valid.mime.types".

while (<MIME>) {
  chop;
  if ($in{ENCTYPE} eq $_) {
    $valid = 1;
  }
}

close MIME;

if ($valid) {
  # Our block of code from above is executed.
} else {
  # The test failed; inform the user and don't create the HTML.
  print "<B>Warning: </B> $in{ENCTYPE} is not a valid choice for ",
        "the MIME Encoding type for a file upload. Please try ",
        "again.<P>";
}
```

As you can see, if the test fails we do not have much recourse, other than to alert the user to try creating the element again with valid data. Since the actual creation stage of the Tool is immediately followed by the toolbar subroutine, the user will get this feedback at the top of a new element selection form.

Another option in a situation like this where you want the user to choose one value from a range of well-defined data, is to narrow the choices in the input field for the option. In this case, we could revamp the option form for file uploading and replace the simple text input with a SELECT containing all the supported MIME types. Wherever possible, this is the preferable way to validate data because it requires far less programming on the back-end.

Protecting Users from Themselves

This example actually suffers from a more difficult problem when it comes to integrating it into an existing form. Since our working template is a complete HTML form, it may not coexist peacefully with the user's larger FORM document. With its own FORM tag and Submit button, its placement could easily disrupt the functionality of the form that has been created to this point. As usual, there are a few ways around this difficulty.

First, you could warn the user on the options form that this particular element may interfere with the overall functioning of the form. Given the way users tend to ignore warnings of this type or at least misunderstand them, this is not the best option but it should always be there anyway if the danger exists.

A second option is to extend the options form and the supporting code to close out the FORM above this particular element with a Submit button and a </FORM> tag and then open another FORM after the file upload widget is completed. This is somewhat presumptuous on the part of the programmer, however, because it assumes you know what the user wants the document to do as a whole.

It also opens other questions, such as how the Tool should handle the FORM tag when it is ending the document, and how our supporting code should handle the ACTION option of the form that follows our widget.

The third option is the best: Find a way to integrate the file upload input into the form at large. This obviates the problems discussed above. Truthfully, as of this writing we have not had time to research what effect a file input field would have on the operation of a form with other inputs, so your guess is as reasonable as ours would be. (You're also as likely as we are to wish for a capability like this!)

Wherever possible, when adding a new element to the Tool, the constraints of the Tool's structure and flow of control should be respected. In addition, the integrity of the document as a whole should be taken into account, so that the end result of introducing a new element is not to break the rest of the user's work.

The same can be said about the most ambitious way for you to extend the Form Generator's functionality: adding a whole new feature.

Adding New Features

We have stated that adding an element to the existing feature set is somewhat akin to learning a new word and incorporating it into your vocabulary. On the other hand, breaking out of the existing features in order to add an entirely new function to the script is a task on a completely different level.

To follow our language metaphor, it's more akin to learning a foreign language than it is to expanding your knowledge of a language you already know. Instead of being able to rely upon the structure already present in *formgen.pl,* we'd need to design an entirely new structure that would coexist with the existing structure. Not easily done, but within the realm of possibility. In this section, we'll examine some principles that might aid you on a quest to extend the core features of the Tool itself.

The realm of potential features that could be added to the Form Generator is virtually limitless, since creating HTML forms and CGIs is so open-ended. The first consideration for any new feature, of course, should be, "Does the user really need this?" You wouldn't want to expend valuable time and energy on building a fur-lined sink or a gas-powered turtleneck, only to find out that nobody's particularly interested in using it!

New Feature Evaluation and Selection

In Chapter 4, "Designing an HTML Form Generator," we briefly noted a number of features that, on closer inspection, were deemed good ideas but difficult to implement. When we get around to revising the Tool to Version 2.0, these would be the first things we'd consider adding.

Often the best things to start adding to a project are those that feel like they're "missing." These are often things that came up during the design process or when actually coding, but were put on the back burner to avoid distractions from the task at hand.

In addition, consider suggestions for "more things they'd like to see" from people who've used the Tool. An outside opinion is always useful in such situations since it brings fresh insight to something that programmers tend to get too close to. However, it's equally important to avoid the tendency to turn a piece of software into an entirely user-driven "feature mill."

In our opinion, it's almost universally true that people will believe, often passionately, that they do want a gas-powered turtleneck, until you give them one. The danger is that your project will end up like so many of the mature consumer software products on the market today: bloated, overly feature-rich, and nearly useless at doing what they were originally designed for.

Once you have a list of potential new features, you'll be faced with the real work of evaluating them for merit and feasibility. The same criteria we applied to the initial design process, discussed in Chapter 4, are applicable at this stage. Since we covered that topic in depth, you can turn to Chapter 4 for a refresher course.

In brief, the considerations that are most important include the time and effort required versus the benefits to the user derived from the new feature. The baseline measurement is: If you think the benefits are worth the effort, then the feature passes the test.

When working with an existing project the way we are now, there is also a variation on a theme we explored in Chapter 4, that of focus. Since we have our core functions operating, we don't face the same risk of distraction getting the project to the point of minimal desired functionality. But when adding features, you do run the risk of obfuscating the existing structure or code to the point where it no longer becomes readable or maintainable.

Even worse, something you add may misdirect the flow of the script so that it loses efficiency or productivity. Or your new code may simply break the Tool completely or cripple a key feature. It's vital, therefore, to test the Tool as you proceed. Your testing shouldn't be limited to new functions only, but should also periodically verify that the rest of the program still behaves the way it was designed.

Our Short List

Those caveats aside, we have our own short list of things we'd like to see incorporated into the Tool. We offer them to you as fuel for the creative mill, and also as an illustration of the principles we mentioned earlier.

Edit Source

Chapter 14, "The Online HTML Editor," covers a tool that allows users to edit the HTML source for a given page over the Web. This kind of direct, hands-on control of the actual meat of the documents created by the Tool would be extremely valuable. There's a slight degree of risk to the integrity of the Tool's output because you would have to open the structure and content of the code-generated source to human hands. This introduces the possibility for a user to inadvertently change some portion of the form that the Tool depends upon to create a working document.

However, the benefits outweigh the risk in this case, and implementing such a feature would be fairly easy, especially with an existing script that does exactly what we want. In terms of interface, the already functioning

View Source button could easily be changed to an Edit Source button, with the block of code that simply displays the document-in-progress replaced with modified code from the HTML editing script discussed in Chapter 14.

Joining a Form Already in Progress

We recognize the possibility that a user would not be able to complete a form in one sitting, but currently there is no ability to save a work-in-progress and resume work on it later. Therefore, it's desirable to give the user a choice when first accessing the *formgen.pl* script to start a new form or pick up work on an existing Tool project.

The interface for this choice could be a SELECT that lists all the currently saved projects, situated on the first page that *formgen.pl* returns to its users.

The most readily discernible risk in this feature is the possibility that someone would grab a document created by someone else. We'd need to create some sort of authentication to ensure that this couldn't happen. Since we capture the user's e-mail address when they start a new form, it's probably easiest to require it again when they wish to resume. The value in the document's HEAD file could then be compared to the submitted value and if they didn't match, the request could be rejected.

In retrofitting the script to handle this capability, the most important aspect is properly initializing the Tool's environment to let it know where the user was when they left off. This entails figuring out how many temporary files are on the server for this particular document and setting the STEP variable to the proper value. For navigation, we could add a separate Resume Document button on the welcome form and then trap that value so that it traverses the desired block of code.

Adopting a Completed Form

To extend the "resuming" function one step further, imagine if you could point at an existing form using a URL, instruct the Tool to retrieve it, and adapt it to its operating environment. The user would then be able to update and maintain existing forms anywhere on the Web.

Depending upon the extent to which we wish to implement this concept, we may find ourselves in the position of having to write an HTML parser to make it function properly. This could be difficult, since HTML is not really designed as a machine-readable format. It's easy enough to parse HTML and translate it into its visual form, but much more difficult to parse it for logical or content structure and meaning.

This would be necessary if, for example, we wished to allow users to retrofit their forms with our table formatting. The Tool would be required not only to find input fields, but also to attempt to locate their labels and to understand what kind of input was required so that we could adjust our formatting accordingly. This could easily turn into a monumental task.

If, however, we simply allowed the user to add to the form or manually edit the source (as per the feature mentioned earlier), we'd have a more manageable task. This approach greatly reduces the usefulness of the feature, though, since the appeal of adding nicely formatted fields to the bottom of an existing script is limited. Still, the user would be able to take advantage of the ability to roll the form into a CGI, and this may be enough to merit its creation.

In interface terms, this feature would logically be added to the welcome form, as a third option alongside the buttons for beginning a new form, or resuming work on an existing one. Once again, an additional button could be added to drop the script into the appropriate block of code.

Data Validation and Error Checking

We also mentioned in Chapter 4 a potential feature that would allow users to specify the parameters for a valid response to any of their input fields. This could be a real boon to the data entry world, where speed and efficiency often depend upon reliable data validation. It's possible to add fields to the option forms of appropriate elements, such as text, numeric input, or large text areas.

Deciding on how users specify what kind of data they're looking for, and what constitutes valid replies, is a tricky problem. We went into this in detail in our brainstorming session in Chapter 4. However, if we offer a limited amount of data validation, we may be able to achieve a trade-off between power and plausibility.

One obvious example would be to give users the option to specify minimum and maximum values allowable on numeric inputs. This is an easily definable range of values, and it would be simple to create a bit of code to act as a template for the conditional statement that we'd need to create.

This brings us to the second hitch—since we'd need to validate the data using Perl code in the supporting CGI, we'll also need a way to get the validation information to the part of the Tool that generates the CGI code. Keep in mind that CGI generation occurs after the user is finished with the form, when the HTML source is encapsulated in a combination of script boilerplate and generated statements. One way to communicate this is to embed an HTML comment where the fields to be validated occur. To make this work, we'd need to adapt the finishing stages of the Tool to look for such comments and turn them into working code.

A prototype for this simple messaging system might consist of HTML source code such as:

```
<!- VALID NAME="AGE" MAX=120 MIN=0 ->
<INPUT TYPE="number" NAME="AGE" SIZE=2 MAX=3>
```

Then, during the phase when HTML source is translated into Perl, the program could watch for a comment containing the keyword VALID, parse for MAX and MIN, and roll it into a conditional that tests the value of the user's submitted data.

This block of code could be inserted in the POST portion of the resulting CGI, which gets run when the user submits data. The end result of the translation from the comment in the HTML and the actual input could look something like this:

```
if (($in{AGE} < $min) || ($in{AGE} > $max)) {
   print "<P><B>The User's submitted AGE value, $in{AGE},",
        " is not valid.</B>";
}
```

With a little work, you may be able to extend this model to more complex data types. The ideal would be to have a library of datatypes such as Name, Zip Code, State, etc., from which users could choose when defining the values they wish to accept as valid. Each would have a predefined range or rules that define validity, and a preconfigured set of tests to make sure the data fit the proper mold.

In our minds, this feature teeters right on the brink of being worthy of the effort required to build it. Perhaps with a little persuading from our users, it may make it into Version 2.0 of the Tool! Tell us what you think.

Renovation: Creating New Structures Within an Existing Framework

For any of these proposed features, a new trail needs to be blazed through the script. None of the existing structures that we examined in our sections on modifying and adding elements are designed to support such features. Therefore, there are no predefined structures in most cases that can be adapted or modified to these ends. However, there are frameworks within which the logical structures of the script reside, and these can and must be used to integrate new ones.

When we discussed the potential new features, you may have noticed that we focused on those points in the script where new code would best be located. The welcome form, the element selection form, and the option forms were all specifically mentioned. These are the logical signposts along the route through the script.

For example, to add another button for a new feature that is accessible from the element selection page, you need only give the button a unique value and then add it to the if/elsif decision tree that controls which block of code gets run. This is the top-level tree, which scans the BUILD variable to determine what the user's next step will be. Locating another conditional in this tree effectively creates a bucket for you in which the response to clicking any new, specific button may be placed.

Back-end processing features, such as data validation, can find a logical and workable home within the code block under the End Document conditional. Scanning for input can further refine the flow of the script in the desired direction.

The point of this postmortem on features is to note that, while adding a new feature does require considerable forethought, planning, and ingenuity, it's not like having to invent gravity. There's an existing framework already in place that you can follow to see how the other features cause the flow of the script to change. Your new feature can sit alongside the Tool's core functions in a peaceful, cooperative way.

If you're having too much trouble fitting a feature into the existing framework, you may need to do some serious reassessment: Is this really a feature that should be in this program? Or are you trying to force a horse to do the work of a pickup truck? Or, if the logical connections are strong enough, is the initial framework the right one? Did you possibly create a starting framework that prevents your program from growing the ways it needs to?

Much like renovating an old house, respecting the structure that's already present is the best path to a successful effort. It's also critical that your renovations don't weaken or remove any support beams that hold the entire structure in place!

SUMMARY!

We hope that you have gained from this chapter not only some useful information about extending the Form Generator, but also about the general principles involved in modifying existing code. We first looked at tracing the path of an existing aspect of a feature and adding additional options and capabilities. Next, we discussed what's involved in adding an additional element to the Tool's features. Finally, we looked at some of the issues involved in adding a brand-new feature to the Tool itself.

Before leaving our discussion of the internal code that makes the Tool work, note that we left out one crucial ingredient to making any of this work. Before you can start applying the techniques we discussed, you must learn to read and understand code. We didn't mention it or cover it because, unfortunately, it isn't a skill you can impart to someone easily. It's the type of ability that must be learned by osmosis, by trial and error, and by staring at lines of real code and thinking, "What is it doing?"

In the next chapter, we'll talk about putting the Tool on your system and making it work in your environment.

MAKING THINGS WORK: INSTALLING AND TESTING YOUR FORMS AND CGIS

*B*y now you know how to create a form with the Form Generation Tool. When you've finished building a form, the Form Generator can produce two distinct types of final output: an HTML form or a CGI with the form embedded in the code. In this chapter, we'll go over the steps required to install and test these forms. They aren't necessarily in their final states, however, and we'll also discuss ways to customize them and add functionality.

RETRIEVING THE FORM

As you've learned, there are four ways to obtain the generated form:

1. Cut-and-paste from the "View Source" Web page.
2. Have the form e-mailed to you.
3. Download the form to your local machine.
4. Have the Tool install the form directly on your server.

Chances are that most of you only have the first three options. The fourth option requires that you be the WebMaster of the server where you're using the tool, or at least that you have write privileges to a portion of either the HTTP document or CGI binary hierarchies.

Many of you will generate the form on another Web server or on your local machine and then upload it to a Web server. We'll also review the steps necessary to accomplish this task.

INSTALLING AN HTML FORM

If you already have a Web site, installing an HTML form should be a familiar task. It's similar to placing an HTML document onto your site, but there are a few additional things you'll want to keep in mind.

Finding a Home

The ultimate destination for your HTML form should be the HTTP document directory on the Web host where it will be served. In most cases, this will be in some part of the Web server's main HTTP document tree. An alternative location might be a *public_html* directory in your personal home directory on your ISP's server. As a "bonus" to access accounts, some ISPs allow you to house Web pages there.

If you aren't the owner of the Web server you plan on using, contact your ISP or system administrator for the location you can use to serve pages. Some ISPs require you to purchase a separate Web host service, in addition to existing account charges.

Should It Have a Home of Its Own?

It's a good idea to group related Web documents, graphics, and forms in the same directory. For instance, all items related to your customer database could be stored in */www/httpdocs/customerdb*. Likewise, you could place all forms in a directory called */www/httpdocs/forms*.

Ownership and Permissions

On a UNIX system, you'll need Read/Write/eXecute permissions for the directory where you install your form. It's also nice to be the owner of that directory, so you can change permissions and make other modifications as needed. If you don't have root access to the server, you'll need to get your sysadmin or ISP to grant you ownership of that directory. We'll provide more information about permission requirements for this directory in the testing section.

What About My NOS?

Many Web hosts today run on network servers other than UNIX. Examples include Windows NT, Novell NetWare, and Macintosh. Some companies already have such client/server systems in place, which means they don't have to commit extra resources and people to maintain a new operating system just for their Web server.

It's often easier for you to update your Web pages using the server's network operating system (NOS), rather than TCP/IP applications such as FTP. But when you do, there will be other access control requirements to consider. To place files under Windows NT, for instance, you'll need to have the Create privilege on the Share you're connecting to, as well as Read/Write/eXecute rights. If this represents more rights than you are currently granted, talk to your network administrator.

Putting It There

Once you have your space designated and have the appropriate permissions, you can put your form there. Depending on the system you're using, there are several ways to do this: copying to an NFS mounted drive or to a drive shared under your NOS, or using FTP. Since all Web servers that run TCP/IP usually can also run an *FTP daemon*, we'll describe how to use FTP to transfer these files.

Using FTP to transfer your Web pages works like this:

- Use an FTP client to connect to the Web server.
- Log on with your ID and password.
- If the current directory isn't already properly set, change to your HTTP document directory (e.g., */www/httpdocs/charlie*). If you get a Permission Denied message, check the directory permissions again or contact your system administrator.

- Upload the documents as Binary. (This will preserve the contents of any graphics files that you may transfer at the same time and won't alter the contents of your text files.)

- *PUT* the file in your HTML directory. Again, if you get a Permission Denied message, check directory permissions or contact your systems administrator.

If you are trying to get your form from a system outside the firewall onto a system inside the firewall, you have to do the opposite of this. Log in to the inside system, *ftp* to the outside system, and do a *GET* instead of a *PUT*.

Making the Form Visible

On a UNIX system, both the form and the directory that contains it need appropriate permissions so that *httpd* can serve the form. One way to do this is make the Web server's group the group for the directory and its files. That is, the *httpd* process runs under a certain user ID, and this ID can be made part of a certain named group (often www and httpd, respectively). This group then needs read access to the directory and file. Alternatively, you can make any user or group own the files and directory, but give the world read access. Examples of both approaches appear in Table 8-1.

Table 8-1

Permission examples for an HTTP document directory and form

HTTP Document Directory	*Owner for Dir and Files*	*Group for Dir and Files*	*Perms for Dir*	*Perms for HTML Docs and Forms*
/www/httpdocs/charlie	charlie	httpd	750	640
/www/httpdocs/singe	singe	managemt	755	644

A Form by Any Other Name

Once your form is in place, you'll want to make sure it has the right ".html" or ".htm" filename. You'll see why this is important when you read the "Troubleshooting" section.

Joining the Group

When uploading a file to your Web space, the owner and group for that file will automatically be set to yours. You may not always wish this to happen. In Table 8-1, for instance, charlie wants all files to be set to the httpd group, rather than whatever group he's a part of, so the Web server can read the files.

Rather than changing the group ID of the file each time you upload it, you can turn on a set group ID permission bit for the directory. To do this, first make sure the group ID of the directory is set to the group ID you want all the files to have, then use the command:

```
chmod g+s directoryname
```

For example:

```
chmod g+s /www/httpdocs/charlie
```

This makes your permissions for that directory appear as follows:

```
drwxrwsr-  3 charlie  httpd      512 Dec  8 16:12 charlie
```

Now, any files charlie uploads to that directory will automatically have their group IDs set to httpd.

TESTING AN HTML FORM

The best way to test your form is to view it with a Web browser—call the URL the same way you want people to call it from the Web. You'll be able to tell right away if it works. In Figure 8-1 you can see what a working form looks like. Ours is a form we created called "afn_survey.html".

Testing the Form Fields

We can also test the form's fields at this time to make sure they're sending the right values and names. NCSA's *httpd* comes with a handy tool for this very purpose, *post-query*, included in the */www/cgi-bin* directory of your *httpd* hierarchy. If you don't use NCSA's *httpd* or can't find that CGI locally, use theirs at:

```
<FORM ACTION="POST"
http://hoohoo.ncsa.uiuc.edu/cgi-bin/post-query
```

To send your data to this form, you need to make it the target for the action of the form:

```
HREF="http://hoohoo.ncsa.uiuc.edu/cgi-bin/post-query">
```

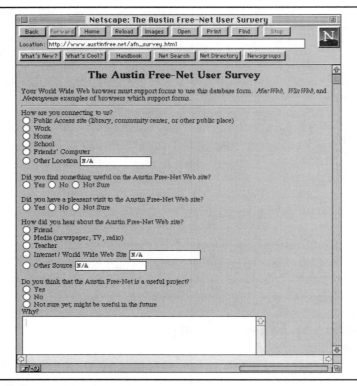

Figure 8-1
A working form that requests information from Austin Free-Net visitors.

Figure 8-2 shows the information that's returned. From this data, you can check the values passed to the script from your INPUT TYPE, NAME, and VALUE fields.

Troubleshooting

There's no reason to expect the first installation of a form to go smoothly. A variety of problems can occur, all of which will eventually show up in your testing. These problems usually fit into one of four categories:

1. Content-Type problems

2. Incorrect or invalid file locations

3. Broken HTML

4. Permissions problems

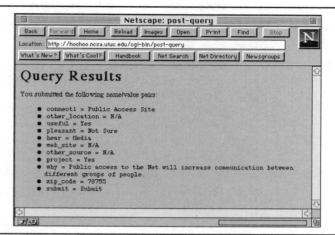

Figure 8-2
Information returned from NCSA's post-query using the form "afn_survey.html".

Content-Type Problems

Content-Type problems occur when a Web server reports to a browser that the form file is of a different MIME type than HTML. This usually manifests itself when the Web browser displays the HTML file as its text source, instead of as a properly formatted HTML document. Figure 8-3 shows an example.

The most common cause for this problem is when the Web server tells the browser to display the file as plain text. A Web server decides how to report a file's type based on its extension. If it can't recognize an extension, it will assign a default type instead. For most Web servers, that default is 'text/plain'.

On NCSA's *httpd* you can check the "mime.types" file and the AddType section of "srm.conf" to see which Content-Types are associated with which extensions, and make sure they're all correct. More likely, though, you made a typo when uploading or renaming the file and didn't give it an ".html" (or ".htm", if appropriate) extension.

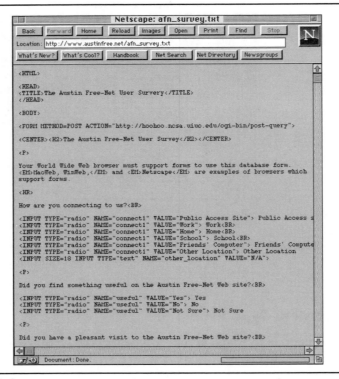

Figure 8-3:
An HTML Form with an incorrect file extension, displayed as 'Content-Type: text/plain'.

Incorrect or Invalid File Locations

For the online community, the "404 Not Found" error message has replaced "the number you dialed is not a working number" as a top pet peeve! On some browsers, such as Netscape, this appears as "File Not Found." If you're lucky enough never to have seen this message, check out Figure 8-4. This message usually indicates that the form file in the URL you specified wasn't found. Either there's a typo in the URL, you named the file incorrectly, or you failed to upload it properly in the first place. You'll want to check out all these possibilities.

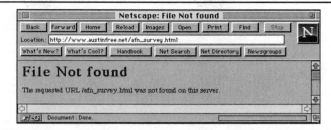

Figure 8-4

A pesky "404 Not Found" error message: The file can't be located.

Broken HTML

If you're using a form straight from the Tool, then there shouldn't be any HTML problems. If you've made changes to the HTML since it was generated, however, there is the possibility that an error of some kind has been introduced.

If you don't see any form elements (input fields, checkboxes, buttons, etc.) when you pull up the form, then the <FORM> tag itself is probably broken. An example of this is depicted in Figure 8-5. Other problems with the HTML code will usually be obvious. You'll see items missing, paragraphs running together, HTML elements continuing further than they should, and other deformations.

Checking your form's input through post-query may also highlight problem HTML areas. For example, if an input tag is incorrectly closed, the input from that area may be posted to the next tag, or the next tag's input could be ignored.

Permissions Problems

When you get a "file not found" or "server can't serve" message, check your file permissions and make sure that the server can write to your file. We discuss file permissions later in the section, "CGI Ownership and Permissions."

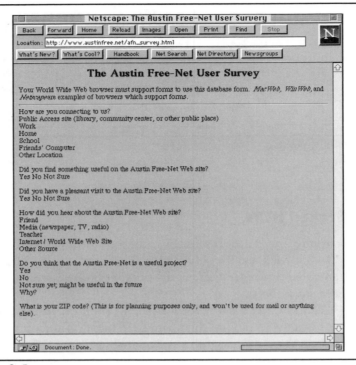

Figure 8-5
A form with a broken <FORM> tag, showing no input fields or buttons.

INTEGRATING THE HTML FORM INTO AN EXISTING HTML DOCUMENT

Most of you already have an existing Web site. But perhaps you've found creating forms and CGIs so intimidating or cumbersome that you haven't yet increased that site's functionality. Or maybe you have "boilerplate" text or graphics you add to all your HTML documents. The Form Generation Tool is designed to help you extend your current Web site. Therefore, it should be just as simple for you to include forms in existing HTML documents as to build new ones.

Using an editor on your local machine or the Web server, you can cut-and-paste your HTML form into the current document. There are a few things you'll want to keep in mind though.

Tag Considerations When Integrating

The main thing that you'll need to do is to strip out the large document elements from the form that should already be in your HTML document. These are <HTML>, <HEAD>, <TITLE>, and <BODY>. Don't forget to strip out their corresponding closing tags (</HTML>, </HEAD>, </TITLE>, and </BODY>) as well. Also, don't forget "global" document settings like <BASEFONT>.

No Forms Within Forms

An HTML form is allowed to have only one ACTION. You cannot have nested forms, that is, an HTML form contained within another form. Only one form per page, please!

In other words, this is bad HTML:

```
<FORM ACTION="http://www.outer.net/cgi-bin/a_form.pl"
  METHOD="POST">
..
<FORM ACTION ="http://www.outer.net/cgi-bin/b_form.pl" METHOD="POST">
..
</FORM>
..
</FORM>
```

By now you know how to create, install, and test your form. To use the form, you must be able to *serve* it so we'll discuss that next.

SERVING THE HTML FORM

Obviously a form isn't all there is to a CGI program. For example, there's no mechanism to compile and save information in an online survey. To give your form a purpose, you'll need two things:

1. a forms library to extract the form data so a CGI can work with it
2. a CGI program to actually do something with the data

Forms Libraries

When you enter data into an HTML form and submit it, the Web browser you're using "packages" it and sends it to the CGI to be "unpacked." In order for a CGI to extract that data and work with it, routines are required to parse the data. Rather than adding the code to do this to each of our CGIs, we can include functions from a *Forms Library* to do it for us.

Where to Find Them

Forms Libraries are pretty common. There are several such libraries, written in a variety of languages. Perl examples include *formlib.pl* and *cgi-lib.pl*. *cgi-lib.pl*, and a variety of other ones, can be found at this NCSA site:

```
ftp://ftp.ncsa.uiuc.edu/Web/httpd/Unix/ncsa_httpd/cgi/
```

formlib.pl can be found at:

```
http://www.cosy.sbg.ac.at/www-doku/tools/bjscripts.html#formlib
```

How to Use Them

Because they must be present at runtime, Forms Libraries need to be included in your code so their functions can be called. The Perl 'require' function permits this to occur. If the library isn't in the same directory as the CGI you're using, then you may need to put its location in the search path stored in the '@INC' array as well.

Once you have included the library, you can use its functions to extract the form data from that package. You should check the library you're using for its list of functions; the function most commonly used in this book is '&GetFormsArgs()'.

Ask Your ISP

If your Web site is on your ISP's server, you may want to contact them to find out which Forms Libraries they already have and where they're located (i.e., their full path specification). You can then research and use the functions from their libraries. Using materials already on their system will save you time, disk space, and associated charges as well.

Your CGI Program

This is the code that actually does something with the form's input data and (hopefully) performs some useful service for your users. For the purposes of this book, we're just going to give you an example of what needs to be included to extract form data for the CGI to use.

INSTALLING THE FORM/CGI COMBINATION

The second possible output type for the Form Generation Tool is a CGI script that includes embedded HTML code. Just as an HTML form allows you to extend your current HTML documents, a CGI form allows you to create complex CGI scripts to perform a multitude of tasks (we'll provide some interesting examples later in this book).

The process of installing a CGI application is similar to installing an HTML form. You may want to review the section "Installing an HTML Form" to see how the processes compare. The main differences are in location and permissions.

Where to Put the Script

Where you put your script depends on the directory where your Web server executes its CGIs. Web servers usually let you specify directory trees for CGI executables. Under NCSA's *httpd*, this is set up in the Server Resource Management file ("srm.conf") using the *ScriptAlias* command. By default, however, there is only one directory set up for CGIs, called */cgi-bin*.

There's also a method to allow CGIs to be executed from any HTTP document directory. Do this by declaring a MIME type to execute files with a certain extension rather than sending them. For example, if we wanted to be able to execute Perl CGIs with the ".pl" extension from any server-readable directory, we'd add the following to our "srm.conf" file:

```
AddType application/x-httpd-cgi .pl
```

Under NCSA's *httpd*, the ExecCGI option should also be enabled in the "access.conf" file for the directory tree where you wish CGIs to be executed. By default, that option is activated for the */cgi-bin/* subdirectory, but other directories can be easily activated as well.

Involving Your Sysadmin or ISP

If you're running your own Web server and have ownership of the entire *httpd* program tree, or if your sysadmin has activated script execution from user-accessible directories, then you'll have no problem uploading your scripts. Otherwise, you'll probably have to get your sysadmin or ISP to put your CGI scripts into the correct directory.

Often, ISPs and sysadmins won't allow scripts to be executed from just any directory. They like to have a look at whatever's being run on their server. Here's why:

- A CGI application is run using the same user ID as the Web server itself. If it contains malicious code, it can wreak all kinds of havoc—including deleting crucial files!

- A poorly written or malicious CGI script could compromise system security by exposing the password file and other configuration files to outsiders.

- Complex CGI applications could cripple a system by using large amounts of memory or CPU cycles.

Ask your systems administrator or ISP how they prefer to handle your scripts. They'll probably want you to mail them in or put them in your home directory, from where they'll copy them to the */cgi-bin* directory.

If you're the sysadmin for your Web server or have been granted the ability to run CGI scripts from your directory, read on about uploading and file permissions.

Uploading the CGI Script

If you recall how to upload an HTML form, then you can also upload a CGI script. If you have ownership of the directory where you'll be running the script, then you'll want to make sure you have write permission in that directory. Simply follow the instructions for uploading an HTML form.

CGI Ownership and Permissions

It's important that *httpd* be able to execute your CGI script. Therefore, *httpd*'s associated user ID needs Read/eXecute privileges to the directory where the script resides, as well as to the CGI script itself. If that ID owns the directory and file, or that ID's group owns them, or if you make both the files and their directory world-readable and executable, everything should work just fine. Which approach you use depends on whether you have root access to the system. If you do, the first option is best; if not, use the second. Table 8-2 summarizes both approaches.

Also, note that if the script writes to other files and/or creates other files, then the *httpd* login must also have write permissions for the other files and/or the directories to contain the new files.

Table 8-2
Ownership and permissions for CGI directories and files

CGI Directory	Owner	Group	Directory Permissions	File Permissions
/www/cgi-bin	www	httpd	750	750
/www/httpdocs/ charlie	charlie	managemt	755	755

Once you have your CGI script loaded onto the server and the permissions set correctly, you can begin testing it.

TESTING THE FORM/CGI COMBINATION

It's atypical for a CGI application to work perfectly immediately after being installed. This is especially true on UNIX systems, where permission and ownership issues are common pitfalls when trying to make programs work.

It's a good idea to test the canned Perl script that the Tool generates before making any modifications. If you didn't make any changes, it should run. The only thing you'll have to worry about are permissions and ownership. If you did make changes, then there may be other snares that could entrap you.

Testing the CGI Script from the Command Line

Before using your browser to test a CGI script, it's a good idea to test it from the command line. Browser errors are often generic and don't help the debugging process much.

If the script works from the command line, it will spit out `Content-Type: text/html`, followed by a stream of the HTML embedded in your CGI. If it doesn't work, it returns an error message that may indicate a permission or ownership problem, a Perl path problem, or some kind of Perl interpretation error.

Permissions/Ownership Problems

The ideal way to test for a permissions problem is to run the script using the same user ID as *httpd*. This should be the same user ID that's used when someone accesses the server from the Web. On most UNIX systems, this is `www`. If you have `root` access to the system, you can use the *su* command to change your user ID to `www`:

```
root@outer.net:/ [5 ] # whoami
root
root@outer.net:/ [6 ] # su www
root@outer.net:/ [1 ] # whoami
www
```

Note that even though we've switched to `www`, our prompt still says we're `root@outer.net`. Because of this and the confusion inherent in running multiple shells, it's easy to be unsure what user ID you're using. Therefore, it's a good idea to use the *whoami* command periodically to make sure you're not suffering from an identity crisis!

Once you're the Web user, try running your script. If there's a permissions problem, you'll get a "Permission Denied" message. Here's what happens when we try to run a CGI called *ch8cgi.pl* as the `www` user, when only `root` has read and execute rights:

```
root@outer.net:/usr/local/www/httpd-1.3/cgi-bin [1 ] # ch8cgi.pl
ch8cgi.pl: Permission denied.
```

Seeing that we have a permissions problem of some kind, a quick look at the file's attributes reveals that `www` doesn't have the execute privilege. We can then use *chown* to grant it the correct ownership rights:

```
root@outer.net:/www/cgi-bin [15 ] # ls -la ch8cgi.pl
-rwxr-x---   1 root     root         3779 Dec 11 00:46 ch8cgi.pl*
root@outer.net:/www/cgi-bin [16 ] # chown www.httpd ch8cgi.pl
```

These are pretty basic UNIX file permissions debugging techniques. Nevertheless, it's important to be aware that permission and ownership issues cause as many problems with CGIs as they do in other areas of UNIX administration. Therefore, always check permissions first whenever problems occur.

What If I'm Not Superuser?

If you're running a CGI script out of your own directory, the easiest thing to do is make the script world-readable/executable. This helps avoid execution problems due to permissions.

The down-side of this approach is that it allows anyone to read and execute the script. You might be able to work something out with your sysadmin or ISP to set the group for your CGI directory to *httpd* and turn on the set group ID bit so that files placed in that directory also belong to the group named *httpd*. You can then change the permissions to *750* so that the rest of the world can't see or run files in that directory.

Problems Accessing Perl

If the script has a problem at runtime, it generally produces a message like "Command not found." Here are some of the reasons for such problems:

- The Perl interpreter isn't included as the first line in the script. Ensure that the first line is something like:

  ```
  #!/usr/local/bin/perl
  ```

- The path or filename to Perl is incorrect. Make sure Perl is actually located in the path specified by the first line in the script. If it's somewhere else, change the first line of the script to reflect its actual location.

- The www user doesn't have permission to run Perl. Check Perl's permissions. It's probably okay to make it world-readable/executable.

Perl Compilation Errors

Perl's runtime environment is good about letting you know when there's a language-related error. When attempting to run the script from the command line, you'll get an alert, the line number where the error occurs, and the next item after the error. For example, when a semicolon is omitted at the end of a statement, Perl complains:

```
outer.net.charlie 64 % ch8cgi.pl
syntax error in file ch8cgi.pl at line 7, next token "print "
Execution of ch8cgi.pl aborted due to compilation errors.
```

Okay, so it doesn't say, "Hey, Biffo, you left out a semicolon!" But it at least gives you a signpost as to where the error occurred. Using this information, you should be able to track down and correct any problems. Actually, it tells you where it first *noticed* the error which could be several lines below where the semicolon was left out.

Testing the CGI from a Web Browser

Once you're able to run the CGI from a command line, test it with a Web browser. If it works, then you should see your form in all its glory and be able to input data as needed. When you submit the form, it should return the form variable names and values inputted.

Our sample CGI, *ch8cgi.pl*, includes all the major form elements: checkboxes, radio buttons, a numeric field, a text field, a text area, a multiple selection menu, and submit and reset buttons. When it's running correctly, you can see these elements, as shown in Figure 8-6.

The CGI generated by the Tool is completely self-contained. It not only includes the form itself, but also includes the code necessary to extract the data entered in the form. This means that the form is also ready to test: The CGI form is scripted to post data to itself, extract it, and display the values that were entered. If we fill in some of the form elements and click the Generate Chapter button, we'll return the variable names and data that were entered, as Figure 8-7 illustrates.

Dealing with the Bad News

If there is a problem with your CGI, your Web browser will likely report a "500 Server Error." This is a catch-all error for any CGI problem, which can be rather confusing. It doesn't tell you that the problem is due to a path error but it's a good idea to check all paths if you see the "500 Server Error." What's more, the tone of the error makes it sound like it's the Web server that's having a problem, rather than the CGI script. Figure 8-8 illustrates this error, in this case generated because of a compilation problem.

Carriage Returns Can Be Nasty Characters

You should be careful when using a DOS or Windows editor to modify your Perl scripts if they're run on a UNIX system. These editors tend to include the Carriage Return character (a.k.a. CR, Control-M, and ^M) in text files. UNIX, on the other hand, uses only the Line Feed character (a.k.a. LF, Control-J, and ^J) to end the current line of text and start a new one.

Including a Carriage Return in a Perl script on a UNIX system will break it, usually causing compilation errors. Scripts viewed with the *vi* editor cause Carriage Returns to reveal themselves as ^M

characters. Once you can see them, you can remove them.

Or, you could create a simple shell (or Perl) script to change Carriage Returns to Line Feeds. Here's a sample shell script that uses the UNIX *tr* command and the hexadecimal values for CR and LF to do the translation:

```
#!/bin/sh
tr '\015' '\012' < $1 > $1".1"
```

Carriage Returns don't seem to cause any ill effects in plain HTML code, other than making it somewhat "messy" to read with the ^Ms at the end of each line.

If you're unable to run a CGI script from your browser because of a permissions or ownership problem, you'll get a "403 Forbidden" error message. When you see one of these, as in Figure 8-9, it's a good idea to check the permissions governing the script in question (if you're having problems, so are your users).

If you've installed and successfully tested your bare-bones CGI or HTML form, it's now time to customize it for your particular site.

MAKING YOUR FORM YOUR OWN

In this section, we'll take a standard form created by the Tool and hot-rod it into something that looks handcrafted and unique. We'll be using marbling as well as sponging techniques, so you'll need some oil and latex paints, a high-speed buffing machine, and some 220 wet and dry silicon sandpaper! Just kidding...

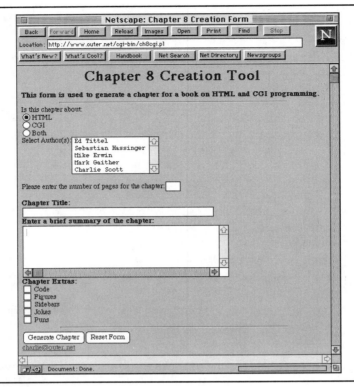

Figure 8-6
The CGI form ch8cgi.pl, containing all the major form elements.

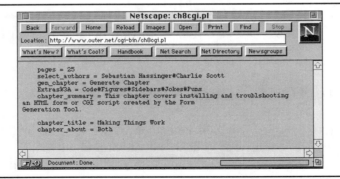

Figure 8-7
Values returned from the ch8cgi.pl form submission.

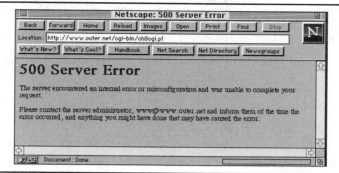

Figure 8-8

A 500 server error generated because of a compilation error.

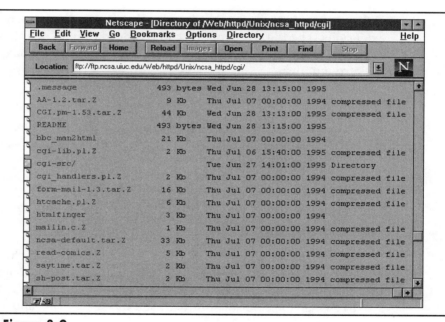

Figure 8-9

A 403 forbidden error message because www didn't have
read/execute permissions to ch8cgi.pl.

Giving It a Touch-Up: Modifications to the Form

All of the basic HTML tags should be in place so that you can modify your HTML form. We'll go through a few example modifications. (And remember we're designing for the high-end browsers like Netscape.)

 Many of these changes won't work with some browsers currently in use: Some are Netscape-specific extensions, and some have been adopted by a few but not all current browsers. In most cases, they'll just be ignored by the browser that doesn't support them, but in cases where it could cause problems (like Tables), it's good to point this out, both in HTML comments and in specific remarks to your audience on the page itself. ▲

Changing Backgrounds

You can change the background color or make it an image using Netscape extensions. The BGCOLOR option can be added to the <BODY> tag, and a hexadecimal value entered for the color. For example, for a black background use:

```
<BODY BGCOLOR="000000">
```

To make the background a tiled image, use the BACKGROUND option in the <BODY> tag. Here's a line that uses a JPEG image as a background:

```
<BODY BACKGROUND="./images/bg2.jpg">
```

Text Modifications

One of the simplest things to modify is text styles. You can change text and link colors, the default font size, and accentuate words by giving them specific font sizes and styles.

To change the color of your text, add the TEXT, LINK, and VLINK (Visited Link) options to the <BODY> tag, using the hexadecimal color values of your choice:

```
<BODY BGCOLOR="#020202" TEXT="#FFFFFF" LINK="#E4B636"
  VLINK="#9291C1">
```

To change the default font size, use the <BASEFONT> tag at the beginning of your document. To increase the default font size by one point, use the following approach:

```
<BASEFONT SIZE="+1">
```

To change the font size of a specific chunk of text, use the <FONT> tag:

```
<FONT SIZE="+1">W</FONT>elcome!
```

You can also change font size by giving the attribute a specific value (FONT SIZE=5) rather than relatively as shown. For all the latest Netscape extensions, check the following URLs:

```
http://home.netscape.com/assist/net_sites/html_extensions.html
http://home.netscape.com/assist/net_sites/html_extensions_3.html
```

Of course you can also add styles to the text, such as boldface, italics, and emphasis, using the standard HTML tags.

Format Changes with Tables

Modifying the tables in your form, and adding tables to set certain things off, is a great way to customize your form. When the Tool generates its tables, it doesn't include any of the fancy stuff, like text alignment and borders. It's simple, however, to add these elements afterwards.

To add a border, locate your <TABLE> tag and add a BORDER option to it with the thickness you desire. To add a medium thickness border use:

```
<TABLE BORDER="4">
```

In the <TD> tag for your table elements, you can add the ALIGN and VALIGN options for horizontal and vertical alignment of the element therein. For example, to align a piece of text in the exact center of the table's cell, use:

```
<TD ALIGN="CENTER" VALIGN="MIDDLE">
```

Souping It Up: Additions to the Form

Because forms are one of the more dynamic parts of the World Wide Web, it makes sense that they should be just as beautiful and cool as any other Web page. You can add whatever you like to a basic form, just as you would to your favorite home page. These additions can also help you meld a form into your current Web site's look-and-feel.

Help Text

It's important to let people know what a form page is for. Providing a textual description is a good first step. For specific items, especially those that are part of the jargon of your particular site, it's good to have hyperlinks from these items to associated help files.

Boilerplate Items

For your form to blend in with your site's overall ambience, add the boilerplate items that appear on your other Web pages. Examples of these items include:

- Logos
- Navigation bars (imagemaps or individual graphics)
- Contact information (such as mailto: links)
- Last date and time the form was updated
- Links to other pages on your site

First and foremost, the goal is to make this page blend in with all the others.

Exotic Data

What we're calling "exotic" data here isn't so exotic anymore. These include things such as Java and Shockwave applets that can add animation and video to your site. Other items might include audio instructions or a Virtual Reality Modeling Language (VRML) model of an item of interest to your users.

Extending the form should be simple with a little knowledge of HTML. Next, we'll talk about extending your CGI program to perform functions upon the data that's entered into its embedded form.

EXTENDING THE CGI PROGRAM

You'll be wanting to extend your CGI program, of course: A script that just returns input values, while useful for debugging, is extremely boring! Now's the time to make your CGI script actually *do* something. It's also time to add customizations to the embedded form, just as we discussed for the preceding plain-vanilla HTML version.

Adding to and Modifying the Embedded HTML Form

Much like you did with the HTML form, you'll want to add extras to your CGI form to make it fit in with the rest of your site. Boilerplate items, exotic data, textual, and background changes can all be implemented here as well.

All of these should be added to the GET portion of the CGI, which is what's run when the script is called without data being posted to it. You'll recognize it as the section filled with print statements containing HTML code. The first line is:

```
print "<HTML>";
```

Check back to the "Making Your Form Your Own" section for pointers on things you can do. Figure 8-10 displays a Tool-generated form that's been enhanced by its creator. Its source is also listed, so you can get your own ideas from it.

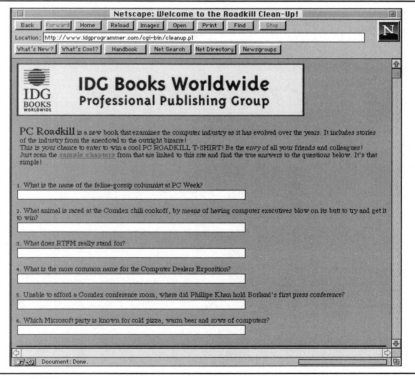

Figure 8-10

A form for the IDG PC Roadkill promotional site, generated with formgen.pl and spruced-up by its creator.

```perl
#!/usr/local/bin/perl
# perl script to both supply and support the cleanup HTML form
# generated by http://www.outer.net//cgi-bin//formgen.pl
# on Fri Dec  8 21:02:33 CST 1995

$| = 1;                   # output NOT buffered
print "Content-Type:\ttext/html\n\n\n",
    "<!DOCTYPE HTML PUBLIC \"-//IETF//DTD HTML 2.0//EN\">\n";


$host = $ENV{SERVER_NAME};
$ENV{SCRIPT_NAME} =~ s/([a-zA-Z0-9\.\-_]+)$//;
$program = $1;
$scriptpath = $ENV{SCRIPT_NAME};


## formlib stuff.

if (($ENV{REQUEST_METHOD} eq "POST") &&
    ($ENV{CONTENT_TYPE}  eq "application/x-www-form-urlencoded")){

# Extract form data - borrowed heavily from
# Brigette Jellinek's formlib.pl.

read(STDIN,$input,$ENV{CONTENT_LENGTH});

  foreach (split("&", $input)) {
     /(.*)=(.*)/;
     $name = $1;
     $value = $2;
     $value =~ s/\+/ /g ;
     $value =~ s/%(..)/pack('c',hex($1))/eg;
     # unescape characters

      if (defined $in{$name}) {
        $in{$name} .= "#" . $value
         } else {
         $in{$name} = $value;
          }
        }


#  print "<PRE>";
#  foreach (keys %in) {
#    print "    $_ = $in{$_}\n";
#    }

#  print "</PRE>";

  print "<CENTER><A
HREF=\"http://www2.outer.net/PCroadkill/PCroadkill.html\">",
     "<IMG WIDTH=306 HEIGHT=148 BORDER=0
SRC=\"http://www2.outer.net/PCroadkill",
     "/graphics/home.gif\"></A></CENTER>";
```

```
} else {

  print "<HTML>";
  print "<HEAD>";
  print "<TITLE>Welcome to the Roadkill Clean-Up!</TITLE>";
  print "";
  print "</HEAD>";
  print "<BODY BGCOLOR=\"#A2AAB8\" LINK=\"#E44B24\">";
  print "<!- Form created by formgen.pl on Fri Dec  8 20:44:10
CST 1995 ->";
  print "<!- For: nina@outer.net ->";
  print "<FORM ACTION=\"http://www2.outer.net/cgi-bin/cleanup.pl\"
              METHOD=\"POST\">";
  print " <P><TABLE>";
  print "<TR>";
  print "<TD><FONT SIZE="5">PC Roadkill</FONT> is a new book that
examines the computer industry as it has ";
  print "evolved over the years. It includes stories about the
industry from the ";
  print "anecdotal to the outright bizarre!<BR>";
  print "This is your chance to enter to win a cool PC ROADKILL
T-SHIRT! Be the envy ";
  print "of all your friends and colleagues!<BR>Just scan the
   <A HREF=\"sample.html\"><STRONG>sample chapters</STRONG></A>
   from that ";
  print "are linked to this site and find the true answers to the
questions below. ";
  print " It's that simple!</TD></TR>";
  print "<TR>";
  print "<TD><P></TD></TR>";
  print "<TR>";
  print "</TABLE><P>";
  print "<FONT SIZE=\"1\">1.</FONT> What is the name of the feline
   gossip columnist at PC Week?<BR>";
  print "<INPUT TYPE=\"text\" NAME=\"q1\" SIZE=\"60\" >";
  print "<P>";
  print "<FONT SIZE=\"1\">2.</FONT> What animal is raced at the
Comdex chili cookoff, by means of having computer executives
blow on its butt to try and get it to win?<BR>";
  print "<INPUT TYPE=\"text\" NAME=\"q2\" SIZE=\"60\" >";
  print "<P>";
  print "<FONT SIZE=\"1\">3.</FONT> What does RTFM really stand
for?<BR>";
  print "<INPUT TYPE=\"text\" NAME=\"q3\" SIZE=\"60\" >";
  print "<P>";
  print "<FONT SIZE=\"1\">4.</FONT> What is the more common name
```

```
            for the Computer Dealers Exposition?<BR>";
            print "<INPUT TYPE=\"text\" NAME=\"q4\" SIZE=\"60\" >";
            print "<P>";
            print "<FONT SIZE=\"1\">5.</FONT> Unable to afford a Comdex
            conference room, where did Phillipe Kahn hold Borland's
            first press conference?<BR>";
            print "<INPUT TYPE=\"text\" NAME=\"q5\" SIZE=\"60\" >";
            print "<P>";
            print "<FONT SIZE=\"1\">6.</FONT> Which Microsoft party is known
            for cold pizza, warm beer and rows of computers?<BR>";
            print "<INPUT TYPE=\"text\" NAME=\"q6\" SIZE=\"60\" >";
            print "<P><P>";
            print "<HR WIDTH=\"100%\" SIZE=\"2\" NOSHADE>";
            print "<FONT SIZE=\"5\">Who you are:</FONT><P>";
            print "  <TABLE>";
            print "<TR><TD ALIGN=\"LEFT\">Name:</TD><TD><INPUT TYPE=\"text\"
                        NAME=\"Name\" SIZE=\"60\" MAXLENGTH =\"60\">
                        </TD></TR>";
            print "<TR><TD ALIGN=\"LEFT\">E-mail:</TD><TD><INPUT
                        TYPE=\"text\" NAME=\"Email\" SIZE=\"60\"
                        MAXLENGTH=\"60\"> </TD></TR>";
            print "<TR><TD>Phone:</TD><TD><INPUT TYPE=\"text\"
                        NAME=\"Phone\" SIZE=\"60\"MAXLENGTH=\"60\">
                        </TD></TR>";
            print "<TR><TD>Address:</TD><TD><INPUT TYPE=\"text\"
                        NAME=\"Address\" SIZE=\"60\" MAXLENGTH=\"60\">
                        </TD></TR>";
            print "<TR><TD>Street/Suite#:</TD><TD><INPUT TYPE=\"text\"
                        NAME=\"Street\" SIZE=\"60\"MAXLENGTH=\"60\">
                        </TD></TR>";
            print "<TR><TD>City/State/Zipcode:</TD><TD><INPUT TYPE=\"text\"
                        NAME=\"City\" SIZE=\"60\" MAXLENGTH=\"60\">
                        </TD></TR>";
            print "<TR><TD>Country:</TD><TD><INPUT TYPE=\"text\"
                        NAME=\"Country\" SIZE=\"60\"MAXLENGTH=\"60\">
                        </TD></TR>";
            print "</TABLE><P>";
            print "<INPUT TYPE=\"submit\" VALUE=\"Clean-up!\" >";
            print "<INPUT TYPE=\"reset\" VALUE=\"Erase-it!\" ><BR><P>";
            print "</FORM>";
            print "<A HREF=\"PCroadkill.html\">| back |</A>";
            print "</BODY>";
            print "</HTML>";
}
```

Customizing Your Form CGI's Action

The CGI forms generated by these tools are as packed with features as a
Swiss Army knife. You'll notice in the Perl code generated by the Tool that
the CGI is self-referential: If data is posted to it, it calls itself. You should
also notice that the extraction code is already part of the script. In other
words, the CGI is application-ready. Just plug in the necessary logic code,
and it's ready to run!

Where to Begin?

The first thing you'll want to do is remove the code that displays the values
entered as preformatted text. Your users don't need to see these values. The
code for *cleanup.pl* that we showed you earlier has already been cleaned up:

```
#  print "<PRE>";
#  foreach (keys %in) {
#    print "    $_ = $in{$_}\n";
#    }

#  print "</PRE>";
```

Now let's go a little further with the CGI. Let's say we want this script to
dump all its data into a tab-delimited file so a database can use it later. To do
this, we can write a quick chunk of code to replace the preceding chunk:

```
open(OUTPUT_FILE, ">>/www/cgi-bin/output/output_file.txt");
foreach (keys %in) {
  print OUTPUT_FILE "$in($_)\t";
}
print OUTPUT_FILE "\n";
close(OUTPUT_FILE);
```

This little plug-in opens a file for data storage called /www/cgi-
bin/output/output_file.txt. It then prints each of the pieces of extracted
form data stored in the $in() variables into the file, followed by a tab.
When it's finished, it prints a newline character to the file, then closes it.
This CGI extension is *extremely* simple. You'll see how to apply more
complex ones in the coming chapters.

Extension by Example

To round things out, we'll go over some other simple customizations to the CGI script's action. This will assist you in creating ready-to-run scripts.

Guestbook

We can take the "write to file" plug-in and expand upon it to create a "Guestbook" for users to sign into. Just generate the form using the Tool, open a file for appending, and send the data the user entered to a file. Instead of tab-delimiting it, you could add a description of the data and format it to be human-readable.

Query/Response Forms

By adding conditional statements, we can generate output based on a user's input. For example, by responding to a series of questions we can decide if they need technical, sales, or marketing support.

Interaction with Another Program

We can use our CGI application to convert the form's data to a type that another (usually third-party) program can use. This is often how databases are accessed from the Web. You'll see an example of this in the Quote Generator that's covered in Chapter 19.

SUMMARY

In this chapter, we've discussed how to install a form and its accompanying CGI generated with the Form Generation Tool. You've learned how to troubleshoot installation and execution problems. Finally, you've explored some of the many possible options for extending these forms to be part of a working application (and to fit into your Web site's overall look-and-feel).

Until now, we've hinted at some of the CGI applications that could be generated using a tool like this. Soon, we'll explore some examples that should lay the groundwork for the kinds of things you can create. But first, we'll investigate the development environment for the Form Generation Tool and explore how you might develop your own applications.

OUR DEVELOPMENT ENVIRONMENT AND SOME USEFUL TOOLS

*T*his chapter briefly documents the development environment that we used to build and test the code for this book. Its purpose is to explain the platforms, operating systems, languages, libraries, and tools we used. We'll also discuss some potential stumbling blocks you may encounter as you try to take our work—and the code we include on the companion CD—and apply it to your own particular circumstances. We conclude with an overview of the most useful CGI-related tools and online information we've been able to find lately, including many that we use ourselves, and others that just looked especially good!

BASIC ASSUMPTIONS

Because we couldn't develop parallel versions of everyone's code that's discussed here (some of which appears on the CD-ROM), we had to make some assumptions about which environment, tools, and programming languages to target for the development efforts and advice you'll find in this book. In the sections that follow, we'll lay out exactly what we assumed, try to explain why we made such outrageous assumptions, and explain how you might use these ideas and capabilities under other circumstances.

For Better or Worse, Our Platform Is UNIX

We'll start this section with our profound and humble apologies to the developers who use a Web server running under OS/2, on some version of Microsoft Windows, or on the Macintosh. In our survey of the current state of the art, we decided that because the overwhelming majority of Web servers in use today run some form of UNIX, that UNIX would be our target development platform.

If you're running UNIX, you'll be pleased to hear that we tested our code on the following versions or implementations:

- 4.3 BSDI
- Linux (Slackware distribution 2.3 and the 1.1.59 kernel)
- AU/X version 3.0.1 (System 5 compatible)
- Sun/OS 4.13 (no Solaris, sorry)

Even if you're not running one of these particular flavors but are using some kind of UNIX on your system, you should be able to take nearly all of the code included with this book—ours and other people's—and use it on your systems without too much effort.

If you've never ported code from one version of UNIX to another, you might want to talk to someone who has. You should also search the USENET newsgroup list for groups that discuss one of the flavors mentioned above, and probably also the flavor you're using. If you don't have a text-only listing of all the newsgroups available from your ISP, you can usually get one just by asking for it. You can then use a text editor with a *search* command to look for UNIX version names (that is, look for *bsd* or *linux* rather than *unix*). Finally, you'll probably want to obtain a manual of system calls for both versions of UNIX involved (the one you're porting from and the one you're porting to) so you can figure out how to translate or kludge the capabilities of the source system on your target of choice.

If you're working on a non-UNIX system, take heart in our inclusion of source code and in the willingness of most authors whose work appears on the Internet to offer the same. Even though most of the authors whose work we included here—including our own—make occasional to heavy use of system functions in their CGI programs, this is merely a hump to get over in most cases, rather than a death knell to the usability of the work that's included here.

Because system calls vary from operating system to operating system, we can't really give you much useful advice on exactly what to do to port our CGI applications to your system. In some cases—most notably, the Macintosh running Mac/OS—it will be necessary to recode everything in AppleScript anyway. In other cases, you should be able to find a Perl variant for your platform that will gladly accommodate the non-system-dependent aspects of the programs for you. The problem remains one of mapping UNIX system calls to those calls supported by your system (or faking your way around them) but this is doable.

In the final analysis, we hope this explains why we've taken so much time in the book to talk about approaches and methods and have used code primarily for illustration. Hopefully, you'll be able to take our ideas and those of the many fine authors whose code we discuss in the book and use them as you see fit in your own programming environment, whatever that may be.

Although *httpd* implementations vary, nearly all of them follow the same approach to accepting input from clients and passing it on to CGI programs. Likewise, nearly all of them handle CGI program output the same way. Working within a standard environment like the Web means there's only so much ugliness and eccentricity that the development community will tolerate, no matter what platform is hosting a server!

Our Language of Choice Is Perl4

Even though Larry Wall and his colleagues have been laboring mightily on Perl5, the object-oriented and entirely worthy successor to Perl4, we've made Perl4 the language of choice for this book.

Here's why. Our Perl4 is actually version 4.036. It's been heavily tested, widely used, and the bulk of the shareware, freeware, and public domain CGIs we located on the Net work for that version. Perl5 is interesting and offers nice new capabilities but it's an object-oriented language that diverges considerably from its Perl4 ancestor.

We do use Perl version 5.001 when we must, and we've observed that moving code from Perl4 to Perl5 is not that hard (as you might expect, since

Perl5 is regarded as a "strict superset" of Perl4). The only major "gotcha" we've found in this process is the need to escape the @ (at sign) character in Perl5 input streams. Otherwise, the interpreter tries to interpret the term to the right of the @ sign as an array reference, with sometimes strange results.

Because there's just not that much code or experience coming out of Perl5 right now, we stuck to the more familiar version. Besides, most of the system administrators we talked to indicated that they would be running both versions in parallel on their systems. Since most of the tools in use today were written for Perl4, we expect parallel use to continue for some time to come.

You'll find that there are lots of other languages used for CGI scripts on the Net—most notably C or some UNIX shell variants—but we chose Perl because of its outstanding string-handling capabilities. And since implementations are currently available for UNIX, Windows NT, DOS, OS/2, and the Mac/OS, your platforms won't be too constrained by our choice of language. We just happen to think it's the most efficient and expedient language for CGI programming available today. You're certainly entitled to think otherwise, and we won't argue with you—we'll simply point out that you shouldn't have too much difficulty translating our Perl code into that language, since it's also pretty easy to learn and understand.

Finally, we chose Perl because of its outstanding debugger, which permits step-by-step execution, halts at predefined breakpoints, and allows variable inspection and interactive value assignment. All of these things make it easier to deal with HTTP's use of *stdin* and *stdout* for handling input and output during program execution.

We've also come to know and love many of the tools and libraries mentioned in this book (most of which are in Perl for some strange reason or another), which have become comfortable and familiar through repeated use. Here again, you can think and use what you want, but we've found the selection of Perl tools and utilities to be consistently superior to others that we've looked at (however cursorily).

Here again, we reemphasize the book's focus on concepts, ideas, and programming approaches, rather than a single-minded concentration on programming details. We think that if you understand the solutions that CGIs are supposed to provide and the common techniques that have been used to implement them, you'll be able to take it from there!

We'll Work with Either CERN or NCSA httpd

Even though there are some significant configuration and structural differences between the two major UNIX implementations of the HTTP daemon, *httpd*, we're equally at home working with both. Both of these systems are well documented and broadly used. You'll find differences between them when it comes to image-handling, mapfiles, configuration details, and directory structures but these are all elements that can be flushed out and dealt with.

Even if you choose a different UNIX or non-UNIX *httpd*, you'll find that it resembles one or the other of these two major variants. Here again, this derives as much from the standard nature of the TCP/IP networking world, where a certain amount of individual variation is tolerated but outright nonconformity is usually ignored. As long as vendors or implementers build other versions, you can rest assured they want them to be used: This, we would argue, guarantees a basic level of conformity that should be comforting.

When systems do diverge from one or the other of these norms, you'll observe that such divergence is heavily documented. Where things are different, the implementers are usually keenly aware of the differences. And because they want you to use their implementation, they're usually happy to let you know how and why, and what needs to be done about it.

This is equally true for the OS/2, Windows NT, Macintosh, and commercial UNIX implementations we've investigated. We've been especially impressed with Chuck Shotton's WebSTAR for the Macintosh (now a Quarterdeck product, which you can visit at *http://www.qdeck.com*). On the Windows NT front, we've seen great results from O'Reilly & Associates' WebSite (*http://www.ora.com*), Process Software's Purveyor (*http://www.process.com*), and Netscape Communications' Netscape Commerce Server (*http://home.netscape.com*).

We Take Good Tools Wherever We Can Get Them!

Most of the programmers involved in this project learned, to their surprise (and sense of synchronicity) that they had begun using *formlib.pl* a library of Perl code for handling HTML <FORM> input, more or less independently, starting about two years ago. Its author, Brigitte Jellinek of the University of Salzburg in Austria, has done a superb job of making forms input easy to accommodate and handle within Perl programs. It remains the common programming denominator across the entire group of authors and writers.

Many other tools or toolsets have come and gone. The best way to decide how usable a library or toolset might be is to force yourself to read its documentation. If that looks interesting, there's no substitute for hands-on experience. That's why using these tools, however briefly, is the only way to honestly evaluate them. Sure, this takes time (sometimes lots of it) and effort, but it's the only way to distinguish a tool that just "looks nice" from one that helps your programming go more smoothly.

We've tried to recommend only those tools that we've used for a while with good results, or those that have been highly rated by other programmers whose opinions we trust. In the final analysis, a live test in your environment is the only way you can decide what to use. If you're willing to spend some time and dig in deeply, you may find your programming skills improving at the same time that your program's capabilities begin to blossom.

As programmers, we can think of no better way to learn than by reading the work of others, both seriously and deeply. Even though you may end up rejecting most of what you examine, you'll have ample opportunities to learn new programming approaches, constructs, algorithms, and techniques.

Putting Theory (and Advice) into Practice

When it comes to building real-life Web services and applications, at some point you have to disengage from the realm of possibility and settle into the real world. This means making platform, operating system, programming language, and other choices that constitute your development environment. Here, we've tried to explain the environment we used to write this book and why we chose it. We've also explained some of the trials and tribulations you might have to go through in order to take a different tack.

At the end of the day, however, the need to provide your users with effective, intelligent Web services is what we hope gives value to this book, no matter how our choices for assembling a development environment differ from yours. Therefore, our primary goal in this book is to help you understand concepts, techniques, and approaches to programming CGI, rather than leading you by the hand through a mass of what could all too easily be irrelevant details.

If we can share a common understanding of the programming process and the kinds of solutions you can provide to your users, you should be able to puzzle out the details for yourself. If not, we'll try to point you to numerous other sources of information and points of view, so that you can illuminate your understanding from many angles and ultimately find the information that will let you proceed to build the solutions you want! In fact, that's what the next section is about.

THE MAJOR CGI LIBRARIES

Actually, the title of this section is something of a misnomer. Since there's no formal rating for CGI libraries, whether major, minor, or otherwise, we're making a brash claim about the collections of code that we're going to cover here. So we'll start by confessing that the section title's just a ploy to pique your interest in some of the better CGI materials we've encountered in our wanderings around the Net.

We'll take you on a tour of a number of interesting CGI collections online—we think you'll agree that they're useful as well. We'll begin the section with some information about how we located these resources in the first place and then proceed to tackle these treasure troves in more or less alphabetical order (by URL, that is). We'll end the chapter with a few well-chosen caveats on reusing other people's work and on deciding whether your own work is worth sharing with others.

Before we explain how we found this stuff, we'd like you to pause a moment and thank your lucky stars—or perhaps the Big Spider herself—that so many individuals and organizations have seen fit to share their hard work and valuable programs with the Internet community. We strongly believe that one of the key factors behind the success of the Internet in general, and the Web in particular, has been the selfless efforts of all the people who've contributed their work to the greater good.

If it weren't for the generosity of others, we wouldn't be able to tell you about the many collections of CGI programs and code you can find on the Web. Not only would that be too bad for us (we'd have nothing to write about), it would also be too bad for you (you'd have to build all the CGI widgets and tools you'd need yourself, instead of being able to stand on the shoulders of the giants who've gone before you)!

Looking for CGI Nirvana

When it comes to locating the real storehouses of knowledge on the Web, there's no substitute for knowing where—and how—to start looking. Fortunately, we have been mired in Web programming long enough to know where and how to look for CGI information. For the benefit of those who may not be similarly mired, we'd like to share some of our favorite techniques with you. If the resources we mention don't include the widget you need, you can prospect for it on your own.

Round Up the Usual Suspects

We're pretty sure that this section heading (cheerfully stolen from the movie, *Casablanca*) appears somewhat out of its original context. In this case, we mean that you should check out the usual jumping-off points for HTML- and CGI-related information searches.

What does this mean? Here's a list of possible answers:

- **Check the "official" information resources.**
  This means looking in the Web pages for the W3C and at NCSA. All of the relevant locations have useful CGI information, including code libraries, specifications, and pointers to other sites. Some of the best relevant URLs are:

  ```
  http://hoohoo.ncsa.uiuc.edu/cgi/
  http://hoohoo.ncsa.uiuc.edu/cgi/interface.html
  http://www.w3.org/hypertext/WWW/Daemon/User/CGI/Overview.html
  ```

- **Use a search engine.**
  We had the best luck with the following search strings: CGI script, CGI program, and CGI library. You, too, can run a search on one or more of these strings at any of the following URLs (if we've omitted your favorite search engine, please forgive us in advance):

  ```
  http://www.yahoo.com/search.html
  http://query1.lycos.cs.cmu.edu/lycos-form.html
  http://nmt.edu/~mfisk/websearch.cgi
  http://www.cs.colorado.edu/home/mcbryan/WWWW.html
  http://home.netscape.com/home/internet-search.html
  ```

- **Consult** "Looking for CGI Resources" in Chapter 2. If we didn't cover it here, we definitely covered it there (take a look, if you haven't already).

Since knowing where to start looking for information is a key ingredient for a successful Web information search, we're glad to help you start off on the right foot. But before you run off to look for yourself, read the rest of this chapter. You may want to hit some of the other resources in here first, instead of finding them on your own!

Ask an Expert!

By all means, if you know somebody who's been hacking CGIs since the WWW was a just a small skein in an out-of-the-way research lab in Switzerland, ask them for input on good CGI resources. They may even share some of their own stuff with you. Other places to ask for pointers should include the relevant newsgroups and mailing lists (see Chapter 2) and Doctor Web (formerly known as the Web Developer's Virtual Library), available at:

```
http:/www.stars.com/Dr.Web/
```

Do Some Reading

There are lots of good resources out there (so we can't tell you how *thrilled* we are that you're reading our book). In addition to the information that these pages contain, you should take a trip to your favorite bookstore and consult titles in any or all of the following areas:

- HTML information, programming, and design
- computer languages, especially Perl, Java, Python, and C
- CGI or Web programming

You'll also find useful information in weekly or monthly computer magazines like *PC Week*, *PC Magazine*, *Internet World*, *IWAY*, *NetGuide*, and others. Please consult Chapter 2 for contact/subscription information on these resources. They all cover the Web regularly and often include useful information on new and interesting CGI libraries, tools, or techniques.

By the time you've waded through all this material, you'll have amassed enough URLs to check to keep you busy for a week. If they're not on the list covered in the sites mentioned in this chapter, you may have undiscovered riches yet to explore!

Some Select CGI Sites

In this section, we'll take you on a tour of some CGI sites on the Web that contain useful pointers, usable code, and/or useful programming information. We'll present these sites by their URLs in alphabetical order, followed by a brief description of their contents, coverage, and value to both budding and experienced CGI programmers.

http://hoohoo.ncsa.uiuc.edu/cgi/interface.html

This is the "front page" for CGI information at the National Center for Supercomputing Applications (NCSA) one of the primary sources for Web server software and technology on the Web today. This site offers a rich collection of information about CGI, including numerous specifications, programming guides, and other documentation. It also includes a large collection of CGI programs, source code, and pointers to other related references.

NCSA maintains a large collection of CGI programs in an FTP archive on its server. The URL for this collection is:

```
ftp://ftp.ncsa.uiuc.edu/Web/httpd/Unix/ncsa_httpd/cgi/
```

Figure 9-1 shows a screenshot from the file listing in this archive, which just scratches the surface of what's available here. You'll find everything from CGIs for forms-handling to online comics retrieval routines—hey, would we kid you about something as important as the comics?

Because of the wealth of information as well as the software that this site contains, we can't recommend it highly enough. Please do check it out.

```
┌─────────────────────────────────────────────────────────────────────────┐
│ ═    Netscape - [Directory of /Web/httpd/Unix/ncsa_httpd/cgi]    │▼│▲│   │
├─────────────────────────────────────────────────────────────────────────┤
│ File  Edit  View  Go  Bookmarks  Options  Directory            Help      │
├─────────────────────────────────────────────────────────────────────────┤
│ Back  Forward  Home │ Reload  Images  Open │ Print │ Find │ Stop │        │
├─────────────────────────────────────────────────────────────────────────┤
│ Location: │ftp://ftp.ncsa.uiuc.edu/Web/httpd/Unix/ncsa_httpd/cgi/ │ ↧ │ N │
├─────────────────────────────────────────────────────────────────────────┤
│  .message          493 bytes  Wed Jun 28 13:15:00 1995                    │
│  AA-1.2.tar.Z         9 Kb     Thu Jul 07 00:00:00 1994 compressed file   │
│  CGI.pm-1.53.tar.Z   44 Kb     Wed Jun 28 13:13:00 1995 compressed file   │
│  README            493 bytes  Wed Jun 28 13:15:00 1995                    │
│  bbc_man2html        21 Kb     Thu Jul 07 00:00:00 1994                    │
│  cgi-lib.pl.Z         2 Kb     Thu Jul 06 15:40:00 1995 compressed file   │
│  cgi-src/                      Tue Jun 27 14:01:00 1995 Directory         │
│  cgi_handlers.pl.Z    2 Kb     Thu Jul 07 00:00:00 1994 compressed file   │
│  form-mail-1.3.tar.Z 16 Kb     Thu Jul 07 00:00:00 1994 compressed file   │
│  htcache.pl.Z         6 Kb     Thu Jul 07 00:00:00 1994 compressed file   │
│  htmlfinger           3 Kb     Thu Jul 07 00:00:00 1994                    │
│  mailin.c.Z           1 Kb     Thu Jul 07 00:00:00 1994 compressed file   │
│  ncsa-default.tar.Z  33 Kb     Thu Jul 07 00:00:00 1994 compressed file   │
│  read-comics.Z        5 Kb     Thu Jul 07 00:00:00 1994 compressed file   │
│  saytime.tar.Z        2 Kb     Thu Jul 07 00:00:00 1994 compressed file   │
│  sh-post.tar.Z        2 Kb     Thu Jul 07 00:00:00 1994 compressed file   │
└─────────────────────────────────────────────────────────────────────────┘
```

Figure 9-1
The FTP Listing for the NCSA CGI archive shows most of the items it contains.

http://www-genome.wi.mit.edu/ftp/pub/software/WWW/cgi_docs.html

This is an outstanding library of forms-handling CGI routines, written in Perl5 by L. Stein of the MIT Human Genome project. This library, known as *CGI.pm*, uses objects to create Web fill-out forms on-the-fly and to parse their contents.

CGI.pm supplied a simple interface for parsing and handling query strings passed to CGI programs. It also offers a set of functions for creating fill-out forms in HTML. Instead of using HTML syntax for forms elements, the document is created by Perl function calls.

In *CGI.pm* all actions occur through a CGI object. When you create an object, it examines the environment for a query string, parses it, and stores the results. You can then ask that object to return or modify query values. CGI objects can handle either POST or GET methods and can correctly distinguish between scripts called from <ISINDEX> documents and form-based documents. *CGI.pm* even allows you to debug your scripts from the command line without worrying about setting up environment variables.

CGI.pm is stored on the server in a UNIX compressed (.Z) format. It can be downloaded via an HTTP file transfer right on the page. Because the compressed version of the library is less than 46 K, it's quick and easy to grab. Figure 9-2 shows the link to the file.

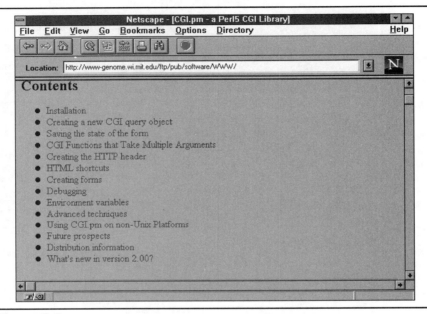

Figure 9-2
The CGI.pm library can be downloaded from a link on this page.

http://www.cosy.sbg.ac.at/www-doku/tools/bjscripts.html

This is a collection of CGI scripts assembled by Brigitte Jellinek, of the University of Salzburg, in Austria. It includes a spiffy guestbook application, some system administration utilities, and some log-file-handling CGIs, in addition to the forms-handling library that won our hearts. Figure 9-3 shows a listing of what Jellinek has to offer.

Figure 9-3
A forms-handling library is just one of the gems in the Jellinek collection.

formlib.pl contains three Perl subroutines that can help you to handle input from HTML forms. For forms that use the POST method, you'll need to use the 'GetPostArgs' routine, and for those that use the GET method, the 'GetFormArgs' should you want to handle both methods at the same time.

All three of these subroutines read and parse the input appropriately, and deliver their arguments in an associative array named "%in". Thus if you had an input field named `color` in your form, and the user entered `red` in that field, you'd find that:

```
$in{'color'} == 'red'.
```

Jellinek also includes a subroutine 'GetPathArgs' to parse arguments passed via the PATH, where she assumes the format will be:

```
/var1=value1/var2=value2...
```

for the path. Here again, results are returned in the associative array, '%in'.

As she notes, this can be quite convenient should you want to access the same program from several forms: some of them general and some of them specialized (perhaps with fixed or hidden values).

http://www.oac.uci.edu/indiv/ehood/perlWWW/

This is a collection of pointers to Perl CGI programs and other tools maintained by Earl Hood, of Convex Computer Corporation in the Dallas, Texas area, another name that pops up frequently in CGI programming circles. This page contains a broad selection of applications, HTML browsers, file conversion programs, widgets, utilities, and other goodies.

Earl's page includes a category called "Development" that features pointers to CGI libraries and archives, including both *cgi-lib.pl* and *CGI.pm* (mentioned elsewhere in this section). It also provides pointers to four other major libraries. Other sections include pointers to a bunch of useful Perl-based tools and widgets; aspiring authors can also contact Mr. Hood to see about getting their own Perl libraries or programs listed.

http://WWW.Stars.com/Vlib/Providers/CGI.html

This collection of CGI resources is part of the Web Developer's Virtual Library project, implemented by Alan Richmond at *stars.com* (also the home of Doctor Web). Here's what *Netsurfer Digest* (April 21, 1995) had to say about this site:

> The WWW Virtual Library section on Web Development has over 1,000 links to sites with information of interest. Whatever you want to know about the World Wide Web can probably be found in one of the sites pointed to by their extensive topical list. This site makes it quick and easy to find sites containing more information.

Their CGI section is no exception to this; it contains pointers to innumerable sources of code, specifications, and other information about CGI. Figure 9-4 only hints at the wealth of information you'll find at this URL.

The Virtual Library listing for CGI includes 27 entries, of which 12 or 13 contain useful CGI code samples, libraries, or programs. It includes almost all of the other resources we cover in this chapter, in addition to the primary sources of documentation and server-specific information.

http://www.w3.org/hypertext/WWW/Daemon/User/CGI/ Overview.html

This URL points to the CERN *httpd* site and includes an in-depth discussion of the CGI interface for that particular server. In addition to providing good background information and implementation details on

CGI, these documents include multiple code samples inline, as well as pointers to numerous example programs.

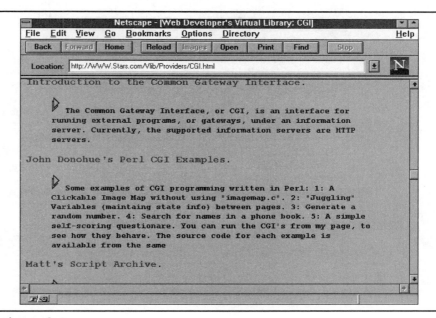

Figure 9-4

The W3 developer's virtual library has an extensive listing of CGI-related topics.

You'll find pointers to a date conversion program (*calendar*) and a Web gateway to the UNIX *finger* command, as well as the nearly ubiquitous *cgi-parse* program (used to parse input variables using the POST method). These pages also include useful installation and server-handling information (specific to the CERN implementation) regarding CGI scripts.

http://atlantis.austin.apple.com/people.pages/carldec/web.dev.pointers.html

This document comprises Carl de Cordova's "Web Development Pointers," which is surely one of the most comprehensive sets of Macintosh-related Web development pointers available anywhere. Figure 9-5 doesn't begin to do justice to the breadth of coverage that this page contains, but it provides pointers to some very interesting AppleScript resources.

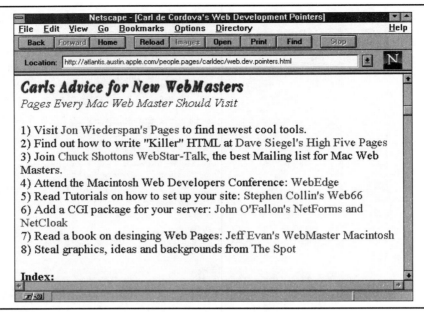

Figure 9-5
Carl de Cordova's Web Developer's page includes pointers to nearly everything development-related for the Macintosh.

In addition to the many AppleScript resources depicted in Figure 9-5, the WebEdge server is host to a large collection of CGIs authored by WebEdge attendees. At this site, you'll find the best collection of Macintosh CGIs available anywhere:

```
http://www.webedge.com
```

http://www.yahoo.com/Computers/World_Wide_Web/

Yahoo stands for "Yet Another Hierarchical Officious Oracle"; it's a database written and maintained by David Filo and Jerry Yang, who style themselves "self-proclaimed Yahoos." This is an inauspicious introduction to one of the real treasures of the World Wide Web. From the *World_Wide_Web* directory at this URL, choose *CGI - Common Gateway Interface*. Figure 9-6 can only hint at the wealth of information and material included in the 42 entries listed here.

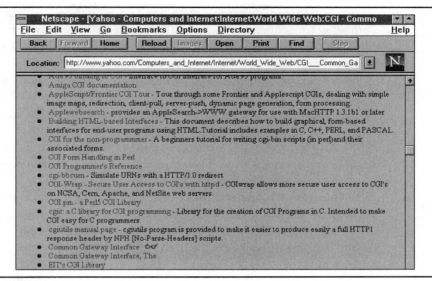

Figure 9-6
The Yahoo listings for "CGI" include a bunch of great code collections.

You'll find that 38 of the 42 entries (at the time of this writing) point to collections of CGI code from platforms ranging from the Amiga to UNIX. And the resources linked herein include only minimal overlap with our own picks, as well as those lists provided by other hotlists and link pages. This collection is worth visiting and revisiting, as you mine the libraries and programs for goodies worth grabbing and reusing!

Using CGI Programs Effectively

We've got to confess that one of the libraries we mentioned in this chapter—namely, Brigitte Jellinek's *formlib.pl* —didn't exactly pop out of any searches. Though we did find her by name on the Web, this library didn't show up on any of our search engines. Instead, her reputation preceded her entry into this book: As we looked through our own CGIs and those of others, her code kept showing up all over the place.

This points to one of the key benefits of joining the Internet community in general, and the fraternity of CGI programmers in particular: Good tools spread like wildfire and become part of what "everybody knows." We don't know who first heard about Brigitte's work, or how we first obtained a copy, but among the authors of this book, "everybody knows" that *formlib.pl* is an invaluable tool. What this should tell you, our gentle reader, is that this Perl program is quite worth checking out. It also suggests that reading lots of CGIs and looking for other common elements may help you to locate other treasures that might not register on the CGI radar any other way.

By exclusion, this also points out another potential gotcha when using CGIs taken off the Net. Not every tool or program is as usable as *formlib.pl*. Sometimes, the work of others takes more time and effort to master and incorporate into your own code than building the equivalent functionality yourself. While you're perusing these libraries, keep reminding yourself of this tradeoff and stay away from things that appear to be hard to understand. If it looks too hard to use, it probably is!

In other words, the best proof of reusability is repeated use in other CGIs. If you stick to the tools that you find used most often by others, you may not live on the bleeding edge of programming technology. But until you become a CGI guru yourself, living on the edge may be a little ambitious anyway.

Besides, there'll come a time, sooner or later, when you have to build or use some brand-spanking new tool, algorithm, or technology because you have no other choice. You can have your fun teetering on the bleeding edge when that happens—in the meantime, stick to those tools and programs that have withstood the use and abuse of your colleagues, and you'll be less likely to wind up bleeding all over your late and broken CGI code!

Publish and/or Perish!

When you've covered all the bases for a particular widget or program and haven't come up with a solution, you may be forced to write a widget or program of your own someday. If that happens to you, it may cause you to think about sharing your work with others and publishing your CGI on the Web.

We think this is a great idea but you have to be certain that what you have to offer is both general and useful enough to be worth publishing. This means that if your widget lets a system administrator assign a new user account name and password, that you take the time to test it on multiple versions of UNIX before you release it to the world. It also means that you'll want to release it privately to a small circle of would-be users and incorporate their feedback before you loose your tool on an unsuspecting world.

Then, when you do publish your CGI program or widget, you can do so with confidence that it works as advertised and that it provides functionality that others can actually use. Anything less, as they say, is simply unacceptable! And when you've published your work, be open to the feedback from users that will come your way and be prepared to refine and improve your work over time. This will keep your widget or program useful, rather than making it obsolete.

SUMMARY

In this chapter, we've discussed our development environment and tools of choice. We also reviewed a number of key Web sites where you'll find CGI programs ready for the taking (if not for the using). We've also tried to point out some useful resources and approaches for finding other sites and code we may not have mentioned.

Hopefully, this combination of tools, goodies, and pointers includes the very CGI widget or program you're looking for. If not, you may have to write the code yourself. If you do, you can think about publishing your own work on the Web when it's written, tested, and ready for prime time.

Don't forget that using "other people's code" is nearly as easy and as much fun as spending "other people's money." Just remember: You don't know where that code has been, so be careful what you use and how you use it. As always, practice "safe computing"!

PUTTING CGI PROGRAMMING TO WORK

*T*he eleven chapters in Part II supply examples, analyses, and basic techniques you'll be able to use when creating your own CGI applications. They also include some pretty nifty Web-based tools and utilities, some of which you'll probably want to install on your own Web server. Each of the chapters begins with a statement of requirements and a resulting design, before exploring its implementation in depth. Once the code is covered, we discuss possible enhancements or improvements to the existing implementation and cover the important details related to installation and use.

Chapter 10 provides a Web-based front-end to DNS administration issues, like domain name requests, and helps to handle tracking of such requests, and the ultimate implementation of the name/address pairs that underlie them. Chapter 11 covers a fax gateway that can deliver faxes to its recipients over the Web. Chapter 12 tackles a Majordomo mailserver front end, with meaningful digressions on LISTSERV and *listproc*, as it provides a tool to help overcome the unbearable stodginess of those systems' interfaces.

Chapter 13 provides a controlled calendaring and scheduling application, while Chapter 14 delivers a Web-based HTML editor (primarily for use with end-user home pages). In Chapter 15, we examine the issues inherent in Web-based commerce and explore the various secure transaction and financial exchange implementations available today.

Chapter 16 provides a set of Web-based tools for managing users on UNIX systems, and Chapter 17 describes a general tool for automating UNIX commands through Web front ends. Chapter 18 takes that idea to heart, as it describes the HTML forms that could handle a range of UNIX system commands. Chapter 19 introduces a Quote Generator designed to provide pricing for a grab-bag of Internet services and connection types, while Chapter 20 concludes the book with a tool that automatically constructs an instruction file, for use with Roy Fielding's wonderful MOMspider Web site profiling tool.

Throughout Part II, our goal is to explore a variety of useful and complex CGI scripts that deliver added functionality to any Web. Along the way, we also seek to demonstrate approaches, techniques, and implementation tricks for building sound, workable Web extensions.

DNS ADMINISTRATION

A ny network administrator who manages an Internet domain can tell you that one of the most difficult services to master is the Domain Name Service (DNS). Although TCP/IP programmers have written DNS applications for other operating systems, the best DNS servers still run on UNIX.

But UNIX (and DNS administration on UNIX systems) is crammed with esoteric configuration files and strict permissions rules with few user-friendly methods for controlling them.

CAUGHT IN A BIND?

When creating DNS records, you'll find yourself updating at least three configuration files, and killing and restarting the *named* DNS daemon. Of course it won't restart if, like most of us, you're prone to the occasional typo in your configuration files. Imagine now that you're an Internet Service Provider administering the primary DNS server for a multitude of customers domains, and you need to update these files several times a week! Wouldn't it be nice to have an easy, reliable method for making modifications?

THE INTERNIC: NOT EXACTLY OLD FAITHFUL

DNS is not the only problem in setting up a domain. If you need to register an Internet domain, then you must process the request through the Internet Network Information Center, commonly known as the InterNIC, or just the NIC. Actually there are many NICs (Network Information Centers) because a NIC is any organization that's responsible for supplying information about any network. For example, there's APNIC (Asia Pacific NIC). Now, however, all the NICs cooperate and the InterNIC is the official information provider of the Internet.

The InterNIC not only registers Internet domains, but is the entity that provides root domain name services for the entire Internet. The InterNIC Registration Services are operated by Network Solutions, Inc. and are partially funded by an NSF grant.

Since October 1995, the InterNIC has also begun to charge for its services. The resources involved in servicing the demand for domain names has far outweighed the NSF operating budget, so the InterNIC is now charging a yearly fee for retention of COM, ORG, and NET second-level domain names (GOV and EDU domains are still covered by the NSF charter).

To register a domain, either fill out an online form on the InterNIC's Web site, or e-mail a domain request to *hostmaster@rs.internic.net*. Then you wait...

Registering a domain with the InterNIC can take anywhere from a couple of days to four weeks. Why the variation? Only the InterNIC really knows, and they're not talking. In fact, chances are you'll never talk to a human being at the NIC. They've got much of it nicely automated and have e-mail forms for nearly every question and request.

The real reason it takes so long to register a domain with the InterNIC comes from the sheer volume of requests they handle. Perhaps charging for domains will reduce the demand and allow them to obtain more resources, but don't count on it! Ultimately, the better your registration request fits their automated system, the less likely it will be that a human has to touch it—and the faster it will be processed.

Another problem for busy DNS admins is administrative: that is, keeping up with the status of the domains you've tried to register. A busy Internet service provider may have dozens of outstanding domain requests at any given time, in various states of acceptance and completion!

If anything, this situation will only be exacerbated by the new procedures just put in place for re-registering domain names, an "inactivity" clause that allows unused names to be reclaimed, and a "surrender" clause that gives the InterNIC the ability to force a name-holder to surrender a name in cases of legal challenge or controversy. Far from simple to begin with, InterNIC Registration Services appear headed for still more complexity!

For more information on InterNIC Registration Services, visit their Web site at:

```
http://rs.internic.net/rs-internic.html
```

SOLUTION: A DNS ADMINISTRATION APPLICATION

Hopefully, we've demonstrated by now that we need a tool both to simplify the actions of both the Byzantine InterNIC registration process and to configure the DNS files for the newly created domain. Using the CGI programming techniques described in earlier chapters, you can create a DNS Administration Application.

DNS Administration Requirements

What would this CGI program need to do? Here are a few basics that would be nice:

- A simple domain request process, so that people who wish to register a domain can do it without knowing the inner workings of the InterNIC or DNS jargon.

- Parse a domain request, package and send it to the InterNIC in their preferred format.

- A domain tracker database for the DNS administrator to manage domains pending registration, those that have failed registration, and those that have succeeded and are currently under the local DNS server's authority.

- Parse mail from the InterNIC to automatically inform the local system's domain tracker database of the request's success or failure.

- If registration is successful, update the DNS zone file and other necessary files.

- Notify the administrative contact of the registration's success or failure.

A program that can handle these activities would bear the brunt of the most difficult and tedious domain registration and management work. Since these functions are pretty generic, the next question is: How can you actually implement these tasks?

Implementation Approaches

There are a variety of methods you could use to implement the functions we've listed. Here are some possible options:

- You could make the entire thing a WWW form-based CGI.

- You could make it all run in the background with no human administrative intervention whatsoever (a scary but plausible thought).

- You could forgo the Web and do it all from a TTY terminal (yuk!).

The DNS administration application we've programmed operates the way it does for a number of logistical, administrative, and human factors reasons. Here's the breakdown of how it works:

- A simple e-mail form gives your customers a way to submit a domain name request to a specified e-mail address on your server.

- Using an HTML form, the DNS administrator examines the form, and if the request seems legitimate, then instructs the program to process its e-mail version: It reformats its contents into the InterNIC's preferred format and forwards that information on to the NIC.

- The database handles subsequent interaction with the NIC, including status tracking, notification of delivery, and updates of the DNS zone files needed to extend your local DNS server.

The rest of this section describes some of these operations in detail.

E-Mail Domain Action Request and Parser

We created a handy e-mail form to request a new domain, request a change in existing domain information, or delete a domain. The user making the request returns the form to your Web server's ID (usually *www*). Once this e-mail has been received, it's parsed to determine if it's a domain action request. If it is, the request is queued for subsequent administrative action.

One benefit of this approach is that most Internet users are already familiar with creating and responding to e-mail. Another is that it acts as a security measure, since the administrator handles the actual processing of the request later on. Finally, it allows anyone to register a domain, whether or not they have access to the World Wide Web.

HTML Forms-Based DNS Tracker Database

The DNS tracker database user interface displays domain requests to be forwarded to the InterNIC, along with requests already outstanding at the InterNIC, domains that failed registration, and domains that completed successfully and are under your DNS' authority. The database is also the coordinating center from which an administrator will send requests to be processed, mark as registered those domains that complete the process successfully, and mark as failed those domains that failed registration. An additional feature has been added, mostly as a convenience—namely, the ability to e-mail domain action requests to users (primarily, to those who request such notification).

HTML forms provide a good user interface to the database. Features such as scrollable lists, value fields, and submission buttons lend themselves nicely to defining the data for the underlying database. Finally, because you can use a WWW browser to administer the database, the database itself can be delivered on the Web, and you can manage it anywhere there's an Internet connection. Of course you'll want to password protect it using an ".htaccess" file (or some more secure alternative), to limit access to authorized users. ▲

The Innards

For the back-end operations of the CGI programs, we chose Perl because it allows us to handle the necessary file updates and UNIX system calls quickly and easily. We could easily have used C instead; for this kind of program, it's mostly a matter of personal preference.

In our implementation, Perl-based CGI scripts do all of the parsing, create all of the HTML forms, modify the DNS zone files and "named.boot" file, and handle mail for the InterNIC and the administrative contact. These scripts drive the entire application, so let's dig into the code!

MAIL-ORDER DOMAINS: PARSE.IN.WWW.MAIL.PL

The script *parse.in.www.mail.pl* was written to handle all incoming mail, both from users requesting domains and from the InterNIC. We'll take each portion of this script step-by-step, starting with the two forms that this program needs: *domreg.form* and *new.dns.form*.

The Domain Registration Form: domreg.form

To begin the domain management process, you first need to create the domain registration request form we mentioned earlier. We've called this form *domreg.form*. It's the form that is mailed to users when they want to make a domain change.

Here's the format we've created that works with our CGIs:

```
DNS or Domain Registration Information Form
Your Org

Last Revision: 10/01/95


To have (Your Org) register a domain and/or provide any DNS
service for that domain, please reply to this mail with the
following information: (Please do not put "same" or "above" for
any field—This is an automated process and needs a
complete record in every field).
Use "N/A" for NIC Handle unless you have one, and please keep
the field tags as they appear below; just add your entries to the
right of the colons.
```

Also, please note that only ONE domain may be requested per form.

```
Domain Name:
Purpose or Description:
Domain Action (New, Modify, Delete):
Organization (Required):
Organization's Street Address:
Organization's City:
Organization's State:
Organization's Zip Code:
Organization's Country:
Administrative Contact (Last, First):
NIC Handle for Contact (if it exists):
Admin Organization:
Admin Street Address:
Admin City:
Admin State:
Admin Zip Code:
Admin Country:
Admin Telephone #:
Admin E-Mail Address:
Billing Contact (Last, First):
NIC Handle for Billing Contact (if it exists):
Billing Organization:
Billing Street Address:
Billing City:
Billing State:
Billing Zip Code:
Billing Country:
Billing Telephone #:
Billing E-Mail Address:
Invoice Type (Email or Postal):#
Please note that we rely upon the speed and accuracy of the
InterNIC, the entity that controls Domain name registration and the
root name servers.

Please contact us regarding inaccuracies or changes.

Thank you,
Your Organization Here
```

As you can see, we supply explicit instructions to the person registering a domain and include a disclaimer that puts the onus for registration time on the InterNIC. Insert your company's name any place where you see Your Org or Your Organization Here. Further instructions are in the code comments for *parse.in.www.mail.pl* discussed later in this chapter.

The New DNS Form Template: new.dns.form

The new DNS form template is essentially the InterNIC domain registration form stripped down to its barest essentials. It will be used as a template to convert a user's domain registration form into the InterNIC's preferred format. Here's a sample of OuterNet's *new.dns.form*:

```
Domain Version Number: 2.0

0.    (N)ew (M)odify (D)elete....:     {ACTION}

1.    Purpose/Description........:     {PURPOSE}

2.    Complete Domain Name.......:     {COMPLETE}

Organization Using Domain Name
3a.   Organization Name..........:     {ORG}
3b.   Street Address.............:     {ADDRESS}
3c.   City.......................:     {CITY}
3d.   State......................:     {STATE}
3e.   Postal Code................:     {ZIP}
3f.   Country....................:     {COUNTRY}

Administrative Contact
4a.   NIC Handle (if known)......:     {ADMIN_HANDLE}
4b.   Name (Last, First).........:     {ADMIN_NAME}
4c.   Organization Name..........:     {ADMIN_ORG}
4d.   Street Address.............:     {ADMIN_ADDRESS}
4e.   City.......................:     {ADMIN_CITY}
4f.   State......................:     {ADMIN_STATE}
4g.   Postal Code................:     {ADMIN_ZIP}
4h.   Country....................:     {ADMIN_COUNTRY}
4i.   Phone Number...............:     {ADMIN_PHONE}
4j.   E-Mailbox..................:     {ADMIN_EMAIL}

Technical Contact
5a.   NIC Handle (if known)......:     MWE2
5b.   Name (Last, First).........:     Erwin, Mike
5c.   Organization Name..........:     OuterNet Connection
Strategies, Inc.
5d.   Street Address.............:     P.O. Box 26633
5e.   City.......................:     Austin
5f.   State......................:     TX
5g.   Postal Code................:     78755-0633
5h.   Country....................:     United States
5i.   Phone Number...............:     512-345-3573
```

```
5j.   E-Mailbox..................:      mikee@outer.net

Billing Contact
6a.   NIC Handle (if known)......:      {BILLING_HANDLE}
6b.   Name (Last, First).........:      {BILLING_NAME}
6c.   Organization Name..........:      {BILLING_ORG}
6d.   Street Address.............:      {BILLING_ADDRESS}
6e.   City.......................:      {BILLING_CITY}
6f.   State......................:      {BILLING_STATE}
6g.   Postal Code................:      {BILLING_ZIP}
6h.   Country....................:      {BILLING_COUNTRY}
6i.   Phone Number...............:      {BILLING_PHONE}
6j.   E-Mailbox..................:      {BILLING_EMAIL}

Primary Name Server
7a.   Primary Server Hostname....:      ns.outer.net
7b.   Primary Server Netaddress..:      204.96.12.2

Secondary Name Server(s)
8a.   Secondary Server Hostname..:      helix.net
8b.   Secondary Server Netaddress:      204.244.2.2

Invoice Delivery
9.    (E)mail (P)ostal...........:      {INVOICE_TYPE}
```

The `Domain Version Number` is required but is important only to the InterNIC: It lets them know what version of their form you are using and aids processing.

All of the fields in curly braces are required for our program and should not be modified in your organization's form. The form should be filled out completely in any case because the NIC expects to use all of the information it contains (e.g., technical contact, primary and secondary DNS addresses, etc.). These are the tags that *parse.in.www.mail.pl* will use later to create a new domain registration form for the specified domain.

The only things that should be modified in this form are the `Technical Contact` and `Primary` and `Secondary Name Server(s)` fields, which should be changed from OuterNet's information to match your own technical contact information, and your primary and secondary name servers.

Common Variables for parse.in.www.mail.pl

We use a set of standard variables throughout the program, so we'll define them first:

```
# make boolean null
$mail_from_nic  = 0;

#  zero-out counter
$header_ct      = 0;

#  Sets up a date variable for use later.
$date           = `date '+%m/%d/%y'`;

#! The user ID that identifies your Web server
$WEB_UID        = "www";

#! Change this to where you want to root your DNS data tree
$DNSROOT        = "/www/cgi-bin/dns/";
$PENDINGDIR     = $DNSROOT."pending/";
$NEWDIR         = $DNSROOT."new/";

#! The NIC template used for submissions. You can name this
#! anything you want, but for consistency, we'd suggest you
#! don't change this.
$DNSTEMPLATE    = $DNSROOT."new.dns.form";
```

Most of these variables are self-explanatory. The ones preceded by comments that begin with #! are the ones that you'll need to change to reflect your system's particular configuration.

Parsing the Mail: Headers and Contents

The *parse.in.www.mail.pl* script is opened from a standard input pipe when mail is received at a specified address (this setup will be explained later in an installation section). The main loop of *parse.in.www.mail.pl* parses the SMTP mail headers until there are none left. While it's thus engaged, it stores each line in a table called $headers. Here's the beginning of that main loop:

```
while (<STDIN>) {
   $headers[$header_ct++] = $_;
```

E-mail headers typically appear in a format like this:

```
From mts@internic.net  Fri Jul  7 00:20:28 1995
Received: from rs.internic.net (rs.internic.net [198.41.0.5]) by
loop (8.6.12/8.6.12) with ESMTP id AAA03624 for <www@outer.net>;
Fri, 7 Jul 1995 00:20:27 -0500
Received: (mts@localhost) by rs.internic.net (8.6.11/InterNIC-RS)
   id BAA24383;
Fri, 7 Jul 1995 01:16:34 -0400
Date: Fri, 7 Jul 1995 01:16:34 -0400
Message-Id: <199507070516.BAA24383@rs.internic.net>
To: WWW Master (OuterNet) <www@outer.net>
From: domreg@internic.net
Subject: Re: [NIC-950707.34] NEW domain for xyz.com
Reply-To: domreg@internic.net
X-MTS-LoopDetect: InterNIC_Registration_Services
In-Reply-To: Your message of Fri, 7 Jul 1995 00:12:32 -0500
   <199507070512.AAA03086@outer.net>
```

From these headers the script decides whether the message is a response from the InterNIC regarding domain registration or a new request that needs to be processed.

The first phase of this decision examines the From: section of the message to see if it's from the InterNIC. If so, the Boolean $mail_from_nic is set to true:

```
if ((/From: domreg@internic.net/)  ||
  (/From: Domain Registration Role Account/) ||
    ((/From:/) && (/\<domreg@internic.net\>/))) {
    $mail_from_nic = 1;
}
```

The next conditional checks to see if the message is a form submitted by a user, rather than the InterNIC. It looks for portions of the Administrative Contact section of the domain registration form, which aren't returned in the NIC's reply. If it finds them, it sets the $mail_form Boolean to true:

```
if ((/NIC Handle for Contact/) || (/Administrative Contact/)) {
  $mail_form = 1;
  if ($mail_from_nic) {
    $mail_form = 0;
  }
}
```

Now that we know if the mail is from the NIC or the user, we need to decide what it concerns. The next part of the Perl script checks the Subject: line for a RE: tag and one of the standard subject lines from a NIC domain addition, modification, or deletion. If one of these subject lines is identified, it's a reply from the NIC and the $nic_reply Boolean is set to true:

```
if ((/Subject: Re: \[NIC\-/) && (/New domain for/)
   && (/URGENT/)) {
   /Subject\: Re\: \[NIC\-(\d+)\.(\d+)\] URGENT\:  New domain for
(.*)/ && ($domain = $3);
   $nic_reply = 1;
}
elsif ((/Subject: Re: \[NIC\-/) && (/New domain for/)) {
   /Subject\: Re\: \[NIC\-(\d+)\.(\d+)\] New domain for (.*)/ &&
($domain = $3);
   $nic_reply = 1;
}
elsif ((/Subject: Re: \[NIC\-/) && (/Modify domain for/) &&
(/URGENT/)) {
   /Subject\: Re\: \[NIC\-(\d+)\.(\d+)\] URGENT\:  Modify domain
for (.*)/ && ($domain = $3);
   $nic_reply = 1;
}
elsif ((/Subject: Re: \[NIC\-/) && (/Modify domain for/)) {
   /Subject\: Re\: \[NIC\-(\d+)\.(\d+)\] Modify domain for (.*)/
&& ($domain = $3);
   $nic_reply = 1;
}
elsif ((/Subject: Re: \[NIC\-/) && (/Delete domain for/) &&
(/URGENT/)) {
   /Subject\: Re\: \[NIC\-(\d+)\.(\d+)\] URGENT\:  Delete domain
for (.*)/ && ($domain = $3);
   $nic_reply = 1;
}
elsif ((/Subject: Re: \[NIC\-/) && (/Delete domain for/)) {
   /Subject\: Re\: \[NIC\-(\d+)\.(\d+)\] Delete domain for (.*)/
&& ($domain = $3);
   $nic_reply = 1;
}
elsif (/Subject: Re: \[NIC\-/) {
   /Subject\: Re\: \[NIC\-(\d+)\.(\d+)\] (.*)/ && ($domain = $3);
   $nic_reply = 1;
   }
```

The final portion of the main loop attempts to match fields in the returned-and-filled-out *domreg.form* to those specified in the code, and then extracts the information after the colon in each entry. The fields listed below and the fields in *domreg.form* must match exactly for this extraction to occur, so any change to one of these files must be duplicated in the others:

```
/>*(\s*)Domain Name\:(\s*)(.*)/ && ($domain_name = $3);
/>*(\s*)Purpose or Description\:(\s*)(.*)/ && ($purpose = $3);
/>*(\s*)Domain Action \(New, Modify, Delete\)\:(\s*)(.*)/ &&
($domain_status = $3);
/>*(\s*)Organization \(Required\)\:(\s*)(.*)/ && ($org = $3);
/>*(\s*)Organization\'s Street Address\:(\s*)(.*)/
    && ($org_addr = $3);
/>*(\s*)Organization\'s City\:(\s*)(.*)/ && ($org_city = $3);
/>*(\s*)Organization\'s State\:(\s*)(.*)/ && ($org_state = $3);
/>*(\s*)Organization\'s Zip Code\:(\s*)(.*)/ && ($org_zip = $3);
/>*(\s*)Organization\'s Country\:(\s*)(.*)/
    && ($org_country = $3);
/>*(\s*)Administrative Contact \(Last\, First\)\:(\s*)(.*)/ &&
($admin_name = $3);
/>*(\s*)NIC Handle for Contact \(if it exists\)\:(\s*)(.*)/ &&
($nic_handle = $3);
/>*(\s*)Admin Street Address\:(\s*)(.*)/ && ($admin_addr = $3);
/>*(\s*)Admin Organization\:(\s*)(.*)/ && ($admin_org = $3);
/>*(\s*)Admin City\:(\s*)(.*)/ && ($admin_city = $3);
/>*(\s*)Admin State\:(\s*)(.*)/ && ($admin_state = $3);
/>*(\s*)Admin Zip Code\:(\s*)(.*)/ && ($admin_zip = $3);
/>*(\s*)Admin Country\:(\s*)(.*)/ && ($admin_country = $3);
/>*(\s*)Admin Telephone \#\:(\s*)(.*)/ && ($admin_phone = $3);
/>*(\s*)Admin E-Mail Address\:(\s*)(.*)/ && ($admin_email = $3);
/>*(\s*)Billing Contact \(Last\, First\)\:(\s*)(.*)/ &&
($billing_name = $3);
/>*(\s*)NIC Handle for Billing Contact \(if it exists\)\:(\s*)(.*)
    / && ($nic_handle_billi.y = $3);
/>*(\s*)Billing Organization\:(\s*)(.*)/ && ($billing_org = $3);
/>*(\s*)Billing Street Address\:(\s*)(.*)/
    && ($billing_addr = $3);
/>*(\s*)Billing City\:(\s*)(.*)/ && ($billing_city = $3);
/>*(\s*)Billing State\:(\s*)(.*)/ && ($billing_state = $3);
/>*(\s*)Billing Zip Code\:(\s*)(.*)/ && ($billing_zip = $3);
/>*(\s*)Billing Country\:(\s*)(.*)/ && ($billing_country = $3);
/>*(\s*)Billing Telephone \#\:(\s*)(.*)/ && ($billing_phone = $3);
/>*(\s*)Billing E-Mail Address\:(\s*)(.*)/
    && ($billing_email = $3);
/>*(\s*)Invoice Type \(Email or Postal\)\:(\s*)(.*)/
    && ($inv_type = $3);
}
```

Making Everything Consistent

Because we'll be working with the domain name in several places throughout the script, we need to translate any uppercase characters in the $domain and $domain_name variables to lowercase. This not only gives us consistency, but will be important in case-sensitive situations, such as when we use the domain name as a UNIX filename. We'll also chop off the top-level domain (MIL, GOV, COM, etc.) for use in later versions of this script:

```
$domain        =~ tr/A-Z/a-z/;
$domain_name   =~ tr/A-Z/a-z/;
@domain_split  =  split('\.',$domain_name);
$top           =  $domain_split[1];
$top           =~ tr/a-z/A-Z/;
```

Processing the NIC's Reply

If we've recognized the message as a reply from the NIC, we must then check for the existence of a file with that domain name in the pending directory. This file should have been created when the request was originally sent. If it exists, we'll append the reply to that file:

```
if ($nic_reply) {
   $FILENAME = $PENDINGDIR.$domain;
   if ( -e $FILENAME ) {
      open(LOGFILE,">> $FILENAME");
      print LOGFILE "\n\n";
      for ($ct=0; $ct<$header_ct; $ct++) {
          print LOGFILE $headers[$ct];
      }
   close (LOGFILE);
   }
}
```

Processing a New Request

Here's the final meat of the code. If there's a registration form to be processed, the script makes sure there isn't already a domain request pending under that name. If there isn't, it creates a new file for the domain under the new domain directory. If there is a pending request under that name, the administrator is flagged to investigate further.

For the file contents, the script feeds the data from *new.dns.form*, substituting the data from the *domreg.form* reply in place of the tags within the curly braces. At the end, it changes the owner of the new domain file to the user specified in $WEB_UID and gives the owner and group read and write permission, while world gets read-only:

```
if ($mail_form) {
   $FILENAME = $NEWDIR.$domain_name;
   unless ( -e $FILENAME ) {
   open (LOGFILE,"> $FILENAME");
   open (TEMPLATE, $DNSTEMPLATE);
   print LOGFILE "\n\n";
   while (<TEMPLATE>) {
         if (/\{ACTION\}/) {
            s/\{ACTION\}/$domain_status/;
         }
         if (/\{COMPLETE\}/) {
            s/\{COMPLETE\}/$domain_name/;
         }
         if (/\{ORG\}/) {
            s/\{ORG\}/$org/;
         }
         if (/\{ADDRESS\}/) {
            s/\{ADDRESS\}/$org_addr/;
         }
         if (/\{CITY\}/) {
            s/\{CITY\}/$org_city/;
         }
         if (/\{STATE\}/) {
            s/\{STATE\}/$org_state/;
         }
         if (/\{ZIP\}/) {
            s/\{ZIP\}/$org_zip/;
         }
         if (/\{COUNTRY\}/) {
            s/\{COUNTRY\}/$org_country/;
         }
         if (/\{ADMIN_HANDLE\}/) {
            s/\{ADMIN_HANDLE\}/$nic_handle/;
         }
         if (/\{ADMIN_NAME\}/) {
            s/\{ADMIN_NAME\}/$admin_name/;
         }
         if (/\{ADMIN_ORG\}/) {
```

```
            s/\{ADMIN_ORG\}/$admin_org/;
        }
        if (/\{ADMIN_ADDRESS\}/) {
            s/\{ADMIN_ADDRESS\}/$admin_addr/;
        }
        if (/\{ADMIN_CITY\}/) {
            s/\{ADMIN_CITY\}/$admin_city/;
        }
        if (/\{ADMIN_STATE\}/) {
            s/\{ADMIN_STATE\}/$admin_state/;
        }
        if (/\{ADMIN_ZIP\}/) {
            s/\{ADMIN_ZIP\}/$admin_zip/;
        }
        if (/\{ADMIN_COUNTRY\}/) {
            s/\{ADMIN_COUNTRY\}/$admin_country/;
        }
        if (/\{ADMIN_PHONE\}/) {
            s/\{ADMIN_PHONE\}/$admin_phone/;
        }
        if (/\{ADMIN_EMAIL\}/) {
            s/\{ADMIN_EMAIL\}/$admin_email/;
        }
        if (/\{BILLING_HANDLE\}/) {
            s/\{BILLING_HANDLE\}/$nic_handle_billing/;
        }
        if (/\{BILLING_NAME\}/) {
            s/\{BILLING_NAME\}/$billing_name/;
        }
        if (/\{BILLING_ORG\}/) {
            s/\{BILLING_ORG\}/$billing_org/;
        }
        if (/\{BILLING_ADDRESS\}/) {
            s/\{BILLING_ADDRESS\}/$billing_addr/;
        }
        if (/\{BILLING_CITY\}/) {
            s/\{BILLING_CITY\}/$billing_city/;
        }
        if (/\{BILLING_STATE\}/) {
            s/\{BILLING_STATE\}/$billing_state/;
        }
        if (/\{BILLING_ZIP\}/) {
            s/\{BILLING_ZIP\}/$billing_zip/;
        }
        if (/\{BILLING_COUNTRY\}/) {
            s/\{BILLING_COUNTRY\}/$billing_country/;
        }
        if (/\{BILLING_PHONE\}/) {
```

```
            s/\{BILLING_PHONE\}/$billing_phone/;
        }
        if (/\{BILLING_EMAIL\}/) {
            s/\{BILLING_EMAIL\}/$billing_email/;
        }
        if (/\{PURPOSE\}/) {
            s/\{PURPOSE\}/$purpose/;
        }
        if (/\{INVOICE_TYPE\}/) {
            s/\{INVOICE_TYPE\}/$inv_type/;
        }
        print LOGFILE;
    }

    close (LOGFILE);
    system("chown $WEB_UID $FILENAME");
    system("chmod 664 $FILENAME");
  }
}
```

Notice that this script doesn't immediately package the domain request and send it to the InterNIC. Indeed it could, but it's much safer to permit the opportunity for human intervention! That's why the request is saved to a file, to be processed later by an administrator. The next script we'll discuss supports this processing.

THE USER INTERFACE: DNS_LINES.PL

The CGI *dns_lines.pl* is a Perl script that presents the DNS information to the administrator via a Web interface. Its purpose is to pull up lists of new, pending, completed, and failed domain requests, and to let the administrator choose how to manipulate them. It also gives the administrator the option of e-mailing a domain registration form to a user.

Like a TV news anchor, it doesn't actually do much DNS work itself, but it does present or pass on the work from the other CGI programs (*parse.in.www.mail.pl, dns_edit.pl,* and *dns_action.pl*). Likewise, when you request something via the Web interface, it doesn't perform that action itself, but sends a request to perform that action to *dns_edit.pl.*

Before we belittle this script, we hasten to add that the user interface portion of the DNS Administration Application is very important because it's what most people deal with. It also makes a large amount of data manageable.

The Necessities

This script requires *formlib.pl,* a shareware library that includes many form-parsing functions. If you don't already have a copy of this excellent library, you can find it at:

> http://www.cosy.sbg.ac.at/www-doku/tools/bjscripts.html

(Note: *formlib.pl* is also included at the beginning of the script.) We also define our date constants here.

Next to be defined are the DNS root directory (in our case */www/cgi-bin/dns*) and the new, pending, done, and failed directories beneath it. All of these directories should be changed to match your configuration, as indicated by the #! in the comment headers. Be sure to take heed of the caveats in the comments about directory ownership.

At the end of this portion, we send all standard error output to a trash area called */dev/null,* instead of a file or TTY device. When you're debugging, though, you may want to write this output to a file because it can provide useful troubleshooting information.

```
$| = 1; # output NOT buffered  (Defaults to stdout)

# get some formatted dates for use later
$datestr    = `date '+%m/%d/%y %H:%M:%S'`;
$logdate    = `date '+%h %d %T 19%y'`;
chop ($logdate);

#####################################################
#! Directory definitions: please change these to match the
#! locations where you wish to store your data files. Make
#! sure that your Web server's UID has access to these
#! directories. For instance, our server runs as user "www" and
#! not as "root"; thus, the following four dirs on our machine
#! are all owned by user "www".
#
#####################################################

$DNSROOT     = "/www/cgi-bin/dns/";  #! Your DNS data root dir
$NEWDIR      = $DNSROOT."new";       #! Incoming request dir
$PENDINGDIR  = $DNSROOT."pending";   #! Issued/pending request dir
$DONEDIR     = $DNSROOT."done";      #! Registered domains dir
$FAILEDDIR   = $DNSROOT."failed";    #! Failed request dir
#####################################################
#
```

```
# You should need to make no alterations beyond here
# (except for debugging).
#
#####################################################
# Redirect stderr to the trash. For debugging, redirect this to a
# file for later perusal (or remove the comment on the open state-
# ment below, and comment out the /dev/null statement beneath it).
#
# open (STDERR,"> /tmp/dns.stderr");
#####################################################

open (STDERR,"> /dev/null");
```

Bring on the Form

The rest of this CGI deals exclusively with presenting its data as an HTML form. To do this, we send a message to the Web browser that it's about to receive some HTML, as opposed to another MIME data type:

```
#####################################################
# PRINT APPROPRIATE WWW HEADER INFORMATION
#
print "Content-Type: text/html\n\n\n";
#
#####################################################
```

Display the Domains

To display the domains, you'll use five subroutines that all perform basically the same functions:

- List the contents of a directory; entries represent domain names created by one of the other scripts.

- Extract the name of each file and its last modification date from the list.

- Print this information to STDOUT, using the HTML <OPTION> format so it appears as a scrollable pick list.

The reason there are five subroutines is so we can create five different lists. Four of these lists are sorted by update time (most recent first) and the other list is sorted alphabetically:

1. New domain requests
2. Domains pending registration
3. Completed domains
4. Failed domain registrations
5. Completed domains sorted alphabetically

All these subroutines use the standard *ls* UNIX command to list the directory. The *get_done_alpha* subroutine uses *ls -l* to list the files alphabetically, while the others use *ls -lt* to list them by date, most recent entry first. ▲

```
######################################################
# GETS THE NUMBER AND DATES OF THE INCOMING REQUESTS
#
# The following 5 functions are all exactly the same, except for
# minor changes to their data sources. We could have built one big
# routine and passed the directory name as an argument, thereby
# saving about 30 lines of code, but cut-copy-and-paste made the
# current code a good example of "cookie-cutter prototyping."
######################################################
sub get_new {
# Loops through "ls's" output
    open (NEWDIR,"ls -lt $NEWDIR |");
    while (<NEWDIR>) {
      $line = $_;
      @lineparts = split;      # split assumes white space
      if ( $lineparts[8] ) {  # Output only if (column 8) exists
        $domain = $lineparts[8];
        $date_reg = $lineparts[5]." ".$lineparts[6]."
".$lineparts[7];
        $outputline = "$date_reg : $domain\n";
        print STDOUT "<OPTION>  $outputline";
      }
    }
# $outputline is a global
  close(NEWDIR);
}

######################################################
# GETS THE NUMBER AND DATES FOR PENDING REQUESTS
```

```perl
#
# For the details, refer to the "get_new" function above.
#
#######################################################
sub get_pending {
  open (PENDINGDIR,"ls -lt $PENDINGDIR |");
  while (<PENDINGDIR>) {
    $line = $_;
    @lineparts = split;
    $elements = $#lineparts;
    if ( $lineparts[8] ) {
      $domain = $lineparts[8];
      $date_reg = $lineparts[5]." ".$lineparts[6]." ".
$lineparts[7];
      $outputline = "$date_reg : $domain\n";
      print STDOUT "<OPTION>  $outputline";
    }
  }
  close(PENDINGDIR);
}
#######################################################
# GETS THE NUMBER AND DATES OF THE COMPLETED REQUESTS
# (sorted by date)
#
# For the details, refer to the "get_new" function above.
#
#######################################################
sub get_done {
  open (DONEDIR,"ls -lt $DONEDIR |");
  while (<DONEDIR>) {
    $line = $_;
    @lineparts = split;
    $elements = $#lineparts;
    if ( $lineparts[8] ) {
      $domain = $lineparts[8];
      $date_reg = $lineparts[5]." ".$lineparts[6]." "
.$lineparts[7];
      $outputline = "$date_reg : $domain\n";
      print STDOUT "<OPTION>  $outputline";
    }
  }
  close(DONEDIR);
}
#######################################################
# GETS THE NUMBER AND DATES OF THE COMPLETED REQUESTS
# (sorted alphabetically)
#
# For the details, refer to the "get_new" function above.
```

```perl
#
#####################################################
sub get_done_alpha {
  open (DONEDIR,"ls -l $DONEDIR |");
  while (<DONEDIR>) {
    $line = $_;
    @lineparts = split;
    $elements = $#lineparts;
    if ( $lineparts[8] ) {
      $domain = $lineparts[8];
      $date_reg = $lineparts[5]." ".$lineparts[6]." "
.$lineparts[7];
      $outputline = "$date_reg : $domain\n";
      print STDOUT "<OPTION>  $outputline";
    }
  }
  close(DONEDIR);
}


#####################################################
# GETS THE NUMBER AND DATES OF THE FAILED REQUESTS
#
# For the details, refer to the "get_new" function above.
#
#####################################################
sub get_failed {
  open (FAILEDDIR,"ls -lt $FAILEDDIR |");
  while (<FAILEDDIR>) {
    $line = $_;
    @lineparts = split;
    $elements = $#lineparts;
    if ( $lineparts[8] ) {
      $domain = $lineparts[8];
      $date_reg = $lineparts[5]." ".$lineparts[6]." "
.$lineparts[7];
      $outputline = "$date_reg : $domain\n";
      print STDOUT "<OPTION>  $outputline";
    }
  }
  close(FAILEDDIR);
}
```

Bringing It All Home

This script's main body prints all of the form's formatting information and calls the domain display subroutines we've just described. It populates the form with data, using convenient scrollable lists. It includes an entry field to enter the user's e-mail address for the domain registration form. Finally, the form includes submission buttons with the options we've created for this program. These options allow you to perform an action on a selected domain or to send the registration form to the address in the e-mail field. OuterNet's form is shown as an example in Figure 10-1.

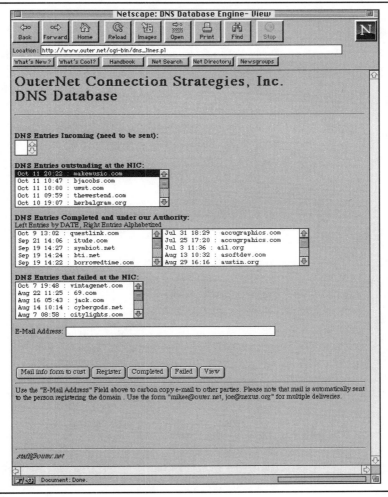

Figure 10-1
OuterNet's DNS admin form.

The source code for the main portion of the form is listed below. Follow along and compare it to what you see in Figure 10-1. Also, jump back to the domain listing subroutines to see how they fill in the gaps.

```
####################################################
# MAIN
#
# Most of what the main function here does is return output to a
$ waiting Web server. It calls "get_new" and "get_pending" along
# with the other subroutines as needed. Note: There are probably
# 10 easier ways to handle input and output than by escaping the
# " (doublequote) character all over the place. We leave this as
# an exercise for our more alert readers!
#
#! Be sure to check the line that calls the "/cgi-bin/dns_edit.pl"
#! script below. If you have changed this CGI's name, modify
#! the line to match your changes.
#
####################################################
{
  print STDOUT "<TITLE>DNS Database Engine- View</TITLE>";
  print STDOUT "<h1>DNS Database</h1>";
  print STDOUT "<HR>";
  print STDOUT "<FORM METHOD=POST ACTION=\"
    /cgi-bin/dns_edit.pl\">";
  print STDOUT
    "<strong>DNS Entries Incoming (need to be sent):
</strong><BR>";
  print STDOUT "<SELECT MULTIPLE SIZE=2 NAME=\"new\">\n";

  do get_new();

  print STDOUT "</SELECT><P>";
  print STDOUT
    "<strong>DNS Entries outstanding at the NIC:</strong><BR>";
  print STDOUT "<SELECT MULTIPLE SIZE=5 NAME=\"pending\">\n";

  do get_pending();

  print STDOUT "</SELECT>";
  print STDOUT
    "<P><strong>DNS Entries Completed and under our Authority:
</strong><BR>";
  print STDOUT
    "Left Entries by DATE, Right Entries Alphabetized<BR>";
  print STDOUT "<SELECT MULTIPLE SIZE=5 NAME=\"done\">\n";
```

```
    do get_done();

    print STDOUT "</SELECT><SELECT MULTIPLE SIZE=5 NAME=\
      "done\">\n";

    do get_done_alpha();

    print STDOUT
      "</SELECT><P><strong>DNS Entries that failed at the
NIC:</strong><BR>";
      print STDOUT "<SELECT MULTIPLE SIZE=5 NAME=\"failed\">\n";

    do get_failed();

    print STDOUT "</SELECT><P>";
    print STDOUT
      "E-Mail Address:<input size=55 type=\"text\" INPUT
NAME=\"email\" VALUE=\"\"><BR>";

    print STDOUT
      "<INPUT TYPE=\"submit\" NAME=\"infomail\" VALUE=\"Mail info
  form to cust\">";
    print STDOUT
      "<INPUT TYPE=\"submit\" NAME=\"Register\" VALUE=\"Register\
      ">";
    print STDOUT
      "<INPUT TYPE=\"submit\" NAME=\"Completed\"
VALUE=\"Completed\">";
    print STDOUT
      "<INPUT TYPE=\"submit\" NAME=\"Failed\" VALUE=\"Failed\">";
    print STDOUT
      "<INPUT TYPE=\"submit\" NAME=\"View\" VALUE=\"View\">";
    print STDOUT "<HR>";
    print STDOUT
      "Use the \"E-Mail Address\" Field above to carbon copy e-mail
to other parties.\ Please note that mail is automatically sent to
the person registering the domain. Use the form \"mikee@outer.net,
joe@nexus.org\" for multiple deliveries.<P><HR>\
<ADDRESS>staff@outer.net</ADDRESS>\n";
    }
```

You'll notice that whenever an action is performed on this form, it passes its submitted information to *dns_edit.pl*. This Perl script is the next program we'll scrutinize.

MY OWN PRIVATE INTERNIC: DNS_EDIT.PL

The *dns_edit.pl* script is the workhorse in this DNS administration suite. It's charged with actually performing most of the functions provided in the form displayed by *dns_lines.pl*. This code is heavily annotated, so we'll break it up into major sections and fill in any gaps in the commentary.

The Standard Fare

You've seen most of the Perl libraries and standard constants listed below in previous pieces of code, so we'll skip the details on those.

The portions you'll need to worry about are the variable and directory definitions, such as $DNS_ROOT. These are the ones you must change to match your configuration. Here again, pay close heed to the ownership warning in the directory definitions section!

```perl
#######################################################
# Set up some variables using the Web server's environment
# variables and include all the PERL libs that might be
# needed.
#
#######################################################

require "/www/cgi-bin/formlib.pl";

&GetFormArgs();   # parse arguments passed from FORM (now in %in)
$ENV{PATH_INFO} ne '' && &GetPathArgs($ENV{PATH_INFO});

require "/www/cgi-bin/debugforms.pl";

#######################################################
# VARIOUS STARTUP VARIABLES
#
#######################################################
# output NOT buffered  (Defaults to StdOut)
$|        = 1;

# Set up some date and time variables for later use
$datestr  = `date '+%m/%d/%y %H:%M:%S'`;
$datestr1 = `date '+%m/%d/%y'`;
$timestr  = `date '+%H:%M:%S'`;
```

```
chop ($timestr);
chop ($datestr1);
chop ($logdate = `date '+%h %d %T 19%y'`);


#####################################################
#! Variable definitions: please change these to match your
#  particular setup. Most of these identifiers are self-
#! explanatory. One thing to remember is that the
#! $PRIMARY_NS and $SECONDARY_NS values need to end with
#! a ".". IE: "outer.net."
#!
#####################################################

#! your primary domain name server (add the root dot)
$PRIMARY_NS       = "ns.outer.net.";
#! your main secondary domain name server (add the root dot)
$SECONDARY_NS     = "helix.net.";
#! the mail address of your dns admin in named db format
$HOSTMASTER       = "hostmaster.outer.net.";
#! the mail address of your dns admin in normal format
$HOSTMASTERMAIL   = "hostmaster@outer.net";
#! the location of your named.boot file (full path)
$NAMED_BOOT       = "/etc/named.boot";
#! the mail address of your Web admininstrator
$WEBMASTERMAIL    = "webmaster@outer.net";


#! the name of your organization
$OURSITE          = "OuterNet";
#! the location of your template
$MAILTEMPLATE     = "/www/cgi-bin/dns/domreg.form";


#####################################################
# Directory definitions: please adjust these to match your data
# files' location. Make sure that the UID for your Web server
# software has access to these directories. For instance, our
# server runs as user "www" and not as "root"; thus, the following
# four dirs on our machine are all owned by user "www".
#
#####################################################

#! Your DNS data root directory
$DNSROOT          = "/www/cgi-bin/dns/";
#! Directory for incoming requests
$NEWDIR           = $DNSROOT."new";
#! Directory for issued and pending requests
$PENDINGDIR       = $DNSROOT."pending";
#! Directory for registered domains
```

```
$DONEDIR        = $DNSROOT."done";
#! Directory for failed requests at the NIC
$FAILEDDIR      = $DNSROOT."failed";
#! Directory of where to find your named db files
$ZONEDIR        = "/usr/local/domain/zone";

######################################################
# Redirect stderr to the trash. For debugging redirect this to
# a file for later perusal, or uncomment the next open statement,
# and comment out the current executable open statement.
#
# open (STDERR,"> /tmp/dns.stderr");
######################################################

open (STDERR,"> /dev/null");

######################################################
# APPROPRIATE WWW HEADER INFORMATION
#
print STDOUT "Content-Type: text/html\n\n\n";
#
######################################################

# &debug;    #! For debugging output uncomment here.
```

Grabbing the Form Data

To effectively use the data passed from our HTML form, we need to extract it from the $in{} placeholders, delivered compliments of *formlib.pl*. By placing them in standard Perl variables, we use them more easily later. We must also split the domain name from the rest of the data in the HTML field.

```
######################################################
# WEB INPUT SETUP
# Parse through the passed variables and poke them into known
# areas for later use. Depending on the state of the system
# when a Web request is made, some of the variables below may
# not be set. The most obvious example is the state of the
# buttons (Register, mail, completed, etc.). Since the user
# can only hit one button at a time, we can determine what
# actions to take based on the state of all the buttons.
#
```

```
##################################################

$new          = $in{new};
@new_split    = split(" ",$new);
# The domain name is listed in the fourth field of our HTML
# display; we grab it by splitting on the whole line.
$new_domain      = $new_split[4];

$pending          = $in{pending};
@pen_split        = split(" ",$pending);
$pending_domain   = $pen_split[4];

$done             = $in{done};
@done_split       = split(" ",$done);
$done_domain      = $done_split[4];

$failed           = $in{failed};
@failed_split     = split(" ",$failed);
$failed_domain    = $failed_split[4];

$Register         = $in{Register};
$infomail         = $in{infomail};
$Completed        = $in{Completed};
$Failed           = $in{Failed};
$View             = $in{View};

$email            = $in{email};
$cust_number      = $in{cust_num};
$account_number   = $in{account_num};
```

Taming "named.boot"

You'll remember that at the beginning of this chapter we discussed the trials involved in configuring DNS on a UNIX system. One of the main gripes we voiced was the number and complexity of the files that had to be updated. The next two subroutines in *dns_edit.pl* relieve us of some of that burden.

The first subroutine, *make_zone,* actually creates a zone file for a domain that has completed registration. It uses a standard template for the zone file and inserts the domain name, primary DNS, secondary DNS, and serial number where appropriate. At the end, it notifies the administrator using the Web browser that the file has been created, then gives it the appropriate UNIX file permissions.

```
############################################################
# MAKES A NAMED DB FILE FOR THE NEW DOMAIN
#
# The function is probably the largest timesaver that we found
# with this system. By making this CGI do all the template work
# for setting up a new domain, you don't have to worry about
# the NIC rejecting your new domain request based on invalid DNS
# server information. Please note that the serial number system
# that we use involves a rotation based on the current date. The
# number is expressed as a digit in the form: 19950101,
# for January 1 1995. If multiple updates occur on one day,
# increment the value by a day or introduce your own system by
# modifying the $serial variable below. The Time to Live Values
# should also be changed to meet your organization's needs. The
# "MOST IMPORTANT HOST" and "HOSTS" areas are for future
# modification when machine "A" recs need to be added.
#
############################################################

sub make_zone_file {
# set the full path to the file
  $zonefile = $ZONEDIR."/".$pending_domain;
# set the serial number for the domain
  $serial = `date '+%y%m%d'`;
  chop ($serial);
  $serial = "19".$serial;

# The rest of this function prints to the file
  open (ZONEFILE, "> $zonefile");
  print ZONEFILE "\$ORIGIN $pending_domain.\
;\
; ------------------------------------------------------------
--------------\
; Primary Domain Configuration Files for $pending_domain.\
; Consult with  $HOSTMASTERMAIL for assistance.\
;\
; ------------------------------------------------------------
--------------\
;       THE Start Of Authority RECORD\
; ------------------------------------------------------------
--------------\
\@    IN    SOA         $pending_domain. $HOSTMASTER \(\
                        $serial          ; serial number\
                        10800            ; secondaries refresh
    \(3 hours\)\
                        1800             ; secondaries retry
      \(1/2 hour\)\
```

```
                              3600000          ; secondaries expire
      \(41 days\)\
                              108000 \)        ; minimum default TTL
      \(30 hours\)\
   ;\
   ; ------------------------------------------------------------
   --------------\
   ;       Name Server Records\
   ; ------------------------------------------------------------
   --------------\
   ;\
                  604800   IN NS   $PRIMARY_NS              ;
   Primary\
                  604800   IN NS   $SECONDARY_NS            ;
   Secondary\
   ;\
   ; ------------------------------------------------------------
   --------------\
   ;       MOST IMPORTANT HOST\
   ; ------------------------------------------------------------
   --------------\
   ;\
   ;\
   ; ------------------------------------------------------------
   --------------\
   ;       HOSTS\
   ; ------------------------------------------------------------
   --------------\
   ;\
   ;";
     close (ZONEFILE);
     print STDOUT "<H3>Updated zone config file: $zonefile.</h3>";
     system("chmod 664 $zonefile");   # UNIX housecleaning
   }
```

When *named* starts, it reads from a configuration file called "named.boot", which tells it where to look for zone files for each domain that it's a primary or secondary for. The next subroutine, *update_named_boot*, does exactly this. It simply appends a domain name, the zone file location information, and whether the host is a primary or secondary for that domain. An easy piece of code, but a great timesaver! Look at the comments for a sample.

```
#####################################################
# UPDATES THE NAMED.BOOT FILE WITH THE NEW ENTRY
#
```

```
# For everything to be kosher with the named server, the
# appropriate entry in the named.boot file needs to be made.
# The following few lines of code append an entry like that shown
# in the following example to the end of the file. The example is
# specific to OuterNet's site and would look different on yours.
#
# ; Borrowed Time, Inc.
# ; Contact: (lordgrey@outer.net)
#  (NIC: [NIC-950909.2380] BTI.NET)
# ;
# primary        bti.net        zone/bti.net
#
#############################################################

sub update_named_boot {
  open (NAMEDFILE, ">> $NAMED_BOOT");
  print NAMEDFILE
    ";\n; $org_name\n; Contact: $admin_name_ \($email_addr\)
\(NIC: $nic_number_\)\n;\n";
  print NAMEDFILE
    "primary\t\t$pending_domain\t\tzone/$pending_domain\n";
  close (NAMEDFILE);
  print STDOUT "<H3>Updated the $NAMED_BOOT file. This zone will
 be available at midnight.</H3>";
}
```

Processing a Domain Request

Remember the file that was created from the mailed-in domain registration
form? Now it's time to actually work with that data. The subroutine
get_new_data does this. It reads the data from the specified fields and stores
it in variables for later use. We'll need that data when we send the final
registration form to the NIC!

```
######################################################
# GETS DOMAIN ACTION INFORMATION FROM THE DNS DATA FILE
#
# In the event of a new registration, and if the user hits the
# "Register" button from the Web interface, this function is
# called (from main below), which then opens the domain file
# containing the data and fills up a whole selection
# of variables to be used in printing out the final registration
# template used by the NIC. The bulk of the data is extracted
# from the datafile by expecting the data to fit a regular
# expression. Typically this is derived from the mail message sent
```

```
# by a domain requester.
#
#################################################
sub get_new_data {
  $datafile = $NEWDIR."/".$new_domain;

# Here we open the data file for reading
  open(NEWFILE, "$datafile");
  while (<NEWFILE>) {
    /0\.(\s*)\(N\)ew \(M\)odify \(D\)elete\.\.\.\.\:(\s*)(.*)/
      && ($ACTION = $3);
    /1\.(\s*)Purpose\/Description\.\.\.\.\.\.\.\.\:(\s*)(.*)/
      && ($PURPOSE = $3);

    if ($ACTION eq "New") {
# These variables hold the value "selected" or a null so that
# the Web pop-up paints right.
      $NEW_SELECTED    = "Selected";
    }
    if ($ACTION eq "Modify") {
      $MODIFY_SELECTED = "Selected";
    }
    if ($ACTION eq "Delete") {
      $DELETE_SELECTED = "Selected";
    }

    /2\.(\s*)Complete Domain Name\.\.\.\.\.\.\.\:(\s*)(.*)/
      && ($DOMAIN = $3);
    /3a\.(\s*)Organization Name\.\.\.\.\.\.\.\.\.\.\.\:(\s*)(.*)/
      && ($ORG = $3);
    /3b\.(\s*)Street Address\.\.\.\.\.\.\.\.\.\.\.\.\.\.\:(\s*)(.*)/
      && ($ADDRESS = $3);
    /3c\.(\s*)City\.\.\.\.\.\.\.\.\.\.\.\.\.\.\.\.\.\.\.\.\.\.\.\:
      (\s*)(.*)/ && ($CITY = $3);
    /3d\.(\s*)State\.\.\.\.\.\.\.\.\.\.\.\.\.\.\.\.\.\.\.\.\.\.\.\:
      (\s*)(.*)/ && ($STATE = $3);
    /3e\.(\s*)Postal Code\.\.\.\.\.\.\.\.\.\.\.\.\.\.\.\.\.\:
      (\s*)(.*)/ && ($ZIP = $3);
    /3f\.(\s*)Country\.\.\.\.\.\.\.\.\.\.\.\.\.\.\.\.\.\.\.\:
      (\s*)(.*)/ && ($COUNTRY = $3);

    /4a.(\s*)NIC Handle \(if known\)\.\.\.\.\.\.\.\:(\s*)(.*)/
      && ($ADMIN_HANDLE = $3);
    /4b.(\s*)Name \(Last\, First\)\.\.\.\.\.\.\.\.\.\.\:(\s*)(.*)/
      && ($ADMIN_NAME = $3);
    /4c.(\s*)Organization Name\.\.\.\.\.\.\.\.\.\.\.\:(\s*)(.*)/
      && ($ADMIN_ORG = $3);
    /4d\.(\s*)Street Address\.\.\.\.\.\.\.\.\.\.\.\.\.\:
```

```
            (\s*)(.*)/ && ($ADMIN_ADDRESS = $3);
   /4e\.(\s*)City\.\.\.\.\.\.\.\.\.\.\.\.\.\.\.\.\.\.\.\.\.\.\.\:
      (\s*)(.*)/ && ($ADMIN_CITY = $3);
   /4f\.(\s*)State\.\.\.\.\.\.\.\.\.\.\.\.\.\.\.\.\.\.\.\.\.\.\:
      (\s*)(.*)/ && ($ADMIN_STATE = $3);
   /4g\.(\s*)Postal Code\.\.\.\.\.\.\.\.\.\.\.\.\.\.\.\.\.\:
      (\s*)(.*)/ && ($ADMIN_ZIP = $3);
   /4h\.(\s*)Country\.\.\.\.\.\.\.\.\.\.\.\.\.\.\.\.\.\.\.\.\:
      (\s*)(.*)/ && ($ADMIN_COUNTRY = $3);
   /4i\.(\s*)Phone Number\.\.\.\.\.\.\.\.\.\.\.\.\.\.\.\.\:
      (\s*)(.*)/ && ($ADMIN_PHONE = $3);
   /4j\.(\s*)E-Mailbox\.\.\.\.\.\.\.\.\.\.\.\.\.\.\.\.\.\.\:
      (\s*)(.*)/ && ($ADMIN_EMAIL = $3);

   /6a.(\s*)NIC Handle \(if known\)\.\.\.\.\.\.\.\:(\s*)(.*)/
      && ($BILLING_HANDLE = $3);/6b.(\s*)Name \(Last\,
      First\)\.\.\.\.\.\.\.\.\.\.\:
      (\s*)(.*)/ && ($BILLING_NAME = $3);
   /6c.(\s*)Organization Name\.\.\.\.\.\.\.\.\.\.\.\.\:(\s*)(.*)/
      && ($BILLING_ORG = $3);
   /6d\.(\s*)Street Address\.\.\.\.\.\.\.\.\.\.\.\.\.\.\:
      (\s*)(.*)/ && ($BILLING_ADDRESS = $3);
   /6e\.(\s*)City\.\.\.\.\.\.\.\.\.\.\.\.\.\.\.\.\.\.\.\.\.\.\.\:
      (\s*)(.*)/ && ($BILLING_CITY = $3);
   /6f\.(\s*)State\.\.\.\.\.\.\.\.\.\.\.\.\.\.\.\.\.\.\.\.\.\.\:
      (\s*)(.*)/ && ($BILLING_STATE = $3);
   /6g\.(\s*)Postal Code\.\.\.\.\.\.\.\.\.\.\.\.\.\.\.\.\.\:
      (\s*)(.*)/ && ($BILLING_ZIP = $3);
   /6h\.(\s*)Country\.\.\.\.\.\.\.\.\.\.\.\.\.\.\.\.\.\.\.\.\:
      (\s*)(.*)/ && ($BILLING_COUNTRY = $3);
   /6i\.(\s*)Phone Number\.\.\.\.\.\.\.\.\.\.\.\.\.\.\.\.\:
      (\s*)(.*)/ && ($BILLING_PHONE = $3);
   /6j\.(\s*)E-Mailbox\.\.\.\.\.\.\.\.\.\.\.\.\.\.\.\.\.\.\:
      (\s*)(.*)/ && ($BILLING_EMAIL = $3);

   /9\.(\s*)\(E\)mail \(P\)ostal\.\.\.\.\.\.\.\.\.\.\.\.\:
      (\s*)(.*)/ && ($INVOICE_TYPE = $3);

   if ($INVOICE_TYPE eq "Email") {
# these variables hold the value "selected" or a null so that
# the Web pop-up paints right.
      $EMAIL_SELECTED   = "Selected";
   }
   if ($INVOICE_TYPE eq "Postal") {
      $POSTAL_SELECTED   = "Selected";
   }
 }
 close (NEWFILE);
}
```

Checking the Request

We said earlier that it's safer for an administrator to double-check a domain request sent by a user before it gets zipped off to the InterNIC. The final subroutine for this script, *register*, formats the domain request into an HTML form that can be edited before it's sent to its final destination. It also allows you to register a new domain directly from the Web, rather than from the e-mail form. The domain registration editing page is shown in Figure 10-2.

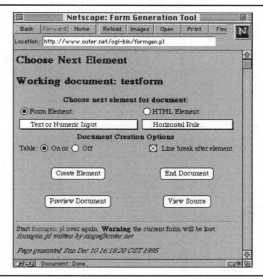

Figure 10-2
The DNS admin registration editing page.

When the Register Domain button is clicked, the final script in the suite, *dns_action.pl*, is called. It's what will actually send the domain request to the NIC.

```
##########################################################
# PRINTS THE OUTPUT HTML POPULATED WITH ALL OF THE RIGHT VALUES
#
# There's not much to this function. It basically draws the end
# product Web page so that the admin can see what transaction
# is about to transpire, and if changes are needed, conduct them
# on the spot before processing fully.
#
##########################################################
```

```
sub register {
  print
#!Change destination in line below to match your site
    "<FORM METHOD=\"POST\" ACTION=\"http://www.outer.net/cgi-
bin/dns_action.pl\">";

  print "<P>Urgent: <INPUT TYPE=\"checkbox\" NAME=\"URGENT\">\n";
  print "<P>0.   (N)ew (M)odify (D)elete....: <SELECT
NAME=\"ACTION\"><OPTION
$NEW_SELECTED>New<OPTION$MODIFY_SELECTED>Modify<OPTION
$DELETE_SELECTED>Delete</SELECT>";
  print "<BR>1.   Purpose/Description.........: <INPUT TYPE=\
"text\" VALUE=\"$PURPOSE\" NAME=\"PURPOSE\" SIZE=\"40\"
 MAXLENGTH=\"80\">";
  print "<BR>2.   Complete Domain Name....: <INPUT TYPE=\"text\"
 VALUE=\"$DOMAIN\" NAME=\"COMPLETE\" SIZE=\"40\" MAXLENGTH=\"80\
">";
  print "<P><B>Organization Using Domain Name</B>";
  print "<BR>3a.  Organization Name.......: <INPUT TYPE=\"text\"
VALUE=\"$ORG\" NAME=\"ORG\" SIZE=\"40\" MAXLENGTH=\"80\">";
  print "<BR>3b.  Street Address.............: <INPUT TYPE=\
"text\" VALUE=\"$ADDRESS\" NAME=\"ADDRESS\" SIZE=\"60\"
 MAXLENGTH=\"80\">";
  print "<BR>3c.  City........................: <INPUT
TYPE=\"text\" VALUE=\"$CITY\" NAME=\"CITY\" SIZE=\"30\"
MAXLENGTH=\"80\">";
  print "<BR>3d.  State.......................: <INPUT
TYPE=\"text\" VALUE=\"$STATE\" NAME=\"STATE\" SIZE=\"15\"
MAXLENGTH=\"80\">";
  print "<BR>3e.  Postal Code................: <INPUT TYPE=\
"text\" VALUE=\"$ZIP\" NAME=\"ZIP\" SIZE=\"15\" MAXLENGTH=\
"80\">";
  print "<BR>3f.  Country....................: <INPUT TYPE=\
"text\" VALUE=\"$COUNTRY\" NAME=\"COUNTRY\" SIZE=\"20\"
MAXLENGTH=\"80\">";
  print "<P><B>Administrative Contact</B>";
  print "<BR>4a.  NIC Handle (if known)....: <INPUT TYPE=\"text\"
VALUE=\"$ADMIN_HANDLE\" NAME=\"ADMIN_HANDLE\" SIZE=\"40\"
MAXLENGTH=\"80\">";
  print "<BR>4b.  Name (Last, First).........: <INPUT TYPE=\
"text\" VALUE=\"$ADMIN_NAME\" NAME=\"ADMIN_NAME\" SIZE=\"40\"
 MAXLENGTH=\"80\">";
  print "<BR>4c.  Organization Name.........: <INPUT TYPE=\"text\"
 VALUE=\"$ADMIN_ORG\" NAME=\"ADMIN_ORG\" SIZE=\"40\"
MAXLENGTH=\"80\">";
  print "<BR>4d.  Street Address.............: <INPUT TYPE=\
```

```
"text\" VALUE=\"$ADMIN_ADDRESS\" NAME=\"ADMIN_ADDRESS\" SIZE=\"60\"
MAXLENGTH=\"80\">";
   print "<BR>4e.  City........................: <INPUT
TYPE=\"text\" VALUE=\"$ADMIN_CITY\" NAME=\"ADMIN_CITY\" SIZE=\
"30\" MAXLENGTH=\"80\">";
   print "<BR>4f.  State.......................: <INPUT
TYPE=\"text\" VALUE=\"$ADMIN_STATE\" NAME=\"ADMIN_STATE\"
SIZE=\"15\" MAXLENGTH=\"80\">";
   print "<BR>4g.  Postal Code................: <INPUT TYPE=\
"text\" VALUE=\"$ADMIN_ZIP\" NAME=\"ADMIN_ZIP\" SIZE=\"15\"
 MAXLENGTH=\"80\">";
   print "<BR>4h.  Country....................: <INPUT TYPE=\
"text\" VALUE=\"$ADMIN_COUNTRY\" NAME=\"ADMIN_COUNTRY\" SIZE=\
"20\" MAXLENGTH=\"80\">";
   print "<BR>4i.  Phone Number...............: <INPUT TYPE=\
"text\" VALUE=\"$ADMIN_PHONE\" NAME=\"ADMIN_PHONE\" SIZE=\"40\"
MAXLENGTH=\"80\">";
   print "<BR>4j.  E-Mailbox..................: <INPUT TYPE=\
"text\" VALUE=\"$ADMIN_EMAIL\" NAME=\"ADMIN_EMAIL\" SIZE=\"40\"
MAXLENGTH=\"80\">";
   print "<P><B>Billing Contact</B>";
   print "<BR>6a.  NIC Handle (if known)....: <INPUT TYPE=\
"text\" VALUE=\"$BILLING_HANDLE\" NAME=\"BILLING_HANDLE\"
SIZE=\"40\" MAXLENGTH=\"80\">";
   print "<BR>6b.  Name (Last, First).........: <INPUT TYPE=\
"text\" VALUE=\"$BILLING_NAME\" NAME=\"BILLING_NAME\" SIZE=\"40\"
MAXLENGTH=\"80\">";
   print "<BR>6c.  Organization Name.........: <INPUT TYPE=\"text\"
VALUE=\"$BILLING_ORG\" NAME=\"BILLING_ORG\" SIZE=\"40\"
MAXLENGTH=\"80\">";
   print "<BR>6d.  Street Address.............: <INPUT TYPE=\
"text\" VALUE=\"$BILLING_ADDRESS\" NAME=\"BILLING_ADDRESS\"
SIZE=\"60\" MAXLENGTH=\"80\">";
   print "<BR>6e.  City.......................: <INPUT
TYPE=\"text\" VALUE=\"$BILLING_CITY\" NAME=\"BILLING_CITY\"
SIZE=\"30\" MAXLENGTH=\"80\">";
   print "<BR>6f.  State......................: <INPUT
TYPE=\"text\" VALUE=\"$BILLING_STATE\" NAME=\"BILLING_STATE\"
SIZE=\"15\" MAXLENGTH=\"80\">";
   print "<BR>6g.  Postal Code................: <INPUT TYPE=\
"text\" VALUE=\"$BILLING_ZIP\" NAME=\"BILLING_ZIP\" SIZE=\"15\"
MAXLENGTH=\"80\">";
   print "<BR>6h.  Country....................: <INPUT TYPE=\
"text\" VALUE=\"$BILLING_COUNTRY\" NAME=\"BILLING_COUNTRY\"
SIZE=\"20\" MAXLENGTH=\"80\">";
   print "<BR>6i.  Phone Number...............: <INPUT TYPE=\
"text\" VALUE=\"$BILLING_PHONE\" NAME=\"BILLING_PHONE\" SIZE=\
```

```
"40\" MAXLENGTH=\"80\">";
  print "<BR>6f.   E-Mailbox..................: <INPUT TYPE=\
"text\" VALUE=\"$BILLING_EMAIL\" NAME=\"BILLING_EMAIL\" SIZE=\
"40\" MAXLENGTH=\"80\">";
  print "<P><B>Invoice Delivery</B>";
  print "<BR>9.   (E)mail (P)ostal..........: <SELECT
NAME=\"INVOICE_TYPE\"><OPTION $EMAIL_SELECTED>Email<OPTION
$POSTAL_SELECTED>Postal</SELECT>";

  print "<HR><INPUT TYPE=\"submit\" NAME=\"register\"
VALUE=\"Register Domain\">",
      "<INPUT TYPE=\"reset\" NAME=\"reset\" VALUE=\"Reset
form\"></FORM>";
}
```

The Main Body

The main portion of this code is where the subroutines are invoked, but it includes several functions of its own. Remember that this script handles the actions taken on the HTML form data created by *dns_lines.pl*. This means it performs one of the five functions below (refer back to Figure 10-1 for the form's appearance):

1. **Mail info form to cust** to send the domain registration template.
2. **Register** to process the registration of a new domain.
3. **View** to look at the domain request and NIC response for a domain.
4. **Completed** to process a domain that has been registered successfully.
5. **Failed** to notify a user the NIC responded the domain could not be registered for whatever reason.

Let's take a look at each function in the order it appears in the script.

Mailing the Domain Registration Form

This function checks to see if the $infomail value exists. If it does, that means that the Mail info form to cust button was selected, and it should e-mail the domain registration template, *domreg.form,* to the parties specified in the e-mail address field. Note that it can be a single e-mail address, or a series of addresses separated by a comma (e.g., *charlie@caffeine.net, etittel@zilker.net*).

Also note that the code makes no checks to ensure that the e-mail address was entered in the proper format. If it doesn't go through, then your Web server's ID will get the bounced mail (and, usually, the login set up as "postmaster" will also get a copy). That's why an important part of the admin's job has to be regular monitoring of bounced e-mail messages, either from the postmaster or *www* accounts. ▲

```
print STDOUT "<TITLE>DNS Database Engine</TITLE><H1>DNS
Administration</H1><HR>";


################################################
# MAIL THE TEMPLATE TO A USER
#
################################################

if ($infomail) {
  system("$MAILER -s 'DNS Registration Form' $email
    < $MAILTEMPLATE");
  print STDOUT "<H2>The Form has been mailed to: $email</H2>";
}
```

Register a Domain

This function prepares to send a domain request off to the NIC. First, it checks to see if the $new variable exists. If it doesn't, then no domain was selected from those waiting for registration, so it calls the *register* subroutine directly. This allows an administrator to process a new registration by entering the information into the form rather than e-mailing it. If a domain was selected from the list, then it calls the *get_new_data* subroutine before calling the *register* subroutine. Feel free to look back at any of them to remind you what they do!

```
################################################
# Register the domain with the NIC, either by getting the info
# from the Web page or by reading a pre-existing file that has
# already been returned. This must conform to the template
# mentioned by $MAILTEMPLATE.
#
################################################

if ($Register) {
  if (!$new) {
    &register();
  }
```

```
    else {
      &get_new_data();
      &register();
    }
}
```

View Domain

This function allows you to keep track of the correspondences between you and the InterNIC regarding a domain. Essentially, it just reads the data file of whatever domain you select and spits it out onto the Web. You'll notice that it doesn't try any fancy formatting, but just prints the raw text using <PRE>...</PRE> tags.

```
##################################################
# VIEW RESULTS
#
# This subsection merely reads the DNS data file on record
# and outputs the results to the user in an HTML document.
#
##################################################

if ($View) {
  $items_selected = 0;

  if ($new) {
    $items_selected++;
    $view_domain = $new_domain;
    $view_file = $NEWDIR."/".$view_domain;
  }
  if ($pending) {
    $items_selected++;
    $view_domain = $pending_domain;
    $view_file = $PENDINGDIR."/".$view_domain;
  }
  if ($done) {
    $items_selected++;
    $view_domain = $done_domain;
    $view_file = $DONEDIR."/".$view_domain;
  }
  if ($failed) {
    $items_selected++;
    $view_domain = $failed_domain;
    $view_file = $FAILEDDIR."/".$view_domain;
  }
```

```
  if ($items_selected > 1) {
    print STDOUT "<H2>Please select only 1 item to view at a
time.</H2>";
  }
  else {
    print STDOUT "<H2>View Domain: $view_domain</H2><HR><PRE>";
    open(VIEWSTREAM, "cat $view_file |");
    while (<VIEWSTREAM>) {
      print STDOUT;
    }
    close (VIEWSTREAM);
    print STDOUT "</PRE>";
  }
}
```

Completed Domain

If you're lucky enough to get an affirmative response from the NIC regarding your registration, you'll select that domain and click the Completed button. If a domain from the pending list has been selected as completed, then the script e-mails the requester that the domain has been registered and updates the appropriate DNS files.

The script actually takes the name, e-mail address, and organization of the registrant from the original request and inserts them where appropriate in the e-mail message. The end result is a very personalized, yet professional, acknowledgment that you don't have to strike a single key to create. We know several sysadmins who wish they could automate every user response like this!

After the message is sent, the script calls on the subroutines *make_zone_file* and *update_named_boot* described earlier.

```
################################################
# COMPLETED DOMAIN ACTION
#
# This subsection is called when the administrator selects a
# domain in the pending area and hits the "Completed" Button
# on the Web page.
#
################################################

if ($Completed) {
  if ($email) {
    $email = ", ".$email;
  }
```

```
    if (!$pending) {
        print STDOUT "<H2>Please select a choice from the outstanding
area</H2>";
    }
    else {
        print STDOUT "<H2>Domain $pending_domain has been successfully
completed</H2>";

# These two lines set the location of the files to capture data
# from and the files to move it into.
        $from = $PENDINGDIR."/".$pending_domain;
        $to = $DONEDIR."/".$pending_domain;

# The following few lines parse out the e-mail address and
# organization from the original text sent to the NIC. These
# variables are then used to mail an appropriate response to the
# registrant.

        $email_addr = `grep '4j.  E-Mailbox.................:' $from
| awk '{print \$4}'`;
        chop($email_addr);
        $org_name = `grep '3a.  Organization Name..........:' $from
| awk '{print \$4, \$5, \$6, \$7}'`;
        chop($org_name);
        $admin_name_ = `grep '4b.  Name (Last, First).........:' $from
| awk '{print \$1, \$2, $3}'`;
        chop($admin_name_);
        $nic_number_ = `grep 'Subject: Re: ' $from | awk '{print
\$3,\$4}' | uniq`;
        chop($nic_number_);
        $nic_number_ =~ s/\n/ /;

# Move the completed domain to the "done" area
        system("mv $from $to");

open (ACKMAIL, "| $MAILER -s 'RE: NEW domain for $pending_domain'
$email_addr$email");
        print ACKMAIL "\n\nThe registration for the domain
\"$pending_domain\" has been processed\n";
        print ACKMAIL "and is currently under $OURSITE's
authority.\n\n";
#! When new domains come online, there is a variety of newsgroups
#! and Websites that will publicize such things, $HOSTMASTERMAIL
#! makes it easy to create and maintain this information.
        print ACKMAIL "Please send e-mail to $HOSTMASTERMAIL for
advertisement of your hosts.\n";
        print ACKMAIL "Note: Your account has been charged for this
```

```
registration unless an \nalternate agreement with $OURSITE has
been made.\n\n";
    print ACKMAIL "Thank you,\n$OURSITE Domain Administration.
($HOSTMASTERMAIL)\n\n";
    close (ACKMAIL);
    print STDOUT "<H3>Successfully sent response: mail has been
sent.</H3>";

    &make_zone_file();
    &update_named_boot();
  }
}
```

Failed Domain Registration

If the InterNIC denied the registration, then you'll click the Failed button. A domain can fail registration for a variety of reasons; the most common is that the domain name requested is already registered to someone else. The NIC has a few other guidelines, such as only one domain per organization (though for larger organizations, like Bellcore, it has proved possible for departments and other subentities to obtain separate domain names, indicating that size also counts with the InterNIC!) and at least currently no domains that contain only numbers, such as 123.com.

As you might guess, the next part of the code moves the pending domain to the failed domain directory. As with completed domains, the failed domain portion also extracts the e-mail address of the registrant to send them a letter saying that the domain failed registration.

```
#######################################################
# FAILED DOMAIN ACTION
#
# This subsection is called when the user selects a domain in
# the pending area and hits the "Failed" Button on the Web page.
# This occurs when the NIC has rejected a domain request for any
# of a number of reasons. Basically, the file is moved to the
# failed directory and a notification mail is sent to the
# requester.
#
#######################################################

if ($Failed) {
  if ($email) {
    $email = ", ".$email;
  }
```

```
    if (!$pending) {
      print STDOUT "<H2>Please select a domain request from the
        Outstanding area</H2>";
    }
    else {
      print STDOUT "<H2>Domain $pending_domain has been successfully
moved</H2>";
      $from = $PENDINGDIR."/".$pending_domain;
      $to = $FAILEDDIR."/".$pending_domain;
      $email_addr = `grep '4j.  E-Mailbox..................:' $from
| awk '{print \$4}'`;
      chop($email_addr);
      print STDOUT "<H3>Mail sent to: $email_addr$email</H3>";
      system("mv $from $to");
open (ACKMAIL, "| $MAILER -s 'RE: NEW domain for $pending_domain
FAILED' $email_addr$email");
      print ACKMAIL "\n\nThe registration for the domain
\"$pending_domain\" has been processed\n";
      print ACKMAIL "and has been rejected by InterNIC. It is
therefore currently NOT under $OURSITE's authority.\n\n";
      print ACKMAIL "The reason for the failure is most likely due
to a pre-existing registration\n";
      print ACKMAIL "by another party. For more information,
consult the WHOIS database at the NIC:\n";
      print ACKMAIL "This resource can be reached by telnetting to:
rs.internic.net.\n";
      print ACKMAIL "\n\nThank you,\n$OURSITE Domain Administration.
($HOSTMASTERMAIL)\n\n";
      close (ACKMAIL);
      print STDOUT "<H3>Sucessfully sent response mail in
notification of the failure.</H3>";
    }
  }

  print "<HR> <ADDRESS>$WEBMASTERMAIL</ADDRESS>\n";
```

To look at our last script, we're going to have to backtrack a little bit to the *register* subroutine in *dns_edit.pl*. Remember that it only creates the domain registration edit form but doesn't actually send the request to the NIC. The program it calls, *dns_action.pl,* does that, and that's where we're headed next.

MAKING THE REQUEST KNOWN: DNS_ACTION.PL

Our last stop before we hit the InterNIC is *dns_action.pl*. This script sends the domain registration form to the InterNIC. But before it does this, it guarantees that the form is in the proper format. We'll go through this script piece-by-piece to show you what it does.

Even More Variables

You've seen most of the variables by now, plus our old friend *formlib.pl*. It's important to keep them fresh in your mind and remember that the ones with the #! in the comments must be changed to suit your system's configuration.

```
require "/www/cgi-bin/formlib.pl";

##################################################
# VARIOUS SETUP VARIABLES
#
##################################################

$|               = 1;

# Sets up a date and time string
$datestr         = `date '+%m/%d/%y %H:%M:%S'`;
$timedate        = `date '+%H%M%S'`;
chop ($datestr);
chop ($timedate);

# parse arguments passed from FORM (now in %in)
&GetFormArgs();
$ENV{PATH_INFO} ne '' && &GetPathArgs($ENV{PATH_INFO});

#! Your DNS data root directory
$DNSROOT            = "/www/cgi-bin/dns/";
#   These two are normally not edited
$PENDINGDIR        = $DNSROOT."pending/";
$NEWDIR            = $DNSROOT."new/";
#! This should = the one in "parse.in.www.mail.pl"
$DNSTEMPLATE       = $DNSROOT."new.dns.form";
#! You'll probably need to edit this
$MAILER            = "/usr/bin/mailx";
#! And this
$HOSTMASTER        = "hostmaster@outer.net";
$INTERNICMASTER    = "domreg@rs.internic.net";
```

This approach relies on using symbolic variables in the code, instead of outright calls to the underlying values involved. We can't overemphasize the value of this approach: If used properly, whenever you install or move a program, you'll only have to edit one set of values, instead of hunting for occurrences throughout all of the files involved. This is probably the nicest thing you can do for yourself as a CGI programmer, and it's even nicer for others who use your code but who may not know all the internals. ▲

Working with the Web Variables

The next portion of the code extracts all of the fields from the WWW domain registration edit form. It also translates the complete domain name into lowercase for the NIC form and the top-level domain into uppercase, the preferred format for the InterNIC's use.

```
##################################################
# PARSE FOR WWW INPUT
#
# Setup information is derived from environment variables passed
# to this script from earlier scripts in this set of programs.
# Most of the Web fields are passed and parsed here.
# You shouldn't need to edit anything that follows this.
#
##################################################

$ACTION            = $in{ACTION};
$TOP               = $in{TOP};
$COMPLETE          = $in{COMPLETE};
$COMPLETE          =~ tr/A-Z/a-z/;
@COMPLETE_SPLIT    = split ('\.',$COMPLETE);
$COMPLETE_TOP      = $COMPLETE_SPLIT[1];
$COMPLETE_TOP      =~ tr/a-z/A-Z/;

if ($COMPLETE_TOP ne $TOP) {
  $TOP= $COMPLETE_TOP;
}

$ORG               = $in{ORG};
$ADDRESS           = $in{ADDRESS};
$CITY              = $in{CITY};
$STATE             = $in{STATE};
$ZIP               = $in{ZIP};
$COUNTRY           = $in{COUNTRY};
```

```
$ADMIN_HANDLE      = $in{ADMIN_HANDLE};
$ADMIN_NAME        = $in{ADMIN_NAME};
$ADMIN_ORG         = $in{ADMIN_ORG};
$ADMIN_ADDRESS     = $in{ADMIN_ADDRESS};
$ADMIN_CITY        = $in{ADMIN_CITY};
$ADMIN_STATE       = $in{ADMIN_STATE};
$ADMIN_ZIP         = $in{ADMIN_ZIP};
$ADMIN_COUNTRY     = $in{ADMIN_COUNTRY};
$ADMIN_PHONE       = $in{ADMIN_PHONE};
$ADMIN_EMAIL       = $in{ADMIN_EMAIL};
$BILLING_HANDLE    = $in{BILLING_HANDLE};

$BILLING_NAME      = $in{BILLING_NAME};
$BILLING_ORG       = $in{BILLING_ORG};
$BILLING_ADDRESS   = $in{BILLING_ADDRESS};
$BILLING_CITY      = $in{BILLING_CITY};
$BILLING_STATE     = $in{BILLING_STATE};
$BILLING_ZIP       = $in{BILLING_ZIP};
$BILLING_COUNTRY   = $in{BILLING_COUNTRY};
$BILLING_PHONE     = $in{BILLING_PHONE};
$BILLING_EMAIL     = $in{BILLING_EMAIL};
$PURPOSE           = $in{PURPOSE};
$INVOICE_TYPE      = $in{INVOICE_TYPE};
$URGENT            = $in{URGENT};

if ($URGENT =~ "on") {
  $URGENT = "URGENT: ";
}
```

Sending the Mail to the NIC

The next part of the code takes the massaged variables extracted from the form and inserts them into the same *new.dns.form* template that we used in *parse.in.www.mail.pl*, in essentially the same way as in that script. It shoots these variables through an open mailer pipe destined for the InterNIC's hostmaster.

The mailer line is interesting because it places the appropriate variables in the subject and addressee fields. Compare that line to the end result of an InterNIC reply:

```
From: domreg@internic.net
To: WWW Master <www@outer.net>
Subject: Re: [NIC-951006.515] URGENT: Modify domain for
  questlink.com
```

Here's the code that makes this happen:

```
#
# Here's our page that details what has just transpired. You'll
# notice that there's a ton of improvement that can be done here,
# especially for a nice wizzy Web site like yours.
#
print STDOUT "Content-Type: text/html\n\n\n";
print STDOUT "<H2>Mail regarding the domain $COMPLETE has been
successfully sent to the NIC. </H2>";

# This sets up the pending domain record in the right dir
$rec_file = $PENDINGDIR.$COMPLETE;


#
#  Probably the line that does the most, this opens a running pipe
#  to the mailer so that the registration form can be sent to the
#  NIC.
#! You'll want to customize this statement to match your site's
#! e-mail configuration.
#
open (MAIL, "| $MAILER -s '$URGENT $ACTION domain for
 $COMPLETE' $INTERNICMASTER $HOSTMASTER");
open (RECORD, "> $rec_file");
open (TEMPLATE, $DNSTEMPLATE);
while (<TEMPLATE>) {
# Each of the following lines replaces the {FIELD} with the value
# retrieved from the Web page. A simple regex sub is performed to
# accomplish the task.
  if (/\{ACTION\}/) {
    s/\{ACTION\}/$ACTION/;
  }
  if (/\{COMPLETE\}/) {
    s/\{COMPLETE\}/$COMPLETE/;
  }
  if (/\{PURPOSE\}/) {
    s/\{PURPOSE\}/$PURPOSE/;
  }
  if (/\{ORG\}/) {
    s/\{ORG\}/$ORG/;
  }
  if (/\{ADDRESS\}/) {
    s/\{ADDRESS\}/$ADDRESS/;
  }
  if (/\{CITY\}/) {
    s/\{CITY\}/$CITY/;
  }
```

```
if (/\{STATE\}/) {
  s/\{STATE\}/$STATE/;
}
if (/\{ZIP\}/) {
  s/\{ZIP\}/$ZIP/;
}
if (/\{COUNTRY\}/) {
  s/\{COUNTRY\}/$COUNTRY/;
}
if (/\{ADMIN_HANDLE\}/) {
  s/\{ADMIN_HANDLE\}/$ADMIN_HANDLE/;
}
if (/\{ADMIN_NAME\}/) {
  s/\{ADMIN_NAME\}/$ADMIN_NAME/;
}
if (/\{ADMIN_ORG\}/) {
  s/\{ADMIN_ORG\}/$ADMIN_ORG/;
}
if (/\{ADMIN_ADDRESS\}/) {
  s/\{ADMIN_ADDRESS\}/$ADMIN_ADDRESS/;
}
if (/\{ADMIN_CITY\}/) {
  s/\{ADMIN_CITY\}/$ADMIN_CITY/;
}
if (/\{ADMIN_STATE\}/) {
  s/\{ADMIN_STATE\}/$ADMIN_STATE/;
}
if (/\{ADMIN_ZIP\}/) {
  s/\{ADMIN_ZIP\}/$ADMIN_ZIP/;
}
if (/\{ADMIN_COUNTRY\}/) {
  s/\{ADMIN_COUNTRY\}/$ADMIN_COUNTRY/;
}
if (/\{ADMIN_PHONE\}/) {
  s/\{ADMIN_PHONE\}/$ADMIN_PHONE/;
}
if (/\{ADMIN_EMAIL\}/) {
  s/\{ADMIN_EMAIL\}/$ADMIN_EMAIL/;
}
if (/\{BILLING_HANDLE\}/) {
  s/\{BILLING_HANDLE\}/$BILLING_HANDLE/;
}
if (/\{BILLING_NAME\}/) {
  s/\{BILLING_NAME\}/$BILLING_NAME/;
}
if (/\{BILLING_ORG\}/) {
  s/\{BILLING_ORG\}/$BILLING_ORG/;
}
```

```perl
     if (/\{BILLING_ADDRESS\}/) {
       s/\{BILLING_ADDRESS\}/$BILLING_ADDRESS/;
     }
     if (/\{BILLING_CITY\}/) {
       s/\{BILLING_CITY\}/$BILLING_CITY/;
     }
     if (/\{BILLING_STATE\}/) {
       s/\{BILLING_STATE\}/$BILLING_STATE/;
     }
     if (/\{BILLING_ZIP\}/) {
       s/\{BILLING_ZIP\}/$BILLING_ZIP/;
     }
     if (/\{BILLING_COUNTRY\}/) {
       s/\{BILLING_COUNTRY\}/$BILLING_COUNTRY/;
     }
     if (/\{BILLING_PHONE\}/) {
       s/\{BILLING_PHONE\}/$BILLING_PHONE/;
     }
     if (/\{BILLING_EMAIL\}/) {
       s/\{BILLING_EMAIL\}/$BILLING_EMAIL/;
     }
     if (/\{INVOICE_TYPE\}/) {
       s/\{INVOICE_TYPE\}/$INVOICE_TYPE/;
     }
     print MAIL;
     print RECORD;
  }
close (MAIL);
close (RECORD);
close (TEMPLATE);
# UNIX housekeeping- mainly for security reasons
system("/bin/chmod 664 $rec_file");

# As the request is processed, the data file is moved from the
# NEW directory to the PENDING one, as illustrated by these few
# system calls.
$from = $NEWDIR.$COMPLETE;
$to = $PENDINGDIR.$COMPLETE;
system("mv $from $to");
# more UNIX tidying-up
system("/bin/chmod 664 $to");
```

Finally this script sends a message to notify the user that a request has been sent. This message is created and sent just as for the completed and failed domains in *dns_edit.pl*. It also warns the user that it may take two to four weeks for the NIC to respond to a registration request (which may be a successful registration, or a rejection of your request).

```
#
# The last section sends a tickle mail back at the person whose
# e-mail address is listed in the form itself. It alerts the
# recipient about the action that has just taken place, and gives
# him or her an opportunity to respond should a problem occur.
#
if ($ADMIN_EMAIL) {
  open (ACKMAIL, "| $MAILER -s '$URGENT $ACTION domain for
$COMPLETE' $ADMIN_EMAIL ");
  print ACKMAIL "\n\nThe registration for the domain \"$COMPLETE\"
 has been submitted\n";
  print ACKMAIL "and is currently pending at the Network
Information Center (NIC)\n";
  print ACKMAIL "for processing. This process can take up to 4
weeks.\n\n";
  print ACKMAIL "We will contact you when the NIC finishes their
 configuration.\n\n";
  print ACKMAIL "Hostmaster\n";
  close (ACKMAIL);
}

print STDOUT "<H2>A Reply from the NIC should follow in about 2
weeks.</H2>";
```

Now that we've seen what each of the scripts involved in our DNS Administration Application does, let's talk about how to install them.

INSTALLING THE DNS ADMINISTRATION APPLICATION

Looking through the comments in the code, you'll see that there are several things that you should change during installation. Among them are the DNS data directories, the hostname, the path to your mailer program, and your Web server's user ID. All of these are marked by a #!.

When installing the DNS Admin Application, these are the variables you should keep in mind. If this is your first installation, you may want to use the defaults we've chosen, to keep errors to a minimum. It's easy to get confused regarding ownership and permissions.

The DNS Data Directories

For proper operation of this CGI you'll need to create a directory structure to store the domain information. The root of this directory structure is defined in $DNSROOT. To keep everything in the same vicinity, we've chosen to place the DNS root beneath the directory where we keep our CGIs: */www/cgi-bin/dns.* Note that for simplicity we chose *dns* as the directory name.

Underneath the DNS root you'll need directories for the new registrations ($NEWDIR), pending registrations ($PENDINGDIR), completed registrations ($DONEDIR), and failed registrations ($FAILEDDIR). Once again, we went the easy route and chose new, pending, done, and failed as the directory names for these variables. The complete structure looks like this:

```
/www/cgi-bin/dns
                /new
                /pending
                /done
                /failed
```

The owner of this structure should be your Web server's user ID, set in the $WEB_UID variable in *parse.in.www.mail.pl.* In OuterNet's case, this user ID is www. The group ID for this directory structure is set to daemon, so that the *sendmail* and *httpd* daemons can make changes in those directories. There shouldn't be a need for anyone except the www user and the daemon to update anything in these directories, so they are given UNIX octal file permissions of 770: i.e., full access for www and the daemon group, and nothing for the rest of the world.

Putting Everything in Its Place

The next step is to put all of the files in their proper places and to give them appropriate permissions. Remember, we've created a total of six files for this application: *parse.in.www.mail.pl, domreg.form, new.dns.form, dns_lines.pl, dns_edit.pl,* and *dns_action.pl.* Where these files are placed, and who is permitted to use them, makes or breaks this program!

Information on the installation of these files can be found in their commentary, but we'll summarize in Table 10-1. The scripts *dns_edit.pl, dns_lines.pl,* and *dns_action.pl* should all be placed where your CGI scripts are normally located. In our case, that's in */www/cgi-bin.* In most default Web server setups, this is in */usr/local/etc/httpd/cgi-bin.*

Understanding UNIX Permissions

In the right-hand column in Table 10-1 you'll see strings of octal numbers that describe UNIX file access permissions. Although the notation is somewhat arcane, it's very precise. Here's how to read these numbers: Each permission consists of three octal digits (a number from 0 to 7), where the first digit covers the owner's rights, the second digit covers group rights, and the third digit cover the world's (or everybody's) rights to the file.

Table 10-1
The location, ownership, and permissions

File	*Location*	*Owner*	*Permissions*
dns_action.pl	/www/cgi-bin	www.httpd	750
dns_edit.pl	/www/cgi-bin	root.httpd	750
dns_lines.pl	/www/cgi-bin	root.httpd	750
domreg.form	$DNSROOT	www.httpd	444
new.dns.form	$DNSROOT	www.httpd	644
parse.in.www.mail.pl	/usr/local/bin	root.root	755

For each digit, convert the octal number into three binary digits (1 or 0, where 1 means allowed, 0 means denied). The leftmost bit indicates read access, the middle bit write access, and the rightmost bit execute access. Thus, the five digits that appear in Table 10-1 can be decoded using Table 10-2.

Table 10-2
A breakdown of file access permissions

Octal	*Binary*	*Indicates*
7	111	read,write, execute
6	110	read, write, no execute
5	101	read, no write, execute
4	100	read, no write, no execute
0	000	no read, no write, no execute

Thus, 444 means that the owner, the group, and the world all have read-only rights (no write, no execute) for the file in question. Similarly, 750 means that the owner has read, write, and execute rights, the group has read and execute rights only, and the world has no rights, to that file.

If you can remember that each of the three digits stands for owner, group, and world (left to right), and that within each digit, each bit stands for read, write, and execute, you'll be able to figure the rest out for yourself! ▲

Pretending You're Someone Else

If you run into a problem in UNIX, first check to see if it's a file permissions issue. The best way to make sure you have the permissions set right is to become the superuser, then use the *su* command to change your ID to someone else. In this case, you'll want to make sure you can write and read in the DNS data directories when you're the www user, and make sure that you can actually run each of the Perl scripts we've described!

Calling the Scripts

The scripts *dns_edit.pl* and *dns_action.pl* both have the distinction of being called by other scripts, so there's really no trick to installing them except proper location. The other two, *parse.in.www.mail.pl* and *dns_lines.pl,* need to be called by other means.

As we've described, *parse.in.www.mail.pl* gets called when a mail message is delivered to your Web server's user ID (www in the OuterNet example). How do we get it to run? We send all incoming mail to that program through a pipe using the *sendmail aliases* file. Thus, you'll need to add *parse.in.www.mail.pl* to the list of addresses after the Web user alias. Here's a sample from OuterNet's *aliases* file:

```
www: webmaster, |/usr/local/bin/parse.in.www.mail.pl
```

The www mail is sent to the webmaster alias and is also piped to the *parse.in.www.mail.pl* file, where it is then parsed. The alias webmaster is another Web user alias that is sent to a real person who can see what's transpiring between users, the DNS admin program, and the NIC. The second, real-person alias can be anyone you wish.

The *dns_lines.pl* script is simply called from the administrator's Web browser. It can be called either directly or through an HTML anchor on another page.

HIGH RISK PROGRAMMING

You may want to include a modicum of security for *dns_lines.pl,* such as using an ".htaccess" file (as in the NCSA implementation of *httpd).* ▲

At this point, you should be able to install the DNS admin suite. If you have problems, go back and check ownership and permissions. You'll probably find you left something out. If things work without an apparent hitch, you're ready to use the DNS application.

USING THE CGI

You probably already have some ideas about using the DNS Admin Application from our discussion. Nonetheless, let's take it step-by-step (refer back to Figures 10-1 and 10-2 to see what the user interface looks like).

The first step is to pull up the *dns_line.pl* CGI in a WWW browser. You can do this directly or from an HTML anchor on another page. Once you see the admin screen, type your e-mail address into the E-Mail Address field. Once it's entered, click the Mail info form to cust button, and within minutes you should have a copy of the domain registration form in your inbox.

Next, fill out the form with your domain information and e-mail it back to your WWW server's user ID. When you go back to the *dns_lines.pl* interface screen, you should see the domain request form you just filled out in the field, DNS Entries Needing to Be Sent.

Select its domain name, then click on the Register button. At this point, you can edit what's going to be sent to the NIC and correct any problems. When you're finished, click the Register Domain button to send the request to the NIC.

Now wait for two or three weeks. Go out and do something fun—like take a cruise to Australia!

When you see the response mail, go back to the *dns_line.pl* administration interface and select the domain from the field, DNS Entries Outstanding at the NIC, then click the Completed button.

Everything else is done for you! The zone files are created and the "named.boot" file is updated with your new entry. Having the DNS entry already set up is important because about three days after registering a domain, the NIC will check to make sure there is a valid DNS entry for it at your site. If there isn't, it will remove the entry from its root name server and you'll have to mail them to add it again. You still keep the domain, but almost no one can get to it until they add it to their name server again!

DNS EXTENSIONS

We've shown you one of the many powerful system administration functions possible with CGI scripting. The DNS Administration Application allows you to easily manage multiple domains, simplifies your dealings with the InterNIC, and avoids some of the sysadmin headaches common with DNS. There are several other options we could add.

One simple option would be to add a way for users to fill out a domain registration form on the Web, rather than sending mail. We've already got the basic tools for this. We could use a version of the form in the *register* subroutine of *dns_edit.pl*. But instead of sending their registration to the NIC immediately, we could pipe it to a script as in *parse.in.www.mail.pl*. It could parse out and append to the user's information, and store it in a file in the new domain directory. Providing an online form would make it easy for users to register a single domain, and having it sent to the new directory for later administrative processing still gives you some degree of security. Some administrators would rather increase the degree of automation; we've found that a human filter between users and official bodies like the InterNIC is almost always a good idea!

Another extension would be to control the listings of domain information supplied by the DNS tracker database to several of the Perl scripts to solicit a cutoff date, and display entries more recent than that date. This would be a relatively easy extension to the code but would require you to parse the database entries by date and forward only those newer than the cutoff for display. Likewise, responses from the InterNIC could be parsed to automatically enter status information, include completed domains, rejected domains, changes, and even, forwarding of the InterNIC's rejection message to the domain's requester. All of this depends on more code for text recognition and capture; the basic methods and principles for which should be clear by now.

Once you have your domain registered, you'll probably want to associate it with a TCP/IP network or subnetwork address. Many administrators allocate IP address spaces and update DNS zone files by hand. A helpful extension to the DNS application suite would do this automatically. When you register a domain, there could be a checkbox on the admin page called `Network Assignment`. If this box is checked, it could read in a field, `Number of Machines`, for the administrator to complete. This information would never be sent to the NIC, but once the registration was complete, it could be used to allocate a network address range for that domain. It would use the `Number of Machines` data field to indicate network size. It could then update the host file with this information, as well as the appropriate DNS zone file.

As you use the DNS Admin Application yourself and have further dealings with the InterNIC and DNS administration, you'll no doubt think of other timesavers.

SUMMARY

As we've said, one of the nice things about CGI applications on the Web is that you can use them from almost anywhere. It's no longer necessary to be tied to a single console in your office. Wouldn't it be nice to have something like the DNS Admin Application for every task you do? If you did, you could perform your job from anywhere on the planet!

These CGI and HTML creation tools will put you on your way to managing much of what you do remotely. But there's still going to be a need for paper you say? Don't bet on it! The WWW FAX gateway we'll describe to you in the next chapter may be the paperless solution.

A CGI-Based Fax Viewer

*F*or over a decade, the business standard for immediate document delivery to and from distant locations (especially overseas) has been facsimile (fax). Because it's an electronic transfer, sending a fax is, by definition, faster than the postal service or overnight package delivery. The biggest failing of fax technology has been its general lack of print and paper quality.

Through Rain, Sleet, and Line Noise

Now, with better compression techniques and plain-paper fax machines supplanting older thermal ones, there's little quality lost between an original and its facsimile. Thus, faxing is becoming more popular than ever before. In this chapter, we'll show you how to deliver faxed information to readers via the World Wide Web.

Everybody's Doing It . . . With Fax Modems

Always popular in offices, fax systems have become more common in homes over the past three or four years. Today, nearly anyone with a personal computer can also send and receive faxes. This is because most modem manufacturers are augmenting their modems to handshake with fax carrier tones.

Practically any 14.4kbps or 28.8kbps modem you purchase today has fax capability and ships with bundled fax software. Even Personal Data Assistants (PDAs), such as Apple's Newton, can accept PCMCIA fax modem cards. Now you can fax from your home, your car, or even a plane!

Benefits of Computer-Based Faxing

Sending and receiving faxes via computer isn't just a novelty: It's a powerful business tool that allows greater freedom of movement away from your office. It's also an inexpensive means for small companies to own a fax system. Let's look at some of the specific advantages of computer-based faxing:

- Incoming faxes are stored electronically on your local hard drive. This means you can look at them and see if they're worth printing, saving paper and expense.

- It's typically cheaper. An InkJet fax machine costs around $800. On the other hand, 14.4kbps fax modems (and software) are bundled with many personal computer packages nowadays, and an InkJet printer costs around $300. If you need to fax hardcopy items (for signatures, pre-printed documents, etc.), a greyscale scanner to digitize these images costs around $250.

- It also saves in phone expenses when you can use your existing Internet connection (typically, a local phone call or dedicated line) rather than directly dialing the other fax machine over traditional long-distance lines.

- You can typically fax directly from the word processing application you're using with built-in Print commands. You no longer have to print out documents and manually feed them into a fax machine.

■ Faxing is also networkable: Much like a network print server saves on printer costs, a network fax server avoids the expense of putting a fax modem and analog line in every office.

Now that we've discussed how fax modems have made faxing easier and more affordable, let's tie this technology into the World Wide Web.

FAXES AND THE WEB

Someday e-mail and the Web may replace fax machines as a primary means of business document delivery. More and more businesses will become connected to the Net, and higher bandwidth options will increase the Net's carrying capacity. Multicasting should allow simultaneous data transmission to multiple destinations, in a fraction of the time it currently takes. Because MIME standards allow the inclusion of multimedia in e-mail and Web documents, technology may deliver things on the Intenet that fax machines can never do!

Another reason to throw out your fax machine is the inability of traditional fax technology to handle color, which is something easily overcome when you're talking between computers instead of between fax machines.

Why Webify a Fax System?

Because users can access the Web from anywhere on the Internet, it makes sense to let them read their faxes using that medium. Just as the Web already delivers many kinds of documents today, it can also deliver graphical versions of fax data as Web graphics, and more.

With the personal fax and network fax server software packages available now, it may seem redundant to build a CGI program that does essentially what they do. However, there are a number of advantages to a Web-based fax gateway that current standalone and network packages can't offer:

■ Administration from multiple locations. You can send, receive, administer, or print faxes anywhere you have an Internet connection and Web browser.

- The ability to customize features specific to your business: Because the fax delivery program is your own CGI, you can tailor it to your particular needs.

- The ability to integrate faxes with other Internet services adds a mechanism for hardcopy follow-up to electronic communications, as well as other advantages. This is something we'll discuss further at the end of the chapter.

As you can see, a fax gateway can be a useful and effective business tool. Therefore, in this chapter we'll be providing you with the framework for a fax gateway, that you can use as-is, or customize with your own services.

What We'll Cover

Here, we'll only cover that portion of the fax gateway that lets us *receive* and *view* faxes. Toward the end of the chapter, we'll briefly discuss the possibilities for *sending* faxes with copy or information that originates on the Web. In fact, the Quote Generator program in Chapter 19 provides an example implementation for sending faxes from within a CGI program. So let's get on with designing the Fax Viewer!

SPECIFICATIONS FOR THE FAX VIEWER

Our minimalist Fax Viewer needs only four parts:

1. Fax Receiver
2. Fax Translator
3. Fax Administration Screen
4. Back-End to the Administration Screen

Let's look at each of these.

The Fax Receiver

The fax receiver needs to:

1. Answer the modem when a call arrives.
2. Acknowledge that the incoming data is a fax.
3. Deposit the fax file into a working directory.

 The programming required to accomplish these three tasks is beyond the scope of this chapter and it's best to use a third-party application. We'll discuss one called *mgetty+sendfax* that integrates nicely with a CGI fax gateway. Judicious use of a search engine on the Web should help you turn up other alternatives, if this one proves unacceptable (or doesn't work on your Web server's platform or OS). ▲

For the record, we developed this package on a Wintel platform for the 2.3 Slackware distribution of Linux. Our normal operating environment also includes AU/X, SunOS, and Solaris, which gives us the ability to test across multiple UNIX versions. For more information about our development environment, and insight into the thinking that goes into some of our development decisions, please consult Chapter 9 of this book.

Suffice it to say here that if you're not using some flavor of UNIX for your CGI development, you'll be less likely to be able to use our code intact. You'll also have to look further afield to find equivalent tools and libraries to match what we're using here, but they can indeed be found, if you'll just keep looking!

The Fax Translator

When fax systems communicate, they send their fax pages in the form of compressed bitmap files. The current format standard for these files is called Group 3 (G3). On computer systems, these files often take a ".g3" extension.

No currently available Web browser can display Group 3 files directly, so this format needs to be translated into something a browser or helper application can handle. There is a variety of tools that can do this, one of which is incorporated into the *mgetty+sendfax* program. The CGI program we're going to write runs its conversion tools against a directory of G3 files (incoming faxes, in other words).

Viewfax to the Rescue

For direct display of datatypes from a browser that doesn't have built-in support, the notion of a "helper application" comes into play. Most of the major browser vendors allow users to configure an association between file extensions and particular applications within the browser, so that if a particular file type shows up that the browser itself can't handle, it can invoke the associated applications with that file as input. For fax messages, a helper application called *viewfax* is available from:

```
ftp:// ftp.leo.org/pub/comp/networking/communication/modem/mgetty
```

As you'll see throughout the rest of this chapter, our CGI delivers more functionality than the average helper application could, which is, of course, why we built it!

A Prime Candidate for a Script

We'll use this program only to call other programs, and we're not concerned about speed. So there's no reason to write it in a language that needs an external compiler or is considered "fast," like C. We could write it in a C or Korn shell script, but we've chosen Perl, not only as a matter of personal preference, but because it's portable across a variety of hardware and software platforms.

The Fax Administration Screen

The fax administration screen's UI needs to display a list of incoming faxes and give the administrator options for what to do with them. Since this is only the groundwork for a fax system, we'll make it do three more things as well:

1. View a fax (with magnification factors).
2. Delete a fax.
3. View a thumbnail fax.

Save the Trees

The first two options are self-explanatory. The last option lets you preview a smaller graphic of the fax and possibly glean what it's about before loading up a full-sized version. This is especially helpful if you're attached over a slow Internet link. Finally, you should also be able to select multiple faxes from the list, so you can view or delete several at once. Of course, you can always use the browser's built-in print functionality to produce hard copies of these faxes whenever necessary (but now, you'll get to examine these files before they're used to kill another tree).

A Choice Blend of HTML and Perl

HTML provides us with the code we need to create the multiple selectable lists and option buttons. It also allows us to distribute the list over the Web. But what about reading the list of incoming faxes?

Again, Perl lets us make system calls to read the fax directory and obtain information from it. Once again, speed isn't important, but portability concerns steered us away from shell scripts.

The Admin Back-End

The back-end for the administration screen must handle fax processing. If a view of a fax or a thumbnail is selected, it needs to create the proper representation, and deliver it to the user. If a delete operation is requested, the back-end must perform that task as well.

You Guessed It: HTML and Perl Again!

For displaying an image on a Web Browser, HTML already gives us all the tags we need. For its part, Perl provides easy file manipulation and access to system calls to perform deletions and other functions.

Let's start looking at the code—we'll go through each of the systems described previously, as well as the third-party applications needed to make them work.

Receiving Faxes: mgetty

Programming a *getty* replacement to receive faxes isn't really a CGI function, so it's beyond the scope of this book. Fortunately, there's already one available for us to use. The *mgetty* application is part of the *mgetty+sendfax* package, created by Gert Doering. It can accept Group 3 faxes over a Class 2 or 2.0 fax modem.

It has been compiled and runs on a variety of UNIX flavors, including AIX, Linux, and Solaris. You can get the source code and documentation at:

```
http://www.leo.org/~doering/mgetty/
```

You may be able to locate other packages similar to *mgetty* that work just as well. We discuss *mgetty* here only as an example of a fax gateway that we've had good luck with.

Translating the Faxes: g3togif.pl

The first script we'll look at is *g3togif.pl*. It converts the G3 faxes received by *mgetty* into GIF files. Once it's a GIF file, we can view it inline with any graphics-capable Web browser.

The code required to make this type of conversion is long and complex. Fortunately, there are third-party utilities to make the transition smoother!

The reason *g3togif.pl* was created is that there is no single third-party utility we know of that can convert a file from G3 to GIF. There are, however, utilities that can perform the necessary intermediate steps. The simplest process we found required three steps:

1. Convert a Group 3 file to a Portable Bitmap file.
2. Convert from Portable Bitmap to PostScript.
3. Convert from PostScript to GIF.

The process looks like this:

```
G3 ---> PBM ---> PS ---> GIF
```

This conversion requires three programs: *g3topbm*, *pnmtops*, and *Ghostscript*. We'll run through what each of them does; how they're used is documented in the code itself.

g3topbm

g3topbm is included in the *mgetty+sendfax* package and gets compiled and installed when you make *mgetty* and *sendfax*. It takes a G3 format file and translates it into an X Windows Portable Bitmap (PBM) file. Once the file is a PBM, it can be converted into a variety of other formats.

pnmtops

pnmtops converts a Portable Anymap File (PNM) into PostScript. PNMs include PBMs, so we can convert our PBM output from *g3topbm* into PostScript now. *pnmtops* is part of the PBMPlus package, which you can find on a variety of UNIX sites. For example, there's a version at:

```
ftp://wuarchive.wustl.edu/graphics/graphics/packages/pbmplus
```

PBMPlus has several dozen other conversion utilities that you can integrate with this and other CGIs.

Ghostscript (gs)

Ghostscript is a versatile public-domain package that lets you manipulate PostScript files in a multitude of ways, one of which converts PostScript files into GIF format. *Ghostscript* is available for most platforms (including MS Windows, OS/2, Mac, and UNIX), and is standard in many Linux distributions. If you don't already have a copy, you can find it at:

```
http://www.cs.wisc.edu/~ghost/ghostscript/obtaina.html
```

Now that you're familiar with the third-party applications we're using, let's move on to the Perl code.

Defining Constants

First, there are two directories we need to work in: where we *get* the faxes from and where we *put* the faxes once we've converted them. The directory where *mgetty* deposits its G3 files is defined as '$FAXDIR'.

You can choose a second directory, which will be defined as '$OUTPUT_DIR'. If your fax server and Web server are one and the same, then the '$OUTPUT_DIR' should be somewhere under your Web server's document root (e.g., */www/httpdocs*). Otherwise, it should be some cross-mounted directory. In our case it's the latter, and we've chosen */home/fax*, which is linked to also appear as */www/httpdocs/fax*.

If '$OUTPUT_DIR' isn't under your Web server's document root, then it should be made known to your Web server by linking, or cross-mounting, so that it appears as though it were under the document root. This can be achieved either through symbolic linking (if you are on the same UNIX file system) or through the UNIX *mount* command (if it's on a different file system or server). As the setting for the following variables indicate, we've chosen */home/fax*, which is linked to also appear as */www/httpdocs/fax* for our fax directory structure:

```
$FAXDIR     = "/usr/spool/fax/incoming/";
$OUTPUT_DIR = "/home/fax/";
```

Our next constants supply the locations and names for the conversion utilities we're using. For converting G3 files to PBM, we have $G3_TO_PBM; for converting PBM files to PostScript, we have $PBM_TO_PS.

```
$G3_TO_PBM  = "/usr/local/bin/g3topbm";
$PBM_TO_PS  = "/usr/local/bin/pnmtops";
```

The constant $PS_TO_GIF describes the location of the file we're using to convert PostScript files to GIF. In this case it's *Ghostscript*, and we'll go ahead and include our command-line options. The -q -dNOPAUSE lets it run in quiet mode, without user interaction. The -r110x110 option is the resolution of the final GIF (110x110 pixels). The -sDEVICE=gifmono tells *Ghostscript* that the final output file should be in monochrome GIF format.

```
$PS_TO_GIF = "/usr/bin/gs -q -dNOPAUSE -r110x110 -sDEVICE=gifmono ";
```

Listing Fax Files

The next step is to list the faxes within our incoming fax directory. We do this by opening a filestream for the long-form `ls` listing of `$FAXDIR`. We include the `-t` option so that faxes are listed from newest to oldest, in reverse chronological order:

```
open (FAXDIR,"ls -lt $FAXDIR/. |");
```

Because the long *ls* listing also produces information we don't need, we separate each line into its constituent parts using the `split` operation:

```
while (<FAXDIR>) {
    $line = $_;
    @lineparts = split;
```

In a UNIX long directory listing, the eighth field is the filename itself. We'll take that filename and prepare it for use in our format conversions. The G3 filename will be stored in `$g3file`. We need to add ".ps" to the end of the intermediate PostScript file and store it in `$psfile`. This is also where we'll assign `$output_gif` to the GIF file, adding ".gif" to it and placing it in `$OUTPUT_DIR`:

```
if ( $lineparts[8] ) {
    $g3file = $FAXDIR.$lineparts[8];
    $psfile = $g3file.".ps";
    $output_gif = $OUTPUT_DIR.$lineparts[8].".gif";
...}
```

Note: We've omitted code that occurs before the closing bracket in this `if` statement (it's actually reproduced later). If you want to see the real source, check the companion diskette.

Getting Rid of the Rabble

There are certain characters that cannot appear in UNIX filenames because they're wildcards or operators of some kind. We need to check for their existence in the output filename and use the Perl pattern substitution operation to remove them:

```
if ( ($output_gif =~ '\#') || ($output_gif =~ '\!') ||
     ($output_gif =~ '\?') || ($output_gif =~ '\*') ||
```

```
($output_gif =~ '\$') || ($output_gif =~ '\%') ||
($output_gif =~ '\&') || ($output_gif =~ )
{
    $output_gif =~ s/\#//;
    $output_gif =~ s/\!//;
    $output_gif =~ s/\?//;
    $output_gif =~ s/\*//;
    $output_gif =~ s/\$//;
    $output_gif =~ s/\%//;
    $output_gif =~ s/\&//;
    $output_gif =~ s/\@//;
}
```

This chunk of code will be useful in all kinds of CGI programs, so you may want to cut it out of its parent file from the diskette, and keep it around for other uses! ▲

The Conversion Experience

This process simply calls our G3 to PBM, PBM to PS, and PS to GIF converters through two *system* calls. The $G3_TO_PBM converter is run on each $g3file. The PBM output is piped directly to the $PBM_TO_PS converter. The resulting $psfile is then run through the $PS_TO_GIF translator, and the final $output_gif is placed in its proper directory:

```
system("${G3_TO_PBM} ${g3file} | ${PBM_TO_PS} > ${psfile}");
system("${PS_TO_GIF} -sOutputFile=${output_gif}−${psfile}");
```

Replacing the lines above with our converters, you'd see the following:

```
/usr/local/bin/g3topbm ${g3file} |
    /usr/local/bin/pnmtops > ${psfile}
/usr/bin/gs -q -dNOPAUSE -r110x110 -sDEVICE=gifmono -
    sOutputFile=${output_gif}−${psfile}
```

Post-Conversion Cleanup

Everybody hates to clean up but if you don't, you'll find yourself drowning in megabytes of PostScript files in your incoming fax queue!

The first thing to do is make your Web server the owner and group for each $output_gif file. In our case it's www and httpd, respectively. You should also make them readable and writable by your Web server, so they can be viewed and deleted later via a Web browser. Then, you'll need to get rid of your intermediate files, $g3file and $psfile, to save space. All of this is handled in Perl with *system* calls.

The last thing to do is close the output stream of the *ls* statement on the incoming fax directory, $FAXDIR:

```
        system("chown www.httpd ${output_gif}");
        system("chmod 644 ${output_gif}");
        system("rm -f ${g3file}");
        system("rm -f ${psfile}");
        }
    }
    close(FAXDIR);
```

Running *g3togif.pl* should convert all incoming faxes to GIF files. Now let's move on to working with these GIF files through a user interface.

The Fax Administration Screen: get_fax.pl

The CGI *get_fax.pl* presents its users with a list of faxes and allows them to operate on them. We decided earlier that these operations would include the following: view a fax (with magnification factors), view a thumbnail fax, and delete a fax. The functions themselves are performed by another CGI. This one just provides an administration UI.

The Startup Variables and Constants

The first thing we need to do is unbuffer STDOUT so we don't have to wait for the buffer to fill before we get output. This helps prevent Web browser timeouts.

Next, we define the place where GIF fax documents are stored. This place should be equal to, or at least a symbolic link to, the '$OUTPUT_DIR' defined in *g3togif.pl*:

```
$|     = 1;                          #  Unbuffer STDOUT.
$FAXDIR = "/www/httpdocs/forms/fax"; #! Where your Fax documents
                                     #! are stored.
```

Next we want to send the appropriate MIME type, text/html, to the Web browser, and direct all errors to STDERR:

```
###############################################################
# APPROPRIATE HEADER INFORMATION
#
print STDOUT "Content-Type: text/html\n\n\n";
#
###############################################################
open (STDERR,"> /dev/null");
```

Reading the Fax Directory

Now we need a subroutine to read in the fax directory to create our list of faxes. The subroutine read_dir opens a datastream from the output from ls. The -lt option means that it's a long file listing, listed in reverse chronological order:

```
sub read_dir {
  open (FAXDIR,"ls -lt $FAXDIR/. |");
```

The output lines are held and split into their component parts. The date, time, and filename for each line are all sent as an <OPTION> on a selectable HTML form list. Remember that the date and time associated with each of these files is the date and time it was converted, not when it was received. After the entire directory has been read, we close the stream.

```
while (<FAXDIR>) {
    $line = $_;
    @lineparts = split;
    $elements = $#lineparts;
    if ( $lineparts[8] ) {
        $faxfile = $lineparts[8];
        $date_conv = $lineparts[5]." ".$lineparts[6]."
           ".$lineparts[7];
        $outputline = "$date_conv : $faxfile\n";
        print STDOUT "<OPTION>  $outputline";
    }
}
close(FAXDIR);
}
```

Lest you be too concerned about the date of conversion versus that of reception, let us remind you that we avoid this problem altogether by sweeping our conversion directories every 15 minutes, unless the system is under heavy load, from a *cron* task we created for that very purpose! ▲

The HTML Form

This portion contains the bulk of the code. It merely sends the HTML tags to the user's Web browser.

Notice that the action performed by this form is to post data to the CGI view_fax.pl, which we'll discuss next.

```
print STDOUT "<HEAD><TITLE>List of Received Faxes</TITLE>";
print STDOUT "</HEAD><BODY>";
print STDOUT "<CENTER><H1>OuterNet's List of Received Faxes</H1></CENTER>";
print STDOUT "<HR>";
print STDOUT "<FORM METHOD=POST ACTION=\"/cgi-bin/view_fax.pl\">";
```

This next portion is our fax list, where we can select multiple items. The options are pulled from running the read_dir subroutine we discussed earlier.

```
print STDOUT "<P><STRONG>Faxes Received:</STRONG><BR>";
print STDOUT "<SELECT MULTIPLE SIZE=5 NAME=\"PENDING\">\n";

do read_dir();

print STDOUT "</SELECT>";
print STDOUT "<P>";
```

Here's where we add the magnification factor options (it defaults to 100%, or actual size):

```
print STDOUT "<P><SELECT NAME=\"MAGNIFICATION\">";
print STDOUT "<OPTION>50%";
print STDOUT "<OPTION>75%";
print STDOUT "<OPTION SELECTED>100%";
print STDOUT "<OPTION>150%";
print STDOUT "<OPTION>200%";
print STDOUT "</SELECT>";
print STDOUT "<P>";
```

Finally, we see the submission buttons that list with the options we designed into this program—namely, View, Thumbnail, and Delete:

```
print STDOUT "<P><INPUT TYPE=\"submit\" NAME=\"DELETE\"
  VALUE=\"Delete\">";
print STDOUT "<INPUT TYPE=\"submit\" NAME=\"VIEW\"
  VALUE=\"View\">";
print STDOUT "<INPUT TYPE=\"submit\" NAME=\"THUMBNAIL\"
  VALUE=\"Thumbnails\"><P>";

print STDOUT "<HR>";
#! Please customize e-mail address below to match local req'mts
print STDOUT "<ADDRESS><A
  HREF="mailto:staff@outer.net">staff@outer.net</A></ADDRESS>\n";
```

This form's user interface is shown in Figure 11-1.

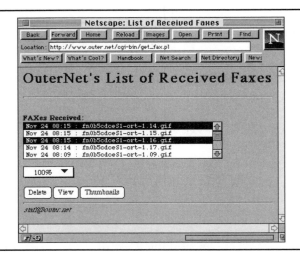

Figure 11-1

A view of the fax administration screen with multiple faxes selected.

Now you have a means to manipulate the fax files you've received. The next script, *view_fax.pl*, implements the options selected from *get_fax.pl*.

THE ADMIN SCREEN BACK-END: VIEW_FAX.PL

The back-end script, *view_fax.pl,* is what actually performs a fax deletion or presents a full-blown fax or thumbnail to the user. As we go through each section, you'll see that this part is actually pretty simple.

Things Required and Optional

The first part of *view_fax.pl* includes required libraries and sets up variables and constants. The only library this script needs is *formlib.pl* to process the HTML form. We've included this one before, so you should be familiar with it.

```
#############################################################
#
# INCLUDE THE FORMS PROCESSING PERL LIBRARY
#
#############################################################

require "/www/cgi-bin/formlib.pl"; #! Location of your /cgi-bin.
#! Please localize to match your own directory structure.
```

We also need to unbuffer STDOUT again (see *get_fax.pl* for an explanation). Next we'll use the *formlib.pl* function &GetFormsArgs() to parse the form arguments passed from *get_fax.pl.* $FAXDIR in *view_fax.pl* should be the same as $FAXDIR in *get_fax.pl.* $LOCAL_FAXDIR tells your Web browser where your fax GIFs are located. It should be the absolute, fully-qualified URL for the directory specified in $FAXDIR.

```
#############################################################
#
#   VARIOUS STARTUP VARIABLES AND CONSTANT DEFINITIONS
#
#############################################################
$|    = 1;          # Unbuffer STDOUT.

&GetFormArgs();    # Parse arguments passed from FORM (now in %in).

#! Where your Fax documents are stored; please modify to match
#! your local configuration.
$FAXDIR = "/www/httpdocs/forms/fax/";
```

```
#! Use this to specify the location of the graphics files; please
#! modify to match your local configuration.
$LOCAL_FAXDIR = "http://www.outer.net/forms/fax/";
```

The $WIDTH and $HEIGHT variables specify the default pixel size for a
viewed fax. $MIN_WIDTH and $MIN_HEIGHT specify the default pixel size for
thumbnail views.

```
$WIDTH      = 612;
$HEIGHT     = 792;

$MIN_WIDTH  = $WIDTH * .2;
$MIN_HEIGHT = $HEIGHT * .2;
```

Parsing Form Data

Here's where we start working with the data sent to us from the HTML
form. First we tell the browser we're sending a standard HTML MIME
type. Then, we save the values sent from the form in the $in{} array to
more manageable fields.

```
#############################################################
# APPROPRIATE HEADER INFORMATION
#
print STDOUT "Content-Type: text/html\n\n\n";
#
#############################################################

$PENDING       = $in{PENDING};
$DELETE        = $in{DELETE};
$VIEW          = $in{VIEW};
$MAGNIFICATION = $in{MAGNIFICATION};
$THUMBNAIL     = $in{THUMBNAIL};
```

Now we need to magnify the pixel sizes of the image by the value
specified in $MAGNIFICATION. We divide the percentage value of
$MAGNIFICATION by 100 to get a magnification factor to multiply $WIDTH
and $HEIGHT.

```
chop($MAGNIFICATION);
$MAGNIFICATION /= 100;
$WIDTH *= $MAGNIFICATION;
$HEIGHT *= $MAGNIFICATION;
```

Finally, for each fax stored in $PENDING we split off the date and time so that we have only the filename:

```
$number_of_faxes = 0;

@entry_split = split("#",$PENDING);
foreach $fax_entry (@entry_split) {
  @fax_split = split(" ",$fax_entry);
  @FAX_FILES [$number_of_faxes++] = $fax_split[4];
}
```

Deleting Faxes

If you elect to delete a fax or group of faxes, then you'll run through this rather simple routine. For each extant fax selected, the program makes a system call to the UNIX *rm* command to remove it. Once finished, it announces that you're done and returns to the *get_fax.pl* admin screen.

```
if ($DELETE) {
    print STDOUT "<STRONG>The following fax file(s)";
    print STDOUT " were processed:</STRONG><HR>";

    for ($ct=0; $ct<$number_of_faxes; $ct++) {

        $path_to_fax = ${FAXDIR}.$FAX_FILES[$ct];
        if (-f $path_to_fax) {
            system("rm -f $path_to_fax");
            print STDOUT "<P>Deleted: $FAX_FILES[$ct]<BR>";
        }
    else {
        print STDOUT "<P>Not Found: $FAX_FILES[$ct]<BR>";
        }
    }
    print STDOUT "<HR>";
    #! Modify to match your /cgi-bin location:
    open(GET_STREAM, "/www/cgi-bin/get_fax.pl |");
    while (<GET_STREAM>) {
        unless ($_ =~ "Content-Type: text/html") {
            print STDOUT;
        }
    }
    close (GET_STREAM);
}
```

Viewing Faxes

If you've elected to view a fax, then that fax is merely displayed by the Web browser using the <IMG WIDTH= HEIGHT= SRC= > HTML tag. This is where the full URL to the fax path comes into play.

```
if ($VIEW) {
     $path_to_fax = ${FAXDIR}.${FAX_FILES[0]};
     $web_path_to_fax = ${LOCAL_FAXDIR}.${FAX_FILES[0]};

#!   Modify to match your location's name:
     print STDOUT "<TITLE>OuterNet FAX Viewer</TITLE>";
     print STDOUT "<CENTER><H2>FAX: $FAX_FILES[0]</H2></CENTER>";

     if ( -f $path_to_fax ) {
          print STDOUT "<HR>";
          print STDOUT "<IMG WIDTH=$WIDTH HEIGHT=$HEIGHT
                        SRC=\"$web_path_to_fax\">";
#!        Modify to match correct e-mail address:
          print STDOUT "<HR>";
 HREF="mailto:staff@outer.net">staff@outer.net</A></ADDRESS>";
}
     else {
          print STDOUT "<HR>";
          print "<STRONG>This fax was not found in the Fax
                 directory</STRONG>";
          print STDOUT "<HR>";
#!        Modify to match correct e-mail address:
          print STDOUT "<ADDRESS><A
 HREF="mailto:staff@outer.net">staff@outer.net</A></ADDRESS>";
}
}
```

A fax displayed within this program is shown in Figure 11-2.

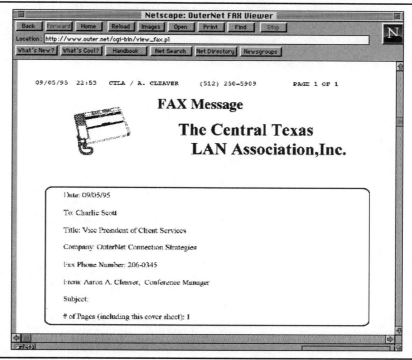

Figure 11-2
A sample fax displayed by view_fax.pl.

Viewing Thumbnails

Viewing thumbnails is much like viewing a fax. However, the $MIN_WIDTH and $MIN_HEIGHT values are used instead of $WIDTH and $HEIGHT. For aesthetic reasons we're displaying them within HTML 3.0 tables. Since we could view many thumbnails at once, we've limited our view to three images on a single line. The formatting for these tables requires some calculation, based on the number of faxes to be displayed.

```
if ($THUMBNAIL) {
    print STDOUT "<STRONG>The following Fax file(s)";
    print STDOUT " were selected:</STRONG><HR>";
    print STDOUT "<TABLE BORDER=5 CELLPADDING=2 ALIGN=CENTER>";
```

```
        print STDOUT "<TH COLSPAN=3>Fax Thumbnails- Line 1</TH><TR
ALIGN=CENTER><P>";

    $inner_ct = 0;
    $line = 1;
    for ($ct=0; $ct<$number_of_faxes; $ct++) {

        $path_to_fax = ${FAXDIR}.$FAX_FILES[$ct];
        $web_path_to_fax = ${LOCAL_FAXDIR}.${FAX_FILES[$ct]};

        if (-f $path_to_fax) {
            if ($inner_ct == 3) {
                $inner_ct = 0;
                $line++;
                print STDOUT "</TR><TH COLSPAN=3>
        Fax Thumbnails- Line $line</TH><TR ALIGN=CENTER><P>";
            }
            print STDOUT "<TD ALIGN=CENTER>
        <FONT SIZE=-1>$FAX_FILES[$ct]<P>";
            print STDOUT "<A HREF=\"$web_path_to_fax\">";
            print STDOUT "<IMG ALIGN=TOP WIDTH=$MIN_WIDTH
        HEIGHT=$MIN_HEIGHT ";
            print STDOUT "SRC=\"$web_path_to_fax\">"
            print STDOUT "</A></FONT></TD>";
$inner_ct++;
        }
    }
    print STDOUT "</TR></TABLE></CENTER><HR>";
}
```

Now that we've covered the four main parts of our Fax Viewer: *mgetty*, *g3togif.pl*, *get_fax.pl*, and *view_fax.pl* we'll describe how to install those pieces!

Figure 11-3 shows several thumbnails on simultaneous display.

INSTALLING THE FAX VIEWER

Remember that there are two separate sets of programs that make up the Fax Viewer: the scripts that we've written and the third-party applications they use. Here, we'll discuss setting up our scripts. For the third-party utilities, use their documentation and *make*files to decide where those items should be placed and what their required file ownership and permissions should be.

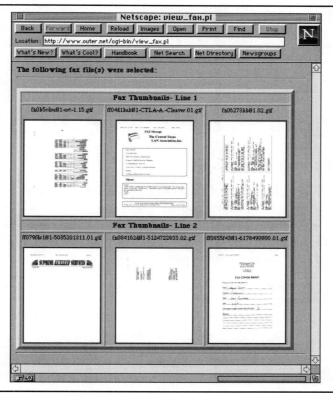

Figure 11-3
A view of several fax thumbnails from the Fax Viewer.

Our CGI Scripts

To install our CGI scripts, *g3togif.pl*, *get_fax.pl*, and *view_fax.pl*, change those variables whose comments begin with a #! to match your system's setup. For instance, you should make '$FAXDIR' point to where your GIF fax files are stored on your system. Likewise, make '$PS_TO_GIF' the path and program name for your chosen PostScript to GIF converter.

Table 11-1 shows the name of each of our scripts, where they should be located, and what their ownership and permissions should be.

Table 11-1

Location, ownership, and permissions for Fax Viewer files

File	Location	Ownership	Permissions
g3togif.pl	/usr/local/bin	root.root	750 or -rwxr-x--
get_fax.pl	/www/cgi-bin	www.httpd	750 or -rwxr-x--
view_fax.pl	/www/cgi-bin	www.httpd	750 or -rwxr-x--

Calling g3togif.pl

The script *g3togif.pl* needs to be called periodically to run through the incoming fax directory and convert the G3 files to GIF. The best way to do this is through the UNIX *cron daemon*. Have *crond* execute the script at whatever interval you wish. For example, we have ours running every 15 minutes using the following line in our *crontab* file:

```
# Runs the Fax coversion on incoming Faxes 8 times an hour.
#
00,08,15,21,30,38,45,51 * * * * /usr/local/bin/g3togif.pl >
   /dev/null;
```

You can also set up *mgetty* to automatically launch a program after it executes. This is an alternative way to run *g3togif.pl*. However, we decided against it because it meant incoming faxes were converted as soon as they came in. Since *g3togif.pl* can take considerable CPU resources, we only want it to run on a specified schedule. ▲

get_fax.pl and view_fax.pl

Since they get called from a URL, both *get_fax.pl* and *view_fax.pl* need to be located where you store your CGI scripts. Both also need to be owned by your Web server's user ID.

You can either call *get_fax.pl* directly from your Web browser, or you can create an HTML "fax Admin" page that contains an anchor to that program. You'll always be accessing *get_fax.pl* first. By the same token, there should never be any need to run *view_fax.pl* by itself.

Understanding UNIX Permissions

In the right-hand column in Table 11-1 you see strings of octal numbers that describe UNIX file access permissions. Although the notation is somewhat arcane, it's very precise. Here's how to read these numbers: Each permission consists of three octal digits (a number from 0 to 7), where the first digit covers the owner's rights, the second digit covers group rights, and the third digit covers the world's (or everybody's) rights to the file.

For each digit, convert the octal number into three binary digits (1 or 0, where 1 means allowed, 0 means denied). The leftmost bit indicates read access, the middle bit write access, and the rightmost bit execute access. Thus, the five digits that appear in Table 11-1 can be decoded using Table 11-2.

Table 11-2
Reading UNIX Permissions

Octal	Binary	Indicates	ls -l
7	111	read, write, execute	rwx
6	110	read, write, no execute	rw-
5	101	read, no write, execute	r-x
4	100	read, no write, no execute	r--
0	000	no read, no write, no execute	---

Thus 444 means that the owner, the group, and the world all have read-only rights (no write, no execute) for the file in question. Similarly, 750 means that the owner has read, write, and execute rights, the group has read and execute rights only, and the world has no rights, to that file.

If you can remember that each of the three digits stands for owner, group, and world (left to right), and that within each digit, each bit stands for read, write, and execute, you'll be able to figure the rest out for yourself!

The fourth column shows the standard -rwxrwxrwx notation that you get on the UNIX command line when you ls -l to see permissions.

The GIF File Directory

Don't forget to create a directory under your Web server's document root for the GIF fax files. In our case, we used */www/httpdocs/forms/fax*. Your Web server's user ID (we use www) must have write privileges to this directory.

The Third-Party Utilities

To make the Fax Viewer complete, you'll need to acquire the third-party tools discussed so far (or some reasonable alternatives): *mgetty*, *g3topbm*, *pnmtops*, and *gs*. You should be able to get them from the URLs we mentioned earlier. You may also want to search for alternatives that might reduce the number of steps in the conversion process.

Where your third-party applications get installed and who owns them will depend on their requirements and the *make*files supplied with the individual packages. Table 11-3 shows where we've placed the tools for our own Fax Viewer. These suggestions may help you debug any UNIX permissions problems.

Remember: The best way to test UNIX permissions problems is to use the *su* command to become the user who needs to be able to run the program.

Table 11-3
Sample location, ownership, and permissions for third-party utilities

File	Location	Ownership	Permissions
mgetty	/usr/local/sbin	root.root	700 or -rwx------
g3topbm	/usr/local/bin	bin.bin	755 or -rwxr-xr-x
pnmtops	/usr/local/bin	bin.bin	755 or -rwxr-xr-x
gs	/usr/bin	root.bin	755 or -rwxr-xr-x

FUTURE DIRECTIONS FOR THE FAX VIEWER

By now you've probably thought of several features you would like to add to this raw Fax Viewer. We have, too, and here are a few of our ideas.

A Print Option

It's nice being able to view your faxes without printing them. However, it's still useful to obtain a hardcopy every now and then. We could add a Print button to the fax Administration Screen that converts our GIF files *back* into PostScript format for printing. This may take a little more processing time than just keeping the original PostScript files around, but it will definitely save hard drive space! If you implement the Print button, you can decide whether to convert again each time you want to print, or to consume more disk space all the time by storing all of the PostScript files.

A Fax Forwarding Option

From the Admin Screen, a fax Forwarding button could allow you to fax a received fax to someone else. It would permit a fax number to be entered, convert the GIF back into G3, and use *sendfax* to send the fax (see Chapter 19, "A Customer Quote Generator," for more on *sendfax* and creating cover sheets).

An E-Mail Option

This would be rather simple to add. From the Admin Screen you could fill in an e-mail address, select your faxes, and click the E-Mail button. It would then send the GIF file as a MIME attachment to the specified e-mail address. This would allow a single person to distribute faxes to a group of people.

SUMMARY

As you can see, there are a variety of ways to customize this fax gateway for your organization. The CGI we've discussed here is highly configurable, and amenable to these and other changes and enhancements.

As we said at the beginning of this chapter, the Web and e-mail may someday replace fax systems. E-mail mailing lists, such as Majordomo, LISTSERV, and *Listproc*, already provide a means for electronic document distribution. However, they are difficult to manage when you are operating multiple lists on a single host. The Mailserver Front-End outlined in the next chapter can help alleviate many of the headaches caused by mailing list management!

Building a Better Interface: Majordomo Administration via the Web

*I*nternet mailing lists (commonly known as "lists") are collections of e-mail addresses used to broadcast messages to a group of subscribers. Mailing lists are used for announcements, discussions, instruction, and general communications. They're analogous to USENET discussion groups, except that they use Internet e-mail for transport instead of the Network News Transport Protocol (NNTP).

The Case for a Facelift

Lists can have subscribers numbering from just a handful to thousands upon thousands. Anyone who has ever owned a list or administered a list server (which typically handles multiple lists on a single machine), can tell you that, at any size, mailing lists always dance on the edge of chaos.

In the life of the typical list owner (the person who manages a particular mailing list), mail bounces; users get confused and send *subscribe* and *unsubscribe* messages to the entire readership instead of to the administrative account; flame wars erupt; the server goes down; or somebody's personal mailbox starts spewing 100K messages every 90 seconds—in short, anything and everything happens.

The life of a list-server administrator (the person who manages the server where the mailing lists reside) is no less interesting. Generally, the same cornucopia of misadventures descends upon the server administrator as on the list owner, but the problems come from list owners rather than subscribers.

What makes running a list so challenging is the continual, day-to-day need to deal with the list server's user interface. As the first mailing list server in existence (on BITNET), LISTSERV set the standard for syntax and conventions. Unfortunately, its interface is neither easy to use nor pleasant to work with, thanks in part to its VAX ancestry. *Listproc*, as a clone of LISTSERV that runs on UNIX servers, is no better. List creation and configuration on these servers entails editing a "config" file, with syntax like this:

```
list ice-weasels ice-weasels@outer.net singe@outer.net \
  password -m 25 -M -c
header ice-weasels {
  X-Mailer:              # Preserve the mailer line.
  X-Organization:        # Save some stuff about the person sending.
}
default ice-weasels{
mail = ack
address = fixed
}
batch 7 8
manager singe@outer.net
password bigsecret
comment  ice-weasels # At night, the ice weasels come.
serverd -l 20 -e -i 300
digest ice-weasels 1000 24
restriction 20
frequency 60
mailmethod system
option bsd_ps
option bsd_mail
option relaxed_syntax
```

This is about as unfriendly as managing a server gets. Now, imagine this many lines and more for each of the twenty-odd lists you support, all jumbled into a single configuration file.

When it comes to list owners controlling their own lists, they're usually limited to requesting lists of current subscribers, subscribing and unsubscribing members through a command-line interface (one command per line, please), approving messages before broadcast, providing descriptions of individual lists, and, in some cases, forcing digest creation, all through an e-mail interface. *Listproc* supports a new, interactive interface that is accessible using a telnet-like client, but still offers only the command-line approach to managing the lists under the server's control.

LISTSERV and *Listproc* enjoyed nearly exclusive control of the mailing list world for a number of years. More recently, there has been a challenger to the mailing list throne, Majordomo. Written in Perl by Brent Chapman (*brent@GreatCircle.COM*), Majordomo delivers numerous advantages over LISTSERV and *Listproc,* but retains some of the most onerous features that are apparently required from list servers.

Majordomo's primary advantage is its development platform. Because it was written almost entirely in Perl, it can theoretically be used on any platform that supports Perl. By contrast, LISTSERV runs primarily on VAXen, and *Listproc* needs to be compiled for your particular flavor of UNIX before it can be used. If *Listproc* hasn't been ported to your flavor, you're in for a real adventure!

Perhaps owing to its dependence on a stress-tested, flexible, interpreted language like Perl, Majordomo seems more stable and reliable than *Listproc.* Majordomo's user and list owner interface is also slightly more friendly. Mistaken commands sent to lists are caught, in most cases, and these commands are quite readable.

Nevertheless, Majordomo still suffers from shortcomings in its interface. Listing, adding, and deleting subscribers entails sending commands via e-mail to the server and awaiting a reply. Only one subscriber can be added or deleted per command line, although multiple command lines can be processed in each e-mail message.

From the list-server administrator's point of view, things aren't much better. Creating a list is a painful chore and requires editing a configuration file almost 300 lines long, including comments. Even worse, a single list can require the creation of 11 or more mail aliases. To change the configuration of an existing list, the list owner must invariably go back and edit that huge, complex file. For list owners, manipulating subscribers requires hand-editing of text files. In short, it sucks!

...And the Web Shall Inherit the Earth

Because mailing lists are primarily Internet-based services, it seems natural that we'd look to the Web for a friendlier medium in which to create a new, improved interface.

Anyone who has been around the Internet for a while might feel threatened when the status quo is rocked so thoroughly by a newcomer protocol like HTTP. And the truth is that *httpd* and HTML *are* changing the Internet as a whole to reflect their own abilities. Bit by bit the entire Internet really is becoming a giant collection of Web sites.

A graphical client/server interface, like that provided over the Web, is the perfect solution to list-server interface problems because of the Web's ability to address the following points:

- The relative flexibility of the back-end, or CGI, portion of the interface allows it to interact with the list-server software with little or no modification to existing programs.

- The graphical, interactive nature of the Web lends itself to the simplicity and manageability that mailing lists so desperately need.

- A single interface can deliver sufficient flexibility to service the needs of users, list owners, and list-server administrators.

- The built-in capabilities of Web servers and clients offer some degree of security and continued control over list servers.

A Web interface to a mailing list server greatly improves usability to end users as well because it insulates them from the details of commands and their syntaxes, while improving access and control for both list owners and list-server administrators.

Pearls Before Perls

Because the fit between mailing lists and the Web is so perfect, there's no reason for us not to pursue the design and creation of an application that embodies that fit. Instead of building an interface to mailing lists as a general class, however, and risking biting off more than we can chew, let's narrow the field to one mailing list in particular. If you noticed that we had fewer complaints about Majordomo in the previous section, you won't be surprised by the package we'll write the CGI for—namely, Majordomo.

In addition to those advantages covered earlier, Majordomo is a natural choice for another reason: we'll be developing the CGI in Perl. Should we need to customize any part of the Majordomo itself, we'll already be speaking the right language. Also, our experience is that Majordomo subscriber lists tend to be smaller than LISTSERV or *Listproc* lists, which makes our design goals easier to meet. Once we have a solid code base, we can stretch out to larger lists, and test performance and reliability under new operating conditions.

Maitre-d: Design Goals

Our previous discussion of interface weaknesses illustrates that the most difficult mailing-list tasks faced by list owners and list-server administrators are manipulating subscribers—adding them to a list, deleting them, or editing their information—creating new lists; and changing the configuration of existing lists.

To set our sights realistically, we used this assessment of the most pronounced weaknesses in list servers to inform our design goals and worked toward correcting them with our CGI package. The result was Maitre-d, a Perl-based CGI that provides a Web front-end to Majordomo for list owners and list-server administrators.

To demonstrate some of the issues you might face when retrofitting a new interface around existing code, we'll take you on a guided tour of the Maitre-d program. At around 1,400 lines, this script is *not* short; but we believe the depth and breadth of the project speaks to many potentials aspects of other possible retrofitting exercises. Without too much effort you should be able to adapt Maitre-d to your own Web site and Majordomo server.

Here's what we cover in the remainder of this chapter:

- We'll begin at the beginning: the first steps taken from abstract design goals to concrete code implementation. We hope to impart a sense of the sometimes painful moments in a programmer's life, before the first keystrokes are on the canvas, and explain the rationale behind the ideas that initially shaped our program design.

- Next is the grand tour of the code, with special attention to the techniques we used both for creating a CGI-mediated Web interface and for suturing that interface onto an existing UNIX-based service.

- Finally, this chapter closes with a discussion regarding the installation of Maitre-d at your own site, both in terms of configuration and possible porting issues.

PRE-CODE BLUES

The most challenging part for any programmer undertaking a project like this is the time spent before a single line of code is ever written. This is the stage that has the most potential to throw you into a funk.

Ideally, your design will lay a foundation upon which you can not only achieve all your stated design goals, but also do so in a way that will be easy to extend and maintain once the initial code is complete. The overriding aim is elegance, an often elusive quality that implies code that finds the path of least resistance from point A to point B. This is not necessarily the most direct path, but most certainly the path that requires the most careful thought, cleverness, and inspiration to find and follow to a successful conclusion.

While we can't claim to have all these programming virtues (that's for someone else to point out, so that we can maintain our humility), we did spend a long while thinking about how to design this program. Ease of use was paramount, as was the flexibility needed to produce a tool aimed at both list owners and server administrators.

Security was an obvious concern, given that we wanted to allow for list creation and modification using Maitre-d via the Web. To validate the list owner and server administrator, we need to force them to log in using an e-mail address and password. The design challenge was how to access that information securely on the server side of the Web transaction, so that a script being run by an authorized WWW user could read in the identification data, but keep that same information hidden from an unauthorized user.

Once validated, the script needed to adjust its behavior depending on the role (list owner or server administrator) of whomever had just logged in. This implied that the script needed to perform its own authentication and not rely on any server-level security system.

In addition, we considered the program's ability to interact with the Majordomo system, specifically to ensure that it knew all the lists currently available to the user, and that it could create new lists and edit existing configurations and subscriber lists.

Finally, in the interests of portability and ease of use, we decided to design Maitre-d as a single Perl script. This meant the script would call itself repeatedly, so we had to modify the script's behavior according to the arguments passed during each call. This also meant we had to make the script capable of running when called via both GET and POST methods, extract its variables properly, and respond accordingly, no matter which method was used.

This last decision represents a deliberate experiment, since most CGI applications consist of a collection of smaller scripts rather than a single large one. There are various reasons for this, chiefly as a response to the connectionless nature of Web applications. Every time the client connects to the script we have to treat it as a separate and discrete event, even if it takes place in the middle of a complex series of client/server transactions.

Every time a script returns information to a client, that information must be complete and must lead the client to the next connection point in the chain, independent of any future actions on the part of the script. That's why it's sometimes simpler when developing a Web application with CGIs, to design each segment of the transactional chain as a separate script, to keep all their behaviors as separate and distinct as their interactions with Web clients will be.

However, each additional script in a package multiplies the complexities of its installation and maintenance. Therefore, it's theoretically desirable to roll the entire package into one script. Our script represents a text of that theory.

The potential downfall in this experiment is a loss of performance or reliability. The finished Maitre-d script weighs in at over 1,400 lines, which is quite a bit larger than the largest piece of the calendar package (covered in Chapter 13). The effects of this script on your system will vary widely depending on the individual system setup and load that you're dealing with, as well as other things that influence perceived speed over the Internet.

TIPTOE THROUGH THE CODE

Developing for the Web is always an adventure. Because it's still a new and constantly evolving venue, the Web's effect on even the most mundane client/server applications can rarely be accurately gauged in advance. The only thing to do is to dive into the code, starting with a skeleton of what you think the script should end up looking like and fleshing out features one by one.

As we went along here, we kept glancing up, reassessing our progress toward our final destination, and making necessary adjustments. Somehow, we arrived at the end, with a smoothly running, finished application, and a complete understanding of the real algorithm it took to solve our initial problem.

We can't imagine that your experiences will be that much different. But in an effort to reveal the development and inner workings of Maitre-d, we'll parallel our developmental path with insightful commentary as much as we can.

Preamble

Our code begins, as all Perl scripts do, with the stuff that instructs the shell to run Perl and feed the remainder of the script to it. In this case we'll be using Perl 4.036. The reason we don't use Perl 5 is simple: The core code for the script began evolving before Perl 5 was widely available. This script should run under Perl 5 just fine, except for the added need to escape the "at" sign (@) in a scalar context (otherwise, Perl 5 will interpret this as an array reference).

```
#!/usr/local/bin/Perl
#! Please change to match Perl's location on your system
#
#  Maitre-d (A Web Front-End for Majordomo)
#
# Copyright (C) 1995 Sebastian Hassinger <singe@outer.net>
# All rights reserved.
```

We've deleted the full copyright notice and other introductory comments. As we jump into the script, look for the standard CGI code: unbuffering output and printing the HTTP headers. This is followed by a number of variable initializations, both localization constants and runtime arguments.

```
$| = 1;                    # output NOT buffered
print "Content-Type: text/html\n\n";
#########################################

open (STDERR, ">>Maitre-d.errors");
```

```
      # Keep track of OS-generated errors.

 #! Change configurations in next 2 lines to reflect your system
 #! setup.
 $host     = "www.outer.net";   # Web host name.
 $mailhost = "mail.outer.net";  # Name used for majordomo host, if
                                # different than the Web server.

 $aliasfile = "/usr/lib/aliases";
    # alias file used by your server's sendmail or equivalent
    # must be made writable by majordomo if you wish to create
    # mail aliases through Web.

 $newaliases = "/usr/ucb/newaliases";
    # full path to program used to rebuild aliases database
 $wrapper = "/usr/local/majordomo/bin/wrapper";
    # full path to majordomo wrapper program - for use in aliases
 $archivepath = "/usr/local/majordomo/archive";
    # full path to archive directory, for same use as above
 $majorodomopath = "/usr/local/majordomo/";
    # full path to majordomo root directory
 $majordomohome = "/home/majordomo";
    # path to majordomo's lists directory
 $maitred = "/cgi-bin/Maitre-d/Maitre-d.pl";
    # URL path to Maitre-d program
 $majordomouser = 30;
 $majordomogroup = 2;
    # numeric uid and gid of majordomo user and group
 $command = $ARGV[0];  # capture command-line arguments
 chop($date = `/bin/date`);
    # for the 'this page created' line at the bottom
```

Initialization and Security

Most of these constants should be changed to reflect your server's OS, the paths to the Majordomo home directory, etc. Please note the path to the mail aliases file. If desired, Maitre-d adds all the necessary aliases to this file for each new mailing list created, and can even rebuild the aliases file as well.

This requires that the HTTP server's user ID have write access to the file. This user is generally *www* and the group *httpd*, so changing the aliases file to include this group and giving the group write access is all that's needed. However, some administrators may get nervous when granting this kind of Web-accessibility to a system-critical file. Given proper security measures, these fears can be allayed.

The script itself handles authentication by comparing the password entered in the Web form against a password from the list's config file, or from the Majordomo server's config file. If these files are readable only by the Majordomo user and the *www* group, you will benefit from operating system ownership and permission security. In addition, we suggest you protect this CGI script with a login name and password (see the next paragraph for the details).

Using the NCSA-based HTTP servers, including *Netsite*, all that's necessary to establish password protection for the CGI is to place an ".htaccess" file in the directory where the script resides. This file specifies those users allowed access to the script when called by GET and POST methods, and specifies where their encrypted passwords reside. This approach lets you give out a common login name and password to all the list administrators or create individual accounts for everyone who needs access, as you see fit.

With both UNIX OS permissions and HTTP user authentication at work, system administrators can feel secure that Maitre-d's features will be used only by those who should be using them.

POST or GET?

In the next chunk of code, we determine whether the script is being called in a form submission context. If it is, we'll extract the form data using our old standby, Brigitte Jellinek's *formlib.pl*.

```
if ($command) { # The command-line arguments flag that this has
                # been called from a form action, therefore, we
                # need to extract form data.

  require "/www/cgi-bin/formlib.pl";
      # This path will need to be changed,if you don't keep
      # formlib.pl in the usual place.
&GetFormArgs();
      # parse arguments passed from FORM (now in %in)
      $ENV{PATH_INFO} ne '' && &GetPathArgs($ENV{PATH_INFO});
  # extract path args
  ...} #additional code deleted to shorten this example
```

For the bulk of the script, we'll be testing for the presence of variables or their values to determine what a user's submission is supposed to do. Once we've checked to see if any of Maitre-d's features are being used, we take care of non-form submissions.

A Simple Menu and a Complex Login

Next, we dip into the first two form submission commands: the admin menu and login authentication. Notice that there isn't a terribly cohesive structure to the chunks of code that represent the various actions Maitre-d can take; that's largely due to the stateless nature of HTTP and CGI.

Since each time the script is run we need to re-identify the user, determine the desires of the user, and correctly process the data that he or she has submitted, there aren't any assumptions or shortcuts we can take through the algorithm. The required structure depends on the order in which we implemented features, and to some degree the flow the data itself dictates for the script. This rough structure is then polished somewhat for logic and readability.

```
if  ($in{ADMIN}) { # display admin menu for list

    $title = "Administer $in{ADMIN}";
    &html_head;

    &admin_menu ("$in{ADMIN}", "$in{OWNER_EMAIL}");
```

The variable $in{ADMIN} represents the name of a submit button that appears on several of the interface forms. When clicked, the associated variable is defined; thus, this if statement will be evaluated as true. The chunk of code executed calls a subroutine that spits out the HTML code for the top of the return page and the administrator's menu. These subroutines let us return the same HTML code from different points in the script.

```
} elsif  ($command eq "login") {
    # Our user has submitted a request to login as either the
    # majordomo owner or administrator. We must now validate
    # the e-mail/password and return admin page or deny access.

    if ($in{LOGIN} eq "owner") { # They checked the majordomo owner
                        # radio button—validate e-mail
                        # address and password for the Majordomo
                        # owner.
open (OWNER, ".majordomo.e-mail");
        # The password file is created specifically for
        # Maitre-d's use. It takes the form:
        # [e-mail address][TAB][password]
        # This file lives in the same directory as the script itself.
    chop ($owner = <OWNER>);
    close OWNER;
```

```
    @owner = split (/\t/, $owner);
      # $owner[0] is now e-mail address, $owner[1] is the password

    if (($in{PASSWORD} eq $owner[1]) &&
      ($in{EMAIL} eq $owner[0])) { # login succeeded
        $title = "Majordomo Owner Administration : $host";
        &html_head;
        &owner_menu ($in{EMAIL});
        # Call the subroutine to return the owner's menu
        # page, with his/her e-mail address as the argument.
  } else {
        # Login failed, return an error page and allow the
        # user to return to the login page.
        $title = "Owner Login Failed";
        &html_head;
        print "<H1>ERROR</H1>\n";
        print "<P><FONT SIZE=+1><B>E-mail address or password ",
          "supplied is incorrect.</B></FONT><P>\n";
        print "<HR>Return to <A HREF=\"http://$host/$maitred",
          "\">login page</A>";
    }
  } else { # logging into a specific list as owner
    open (PASS, "$majordomohome/$in{LOGIN}.config");
      # open list's config file to retrieve list's password
    while (<PASS>) {
      if (/admin_passwd\s*=\s*(.*)$/) {
        # found line with password, extract it
        $password = $1;
      }
    }
    close PASS;
    open (MANAGER, ".$in{LOGIN}.e-mail");
    # Here's the Maitre-d specific config file; it contains
    # the list owner's e-mail address—this is necessary since
    # the owner's e-mail address does not appear in the
    # Majordomo list config file. Each list that you wish to
    # administer via the Web needs a file in the Maitre-d
    # directory that contains the list admin's e-mail address.
    # Without it, the administrator can't log into Maitre-d.

    chop ($manager = <MANAGER>);
    close MANAGER;
    if ($password eq $in{PASSWORD} &&
      ($in{EMAIL} eq $manager)) { # login succeeded
      $title = "Logged into $in{LOGIN}";
      &html_head;
      &admin_menu($in{LOGIN}, $in{EMAIL});
        # Call the subroutine to display the admin menu.
```

```
    } else { # login failed
     $title = "Login for $in{LOGIN} failed";
     &html_head;
     print "<FONT SIZE=+1>E-mail address or password",
       "incorrect</FONT><P><B>Login ",
       "Failed</B><HR><I>Return to",
       "<A HREF=\"http://$host/cgi-bin/Maitre-d/",
       "Maitre-d.pl\">Majordomo Login</A></I>";
    }
   }
```

Authentication is handled in a straightforward manner: by reading the appropriate file, either the ".majordomo.e-mail" file, or the "<listname>.config" and ".<listname>.e-mail" files, and comparing the contents against the submitted e-mail and password. If they match, the user is handed either the owner menu (see Figure 12-1) or the list administrator's menu (see Figure 12-2), as appropriate. If they don't match, an error message is returned instead.

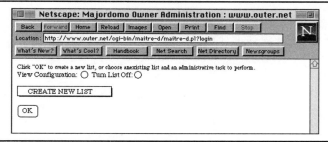

Figure 12-1

Maitre-d's Majordomo owner menu allows you to create a new list, view the config file of an existing list, or disable a list.

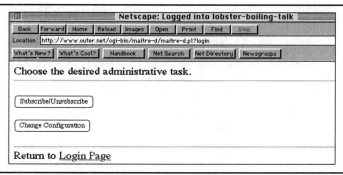

Figure 12-2

Maitre-d's list administrator menu provides task options for existing lists.

Majordomo Owner Commands

All the commands that the Majordomo owner can possibly submit are handled by the following section of code. The form that is presented to the Majordomo owner has a submit button named OWNER, so our test for that variable tells us if that is the form the CGI is being run from.

The owner menu allows for the creation of new lists, the viewing of config files for existing lists, or disabling lists. Which of these three actions is requested is tested first by checking the value passed from the form's select input. If the user selected Create New List, then the proper actions for list creation will be initiated. If an existing list name is selected instead, the radio buttons for viewing a list's configuration or disabling a list are tested to see if they're checked. If one or another radio button is selected, the appropriate actions are taken.

```
} elsif ($in{OWNER}) {
# Handle majordomo owner commands—create new lists, view
# config files for existing lists, or temporarily disable lists.

if ($in{LISTNAME} eq "CREATE NEW LIST") {
# Code chunk to start creating a new list.

$title = "Creating new list";
&html_head;
# Subroutine that outputs the top of the return page.

print "<FORM ACTION=\"http://$host/cgi-bin/Maitre-d/",
    "Maitre-d.pl?genlist\" METHOD=\"POST\">\n";
# Notice our FORM ACTION points back at Maitre-d again
# with the argument "genlist" to trigger the list
# creation behavior.
```

With our form set up, we'll spit back the HTML form inputs to capture the list creation data (see Figure 12-3).

The next chunk of code captures the basic information about the list—its name, its owner's e-mail address, etc. Then we give the owner checkboxes to indicate whether Maitre-d should generate aliases for the list, a list archive, or a digest for the list. Following that, we assign the default list-configuration values to the variables that fill out the configuration form. Thus, when we present the list configuration form to the owner, it will arrive with the defaults already supplied. Finally, we call the subroutine that presents the form for all remaining list options.

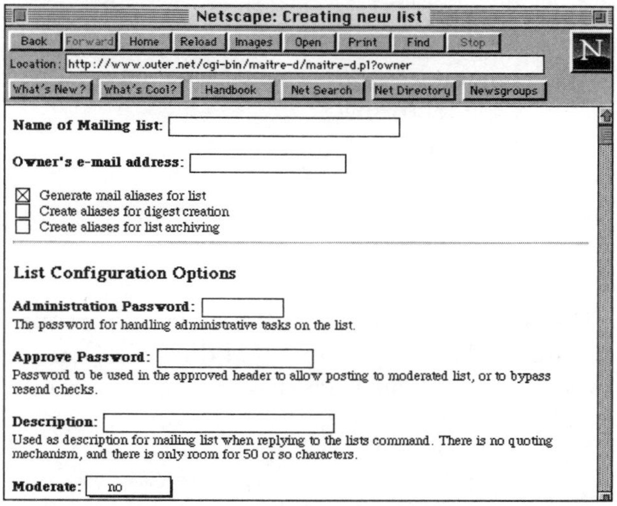

Figure 12-3

Maitre-d's list creation form.

```
print "<B>Name of Mailing list:</B> <INPUT TYPE=\"text\"",
    " NAME=\"LISTNAME\" SIZE=\"30\" MAXLENGTH=\"40\">",
    "<BR><P>";
print "<B>Owner's e-mail address:</B> <INPUT TYPE=\"text\"",
    " NAME=\"OWNER_EMAIL\" SIZE=\"20\" ",
    "MAXLENGTH=\"20\"><P>";
print "<INPUT TYPE=\"checkbox\" ",
    "NAME=\"MAKEALIASES\" CHECKED>";
print " Generate mail aliases for list<BR>";
print "<INPUT TYPE=\"checkbox\" NAME=\"DIGESTLIST\" >";
print " Create aliases for digest creation<BR>";
print "<INPUT TYPE=\"checkbox\" NAME=\"ARCHIVELIST\" >";
print " Create aliases for list archiving<BR>";

# Set up list defaults to pass to the list config subroutine.

$MODERATE = "no";
$SUBSCRIBE_POLICY = "open";
$PRIVATE_GET = "no";
$PRIVATE_INDEX = "no";
$PRIVATE_INFO = "no";
$PRIVATE_WHICH = "no";
$PRIVATE_WHO = "no";
$ADMINISTRIVIA = "yes";
```

```
$DATE_INFO = "yes";
$DEBUG = "no";
$DIGEST_ISSUE = 1;
$DIGEST_VOLUME = 1;
$MAXLENGTH = 40000;
$MUNGEDOMAIN = "no";
$PRECEDENCE = "bulk";
$PURGE_RECEIVED = "no";
$STRIP = "yes";
&configure_list;
```

The next command we must handle is the request to redisplay the owner menu. This may be called at the end of various owner actions; for example, once the owner finishes creating a new list, he or she can select a button that leads back here.

```
} elsif ($in{OWNER} eq "Majordomo Owner Page") {

&owner_menu ($in{OWNER_EMAIL});
  # redisplay owner menu
```

The view config option gives the Majordomo owner an easy way to check the status of a given list, including password examination. This allows the Majordomo owner to backtrack to the login form (we'll get to that portion of the code later) and log in as the owner of a list, with all associated privileges. For us, this represented a graceful way out of trying to duplicate all the list owner features for the Majordomo owner.

```
} elsif ($in{LISTADMIN} eq "view config") {

$title = "Configuration file for $in{LISTNAME}";
&html_head;

open (CONFIG, "$majordomohome/$in{LISTNAME}.config");
  # open list's config file for reading

print "<H3>$in{LISTNAME} Configuration</H3><PRE>";

print while <CONFIG>;

close CONFIG;

print "</PRE>";

print "<FORM ACTION=\"http://$host$maitred?owner\" METHOD=",
```

```
          "\"POST\">\n";
print "<INPUT TYPE=\"hidden\" NAME=\"OWNER_EMAIL\" VALUE=",
          "\"$in{OWNER_EMAIL}\">\n";
print "<HR>Return to <INPUT TYPE=",
          "\"submit\" NAME=\"OWNER\" VALUE=\"Majordomo",
          " Owner Page\">";
print "</FORM>\n";
          # The preceding is a mini-form used to return
          # the owner to the menu code we just saw above. The
          # hidden input field is used to pass the owner's
          # e-mail address, as an added security precaution.
```

Disabling Lists

Anyone who's owned a mailing list, or even been a subscriber for any appreciable amount of time, has experienced the problem that is addressed by our next feature. Either through some glitch in the complex collection of Internet mail delivery systems, or a bug in a digest or other program that monitors the list, a message may be sent repeatedly to every recipient on the list.

This can be an extreme annoyance, or even a hazard to other systems, because such messages can quickly clog hard drives and interrupt other services. To allow the Majordomo owner to quickly resolve such a situation, Maitre-d offers the ability to disable a list in a way that is easily reversible once the offending mail bomb is defused. It does this by making the subscriber list and config file invisible, using the UNIX "dotfile" convention for making files disappear. Because Majordomo uses *sendmail* (or some equivalent) to access the subscriber list, and it uses the UNIX file system, the list mail alias will expand out to zero recipients and no messages will be delivered!

Once the situation is resolved, re-enabling the list is simple: remove the leading period from any file in the Majordomo list directory that contains a list name. Now when *sendmail* expands the list alias, it can find the subscriber file and send messages out to the entire list.

We decided against rolling this re-enablement into the feature set of Maitre-d for the following reason: When this type of situation develops, it's usually necessary to manually clean up queue files, archives, and the like before re-enabling a list. Therefore, the Majordomo owner will be at the UNIX command line, troubleshooting and ironing out problems, at a time when the list can be turned back on. It would be more inconvenient to force a return to the Web interface to turn the list back on than to do it manually.

```perl
} elsif ($in{LISTADMIN} eq "turn off") {
    # Temporarily disable the list by moving the files to
    # invisible files of the same name (i.e., "subscribers"
    # to ".subscribers").

    $title = "Disable $in{LISTNAME}";
    &html_head;

    opendir (LISTS, "$majordomohome");
    while ($file = readdir LISTS) {
        # Using opendir and readdir in Perl is a very
        # efficient way to retrieve the contents of
        # a directory. Each file is assigned to $file in
        # turn.

        if ($file =~ /^$in{LISTNAME}/) {
            # Read through the files in the Majordomo list
            # directory. When we find the files that begin
            # with the list's name (i.e., <listname>,
            # <listname>.config), rename the file to an
            # "invisible" version with the same name.

            print "Moving <B>$file</B> to ",
              "<B>.$file</B><BR>";
            rename ("$majordomohome/$file",
                  "$majordomohome/.$file");
        }
    }
    closedir LISTS;
    print "<FORM ACTION=\"http://$host$maitred?owner\" METHOD=",
        "\"POST\">\n";
    print "<INPUT TYPE=\"hidden\" NAME=\"OWNER_EMAIL\" VALUE=",
        "\"$in{OWNER_EMAIL}\">\n";
    print "<HR>Return to <INPUT TYPE=",
        "\"submit\" NAME=\"OWNER\" VALUE=\"Majordomo ",
        "Owner Page\">";
    print "</FORM>\n";
    # once again, the mini-form that leads back to the owner
    # menu
}
print "<HR>Return to <A HREF=\"http://$host/cgi-bin/Maitre-d",
    "/Maitre-d.pl\">Majordomo Login Page</A>.";
# After this action we give the owner the option to jump back to
# the Maitre-d login page, in case he/she needs to perform list
# owner duties.
```

Generating a New List in Majordomo

Once all the core list definitions and list configuration options have been set, the submit button at the bottom of the form leads to this next section of code. If you recall, the FORM ACTION on the list generation form above calls Maitre-d, in the closest thing to recursion that exists in CGIs, with the command-line argument genlist. This value becomes the trigger for the following conditional:

```
} elsif ($command eq "genlist") {
  # Generate list aliases and config file from values entered in
  # a form.

  if (-e "$majordomohome/$in{LISTNAME}.config") {
    # Check to see if a list already exists with this name.

    $title = "List $in{LISTNAME} Already Exists";
    &html_head;
    print "<H1>ERROR</H1>",
        "<FONT SIZE=+2>Mailing list with name: ",
        "<B>$in{LISTNAME}",
        "</B> already exists.</FONT><P>",
        "<B>Cannot overwrite list. Try again ",
        "with a different name.</B>";
```

After handling error correction, we move on to the meat of creating a new list. First, we take care of the business of mail aliases. Majordomo uses a large number of mail aliases for the operation of any given list. This is a clever way to make *sendmail* do a lot of the grunt work of operating a mailing list with its proven, robust capabilities, but mail aliases are also a real pain to create by hand.

If the owner checked the box for generating aliases for the list and, optionally, the ones for the list's archive and digest, we use the basic values provided, such as its name and its owner's e-mail address, to modify a standard alias boilerplate. If you prefer a different format for Majordomo aliases, feel free to substitute it in place of our own in the lines that follow.

```
} else { # This is a new list after all, let's create it.

  $title = "$in{LISTNAME} Created";
  &html_head;

  print "<FORM ACTION=\"http://$host$maitred?",
      "owner\" METHOD=\"POST\">\n";
```

```
# This form leads back to the owner menu again.

if ($in{MAKEALIASES}) {
  # If the creator has requested mail aliases by
  # clicking on the checkbox, generate
  # standard majordomo aliases.

  $OWNER_EMAIL = $in{OWNER_EMAIL};
  $LISTNAME = $in{LISTNAME};

  if ($in{SENDER}) { # If the creator specified a value
       # for sender, use it in the aliases.

    $SENDER = $in{SENDER}
  } else { # otherwise use default sender,
      # "owner-<listname>"

    $SENDER = "owner-" . $LISTNAME
  }

  $outgoing = "";
  $file_counter = 0;

  while (-e "aliases-$file_counter") {
    # Store the aliases in a temporary file, taking
    # care not to overwrite the temp file of any
    # other lists being created.

    $file_counter++;

  }

  &lock_file ("lock", "aliases-$file_counter");
    # Lock aliases file before proceeding.

  open (ALIASES, ">aliases-$file_counter");

  print ALIASES "# Aliases generated for $LISTNAME by",
    " Maitre-d.pl on $date\n",
    "$LISTNAME-owner:$OWNER_EMAIL\n",
    "$LISTNAME-approval:$LISTNAME-owner\n",
    "$SENDER:$LISTNAME-owner\n",
    "$LISTNAME:\"|${wrapper} resend -p ",
    "$in{PRECEDENCE} ",
    "-l $LISTNAME -h $mailhost $LISTNAME-",
    "outgoing\"\n",
    "$LISTNAME-request:\"|${wrapper} majordomo ",
```

```
  "-l $LISTNAME\"\n";

if ($in{ARCHIVELIST}) {
  # user wants list to be archived, generate
  # archive aliases

  print ALIASES
    "$LISTNAME-archive: \"|${wrapper} ",
    "archive.pl -f $archivepath/$LISTNAME -m ",
    "-a\"\n";

  $outgoing = ", $LISTNAME-archive, \"| $wrapper".
      " digest.pl -r -C -l\"";
    # Append to the outgoing variable for
    # creating the outgoing alias at the end.
}

if ($in{DIGESTLIST}) {
  # Owner wants a digest created; generate
  # appropriate aliases.

  print ALIASES "$LISTNAME-digest:$LISTNAME\n",
   "$LISTNAME-digest-outgoing: :include:",
   "$majordomohome/",
   "$LISTNAME-digest\n",
   "$LISTNAME-digest-request: ",
   "\"|$wrapper request-",
   "answer $LISTNAME-digest\"\n",
   "$LISTNAME-digest-approval:",
   "$LISTNAME-approval\n";

  $outgoing .= ", $LISTNAME-digest ".
      "$LISTNAME-digest-outgoing";
    # Append digest info to outgoing variable
    # for the final alias.
}
print ALIASES "$LISTNAME-outgoing: :include:",
 "$majordomohome/$LISTNAME$outgoing\n";
      # Last alias is standard majorodomo
      # listname-outgoing with the addition of
      # the archive and digest values, if
      # existing.

close ALIASES;

&lock_file ("unlock", "aliases-$file_counter");
```

```
open (ALIASES, "aliases-$file_counter");
  # Open aliases file for reading - to provide
  # feedback to the list's creator.

print "<H3>Majordomo mail aliases</H3><PRE>";

print while <ALIASES>;

print "</PRE>";

close ALIASES;

if (-w "$aliasfile") {
# If alias file is writable by the user www, offer to
# add the aliases to the file.

  print "<HR><B>If desired, the aliases can be",
    "added to the $aliasfile and the alias ",
    "database can be rebuilt.</B><BR>",
    "<INPUT TYPE=\"hidden\" NAME",
    "=\"FILENUM\" VALUE=\"$file_counter\">\n";
  print "<INPUT TYPE=\"submit\"",
    " NAME=\"WRITEALIASES\" ",
    "VALUE=\"Make Mail Aliases\"><BR>";
} else {
  # Alias file not writable; warn user to add them
  # manually for list to work.

  print "<H3>Alias file ($aliasfile) is not",
    "writable.";
  print "</H3><B>You must add the above aliases ",
    "to the mail aliases file ",
    "manually.</B>\n<BR>";

  unlink "aliases-$file_counter";
    # We can delete the aliases file since we
    # can't do any more with it.
  }
}
```

With the aliases generated, we can turn to creating the list so that Majordomo itself knows it exists. A Majordomo list consists of two files: a subscriber file, named the same as the list itself, and a configuration file, named "<listname>.config". First we cover the subscriber file, so that an empty file exists, and next we write out all the configuration option values into the format of the Majordomo mailing list config file.

```
open (SUBSCRIBERS, ">$majordomohome/$in{LISTNAME}");
close SUBSCRIBERS;
# Touch list's subscriber file to make sure it exists.

&secure_file ("$majordomohome/$in{LISTNAME}");
# Change user and group permissions to make it work.

&write_to_config;
    # Write values out to list's config file—this is a
    # subroutine since the config file needs to be written
    # out when the list owner changes its values, as well.

print "<HR><H3>Majordomo Config file for ",
  "$in{LISTNAME}</H3><PRE>";

open (CONFIG, "$majordomohome/$in{LISTNAME}.config");
    # Now that the config file has be written, echo new
    # config values back to user.

print while <CONFIG>;
close CONFIG;

print "</PRE><HR>";

print "<INPUT TYPE=\"hidden\" NAME=\"OWNER_EMAIL\" VALUE=",
    "\"$in{OWNER_EMAIL}\">";
print "<HR>Return to <INPUT TYPE=",
    "\"submit\" NAME=\"OWNER\" VALUE=\"Majordomo",
    " Owner Page\">";
print "</FORM>";

} # end creating new list
```

Now our basic list creation is done. Please notice that there were two buttons that lead off the list creation feedback page (see Figure 12-4).

The standard miniform with a button that leads back to the owner menu is situated at the bottom of the page. In addition, there's a button that leads to a completely different action on Maitre-d's part. This button is located at the bottom of the alias generation list and causes Maitre-d to add new aliases to the master aliases file and to rebuild the database from this file. We'll look at this section of code next.

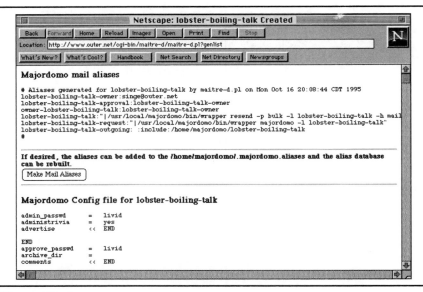

Figure 12-4
The list creation feedback page.

Also Known as Aliases

The alias creation code is tricky because the data it handles is sensitive and because of UNIX localization issues. In addition to the usual file lock, we also copy the current mail aliases file to a backup before modifying it. If some unforeseen event occurs that corrupts the modified file, the administrator always has an unmodified copy as a backup.

We use variables in place of file and program names (such as the alias file and the command for building a new aliases database) to handle the differences from one UNIX's aliases system to the next. In addition, we attempt to represent the method in which the database is rebuilt in as abstract a way as possible, to allow leeway for different implementations.

For example, even though it was written for a standard aliases file and a *newaliases* program for rebuilding the database, we've adapted Maitre-d to run on a site where the Web and mail servers are two different machines, running different operating systems. In this case, a small Perl script was added to be executed by Maitre-d on the Web server. It in turn runs *newaliases* in a *remsh* process, conveying the run-time messages from that program back to Maitre-d.

```
} elsif ($in{WRITEALIASES}) {

    # add aliases to $aliasfile and rebuild database (assumes
    # sendmail is being used, or equivalent)
    &lock_file ("lock", $aliasfile);
    open (BAKUP, ">aliases.bak");
    open (ALIASES, "$aliasfile");
    print BAKUP while <ALIASES>;
      # Create a backup of the alias file, in case of errors when
      # database is created from the edited file.
    close BAKUP;
    close ALIASES;
    &lock_file ("lock", "$aliasfile");

    open (MAILALIASES, ">>$aliasfile") || die "ARG";
    open (LISTALIASES, "aliases-$in{FILENUM}");
      # Open the temporary aliases file in the Maitre-d directory
      # using the file number passed to the script from the form
      # arguments—we embedded the file's identifying number in
      # a hidden input in the form that called the script to
      # create the aliases.
    print MAILALIASES while <LISTALIASES>;
      # add generated aliases to mail alias file
    close MAILALIASES;
    close LISTALIASES;
    unlink "aliases-$in{FILENUM}";
      # delete temporary file
    open (REBUILD_DB, "$newaliases |");
      # Rebuild mail aliases database using user-supplied command.

    while (<REBUILD_DB>) {
      # Watch for errors when rebuilding—assumes sendmail-style
      # error messages—i.e., starts with "line n:".
      if (/line [0-9]+:/) { # error message
        print "<B>ERROR</B> $_<BR>";
        $aliaserror = 1;
      }
    }
    close REBUILD_DB;
    if ($aliaserror) {
      # If an error occurred, inform user and restore backup mail
      # aliases file.
      rename ("aliases.bak", "$aliasfile");
      system ("$newaliases &");
      print "<HR><FONT SIZE=+2>Aliases not added due to errors.",
          "</FONT>";
```

```
} else {
  print "<FONT SIZE=+2>Aliases added to $aliasfile and",
    " database rebuilt."; "</FONT>";

}
print "<FORM ACTION=\"http://$host$maitred?owner\" METHOD",
  "=\"POST\">";
print "<INPUT TYPE=\"hidden\" NAME=\"OWNER_EMAIL\" VALUE=",
  "\"$in{OWNER_EMAIL}\">";
print "<HR>Return to <INPUT TYPE=",
  "\"submit\" NAME=\"OWNER\" VALUE=\"Majordomo Owner ";
print "Page\"></FORM>";
```

This concludes the Majordomo owner portion of our program. At this point we've covered login authentication, the owner menu, creating a new list, viewing the configuration of an existing list, and temporarily disabling a list. We also dipped into the list administrator's territory with the appearance of the code to authenticate list administrators and to call their menu. Next we'll delve deeper into the portions of the script that serve the needs of the list administrator.

List Administrator Tasks

Separate from all the Majordomo owner tasks we've covered until now, Maitre-d also provides an interface for the owner of a particular list. Our design goals included providing an interface for changing the configuration of one's list, and also for subscribing and unsubscribing users. Therefore, a list owner logs in using the same authentication method that the Majordomo went through and is then presented a menu of these two activities. We'll first take a tour through the code that handles subscribing and unsubscribing users to a given list. This is accessed after the list owner has logged in and been verified and has clicked on the Subscribe/Unsubscribe button. In fact, it's this string value that makes the conditional evaluate as true and causes the code to execute.

The first action the code takes is to check to see if its own variables have been submitted with suitable values. This sounds odd, until you understand that the sub/unsub code actually performs both data entry and database manipulation. That is, the code presents an interface for the list owner to add or delete subscribers only after it has checked to see if any subscribers need adding or deleting from the previous form submission. The button at the bottom of the sub/unsub section leads back to itself, with fields defined with the e-mail addresses to add or delete from the list.

Once addresses are added to or deleted from the list's file, the current subscriber list is read in from the file and displayed in a SELECT. Allowing multiple selections means that the form allows the list administrator to delete many subscribers with a single button push.

```
} elsif ($in{ACTION} eq "Subscribe/Unsubscribe") {
# Handle list owner subscribe/unsubscribe requests.

$title = "Subscribe / Unsubscribe Users";
&html_head;

print "<H3>Select one or more subscribers from list below",
    " and click Delete to unsubscribe. Type new ",
    "subscribers' addresses in the area below one at a ",
    "time and click <I>Add</I> to subscribe.</H3><P>";

if (($in{SUBSCRIBER} =~ /^.*@.*\..*$/)
  && ($in{SUBMIT} eq "Add")) {
  # If these form inputs contain valid data, this section
  # of code is being called by itself, and there are
  # subscribers to add to the list.

  if (open (SUBS, ">>$majordomohome/$in{LISTNAME}")) {
    # If we are able to open the list's subscriber file
    # for appending, print the contents of the form input
    # to the end of the list.

    print SUBS $in{SUBSCRIBER}, "\n";
    close SUBS;
    print "Subscriber $in{SUBSCRIBER} added ",
      "successfully.<P>";
  }

} elsif (($in{SUBSCRIBERS}) && ($in{SUBMIT} eq "Delete")) {
  # If, on the other hand, the delete button was clicked and
  # addresses are selected, remove the addresses from the
  # list's subscriber file.

  open (SUBS, "$majordomohome/$in{LISTNAME}");
  open (NEWSUBS, ">$in{LISTNAME}.newsubs");
    # Open a temporary new file to write the modified
    # subscriber list to.

  while (<SUBS>) {
```

```
chop;
if (($in{SUBSCRIBERS} eq $_) ||
   ($in{SUBSCRIBERS} =~ /(^|#)$_(#|$)/)) {
   # If the current address matches the list of
   # subscribers to be deleted, don't print it
   # to the new file.

   print "$_ deleted.<P>"

} else {

   print NEWSUBS $_, "\n";
   # Keep this subscriber, print address to the
   # new file.
   }
}

close SUBS;
close NEWSUBS;

system ("cp $in{LISTNAME}.newsubs" .
   " $majordomohome/$in{LISTNAME}");
unlink "$in{LISTNAME}.newsubs";


}
```

The last two lines of code copy the new file to the actual subscriber file, and with that we are done adding or deleting members as requested in the previous iteration of the form. Next we'll return the form itself.

An Informal Contest

A final note about the last two lines of code—for some reason, Perl has no internal function for copying files (at least none we know of). Perl's *rename* function is analogous to the UNIX *mv*, and, as such, does not work across file systems. So, if anyone can find a built-in Perl function that does the same work as *cp*, we'll try to make it worth your trouble in some way (not to mention how grateful we'll be—this seemingly trivial function, or rather its absence, makes the use of a system call necessary, and that makes the script much less portable). To be fair, there's a way to get away from the system call, by opening two file handles and printing from one to the other, but that seems like overkill for such a simple action.

The next portion of code builds the add/delete form for the list administrator (see Figure 12-5). This is in fact the only portion of code that actually executes the first time the "Subscribe/Unsubscribe" button is checked, since there won't otherwise be any data for the previous block of code to manipulate.

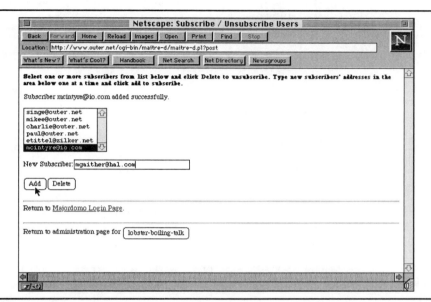

Figure 12-5
The Subscribe/Unsubscribe form interface.

```
open (SUBS, "$majordomohome/$in{LISTNAME}");

print "<FORM METHOD=\"POST\" ACTION=\"http://$host",
    "$maitred?post\">";
print "<INPUT TYPE=\"hidden\" NAME=\"LISTNAME\"",
    "VALUE=\"$in{LISTNAME}\">";
print "<INPUT TYPE=\"hidden\" NAME=\"OWNER_EMAIL\"",
    "VALUE=\"$in{OWNER_EMAIL}\">";
print "<INPUT TYPE=\"hidden\" NAME=\"ACTION\"",
    "VALUE=\"Subscribe/Unsubscribe\">";
# Our file is open for reading, our form is set up, and our
# hidden inputs are in place, we're ready to roll.

while (<SUBS>) {
  chop;
  $count++;
```

```
      $subscribers[$count] = $_;
      # Count the subscribers and load them into an array.
   }
   if ($count > 0) {

      if ($count > 20) { $size = 20 } else { $size = $count }
      # Set select size by number of subscribers, up to a maximum
      # of twenty.
      print "<SELECT NAME=\"SUBSCRIBERS\" SIZE = \"$size\" ",
         "MULTIPLE>";
      # Fill our select with the contents of the array.
      for ($loop = 1; $loop <=$count; $loop++) {
         print "<OPTION>$subscribers[$loop]";
      }
      print "</SELECT><P>";
   }
   print "New Subscriber:<INPUT TYPE=\"text\" NAME=\"SUBSCRIBER\"",
      " SIZE=\"30\" MAXLENGTH=\"70\"><P>";
   # This is the input field for capturing the address of a new
   # subscriber.
   print "<INPUT TYPE=\"submit\" NAME=\"SUBMIT\" VALUE=\"Add\">",
      "<INPUT TYPE=\"submit\" NAME=\"SUBMIT\" VALUE=\"Delete\">";
      # Two submit buttons for this form—one for add and one for
      # delete.
   print "</FORM>";
   print "<HR>Return to <A HREF=\"http://$host/cgi-bin/Maitre-d",
      "/Maitre-d.pl\">Majordomo Login Page</A>.";
   print "<FORM ACTION=\"http://$host$maitred?",
      "login\" METHOD=\"POST\">\n";
   print "<INPUT TYPE=\"hidden\" NAME=\"OWNER_EMAIL\" VALUE=",
      "\"$in{OWNER_EMAIL}\">";
   print "<HR>Return to administration page for <INPUT TYPE=",
      "\"submit\" NAME=\"ADMIN\" VALUE=\"$in{LISTNAME}\">";
   print "</FORM>";
```

The miniform at the bottom of the form interface code should look familiar: it's the list admin's equivalent of the button that the list owner clicks to return to the owner menu. In a similar fashion, this submit button returns the list administrator to the admin menu.

Edit List Configuration

It's fairly common for a list administrator to want to change some aspect of the list's configuration options. This can range from something as subtle as changing the reply-to to the sender (instead of the whole list) or as profound as changing the list from unmoderated to moderated.

In any case, it nearly always requires the server administrator's intervention to accomplish any change, due to permissions and security issues, or a lack of UNIX expertise on the list owner's part. The result is a ceaseless stream of requests for minor modifications that are often more trouble than they're worth.

With Maitre-d, we wanted to change this and allow the list owner to edit configuration values of the list directly. To do this, we read in and parse the list's configuration file and assign its values to corresponding variables. These variables supply the values that are inserted into the list configuration form: They're easily readable, understandable, and editable in that context. Once they've been modified to the list administrator's liking, the form is submitted and the configuration file is rewritten to reflect any changes.

```
} elsif ($in{ACTION} eq "Change Configuration") {
# Change configuration for a given list.
$title = "Change List Configuration";
&html_head;
print "<FORM ACTION=\"http://$host/cgi-bin/Maitre-d/",
    "Maitre-d.pl?changelist\" METHOD=\"post\">\n";
print "<INPUT TYPE=\"hidden\" VALUE=\"$in{LISTNAME}\" ",
    "NAME=\"LISTNAME\">\n";
print "<INPUT TYPE=\"hidden\" NAME=\"OWNER_EMAIL\" ",
    " VALUE=\"$in{OWNER_EMAIL}\">\n\n";
```

These two hidden form inputs conserve the authenticated state of the script—that is, they keep the list administrator logged into the list. One note about these hidden inputs: We use them in a number of areas in our scripts, to pass the client's state across the CGI.

However, Netscape has proposed an HTTP extension that may supersede this method. The proposal is for a feature called HTTP "cookies," which would be packages of variable names and values with additional information, such as an expiration date and the document hierarchy to which the cookie applies. This level of functionality duplicates our own use of hidden inputs with only a slight advantage, but the cookie proposal contains an ability to specify a need to connect with a secured server. This would be a major boon to the design of client/server CGI applications.

For the next section, we follow a dull, repetitive pattern of parsing the configuration file using a huge if/elsif statement and numerous regular expressions. As each configuration value is isolated, we assign it to the variable used to fill in the configuration form.

```perl
open (CONFIG, "$majordomohome/$in{LISTNAME}.config")
|| print "<B>Can't open config file for $in{LISTNAME}</B><BR>";

while (<CONFIG>) {

  if (/^admin_passwd\s*=\s*(.*)/) {
    $ADMIN_PASSWD = $1
  }

  elsif (/^administrivia\s*=\s*(.*)/) {
    $ADMINISTRIVIA = $1;
  }

  elsif (/^advertise/ || $advertise) {
  # This next parse is the only deviation from the two above.
  # "advertise" is a multi-line config option that ends with
  # the string "END." We parse it by adding each line to the
  # $ADVERTISE variable until we find "END".

      if (/END/) {
        if ($advertise) {
          $advertise = 0;
        } else {
          $advertise = 1;
        }
      } else {
        $ADVERTISE .= $_;
      }
  }
  elsif (/^approve_passwd\s*=\s*(.*)/) {
    $APPROVE_PASSWD = $1
  }

  elsif (/^archive_dir\s*=\s*(.*)/) {
    $ARCHIVE_DIR = $1;
  }
  elsif (/^comments/ || $comments) {
      if (/END/) {
        if ($comments) {
          $comments = 0;
        } else {
          $comments = 1;
        }
      } else {
        $COMMENTS .= $_;
      }
  }
```

```perl
elsif (/^date_info\s*=\s*(.*)/) {
  $DATE_INFO = $1
}
elsif (/^debug\s*=\s*(.*)/) {
  $DEBUG = $1
}
elsif (/^description\s*=\s*(.*)/) {
  $DESCRIPTION = $1
}
elsif (/^digest_archive\s*=\s*(.*)/) {
  $DIGEST_ARCHIVE = $1
}
elsif (/^digest_issue\s*=\s*(.*)/) {
  $DIGEST_ISSUE = $1
}
elsif (/^digest_name\s*=\s*(.*)/) {
  $DIGEST_NAME = $1
}
elsif (/^digest_rm_footer\s*=\s*(.*)/) {
  $DIGEST_RM_FOOTER = $1
}
elsif (/^digest_rm_fronter\s*=\s*(.*)/) {
  $DIGEST_RM_FRONTER = $1
}
elsif (/^digest_volume\s*=\s*(.*)/) {
  $DIGEST_VOLUME = $1
}
elsif (/^digest_work_dir\s*=\s*(.*)/) {
  $DIGEST_WORK_DIR = $1
}
elsif (/^maxlength\s*=\s*(.*)/) {
  $MAXLENGTH = $1
}
elsif (/^message_footer/ || $message_footer) {
    if (/END/) {
      if ($message_footer) {
        $message_footer = 0;
      } else {
        $message_footer = 1;
      }
    } else {
      $MESSAGE_FOOTER .= $_;
    }
}
elsif (/^message_fronter/ || $message_fronter) {
    if (/END/) {
      if ($message_fronter) {
```

```
                $message_fronter = 0;
              } else {
                $message_fronter = 1;
              }
          } else {
            $MESSAGE_FRONTER .= $_;
          }
      }
      elsif (/^message_headers/ || $message_headers) {
          if (/END/) {
            if ($message_headers) {
              $message_headers = 0;
            } else {
              $message_headers = 1;
            }
          } else {
            $MESSAGE_HEADERS .= $_;
          }
      }
      elsif (/^moderate\s*=\s*(.*)/) {
        $MODERATE = $1
      }
      elsif (/^mungedomain\s*=\s*(.*)/) {
        $MUNGEDOMAIN = $1
      }
      elsif (/^noadvertise/ || $noadvertise) {
          if (/END/) {
            if ($noadvertise) {
              $noadvertise = 0;
            } else {
              $noadvertise = 1;
            }
          } else {
            $NOADVERTISE .= $_;
          }
      }
      elsif (/^precedence\s*=\s*(.*)/) {
        $PRECEDENCE = $1
      }
      elsif (/^private_get\s*=\s*(.*)/) {
        $PRIVATE_GET = $1
      }
      elsif (/^private_index\s*=\s*(.*)/) {
        $PRIVATE_INDEX = $1
      }
      elsif (/^private_info\s*=\s*(.*)/) {
        $PRIVATE_INFO = $1
      }
```

```
    elsif (/^private_which\s*=\s*(.*)/) {
      $PRIVATE_WHICH = $1
    }
    elsif (/^private_who\s*=\s*(.*)/) {
      $PRIVATE_WHO = $1
    }
    elsif (/^purge_received\s*=\s*(.*)/) {
      $PURGE_RECEIVED = $1
    }
    elsif (/^reply_to\s*=\s*(.*)/) {
      $REPLY_TO = $1
    }
    elsif (/^resend_host\s*=\s*(.*)/) {
      $RESEND_HOST = $1
    }
    elsif (/^restrict_post\s*=\s*(.*)/) {
      $RESTRICT_POST = $1
    }
    elsif (/^sender\s*=\s*(.*)/) {
      $SENDER = $1
    }
    elsif (/^strip\s*=\s*(.*)/) {
      $STRIP = $1
    }
    elsif (/^subject_prefix\s*=\s*(.*)/) {
      $SUBJECT_PREFIX = $1
    }
    elsif (/^subscribe_policy\s*=\s*(.*)/) {
      $SUBSCRIBE_POLICY = $1
    }
} # end while

close CONFIG;

&configure_list;

# The subroutine called above inserts the variables extracted
# from the config file into the form used to enter or edit
# these values.
```

Writing Changes to the Configuration File

Once the list administrator finishes editing the list's configuration file in our handy-dandy form, the changed values are submitted and the configuration file is rewritten. This is accomplished with yet another subroutine, since the same code is used when creating a new list or editing an existing one.

```
} elsif ($command eq "changelist") {
# Change existing list's configuration.

&write_to_config;
# Write form values to configuration file.

$title = "$in{LISTNAME} Configuration File Changed";
&html_head;
print "<FONT SIZE=+2>Configuration changes made to list</FONT>",
    "<BR><BR>";

open (CONFIG, "$majordomohome/$in{LISTNAME}.config");
# Kick the new config file back to the user, so he or she can
# verify the changes have been made.

print "<PRE>";
print while <CONFIG>;
print "</PRE>";
close CONFIG;

print "<FORM ACTION=\"http://$host$maitred?",
    "owner\" METHOD=\"POST\">\n";
print "<INPUT TYPE=\"hidden\" NAME=\"OWNER_EMAIL\" VALUE=",
    "\"$in{OWNER_EMAIL}\">";
print "<HR>Return to administration page for <INPUT TYPE=",
    "\"submit\" NAME=\"ADMIN\" VALUE=\"$in{LISTNAME}\">";
print "</FORM>";

} # end changelist
```

No More Forms!

With the change configuration code out of the way, we've handled all cases in which a button click may have called Maitre-d. More accurately, we've handled all instances in which Maitre-d can be called by itself.

That done, we turn next to the code that gets called if *no* form data is present. In other words, if the script is called by a simple URL, with the GET method, our script falls through all the conditionals above and reaches this point.

This returns the login screen (see Figure 12-6) for the Majordomo owner and list administrators alike.

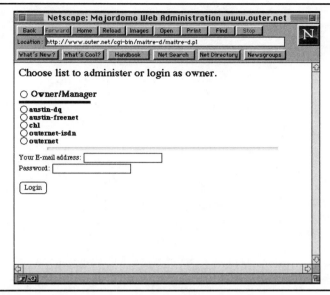

Figure 12-6
The Maitre-d login screen.

```
} else { # No command-line arguments, give welcome/login page.

$title = "Majordomo Web Administration $host";
&html_head;
print "<FORM ACTION=\"http://$host$maitred",
    "?login\" METHOD=\"POST\">\n";
print "<FONT SIZE=5>Choose list to administer or log in",
    "as owner.</FONT><BR><BR>\n";
print "<INPUT TYPE=\"radio\" NAME=\"LOGIN\" VALUE=\"owner\">\n",
    "<B><FONT SIZE=4>Owner/Manager</FONT></B>\n";
print "<HR WIDTH=25% SIZE=4 ALIGN=Left NOSHADE>\n";

open (LISTS, "/bin/ls $majordomohome |");
$count = -1;
# In order to build the login radio buttons and labels for each
# of the existing lists, we open a handle for the file listing
# of the majordomo list directory. Each list found will be added
# to an array and an appropriate form input created.
while (<LISTS>) {
  chop;
  if ($_ =~ /(.*)\.config$/i) {
    $count ++;
    $listolists[$count] = $1
```

```
    }
  }
  close LISTS;

  for ($i = 0; $i <= $count; $i++) {
    print "<INPUT TYPE=\"radio\" NAME=\"LOGIN\"",
        " VALUE=\"$listolists[$i]\" >";
    print "<B>$listolists[$i]</B><BR>\n";
  }

  print "<HR WIDTH=80% SIZE=4 ALIGN=Center>\n";
  print "Your E-mail address: <INPUT TYPE=\"text\" ",
      "NAME=\"EMAIL\" SIZE=20 MAXLENGTH=40><BR>\n";
  print "Password: <INPUT TYPE=\"password\" NAME=\"PASSWORD\" ",
      "SIZE=20 MAXLENGTH=20><BR>\n";
  # The person logging in must enter his or her e-mail address
  # and password in order to be authenticated.
  print "<BR>\n";
  print "<INPUT TYPE=\"submit\" VALUE=\"Log in\" ></FORM>\n";
  print "</BODY>\n ";
  print "</HTML>\n ";
}
```

And with that, Maitre-d is done. All that remains are the subroutines that are called from various points in the preceding code.

Head of the Class

The following subroutine should be familiar from the many times you saw it called in the preceding code. It takes a string as an argument and sets up the top of the HTML document, including the TITLE tagged text.

```
sub html_head {
  print "<HTML>\n ";
  print "<HEAD>\n";
  print "<TITLE>";
  print "$title";
  print "</TITLE>\n";
  print "</HEAD>\n ";
  print "<BODY> \n";
}
```

Nothing too fancy, but it fulfills the basic requirements for a subroutine, and obviates the need to repeat the same code over and over again.

The Seventh Wonder of the HTML World

Forms are great—what's great about them is that we took a large, commented configuration file and turned it into a much more manageable entity. With the commentary from the original configuration file intact, the form is self-documenting, and because the structure of form inputs applies to it, we can handle error-checking before accepting the data from the user.

This subroutine is called from both the area where lists are created, and where an existing list's configuration is modified. In the first case, the form is populated with the default values; in the second, it's filled out with the list's values as parsed from the configuration file.

```
sub configure_list {

    print "<HR><H3>List Configuration Options</H3>";
    print "<B>Administration Password: </B><INPUT TYPE=\"text\"";
    print "NAME=\"ADMIN_PASSWD\"";
    print "SIZE=\"10\" MAXLENGTH=\"20\" VALUE=\"$ADMIN_PASSWD\" > ";
    print "<BR>\nThe password for handling administrative tasks on";
    print " the list.<P>\n\n";
    print "<B>Approve Password: </B><INPUT TYPE=\"text\"";
    print "NAME=\"APPROVE_PASSWD\"";
    print "SIZE=\"20\" MAXLENGTH=\"30\" VALUE=\"$APPROVE_PASSWD\">";
    print "<BR>\nPassword to be used in the approved header for";
    print " posting to moderated list, or to bypass resend checks.";
    print "<P>\n<B>Description:</B> <INPUT TYPE=\"text\"";
    print "NAME=\"DESCRIPTION\" SIZE=\"30\"";
    print "MAXLENGTH=\"50\" VALUE=\"$DESCRIPTION\">";
    print "<BR>\nDescription for mailing list when replying";
    print " to the lists command. There is no quoting mechanism, ";
    print "and there is only room for 50 or so characters.<P>\n";
    print "<B>Moderate:</B> <SELECT NAME=\"MODERATE\" SIZE = \"1\"";
    print "VALUE=\"$MODERATE\">";
    print "<OPTION>no";
    print "<OPTION>yes";
    print "</SELECT>";
    # Please note: preceding statement is a SELECT, this makes "no"
    # the default because it occurs first in the list of options.
    print "<BR>\nIf yes, all postings to the list must be approved";
    print " by the moderator. <P>\n";
    print "<B>Subject prefix:</B> <INPUT TYPE=\"text\"";
    print "NAME=\"SUBJECT_PREFIX\"";
    print "SIZE=\"20\" MAXLENGTH=\"40\" VALUE=\"$SUBJECT_PREFIX\">";
    print "<BR>\nWord will be prefixed to the subject line, if ";
    print "it is not already in the subject. The text is expanded ";
```

```
print "before being used. The following expansion tokens are :";
print " defined \$LIST - the name of the current list,";
print " \$SENDER - the sender as taken from ";
print "the fromline, \$VERSION, the version of majordomo.";
print "<P>\n";
print "<B>Subscribe policy:</B> <SELECT ",
  "NAME=\"SUBSCRIBE_POLICY\"";
print "SIZE = \"1\"";
print "VALUE=\"$SUBSCRIBE_POLICY\">";
print "<OPTION>open";
print "<OPTION>closed";
print "<OPTION>auto";
print "</SELECT>";
# Please note: the preceding statement is a SELECT, which makes
# "open" the default because it is the first option.
print "<BR>\nOne of 3 possible values: open, closed, auto.  ";
print "Open allows people to subscribe themselves to the list.";
print " Auto allows anybody to subscribe anybody to the list ";
print "without maintainer approval. Closed requires maintainer";
print " approval for all subscribe requests to the list.";
print "<P>\n";
print "<B>Private get:</B> <SELECT NAME=\"PRIVATE_GET\" SIZE =";
print "\"1\" VALUE=\"$PRIVATE_GET\">";
print "<OPTION>no";
print "<OPTION>yes";
print "</SELECT>";
# Please note: the preceding statement is a SELECT, which makes
# "no" the default, because it occurs first in the options list.
print "<BR>\nIf set to yes, then the requestor must be on the ";
print "mailing list in order to get files.";
print "<P>\n";
print "<B>Private index:</B> <SELECT NAME=\"PRIVATE_INDEX\"";
print " SIZE =\"1\" VALUE=\"$PRIVATE_INDEX\">";
print "<OPTION>no";
print "<OPTION>yes";
print "</SELECT>";
# Please note: the preceding statement is a SELECT, which makes
# "no" the default, because it occurs first in the options list.
print "<BR>\nIf set to yes, then the requestor must be on the ";
print "mailing list in order to get a file index.";
print "<P>\n";
print "<B>Private info:</B> <SELECT NAME=\"PRIVATE_INFO\"";
print " SIZE =\"1\" VALUE=\"$PRIVATE_INFO\">";
print "<OPTION>no";
print "<OPTION>yes";
# Please note: the preceding statement is a SELECT, which makes
# "no" the default, because it occurs first in the options list.
```

```
print "</SELECT>";
print "<BR>\nIf set to yes, then the requestor must be on the";
print " mailing list to use the info <list> command.";
print "<P>\n";
print "<B>Private which:</B> <SELECT NAME=\"PRIVATE_WHICH\" ";
print "SIZE =\"1\"";
print "VALUE=\"$PRIVATE_WHICH\">";
print "<OPTION>no";
print "<OPTION>yes";
print "</SELECT>";
# Please note: the preceding statement is a SELECT, which makes
# "no" the default, because it occurs first in the options list.
print "<BR>\nIf set to yes, then the requestor must be on the";
print " mailing list to get info from that list.";
print "<P>\n";
print "<B>Private who:</B> <SELECT NAME=\"PRIVATE_WHO\" SIZE =";
print "\"1\" VALUE=\"$PRIVATE_WHO\">";
print "<OPTION>no";
print "<OPTION>yes";
print "</SELECT>";
# Please note: the preceding statement is a SELECT, which makes
# "no" the default, because it occurs first in the options list.
print "<BR>\nIf set to yes, then the requestor must be on the ";
print "mailing list in order to use the who command.";
print "<P>\n";
print "<B>Message footer:</B> <TEXTAREA NAME=\"";
print "MESSAGE_FOOTER\" COLS=\"72\"";
print " ROWS=\"4\">$MESSAGE_FOOTER</TEXTAREA>     ";
print "<BR>\nText to be appended at the end of all messages ";
print "posted to the list. The text is expanded before being ";
print "used. The following ";
print "expansion tokens are defined: \$LIST - the name of the";
print " current list, \$SENDER - the sender as taken from";
print " the from line, \$VERSION, the version of majordomo.";
print " If used in a digest, no expansion tokens are";
print "provided.<P>\n";
print "<B>Message fronter:</B> <TEXTAREA ",
  "NAME=\"MESSAGE_FRONTER\"";
print "COLS=\"72\" ROWS=\"4\">$MESSAGE_FRONTER</TEXTAREA>";
print "<BR>\nText to be prepended to the beginning of all ";
print "messages posted to list. The text is expanded before";
print "being used. The following expansion tokens are defined:";
print " \$LIST - the name of the current list, ";
print "\$SENDER - the sender as taken from the from line, ";
print "\$VERSION, the version of majordomo. If used in a ";
print " digest, only the expansion token _SUBJECTS_ is";
print ""available, and it expands to the list of message ";
```

```
print " subjects in the digest <P>\n";
print "<B>Message headers:</B> <TEXTAREA ",
    "NAME=\"MESSAGE_HEADERS\"";
print "COLS=\"72\" ROWS=\"4\">$MESSAGE_HEADERS</TEXTAREA>";
print "<BR>\nThese headers will be appended to the headers of ";
print "the posted message. The text is expanded before being ";
print "used. The following expansion tokens are defined:";
print "\$LIST - the name of the current list,";
print " \$SENDER - the sender as taken from the from line,";
print " \$VERSION, the version of majordomo.<P>\n";
print "<B>Administrivia:</B> <SELECT NAME=\"ADMINISTRIVIA\"";
print " SIZE =\"1\" VALUE=\"$ADMINISTRIVIA\">";
print "<OPTION>yes";
print "<OPTION>no";
print "</SELECT>";
# Please note: the preceding statement is a SELECT, which makes
# "yes" the default, because it occurs first in the options list.
print "<BR>\nLook for administrative requests (e.g.";
print " subscribe/unsubscribe) and ";
print "forward them to the list maintainer instead of the";
print " list.<P>\n<P>\n";
print "<INPUT TYPE=\"submit\" NAME=\"SUBMIT\" VALUE=\"Write ";
print "Configuration\">";
print "<INPUT TYPE=\"reset\" VALUE=\"Reset Form\"><BR>";
print "<B>Unless you really know what you're up to,";
print " don't bother messing around below this line:</B>";
print "<HR SIZE=10><B>Advertise:</B> <INPUT TYPE=\"text\"";
print "NAME=\"ADVERTISE\"";
print "SIZE=\"20\" ROWS=\"4\" MAXLENGTH=\"80\"";
print "VALUE=\"$ADVERTISE\">";
print "<BR>\nIf the requestor e-mail address matches one of ";
print "these regexps, then the list";
print " will be listed in the output of a lists command.";
print " Failure to ";
print "match any regexp excludes the list from the output. The";
print " regexps under noadvertise override these regexps.<P>";
print "<B>Configuration File Comments:</B> <TEXTAREA ";
print "NAME=\"COMMENTS\" ROWS=\"5\" COLS=\"80\">";
print "$COMMENTS</TEXTAREA><P>\n";
print "<BR>\nComment string that will be retained across ";
print "config file rewrites.";
print "<P>\n";
print "<B>Date in Info:</B> <SELECT NAME=\"DATE_INFO\"";
print "VALUE=\"$DATE_INFO\" SIZE = \"1\">";
print "<OPTION>yes";
print "<OPTION>no";
print "</SELECT>";
```

```
# Please note: the preceding statement is a SELECT, which makes
# "yes" the default, because it occurs first in the options list.
print "<BR>\nPut the last updated date for the info file at ";
print " the top of the info file rather than having it";
print " appended with an info command.";
print "This is useful if the file is being looked at by some ";
print "means other than majordomo (e.g., finger).";
print "<P>\n<B>Debug:</B><SELECT NAME=\"DEBUG\" SIZE = \"1\"";
print "VALUE=\"$DEBUG\">";
print "<OPTION>no";
print "<OPTION>yes";
print "</SELECT>";
# Please note: the preceding statement is a SELECT, which makes
# "no" the default, because it occurs first in the options list.
print "<BR>\nDon't actually forward message, just go through ";
print "the motions.<P>\n";
print "<B>The issue number of the next issue:</B> <INPUT ";
print "TYPE=\"text\" NAME=\"DIGEST_ISSUE\" SIZE=\"2\"";
print " MAXLENGTH=\"4\" VALUE=\"$DIGEST_ISSUE\"><P>\n";
print "<B>The current volume number:</B> <INPUT TYPE=\" ";
print " number\" NAME=\"DIGEST_VOLUME\" SIZE=\"2\" ";
print " MAXLENGTH=\"4\" VALUE=\"$DIGEST_VOLUME\"><P>\n";
print "<B>Digest Subject:</B> <INPUT TYPE=\"text\" ";
print "NAME=\"DIGEST_NAME\" SIZE=\"30\" ";
print "MAXLENGTH=\"50\" VALUE=\"$DIGEST_NAME\">";
print "<BR>\nThe subject line for the digest. This string has ";
print "the volume and issue appended to it.";
print "<P>\n<B>Maximum Length:</B> <INPUT TYPE=\"number\"";
print " NAME=\"MAXLENGTH\"";
print " VALUE=\"$MAXLENGTH\" SIZE=\"7\">";
print "<BR>\nThe maximum size of an unapproved message in";
print "characters. When used with digest, a new digest will be";
print "automatically generated if the size of the digest ";
print "exceeds this number of characters.";
print "<P>\n<B>Mungedomain:</B> <SELECT NAME=\"MUNGEDOMAIN\" ";
print "SIZE =\"1\" VALUE=\"$MUNGEDOMAIN\">";
print "<OPTION>no";
print "<OPTION>yes";
print "</SELECT>";
# Please note: the preceding statement is a SELECT, which makes
# "no" the default, because it occurs first in the options list.
print "<BR>\nIf set to yes, a different method is used to ";
print "determine a matching address. When set to yes, ";
print " addresses of the form user@dom.ain.com are ";
print " considered equivalent to addresses of the form
print " user@dom.ain.com. This allows a ";
print "user to subscribe to a list using the domain address";
```

```
print " rather than the address assigned to a particular";
print "machine in the domain. This keyword affects the ";
print "interpretation of addresses for subscribe, ";
print "unsubscribe, and all private options.";
print "<P>\n";
print "";
print "<B>Noadvertise:</B>  <TEXTAREA NAME=\"NOADVERTISE\"";
print "ROWS=\"4\" COLS=\"80\">$NOADVERTISE</TEXTAREA>";
print "<BR>\nIf the requestor name matches one of these ";
print "regexps, then the list will not be listed in the output ";
print "of a lists command.";
print "Noadvertise overrides advertise.";
print "<P>\n";
print "<B>Precedence:</B> <INPUT TYPE=\"text\" ",
  "NAME=\"PRECEDENCE\"";
print " SIZE=\"20\" MAXLENGTH=\"20\" VALUE=\"$PRECEDENCE\">";
print "<BR>\nPut a precedence header with value <value> ";
print "into the outgoing message.";
print "<P>\n";
print "<B>Purge received:</B> <SELECT NAME=\"PURGE_RECEIVED\" ";
print "SIZE= \"1\"";
print " VALUE=\"$PURGE_RECEIVED\">";
print "<OPTION>no";
print "<OPTION>yes";
print "</SELECT>";
# Please note: the preceding statement is a SELECT, which makes
# "no" the default, because it occurs first in the options list.
print "<BR>\nRemove all received lines before resending the ";
print "message.<P>\n<B>Reply to:</B>  <INPUT TYPE=\"text\" ";
print "NAME=\"REPLY_TO\" SIZE=\"20\" ";
print "MAXLENGTH=\"40\" VALUE=\"$REPLY_TO\">";
print "<BR>\nPut a reply-to header with value <value> into the";
print "outgoing message. If the token \$SENDER is used, then ";
print "the address of the sender ";
print "is used as the value of the reply-to header. This ";
print "is the value of the reply-to header for digest lists.";
print "<P>\n";
print "<B>Resend host:</B> <INPUT TYPE=\"text\"";
print "NAME=\"RESEND_HOST\" SIZE=\"20\" ";
print "MAXLENGTH=\"40\" VALUE=\"$RESEND_HOST\">";
print "<BR>\nThe host name that is appended to all address ";
print "strings specified for resend.";
print "<P>\n";
print "<B>Restrict post:</B> <INPUT TYPE=\"text\" ";
print "NAME=\"RESTRICT_POST\" SIZE=\"20\" ";
print "MAXLENGTH=\"40\" VALUE=\"$RESTRICT_POST\">";
print "<BR>\nIf defined only addresses listed in one of ";
```

```
print " the files (colon or space separated) can post to the";
print " mailing list. This is less useful than it seems it ";
print " should be since there is no way to create these files ";
print " if you do not have access to the machine running ";
print " resend. This mechanism will be replaced in a future";
print " version of majordomo/resend.<P>\n";
print "<B>Sender:</B> <INPUT TYPE=\"text\" NAME=\"SENDER\"";
print " SIZE=\"20\" ";
print "MAXLENGTH=\"40\" VALUE=\"$SENDER\">";
print "<BR>\nThe envelope and sender address for the resent ";
print "mail. Leave blank for the default, <listname>-owner.";
print "This string has \"@\" and the value of resend_host ";
print "appended to it to make a complete address. ";
print "For majordomo, it provides the sender address for";
print "the welcome mail message generated as part of the ";
print "subscribe command.";
print "<P>\n<B>Strip:</B>  <SELECT NAME=\"STRIP\" SIZE = \"1\"";
print " VALUE=\"$STRIP\">";
print "<OPTION>yes";
print "<OPTION>no";
print "</SELECT> ";
# Please note: the preceding statement is a SELECT, which makes
# "yes" the default, because it occurs first in the options list.
print "<BR>\nWhen adding address to the list, strip off all ";
print "comments etc., and put just the raw address in the list ";
print "file. In addition to the keyword, if the file ";
print "<listname>.strip exists, it's the same as specifying a ";
print "yes value. That yes value is overridden by the value ";
print "of this keyword.<P>\n";
print "<INPUT TYPE=\"submit\" NAME=\"SUBMIT\" VALUE=\"Write ";
print "Configuration\">";
print "<INPUT TYPE=\"reset\" NAME=\"Reset Form\" ",
   "VALUE=\"reset\">";
print "</FORM>\n";
}
```

We did mention that it was a long form, didn't we? It may be somewhat cumbersome in a browser, but be assured it's a vast improvement over editing the standard Majordomo configuration file!

Committing the Configuration File to Disk

Once you've slogged through the above form and adjusted the values to your liking, the sections of code that handle creating new lists and changing existing lists both call the following subroutine in order to write the values out to the proper format for Majordomo:

```perl
sub write_to_config
{
  if ($in{LISTNAME} && $in{ADMIN_PASSWD} && $in{APPROVE_PASSWD}
    && $in{OWNER_EMAIL}) {
    # Error correction—if the list's name, passwords, or
    # owner's e-mail are missing, the config file will be
    # rejected.

    &lock_file ("lock", ".$in{LISTNAME}.e-mail");
    open (EMAIL, ">.$in{LISTNAME}.e-mail") ||
      print "Can't write to .$in{LISTNAME}.e-mail:$!<BR>\n";

    print EMAIL $in{OWNER_EMAIL}, "\n";
    close EMAIL;
    # This creates or updates the Maitre-d support file—the
    # place where the owner's e-mail address is stored.

    &secure_file (".$in{LISTNAME}.e-mail");
    &lock_file ("unlock", ".$in{LISTNAME}.e-mail");


    &lock_file ("lock", "$majordomohome/$in{LISTNAME}.config");

    open (CONFIG, ">$majordomohome/$in{LISTNAME}.config") ||
      print "Can't write to $in{LISTNAME}.config:$!<BR>\n";

    print CONFIG  \
        "admin_passwd      =      $in{ADMIN_PASSWD}\n",
        "administrivia     =      $in{ADMINISTRIVIA}\n",
        "advertise         <<     END\n",
        "$in{ADVERTISE}\n",
        "END\n",
        "approve_passwd    =      $in{APPROVE_PASSWD}\n",
        "archive_dir       =\n",
        "comments          <<     END\n",
        "$in{COMMENTS}\n\n",
        "END\n",
        "date_info         =      $in{DATE_INFO}\n",
        "debug             =      $in{DEBUG}\n",
        "description       =      $in{DESCRIPTION}\n",
        "digest_archive    =      $in{DIGEST_ARCHIVE}\n",
        "digest_issue      =      $in{DIGEST_ISSUE}\n",
        "digest_name       =      $in{DIGEST_NAME}\n",
        "digest_rm_footer  =      $in{DIGEST_RM_FOOTER}\n",
        "digest_rm_fronter =      ",
        "$in{DIGEST_RM_FRONTER}\n",
        "digest_volume     =      $in{DIGEST_VOLUME}\n",
```

```perl
                "digest_work_dir   =   $in{DIGEST_WORK_DIR}\n",
                "maxlength         =   $in{MAXLENGTH}\n",
                "message_footer    <<  END\n",
                "$in{MESSAGE_FOOTER}\n",
                "END\n",
                "message_fronter   <<  END\n",
                "$in{MESSAGE_FRONTER}\n",
                "END\n",
                "message_headers   <<  END\n",
                "$in{MESSAGE_HEADERS}\n",
                "END\n",
                "moderate          =   $in{MODERATE}\n",
                "mungedomain       =   $in{MUNGEDOMAIN}\n",
                "noadvertise       <<  END\n",
                "$in{NOADVERTISE}\n",
                "END\n",
                "precedence        =   $in{PRECEDENCE}\n",
                "private_get       =   $in{PRIVATE_GET}\n",
                "private_index     =   $in{PRIVATE_INDEX}\n",
                "private_info      =   $in{PRIVATE_INFO}\n",
                "private_which     =   $in{PRIVATE_WHICH}\n",
                "private_who       =   $in{PRIVATE_WHO}\n",
                "purge_received    =   $in{PURGE_RECEIVED}\n",
                "reply_to          =   $in{REPLY_TO}\n",
                "resend_host       =   $in{RESEND_HOST}\n",
                "restrict_post     =   $in{RESTRICT_POST}\n";
      if ($in{SENDER}) {
        # If a sender is specified, use it.

          print CONFIG "sender            ",
                "=   $in{SENDER}\n"
      } else {
        # No sender specified, create default.

          print CONFIG "sender            ",
                "=   owner-$in{LISTNAME}\n"
      }

      print CONFIG "strip             =   $in{STRIP}\n",
        "subject_prefix    =   $in{SUBJECT_PREFIX}\n",
        "subscribe_policy  =   $in{SUBSCRIBE_POLICY}\n";

    close CONFIG;

    &lock_file ("unlock","$majordomohome/$in{LISTNAME}.config");
    &secure_file ("$majordomohome/$in{LISTNAME}.config");
  } else { # invalid data
```

```
       print "<H1>ERROR IN LIST DATA</H1>";
       print "<B>Go back and re-enter list data.</B><P>";
       exit;
     }
 }
```

Bits and Pieces

These last chunks of code do small administrative tasks; they're called from many points within the rest of the script. lock_file and secure_file are simple ways to ensure that only one person writes to a file at any given time, and that the file has the proper permissions once it is written. admin_menu and owner_menu build the menus for those two classes of users, respectively.

```
sub lock_file
{
  @lock = $_;
    # Gets passed the full path to the file to lock and the
    # argument "lock" or "unlock".

  $toggle = $lock[0];
  $filetolock = $lock[1];

  if ($toggle eq "lock") {

    $sleep_timer = 0;

    while (-e "$filetolock.LCK") {
      sleep 1;
      $sleep_timer++;
      # Count the number of seconds we've waited.

      if ($sleep_timer > 15) {
      # If we wait more than 15 seconds, assume a dead
      # process and unlock the file so we can proceed.

        &lock_dayfile("unlock", "$filetolock")
      }
    }
    open (LOCK, ">$filetolock.LCK");
    close LOCK;

  } elsif ($toggle eq "unlock") {
```

```perl
        unlink "$filetolock.LCK" ||
          print "Can't unlock $filetolock:$!\n";
     }
}

sub admin_menu {  # Passed the list name and the administrator's
                  # e-mail address.

   $listname = $_[0];
   $email = $_[1];

   print "<H2><FONT SIZE=+2>Choose the desired administrative",
       " task.</FONT></H2><HR>";
   print "<FORM ACTION=\"http://$host/cgi-bin/Maitre-d/",
       "Maitre-d.pl?admin\" METHOD=\"POST\">";
   print "<INPUT TYPE=\"hidden\" VALUE=\"$listname\" ",
       "NAME=\"LISTNAME\">";
   print "<INPUT TYPE=\"hidden\" VALUE=\"$email\"",
       " NAME=\"OWNER_EMAIL\">";
   print "<P><INPUT TYPE=\"submit\" NAME=\"ACTION\" ",
       "VALUE=\"Subscribe/Unsubscribe\">";

   print "<P><INPUT TYPE=\"submit\" NAME=\"ACTION\" ",
       "VALUE=\"Change Configuration\">";
   print "<P><HR>Return to <A HREF=\"http://$host$maitred\">",
       "Login Page</A>";
   print "</FORM>\n";
}

sub owner_menu { # Passed owner's e-mail address.

   $owner_email = $_;
   print "<FORM ACTION=\"http://$host$maitred?owner\"";
   print "METHOD=\"POST\">\n";
   print "<INPUT TYPE=\"hidden\" NAME=\"OWNER_EMAIL\" ",
     "VALUE=\"$owner_email\">\n";
   print "<FONT SIZE=2>Click \"OK\" to create a new list, or ";
   print "choose an existing list and an administrative task to ";
   print "perform.</FONT>\n<BR>";
   print "View Configuration: ";
   print "<INPUT TYPE=\"radio\" NAME=\"LISTADMIN\" VALUE=\"view ";
   print "config\">\nTurn List Off:";
   print "<INPUT TYPE=\"radio\" NAME=\"LISTADMIN\" VALUE=\"turn ";
   print "off\">\n<BR><BR>\n";
   print "<SELECT NAME=\"LISTNAME\">\n";
   print "<OPTION> CREATE NEW LIST\n";
   open (LISTS, "/bin/ls $majordomohome |");
```

```
$count = -1;
while (<LISTS>) {
  # Build select of listnames from the directory listing.
  chop;
  if ($_ =~ /(.*)\.config$/i) {
    $count ++;
    $listolists[$count] = $1
  }
}
close LISTS;

for ($i = 0; $i <= $count; $i++) {
  print "<OPTION>$listolists[$i]\n";
}

print "</SELECT> \n";
print "<P><P>\n";
print "<INPUT TYPE=\"submit\" VALUE=\"OK\" NAME=\"OWNER\">\n";
print "</FORM>\n";
}

sub secure_file {

  # Passed complete path to file, change permissions to secure it.
  local ($file) = $_;
  chown ($majordomouser, $majordomogroup, $file);
  chmod 0440, "$file";
}
```

Summary

Version 1.0 of Maitre-d, like all good software, is long on concept and somewhat short on features. We fulfilled our design specifications, but in writing the code we noticed several places where the feature set could be enhanced. Allowing the owner to delve directly into list configuration files would be a start, as would adding a capability for non-administrators to view lists, subscribers, information about lists, and to subscribe and unsubscribe themselves from lists.

Our experiment with a long Perl script as a CGI is still inconclusive. It's difficult to gauge the performance since what Maitre-d does is unlike what other, component-based CGI applications do. In our experience we did find that writing, installing, and maintaining a single long script was easier than working with a suite of smaller scripts, so that in itself may be justification for this approach. The conclusions we draw are like the rest of the CGI development world: no hard and fast rules, just another option that may or may not lend itself well to your particular project.

The length of the script is secondary to its utility, however. In our humble opinion, Maitre-d adds a substantial amount of value to a Majordomo and Web site. Its ease of use, the speed with which new lists can be created, and the burden that it removes from the Majordomo owner—all speak to its worth as member of your suite of CGI applications. We hope you have a similar experience as you experiment with Maitre-d on your own home turf.

WEB-BASED CALENDARING AND SCHEDULING

*W*hile there's always been lots of talk about the Internet, a new and complementary term is gaining currency in networking circles: *Intranet*, or a restricted collection of networks, typically within a single company or organization. Unlike the *Inter*net which is unrestricted and available to anyone with access to a computer, a modem, and an ISP, *Intra*nets are designed to function within a set of confines to service a particular user community. Only those invited or included can typically partake of an Intranet's offerings.

USING THE WEB'S AVAILABILITY

In this kind of situation, the Web functions not just as an information distribution tool, but also as a shared means of communication among the members of a particular workgroup, department, or company. In addition to using an Intranet Web server to distribute forms, to disseminate information, or to maintain a dynamic set of documents and data, such a server can also take advantage of its users' shared access to let them exchange information and coordinate activities.

Today, a number of such Web-based applications are already available, including conversational facilities where users can interactively exchange information that resemble familiar facilities like Internet Relay Chat (IRC) services, or guestbooks, where visitors can register their stop-offs at a Web site, and leave remarks for other visitors to ponder or questions for the site administrator. As the popularity of Intranets grow, we expect that the popularity of these kinds of collaborative applications will follow and that many more examples of this genre will become available.

In this chapter, we're going to explore an interactive Web-based calendaring and scheduling program. This program simply and efficiently exploits the hierarchical nature of file systems to model the equally hierarchical nature of calendars. Because it's available to anyone with access to a given Web server, it works well as the focal point for a shared calendar of events and schedule of activities.

While there are numerous calendaring and scheduling programs already available in the marketplace, no one has implemented a freeware version like ours that exploits the power and accessibility of the Web. While the application itself may not be a new idea, it's a new implementation with an interesting twist. It permits users across many platforms to share a common view of a calendar and its associated schedule, as long as they have an HTML 2.0-compliant Web browser and access to the server where the calendar lives.

RALLY 'ROUND THE CALENDAR

Any group that interacts regularly has to have a shared sense of purpose and must often have a shared sense of time and activities as well. Calendaring and scheduling programs have proven to be popular software tools because they present a single view of a group's time and activities and provide a master schedule around which to plan and work.

Most current calendaring implementations require client software to be installed on each workstation on a network, and on mobile or home-based machines, to access a shared calendar database. This requires separate software for DOS, Windows, UNIX, and Macintosh machines and access to a proprietary database under the control of the server-side of the program and the administrators who manage it.

The beauty of a Web-based implementation, beyond platform independence, is that it requires no additional software on client machines, as long as they already have Web access. The client browser handles platform dependencies by displaying HTML documents dished out by the Web server; CGI programs on the Web server handle the underlying data and administration.

Even though calendaring is a well-understood application, it's important that all users be able to view calendars for any given month and to get details on any given day. The format needs to be attractive and readable (and it's nice if the calendars can be printed for offline use). There has to be a mechanism for scheduling and displaying events. Also, because things change all the time, the ability to reschedule, add, or delete events is as important as the ability to schedule them in the first place.

SOLUTION: THE WEB-BASED CALENDAR

The introduction of the HTML <TABLE> tag provides a nearly irresistible method for creating attractive, easy-to-read calendars. As Figure 13-1 for December 1995 indicates, HTML tables can build a legible and flexible layout for calendar information.

Within this HTML calendar environment, each of the days of the month can act as a hyperlink to a subsidiary document that shows any events for that day. If the day is devoid of scheduled events, clicking on it produces the HTML document (depicted in Figure 13-2), which acts as the "user control center" for this program. The "no events" display for 12/29/95 takes users to a six-month sliding calendar display (two months back and three months forward), with options to obtain help, request an event, or log in as the calendar administrator.

On the other hand, if a day does have an event scheduled, the display looks like that shown in Figure 13-3. Notice that this day features not one, but two "Long Boring Meetings," which are the kind we usually do our best to avoid. Notice that the same selection menu that appears by itself on the "no events" display shows up at the bottom of this one, too.

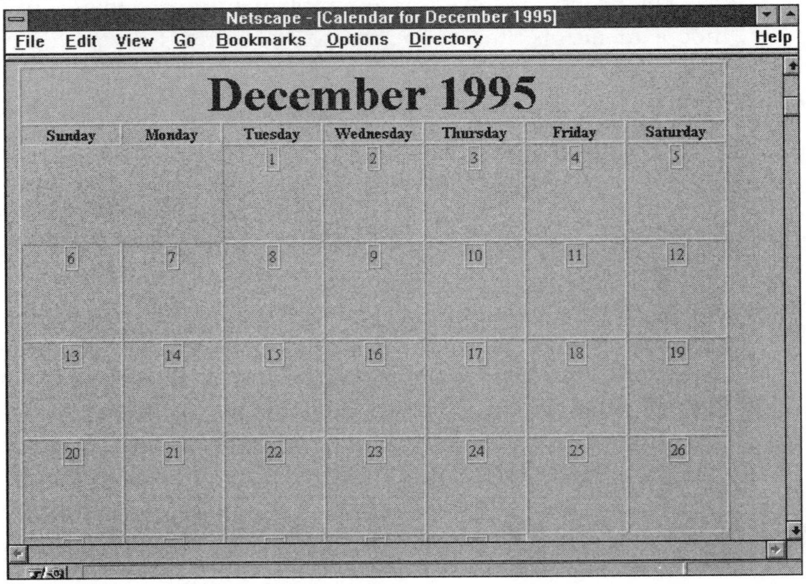

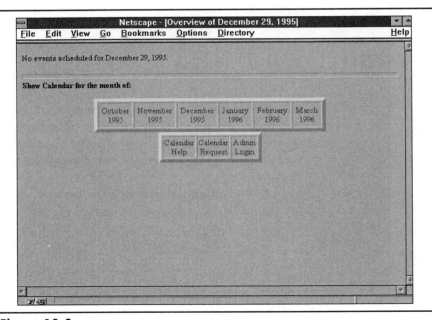

Figure 13-1
The December 1995 calendar looks like the "real thing" on your wall.

Figure 13-2
If nothing's scheduled for a particular day, the program presents a menu of other calendars and some activity choices.

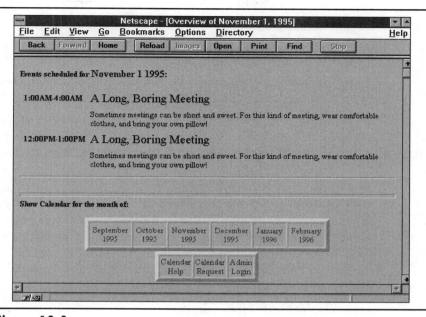

Figure 13-3
On days when events are scheduled, the menu of selections appears beneath that day's list of events.

Designing a Web-Based Calendar

Obviously, we didn't wave a magic wand or invent this program out of nothing; rather, we first sat down at a group meeting to decide what features our calendaring program would need. The list of features that emerged from our discussion—which we'll cheerfully admit was shaped by such excellent programs as CE Software's CalendarMaker and a handful of scheduling programs that we've used over the years—started out long but got shorter as we realized the work that would be involved.

Here's the list:

- Create a single, shared calendar and schedule system, available to the entire group.

- Generate calendars by month, with most of the display on a single screen, with years from 1900 to 2100, inclusive.

- Create and maintain a list of the kinds of events that may be scheduled.

- Associate events with particular days and time slots.

- Separate calendar and schedule access by end users, from calendar and event creation and maintenance by an administrator.

- Make sure that the underlying implementation is simple, understandable, and compact (at an ISP like ours, disk space is always at a premium, so we want to make sure we don't take up too much space).

This relatively modest list of requirements actually resulted from paring down a more ambitious list. Many of the items that were removed from our initial "wish list" will appear at the end of this chapter, where we present ideas for future enhancements.

The Roles of the Game

To state these requirements in somewhat different terms, we recognize two roles that are important to this application:

1. The end user, who examines calendars and schedules, and who can request types of events to be defined, and individual events to be scheduled, rescheduled, or deleted

2. The administrator, who controls the list of defined events, and who can schedule, reschedule, or delete individual events

There's actually no compelling reason why end users couldn't manage event definition, or handle individual events themselves. It's just that we've learned from prior experience that somebody has to be made responsible for maintaining group information; otherwise, it will probably fall into disrepair and the system won't be used. Likewise, since many people may depend on this data to help them set their own individual calendars and to schedule other events, we believe that central control over the calendar is desirable.

When you implement the suite of programs that handle these tasks, you may choose to do things differently. For instance, the program's default operation is not to require the administrator to enter a password. This means anyone can become the administrator, simply by clicking the Admin Login button on the end-user screens. If you want to establish control over Admin access, you'll have to protect the necessary files with an ".htaccess" password file, to force administrators to supply their passwords and to allow only those with valid passwords to perform administrative tasks.

For both roles, the ability to review any monthly calendar or daily list of activities is critical, as is the ability to view the current list of supported event types. For end users, our refusal to let them define event types or schedule individual events means we have to give them a mechanism to make requests. For administrators, this means that a way to recognize and handle incoming requests is critical and that a way to notify end users about actions on requests is equally important.

That's why a great deal of the infrastructure in the calendar software is devoted to communications: requests from end users to the administrator and replies from the administrator to end users. This corresponds to a somewhat "disconnected" notion of asynchronous operations that works well for data that is generally available but centrally controlled.

Organizing the Data

There's also a compelling need for at least two kinds of information containers:

1. A container for event types, to get them collected and organized for display (and further definitions)

2. A set of containers for calendars (and, ultimately, for scheduled events)—our understanding of the basic structure of a calendar pointed us to three kinds of containers:

   a. The basic unit for the calendar is the year. We decided to scale back our original requirements to support calendars for the years from 1980 through 2100.

   b. Each calendar is typically divided into months. Because we've identified an attractive monthly calendar display as a design goal for this software, it's a pretty important container for our purposes.

   c. Each month is divided into a fixed number of days, depending on the month, and the month and year for February. Our calendar program has to be smart enough to know how to deal with leap years and leap centuries as well.

At the top level of this directory tree (with the year containers and events container), you'll also find a notification message file and the list of group members to notify when events are added, changed, or deleted from the calendar.

The principal designer of this program had a stroke of insight that allowed him to greatly simplify the storage of data for any given calendar. The program only builds calendars for the current year, plus the preceding and following years, unless requested otherwise. Also, for each year the program automatically builds only a set of monthly calendars. Daily entries are created only when an event is scheduled for a particular day. This means that:

- Most calendars won't have as many entries as days in the year, for space savings.

- Years and months need to be calculated only once, after which they can be stored as part of the structure of the calendar itself.

In fact, this realization is where the stroke of insight really struck. The designer realized that a year is nothing more than a number, and that its months, once calculated, are nothing more than a range of numbers from one to the last day of the month (whatever that might be). The only real data that has to be captured and maintained is the list of scheduled events, with their corresponding start and end times, for those days that actually contain events.

Our crafty designer quickly realized that the file system itself could be used to model the calendar, and the amount of data required could thereby be greatly minimized. Thus, the directory named *1995* would be the parent container for a series of directories named *January*, *February*, *March*, etc. The only data that has to be associated with this structure is the number of days for February in that year, because all the other months always have the same number of days.

Finally, under any month container, files named after those days with scheduled events would be listed (e.g., "4", "11", "18", and "25", would indicate a month that featured four weekly meetings). Only those files would actually contain data that needs to be read and displayed; the rest of the calendar structure can be elicited by parsing and massaging the directory structure under which the event file lives, as shown in Figure 13-4. (Note: Directories end with a trailing forward slash / in this and subsequent directory listing figures.)

Year Dir	Month Dir	Day Files
96/	January/	
		12
		21
	February/	
		4
		11
		18
		25

... ...

Figure 13-4
The bulk of the calendar information is captured in the directory structure for a given year's calendar entries.

Writing calendar code takes some study and preparation. We were fortunate in that our version of Perl (5.001) includes a time calculation library, *timecalc.pl*.

The event type information stored in the *events/* directory is far more random and is simply organized into two kinds of files:

1. A master list of events is kept in a file named "eventslist".

2. Each entry in the "eventslist" file has a corresponding number that maps to a file named "detail.<number>" (e.g., "detail.1" for the first declared event type, "detail.2" for the second declared event type, etc.). This is where the description information for the event type is stored.

This structure leads to the kind of file organization depicted in Figure 13-5, where a number of "detail..." files precede the "eventslist" file that contains a master list of all the various detail files that it references (from name to number).

    . . .

        events/

            detail.1

            detail.2

            detail.3

            detail...

            eventslist

Figure 13-5
*The "events/" directory includes numerous detail files and a
single master "eventslist" file.*

This approach is entirely open-ended and leaves the number of types of
events (and their descriptions) entirely in the hands of the local calendar
administrator.

Situating End-User and Administrative Elements

Because of the need for administrative and end-user roles in this calendaring
environment, we need to support two different kinds of access to the
information involved. It also requires a fairly complex flow of information
among the components that display and manage the underlying collection
of files and directories that define the events, the calendar, and the daily
schedules for our group's activities.

The basic elements of the system are two Perl programs, *cal.pl* and
request_event.pl. *cal.pl* is the basic workhorse in this outfit: Its job is to
organize and display calendars, based on the contents of the chosen
year/month directory. (*cal.pl* produced Figures 13-1 through 13-3.)
request_event.pl defines the mechanism whereby end users can ask the
calendar administrator to define a new event type or to schedule a
particular type of event at a given day and time.

There's a separate implementation of the main calendar script, *cal2.pl*,
for administrators to use. There's also a calendar administration program,
caladmin.pl, for strictly administrative tasks, which in turn calls
create_event.pl to define new event types when needed (or modifies existing
ones). And when such administrative changes occur, *notify.pl* reads the
notification list (in the file "notifylist") and sends a notification to each
listed recipient therein.

Figure 13-6 documents this overall file structure and assumes the existence of a directory named *www-root* as the root of the Web server's files, with a subdirectory beneath that named *cgi-bin* where scripts generally reside for system-wide use. For example, this is where the end-user scripts, *cal.pl* and *request_event.pl,* might ordinarily reside, making them generally available for public access.

For Intranets, this is perfectly acceptable usage, but if your Web server also serves the public at large on the Internet, you might want to move them into a password-protected subdirectory to prevent outsiders from inadvertently blundering across your calendar and schedule. That's why we show them underneath the */calendar* directory, along with the *admin/* and *data/* subdirectories.

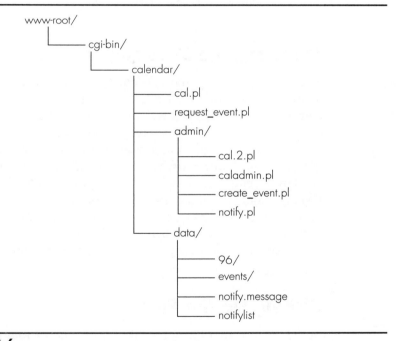

Figure 13-6
A more or less complete picture of the calendar directory tree, as it appears on our web server.

Note further that the *calendar* subdirectory beneath *cgi-bin* contains an administrative subdirectory (*admin*) and the set of data files for the calendars and events in use (*data*). Although only a 1996 directory is shown in this figure (96), there could be additional years (with their subsidiary months) at the same level of the file tree here. Also, the structure beneath the 96 subdirectory isn't shown (for brevity), but is the same as that shown in Figure 13-4; likewise for the *events* subdirectory (see Figure 13-5).

The positioning of calendar elements is important for reasons of security and control. By separating administrative components from data components, we can control who's allowed to run administrative elements by their file permissions or by assigning an ".htaccess" file and associated passwords to that separate directory.

Keeping the data separated allows the Perl scripts to manipulate the data and prevents end users from messing with the files. This will keep their contents pristine and lets us take advantage of what otherwise might be an overly simplistic set of data structures.

Modeling the Data Flows

The keys to setting up the calendar in the first place are the three administrative programs: *cal2.pl*, which provides the overall administrative controls and display characteristics, and which calls *caladmin.pl* to perform calendar administration and *create_event.pl* to perform event type definition or modification work. When event creation or modification work is complete, *create_event.pl* calls *notify.pl* to send notifications to targeted end users.

On the end-user side, *cal.pl* is the primary interface to the program and displays calendars and event information. When users want to request new event types, or events to be scheduled, they'll use *cal.pl* to call *request_event.pl* on their behalf, which will issue their requests for the administrator. This overall information flow is depicted in Figure 13-7.

Picking Up the Pieces

In the sections that follow, we'll examine the various components that make up our Perl-based calendaring program. As with the other programs in this book, we'll be examining these programs through excerpts that help to trace the flow of data and control. For the complete versions of these programs, please consult the contents of the *Chap13* directory on the companion disk that ships with the book. Here we'll step through these programs in their order of presentation, beginning with *cal.pl* and *request_event.pl*, followed by *cal2.pl*, *caladmin.pl*, *create_event.pl*, and *notify.pl*. Following this discussion, we'll review some possible enhancements or additions that could improve the program's usability or appearance, at the cost of more programming effort on your part.

As a whole, the calendar system should be installed by recreating the directory structure we've already reviewed in this chapter on your Web server and copying the various ".pl" files into their respective locations. The files in the */calendar/data* directories will be automatically created by these programs, so there's no need to set them up in advance. The permissions for all the files and directories beneath the *cgi-bin* subdirectory should then be set to 755.

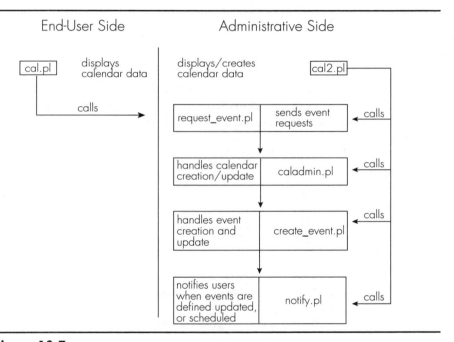

Figure 13.7
The information flows from Users to Administrators, and from Administrators to Users, in the calendar program, all based on a shared calendar of events.

cal.pl

cal.pl is the first part of the calendar program that most users will see. It also provides entry points to the administrative side of the program and for entering users' requests.

In terms of usage, *cal.pl* should be called from a Web client, probably as the underlying URL for a hyperlink reference. On our site, this could mean embedding a valid URL for the program in an HTML document (e.g., <A HREF="http://www.outer.net/cgi-bin/calendar/cal.pl">) or entering the URL directly into a browser's "Open" dialog box.

By default, the program returns the current month for the current year (as defined by the system's date/time setting). The program also supports URL-encoded access to other years and months, using the GET method with the general format:

```
.../cal.pl?<two-digit year>+<complete month name>
```

Thus, the invocation:

```
.../cal.pl?95+October
```

would produce the October 1995 calendar.

The program begins with a section of special constants, designed to help localization for specific sites, as follows:

```
$host = "www.outer.net";
#! Redefine to match the domain name for your Web server.
$calendar_name = "calendar";
#! Redefine to change program name if desired (not necessary).
$path = "/www/cgi-bin";
#! Redefine to provide absolute path on host to CGI directory.
$program = "cal.pl";
# Identifies program; more for developer info than anything else.
$request = "request_event.pl";
# Identifies program called to request event definition, schedule,
# etc.; again, more for developer info than anything else.
$debug = 0;
#! During development, activate to turn on debug output.
```

Next we define arrays to assign numbers to months, based on their names, and to provide full-length month names to use when constructing our on-screen calendars:

```
%month_number = (  "January", "1", "February", "2", "March", "3",
        "April", "4", "May", "5", "June", "6", "July", "7",
        "August", "8", "September", "9", "October", "10",
        "November", "11", "December", "12");
        # Used for converting month name to number
        # to pass as an argument to the UNIX utility "cal" - using
```

```
                       # an associative array allows us to quickly retrieve the
                       # month's number by the name.
       @month_long = ( "January", "February", "March",  "April", "May",
                       "June", "July", "August", "September", "October",
                       "November", "December" );
                       # Array of full-length month names to construct calendar
                       # navigator at bottom of calendar.
```

Next, we take care of some housekeeping and make sure the output between the CGI script and the browser isn't buffered, so a loss of connection won't mean loss of data. We also output the HTML document header for the calendar we'll be building, to keep the connection to the browser active (by sending it some data). Finally, we check the $debug variable, to see if debug output should be emitted at this point.

Command-line arguments, passed by the HTTP GET method, arrive via the @ARGV array in Perl, so they'll be stripped out and inserted into variables with more meaningful names:

```
$year = $ARGV[0];
$month = $ARGV[1];
$day = $ARGV[2];
$item_number = $ARGV[3];
# If ARGV[3] is defined, user is looking for a single item on a
# given day.
```

But if no year and month is supplied, we take the default of determining the current year and month by operating on system data. Only if an item number is supplied will its corresponding overview information be furnished to the user, as follows:

```
if ($item_number) {
  open (DAY, "data/$year/$month/$day");
# First we'll open the day's data file for reading. All events
# are stored in a data file in the /data directory, with a
# hierarchy constructed from the year and month, with a file for the
# day in question.

  $line_number = 0;  # initialize line counter
  while (<DAY>) {
    # Roll through the DAY file, looking for the line number
    # passed on the command line.
    $line_number++;
    if ($line_number == $item_number) {
    # We found our line, capture data contained therein.
```

```
        @line = split;
        # Split input line on whitespace and stuff into @line array.
        # Reconstruct data into variables with meaningful names.
        $eventname = join (' ', @line[3..($#line)]);
        # Join all elements (third to end) to form event's short name.
        $time = $line[2];
      }
    }
    close DAY;             # closes data file
    $title = $eventname;   # set variable $title for html_head
    &html_head;            # subroutine that handles HTML document header
```

Having read or constructed the necessary data, we can now step through the HTML document's header, based on boilerplate information contained in another file (named HEADER):

```
    if (open (HEADER, "data/day.header")) {
    # This allows the calendar owner to set the data directory that
    # will be output at the top of each returned page. This can
    # be either plain text or HTML. The open function returns zero
    # if it cannot open the file and the header will be skipped.
      print while (<HEADER>);
      close HEADER;
```

The real action occurs in the next section, where the body of the document is printed, using the newly defined syntax for HTML <TABLE> elements and contents:

```
    print "<P><B>Event scheduled for <FONT SIZE=+1>$month $day,"
          "19$year:</FONT></B><BR>\n";
    # We'll use a table to format the time, name and detailed
    # description of the event.
    print "<TABLE CELLPADDING=2 CELLSPACING=2>\n";
    print "<TR>";
    print "<TD><B>$time</B></TD>\n";
    print "<TD><FONT SIZE=+2>$eventname</FONT></TD></TR>";
    print "<TR><TD></TD><TD>";
    # Now retrieve the detail file for the event specified (we
    # retrieved the number from the day's data file) and dump it into
    # the current table cell.

    open (DETAILFILE, "data/events/detail.$line[1]");
    print while (<DETAILFILE>);
    close DETAILFILE;

    print "</TD>\n";
```

```
print "</TR><P>\n";
print "</TABLE><HR>\n";

# We handle the footer just like the header: if it's available,
# we add it to the bottom of the document.
if (open (FOOTER, "data/day.footer")) {
  print while (<FOOTER>);
  close FOOTER;
}
```

Otherwise, we'll traverse the `elseif` that follows, which indicates that no event detail has been supplied, but that a single day's overview has been requested. A day overview is similar to the overview of a single event just covered, except that all the events for the requested day will be displayed.

```
} elsif ($day) {
  $title = "Overview of $month $day, 19$year";
  &html_head;
  # Set up the top of the page, as with a single event.

  if (open (HEADER, "data/day.header")) {
# header supplied from the same template as before.
    print while (<HEADER>);
    close HEADER;
  }

  if (-e "data/$year/$month/$day") {
# If the day's data file exists, we can open the file and
# summarize its contents.
    print "<P><B>Events scheduled for <FONT SIZE=+1>$month $day",
          " 19$year:</FONT></B><BR>\n";
    print "<TABLE CELLPADDING=2 CELLSPACING=2>\n";

    open (DAY, "data/$year/$month/$day");
    while (<DAY>) {
# Print events by splitting input line into elements separated
# by spaces, constructing the event's name and time; then
# printing the data in the table cell.
      @line = split;
      $eventname = join (' ', @line[3..($#line)]);
      $time = $line[2];

      print "<TR>";
      print "<TD><B>$time</B></TD>\n";
      print "<TD><FONT SIZE=+2>$eventname</FONT></TD></TR>";
      print "<TR><TD></TD><TD>";
```

```
open (DETAILFILE, "data/events/detail.$line[1]");
# Open detail file and print it in a table cell.
print while (<DETAILFILE>);
close DETAILFILE;

print "</TD>\n";
print "</TR><P>\n";
}
close DAY;
print "</TABLE><HR>\n";
```

The next logical case to cover occurs when there's a day specified, but no data file exists (which means that no events have been scheduled for that day). This results in a message sent to the user, with a standard footer to close off our on-the-fly-generated HTML page:

```
} else { # no data file, no events scheduled
  print "No events scheduled for $month $day, 19$year.<P>";
}
if (open (FOOTER, "data/day.footer")) {
  print while (<FOOTER>);
  close FOOTER;
}
```

The next case is where neither an event nor a date is specified; this results in the display of the calendar for the specified month (or the current month, as the default). In many ways it's the primary display for this entire set of programs. In the next section we call a UNIX system function named *cal* to provide a calendar map, and then parse it to convert it to an equivalent HTML table:

```
} else { # no event number or date specified, give entire month
  $title = "Calendar for $month 19$year";
  &html_head; # set up top of page
  # set up top of calendar
  print "<TABLE BORDER CELLPADDING=0 CELLSPACING=1>";
  print "  <TR>";
  print "    <TH COLSPAN=7><FONT SIZE=+5>$month
19$year</FONT></TH><TD></TD>";
  print "  </TR>";
  print "  <TR>";
  print "    <TH WIDTH=80>Sunday</TH>";
  print "    <TH WIDTH=80>Monday</TH>";
  print "    <TH WIDTH=80>Tuesday</TH>";
  print "    <TH WIDTH=80>Wednesday</TH>";
```

```perl
print "    <TH WIDTH=80>Thursday</TH>";
print "    <TH WIDTH=80>Friday</TH>";
print "    <TH WIDTH=80>Saturday</TH>";
print "  </TR>";
# Go grab calendar data now - feed contraction for month and
# last two digits of year to the UNIX utility "cal" and pipe
# the output back into our filehandle. cal returns an ASCII
# calendar for the month specified, we'll parse it and
# convert it to a Netscape table.
#! Note: localize invocation of system function cal.
open (MONTH, "/usr/bin/cal $month_number{$month} $year |");
# The cal output is formatted with a space between each day
# padded to 2 spaces if necessary, to wit:
#
#      September 95
#  S  M Tu  W Th  F  S
#         1  2  3  4  5
#  6  7  8  9 10 11 12
# 13 14 15 16 17 18 19
# 20 21 22 23 24 25 26
# 27 28 29 30
#
# We discard the first two lines and then parse the numbers
# out of the remaining lines of text.
while (<MONTH>) {
  if (/^[0-9 ]*$/) {
  # Only process line if it contains numbers or spaces.
    chop;
    # Discard line feed on end of line.
    @line = split ('');  # split line into an array
    for ($pointer=0; $pointer <= $#line; $pointer+=3) {
    # Walk the line three spaces at a time, to grab each number.
      $day = $line[$pointer] . $line[$pointer+1];
      # The date can be reconstructed by joining the current
      # array cell and the next one in order.
      $day += 0;
      # This is a kludge to force Perl to consider the
      # variable's contents a number, by adding zero.

      if ($debug) { print $pointer, $day; } # debug code
      if (($day >= 1) && ($day <= 31)){ # code real dates
        $days++;
      } elsif (($day < 1) && ($days < 1)) {
      # If the date value is less than 1 and we haven't counted
      # a single day yet, we must be in the leading blanks; i.e.,
      # the month doesn't start in the 1st week of the calendar.
      # We count these blanks for formatting our table later.
        $leading_blank++
      }
```

```
        } # end for loop
      } # end if valid line
    } # end while
close MONTH;
```

Having grabbed the data for the month's calendar, placed it into an appropriate array, and positioned the elements to correspond to conventional Sunday through Saturday layout and spacing, we'll now emit that data in table format with the appropriate amount of blank cells leading up to the beginning of any month:

```
if ($leading_blank) { print "<TD HEIGHT=80",
      "COLSPAN=$leading_blank></TD>\n" }
# The preceding prints an empty cell spanning the number of blanks
# we counted in the calendar, if we counted any at all.

$week = $leading_blank;
# $week is our counter for the number of cells in each row. Here
# it is initialized for the first row with the number of blank
# cells we just created.

for ($loop = 1; $loop <= $days; $loop++) {
# Now we run though the month, from 1 to the number of days we
# counted from the "cal" function for this month, creating a
# cell for each one.
  print "  <TD HEIGHT=80 ALIGN=center VALIGN=top>\n";
  print "    <TABLE BORDER CELLPADDING=1 CELLSPACING=0>\n";
  print "      <TR>\n";
  print "        <TD><A HREF=\"http://$host/cgi-bin/$calendar_name",
      "/$program?$year+$month+$loop\">$loop</A></TD>\n";
  # This link allows the date to be clicked and the overview for
  # the entire day to be retrieved. The link refers back to this
  # CGI with command-line arguments for the year, month, and day.
  print "      </TR>\n";
  print "    </TABLE>\n";
```

At this point, we check for the existence of a data file associated with individual days of the month. If one exists, we open it and grab its contents for an abbreviated display on this calendar. Otherwise, we continue and print out the cell without any contents (no events scheduled).

```
if (-e "data/$year/$month/$loop") {
  open (EVENTS, "data/$year/$month/$loop");
  $line_number = 0;
  while (<EVENTS>) {
```

```
            $line_number++;
            # This counter keeps track of the line number for a
            # particular event.
            @line = split;
            # Split the current line into an array.
            $timestamp = $line[0];
            # Assign more meaningful variable names.
            $eventnum = $line[1];
            $time = $line[2];
            $description = join(' ', @line[3..($#line)]);
            print "<FONT SIZE=-1><B>$time</B></FONT><BR><A HREF=",
                "\"http://$host/cgi-bin/$calendar_name/${program}",
                "?$year+$month+$loop+$line_number\">",
                "$description<BR></A>\n";
                # This prints the event's time and a link to the
                # overview of the event itself - it refers back to
                # cal.pl with the command-line arguments needed to
                # retrieve the day's data file and the right line item.
          }
       close EVENTS;
       }
    print "  </TD>\n"; # Close out the day's data cell.
    $week++; # Increment our cell counter.
    if ($week > 6) { # iIf we have printed 7 cells, the week's over.
      print "<TR>\n</TR>\n"; # Close out the row.
      $week = 0          # Reinitialize the week counter.
    }
  } # end for
  print "</TABLE>\n";
  # the for loop done, we can close out the table
} # end month overview.
```

This concludes the large `if...elseif` statement that makes up the bulk of this program. Now that it's complete, it's time to compose the button of the calendar display, namely, the footer that's common to the various displays that *cal.pl* can generate. To begin with, we'll set up the monthly navigation buttons at the bottom of each page (two months back from the chosen month through three months into the future):

```
print "<P><HR SIZE=+6>\n";
# Set off the navigator with a horizontal rule.
print "<B>Show Calendar for the month of:</B><P>\n";
print "<CENTER>\n";
print "<TABLE BORDER=5 CELLPADDING=5>\n";
print "<TR ALIGN=center>\n";
```

```
for ($choice = $month_number{$month}-3; ($choice <
$month_number{$month}+3); $choice++){
# The navigator is built by rolling back from the current month
# and looping back up to it and beyond, to the other side of its
# value.
if ($choice > 11) { $calyear = $year+1; $number = $choice-12;}
# If our loop value is over the month array length, increment
# year and roll the month back over to the beginning of the year
# by subtracting 12.
elsif ($choice < 0) { $calyear = $year-1; $number = 12 + $choice;}
# If we decrement past the beginning of the calendar year,
# decrement year and roll the month over to the end of the
# calendar by adding 12.
else { $number=$choice; $calyear = $year }
# If we're not out of the month array, pass the month value and
# year value without changes.
#! Note: HREF link below will need to be localized for your server.
print "<TD><A HREF=\"http://$host/cgi-bin/$calendar_name/$,"
      "{program}?$calyear+$month_long[$number]\">$month_long",
      "[$number]<BR>19$calyear</A></TD>\n";
# The actual link is printed in the cell, with our modified
# month and year values as command-line arguments.
print "</TR>\n";
print "</TABLE>\n";


}
```

Next we present other choices for the calendar system, a set of the other command options open to the user, such as retrieving the Help file, submitting a request, or switching into administrative mode:

```
print "<TABLE BORDER=5 CELLPADDING=2>\n";
print "<TR ALIGN=center>\n";
print "   <TD><A HREF=\"http://$host/cgi-bin/$calendar_name/",
      "calendar_help.html\">Calendar<BR>Help</A></TD>\n";
# Link to our help document.
print "   <TD><A HREF=\"http://$host/cgi-bin/$calendar_name/",
      "$request?$year+$month+$days\">Calendar<BR>Request",
      "</A></TD>\n";
# Link to the script for submitting event requests.
print "   <TD><A HREF=\"http://$host/cgi-bin/$calendar_name/",
      "admin/cal2.pl?$year+$month\">Admin<BR>Login</A></TD>\n";
# Link to the admin version of the calendar (password protected).
print "</TR>\n";
print "</TABLE>\n";
# End calendar system buttons.
```

That's it for the buttons at the bottom of the page. All that's left is to close out our HTML document, as follows:

```
print "</CENTER>\n";
print "<P>\n";
print "</BODY>";
print "</HTML>\n";
```

The only code that's left for cal.pl is the html_head subroutine, which outputs a standard HTML header and the beginning of the document with its title. It's used as a standard document heading, and also sends enough information to the user's browser while the rest of the page is being built, to keep the connection alive and running until the other processing is complete:

```
sub html_head {
  # This is called from each of cal.pl's possible output options,
  # that is, from the month, day, or event overviews. It outputs a
  # standard HTML header and the beginning of the document with
  # the title as specified in the $title variable.

  print "<!DOCTYPE HTML PUBLIC \"-//IETF//DTD HTML 2.0//EN\">\n";
  print "<HTML>\n";
  print "<HEAD>\n";
  print "<TITLE>$title</TITLE>\n";
  print "<BASE HREF=\"http://$host/cgi-bin/$calendar_name/",
    "cal.pl\">\n";
print "</HEAD>\n";
  print "<BODY>\n";
}
```

That's all there is to *cal.pl*: a complex if...elseif conditional that evaluates what the user wants to see, and formats its output accordingly. Yet this program is the hub for all the others that will follow.

request_event.pl

request_event.pl is accessed from a button on *cal.pl*'s control bar, at the bottom of its display page. This program is designed to let users request a time, a day, and an event for the calendar administrator to schedule. Once completed, the form is submitted back to itself (to the *request_event.pl* script) with an additional command-line argument. This argument instructs the script to extract the form's POSTed variable values and record the event in a wait queue, for a response from the calendar administrator later on.

Figure 13-8 shows the one and only screen that you'll see from *request_event.pl*. The real action is on the upper half of the screen. That's where you define the day of the month for the event, its start and stop times, the type of event involved, and the e-mail address for subsequent notification. As we step through the code for this program, you'll learn the details about how each of these fields on the form is handled.

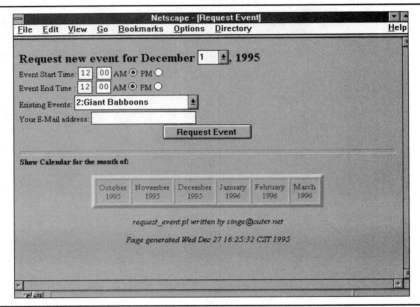

Figure 13-8:
The request_event.pl form lets users specify all the particulars for the event they wish to schedule.

The program begins with the same set of constants and calendar definitions used in *cal.pl*. Following that the $ARGV array is checked for the input values that will be used to drive this program:

```
$year = $ARGV[0];
$month = $ARGV[1];
$day = $ARGV[2];
```

We'll use each of these to help control the subsequent behavior of the program. We begin our work with a check on the date for the event; if none is assigned we arbitrarily pick the value 31:

```
if (!$day) { # No day value was passed from cal.pl.
  $day = 31
} # We'll artificially assign the value, erring on the side of too
  # many days for months under 31, but it's better to have something in
  # this instance than no value at all.
```

Next, we set the context for reading data files, make sure that Perl's output isn't buffered (to prevent data loss if our user's connection to the server should fail), and establish the HTTP header and the HTML document <HEAD> section for the event request page that's currently under construction:

```
# Change to calendar's home directory for access to data files.
chdir "$path/$calendar_name";
$|=1;  # output not buffered
print "Content-type:\ttext/html\n\n\n";
# Return necessary http HTML document header.
# Set up top of document - SGML prologue, HTML, and head tags.
# These remain consistent across both of the script's possible
# sets of actions.
print "<!DOCTYPE HTML PUBLIC \"-//IETF//DTD HTML 2.0//EN\">\n";
print "<HTML>\n";
print "<HEAD>\n";
```

Next, we check a value for $ARGV that we didn't explicitly define at the outset of this program; $ARGV[3] indicates whether the document is being called from itself (through the user's selection of the Request Event button). We also use Brigitte Jellinek's *formlib.pl* to check for errors, while we extract the input data from the user's submission of the form:

```
if ($ARGV[3] eq "post") { # Here's that command-line flag.
  print "<TITLE>Request Recorded</TITLE>\n";
  print "</HEAD>\n";
  print "<BODY>\n";
  # Here's where we extract form data using Brigitte Jellinek's
  # formlib, a perl library that contains subroutines that
  # error-check and extract form data.
  require "$formlib";  # Load up our Perl library.
  &GetFormArgs();      # Call subroutine to extract field names
                       # and values—this also provides error-
                       # checking.
```

After a block of debugging code, to enable verbose reporting of the program's behavior (which we'll omit here), we next check the e-mail address that the user supplies. We only accept event requests that include a string that resembles a real Internet-style e-mail address (meaning, we test for an @ sign that's surrounded by other characters). Note: If you are in a company where mail is processed through central aliases in mail-handling (thus, you don't need to type a domain name following your login because all employees are on the same "virtual" mail server), you may want to customize this code.

If we're satisfied that this is a bona-fide address, we proceed to process the request, as follows:

```
if ($in{EMAIL} =~ /.*\@.*/) { # Valid e-mail exists.
    @eventlist = split (':', $in{EVENTLIST});
        # Split our event number and event name into an array (this
        # is the value supplied by the user for our select field on
        # the event request form).

    open (REQUESTS, ">>data/event.requests");
        # Open the request queue for writing.

    print REQUESTS "$year:$month:$in{DAY}\t$in{EMAIL}\t",
        "$in{STARTHOUR}:$in{STARTMINUTE}$in{STARTAMPM}-",
        "$in{ENDHOUR}:$in{ENDMINUTE}$in{ENDAMPM}\t$in{EVENTLIST}\n";
        # Print the request to the queue using the variables we
        # created and assigned values to, as well as the remaining
        # raw environment variables.

    close REQUESTS;
        # Finished writing to the data file, close it.
        # Note hard-coding of 19 century prefix below; this will need
        # to be changed for the next century, and to further generalize
        # the program!
    print "Your request:<BR>",
        "<B>$eventlist[1] on $month $in{DAY} 19$year, at ",
        "$in{STARTHOUR}:$in{STARTMINUTE}$in{STARTAMPM}-",
        "$in{ENDHOUR}:$in{ENDMINUTE}$in{ENDAMPM}</B><BR>\n",
        " has been entered in the queue. You will be notified ",
        "when the administrator examines it.<P>",
        "<A HREF=\"http://$host/cgi-bin/$calendar_name/",
        "request_event.pl?$year+$month+$day\">",
        "Request another event</A><BR>";
    # Notify the user of our script's actions, echo the event
    # request back to the requestor, and create the link back to
    # the request portion of the script should the user want to
    # make another request.
```

The next branch of the program is reachable only if the e-mail address is invalid, so we'll reject the event request and give the user the option of returning to the event request form, to try again:

```
} else {
  print "<H2>Data error!</H2>";
  print "<P><FONT SIZE=+2><B>You must supply a valid e-mail",
        "address with your request.</B></FONT></P>";
  print "<P><A HREF=\"http://$host/cgi-bin/$calendar_name/",
        "$program?$year+$month+$day\">";
  print "Return to request page</A></P>";
}
```

If we fall into the next else branch of the program, which indicates that this is a "fresh" invocation by the user (using the GET method), we deliver a blank form for the user to fill out. In this section of code, we'll take you as far as building the select list for the number of days in the month, from the Request New Event... line in the form shown in Figure 13-8:

```
\} else {
  print "<TITLE>Request Event</TITLE>\n";
  print "</HEAD>\n";
  print "<BODY>\n";
  print "<FORM ACTION=\"http://$host/cgi-bin/$calendar_name/",
        "$program?$year+$month+$day+post\" METHOD=POST>\n";
  # Our form action line names the script itself, with the
  # addition of the command-line argument "POST," so that the
  # script knows it should extract the form data.

  print "<FONT SIZE=5><B>Request new event for $month ";
  print "<SELECT NAME=\"DAY\" VALUE=\"1\">";
  # The month and year are provided as command-line arguments, and
  # the preceding line begins to set up the SELECT that allows the
  # user to specify the desired day.
  for ($i=1; $i<=$day; $i++) {
    print "<OPTION>$i\n";
  } # This loop creates option lines for 1 to the number of days
    # in the current month (passed on the command line).
  print "</SELECT>, 19$year</B></FONT><BR>\n";
  # Closes out the SELECT statement for days of the month.
```

Next, we'll handle the widgets that allow users to specify the start and stop times for the event, as follows:

```
print "Event Start Time: ";
# Set up form inputs to capture the user's desired start time
# and end time.
print "<INPUT TYPE=\"number\" NAME=\"STARTHOUR\" VALUE=\"12\" ",
    "SIZE=2 MAX=2>:\n";
print "<INPUT TYPE=\"number\" NAME=\"STARTMINUTE\" VALUE=\"",
    "00\" SIZE=2 MAX=2>\n";
print "AM<INPUT TYPE=\"radio\" NAME=\"STARTAMPM\" VALUE=\"AM\"",
    "CHECKED>\n";
print "PM<INPUT TYPE=\"radio\" NAME=\"STARTAMPM\" VALUE=\"PM\""
    "><BR>\n";
print "Event  End Time : ";
print "<INPUT TYPE=\"number\" NAME=\"ENDHOUR\" VALUE=\"12\" ",
    "SIZE=2 MAX=2>:\n";
print "<INPUT TYPE=\"number\" NAME=\"ENDMINUTE\" VALUE=\"00\" ",
    "SIZE=2 MAX=2>\n";
print "AM<INPUT TYPE=\"radio\" NAME=\"ENDAMPM\" VALUE=\"AM\" ",
    "CHECKED>\n";
print "PM<INPUT TYPE=\"radio\" NAME=\"ENDAMPM\" VALUE=\"PM\">",
    "\n";
print "<BR>\n";
# The important thing to notice is the escaped quotation marks
# for the default values of the fields (e.g., NAME=\"ENDAMPM\").
```

The next order of business is to check the list of already defined events. If this list exists, it must be used to create a SELECT list to let the user pick a valid value:

```
if (open (EVENTS, "data/events/eventslist")) {
  # If pre-existing events exist, open the data file and
  # create a select out of it.
  print "Existing Events: \n";
  while (<EVENTS>) {
    if (/^1:/) { # If we're on the first event in the
                 # list, chop it, print the select line,
                 # and use the first event as the default
                 # value.
      chop;
      print "<SELECT NAME=\"EVENTLIST\" VALUE=\"$_\">\n";
    } else {   # Otherwise, the select already exists and we only
               # need to print the current line as an OPTION.
      print "<OPTION>$_";
    }
  }
  close EVENTS;            # Close the data file.
  print "</SELECT>\n<BR>"; # Close the SELECT.
```

Next, we need to deal with the unlikely situation where a user wants to request an event, but no event types have been defined (we'd strongly recommend that any administrator who installs this program include at least a basic collection of event types before making the program publicly available):

```
} else {
    # If we did not find the data file containing the existing
    # event names, the user can't request an event, since a user
    # can't request a new event type (an event that the
    # administrator hasn't already created for the calendar).
    print "No pre-existing events available. <BR>\n";
}
```

Then it's just a matter of providing the HTML for the remaining text entry box for the user's e-mail address and for the Request Event button:

```
print "Your E-Mail address:  <INPUT TYPE=\"text\" ",
    "NAME=\"EMAIL\"><BR>";
# space provided for the user's email address
print "<CENTER><INPUT TYPE=\"submit\" NAME=\"CREATE\" ",
    "VALUE=\"Request Event\"></CENTER>";
# our submit button, that calls the script recursively
print "</FORM>\n";
```

At this point, we've exhausted all the different paths this script can take. From here on out, we'll finish off the return page with the basic elements that occur at the foot of our calendar system's pages. To begin with, this means setting up a calendar navigator at the bottom of the page. Because this code is duplicated from *cal.pl*, we won't reproduce it here. Then, we simply need to close out the bottom of the page:

```
print " </TR>\n";
print "</TABLE>\n";
print "<P>\n";

print "<HR";
chop ($date = `/bin/date`);
print "<HR><ADDRESS>$program written by singe\@outer.net<P>Page ",
    "generated $date</ADDRESS>";
print "<P>\n";
print "</BODY>\n";
print "</HTML>\n";
```

This concludes the *request_event* script. It's funny how many lines of code a short HTML page can require, isn't it? Next, we switch over to the administrative side of the calendar system, as we tackle *cal2.pl*, *caladmin.pl*, *create_event.pl*, and *notify.pl*, in that order.

cal2.pl

This program is nearly identical to *cal.pl* except that it generates event calendars for administrative use, rather than providing an end-user view of the data involved. Calendars may be navigated month by month, or an overview for any particular day may be displayed. This script also contains links to the administrative scripts that create and edit events (*create_event.pl*), back to the user calendar (*cal.pl*), or to the help file. The main screen for this module appears in Figure 13-9, which shows the kinds of administrative tasks it can support in the row of buttons at mid-screen.

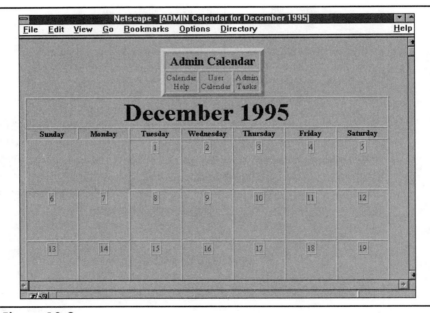

Figure 13-9

The Chief Administrative Functions in cal2.pl appear in the row of buttons mid-screen ("Calendar Help," "User Calendar," and "Admin Tasks").

Once again, we begin with the same set of constant definitions, the calendar arrays, debug controls, and assignment of $ARGV values to named variables. This time we leave the output buffered to limit potential security problems (since this is an administrative utility, after all). Once again, we also reset the relative directory reference for the program, so it can access the calendar data files.

The real action in the program begins when we start to tackle event administration. To start with, if the year and month aren't supplied as input parameters, we ask our local operating system to tell us what month and year it is:

```
unless ($year && $month) {
# If no year and month supplied, make the OS indicate the current
# year and month. Modify next line to your local dir structure.
  chop($datestring = `/bin/date '+%y %m'`);
 @date = split (' ', $datestring);
  $year = $date[0];
  $month = $month_long[$date[1]-1];
  # Use predefined array to find month's name from its number.
}
```

Next, we use the day information (if provided) to present an overview of the events already scheduled for the designated day, in the form of an HTML table:

```
if ($day) {
# If supplied with a day value, give overview for that day.
# Note again that the "19" century prefix is hard-coded; you'll
# need to generalize or change this output for the next millenium!
  $title = "$month $day 19$year - Event Summary";
  &html_head;
  if (open (HEADER, "data/day.header")) {
# Print predefined header file.
    print while <HEADER>;
    close HEADER;
  }
  if (-e "data/$year/$month/$day") {
    print "<B>Events scheduled for <FONT SIZE=+1>$month $day ",
        "19$year:</FONT></B><BR>\n";
# Note again that the "19" century prefix is hard-coded; you'll
# need to generalize or change this output for the next millenium!
print "<TABLE CELLPADDING=2 CELLSPACING=2>\n";
    open (DAY, "data/$year/$month/$day");
    while (<DAY>) {
```

```
@line = split;
$eventname = join (' ', @line[3..($#line)]);
$time = $line[2];
print "<TR>";
print "<TD><B>$time</B></TD>\n";
print "<TD>$eventname</TD></TR>\n";
print "<TR><TD></TD><TD>\n";
# NOTE: when we print HTML code in a script like this,
# it's good form to add \n line feeds where appropriate. The
# HTML client will ignore them, but if you ever have to poke
# through the generated HTML source for debugging purposes,
# you'll hate it a lot less if it's somewhat readable.
    open (DETAIL, "data/events/detail.$line[1]");
print while <DETAIL>;
close DETAIL;

print "</TD>\n";
print "</TR><P>\n";
}
close DAY;
print "</TABLE><HR>\n";
```

Otherwise, if no data file is found for that day, no events have been scheduled. In that case, there's nothing to edit:

```
} else {
# If no data file is found, no events are scheduled.
print "No events scheduled for $month $day, 19$year.<P>";
# Note again that the "19" century prefix is hard-coded; you'll
# need to generalize or change this output for the next millenium!
}
```

Immediately after handling these alternatives, the program prints any predefined footer information that may exist for the page. In most cases, this consists of the two rows of buttons, one for the six-month range around the current month, the other with activity choices for the program's user.

If a particular day has not been supplied, the program presents an entire month's overview (just like *cal.pl* does) to let the user pick the next action. In this next section, which we take as far as showing the entire monthly calendar, you'll begin to see some differences between this program and *cal.pl*, as the in-line comments will indicate:

```
} else { # give entire month overview
$title = "ADMIN Calendar for $month 19$year";
# Note again that the "19" century prefix is hard-coded; you'll
```

```
# need to generalize or change this output for the next millenium!
&html_head; # set up top of page
  # Here's the first real difference between the admin and user
  # calendars. We're about to construct a table with the admin
  # commands accessible from the calendar as a whole. We believe
  # the administrator is less interested in the actual calendar,
  # having set up the events, and is more concerned with admin
  # duties. Hence, the placement of links to admin CGIs above the
  # calendar itself.
  print "<CENTER>";
  print "<TABLE BORDER=5 CELLPADDING=2>\n";
  print "<TH COLSPAN=3><FONT SIZE=+2>Admin Calendar</FONT></TH>\n";
  print "<TR ALIGN=center>\n";
  print "  <TD><A HREF=\"http://$host/cgi-bin/$calendar_name/",
        "calendar_help.html\">Calendar<BR>Help</A></TD>\n";
  # Link to Help file.
  print "  <TD><A HREF=\"http://$host/cgi-bin/$calendar_name/",
        "cal.pl?$year+$month\">User<BR>Calendar</A></TD>\n";
  # Link back to the user version.
  print "  <TD><A HREF=\"http://$host/cgi-bin/$calendar_name/",
          "admin/caladmin.pl?$year+$month+1+ov\">Admin<BR>Tasks</A>",
          "</TD>\n";
  # Link to caladmin, main script for administrative tasks.
  print "</TR>\n";
  print "</TABLE></CENTER>\n";
  # Now we construct the calendar itself.
  print "<TABLE BORDER CELLPADDING=1 CELLSPACING=1>";
  print "  <TR>";
# Note again that the "19" century prefix is hard-coded; you'll
# need to generalize or change this output for the next millenium!
  print "    <TH COLSPAN=7><FONT SIZE=+5>$month 19$year</FONT>",
          "</TH>";
  print "  </TR>";
  print "  <TR>";
  print "    <TH WIDTH=80>Sunday</TH>";
  print "    <TH WIDTH=80>Monday</TH>";
  print "    <TH WIDTH=80>Tuesday</TH>";
  print "    <TH WIDTH=80>Wednesday</TH>";
  print "    <TH WIDTH=80>Thursday</TH>";
  print "    <TH WIDTH=80>Friday</TH>";
  print "    <TH WIDTH=80>Saturday</TH>";
  print "  </TR>";
  #! Grab data from UNIX cal system call (need to localize).
  open (MONTH, "/usr/bin/cal $month_number{$month} $year |");
  while (<MONTH>) {
    if (/^[0-9 ]*$/) {
      chop;
```

```
      @line = split ('');
      for ($pointer=0; $pointer <= $#line; $pointer+=3) {
        $day = $line[$pointer] . $line[$pointer+1];
        $day += 0;
        if ($debug) { print $pointer, $day; }
        if (($day >= 1) && ($day <= 31)){
          $days++;
        } elsif (($day < 1) && ($days < 1)) {
          $leading_blank++
          # Count the leading blanks in the first week.
        }
      }
    }
  }
  close MONTH;
```

By this point, we've displayed the calendar for the designated month, having obtained the number of days and their calendar positions from the UNIX *cal* command, and formatted them nicely into an equivalent HTML <TABLE> structure. Next, we'll invoke the *caladmin.pl* script to obtain an administrative overview of the day that the program is currently focused on, and conclude the output of the current monthly calendar to boot:

```
  if ($leading_blank) {
    print "<TD HEIGHT=80 WIDTH=80 COLSPAN=$leading_blank></TD>";
  }
  $week = $leading_blank;
  for ($loop = 1; $loop <= $days; $loop++) {
    print "  <TD HEIGHT=80 VALIGN=top ALIGN=center>\n";
    print "    <TABLE BORDER CELLPADDING=1 CELLSPACING=0>\n";
    print "      <TR>\n";
    print "        <TD><A HREF=\"http://$host/cgi-bin/",
          "$calendar_name/admin/caladmin.pl?$year+$month+$loop",
          "+ov\">$loop</A></TD>\n";
    # The preceding links to caladmin, which returns an
    # administrative overview for the current day.
    print "      </TR>\n";
    print "    </TABLE>\n";
    if (-e "data/$year/$month/$loop") { # Read in day's data file.
      open (EVENTS, "data/$year/$month/$loop");
      while (<EVENTS>) {
        @line = split;
        $timestamp = $line[0];
        $eventnum = $line[1];
        $time = $line[2];
        $description = join(' ', @line[3..($#line)]);
```

```
      print "<FONT SIZE=-1><B>$time</B></FONT><BR><A HREF=",
          "\"http://$host/cgi-bin/$calendar_name/admin",
"cal2.pl?$year+$month+$day\">$description</A><BR>\n";
          # Print the time of the event and the description, with
          # a link to the overview for the entire day.
        } # End while EVENTS.
        close EVENTS;
      } # end if
      print "</TD>\n";
      $week++;
      if ($week > 6) {
        print "<TR>\n</TR>\n</TABLE>\n";
$week = 0
      }
    } # end for loop
```

Now, we've completed most of *cal2.pl*'s work; all that's left to do is to complete the HTML screen form. Since this is virtually identical to *cal.pl*, we'll simply declare victory and proceed to the next program (if you want to see the details, please consult the listing in the *Chap13* directory on the disk that accompanies this book).

caladmin.pl

caladmin.pl is the core of the administrative side of our calendar system. It provides a front end for basic administrative tasks, and presents an overview of any chosen day's events. *caladmin.pl* also provides methods for creating new events, for editing or deleting existing events, and for reviewing event requests. It also provides a link back to *cal.pl* (the end-user calendar). Overall, this script's behavior is controlled by its method of invocation (GET or POST) and the variables that are passed when it is invoked. For a view of the initial calendar administration screen, please see Figure 13-10.

It begins with the standard constants, arguments, and directory context that you've seen in the other programs. The real action begins when the program tests its method of invocation, to decide whether it needs to process input variables from the screen form that drives its activity:

```
$command = $ARGV[3];
# The command-line argument can affect the script's behavior.
if ($command eq "post") {
# If the command passed to the script is "post," load up the
# formlib library and extract the form variables.
```

```
#! Localize directory spec for Brigitte Jellinek's library.
  require "/www/cgi-bin/formlib.pl";
  &GetFormArgs();
}
```

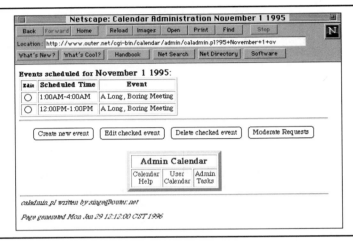

Figure 13-10
The opening calendar administration screen shows the basic event management commands: create, edit, delete, and moderate requests.

After this block of code, you'll observe that the output is left unbuffered, and that the standard HTTP header is emitted, as well as the standard HTML 2.0 prolog line. Since we've seen this before, we'll skip ahead to the next chain of if...elseif statements, which handle the individual administrative tasks for this program, starting with the overview (ov) command:

```
if ($command eq "ov") {
  # When called from the admin calendar, the "ov" command requests
  # an overview of a specified day.
  print "<HTML>\n";
  print "<HEAD>\n";
  print "<TITLE>Calendar Administration $month $day 19$year\n";
# Note again that the "19" century prefix is hard-coded; you'll
# need to generalize or change this output for the next millenium!
  print "</TITLE>\n";
  print "<BASE HREF=\"http://$host/cgi-bin/$calendar_name/",
        "admin/caladmin.pl\">\n";
  print "</HEAD>\n";
  print "<BODY>\n";
```

```perl
    print "<FORM ACTION=\"http://$host/cgi-bin/$calendar_name/",
        "admin/caladmin.pl?$year+$month+$day+post\" METHOD=POST>",
        "\n";
# The overview page contains a form that refers back to itself
  # with the "post" command-line argument.
if (-e "data/$year/$month/$day") {
    # Check for a data file for the day, if it exists, we'll
    # read it in and display it for the administrator.
    print "<B>Events scheduled for <FONT SIZE=+1>$month $day ",
        "19$year:</FONT></B><BR>\n";
# Note again that the "19" century prefix is hard-coded; you'll
# need to generalize or change this output for the next millenium!
    open (EVENTS, "data/$year/$month/$day");
    # Open the data file.
    print "<TABLE BORDER CELLPADDING=2 CELLSPACING=2>\n";
    # The events will be formatted in a table for maximum
    # readability.
    print "<TH><FONT SIZE=-2>Edit</FONT></TH>",
        "<TH>Scheduled Time</TH><TH>Event</TH>\n";
    # Set up our headers to identify the table's columns.
    while (<EVENTS>) {
      $line_number++;  # count events for identification
      print "<TR>";  # start a new row
      @line = split; # first element in line is timestamp
      $eventname = join (' ', @line[3..($#line)]);
        # Join elements from item 3 to the end of the array
        # to form the event's name.
      $time = $line[2];
      print "<TD><INPUT TYPE=\"radio\" NAME=\"ITEM\" VALUE=\"",
          "$line_number\"></TD>\n";
          # This radio button flags the event to be edited or
          # deleted—it is given the same field name for each of
          # the day's scheduled events, with the field's value set
          # by the item's numerical position in the data file. That
          # is, the 3rd event read from the file is assigned the
          # value "3".
      print "<TD>$time</TD>";
      print "<TD>$eventname</TD>\n";
      print "</TR>\n";
    }
    close EVENTS;
    print "</TABLE><HR>\n";
}
```

This sets up a screen form that lets the administrator select those elements for further interaction, in the context of an entire day's schedule. At this point, it makes sense to provide controls for the activities that the program supports. That's what the next block of code supplies for the ov task:

```
print "<CENTER><TABLE CELLPADDING=2 CELLSPACING=2>\n";
print "<TD><INPUT TYPE=\"submit\" NAME=\"CREATE\" ",
    "VALUE=\"Create new event\"></TD>\n";
print "<TD><INPUT TYPE=\"submit\" NAME=\"EDIT\" ",
    "VALUE=\"Edit checked event\"></TD>\n";
print "<TD><INPUT TYPE=\"submit\" NAME=\"DELETE\" ",
    "VALUE=\"Delete checked event\"></TD>\n";
print "<TD><INPUT TYPE=\"submit\" NAME=\"REQUEST\" ",
    "VALUE=\"Moderate Requests\"></TD>\n";
print "</TABLE></CENTER>\n";
print "</FORM>";
} # Eend overview.
```

The next block of code moves on to the create task. If the variable stored in $in{CREATE} exists, two assumptions are allowed:

1. The script has been POSTed to from a form, and this information is extracted form data (handled by *formlib.pl* earlier in the program).

2. The form we're processing was submitted when the user chose the Create New Event button.

This leads the program to present the administrator with the form necessary to create a new scheduled event, or to define a new event type:

```
elsif ($in{CREATE}) {
    print "<HTML><FORM METHOD=\"POST\" ACTION=\"http://$host",
        "/cgi-bin/$calendar_name/admin/create_event.pl",
        "?$year+$month+$day\">\n";
        # Our form action points at the active half of caladmin's
        # interfaces—create_event.pl, passing the ubiquitous
        # year, month, and day as command-line arguments as well as
        # POSTing all the form's data to the script.
    print "<HEAD>\n";
    print "<TITLE>Calendar Administration - Create Event</TITLE>\n";
    print "</HEAD>\n";
    print "<BODY>\n";
    print "<FONT SIZE=5><B>Create new event for $month $day,",
        " 19$year</B></FONT><BR>\n";
    # Note again that the "19" century prefix is hard-coded; you'll
    # need to generalize or change this output for the next millenium!
    print "Event Start Time: ";
```

At this point, we'll skip the rest of the event start and stop time specification code, since it's the same as in *request_event.pl*. We'll resume with the code that lets the user choose an event:

```
if (-e "data/events/eventslist") {
  # Now we'll create the select that allows the user to choose
  # an event. This too should look familiar from the
  # event_request.pl script, with one exception: the default
  # selection is "New Event..." which will cause a new
  # type of event to be created.
  open (EVENTS, "data/events/eventslist");
  print "Existing Events:<BR> <FONT SIZE=-1>(if choosing",
      " \"New Event\" please supply short name for event as ",
      "it should appear on the calendar.</FONT><BR>\n";
  print "<SELECT NAME=\"EVENTLIST\">\n";
  print "<OPTION>New Event...\n";
  while (<EVENTS>) {
    # We're printing the whole eventlist entry, which is
    # in the form <event number>:<event name>. We provide
    # it all for the benefit to the administrator in
    # keeping track of events he or she has created, but
    # more importantly, because create_event.pl needs the
    # information in order to do its work.
    print "<OPTION>$_";
  }
  close EVENTS;
  print "</SELECT>\n";
} else { # If an eventlist doesn't exist, the administrator
         # will only be faced with the option of supplying a
         # brand-new event.
  print "Short name for event (as it should appear on the",
      " calendar): <BR>\n";
}
print "<INPUT TYPE=\"text\" NAME=\"SHORTNAME\" ",
    "VALUE=\"\" SIZE=\"30\" MAX=\"50\">\n";
# This text input allows the administrator to specify the
# name of a new event type, if one is being created.
print "<P><P>\n";
print "<P><B>Note:</B>If creating a new event, you must supply a",
    " detailed description of the event.<BR>\n";
print "<P>To type in a detailed description, make sure the radio",
    " button is on, and type in the space provided.<BR>";
print "<INPUT TYPE=\"radio\" NAME=\"DETAILFILE\" ",
    "VALUE=\"NONE\" CHECKED>\n";
# This radio button is checked because it is presumed that
# the administrator will want to type the detail file
```

```
      # in him/herself in most instances.
      print "<TEXTAREA NAME=\"LONGDESC\" ROWS=\"5\"",
          " COLS=\"80\"></TEXTAREA>\n";
      print "<BR></P>\n";
      print "<P>If a detail file exists on the local file system, click",
          " radio button and type in path to file:<BR>";
      print "<INPUT TYPE=\"radio\" NAME=\"DETAILFILE\" ",
          "VALUE=\"EXISTS\">\n";
      # If the user checks this radio button, the event's detail file
      # exists on the local file system and the path to retrieve it
      # will be supplied in the next text input.
      print "<INPUT TYPE=\"text\" NAME=\"PATHTODETAIL\" ",
          "VALUE=\"\" SIZE=\"55\" MAXLENGTH=\"80\">\n<BR><P>";
      print "<CENTER><INPUT TYPE=\"submit\" NAME=\"CREATE\" ",
          "VALUE=\"Create event\"></CENTER>";
      # Please note the submit button's NAME, which gets passed to
      # create_event.pl along with the rest of the form's data. This
      # is a Netscape peculiarity, so if tables become more universal
      # and named submit buttons do not, message passing would have to
      # be handled differently, as with hidden fields.

  } # end create command
```

Next, we proceed to the EDIT command, which determines what the administrator wishes to edit, retrieves that item, and provides a filled-in set of fields that the administrator can edit to meet his or her requirements. The conclusion of the edit cycle occurs when a submit button causes the updates to be inserted into the underlying data files.

```
  elsif ($in{EDIT}) {
      # The form action statement leads to create_event.pl with the
      # year, month and day supplied on the command line.
      .
      print "<HEAD>\n";
      print "<TITLE>Calendar Administration - CHANGE</TITLE>\n";
      print "</HEAD>\n";
      print "<BODY>\n";
      print "  <HTML><FORM METHOD=\"POST\" ACTION=\"http://$host/cgi",
      "-bin/$calendar_name/admin/create_event.pl?$year+$month+$day",
      "\">\n";

      if ($debug) { require "/www/cgi-bin/debugforms.pl";&debug }

      print "<H2><FONT SIZE=5><B>Edit event #$in{ITEM} for $month $day,",
          "19$year</B></FONT></H2><BR>\n";
  # Note again that the "19" century prefix is hard-coded; you'll
```

```
# need to generalize or change this output for the next millenium!
        # The value of the variable $in{ITEM} will reflect the
        # number of the item chosen by the user to edit on the
        # initial overview page. This number in turn corresponds
        # to the line number the event can be found on in the
        # day's data file, and will be used to retrieve the
        # event's data.

    # Lock the day's data file for changes (this prevents duplicate
    # changes to the same data file, should 2 administrators try to
    # grab it at the same time).
    while (-e "data/$year/$month/$day.LCK") {
      sleep 1;
    }
    open (LOCK, ">data/$year/$month/$day.LCK");
    close LOCK;
    system ("cp data/$year/$month/$day data/$year/$month/$day.bak");
      # This is a precaution, so that, if the scripts fails for some
      # reason, we have one layer of "undo" capability.
    open (DAY, "data/$year/$month/$day") || die $!;
    open (NEWDAY, ">data/$year/$month/$day.new");
    # Open the existing data file for reading, and a <data file>.new
    # file for writing. In both instances, we couch the open stmt in
    # an OR expression, so if the open fails, the latter half of the
    # statement will be evaluated, causing the script to die and the
    # last system error received ($!) to be printed to stderr.
    $index = 0;
    while (<DAY>) {
      chop;
      $index++;
      if ($index == $in{ITEM}) {
      # If the line number matches the item number requested,
      # capture the data from that line and *do not* print that line
      # to the new data file.
        @item = split;
      } else {
      # It isn't the line we want to edit, so print it to the new
      # data file.
        print NEWDAY $_, "\n";
      }
    }
    close DAY;
    close NEWDAY;
```

At this point, we have the original data file in pristine condition and the new data file with all its original lines, except for the one we want to modify. This is how we effectively remove the line, so that an edited version can be reinserted as an update. Next, we'll handle the edits for the line to be changed, starting with some debug code:

```perl
if ($debug) {
  $editline = join(' ', @item);
  print "<P>Editing line: $editline</P>";
}
$eventnum = $item[1];
$eventname = join (' ', @item[3..($#item)]);
@timeinfo = split ('-', $item[2]);
# Start time is timeinfo[0], end time is timeinfo[1]: each
# variable contains a time like 9:45AM.

# Now let's deal further with time - start time first.
$timeinfo[0] =~ s/([AP]M)$//;
# Strip off AM or PM using the regular expression, which stores
# it in $1.
$startampm{"$1"} = " CHECKED ";
# Use the AM or PM we just matched and captured to set the
# appropriate radiobox in the time selection portion of the form.
@starttime = split(':', $timeinfo[0]);  # split hours from minutes
# Now end time, same stuff.
$timeinfo[1] =~ s/([AP]M)$//;
$endampm{"$1"} = " CHECKED ";
@endtime = split(':', $timeinfo[1]);
```

At this point, we reuse the same block of code that we examined in *request_event.pl* to display start and end times for the event. We'll skip that piece and move directly into this program's event list display code. This is the same as the Create New Event interface covered earlier, except that since we're editing an already defined event, we make sure to insert its original definitions in the SELECT entries in this form (that way, if an element is unchanged, it will retain its prior definition).

```perl
if (-e "data/events/eventslist") {
  open (EVENTS, "data/events/eventslist");
  print "<P>Existing Events: <BR>",
      "<FONT SIZE=-1>(if choosing \"New Event\" please ",
      "supply short name for event as it should appear on ",
      "the calendar.<FONT><BR>\n";
  print "<SELECT NAME=\"EVENTLIST\">\n";
  print "<OPTION>$eventnum:$eventname\n";
  while (<EVENTS>) {
    unless (/$eventnum/) { # If the line matches on our edit
                # line's event number, then we won't
```

```
                        # print it, since it already came
                        # at the top of the select.
            print "<OPTION>$_";
        }
    }
    close EVENTS;
```

Next, we'll present the New Event option, in case the administrator wants to replace the selected event with a new type of event altogether. This opens up the possibility that a new event will be defined and handles necessary housekeeping of the underlying description files. Then we close up open files and conclude the EDIT option's HTML page display.

```
    print "<OPTION>New Event...\n";
    print "</SELECT><BR>\n";
} else {
    print "<P>Short name for event (as it should appear on the ",
        "calendar): <BR>\n";
}
print "<INPUT TYPE=\"text\" NAME=\"SHORTNAME\" VALUE=\"\" ",
    "SIZE=\"50\" MAXLENGTH=\"50\">\n";
print "<BR>\n";
# For a variety of reasons, it is difficult to determine whether
# a detail file needs to be changed or not, we offer up a checkbox
# to the administrator to check if he/she wishes changes.
print "<P>If you wish to change the detailed description of an ",
    "existing event, check the box below and provide the new ",
    "description below.<BR>";
print "<P><B>Changing Detailed Description:</B> <INPUT TYPE=\"",
    "checkbox\" NAME=\"CHANGEDESC\"><BR>\n";
print "If creating a new event, you must supply a detailed ",
    "description of the event.\n";
print "If a detail file exists, click radio button and type in ",
    "path to file:<BR>";
print "<INPUT TYPE=\"radio\" NAME=\"DETAILFILE\" VALUE=\"EXISTS",
    "\"> \n";
print "<INPUT TYPE=\"text\" NAME=\"PATHTODETAIL\" VALUE=\"\" ",
    "SIZE=\"55\" MAXLENGTH=\"80\">\n<BR>";
print "If you wish to type in a detailed description, click",
    " the radio button and type in the space provided.<BR>";
print "<INPUT TYPE=\"radio\" NAME=\"DETAILFILE\" ",
    "VALUE=\"NONE\" CHECKED>\n";
open (DESCRIPTION, "data/events/detail.$eventnum");
print "<TEXTAREA NAME=\"LONGDESC\" ROWS=\"5\" COLS=\"80\">";
print while <DESCRIPTION>;
close DESCRIPTION;
```

```
print "</TEXTAREA>\n";
print "<BR>\n";
print "<CENTER><INPUT TYPE=\"submit\" NAME=\"CHANGE\" VALUE=\"",
    "Change event\"></CENTER>";
unlink "data/$year/$month/$day.LCK";  # Remove the lock file.
```

The next operation, delete, closely parallels the edit operation, as the next block of code will attest:

```
} elsif ($in{DELETE}) {
print "  <HTML>\n";
print "<HEAD>\n";
print "<TITLE>Calendar Administration - DELETE</TITLE>\n";
print "</HEAD>\n";
print "<BODY>\n";

if ($debug) { require "/www/cgi-bin/debugforms.pl";&debug }
print "<H2><FONT SIZE=5><B>Deleting event #$in{ITEM} for $month ",
    "$day, 19$year</B></FONT></H2><BR>\n";
  # Lock the day's data file for changes.
while (-e "data/$year/$month/$day.LCK") {
  sleep 1;
}
open (LOCK, ">data/$year/$month/$day.LCK");
close LOCK;

system ("cp data/$year/$month/$day data/$year/$month/$day.bak");
open (DAY, "data/$year/$month/$day") || die $!;
open (NEWDAY, ">data/$year/$month/$day.new");
$index = 0;
while (<DAY>) {
  chop;
  $index++;
  if ($index == $in{ITEM}) {
  # If the line number matches, we capture the data but don't
  # write it to the new data file.
    @item = split;
  } else {
    print NEWDAY $_, "\n";
  }
}
close DAY;
close NEWDAY;
if (-s "data/$year/$month/$day.new") {
# New data file has non-zero size - there is data left in the
# data file even after deleting the file, so we'll copy the new
# data file back to the real data filename.
```

```
      rename ("data/$year/$month/$day.new", "data/$year/$month/$day")
          || die "Can't change file : $!";
    } else {
      # File is empty, delete both the new file and the actual file.
      unlink("data/$year/$month/$day.new","data/$year/$month/$day");
    }
    unlink "data/$year/$month/$day.LCK";
    # End deleting event from day's data file.
```

The final option is to moderate user request for events. This consists of presenting an overview of pending requests from a request queue, which allows the administrator to mark events for deletion or approval. This is presented within an HTML form, which provides display and selection capabilities, where the administrator can approve or deny pending requests.

```
    } elsif ($in{REQUEST}) {
  print "<HTML>\n";
    print "<HEAD>\n";
    print "<TITLE>Calendar Administration - Approve Requests</TITLE>\n";
    print "</HEAD>\n";
    print "<BODY>\n";
    if ($debug) { require "/www/cgi-bin/debugforms.pl";&debug }
    print "<BASE HREF=\"http://$host/cgi-bin/$calendar_name",
        "/admin/caladmin.pl\">\n";
  print "</HEAD>\n";
    print "<BODY>\n";
    print "<FORM ACTION=\"http://$host/cgi-bin/$calendar_name",
        "/admin/create_event.pl?$year+$month+$day\" METHOD=POST>\n";
    if (-e "data/event.requests") {
      print "<H2><FONT SIZE=+2><B>Events Requested</FONT></B></H2><BR>\n";
      print "<TABLE BORDER CELLPADDING=2 CELLSPACING=2>\n";
      print "<TH><FONT SIZE=-2>Approve</FONT></TH>",
          "<TH><FONT SIZE=-2>Deny</FONT></TH>",
          "<TH>Scheduled Day</TH>",
          "<TH>Scheduled Time</TH>",
          "<TH>Event</TH>",
          "<TH>Requestor's E-mail</TH>\n";
      open (REQUESTS, "data/event.requests");
      while (<REQUESTS>) {
        $line_number++;
        print "<TR>";
        @line = split; # First element in line is date.
        @date = split (':', $line[0]); # year, month, day
        $email = $line[1];
        $time = $line[2];
        $eventname = join (' ', @line[3..($#line)]);
```

```
        $eventname =~ s/^[0-9]+://;
        print "<TD><CENTER><INPUT TYPE=\"checkbox\" ",
          "NAME=\"APPROVE\" VALUE=\"$line_number\"></TD>\n";
        print "<TD><CENTER><INPUT TYPE=\"checkbox\" ",
            "NAME=\"DENY\" VALUE=\"$line_number\"></TD>\n";
        print "<TD>$date[1] $date[2] 19$date[0]</TD>\n";
    # Note hard-coding of 19 century prefix below; this will need
    # to be changed for the next century, to further generalize
    # the program!
            print "<TD>$time</TD>\n";
        print "<TD>$eventname</TD>\n";
        print "<TD><A HREF=\"mailto:$email\">$email</A></TD>";
        # Create link to mail to the event requestor should
        # the administrator so desire.
        print "</TR>\n";
    }
    close REQUESTS;
    print "</TABLE><HR>\n";
  }
    print "<INPUT TYPE=\"submit\" NAME=\"VALIDATE\" VALUE=\"Approve/Delete
Requests\">";
    print "</FORM>";

  } # End moderate requests command.
```

As usual, we close this program with the administrative navigation tale, which presents the buttons for subsequent actions. Since it is identical to the conclusion of *cal2.pl*, we'll forgo this section of code and proceed straight on to our next program, *create_event.pl*.

create_event.pl

This program is the back-end workhorse for event creation to *caladmin*'s user interface; that is, *create_event.pl* is only called from *caladmin.pl*. When data is captured to create a new event, it gets passed to *create_event.pl*, which collects and records the necessary information. If edited data for an existing event is passed instead, *create_event* finds the original data, deletes the previous version for the designated event, and inserts the changed information into the file in its place.

This program requires the *timecalc.pl* Perl library, just like *request_event* (and for much the same reason). It also handles form data (from *caladmin*), so it requires Brigitte Jellinek's *formlib.pl* as well. In the program's preamble therefore, you'll see require statements for both libraries. In this program the data isn't buffered (to prevent data loss); you'll also find the same symbolic constants, calendar data arrays, directory context changes, and input arguments (from the $ARGV array) that you've seen in other programs in the calendar system.

The real action for this program begins if the Create button was selected to define a new event using the input data passed into the program, as follows:

```
if ($in{CREATE}) {
  print "<TITLE>Calendar Administration - Create Event $month ",
    "$day 19$year\n";
  print "</TITLE>\n";
  # Following line should be localized.
  print "<BASE HREF=\"http://www.outer.net/cgi-bin/$calendar",
    "_name/admin/$program\">\n";
print "</HEAD>\n";
  print "<BODY>\n";
  if ($debug) { require "/www/cgi-bin/debugforms.pl"; &debug }
  # With the HTML document header and debugging code out of the
  # way, we'll start extracting and interpreting data.
  if (!($in{EVENTLIST}) || ($in{EVENTLIST} =~ /New Event.../)) {
  # If the EVENTLIST select doesn't exist or it has the value
  # "New Event...", we'll run the subroutine that creates a
  # new event type. We'll cover the subroutine at the end of this
  # section.
    &create_event_type;
  }
```

If we're not creating a new event, we must be editing an existing one, so that's what the next block of code handles:

```
else { # Use existing event from the select field's value.
  @eventrecord = split (':', $in{EVENTLIST});
  # Now event id is item 0, short description is item 1.
  $eventnum = $eventrecord[0];
  $shortname = $eventrecord[1];
  # more meaningful variable names
}
# Lock the data file before inserting the event.
while (-e "data/$year/$month/$day.LCK") {
  sleep 1;
}
open (LOCK, ">data/$year/$month/$day.LCK");
close LOCK;
&record_event;
```

```
# With the variable names set, call the subroutine that
# actually inserts the event into the data file. We'll discuss
# this subroutine at the end of this section.
unlink "data/$year/$month/$day.LCK";
```

Next, we respond to the change command that indicates that the user has finished editing the event information and wishes to replace the old version with the (edited) new one. Notice the contortions we must go through to avoid creating spurious or incomplete changes, and the extra levels of protection we've built in with backup files for all changes (if anything untoward ever happens to a data file or to the eventslist, the administrator can roll back to a working version with a couple of well-placed file rename operations).

```
} elsif ($in{CHANGE}) {
   # Note hard-coding of 19 century prefix below; this will need
   # to be changed for the next century, and to further generalize
   # the program!
   print "<TITLE>Calendar Administration - Change Event $month",
      " $day 19$year\n";
   print "</TITLE>\n";
   print "<BASE HREF=\"$host/$calendar_name/admin/$program\">\n";
print "</HEAD>\n";
   print "<BODY>\n";
   # We're about to mess with the data file, we'll lock it now.
   while (-e "data/$year/$month/$day.LCK") {
     sleep 1;
   }
   open (LOCK, ">data/$year/$month/$day.LCK");
   close LOCK;
   rename ("data/$year/$month/$day.new", "data/$year/$month/$day")
        || die "Can't rename: $!";
   # The ".new" suffixed file is the file with the changed line
   # removed. We use it to replace the existing data file, since
   # we are just about to reinsert the changed line. We use this
   # 2-part editing so that, if the administrator begins to change
   # an event in caladmin but then never hits the change button,
   # the data file is never changed.
   if ($in{EVENTLIST} =~ /New Event.../) {
   # If the "New Event" select was submitted, we'll take the
   # data selected and create a new event type.
     &create_event_type;
   } elsif ($in{SHORTNAME}) {
     # It's not a new event but we have a shortname supplied —
     # this indicates the administrator wishes to change the way
```

```perl
# the short name of the event appears in both the day's data
# file and the event listing data file.
@eventlisting = split(':', $in{EVENTLIST});
# We now have the number:shortname in items 0 and 1
if ("$eventlisting[1]" ne "$in{SHORTNAME}") {
# Double check the submitted event name to make sure
# it is truly different from the name in the data
# file. If it is, change it in the event listing file.
  while (-e "data/events/eventslist.LCK") {
    sleep 1;
  }
  open (LOCK, ">data/events/eventslist.LCK");
  close LOCK;
  open (LISTING, "data/events/eventslist") ||
    die "Can't open events list: $!";
  open (NEWLISTING, ">data/events/eventslist.new");
  # Open the file for the edited version of the eventslist.
  while (<LISTING>) {
    chop;
    @listing_value = split (':', $_);
    if ($listing_value[0] == $eventlisting[0]) {
    # Look at the submitted event number and the event
    # number from the data file to find the event whose name
    # we need to edit. If the numbers match, print the new
    # version to the new events data file.
      print NEWLISTING "$listing_value[0]:$in{SHORTNAME}\n";
    }
    else {
    # Otherwise, print the line straight through.
      print NEWLISTING "$_\n";
    }

  }
  close LISTING;
  close NEWLISTING;
rename ("data/events/eventslist","data/events/eventslist.bak");
rename ("data/events/eventslist.new","data/events/eventslist");
# Move the current event listing data file to a backup file,
# and then move the new listing file to the actual filename.
  unlink "data/events/eventslisting.LCK";
  # Remove lock file.

  $eventnum = $eventlisting[0];
  $shortname = $in{SHORTNAME};
  # Assign our values to the variables for use by the rest
  # of the script.
} # End change event short name.
```

In the next `else` statement, we handle the case where information isn't changed or newly created and can be used as-is:

```
} else {
  @eventlisting = split(':', $in{EVENTLIST});
  # We now have the number:shortname in items 0 and 1.
  $eventnum = $eventlisting[0];
  $shortname = $eventlisting[1];
  if ($debug) {
    print "Event number $eventnum\tEvent name:",
        " $shortname<BR>"
  }
  if ($in{CHANGEDESC}) {
  # Not new event, but user has indicated changes to
  # detailed description, rewrite file from the data
  # submitted in the form.
    &create_detail_file;
  }
} # End using existing even.t
```

At this point, we're nearly finished with event manipulation, so the program must construct the new (replacement) line for the day's data file and insert it back into that file. This consists of a call to the `record_event` subroutine and a release on the data file's outstanding lock:

```
&record_event;
unlink "data/$year/$month/$day.LCK";
} # finished changing event
```

Now, we're ready to provide the logic to let the administrator approve or reject pending event requests from users. This consists of setting up another screen form, loading it with request data, and providing action buttons (Accept or Deny) for the administrator to choose for each one:

```
elsif ($in{VALIDATE}) {
  print "<TITLE>Calendar Administration - Validate ",
      "Event Requests</TITLE>\n";
  print "<BASE HREF=\"$host/cgi-bin/$calendar_name/admin/",
    "$program\">\n";
  print "</HEAD>\n";
  print "<BODY>\n";
  if ($debug) { require "/www/cgi-bin/debugforms.pl"; &debug }
  # Read the event requests data file into an array in to carry
  # out the moderate actions—record or delete them.
  while (-e "data/event.requests.LCK") {
```

```perl
  sleep 1;
}
open (LOCK, ">data/event.requests.LCK");
close LOCK;
open (REQUESTS, "data/event.requests") ||
  die "Can't open event.requests : $!";
$loop = 0;
while (<REQUESTS>) {
  $loop++;
  chop ($request[$loop] = $_);
}
close REQUESTS;
@deny = split ('#', $in{DENY});
@approve = split ('#', $in{APPROVE});
# Extract deny and approve actions to arrays, split on the "#"
# characters, which HTML 2.0 uses to join multiple field values.
for ($i = 0; $i <= $#deny; $i++) {
# Run through the deny actions, recording the event-numbers of
# all events to be denied in an associative array.
$decision{"$deny[$i]"} = "deny";
}
for ($i = 0; $i <= $#approve; $i++) {
  # Same deal with the approval - capture the event-numbers of
  # the events to be approved.
  $decision{"$approve[$i]"} = "approve";
}
open (REQUESTS, ">data/event.requests");
for ($i = 1; $i <= $#request; $i++) {
  # Run through moderate array & execute appropriate actions.
  if ($decision{"$i"} eq "approve") {
  # Check the value associated with the item's number. If it is
  # "approve," extract the necessary data, assign them to the
  # appropriate variable names, and record a new event.
    print "Approving $i: $request[$i]<BR>";
    # Extract data and massage into the variables needed for
    # subroutine record_event().
    @line = split (/\s/, $request[$i]);
    # First separate data into whitespace-separated cells
    # in the @line array.
    @date = split (':', $line[0]);
    # Date array is created by splitting the first cell in
    # the line array on the colon.
    $year = $date[0];
    $month = $date[1];
    $day = $date[2];
    $email = $line[1];
    $shortname = join (' ', @line[3..($#line)]);
```

```
$shortname =~ s/^([0-9]+)://;
# Cut the event number and the colon off the event list
# value, preserving the event number value inside the
# parentheses.
$eventnum = $1;
# Assign event number to meaningful, permanent variable name.
@timeinfo = split ('-', $line[2]);
# Start is timeinfo[0], end is timeinfo[1].
```

Here we'll skip the handling of start and end times for the event, which we've seen before, and the related debug code. We'll pick up with the call to the `record_event` subroutine that does the real work. After that, cleanup for undecided events is handled (that is, events that are neither accepted nor denied):

```
        &record_event;
    } elsif ($decision{"$i"} eq "deny") {
        print "Deleting $request[$i]<BR>";
        # No action req'd—event won't be copied to new request file.
    } else {
        print "Retaining $request[$i]<BR>";
        print REQUESTS $request[$i], "\n";
        # Print the undecided request back to the new data file.
    }
} # End for.
close REQUESTS;
if (-z "data/event.requests") { unlink "data/event.requests" }
unlink ">data/event.requests.LCK";
} # End validate.
```

This ends the real processing logic of this program. The remaining code recapitulates the common elements that appear at the bottom of most screens within the calendar system. We'll therefore skip ahead to a brief description of the program's subroutines.

These bits of code are written as subroutines because they're called from multiple points within the same program. When that happens, it's easier to write the code once and call it many times than it is to repeat (and have to test) the same code over and over again. For this program, we've defined four subroutines:

1. `create_detail_file`
   Given an event number and the descriptive data from the form where it's defined, this subroutine creates a new detailed description file for the event (which takes the form "detail.<event number>".

2. `create_event_type`

   This routine creates an entry in the master eventslist for a newly defined event type. It handles a variety of possible errors (missing or invalid data), assigns the new event number, and inserts the newly defined type name at the tail of the master list.

3. `error`

   Provides a centralized error-handling facility, which provides a general way to send error messages to the user (this is a common tool used in many programs that accept interactive input).

4. `record_event`

   As we mentioned several times in our discussion of create_event, the record_event subroutine does much of the real work in this program. It handles identifying the event's start and stop times, sorts new events into existing lists, handles entries with identical timeslots, and manages the day's data file along the way.

That concludes our discussion of *create_event*. The next program on our docket is the final member of the calendar system, *notify.pl*, the script that handles user notification regarding event requests.

notify.pl

This program's job is to handle the aftermath of the administrator's review of the pending event request queue (i.e., what's under the Moderate Requests button from *caladmin.pl*). As such, it reads the "notifylist" file and sends information about the status of requests that have been accepted or denied during the administrator's most recent review.

As usual, the program begins with the normal symbolic constant definitions and accesses six arguments from the Perl input $ARGV array. In addition to calendar information, it also grabs an event number and its corresponding timestamp and command, where appropriate. It also handles data from several of *caladmin*'s forms, so it requires the *formlib.pl* library.

The real action begins after this program's corresponding HTML page, "Event Notification in Progress," is started with the code for the notify process, as it steps through all the entries in the NEWNOTIFY array:

```
@notify = split ('#', $in{NOTIFY});
@newnotify = split (/\n/, $in{NEWNOTIFY});
$totaloop = $#notify;
open (NOTIFYLIST, ">>data/notifylist");
```

```
     for ($o = 0; $o <= $#newnotify; $o++) {
      unless (($newnotify[$o] =~ /Real Name\[TAB\]/) ||
          ($newnotify[$o] =~ /^\s*$/)) {
        $newnotify[$o] =~ s/\r//;
        print NOTIFYLIST $newnotify[$o], "\n";
        @notify = @notify, "$newnotify[$o]";
        $totaloop++;
      }
     }
     close NOTIFYLIST;
```

Next, the program finds the time slot and the event's short name (from
the description data in the various detail files):

```
     open (DAY, "data/$year/$month/$day");
     while (<DAY>) {
       @line = split;
       if (($line[0] == $timestamp) && ($line[1] == $eventnum)) {
         $time = $line[2];
         $shortname = $line[3];
       }
     }
```

Next, the program handles sending messages to all the recipients for
events that have had actions assigned to them. Notice the initial substitution
operation, which cleans out possibly spurious or harmful characters before
creating e-mail messages to the proper recipients (this should prevent any
unpleasant surprises from showing up by mail):

```
     for ($index = 0; $index <= $totaloop; $index++) {
       $notify[$index] =~ s/([a-zA-Z0-9\.]+\@[a-zA-Z0-9\.]+)//;
       $email = $1;
       $name = $notify[$index];
       print "$index: $name, $email<BR>";
       open (MAIL, "|$mail_command $email");
       print MAIL "$shortname has been scheduled at ",
               "$month $day, 19$year.\n";
       print MAIL "\n-\n";
       open (MESSAGE, "data/notify.message") ||
         print "No notify.message in data directory";
       while (<MESSAGE>) {
         print MAIL
       }
       close MAIL;
       close MESSAGE;
```

```
      print "Notified $name $email<BR>\n";
    } # end for
    print "done.<BR>\n";
```

Next, the program supplies the administrator with a list of individuals (taken from the "notifylist" file), who can be chosen to receive notification about their recent event request actions. This includes the code for adding new recipients, when necessary:

```
    } else {
      $title = "Event Notification";
      &html_head;
      print "<FORM ACTION=\"http://$host/cgi-bin/$calendar_name",
          "/admin/notify.pl?$year+$month+$day+$eventnum+$timestamp",
          "+notify\" METHOD=post>";
      if (-e "data/notifylist") {
        print "<H2><FONT SIZE=4><B>Select people to be notified by ",
            "e-mail:</B></FONT></H2><BR>\n";
        open (NOTIFYLIST, "data/notifylist");
        $loopy = 0;
        while (<NOTIFYLIST>) {
          chop ($notify[$loopy] = $_);
          $loopy++
        }
        close NOTIFYLIST;
        $window_size = $loopy;
        if ($window_size > 10) { $window_size = 10;}
        print "<SELECT NAME=\"NOTIFY\" COLS=40 SIZE=$window_size ",
            "MULTIPLE>\n";
        for ($valv=0; $valv < $loopy; $valv++) {
          print "<OPTION>$notify[$valv]\n";
        }
        print "</SELECT>\n";
      }
      close NOTIFYLIST;
      print "<P><BR>Enter new names and e-mail addresses to be ",
          "notified:<BR>\n";
      print "<TEXTAREA NAME=\"NEWNOTIFY\" ROWS=5 COLS=40>\n";
      print "Real Name[TAB]e-mail address (one name per line)\n";
      print "</TEXTAREA><BR>\n";
      print "<INPUT TYPE=\"submit\" VALUE=\"Notify Participants\">";
      print "</FORM>";
    } # end enter people to notify
```

This ends the body of the program, except for a few basic lines of HTML to close off the page that's been under construction. The only other piece that's missing is the subroutine named `html_head`, which provides a common header to all the various pages created in the branches of code for this program. Because it's just a series of simple print statements, we'll skip a review of it here.

That concludes our review of the internals of the calendar system. Next, we'll talk about installation and use and then proceed to cover some suggestions for possible enhancements or improvements.

Installing the Calendar System

These programs were purposely designed to make them easy to install and use, especially in view of the number of elements involved. Two basic steps are required for installation:

1. *Localization of the code*
   As we discussed these programs, we kept referring to a shared block of predefined constants at the head of each one. This consists of some or all of these variables:

   a. $calendar_name: states a local name for the calendar

   b. $calendar_program: names user calendar program (*cal.pl*)

   c. $formlib: specifies path to *formlib.pl* library

   d. $host: identifies the domain name for the Web server

   e. $mail_command: specifies the local mail sending program

   f. $path: points to the root for the calendar scripts

   g. $program: identifies the current program (for debug)

   Each of these constants must be located and an appropriate local value inserted on the right-hand side of the assignment statement where it's first referenced, in order for these programs to work.

2. *Situation in the correct directory structure*

   Earlier in this chapter we recommended that a */calendar*subdirectory be created beneath your server's basic CGI directory (e.g., */www/-cgi-bin/calendar*). This directory is where *cal.pl* and *request_event.pl* must be placed. Beneath */calendar* we specified two sibling directories, *admin* and *data*. These must also be created, then the remaining Perl scripts (*cal2.pl, caladmin.pl, create_event.pl, and* *notify.pl*) must be placed in the *admin* directory. The suite of programs will take care of the rest, including creation of the "eventslist" and "notifylist" files, as well as the detail files and calendar data files.

Once you've followed these two steps, you'll want to test the installation to make sure it works. Next, you'll want your calendar administrator to create a basic list of event types (may we suggest "group meeting," "customer meeting," and "review" as some nice, generic terms to begin with). Remember, without a list of defined events, users won't be able to request anything!

The Calendar Suggestion Box

As we began to use this program widely in our own business, we quickly realized that there were many potential areas for improvement and enhancement with this program. Nevertheless, this version is used every day in our work group and provides a functional backbone for our activities, calendars, and shared schedules. Here's a list of possible improvements or extensions that we came up with:

1. Currently, the program handles only one calendar and schedule. For larger organizations, or for situations where individuals want a personal calendar and schedule separate from the group's, it would make sense to extend this program to recognize and manage multiple sets of data. This would require a richer directory structure than the current implementation and would benefit from a master index file where the program could locate the various elements it needs to handle (much like the "eventslist" file currently provides the keys into the detail files for events).

2. The program works well on-screen but, other than printing from within a browser, offers little or no output capabilities. For those with DayRunners, Franklin Planners, DayTimers, or any of the other paper-based organizers, some way to print pages formatted to fit those environments would be appreciated. This would be especially useful for staffers who must travel or work remotely, who may be less able to access the Web pages than their office-bound counterparts.

3. The program offers none of the sophisticated scheduling tools available from its platform-dependent (but more powerful) counterparts. This includes things like finding the next time everyone's available for a group meeting, requesting multiple time slots (a main request and alternates), scheduling conference rooms and other meeting places, and other meeting planning tools.

Beyond these suggestions, there's plenty of room to spruce up the interface: there's no reason why icons or other graphics couldn't take the place of short event names, or why other graphical elements couldn't find their way into the data presentation. Even so, we think you'll find this set of programs accessible and, even better, immediately useful.

SUMMARY

In this chapter, we reviewed a calendar and scheduling system that combines the broad accessibility and availability of the Web with a facility for managing and coordinating events among a group of participants. Along the way, we visited several interesting programming issues, including the use of locks to control access to shared resources, techniques for calculating and handling calendar and time displays, and repeated demonstrations of generating HTML documents on-the-fly. In the next chapter, we'll examine the ins and outs of using the Web itself to edit HTML documents, for easy tweaking of a home page and its contents.

THE ONLINE HTML EDITOR

14

*B*y now, you may be under the impression that we'd like to replace every aspect of computing with a Web/CGI-centric model. This is only partly true. Actually, we'd like to replace every aspect of human experience with its Webified counterpart!

In all honesty, if our enthusiasm for the Web-based model of computing seems like overkill, it's merely because we feel like kids with a new set of really cool building blocks. The territory is so new and undiscovered that it's difficult to resist the temptation to try everything, Web-style. The true impact of HTTP on the computer industry is not fully understood, so every application of this technology in some other area of computing has revolutionary potential.

It's with this kind of exploratory spirit, then, that we venture into the projects you see in this book. They're ideas we thought were intriguing, hopefully useful, and, best of all, potentially inspiring.

WEB INTROSPECTION

In this chapter, we present a Web-based HTML editor, not to replace the full-fledged word processing system that's already on your desktop, but to provide simple editing capabilities "in place." This eliminates the need to download files to your PC, open them with an editor, make necessary changes, and upload them again.

We'd like to draw an analogy to *vi*, the venerable UNIX text editor. Many is the time we've laboriously created HTML pages, uploaded them, and then found one tiny error. Rather than go through the download/edit/upload cycle we invariably turn to *vi*, open the file where it sits on the server, make the change, and save the file for further use.

This convenience presupposes *telnet* or *rlogin* access to the host where the file resides, and at least a passing familiarity with UNIX and *vi*. For those of you with such knowledge, it's no big deal; for those of you who haven't mastered these areas, it can be a very big deal indeed.

On the other hand, our project requires merely that the user have access to the Web and that he or she can type. The file is edited within an HTML form, then written back to the disk. While it lacks the bells and whistles of the HTML document creation programs, our script is entirely capable of making small, time-consuming edits.

Important Considerations

To make this tool, called "The Renovator," useful, we'll need to analyze its features and potential weaknesses.

As with every aspect of the Internet these days, the first concern is security. If you are going to run a CGI program on your server that reads and writes files, you will surely want assurances that it cannot be used to wreak havoc on your server. The potential destruction that a badly designed Web editor could wreak is immense, as are the potential breaches of privacy.

For that reason, when we first prototyped this script, we wrote it with hardwired paths and permissions, so that it would be able to make changes to only a single document on our test server. Furthermore, we buried it in a directory with an ".htaccess" file that allowed only authorized users to GET or POST files.

The prototype was useful for a number of reasons. It allowed us to experiment with different approaches to interface and features. For a short time, we played around with parsing the file to be edited into separate components. We would find and separate out the document's <HEAD>, <BODY>, and <ADDRESS> components into separate form fields. We soon saw that this really didn't add much value unless we went whole-hog and parsed the individual lines of HTML for things like table cells, form fields, etc., which was far beyond the scope of the project.

In fact, the approach we settled on was as simple as possible: Load the entire page into a large <TEXTAREA> field and allow the user to edit the whole thing at once.

After some more experimentation, we settled on the rest of our simple interface and feature set, and set to work on the most important feature: making the script work for any number of users.

Security

If we left the HTML editor in its prototype state, it wouldn't be very useful at all. Personalized for a single user/single file, it would need to be duplicated, placed in a separate directory with access control, and edited before it would work for anyone else. However, there are ways of extending its flexibility without jeopardizing its security.

Our primary problem is one of permissions. It's trivial to allow multiple authenticated users to access the directory that contains the script, simply by adding them to the ".htaccess" file and making sure they have an entry in the password file (we'll cover this in detail later). The problem arises from the fact that, once the script is running, the user acquires the same effective user ID as that of the Web server. This is most often the *www* ID, but could even be *root* on some systems! Running a script that reads and edits files under that user ID could potentially allow the user read/write permissions to files the administrator wants to protect.

These files can include everything contained within the document root directory, CGI root directory, server logs, configuration files, and authentication files. This unleashes considerable destructive potential.

However, if we could limit each individual user of the editor to the page or pages that they *should* be allowed to access, our problem would be solved. This information could be stored in a protected configuration file for the script on a per-user basis and then read in when the user logged in. When a user authenticates him- or herself to an HTTP server in a CGI context, the environment variable 'REMOTE_USER' gets set to the login name they use. Therefore, our script could use this as a way to look up the page they have permission to edit.

It's much simpler to implement this method with an access system that limits each user to a single page. Once our proof of concept is completed with the first version of the editor, it could be adapted to allow a user access to a collection of files. If we are going to pursue this "single file for a single user" model, you may think we will be seriously limiting the usefulness of the script.

Another approach would be to limit the range of filenames that a single user could access—for example, a user with a login of karen would be limited to files that begin with "karen" in their filenames. This is an easy extension that enables access to multiple files, while preventing users from stepping on one another's files and permissions. The only thing it doesn't guard against is overuse of system resources.

However, we think it's fairly likely that a user on the average Web server will have a single home page that is the focus of most of his or her tweaking and editing activities. Therefore, if we target those users and position the script as a "home page editor," it can provide significant value even at this stage of development.

DEVELOPING THE EDITOR

We prototyped and tested the editor in a hardwired, single-user/single-file mode. The prototype was a typical quickie Perl script, complete with cut corners that made it platform- and even site-specific, chock full of undocumented, obfuscated code.

Once we were happy with the initial version, development started on a release version. This entailed cleaning up for readability and portability, as well as opening up the structure of the script for multiple users and multiple pages.

We also took the opportunity to roll the edit form and the supporting CGI into one script, following the model used for the Form Generator's output. This was an ideal script for such adaptation because it's relatively small and the form itself needs some built-in Perl code to load the appropriate file into the TEXTAREA in the HTML form.

Without further ado, let's take a stroll through the code, highlighting the aspects of the script that are most important and instructive.

Setup and Initialization

As always, we begin with the preamble necessary to set up a proper CGI:

```
$| = 1;                    # output NOT buffered
print "Content-Type:\ttext/html\n\n\n";
```

We've all seen the preceding two lines by this time in numerous other CGIs. We won't bore you by explaining their function again. Next comes the initialization of the variables necessary for the script to run:

```
$host = $ENV{SERVER_NAME};
$ENV{SCRIPT_NAME} =~ s/([a-zA-Z0-9\.\-_]+)$//;
$program = $1;
$scriptpath = $ENV{SCRIPT_NAME};
chop ($date = `/bin/date`);
# Modify next two lines to match local pathnames.
$docroot = "/www/httpdocs/";
$config_file = "/www/auth/users.homepages";
```

The last two variables are the only ones you may need to modify to make the script run on your server. The first, $docroot, is set to the directory that your HTTP server uses as its document root; in other words, the directory you get to when you submit a URL with no path. On our server, requesting the URL *http://www.outer.net/* returns the index for the directory */www/httpdocs*.

The second variable, $config_file, is the path and name of the file that contains the security configuration file. We suggest a secure location, such as your server's authentication directory.

The variables above these two are all initialized from the CGI's environment variables. This is a product of the Form Generator's "roll into Perl script" option. We must say that this particular feature of the Form Generator is particularly useful. The only reason it wasn't incorporated into more projects in this book was that it came fairly late in the Tool's development cycle. It greatly reduces the work an administrator needs to do to get the script to work and also reduces the script's overall vulnerability. Its name or path can be changed without changing its functionality.

Debugging Tools

The next line of the script reads simply:

```
$debug = 0;
```

We kept this development tool in the script to give you another example of useful CGI debugging. We've often said that developing and debugging CGI applications includes some special challenges, because there's no easy way to get inside the browser/server/script transactions.

Unlike writing code to run locally on your machine, you cannot step through CGI code in a real-world environment. Until someone comes up with a Perl debugger that can simulate a browser posting form data and a server calling the script, this kind of *ad hoc* measure will have to do.

When the variable is set to 1 and a browser posts data to the script, a conditional statement will evaluate as true and a subroutine will be run. This subroutine currently contains a simple dump of all the pertinent environment variables and their values. Although the subroutine actually is situated at the bottom of the script, we quote it here for relevancy's sake:

```
sub show_env {

print <<"EOM";
<PRE>

        ====== ENVIRONMENT VARIABLES ======
        argc is $ac
        argv is '$av'

        SERVER_SOFTWARE   = $ENV{SERVER_SOFTWARE}
        SERVER_NAME       = $ENV{SERVER_NAME}
        GATEWAY_INTERFACE = $ENV{GATEWAY_INTERFACE}
        SERVER_PROTOCOL   = $ENV{SERVER_PROTOCOL}
        SERVER_PORT       = $ENV{SERVER_PORT}
        REQUEST_METHOD    = $ENV{REQUEST_METHOD}
        HTTP_ACCEPT       = $ENV{HTTP_ACCEPT}
        PATH_INFO         = $ENV{PATH_INFO}
        PATH_TRANSLATED   = $ENV{PATH_TRANSLATED}
        SCRIPT_NAME       = $ENV{SCRIPT_NAME}
        QUERY_STRING      = $ENV{QUERY_STRING}
        REMOTE_HOST       = $ENV{REMOTE_HOST}
        REMOTE_ADDR       = $ENV{REMOTE_ADDR}
        REMOTE_USER       = $ENV{REMOTE_USER}
        AUTH_TYPE         = $ENV{AUTH_TYPE}
```

```
CONTENT_TYPE       = $ENV{CONTENT_TYPE}
CONTENT_LENGTH     = $ENV{CONTENT_LENGTH}


============================================================
</PRE>
EOM
}
```

You can see that we've taken advantage of a *here* document to avoid the long print statements we generally use in CGI applications. This is appropriate because we have a large block of <PRE> tagged text, and it will display exactly the way it appears in the *here* document, except that the names of the variables will be replaced by their values.

Also, keep in mind that this kind of debugging subroutine can be expanded upon to any degree. For example, it could be used to dump extracted field names and values back to the browser. Or, it could be used to check if a part of your code is manipulating the user's data correctly, by printing the code's intermediate steps during processing.

Unfortunately, the overall behavior of the script cannot be changed, due to the nature of HTTP and CGI, so advanced debugging techniques, such as starting and stopping the execution of the script at will, are out of reach for this kind of application.

Determining the Script's Mode

With the script's operating environment initialized, we can now determine the method used to call the script. Because we designed the CGI with the Form Tool, it serves both to provide the interface for the editor via a form and to support edit-handling for the user when completed.

The Renovator determines its mode of operation by examining the method by which it was accessed. When it's called by a simple URL, either from a mouse click on a link to its URL or by manual input, it assumes a default method of GET and returns the edit form. When the form is submitted, the method can be identified as POST, and the edited data handled appropriately.

The script's mode of operation is determined by a single conditional statement that checks both the access method and if there is URL-encoded data submitted:

```
if (($ENV{REQUEST_METHOD} eq "POST") &&
   ($ENV{CONTENT_TYPE}  eq "application/x-www-form-urlencoded")){
```

Obviously, this statement is set up to evaluate true if the script is called from its form, but this belies the script's logical function. Logically, it would operate in the non-POST mode, serving a form to the authenticated user first, and then operate upon submitted data second. Therefore, we'll reverse the order in which we look at the conditional's two blocks of code, to match this sequence.

Supplying the Editor Interface

If the Boolean statement above evaluates as false, the script drops down to the block of code contained within the else block. This retrieves the configuration file, finds the path to the file the user may edit, and then presents that file to the user in the editing environment.

Please note that the script presupposes the presence of an ".htaccess" file in its directory. To be more accurate, it does not presuppose that precise file, but rather it assumes that your server has restricted access to the script and that users must be authenticated in order to run it.

A further requirement of this authentication method is that it set the CGI environment variable 'REMOTE_USER' to the name used to gain access. By way of shorthand, we refer to this entire system as *.htaccess* because this is a common method for providing precisely such authentication. NCSA HTTP servers use it, as do its many offshoots, or some variation thereof. Whatever your particular server supports, if it fulfills the two requirements described above, it should work with the Renovator script.

The script will fail if 'REMOTE_USER' is not set correctly, which bespeaks an additional level of security. From the average browser there is no way to spoof the value of this variable because it is set on the server side. Therefore, if the user ID fails to match some entry in the configuration file, no editable source file will be opened and presented to the user.

A quick tour through this block of code illustrates how the authentication information, config file, and form elements are used to build the editor.

The following block of code calls the debug subroutine we brought to your attention earlier. During development, we used it to verify that our authentication scheme indeed set those environment variables that we required:

```
if ($debug) {
    &show_env
}
```

This one line is the key to our security measures in this script:

```
$user = $ENV{REMOTE_USER};
```

The $user variable is used to access the appropriate HTML document. With our configuration file open:

```
open (HOMEPAGES, "$config_file");
```

we now have access to a list of users and the files each one is authorized to edit. This config file is expected to take the form:

```
username<whitespace>/path/to/file
singe       /singe/home.html
```

There are two important points to note about this file. The whitespace between name and path can be any number of spaces or tabs; the path should be the URL path (i.e., the path relative to the server's document root). This means that the entry should look like the path component of the URL for the file. In other words:

```
http://www.outer.net/singe/home.hmtl
```

should result in the sample entry for singe, with a path of /singe/home.html. This is the case regardless of where the file physically resides on the server. You must supply the path that the HTTP server takes to get to the file, not the file's location within the server's file system.

The next block of code serves a single purpose, to find the user's entry in the file:

```
while (<HOMEPAGES>) {
    chop;
    @homepage = split;
    if ($user eq $homepage[0]) {
        $homepath = $homepage[1];
    }
}
```

Here, we take advantage of some Perl shorthand, using the default values for the split function to populate our @homepage array. With its default behavior, split separates the contents of the scratch space, where each line of the document is stored individually as it gets read from the file, into data elements based on the existence of any amount of whitespace between elements.

If our $user variable matches the first element of the @homepage array, we know we've found both our user and the page she or he is allowed to edit. Therefore, we preserve the current value for the second element of the array in the variable $homepath. Keep in mind that multiple entries for a single username result in preservation only of the last entry (which will be the only one that's acted upon).

Our next action is to test the $homepath variable to see if it was defined during our romp through the configuration file:

```
if ($homepath) {
```

If it isn't defined, the Boolean evaluates as false and we'll know the user may have been authenticated by the server but has not yet been assigned a page to edit. If this is the case, the following error message is returned to the user:

```
    } else { # no entry for user in config file
print "<H2>Sorry!</H2><P><FONT SIZE=4>There is no entry ",
        "for $user in the renovator's config file.</FONT>",
        "<P>Contact your sysadmin for help.";
}
```

Barring an administrator's oversight or a curious and lucky hacker, this error message should never appear. The user's entry should be found and the $homepage variable initialized. We'll jump back up from the else statement and dive into the code block that runs if the $homepath variable is defined:

```
$homepath =~ s/\/$//;
```

This regular expression-based substitution statement is here for robustness. We recognize that it isn't always easy to enter error-free data into a text file, and in experimenting with the config file ourselves, we found that a common mistake was to add a trailing slash to the file entry. Therefore, this simple command will find such a slash and remove it, as a safeguard against our own feeble human brains.

Now we attempt to open the document named in the configuration file for the current user:

```
open (HOME, "$docroot$homepath") || print "<H2>Can't ",
        "find $user's home page at $homepath</H2>" && die;
```

If it fails to open, we spit an error message back at the browser and then exit the script.

Provided the file does open, however, we come to the point in the script when we must set up the return page and, on it, the interface for the editor. We'll start with the regular niceties like <TITLE>:

```
print "<TITLE>The Renovator</TITLE>\n";
print "<H1><B><FONT SIZE=6>The Online HTML ",
      "editor</FONT></B></H1>\n";
print "<P><FONT SIZE=4>Any changes made to the HTML ",
      "document below will be written to the file http://",
      "$host/$homepath when you click the 'Edit' button ",
      "below.</FONT>\n";
```

With this preamble out of the way, we now get to the real meat of the interface. First we'll set up the FORM tag so that it calls the Renovator CGI again using the POST method:

```
print "<FORM METHOD=\"POST\" ",
      "ACTION=\"http://$host$scriptpath$program\">";
```

As you can see, we specify POST for the METHOD option, as with most HTML forms. We also specify the ACTION URL using the variables we extracted in the initialization stage to rebuild the script's URL. The next line sets up the form field that acts as the editing window:

```
print "<TEXTAREA NAME=\"HOMEPAGE\" ROWS=24 COLS=70 ",
      "WRAP=SOFT>\n";
```

It is a large TEXTAREA that we fill with the contents of the file to be edited. We're taking advantage of the new TEXTAREA option for soft-wrapping the text, to make it more readable. Previously, each line of text would run as far to the right as it could, often off the edge of the TEXTAREA window, making it difficult to read or edit.

We honestly do not know how this new "Netscapism" will affect other browsers when they view this page. Historically, most custom options have been ignored or, at worst, have caused the tag they're embedded in to not display. If you have users seeking to use the script with non-Netscape browsers and they have difficulties, remove the WRAP option. Our motivation for using it derives from the tremendous benefits the script received from its use (however, we've been informed that older versions of Mosaic will have problems with this; simply ignore the tag).

A final word about WRAP: Its best characteristic is that it behaves exactly as it should. In SOFT mode, it wraps the text by inserting line breaks that are stripped when the user submits the data. There is also a HARD mode that does not strip the breaks, but instead produces a text area forced to wrap to the size you set. Hurrah!

The script now reads, line-by-line, the entire edit file to be inserted into the TEXTAREA. Along the way, it performs various manipulations on the source text to make the editor work properly. We'll look at these small manipulations next, one at a time:

```
while (<HOME>) {
    if (/<\/TEXTAREA>/) {
```

If we find a tag in the source file that ends a TEXTAREA, we could be in trouble. Because we assume that the entire file will reside inside a single TEXTAREA in order for the user to be able to edit it, anything threatening that TEXTAREA threatens the script as a whole.

After an HTML browser sees the tag that begins a TEXTAREA, it ignores all else but the </TEXTAREA> tag. When it encounters that tag, it ends the current window by closing the TEXTAREA. If this happens to occur in the middle of a form the user wishes to edit, the rest of the file is dumped into the browser's window in an uneditable state.

Therefore, our first manipulation is to look for </TEXTAREA> in the source file and, if encountered, substitute it like this:

```
s/<\/TEXTAREA>/<- <\/TEXTAREA> ->/
```

This embeds the </TEXTAREA> tag inside an HTML comment, which the browser ignores. We can undo this transformation when we make the user's edits real on the other side of this script, so as not to disrupt the file's HTML integrity.

If, on the other hand, we encounter a line that looks like the Renovator's tag line, we want to make sure the update information is current:

```
} elsif (/last modified .* by/) {
```

We'll do this by substituting an up-to-date line for the old one:

```
$_ = "<I><FONT SIZE=1>last modified $date by <A ".
    "HREF=\"http://$host$scriptpath$program\">".
    "$program</A></FONT></I>\n";
$modline = 1;
```

You'll notice that we built the new line and instead of printing it, we assigned it to the scratch variable, $_. We did this because filling the TEXTAREA is accomplished by printing this variable into it, so in effect we're editing the line in place.

The second line in this section flags a Boolean that tells the rest of the script that we've found the tag line and modified it.

Here is the extremely simple statement that sends the source file into the TEXTAREA bucket, one line at a time:

```
        }
                print
        }
```

This statement also relies on the default behavior of Perl's print function. With no filehandle, list of strings, or variables specified, print outputs the contents of $_ to STDOUT. This filehandle name denotes a CGI's route back to the browser.

If we didn't find a line that reads last modified... with the date and by the program's name, then the Boolean variable $modline won't be defined, and the following Perl statement evaluates as true:

```
        if (!$modline) {
```

When this happens, the script proceeds to insert the line at the end of the document's window:

```
        print "<I><FONT SIZE=1>last modified $date by <A ",
            "HREF=\"http://$host$scriptpath$program\">",
            "$program</A></FONT></I>\n";
    }
```

We've now finished dumping content into the TEXTAREA window for editing. We can close the window and set up the rest of the form so that it's ready for editing and submission:

```
        print "</TEXTAREA>\n<P>\n";
        print "<INPUT TYPE=\"hidden\" NAME=\"PATH\" ",
            "VALUE=\"$homepath\">\n";
```

The hidden field is used to pass the user's authorized file to the POST side of this script to avoid having to read in the configuration file and parse it again.

This portion of the script is finished. The last two `print` statements create the SUBMIT button and a brief footer at the bottom of the page:

```
print "<INPUT TYPE=\"submit\" NAME=\"Change Page\" ",
      "VALUE=\"edit\">\n";
print "</FORM><ADDRESS>The Renovator written by <A HREF=",
      "\"http://www.outer.net/\">singe@outer.net</A>",
      "</ADDRESS>";
}
```

The end result is an editor window within a Web browser window that looks like Figure 14-1.

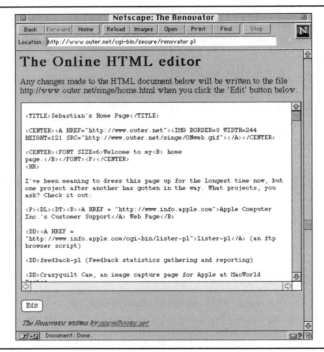

■ Figure 14-1
The online editor's interface.

The next step is for the user to edit the file's source and when finished, the SUBMIT button is clicked, and the data is passed off the script again, this time using the POST method.

Extracting Data and Modifying the Original File

Now that the script has been called again, by the form it spawned, we have a different job to do. The script must extract the form data to determine the file's path and the edited contents of the file. From there, it replaces the current version of the file with the edited version, and we're done!

The first step is to extract the data. Remember, we've just dropped down into this block of code because our top-level conditional statement evaluates as true. This tells us that the script was indeed called via POST, but also that there is URL-encoded data waiting for us on standard input. The next section of code is designed to read that data and extract field name/value pairs.

The read function accepts a precise number of bytes from the filehandle named, in this case STDIN. The data is stored in the variable named as the second parameter, $input:

```
read(STDIN,$input,$ENV{CONTENT_LENGTH});
```

Next is a shorthand way of splitting the input data on the URL-encoding separator character, &, and feeding each of the resulting members of the list through the code encapsulated by the foreach statement:

```
foreach (split("&", $input)) {
```

We capture the data on either side of the equal sign using the parentheses inside the regular expression, then assign them to more decipherable variable names, here $name and $value:

```
/(.*)=(.*)/;
$name = $1;
$value = $2;
```

Plus signs are substituted with spaces throughout the data:

```
$value =~ s/\+/ /g ;
```

The next line uses extended regular expression rules in combination with the pack and hex functions to translate the hex values for meta-characters back into their character representations:

```
$value =~ s/%(..)/pack('c',hex($1))/eg;
```

An example is the space character; when URL-encoded, it's represented as %20, where the percent sign is used to flag the presence of a hexadecimal number representing a character. The left-hand side of the regular expression scans for the percent sign and captures the two characters following it in $1 using the parentheses.

The right-hand side of the regular expression feeds the hex value into hex, which returns the decimal value. This is then fed to pack with the c, or "unsigned character" template. pack is a way to coerce data from one format to another, here from decimal ASCII values to true character representations for those values. %20 captured on the left-hand side ends up being replaced with " " by the end of the line.

A simple two-branched conditional checks to see if this field name has previously received a value:

```
if (defined $in{$name}) {
$in{$name} .= "#" . $value
        } else {
             $in{$name} = $value;
        }
    }
```

If so, the current value is added to the previous value, separated by a #. If it hasn't been previously defined, the field name is used as a key for an associative array pair, and the value is used as the value for that pair.

We'd like to mention yet again that the preceding form data code was adapted liberally from Brigitte Jellinek's *formlib.pl*. Hers was one of the first code libraries to support the type of manipulation we perform in this script. It's safe to say that we may never have successfully conquered CGIs if she hadn't made her code so useful and so broadly available.

If you're still interested in debugging, now would be an excellent time to insert your script in motion. You could set it to print all the field names and values so that you can get a picture of the browser/server/client transaction.

This Old Home Page

The previous stage in our code dealt with collecting data; the next stage will put that data to use. We're ready for the changed home page to be written out to disk. Because we already know that the user is authenticated and we have the path to the file, all that remains before writing it out is to make a backup.

For convenience, we create a new variable with the contents of both $docroot and $in{PATH} concatenated together:

```
$path = $docroot . $in{PATH};
```

Together they create an absolute path to the file on the server. We'll use the full path first to create the backup, then to write over the old version:

```
open (OLDHOME, "$path");
open (BACKUP, ">$path.backup") || print "<H2>Error: Can't open",
        "         $path.backup for writing: $!</H2>" && die;
print BACKUP while <OLDHOME>;
close BACKUP;
close OLDHOME;
```

With our backup complete, we can safely overwrite the old version. The first step is to reverse the commented-out </TEXTAREA> tags. We do this by scanning the contents of the <TEXTAREA> input field and reversing the substitution we performed when originally placing the file's contents in a <TEXTAREA>:

```
while ($in{HOMEPAGE} =~ /<− <\/TEXTAREA> −>/) {
    $in{HOMEPAGE} =~ s/<− <\/TEXTAREA> −>/<\/TEXTAREA>/;
}
```

With the TEXTAREA restored, we can now open a filehandle to write to the file's name:

```
open (HOME, ">$path") || print "<H2>Can't open home page at",
                                "$path!</H2>" && die;
print HOME $in{HOMEPAGE};
print $in{HOMEPAGE};
```

We'll echo the field contents at the same time to both the new file's home page and the user's browser. In this way, the user gets a preview of the form/document and can decide how the edits turned out.

Keep in mind here that what the user sees is not really the page, just its HTML source. To see changes on the actual document, the user must force the browser to reload the entire page from the server, not from internal cache.

The final element on the page is a blurb that reminds users to reload and provides a link to do the reload:

```
print "<P><B>Goto <A HREF=\"http://$host/$in{PATH}\">real home",
    " page</A>. Remember to reload!";
```

This link is built from information gleaned from environment variables, as well as the URL path to the edited file provided by the editor form. As anyone who plays with HTML and CGIs knows, coercing a browser into actually loading the contents of a page from the server can be difficult. It sometimes seems that some browsers are so optimized for cached retrieval that they have lost the ability to do anything else!

This poses a challenge to an administrator or a developer because users may edit files online, then "reload" the old version of the page from their cache and complain that the editor doesn't work.

The good news is that the Macintosh beta of Netscape 2.0 has an undocumented feature: Hold down the "Option" key on your keyboard and the "Reload" option under the "View" menu becomes "Super Reload." This forces the browser to contact the server and truly reload the page.

With that, we've completed our tour of the script's source code. As you can see, supplying an online text editor is really not very difficult, at least at this basic level. The primary concerns are security-related and we believe that with this script, we've created a fairly secure environment.

What if you wanted to extend the editor's functionality? In the next section we'll look at the potential directions such enhancements might take.

EXTENDING THE EDITOR

Obviously, dumping raw HTML source into a TEXTAREA window does not qualify our editor for a "bells and whistles" award. This is most definitely a bare-bones editing environment, but that doesn't mean it has to stay that way.

Text and HTML editors on desktop computers today are famous (and in some cases infamous) for the number of features they possess. On first considering which direction to take with our editor, you might think that we should emulate one of the big-time editors and start throwing features into the mix. This is not a workable approach for several reasons.

First, it isn't always possible to implement features that work in a desktop context in a Web client/server context. In other chapters, we've looked at the various limitations of both HTML and HTTP and should be well versed by now in what we can and can't expect the Web to do. In a pure HTTP/HTML operating environment, all features must be implemented using a call-and-response structure, where actions and choices on the client's end are relayed to the server, which acts upon the input received. The resulting output is redelivered to the client, and the user sees the end product of the original input.

Clearly this model doesn't easily support dynamic editing features, such as formatting or spell-checking on-the-fly. The introduction of development tools such as Java and JavaScript in the near future may make the environment more flexible, but in the meantime we must work with what's available.

Constraints notwithstanding, with careful thought and consideration, we can still add functionality to the editor that adds value for the end user. The key phrase to remember is "add value for the end user" because this should be our primary consideration when adding features. There is little point in throwing features randomly into the CGI program simply because they are possible. Rather, the best approach is to brainstorm a whole array of things that our users will find valuable and useful.

Advanced Parsing

We mentioned in an earlier section our decision not to parse the script at all when presenting it to the user for editing. The current version of the script follows this behavior: It dumps the entire file into one big TEXTAREA window, then lets the user deal with it in its raw form. However, if this is to be an HTML editor, there are many manipulations we could perform on the file before it's displayed.

Earlier, we discussed separating the document's <HEAD>, <BODY>, and <ADDRESS> sections into separate editing windows. This may be of some small value in itself, but you could make it more interesting if you also provide parsing within these structures. If, for example, the HEAD-editing portion of the tool also provided fields for the BODY tag options, such as custom background, text color, link color, etc. (filled out with the user's values if they exist), it would be much simpler to customize the file quickly.

This concept could be extended to a few other key tags, particularly ones with multiple options. The IMG tag, for example, with its dimension, border, alignment, and other options, would be a good candidate. But there's a risk in adding this compartmentalized approach to our interface. We may over-complicate the editor and make it more difficult to see the overall flow of the document if too many of the tags are separated out from the bulk of the text. If we could offer this as an alternate view, it might mitigate the potential clutter.

In fact, if you had such a segregated view available, you could take the parsing concept to the limit, separating each element into a separate entity, with inputs for each of the tag's options. This would actually be a good approach to the feature we talked about including in the Form Generator Tool, in the first section of the book. We talked about how the Tool might be able to load an existing form for editing. If you took this approach, parsing and separating each element from the others, and supplying a custom interface for each one that enabled users to see at a glance how its options were currently set (as well as change them on-the-fly), you could add significant value to that tool.

The difficulty in adding this functionality comes from HTML's design for human- rather than machine-readability. What this means is that there's a lot of leeway about what constitutes a valid HTML file. Therefore, our parsing engine would have to be fairly sophisticated to properly interpret any (and every) possible HTML document.

That engine would make the most sense if it was contained within subroutines that could be used to filter the file as it was being sent back to the browser. That way, you could have control over whether the file was parsed, depending on the user's wishes.

The new Frames implementation in Netscape may enable the adventurous reader to create this, as described, and view the parsed and unparsed views simultaneously. This would help the editing process considerably.

Preferences

The discussion of a "parsed view" strongly suggests another area that is ripe for feature enhancement. If you had a toolbar area at the bottom of the large editor window you could provide a form interface (including buttons) to lead to the parsed and separated views of the file, or back to the simple editor window.

In addition, you could offer the user fields to specify the size of the TEXTAREA window, the WRAP mode, and other characteristics of the editing environment. When submitted, these option values could be used to recreate the form that is presented to the user on-the-fly, so that they would see such changes immediately.

If you wanted to get really involved in the preferences concept, you could actually record a user's preferences in the editor's configuration file. We already have an entry for the user specifying the file to be edited, so there's no reason why you couldn't use that entry for more data. In this way, you could preserve the state of the editor when a user finishes an editing session.

Access to Multiple Files

Finally, we get to the most obvious feature that is currently missing from the editor: access to multiple files. While it's true that many users on a Web server have a single home page that they spend most of their time editing, some home pages are split across a number of files in a directory. In addition, any Web server has a small number of people who need to maintain a large number of files located all over the place.

We originally constrained the scope of the editor to access a single file per user for security reasons, but if we did our job right, the design of the editor could be made more flexible without jeopardizing the server's security. The best way to do this would be to adapt reading the configuration file so that a user's entry could be a path to a single file or a whole directory, linked to a particular kind of filename, or some other control method.

This way, the administrator can be more flexible about who gets access to what parts of the server. If users have an entire directory to themselves, as is sometimes the case, this directory could be listed in their configuration information, rather than just a single file.

If we modify the configuration file, we'll have to modify the behavior of the script as well. Instead of loading right up to the editing window with the file in it, we'll have to provide some way to select the file the user wants to edit.

One way to handle this would be to create a different form interface, generated only when a user has access to a directory (rather than a single file). This interface could be adapted from the toolbar we talked about adding to the bottom of the editing environment. The toolbar not only allows users to select a file they have permission to access, but also to set environment preferences, before launching into the editor form.

The interface for selecting a form could be as simple as a pop-up menu that lists all the files in the target directory. There would have to be several code widgets to handle this properly. First, non-text files should be filtered out. The easiest way to do this would be to use the UNIX *file* command to determine the file's content type and to include or exclude it as circumstances dictate. More filtering should be done to exclude files that the

HTTP server user can't write to, to prevent a situation where a user edits a file and then cannot submit the changes.

Additionally, if there's a directory within the target directory and the user selects it, the script should be smart enough to return the toolbar/file-browser form again, this time with a pop-up of the new directory's contents. You may want to consider barring access to subdirectories, because it reintroduces our fears about security breaches.

If a user creates a soft (symbolic *ln -s*) link to a directory they shouldn't have access rights to, the browser could possibly permit them to edit files they shouldn't be touching. One way around this is to require that any subdirectories in the target directory be owned by the user's login ID before access is allowed. Whatever approach you take needs to be considered carefully, especially for these kinds of potential security breaches.

SUMMARY

We've discussed at length the potential security concerns this script raises. We've also seen the inner workings of the editor script and potential uses and enhancements to the Tool. We think that the online editor represents value significant enough to offset its potential dangers. Whether you install it on your Web server is obviously your call.

Our own rule of thumb with these kinds of issues is generally to try risky software ourselves, making sure to install it as securely as possible. As with all security issues, the key is good management. Controlling who is included in access and configuration files and what they're given access to are sufficient safeguards.

The important lesson to learn from this entire exercise is that there's a tremendous number of common, everyday applications that can be adapted to the Web's peculiar client/server model. The potential gains from adopting this approach, and its potential results, are truly staggering.

WEB COMMERCE OPTIONS

*O*ne of the hottest Internet topics today is the World Wide Web as a marketplace. If you look at any issue of a Net-related magazine, from industry snoops like *Communications Week* to the more mainstream *Internet World*, you'll probably find several articles on the Web as a mall or some other kind of "shopping experience."

Some of the Net's seasoned citizens (those who used it even before the Web was invented) see its commercial use as the end of an era for the Internet. It's a place where people have been able to speak their minds or download public domain software that was often better than its commercial counterparts.

IS THE NET ZONED COMMERCIAL?

Until recently, "credit authorization" and "retail price" weren't part of the Net vocabulary. Some people feel that the entire Net will be for sale someday; that entire internetworks will be broken off from others; and that you'll have to pay if you want access to the "good stuff." They feel that the glory of the Internet is quickly being replaced by a carnival, where you have to pay for each ride.

For other people and companies, the entire reason they're getting on the Internet is for profit, not fun. They view the Internet as a fantastic new marketing medium—a great way to make your name known globally, usually for a fraction of normal advertising costs.

In Austin, Texas, for example, there are at least two dozen companies that have sprung up *specifically* to do online marketing. When you throw in the advertising and marketing firms that are expanding onto the Web, Internet Service Providers with Web design departments, freelancing students, and moonlighters doing Web work for profit, there are probably a couple hundred "Web Page Developers" for hire in most towns the size of Austin!

Web Commerce: A Hypermall or Just Hype?

Regardless of how you feel about sales on the Internet, be warned that it's going to happen. As a matter of fact, it already has. Various Web sites now permit you to purchase items online via credit card. Some offer secure financial transactions, while others don't.

Some Web Presence Providers, such as HyperMall, iMALL, or First Virtual's Infohaus, are launching Web shopping malls to handle online sales. All of these are run by companies running Web servers that allow secure financial transactions. iMALL does it by running a secure Web server, shown in Figure 15-1. (Notice the unbroken key signifying that transactions between our Netscape browser and their Netscape Commerce server are secure. We'll talk more about this later.) First Virtual operates by acting as a financial clearinghouse—a trusted go-between for the buyer and seller. We'll discuss both of these transaction methods later in the chapter. In the meantime, you can visit Infohaus at:

```
http://infohaus.com/
```

iMALL at:

```
http://www.imall.com
```

and HyperMall at:

```
http://www.hypermall.com
```

Figure 15-1
iMALL's main entrance. Notice iMALL uses a Secure Service.

Hasn't This Been Done Before?

Online sales are really nothing new. CompuServe's Electronic Mall has been open for business for about a decade, and the other major online services also have vendors doing financial transactions. The companies doing business on these services have nominal success. They make enough online sales to keep them there, but it's by no means their primary storefront. So what's the big fuss about doing sales on the Net?

One World, One Net

The biggest attraction is that the Net is global. Putting your storefront on CompuServe or America Online means that only subscribers to those services can get to you—making your product available on the Internet expands your accessibility to a whole worldful of shoppers.

Not only will AOL and other Internet-gatewayed online service subscribers be able to reach your site, but so will students with university accounts, and people with access at work. This potential outreach is what has people buzzing about Web commerce.

So Why Hasn't It Caught On?

Although there are thousands of companies with Web presences these days, only a small fraction of them handle online sales. Why is this? It all boils down to the bottom line.

When a business establishes itself on the Web, the initial setup of its site is usually quick, dirty, and cheap. In fact, some employees might be willing to do it for free as an after-hours project. Then, one of two things happens:

1. The site is scarcely visited and doesn't seem to generate any exposure. Solution: Hire a Web design company to beautify the pages, add more multimedia, and market the site aggressively.

2. The site becomes decently popular. Great, right? Unfortunately its popularity consumes your total ISDN bandwidth, crippling your server, and now all of your company's divisions want periodically updated pages on the site. Solution: Get a T1 connection, double your server's RAM, and hire a full-time WebMaster.

Both solutions are the same: Throw money at the site. The only other option is to shut it down.

Most companies with Web presences are either still in the "quick, dirty, and cheap" stage, or they've just come to the crossroads described above. The Web remains unproven as an advertising and marketing medium, and only a small portion of companies with Web presences are currently willing to gamble on it as a sales tool.

But don't worry: Many already do, and eventually most will! These organizations' caution is warranted, but the Web as a medium for commerce will prove itself soon enough.

The Security Question

Many Internet and Web pundits have stated the theory that the reason more companies aren't selling on the Web derives more from security concerns than fiscal prudence. This is probably true for some businesses, thanks in part to the paranoia generated by these pundits themselves, but it doesn't explain the entire phenomenon.

The chief fear when purchasing over the Net is that sales information might be intercepted by an illegitimate party while in transit between the buyer's and seller's systems. The picture painted by the media is that of cabals of rabid hackers "sniffing" the Net for packets of data containing credit card numbers. This is a real possibility that shouldn't be ignored, and measures to prevent and punish this type of "data-jacking" should be enforced. But how much of this concern represents technophobia overshadowing common sense and how much of it is justified?

Is the Paranoia Misplaced?

The average consumer puts his or her credit card information at risk several times a day, without even thinking about it. There's the obvious possibility of a card being stolen from your wallet. There's also the chance that a dishonest sales clerk might copy and illicitly use your card information.

Have you ever made a credit card purchase from a cordless or cellular phone? Someone with an inexpensive scanner could pick up your phone's frequency and obtain your card information that way. Then there's "trashing": Going through the trash at a location where card transactions produce throwaway slips and receipts to obtain credit card numbers and other information.

Our point is that it's no easier to obtain credit card information over the Internet than it is anywhere else. In fact, it's more difficult: It takes technical savvy and the right software to sniff Internet packets, while anyone can rummage through the garbage at your local gas station.

One Benefit of Paranoia

In saying that insecure credit transactions over the Net aren't as risky as many others, we realize that we're comparing bad to worse. We're by no means saying that everything's fine the way it is and that the development of secure financial services should halt.

Airlines have long said that they're the "safest way to travel." With current advances in Web security, it may soon be said that the Web is the "safest way to pay with credit." Various encryption measures implemented by secure Web browsers and servers will make the data they send and receive nearly impossible to decode by a third party, even if intercepted.

In addition, if credit card data could be sent from buyer's to seller's systems securely, card processing could take place directly from the seller's system to the credit card company (either using the same type of security over the Internet, or through a private network). This approach eliminates human intermediaries from any access to credit information.

Implementing Commerce in Your Web Development

As a Web programmer, what do you need to know about Web commerce? The first thing to know is that many businesses are interested in making the Web a point-of-sale for their products. If you're programming a site for a business, chances are good that sooner or later they'll want the option of selling their wares online.

The second thing to realize is that businesses and the public are deeply concerned about Web transaction security. Whether this is overblown or not, they don't want to put themselves at unnecessary financial and legal risk.

The third thing is to know your options. The two Web commerce options discussed in this chapter are:

1. Web commerce via secure communications
2. Web commerce via a trusted third party

While this is not a complete list, it represents the best of what's available today. For more information on this topic, visit your favorite search engine with the keywords "Internet commerce" or "Web commerce" and gape at the flood of information that results!

Secure Communications

Many businesses already have systems in-house to process cards with major credit card companies. These are usually either custom-crafted or provided by the card companies themselves. But there's still the issue of getting the credit card data from the buyer's browser to the business's Web server. Here, we're concerned about transmission of this information.

There are two major proposed secure transmission standards for Web information. The first is Secure Hypertext Transfer Protocol (S-HTTP), which encrypts the HTTP message itself. The second is Secure Sockets Layer (SSL), which layers security at the socket-level, *beneath* the HTTP application protocol. We'll cover both approaches, beginning with a little background coverage of the authentication, encryption, and data integrity techniques that they use.

S-HTTP and SSL are not mutually exclusive. In fact, they can complement each other by using S-HTTP over SSL. Because of this, we'll discuss the costs and benefits of using secure communications as a whole, rather than comparing and contrasting individual methods.

A Trusted Third Party

A trusted third party acts as an intermediary between buyers and sellers and becomes a clearinghouse for their transactions. Here's an example: Both buyers and sellers set up "accounts" with the third party. Only the third party has access to their true financial information (i.e., the buyer's credit card information and the seller's checking account information).

When buyers want to purchase something, they give the seller their third-party account numbers. The seller reports these numbers and the amount of the transaction to the third party, and the third party verifies with the buyers via e-mail that they do want their transactions to be processed. If they do, the third party charges the buyer's credit card and deposits the money in the seller's checking account. No encryption techniques or special clients are necessary; all related communications can even occur via e-mail.

The example described above is actually the First Virtual Internet Payment System (FVIPS), created by First Virtual Holdings—pioneers in this method of Internet commerce. We'll discuss FVIPS further and focus on its pros and cons. We'll also step through a CGI script created using the Form Generation Tool that sets up a sample commerce form, processes the information, and sends it to the First Virtual API for verification and billing. Finally, we'll compare the trusted third-party method to the secure communications method.

SECURE COMMUNICATIONS

As we've said, many companies already have an in-house custom system for processing financial transactions. With these businesses, the issue is not *how* to accept payment methods, such as credit cards, but the *transmission* of the payment information over the Internet.

As we've said, with a packet sniffer, anyone can capture and break down TCP/IP packets on the Internet and obtain the data therein. In many ways, such individuals would have to be in the right place at the right time. Someone with a SLIP connection in San Francisco can't just "see" the transactions between iMALL and a buyer in New Jersey. To capture these packets, snoopers must have physical or remote access to a system on the buyer's network, the iMALL's network, or one of the networks in between.

But since the possibility of an anonymous eavesdropper does exist, the security of the data communication is paramount in Web-based financial transactions.

Ensuring Secure and Reliable Communications

For this level of security to exist without the possibility of tampering, there must be three components involved: authentication, encryption, and integrity.

Authentication

Authentication gives an assurance that the person you think you're communicating with is indeed that person. For secure Web transactions, it lets the client verify the identity of the server, and the server that of the client. It does this using a *digital signature* that's based on pubic key cryptography techniques.

Encryption

Encryption provides security by scrambling a message before transmission, which the recipient then unscrambles. If the message is intercepted, then the encryption should be robust enough to prevent it from being decoded by the interceptor. Public key cryptography is the current method of choice for encryption.

Integrity

Integrity verifies that the contents of a message arrives at its destination in the same form as sent. This may also be accomplished with public key cryptography, because it's assumed that if the signature isn't broken, the message must be the one that was sent.

All three of these items—authentication, encryption, and integrity—are necessary for secure, verifiable transactions between two systems.

So What Is Public Key Cryptography?

Like any encryption technique, public key cryptography attempts to provide a secure method of data encryption using a *key* system. The key is a code that is used to encrypt and decrypt the information in a communication. Until public key standards were developed, a secret key-pair had to be shared between two holders. Such is the case with the Data Encryption Standard (DES), which we'll discuss first.

Secret Key Cryptography and DES

DES is a shared secret-key encryption system originally developed by IBM. It was declared a standard by the United States government in 1977 and has since become the most widely used encryption scheme in the world. One of its most common implementations is in the *crypt* program on UNIX systems, which provides encryption for passwords.

DES has never really been "broken," and transactions between two parties using it are still considered safe. But there are a couple of issues that make it unwieldy at best for secure Web commerce transactions.

Problems with Sharing Secret Keys

For two parties to exchange DES-encrypted communications with one another, both must have access to the same secret key for encryption and decryption. Each party must trust the other not to reveal this key to anyone else. This trust-based environment may be fine for communication between two users, or even between parties on a small network of users. But for moderate to large networks, or the Internet, it has three drawbacks:

1. For secure communications among several different parties, you'll need separate secret keys to be shared between you and each of the other parties. This can become unmanageable for large numbers of users.

2. Because a secret key must be shared with DES, there must be some kind of prior relationship between the parties involved in which they create the agreed-upon key. In a Web commerce environment, this would mean that a prospective buyer must contact the vendor and agree upon a key before any transaction could take place.

3. To share a secret key, some type of contact must take place. For key sharing among a large number of users, making this transaction secure is next to impossible. In a Web commerce situation, for instance, you wouldn't want to share a secret key via Internet e-mail because someone could intercept the e-mail and obtain the key. You could encrypt the message containing the key, but that would still require some type of contact in order to obtain that key.

Problems with Authentication

Since you and other parties share the same secret key, this makes it impossible to tell which member of this group may have modified data. There's no unique "digital signature" for each party.

Let's look at a Web commerce example: Let's say your position in a company requires that you occasionally make stock purchases from a stockbroker's secure Web site. There's another employee who's also granted this access in case you're out. Using DES encryption you, the other employee and the stockbroker's server must share the same secret key.

One day you come back from lunch and find that thousands of dollars had been placed on a penny stock that plummeted. You're surprised to see that the Web's feedback form shows your name on the transaction because you know you didn't make it. You suspect the other employee, but how can you prove it, since both of you have access to the same key? With a single shared key, it becomes all too easy to forge something in someone else's name.

For more information on the DES cryptography standard, check out what RSA has to say about it in its "FAQ About Today's Cryptography":

```
http://www.rsa.com/rsalabs/faq/faq_des.html
```

The RSA Public Key Cryptosystem (PKC)

These problems with authentication and sharing keys among large number of users have since been addressed. In 1977 Ronald Rivest, Adi Shamir, and Len Adelman invented the *RSA Public Key Cryptosystem* while at the Massachusetts Institute of Technology. They since founded RSA Data Security, Inc. and its research arm, RSA Labs, to further develop PKCs and other data security methods. ("RSA" is a combination of the creators' last-name initials.)

RSA is a for-profit company, and its product is the algorithm used in its patented public key cryptosystem. It sells this algorithm, known as the *RSARef*, or the C libraries to implement it, to companies such as Netscape, IBM, and Microsoft that wish to implement a PKC in their products.

The RSARef is free from RSA, if you're using it only for educational and testing purposes (i.e., you're not going to release any product, free or otherwise, that uses the technology). Both S-HTTP and SSL use the RSA Public Key Cryptosystem.

How the RSA PKC Works

The RSA Public Key Cryptosystem uses a pair of matched keys instead of just one shared key. A user will have both an RSA Public Key and an RSA Private Key. A user makes the Public Key public information, usually by posting it where anyone can get to it, such as on the Web. The user's RSA Private Key will be kept secret by the user.

Here's an example: When Nicholas wants to send Anna a private message, he'll use Anna's public key to encrypt it. Once encrypted, it can only be decrypted by Anna's private key. For the FAQ on the RSA Public Key Cryptosystem, see the following document:

```
http://www.rsa.com/rsalabs/faq/faq_rsa.html
```

Nicholas can also scramble a message using his private key, which Anna can unscramble by using his public key. Why would he want to do this? While not useful as a means to send secure data *per se*, private key encryption is useful as a way to authenticate that something actually came from the purported sender. If Anna can decrypt a piece of data using Nicholas' public key, then she knows that it *had* to have been created with his private key. Only Nicholas himself should have access to his private key, so the data had to come from him. This is what supports the notion of a digital signature.

The RSA Digital Signature

To create a digital signature, a document is sent through a hashing algorithm that generates a *message digest*. (Examples of Message Digest algorithms are RSA's MD2 and MD5.) The user then encrypts the message digest using his or her private key.

When a document is received, the recipient also sends it through a hashing program to calculate the message digest. The recipient then decodes the sender's digital signature using his or her public key and compares the message digest contained therein to the one the recipient generated. If they match, then the recipient can be assured that the document wasn't tampered with in transit, because only the original sender can use their private key for encryption.

Digital ID

The one hole in a digital signature is that the recipient can't be sure that even the public key received with a message really belongs to its claimed owner. For example, I could create public and private keys authenticating myself as "Jerry Smith," but they only prove that the messages are from a person calling himself Jerry Smith. The way around this is through Digital ID.

A *Digital ID* is someone's public key that has been "digitally signed" by someone trusted to do so; for instance, a security director, a network administrator, or a service that's been set up to process Digital IDs.

One such service is VeriSign, a company set up by RSA Data Services specifically to provide authentication for digital signatures. Having such trusted parties sign your digital signature means that you are in real life who you say you are in cyberspace. It's much like having a Notary Public witness a physical signature. VeriSign has already created Digital IDs for the likes of Netscape, IBM, Apple, and CompuServe. For more information about their services, and Digital IDs in general, visit them at:

```
http://www.verisign.com
```

When Anna sends a message digest encrypted with her private key to Nicholas, she includes her Digital ID with it. Her Digital ID is signed by VeriSign, so Nicholas uses their public key to decrypt it. That verifies that it's really hers, so he then uses her now decoded public key to decrypt the message digest. He then verifies the decrypted message digest against the one he gets from his hashing algorithm.

All of this sounds complex because we have users performing these tasks. However, it can all be incorporated into a security-aware application so everything takes place automatically, as is the case with both S-HTTP and SSL.

Now that you've got the cryptography background, let's get into its application using these two security techniques!

SECURE HYPERTEXT TRANSFER PROTOCOL (S-HTTP)

The first secure communications method we'll explore is S-HTTP. This approach is promoted by Enterprise Integration Technologies (EIT), a company that provides and enables electronic commerce. It's essentially HTTP with security enhancements, geared exclusively toward Web transaction security.

The Design of S-HTTP

Work on S-HTTP has been underway since 1994, and it's currently at version 1.1. Though an Internet Engineering Task Force draft has been created, it's still considered a work-in-progress, and no formal RFC or stamp of approval has been given by a standards committee. You can download the current Internet specification draft on EIT's anonymous ftp site at:

```
ftp.eit.com/pub/standards/drafts/shttp.txt
```

If you go searching for information on S-HTTP, you'll want to use "S-HTTP" as your search string, rather than "S-HTTP." For some reason, we couldn't find anything when using the hyphen in the name on our favorite search engines, but eliminating the hyphen turned up a mountain of stuff!

Message-Based Security

S-HTTP offers what is called *message-based security*. That is, the content and sender of an HTTP message is verifiable by the recipient. This message is contained within the S-HTTP protocol itself, encoded as it goes out, and decoded as it's received. This approach is similar to Privacy Enhanced Messaging (PEM) and some MIME efforts. As we'll see, SSL uses a different approach by installing security *underneath* the HTTP protocol rather than *within* it.

Encryption, Authentication, and Integrity Support

S-HTTP 1.1 currently offers support for both RSA's Public Key Cryptosystem Standard Level 7 (PKCS-7) and Privacy Enhanced Messaging (PEM), but it doesn't have to be limited to these two. It can provide a secure transaction through data signature, authentication, and encryption.

You can use any combination of these services, or none of them at all. Several types of key management systems are allowed, including shared secret keys (as with DES), public key exchange, and Kerberos ticket distribution. Although S-HTTP supports the option of using specific public keys, it doesn't require it. Someone using an S-HTTP-aware browser can have a secure session without knowing the public key of the connection point or their own public key.

S-HTTP Implementation as an End User

Much of S-HTTP's implementation takes place at the S-HTTP browser and *S-HTTPd* server. You don't need to make any changes to HTML or any other message type to make S-HTTP work: It's all in the application's transport protocol. If you're viewing information on an *S-HTTPd* server via an S-HTTP-compliant browser, you shouldn't notice anything strange or new about secure documents.

With Netscape, it's easy to tell when communications are secure or not: There's a key icon in the bottom left-hand corner of the browser window. When it's broken, communications are insecure; when it's whole, some form of secure communications are in use. Don't send any credit card or other sensitive information unless your key is complete!

S-HTTP Implementation as a Web Developer

S-HTTP is a highly configurable security protocol. Not only can you specify what types of encryption will be used, but what order they'll be negotiated, and what specific algorithms must be used. You can also specify a prearranged key to use in a transaction, and which message digest algorithm to use for digital signatures (check the Internet draft specification for S-HTTP mentioned earlier for more information on all of its features).

For our purposes, we'll cover three S-HTTP configuration headers: Content-Privacy-Domain, Content-Type, and Content-Transfer-Encoding.

Content-Privacy-Domain

The Content-Privacy-Domain header sets which type of encryption protocol will be used. It can be either PKCS-7 or PEM, both of which were described earlier.

Content-Type

In regards to S-HTTP, Content-Type means the same thing as it does in HTTP. The important thing is to make the Content-Type whatever the message content will be after it has been completely decoded.

Content-Transfer-Encoding

Content-Transfer-Encoding describes which encoding method you'll use with your encryption algorithm. For PKCS-7 it can be either BASE64, 8BIT, or BINARY; BASE64 is the most secure encryption and BINARY the least. For PEM it can only be 7BIT.

S-HTTP Web Servers and Browsers

If you're expecting to see a list of free S-HTTP-compliant Web servers and browsers in this section, then you'll be sorely disappointed! There are very few products implementing S-HTTP at this time, and all of them require some sort of payment.

Although the S-HTTP specification is in the public domain, the public key cryptosystem algorithm they use still belongs to RSA and requires licensing of the RSARef from RSA.

Secure NCSA httpd and Mosaic: Members Only!

Much of the development in servers and browsers that supports S-HTTP has been done by an organization called CommerceNet. CommerceNet was founded by EIT, RSA, and NCSA to help implement and improve the S-HTTP specification. It has a member base that includes Internet juggernauts such as Netscape, America Online, and CompuServe, as well as financial institutions like Citibank, MasterCard, and First Interstate. For more information on CommerceNet, see their Web site:

```
http://www.commerce.net
```

EIT, NCSA, and RSA all contributed to creating S-HTTP enhanced versions of both NCSA's *httpd* Web server and NCSA's Mosaic Web browser for CommerceNet. Unfortunately for most of us, you have to be a CommerceNet Sponsoring Member to use the server and browser, or a CommerceNet Associate Member to use only the browser. The price tag for Sponsoring Membership is $35,000 per year. For an Associate Member it's $5,000 per year. In other words, you better *really* want to engage in Web commerce. If you're still interested, the Secure NCSA *httpd* home page is at:

```
http://www.commerce.net/software/Shttpd/
```

and Secure NCSA Mosaic's page is at:

```
http://www.commerce.net/software/SMosaic/
```

Open Market's Secure WebServer

CommerceNet member Open Market sells its own Secure WebServer for a variety of UNIX flavors, including BSD, AIX, SunOS, and Solaris. Their package implements both S-HTTP and SSL and costs $4,995. You can get an overview and learn more about its technical specifications at:

```
http://www.openmarket.com/products/secureweb.html
```

CompuServe's S-HTTP Offerings

Another CommerceNet member, CompuServe, offers both an S-HTTP enhanced server and browser. The server is marketed as the "Internet Office Web Server" and used to be Spry's "SafetyWEB." The S-HTTP-aware version sells for $1,999 and is available for Windows NT and many UNIX flavors (including Solaris, BSD, and Linux). You can view the data sheet at:

```
{ http://www.compuserve.com:80/prod_services/corp_solutions/ioff_server/
{ ioff_server.html
```

The SPRY Mosaic browser that's included in CompuServe's "Internet in a Box 2.0" kit includes support for S-HTTP. Internet in a Box retails for around $89 and can be found at many software and book stores. Its spec sheet is located at:

```
http://www.compuserve.com:80/prod_services/consumer/ibox/ibox.html
```

THE SECURE SOCKETS LAYER (SSL) PROTOCOL

The Secure Sockets Layer (SSL) Protocol is being touted by Netscape Communications Corporation as a reliable and secure means for applications communication. Unlike S-HTTP, which is a protocol for a specific application, SSL is a secure layer *underneath* an application protocol. This means that SSL can be implemented not just for HTTP, but for NNTP (news), FTP, and Telnet as well. It also means that you can transport Secure HTTP over SSL, for an additional layer of security.

The Design of SSL

The SSL specification is currently at version 3.0 and, like S-HTTP, is still an Internet draft. It hasn't yet been given a nod by the IETF or other standards organizations. You can find the latest specification draft at Netscape:

```
http://home.netscape.com/newsref/std/SSL.html
```

The SSL specification is free for anyone to use and develop into their applications. To use Netscape's SSL C library (called *SSLRef*), you must get permission from Netscape. If you plan on using it for commercial purposes, you'll have to purchase their license.

Connection-Based Security

Whereas Secure HTTP provided a means to secure the *message* within an HTTP transfer, SSL lets you secure the *application protocol* within a connection. The SSL protocol itself is composed of two layers:

1. The SSL Record Protocol: It's the lowest-level SSL protocol that rests upon a reliable transport protocol such as TCP. Its purpose is to encapsulate the higher-level protocols.

2. The SSL Handshake Protocol: It provides the authentication between the server and client and negotiates an encryption method and keys. Once this is completed, the application protocol can begin transmission.

Encryption, Authentication, and Integrity Support

SSL encrypts data using a secret shared key which is derived by the SSL Handshake protocol at connection time. This key is used in conjunction with a symmetric encryption algorithm, such as DES or RC4. SSL achieves authentication through the use of a public key cryptosystem such as RSA or DSS. For their secure Commerce Server, Netscape uses the RSA PKCS. Integrity is ensured through the use of a digital signature on hashed messages using algorithms such as MD5.

Implementing SSL

Unless you plan on writing your own SSL-compliant Web server or browser, there's not much that you need to know about implementing SSL as a Web programmer. Essentially you just use a browser and server that supports SSL and leave your HTML and CGIs as-is.

SSL Web Servers and Browsers

In the S-HTTP section we've already seen a couple of Web servers that support SSL: OpenMarket's Secure WebServer and CompuServe's Internet Office. There is also, of course, Netscape's Commerce Server. But SSL is distinguished from S-HTTP in that there is a free SSL library available.

Netscape's Commerce Server and Navigator

Netscape's Commerce Server was the first Web server to utilize SSL. It's available for the higher-end UNIX platforms, such as Solaris, OSF/1, AIX, IRIX, and BSDI, for $2,995. It's also available for both the Alpha and Intel versions of Windows NT 3.5 for $1,295. You can learn more about the Commerce Server at the following URL:

```
http://home.netscape.com/comprod/netscape_commerce.html
```

The Netscape Navigator is the most popular Web browser for a variety of reasons. The biggest reason is that it's jam-packed with features and extensions. One of these features is the ability to use SSL without purchasing an add-on or a "commerce edition."

You can usually get the latest version of Netscape for free from Netscape's site. But if you want support, you have to pay for it. At press time, the latest free version of Netscape was 2.0 beta 3. The latest commercial versions were 1.2 for Windows 3.1 and 95, and 1.1 for Macintosh and UNIX systems. Netscape sells fully supported commercial versions for $39 each. You can download your preferred free version of Netscape from:

```
http://home.netscape.com/comprod/mirror/index.html
```

SSLeay: a (Sort of) Free Implementation of SSL

SSLeay is the first free implementation of Netscape's SSL standard. It was created by Australian Eric A. Young (the "eay" in SSLeay) using only publicly available documentation on the specification. For more information, check the FAQ at:

```
http://psych.psy.uq.oz.au/~ftp/Crypto/
```

The libraries for implementing SSLeay are distributed as source code. Theoretically, you should be able to use these libraries to make any Internet application SSL-enhanced. The source code and documentation are available from:

```
ftp.psy.uq.oz.au:/pub/Crypto/SSL
```

SSLeay is a full-featured SSL protocol that supports the most popular encryption algorithms, including: DES, RSA, RC4 (another RSA scheme), and IDEA (an algorithm used by Pretty Good Privacy (PGP).

Is SSLeay Legal?

When you read the SSLeay FAQ, you get the idea that not even its authors are quite sure if it's legal. The answer seems to be: If you're outside the United States, then it probably is. If you're inside the United States, there could be legal snags.

Since SSLeay's SSL protocol was created basically from scratch, Eric Young doesn't owe any licensing fees to Netscape for SSLRef or anything else. SSLeay does use the RSA public key cryptosystem algorithm, however. In Australia this isn't a problem because the RSA patent only applies within the U.S.

If you're using SSLeay within the United States, you'll need to get the RSARef licensing agreement from RSA. If you're using it for non-commercial purposes (e.g., research) you might be able to get it free; otherwise, you'll have to pay. You might have the same issue using RC4 inside the U.S.

For an interesting and amusing look at the legal entanglements surrounding SSLRef, RSARef, and creating a free SSL Web server, visit Alex Tang's Neverending Saga page:

```
http://petrified.cic.net/~altitude/ssl/ssl.saga.html
```

Browsers and Servers

Eric Young's cohort, Tim Hudson, has already patched SSLeay to several applications. Many of these are described and linked to on the previously cited SSLeay home page. Among them are NCSA's *httpd* 1.3 and Mosaic 2.6, available from:

```
ftp.psy.uq.oz.au:/pub/Crypto/SSLapps
```

Again, if you're in the U.S., you'll be restricted by the RSA patent and must obtain the RSARef license to use these. But if you have the agreement, you'll have an SSL Web server and browser!

If you set up the SSLeay NCSA *httpd*, don't expect it to necessarily work with the Netscape browser. The Netscape Navigator trusts only four hardcoded Certificate Authorities (CAs, or Digital IDs) for secure transactions and doesn't allow the user to configure their own. A future version of Netscape is rumored to support this, but as of yet, it doesn't.

So in order to use the Netscape Navigator with your SSLeay-patched server, you'll have to purchase a CA from VeriSign or Netscape (i.e., get them to sign your server's digital signature) which costs between $200 and $300.

The SSLeay NCSA Mosaic is configured to ignore server CAs, so you lose a level of security, but it can interoperate with Netscape's Commerce Server. Another Web server that uses SSLeay is Apache-SSL, but it deserves a section of its own.

Apache-SSL

Apache-SSL is the creation of the Community ConneXion, a California-based organization dedicated to preserving privacy on the Internet. Apache-SSL draws upon the efforts of the Apache *httpd* Server Project and Eric Young's SSLeay. They've also licensed RSARef and gotten a CA from VeriSign, so the Netscape Navigator will work with Apache-SSL.

The Community ConneXion is running the Apache-SSL server themselves, as you can see in Figure 15-2. Notice the unbroken key in the lower left-hand corner signifying a secure SSL connection between our browser and their server. You can visit their URL yourself at:

```
http://www.c2.org
```

Obtaining Apache-SSL

Apache-SSL is completely free for non-commercial use. You can obtain it from:

```
http://www.c2.org/apachessl/
```

The commercial version of Apache-SSL hasn't been released yet, and there's no launch date set. There are apparently still various legal issues that need to be taken care of before it can be available for commercial use. The Apache-SSL Web page claims that, when released, it will sell for $495—about one-third the price of other secure Web servers!

Figure 15-2
The Community ConneXion Web site that uses Apache-SSL.

WHICH PROTOCOL SHOULD YOU USE?

In this chapter, we've looked at both Secure HTTP and Secure Sockets Layer as Web commerce options that ensure a secure connection between the buyer and seller. Secure HTTP has the advantage of being highly extensible and offering a stronger security algorithm. SSL, on the other hand, is extremely transparent and can be used to provide secure connections for application protocols besides HTTP.

As a Web developer, which security scheme should you use for your Web commerce server? Cost considerations aside, the answer is "both."

It's best to get a server, such as Open Market's Secure WebServer or CompuServe's Internet Office, that supports both S-HTTP and SSL. That way, your server can operate securely with browsers that support only one or the other, and also have the advantage of two security layers with browsers that support both.

Speed: The One Disadvantage Both Have

Because on-the-fly encryption and authentication occur each time you request information from a secure Web server, it's going to be slightly slower than the same data coming from an unsecured connection. The typical performance loss is between 5% and 25% and applies to both S-HTTP and SSL.

So Which Protocol Is Winning?

Both EIT/CommerceNet and Netscape routinely reaffirm their commitments to open standards on the Internet, including secure commerce transactions. But while both SSL and S-HTTP are still up for grabs as Internet standards by the IETF, you don't see either company trying to implement each other's protocol. Both may be committed to open standards, but each one wants to set that standard.

In comparisons of S-HTTP and SSL by both companies, each one is slanted more toward its own standard. EIT sees SSL as more vulnerable than S-HTTP, because it uses a smaller encryption key and isn't as configurable. Netscape recognizes S-HTTP's power involving the Web, but sees it as limited because it's usable *only* with the Web, while SSL works with other Internet protocols.

Customers should be the real winners in this case: Because everyone's touting S-HTTP over SSL as the more secure connection method (even EIT and Netscape acknowledge this), servers and browsers that implement both will be the most popular.

TRUSTED THIRD-PARTY WEB COMMERCE

As we described earlier in this chapter, trusted third-party Web commerce enables sales to take place over the Internet simply and without encryption. In other words, you don't need a secure Web browser or server, or any other application-specific hardware or software, to conduct safe electronic commerce over the Internet.

First Virtual Holdings, Inc. has been a pioneer in the area of trusted third-party Web commerce since 1994, so we'll focus on their efforts.

How Does First Virtual Do It?

First Virtual acts as a commerce clearinghouse, able to charge to buyers' credit cards and deposit in sellers' checking accounts. But the reason that these transactions don't need connection-level security measures is that this financially sensitive information never traverses the Internet during account creation or a sale. How is this possible?

We'll describe their approach in the next two sections.

Setting Up an Account

First Virtual makes the process of setting up an account for buying or selling as easy as possible. Anyone can be a buyer, seller, or both. First Virtual places the onus of non-payment on the merchant, so they don't require credit approval to be a seller. All a buyer needs is a MasterCard or Visa number, and a United States checking account for selling. Here are the steps involved:

- Locate an application form to fill out. You can fill one out via e-mail, telnet, or an HTML form (we'll focus on the latter here). The URL for the application is:

  ```
  http://www.fv.com/newacct/index.html
  ```

- The form asks you for your name, address, phone number, e-mail address, and an initial personal identification number (PIN, a.k.a. account number) choice. Note that no financial information is sent on this form.

- You receive instructions by e-mail on how to activate your First Virtual account.

- If you wish to be a buyer, call the 800 number supplied in the message. To activate your account, use a touch-tone phone to enter your credit card number and expiration date, as well as the application number in the e-mail. Your credit card is charged a $2 processing fee.

- If you wish to be a seller, snail mail First Virtual a check for $10 (this is the seller setup fee), drawn upon the account you want First Virtual to deposit into. On the check, write your application number.

- When your account has been activated for buying or selling, you'll receive a response via e-mail. You're now ready for your Web shopping spree!

Remember, no financial information is ever transmitted across the Internet during the application process. First Virtual prides itself on this security aspect—the server they keep the credit card numbers on isn't even connected to the Internet.

Your First Virtual account number, however, was transmitted. What's to keep someone else from using it as they would your credit card number? The next section explains this.

Conducting a Sale

Let's step through what happens when a transaction occurs using the First Virtual Internet Payment System (FVIPS). Our example begins on a commercial Web server set up for First Virtual payment:

1. A buyer connects to a Web site with a patent search engine that costs $10 per search. Before the search can begin, she's required to input her First Virtual account number and her search criteria. She does so and submits the data.

2. A CGI is run to check with First Virtual to see if her First Virtual Account is valid. If so, the patent search is run.

3. When the search is successful, another CGI is run to report the $10 charge to her account by the seller to First Virtual.

4. First Virtual uses the information sent by the seller to create a verification letter for the buyer (the seller doesn't get a carbon copy). The verification letter take the form of an e-mail message that lets the buyer respond whether she wants to accept, deny, or declare the charges fraudulent. This letter is another step in the security process because it lets the buyer deny charges that she didn't make. However, it also means that she can say no to charges even though she used the service. The seller can complain, and the buyer may get her account revoked, but this does nothing to help the seller get its money.

5. If the buyer accepts the charges, her credit card is charged and the seller is sent e-mail saying that the buyer accepted the charge. For each product sale, First Virtual charges the seller a 29 cent transaction fee, plus 2% of the selling price. So for your $10 patent search, First Virtual makes 49 cents. First Virtual also charges sales tax to buyers when the charges are posted to their credit cards.

6. After what First Virtual considers a "reasonable amount of time" as defined by their terms and conditions, they will deposit your sales revenue into your checking account. For this deposit they charge $1 to cover costs.

Again the thing to note is that no "real-world" financial information ever crosses the Internet. The buyer never has to give her credit card number directly to the seller.

Web Commerce Programming Using First Virtual

First Virtual has set up their Internet Payment System to accept transactions from a variety of applications, including e-mail, telnet, FTP, and the World Wide Web. They already have a variety of CGIs pre-cooked for you to use with their service. Among them are:

■ *Emailpayform*, which allows you to take payment over an HTML e-mail form.

■ *Member*, which accepts organization membership fees over the Web.

■ *Websale*, which allows you to charge for specific documents on your Web site.

For more information on these, see the "Selling Information over the WWW" page at First Virtual:

```
http://www.fv.com/tech/www.html
```

Rather than be limited by these pre-cooked scripts, we'll explore using the First Virtual Application Programming Interface (FV-API) in conjunction with CGIs to provide a powerful platform for Web commerce.

In this section you'll learn how to incorporate First Virtual's Internet Payment System into a Web commerce platform. First we'll discuss their commerce transaction protocol. Next we'll talk about FV-API for Web transactions. Finally, we'll go through a simple Web commerce CGI application created by the Form Generation Tool that uses their API.

First Virtual's Green Commerce Model of Internet Financial Transactions

There are several methods that may be used to make a First Virtual transaction. Their electronic payment scheme, called the Green Commerce Model, allows you to make commerce transactions through e-mail, FTP, WWW, or practically any other Internet application. It does this through the use of a MIME type that First Virtual created, *Application/ Green-Commerce*.

In other words, First Virtual doesn't care how you get the information to their server, as long as it's in the format of the Application/Green-Commerce MIME type. More information on the Green Commerce Model and the Application/Green-Commerce MIME type can be found through First Virtual's technical information page:

```
http://www.fv.com/tech/index.html
```

First Virtual's API

Rather than using the Application/Green-Commerce MIME type coding directly in our CGI program, we're going to interface it with the First Virtual API. This provides a simplified method for carrying out transactions with First Virtual.

The First Virtual API is a collection of programs that makes dealing with First Virtual easier. The program we're concerned with is called *fv*.

Where to Get It

The FV-API is available in C source-code from First Virtual. It can be compiled on almost any UNIX system with a little work, but is especially easy to set up on Linux, SunOS, and Solaris. First Virtual plans on making this API available for other platforms, such as Windows NT, but doesn't have any firm release dates at present. The document on obtaining, compiling, and installing the FV-API is at:

```
http://www.fv.com/tech/fv-api.html
```

What *fv* Does

Since First Virtual was originally created as a means to charge people for information on the Internet, you can configure what you want to charge for an information file in a hidden configuration file. The *fv* API is able to read this configuration file.

You can also use *fv* to perform a variety of functions against a First Virtual account: You can check on the status of an account, you can bill a specified amount to that account, or you can bill the account for a specific file. The complete syntax is listed below:

```
draconis:~> fv
fv usage:
  To check the status of an FV Account-ID:
    fv [-f .$] check 'First Virtual Account ID'
    fv checkat server_address 'First Virtual Account ID'
      (Returns invalid/seller-only/active/suspended/unavailable)
  To find out how much a file is configured to cost:
    fv [-f .$] costof filename
  To submit a bill for the contents of a file:
    fv [-f .$] chargefor filename 'FV Account ID' ['Description']
  To submit a single charge (a bill):
    fv [-f .$] bill buyer seller amount 'Description'
      (Returns ok/unavailable/error)
  To submit an arbitrary transfer-request transaction
    fv trstdin [serverip emailaddr emailprog xferpref] <packet >result

 Either /.$ or ./.$ must exist and be properly formatted
 for initialization purposes, or use the -f option.
```

When *fv* is run correctly, it opens up a socket (the default is 440) with a First Virtual server using the Simple Green Commerce Protocol (SGCP). It takes the command-line arguments given to it and translates it into the equivalent Application/Green-Commerce MIME type commands.

When a response is received from the server, it takes the MIME response and returns a simple word or phrase (such as "active") to describe it. More on *fv*'s commands and the FV-API in general can be found on its specification sheet:

```
http://www.fv.com/tech/fv-api-spec.html
```

As you can see, *fv*'s simple command-line interface and short return values make it amenable to a front-end such as a Web form or CGI. That's exactly what we're going to add to it next!

A Sample Commerce CGI

We have used the Form Generation Tool to assist in programming a sample commerce CGI interface that uses FV-API for transactions. It has been created with a specific example in mind, and is by no means a ready-to-run, full-featured commerce application. We created it just to show you how easy it can be to incorporate the FV-API into your CGI programs.

The Application's Design

Let's say we have a product that we want to sell called "The Perl Hacker T-Shirt." It's really just a basic t-shirt but comes pre-soiled with cappuccino and pizza stains. It's also curved inwards at the stomach to better match the posture of the typical Perl programmer—that is, happily hunched over the keyboard!

We need to create a Perl CGI that encapsulates an HTML form to allow a user to enter their name, shipping information, t-shirt size, and First Virtual account number. When the form is posted-to with data, the account number is validated with First Virtual. If the account is invalid or the server is unavailable, then an error document is returned. If it is an active account, then the ordering information is saved to a file and the account is charged for the t-shirt, based on size.

The Code

Rather than go through the entire code step-by-step, we'll just list it with its comments and add more comments in the areas where we feel it's necessary. You should be able to understand the portions generated directly by *formgen.pl* by now, so large parts of this CGI will go by without commentary. Once you've gone through it, you should be able to implement your own commerce CGI with the FV-API, using the example below as a guide:

```perl
#!/usr/local/bin/perl
# Please customize this reference to match local conditions.
#
# perl_hack_tshirt.pl—A sample CGI Interface for First Virtual
#                       transactions.
#
# Copyright (C) 1995 Charlie Scott (charlie@outer.net)
# All rights reserved.
# FIRST VIRTUAL (TM) and the FIRST VIRTUAL logo are service marks
# of First Virtual Holdings Incorporated.
#    perl_hack_tshirt.pl
#
```

```
# Created: Wed Dec 20 22:06:52 CST 1995
#
#    Revision History:
#
#    Version 1.0      Script Created.
#
# PURPOSE:       This script provides an HTML form interface for an
#                online t-shirt sale. When posted, it extracts the
#                entered data and checks the user's First Virtual
#                account information. If valid, it adds the user's
#                information to an order file and charges their
#                First Virtual account.
#
# INSTALLATION: To configure this script, edit all lines in the
#                next section that have "#!" as comments to their
#                immediate right.  This script needs to be installed
#                in your Web server's bin directory, typically
#                "cgi-bin". You'll also need the First Virtual API
#                "fv" to use this script, available at
#                ftp://ftp.fv.com. You will also need to create a
#                file called fv.conf that contains the
#                configuration information.
#
# USAGE:         This script is called directly by the user's Web
#                browser.
#
###################################################################
# Perl script to both supply and support the perl_hack_tshirt HTML
# form generated by http://www.outer.net/cgi-bin/formgen.pl on Wed
# Dec 20 14:11:37 CST 1995


$| = 1;                 # output NOT buffered
print "Content-Type:\ttext/html\n\n\n",
       "<!DOCTYPE HTML PUBLIC \"-//IETF//DTD HTML 2.0//EN\">\n";

$host = $ENV{SERVER_NAME};
$ENV{SCRIPT_NAME} =~ s/([a-zA-Z0-9\.\-_]+)$//;
$program = $1;
$scriptpath = $ENV{SCRIPT_NAME};

## formlib stuff

if (($ENV{REQUEST_METHOD} eq "POST") &&
   ($ENV{CONTENT_TYPE}   eq "application/x-www-form-urlencoded")){

# Extract form data - borrowed heavily from
# Brigette Jellinek's formlib.pl.
```

```
read(STDIN,$input,$ENV{CONTENT_LENGTH});

foreach (split("&", $input)) {
  /(.*)=(.*)/;
  $name = $1;
  $value = $2;

  $value =~ s/\+/ /g ;
  $value =~ s/%(..)/pack('c',hex($1))/eg;
  # unescape characters

  if (defined $in{$name}) {
    $in{$name} .= "#" . $value
  } else {
    $in{$name} = $value;
    }
  }

  # THIS IS WHERE formgen.pl ENDS AND perl_hack_tshirt.pl BEGINS.
  # Put array variables into cleaner ones.

  $FullName = $in{FullName};
  $StreetAddress = $in{StreetAddress};
  $City = $in{City};
  $State = $in{State};
  $Zip = $in{Zip};
  $Phone = $in{Phone};
  $FVAcct = $in{FVAcct};
  $Small = $in{Small};
  $Medium = $in{Medium};
  $Large = $in{Large};

  #! Your FV Config File for Web Transactions Location
  $FV_CONFIG = "/www/conf/fv.conf";

  #! The Seller's FV Account Number
  $FV_SELLER = "12345678";
```

The next part is our first instance of calling *fv*. Here we're using it to check the account's validity. When we get the response, we chop it down to only the first word:

```
# Check the inputted FV account number.
$FV_CHECK = `/usr/local/bin/fv -f ${FV_CONFIG} check
    ${FVAcct}`;
chop($FV_CHECK);
```

```
($FV_CHECK, $Remainder) = split("\r\n\t\ ", $FV_CHECK,2);
```

If the account is good (i.e., "active"), then we continue with the processing. We get the dollar amount to charge for the t-shirt from its size:

```
    if ($FV_CHECK eq "active") {
if ($Small) {
        $CHARGE = 10;
    } else {
      if ($Medium) {
        $CHARGE = 12;
      } else {
        $CHARGE = 15;
      }
    }
```

Our next step is to open a file in which to place order information. We'll store the information in a tab-delimited format to be used later by a database. Supposedly, our shipping department would have access to this file in order to send the shirts to the customers.

After "processing" the order, we use the *fv* program again to bill the buyer's First Virtual account:

```
# Open order processing file, write to it, and close.
open(ORDERS,">>/www/cgi-bin/perl_hack_tshirt.orders");
print ORDERS "$FullName\t";
print ORDERS "$StreetAddress\t";
print ORDERS "$City\t";
print ORDERS "$State\t";
print ORDERS "$Zip\t";
print ORDERS "$Phone\t";
print ORDERS "$FVAcct\t";
print ORDERS "\$$CHARGE\t";
close(ORDERS);

print "<TITLE>Your Order Has Been Processed</TITLE>\n";
print "<H1>Your Order Has Been Processed</H1>\n";
print "<P>";
print "Your <B>FIRST VIRTUAL</B> account will be charged",
  "\n";
print "<B>\$$CHARGE for this transaction. Your T-Shirt \n";
print "is on its way!\n";

# Charge the account.
system("fv -f $FV_CONFIG bill $FVAcct $FV_SELLER $CHARGE
        \"T-Shirt\"");
```

Everything within the following else condition is what happens when the account is anything but active. It's essentially a generic error condition.

We do go a bit further, however, by reporting specific error messages for some of the responses.

```
} else {

    print "<TITLE>First Virtual Transaction Failed</TITLE>\n";

    if ($FV_CHECK eq "unavailable") {

        print "<H1>FV Server Unavailable!</H1>\n";
        print "The First Virtual Commerce Server is
            unavailable.\n";
        print "Please try again later.\n";
    } else {
        print "<H1>FV Account Invalid</H1>";
        print "The First Virtual Account you entered is not
            valid\n";
        print "for online purchases at this time.\n";

        if ($FV_CHECK eq "suspended") {
            print "Your account has been suspended. Please \n";
            print "contact First Virtual for information.\n";
    } else {

            if ($FV_CHECK eq "seller-only") {
              print "Your account is not authorized for \n";
              print "purchases. You need to activate it \n";
              print "as a Buyer account with First Virtual.\n";
            } else {
                print "If you entered it correctly, please\n";
                print "contact First Virtual about your \n";
                print "account's status.\n";
            }
        }
      }
    }
}
```

The last portion is the embedded HTML code we created using the Form Generation Tool. Figure 15-3 presents a view of the final GUI.

```
} else {

    print "<!DOCTYPE HTML PUBLIC \"-//IETF//DTD HTML
        2.0//EN\"><HTML>\n";
    print "<HEAD>\n";
    print "<TITLE>Perl Hacker T-Shirt Order Form</TITLE>\n";
```

```
print "\n";
print "</HEAD>\n";
print "<BODY>\n";
print "<!- Form created by formgen.pl on Wed Dec 20 13:36:08
      CST 1995 ->\n";
print "<!- For: charlie@outer.net ->\n";
print "<FORM ACTION=\"http://www2.outer.net/cgi-bin/
      perl_hack_tshirt.pl\" METHOD=\"POST\">\n";
print "<H1 ALIGN=\"Center\">Perl Hacker T-Shirt Order
      Form</H1>\n";
print "<BR>\n";
print "<P>\n";
print "Please enter all information in the form below. If you
      don't \n";
print "give us your address, we won't know how to send you the
      T\n";
print "Shirt! Don't forget to input your FIRST VIRTUAL",
      " account\n";
print "number!<BR>\n";
print "<HR ALIGN=\"Center\">\n";
print "<B>Please enter your full name:</B><BR>\n";
print "<INPUT TYPE=\"text\" NAME=\"FullName\" SIZE=\"30\"
      MAXLENGTH=\"50\" >\n";
print "<BR>\n";
print "<B>Please enter your street address:</B><BR>\n";
print "<INPUT TYPE=\"text\" NAME=\"StreetAddress\" SIZE=\"50\"
      MAXLENGTH=\"60\" >\n";
print "<BR>\n";
print "<B>Please enter your city, state, and ZIP:</B><BR>\n";
print "<INPUT TYPE=\"text\" NAME=\"City\" SIZE=\"15\"
       MAXLENGTH=\"20\" >\n";
print ",\n";
print "<INPUT TYPE=\"text\" NAME=\"State\" SIZE=\"2\"
      MAXLENGTH=\"2\" >\n";
print "<INPUT TYPE=\"text\" NAME=\"Zip\" SIZE=\"12\"
      MAXLENGTH=\"12\" >\n";
print "<BR>\n";
print "<B>Please enter your phone number:</B><BR>\n";
print "<INPUT TYPE=\"text\" NAME=\"Phone\" SIZE=\"12\"
      MAXLENGTH=\"12\" >\n";
print "<BR>\n";
print "<P><BR>\n";
print "<B>FIRST VIRTUAL Account Number:</B><BR>\n";
print "<INPUT TYPE=\"password\" NAME=\"FVAcct\" >\n";
print "<BR>\n";
print "<P><BR>\n";
print "<B>Select t-shirt size:</B><BR>\n";
```

```
print "<TABLE>\n";
print "<TR>\n";
print "<TABLE>\n";
print "<TR>\n";
print "<TD ALIGN=RIGHT><INPUT TYPE=\"radio\" NAME=\"\"
      VALUE=\"Small\" CHECKED></TD>\n";
print "<TD>Small (\$10)</TD>\n";
print "</TR>\n";
print "<TR><TD ALIGN=RIGHT><INPUT TYPE=\"radio\" NAME=\"\"
      VALUE=\"Medium\"></TD>\n";
print "<TD>Medium (\$12)</TD>\n";
print "</TR>\n";
print "<TR><TD ALIGN=RIGHT><INPUT TYPE=\"radio\" NAME=\"\"
      VALUE=\"Large\"></TD>\n";
print "<TD>Large (\$15)</TD>\n";
print "</TR>\n";
print "<TR>\n";
print "</TR>\n";
print "</TABLE>\n";
print "<HR ALIGN=\"Center\">\n";
print "<TABLE>\n";
print "<TR>\n";
print "<INPUT TYPE=\"submit\" NAME=\"Submit\" VALUE=\"Submit
      Order\"><BR>\n";
print "</TR>\n";
print "</TABLE>\n";
print "</FORM>\n";
print "</BODY>\n";
print "</HTML>\n";
}
```

Benefits and Drawbacks of Trusted Third-Party Systems

By examining First Virtual's model of a trusted third-party Web commerce system, we're sure you can see some advantages and disadvantages to using them.

Benefits

The biggest benefit of this system is that it's inexpensive compared to secure communication-based commerce systems. There's not special hardware or software you have to buy. You don't have to worry about being compatible with a certain browser. You can become a First Virtual merchant for just $10, and easily implement their protocol in your current Web system using their FV-API.

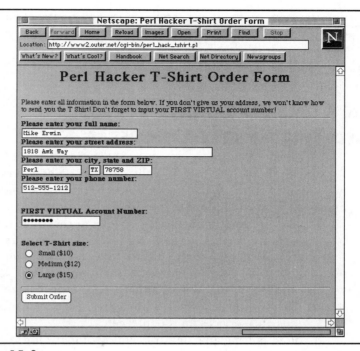

Figure 15-3
Our "Perl Hacker T-Shirt" ordering and first virtual payment form.

Another plus is that it essentially lets you "accept" credit cards through First Virtual. This isn't a big deal to large companies. For small companies, finding a credit card clearinghouse that will accept you as a merchant can be difficult, especially if you don't have walk-in business.

Drawbacks

One annoying thing about the third-party system is having to get a third party involved at all. What it means is that you're only going to be able to do business with other people who have First Virtual accounts. Or, you're going to have to convince others who want to purchase things from you that it will benefit them to get one. With direct credit card purchases, you don't have this limitation.

The second drawback is, while it makes it easy to become a Web merchant, the fact is that First Virtual assumes no financial burden for non-payment by the buyer. This could end up putting the seller at great financial risk. Even First Virtual suggests that you don't use their system if non-payment by the buyer would cause you financial hardship. Also, none of it is guaranteed or insured should *anything* go wrong with First Virtual's equipment. It is not a bank.

SECURE COMMUNICATIONS VERSUS TRUSTED THIRD-PARTY COMMERCE

Which one should you use? It really depends on how serious you are about making sales on the Web—which could be translated into: How much money are you willing to put into it?

Trusted third-party commerce, at least at this stage in the game, should be used only for small-scale sales for low dollar amounts. This is due to the risk of non-payment, but also has to do with the amount of sales that may occur. If you plan to sell hundreds of items on the Web per day, then the fees you pay to First Virtual will eventually eclipse the cost of a secure Web server. This method is best for a small business that wants to sell only a few of its goods and services on the Internet.

If you're putting an extensive catalog of items for sale on the Web, or the goods or services you sell are expensive, consider using secure communications. This means that you'll have to get a secure Web server and find a way to process the credit information once received.

If you're a medium-sized or larger business, or one with a heavy Internet presence, secure communications will probably be best for you.

SUMMARY

In this chapter, we discussed the need for Web commerce solutions that are safe from fraud. We then covered two options for Web commerce: secure communications using the Secure Sockets Layer and Secure HTTP protocols, and a trusted third-party commerce model with First Virtual as the prime example. Within both, we discussed philosophies, methods, and implementations, with a slant toward Web programming.

There's no way we could have covered everything on these topics, but we tried to give you enough information to get you primed in using these Web commerce approaches for yourself. We have no doubt that, as a Web programmer, you'll *need* to use them sometime in the near future.

The best thing for you to do is keep abreast of the latest developments in Web commerce from magazines and USENET groups, such as:

```
comp.infosystems.www.announce
```

Other places to check often are the URLs listed in this chapter. Many of them are constantly developing new standards and products for electronic commerce. Both Netscape and Microsoft, for instance, are working out deals with major credit card companies to include credit card processing in their Web server software.

Now we'll go from the exciting development of secure Web commerce to a problem that has challenged systems administrators for over two decades: UNIX account management!

A Web-Based Unix Account Manager

*L*ike the DNS Administration Tool, the CGI program in this chapter is another way to simplify UNIX system administration duties. Sysadmins can tell you that editing a password file by hand to make account changes is never what you'd call "fun." You may have to make permission changes to the "passwd" file, locate the proper field to add or modify, and use an editor such as *vi* or *ed* to make the changes. For some administrators who aren't familiar with UNIX but need to run it on their network, this can be difficult. A UNIX guru would say you can do it in your sleep (given the working hours of the typical UNIX hacker, many of us do), but that's small comfort to the uninitiated. In this chapter, we try to do a bit more to help out!

UNIX ACCOUNT MANAGEMENT: A CHALLENGE FOR NEWBIES AND GURUS ALIKE

Even UNIX wizards can make mistakes, and the password file is *not* something you want to screw up. If you change file permissions so that the world can't read it, your users will find they can't log in. Extra spaces or newlines can also cause problems for specific users. Hidden control characters can split the "passwd" file down the middle, so that half your users won't be able to log in. Therefore, you can see that even a supreme sysadmin would like something foolproof to perform the task, if only to keep from losing face (or more sleep).

"Pay No Attention to the Man Behind the Curtain!": UNIX Wizardry Revealed

A big part of being a UNIX wizard is making difficult things look easy. That's exactly what this book is about—making the complexities of Web programming seem like a piece of cake. Whether it's creating a CGI application, DNS administration, or a calendar/scheduling system, if it needs to get done, then we're giving you the power to do it.

The reason gurus seem so capable is that they have tools to help them take care of the daily grind of administration. They probably already have an applet (secret weapon) to manage user accounts. It could be a shell script that comes with their UNIX software (such as *adduser*), a program they wrote themselves, or some kind of X Windows-based server management software. We're going to give you your own secret weapon—using the Form Generation Tool, we'll create a Web-based UNIX Account Manager to handle many of these administrative tasks.

What We're Dealing with

In this chapter, we'll explore the benefits of a Web-based UNIX Account Manager versus the other types of tools already available. We'll outline the capabilities we would like this application to have and describe how to develop them.

Then we'll step through the code of our Account Manager, detailing the most important sections and describing why it works the way it does. Then we'll discuss installation procedures, emphasizing security issues. We'll conclude with enhancements that could be made to the Account Manager, if you wanted to increase its capabilities or spruce up its interface.

CURRENT USER MANAGEMENT TOOLS VERSUS A WEB-BASED TOOL

As we've said, there are a variety of user management utilities already available for UNIX systems. Some come with the operating system; others may be third-party shareware or commercial packages; and still more have been written by an erstwhile sysadmin. These packages can be broken down into three types:

1. Command-line interactive tools
2. Menu-driven terminal tools
3. X Windows GUI tools

There are benefits and costs associated with each of these types, and we'll compare them with our Web-Based Account Manager.

Command-Line Interactive Tools

This is probably the primal species of UNIX account managers. Command-line tools are simple programs or shell scripts that either take command-line arguments to create an account, or guide their users through an interactive session online.

adduser

The most common command-line tool is called *adduser*, available for almost every flavor of UNIX. If your OS didn't come with a version, then you can probably find one on the Internet, or port one over from a different system.

In the Slackware Linux 2.3 distribution, *adduser* is a C program that interactively queries for information about the users it creates. It also provides default suggestions, such as the next available UID number, and what shell should be used. It even goes through the trouble of creating the user's home directory. Here's a sample of an interactive session with Linux's *adduser*:

```
austinfree:/sbin# adduser
Adding a new user. The username should not exceed 8 characters
in length, or you may run into problems later.
Enter login name for new account (^C to quit): pretzel
```

```
Editing information for new user [pretzel]
Full Name: Penelope Retzel
GID [100]:
Group 'users', GID 100
First unused uid is 501
UID [501]:
Home Directory [/home/pretzel]:
Shell [/bin/bash]:
Password [pretzel]:
Information for new user [pretzel]:
Home directory: [/home/pretzel]
Shell: [/bin/bash]
uid: [501] gid: [100]
Is this correct? [y/N]: y
Adding login [pretzel] and making directory [/home/pretzel]
Adding the files from the /etc/skel directory:
././.kermrc -> /home/pretzel/././.kermrc
././.less -> /home/pretzel/././.less
././.lessrc -> /home/pretzel/././.lessrc
././.term -> /home/pretzel/././.term
././.term/termrc -> /home/pretzel/././.term/termrc
austinfree:/sbin#
```

Under Apple's breed of UNIX, A/UX, *adduser* is a Korn shell script that can create a new account through an interactive session. It can also take command-line arguments, so you can pass it information from another program or script. Here's a listing of the options it takes:

```
outer.net.charlie 9 # adduser -h
getopt: option requires an argument—h
usage: adduser [-r real-name] [-a address] [-x extension] [-p home-phone]
[-g group] [-d dir | -h home] [-s shell] [-u uid | -U UID] [-i] [-c] [-P
encrypted-password] name
```

Look familiar? It's essentially the same information we saw in the Linux *adduser* program. The command line is something less than user-friendly, but it allows you to send information from another program, perhaps an employee database or a CGI program. The command-line interface means that it can also be run from telnet, therefore from anywhere you can connect to your UNIX system.

Limitations of *adduser*

The most obvious limitation of *adduser* is that it can only be used to create accounts, not to change or delete an existing account. The second shortcoming is that it is solely command-line oriented: There's no GUI for it, unless you create one.

Menu-Driven Terminal Tools

A menu-driven terminal tool uses the properties of your terminal to allow cursor movement and menu selection. Many of you may be familiar with the mail program *Pine* and other such interfaces. These utilities use a library called *curses* that contains functions for cursor movement.

Current Uses of Menu-Driven Terminal Tools

Menu-driven terminal tools have gone somewhat out of vogue lately. They were common on versions of XENIX several years ago, but have never been prevalent on major UNIX platforms. Most terminal-based user management tools that are still in use are proprietary. They are usually designed to assist someone administering a UNIX system at a particular company and will set up accounts the way that company and that administrator prefers.

Like *adduser*, you can use a menu-driven tool from any system on which you can telnet to a UNIX box—as long as you can emulate one of the terminal types it can use.

Limitations of Menu-Driven Terminal Tools

Although the menu interface brings us closer to GUI operation, it's still clumsy compared to other GUIs. The *curses* library helps you create fields and selectable menus, but doesn't have ready-to-use GUI niceties like buttons, checkboxes, or pull-down menus. When it comes to ease-of-use, HTML forms are superior to any other UI library.

Another limitation of menu-driven tools is their proprietary nature—that is, they may not be directly portable to other UNIX systems. Some systems do not have the library you need, or you might have to recompile it for your system.

The final limitation is that there are no good freeware versions out there for you to use (at least none that we found). As noted earlier, most of these management tools are proprietary, so you'll have to create your own.

X Windows GUI Tools

There is also a smattering of GUI administration tools for UNIX for the X Windows environment. An example of this is *OpenView* from Hewlett-Packard, though there are several others that may come with your version of X. Information on OpenView can be found at:

```
http://www.dmo.hp.com/nsmd/ov/main.html
```

There are also several shareware X user account managers. Michael McNeil has created one for Linux users running X11 Release 6 and Motif called *xusermgr*. You can download it at this URL, preferably in the wee hours since this is a very busy site:

```
ftp://sunsite.unc.edu/pub/Linux/X11/xutils/
```

If you attempt to log in and it's busy, you'll be greeted with a list of over 40 "mirror sites." You can usually get to these and download the materials you need. Since these sites duplicate (or mirror) the sunsite ftp server more or less exactly, you can use the same directory specification (e.g., */pub/Linux/X11/xutils/*) to locate the materials you need.

Uses of X Windows Tools

X Windows user management utilities are typically quite slick; i.e., full-featured and easy to use. A good one will allow you to add, change, and delete user information, including name, group, password, home directory, and shell. It will also use the best choice of GUI elements to allow you to do this. For instance, it will give you a pull-down menu of shell choices rather than just having you type one into a field.

Limitations of X Windows Tools

The only problem with X Windows tools is X Windows itself. You'll have to run X Windows on your UNIX systems to use the account manager, which can be a resource burden. What if you're away on a trip and need to dial in to perform user management, and all you have with you is a Macintosh PowerBook? To administer your UNIX accounts from a non-UNIX system, you'll also have to run an X Windows server to use the tool. X Windows packages for Microsoft Windows, OS/2, or MacOS can be expensive—up to $300 per license!

Why Not Use the Web?

Now that you've seen some of the advantages and disadvantages of UNIX account management packages, let's move on to our project: designing a Web-based UNIX Account Manager. We'll explore why a CGI application might be the best solution for UNIX account maintenance.

A Simple GUI

HTML forms afford a simple method for programming a GUI interface. You don't have to learn the application programming interface calls for a certain library, compile a library into your program, or worry about that library being incompatible across platforms. With the help of the Form Generation Tool, you can design and implement a form into a CGI script even more quickly.

Because there's a Web browser for every major computer platform, you can be assured that whatever machine you're on, you'll be able to perform user management.

A Flexible and Portable CGI Language

As with the other CGI applications in this book we chose to program this one in Perl. The usual reasons apply: It's highly portable, available on most UNIX systems, and easy to implement. Much of what this script does involves parsing text files, something that Perl was designed for in the first place. Finally, it's so easy to understand that it's almost self-documenting.

It Can Be Accessed Globally

Firewalls and other security measures aside, because our Web-based Account Manager uses Internet technology, an Internet server that's running it should be accessible from any other Internet machine running a Web browser. This means you can administer your user database from anywhere in the world.

Are There Any Limitations?

There are very few limitations because you'll be creating your own code. You can write the Web-Based Account Manager to modify your user accounts in any way you see fit. This feature makes it nicer than third-party tools you typically aren't allowed to alter.

It would be nice to say that the Web-based Account Manager is the perfect solution, but there is a disadvantage to this approach—namely, security risks. By creating another means to manipulate user accounts, you've added a door for others to gain access to this information.

While there are several measures that can help protect an unauthorized user from gaining access to your Web-based user database, there are no doubt equally as many ways to get around them! The more doors you have to your house, the greater the chance you'll overlook one. Nevertheless, we'll try to address security issues directly in the latter part of this chapter.

DESIGNING OUR WEB-BASED UNIX ACCOUNT MANAGER

The first step in creating our Account Manager is to create a design that documents the features and functions we'd like it to have. Ideally, it should be able to do the things that *adduser* and *xusermgr* can do, plus provide the access and interface benefits of the Web. Using this as a guideline, here are some of the essential features we would include:

- Add a user.
- Delete a user.
- Change user information at the field level. For instance, you can change a user's default shell without having to remove and recreate the user.
- Change or delete several accounts at once.
- Perform any of the above items from a friendly GUI.

From our guidelines, we can infer that this application will need two major components:

1. A graphical user interface
2. A back-end program to perform account changes

Crafting the GUI: Should It Be Static or Dynamic?

Obviously, our GUI will be Web-based. We can use the HTML FORM elements to create an interface with drop-down menus, selectable line-items, and input fields.

One way to do this is using a static HTML FORM document that calls a script to process the information. We might find this sufficient for managing accounts on a system with a small population of users.

But let's say we're managing accounts on a large university system, where there are hundreds of students, faculty, and staff with accounts. In addition, they could belong to several dozen groups. Rather than memorizing all the group names, wouldn't it be nice to have a pull-down menu of this information?

If our HTML document is static, we'd need to update it with a new group each time one is added to the "/etc/group" file. This would be tedious and open to mistakes (especially if there are several sysadmins working more or less independently).

Our solution is to make the document dynamic, by embedding the HTML within a CGI script. This lets us create a subroutine to read in the "/etc/group" file and make each line an option in a pull-down menu. The same thing could be done for "/etc/shells". In our case, we'll also use the CGI script to display the "/etc/passwd" file itself and present you with a list of users to modify. To do all of this, we've created a script called *view_user.html.pl*.

The Back-End Script

Our back-end script, *change_user.pl*, makes the changes to the form information delivered by *view_user.html.pl*.

All user account information on a UNIX system must be reflected in a password file, and it's risky to let a script act directly upon the password file. What we'll do instead is create a clone of the password file on which the script will perform its changes. Then, for the changes to take effect, the clone file will have to be copied over the original. This intermediate step permits a sysadmin to inspect the file's contents and make doubly sure no inadvertent mistakes have been introduced.

Now that we've described the two major scripts involved in our Account Manager, let's look at the code.

MANAGING UNIX USER ACCOUNTS: VIEW_USER.HTML.PL

The first script we'll look at is *view_user.html.pl*, which parses the password file and presents its information as an HTML table. The user can then select a series of accounts and perform actions upon them, such as add, delete, or change entries. In other words, this Perl script sets up the GUI for our Account Manager.

Configuration Values and Other Building Blocks

We first need to specify our setup variables and constants for this CGI. These consist of the files we'll be working with, plus a few descriptive items and paths to helper scripts.

The first section contains items that you'll need to change to reflect your system configuration, namely the location of the password, group, and shells file on your UNIX box, as well as a description of your site to be used in the GUI. The first three can usually be found in the *etc* directory. The last is one you make up on your own, but it's often a good idea to use the hostname.

```
###############################################################
#
# Setup and configuration area. Most of the user-configurable parts
# are contained in this section.
#
###############################################################

$PASSWD_FILE    = "/etc/passwd"; #! Full path to the passwd file
$GROUPS_FILE    = "/etc/group";  #! Full path to the group file
$SHELLS_FILE    = "/etc/shells"; #! Full path to the shells file
$SITENAME       = "OuterNet";    #! A description of this site
```

The next three items are startup defaults that don't need changing. We'll discuss them later.

```
###############################################################
#
# More Setup and Configuration, various variables. No user-
# servicable parts beyond this point.
#
###############################################################
$user_count    = 0;
$shell_list    = "<OPTION SELECTED>None ";
$group_list    = "<OPTION SELECTED>None ";
```

The final constant contains the path of the program used to create a random, eight-character password. Later in the chapter, we'll discuss how and why this program gets called. Suffice it to say that this program can be either a third-party program or a script you write yourself. It can be as simple or as complex as needed.

The program we use generates a password by combining two words from a word list and varying the case of the characters on each word. But one that generates an eight-character random number would be sufficient for some systems. The constant's label of $clear_text was chosen to remind you that when you enter the password, it's not encrypted immediately:

```
# We have a short program that creates suitable passwords. In short
# an 8 character random number generator can be substitued
# perfectly.
#
$clear_text = '/www/cgi-bin/mk.passwd.pl';  #! Replace this
chop ($clear_text);
```

Join the Club: Displaying Available Groups

The first subroutine in *view_user.html.pl* creates a popup menu list of the groups to which a user can belong. This prevents you from having to know all group ID numbers or names yourself. This feature alone outdoes anything *adduser* can do.

The subroutine get_groups opens the file we specified as the group file and steps through each line. It's smart enough to skip the pound sign (#) that denotes comments and the plus sign (+) that appears at the end of a group file on a server that's using NIS (*Network Information Service*), also known as *yp* (yellow pages) service.

```
################################################################
#
# get_groups
#
# To present the user with a nice popup list of the available
# groups, we open the /etc/groups file and, after removing the
# system admin groups such as root and daemon, we build an HTML
# <SELECT> list for the user to use.
#
################################################################

sub get_groups {
  open(GROUPS_FILE,"$GROUPS_FILE");
  while (<GROUPS_FILE>) {
    unless (/\#/ || /\+/) {  #! forget about #s and +s
```

The next line splits the group line at the colon, so it can parse out the group name and the group number. The character between them is an asterisk, which isn't used.

A check is then made to see if the group number is less than or greater than ten. If it is, then it will add the group name and number to a group list, with the HTML form <OPTION> tag. We ignore groups with a number of less than ten for security reasons. Group 0 is reserved for *root*, and 1 through 9 are typically for system processes such as *sys*, *daemon*, and *bin*.

At the end, we close the groups file to finish our business with it.

```
    ($group_name,$na,$gid_num) = split(/:/);
    if ($gid_num > 10) {
      $group_list .= "<OPTION>".$gid_num." ".$group_name;
    }
  }
}
close (GROUPS_FILE);
}
```

Sonny Selects Shells with a Sun Station

A rather silly tongue twister to head a section on a simple subroutine. The get_shells subroutine does the same type of thing that get_groups does: It presents the Web user with a list of available shells to select from and opens the "/etc/shells" file, which contains a list of shells allowed to be run on the UNIX system. There's only one item per line, so we don't have to parse it any further. It takes in each line and skips the ones that contain the comment character (#). At the beginning of the others it prepends the HTML <OPTION> tag. Last, it closes the shells file.

```
###############################################################
#
# get_shells
#
# To present the user with a nice popup list of the available
# shells, we open the /etc/shells file and, after removing the
# comment lines (#) we build an HTML <SELECT> list for the user to
# use.
#
###############################################################
sub get_shells {
  open(SHELLS_FILE,"$SHELLS_FILE");
  while (<SHELLS_FILE>) {
    unless (/#/) {
      $shell_list .= "<OPTION>".$_;
    }
  }
  close (SHELLS_FILE);
}
```

Displaying the Account Information

The `get_passwd_entries` subroutine reads in the password file itself and parses through the information. It then displays it in an HTML form, adding a checkbox for line item selection. We'll go through the more important pieces bit by bit.

```
###########################################################################
#
# get_passwd_entries
#
# This function reads in the password file and prints the output
# to a table. Most of the information concerning a single
# account is for viewing, except for the first column (marked by a
# checkbox), which is used to select entries for various actions.
# The buttons displayed below are how these actions get chosen.
#
###########################################################################
sub get_passwd_entries {
  open(PASSWD_FILE,"$PASSWD_FILE");
  while (<PASSWD_FILE>) {
```

When we read in a password line, we split it into its component fields and store each in a variable:

```
$passwd_line = $_;
/^(([^:]+)/;
($user,$crypt_passwd,$uid,$gid,$gcos,$home,$shell) = split(/:/);
```

Next we display each user, as long as it's not *root* (using UID 0) or has no "asterisked-out" password. That is, in place of an encrypted password there's a * or an x, which indicate either TCB (Trusted Computing Base) or shadow password file storage of passwords for those logins. These are additional security measures, so that *root*'s information can't be modified, nor the information for those user IDs that system processes use (which often have asterisks instead of passwords). It's also a good idea to exclude those logins marked "NOLOGIN" in the password field, since they've been excluded from login use.

Each set of user information is displayed as a table of parsed password fields. Each line also has a checkbox added at its beginning. The value it returns is the user ID number displayed on that line. This information is used whenever a user's account information is modified. At the end, we close the password file:

```
    if (($uid != 0) && ($crypt_passwd ne "*")) {
      $user_count++;
      print STDOUT "<TR><TD><INPUT TYPE=\"checkbox\" NAME=\"selection\"
VALUE=\"${uid}\"></TD>";
      print STDOUT "<TD>$user</TD>";
      print STDOUT "<TD>$crypt_passwd</TD>";
      print STDOUT "<TD>$uid</TD>";
      print STDOUT "<TD>$gid</TD>";
      print STDOUT "<TD>$gcos</TD>";
      print STDOUT "<TD>$home</TD>";
      print STDOUT "<TD>$shell</TD></TR>\n";
    }
    }
    close (PASSWD_FILE);
}
```

Calling the Functions in the Main Body

The main body of *view_user.html.pl* is where we tie all of the subroutines
together. It's also where the principle HTML output is created and where
the SUBMIT and RESET buttons for our form are created.

The beginning of this section simply calls the &get_shells() and
&get_groups() subroutines we wrote earlier to display the popup menus of
shells and groups.

```
#######################################################################
#
# main
#
# This function is where most of the HTML output is produced.
# First we call the get_shells function and the get_groups
# function to populate our popup boxes with the appropriate
# choices.
#
#######################################################################
{
  &get_shells();
  &get_groups();
```

Next, we generate the majority of our HTML. First we have to send to
the browser the 'Content-Type: text/html' to instruct it to translate the
ensuing data as HTML. Then we begin the HMTL output, treating the
$SITENAME constant we defined earlier.

Password File Account Information

Some of you may not be familiar with the format of a UNIX password file. The standard UNIX "passwd" file has entries that look like this:

```
mike:6DjBhlJh29wxA:89:110:Mike Erwin:/home/mike:/bin/csh
```

Its fields are delimited by a colon. Descriptions for each field, going from left to right, can be found in Table 16-1.

Table 16-1
The names, variables, and description of password field items

Item Name	Variable	Description
User Name	$user	The user's unique 8-char name.
Encrypted Password	$crypt_passwd	The user's password after encryption.
User ID Number	$uid	The numeric equivalent to the user name (should be a unique number).
Group ID Number	$gid	The numeric equivalent of the group name. This is the default group the user belongs to. For others, you must add the user to the individual group in the "group" file.
GECOS* (General Electric Comprehensive Operating System) Field	$gcos	General descriptive information for the user, such as full name, office, and phone number (usually just the user's full name).
Home Directory	$home	The default directory where the user gets dropped after logging in. This can be a directory the user owns, or any drop space the user has permissions to.
Default Shell	$shell	The default shell the user will be given after logging in. Whatever it is, it must be listed in the "shells" file.

* This strange acronym exists because in UNIX's early days at Bell, this field was used to hold information about machines that ran GCOS, an operating system originally developed by GE. The UNIX systems used these machines for print spooling and other tasks. Though the field serves a different purpose now, the name stuck.

Next comes the <FORM> tag. This form's ACTION is to call the *change_user.pl* CGI on *www.outer.net*. The *change_user.pl* script, which we'll dig into later, is what actually makes changes to the "passwd" file. You'll need to change this URL to the location for your *change_user.pl* script:

```
print STDOUT "Content-Type:\ttext/html\n\n\n";
print STDOUT "<HTML><HEAD><TITLE>Users and Groups on
${SITENAME}</TITLE></HEAD>";
print STDOUT "<BODY>";
print STDOUT "<FORM ACTION=\"http://www.outer.net/",
    "cgi-bin/change_user.pl\" METHOD=\"POST\">\n";
print STDOUT "<H2>Users and Groups on ${SITENAME}</H2><HR>\n";
```

Next come the submission buttons for the form. We have a button for every feature allowed: Add, Change, and Delete. The value of the button clicked is sent to *change_user.pl*, so that it knows what action to perform:

```
print STDOUT "<INPUT TYPE=\"submit\" NAME=\"Change\"
VALUE=\"Change\">\n";
print STDOUT "<INPUT TYPE=\"submit\" NAME=\"Delete\"
VALUE=\"Delete\">\n";
print STDOUT "<INPUT TYPE=\"submit\" NAME=\"Add\" VALUE=\"Add\">\n";
```

The next portion sets up a table of input fields for user information that can be changed. We're allowing the following items to be manipulated:

- User name
- User ID
- Group ID (retrieved from the $groups_list)
- User information
- Home directory
- Shell (retrieved from the $shells_list)
- Password, which a second input box will verify has been typed in correctly. Its input type is set to 'PASSWORD' so that onlookers can't see what's being typed in. The default value is the random password generated by the program specified in $clear_text.

Go through each piece of the embedded HTML below to see which variable goes with which field:

```
print STDOUT "<HR><STRONG>Enter information in the fields you would like to
change:</STRONG><P>";
print STDOUT "<TABLE CELLPADDING=0 CELLSPACING=0>";
```

```
print STDOUT "<TH>Description</TH><TH>New Value</TH>";
print STDOUT "<TR><TD>New User Name:</TD>";
print STDOUT "<TD><INPUT SIZE=20 MAXLENGTH=20 TYPE=\"TEXT\" INPUT
NAME=\"new_user\" VALUE=\"\"></TD></TR>";
print STDOUT "<TR><TD>New User ID:</TD>";
print STDOUT "<TD><INPUT SIZE=20 MAXLENGTH=20 TYPE=\"TEXT\" INPUT
NAME=\"new_uid\" VALUE=\"\"></TD></TR>";
print STDOUT "<TR><TD>New Group ID:</TD>";
print STDOUT "<TD><SELECT NAME=\"new_gid\"> ${group_list}
</SELECT></TD></TR>";
print STDOUT "<TR><TD>New User Information:</TD>";
print STDOUT "<TD><INPUT SIZE=20 MAXLENGTH=20 TYPE=\"TEXT\" INPUT
NAME=\"new_gcos\" VALUE=\"\"></TD></TR>";
print STDOUT "<TR><TD>New Home Directory:</TD>";
print STDOUT "<TD><INPUT SIZE=20 MAXLENGTH=20 TYPE=\"TEXT\" INPUT
NAME=\"new_home\" VALUE=\"\"></TD></TR>";
print STDOUT "<TR><TD>New Shell:</TD>";
print STDOUT "<TD><SELECT NAME=\"new_shell\"> ${shell_list}
</SELECT></TD></TR>";
print STDOUT "<TR><TD>Password:</TD>";
print STDOUT "<TD><INPUT SIZE=20 MAXLENGTH=20 TYPE=\"PASSWORD\" INPUT
NAME=\"password\" VALUE=\"$clear_text\"></TD></TR>";
print STDOUT "<TR><TD>Verify Password:</TD>";
print STDOUT "<TD><INPUT SIZE=20 MAXLENGTH=20 TYPE=\"PASSWORD\" INPUT
NAME=\"password2\" VALUE=\"$clear_text\"></TD></TR>";
print STDOUT "</TABLE><P>\n";
```

The next line displays the password stored in $clear_text so that the administrator can see it:

```
print STDOUT "The Password: <STRONG>$clear_text</STRONG> has been already
entered above.<BR>\n";
```

The last portion of the code sets up the user information display. It creates a bordered table around the password fields parsed by &get_passwd_entries() and describes them with column headings:

```
print STDOUT "<HR><TABLE BORDER CELLPADDING=2 CELLSPACING=2>";
print STDOUT "<TH><FONT SIZE=-2>Select</FONT></TH><TH>User</TH>",
    "<TH>Encrypted Password</TH>";
print STDOUT "<TH>UID</TH><TH>GID</TH>";
print STDOUT "<TH>GCOS Fields</TH><TH>Home Directory</TH>",
    "<TH>Shell</TH>";
  &get_passwd_entries();
  print STDOUT "</TABLE><HR>\n";
  print STDOUT "</BODY></HTML>\n";
}
```

Figure 16-1 depicts the final product of the *view_user.html.pl* code. We have a slick (and quick) user interface for managing user information in a UNIX password file.

Now that we've got our GUI for displaying account information, we need to actually do something with the selections we make. The next script, *change_user.pl*, uses the form data we've entered to take the appropriate action on the password file. Once you're up and running, it will be rare that you have to touch a password file by hand!

THE SYSADMIN'S RIGHT HAND: CHANGE_USER.PL

Now that we've decided what changes we want to make to the UNIX accounts database, our account management tool needs to actually make the corresponding changes to the password file. The Perl script *change_user.pl* contains the routines to do this. As you remember, this CGI is called by *view_user.html.pl*'s form action. We'll step through each part and go over how it uses the data to make these changes.

Preparing the CGI for Webspeak

In order to use the data passed by the form, we need to extract it from the "packaged" return from the browser. Again, we'll use the &GetFormArgs() routine from *formlib.pl* to place them in the %in array.

```
###################################################################
#
# Web setup and configuration.  Here we parse out the environment
# variables found to control which options need to be handled. We
# also set up some variables for ease of use as well as assign the
# various actions when an associated button was clicked (Add,
# Change, Delete).
#
###################################################################

require "/www/cgi-bin/formlib.pl";
$| = 1;              # output NOT buffered
&GetFormArgs();      # Parse arguments passed from FORM (now in %in).
$ENV{PATH_INFO} ne '' && &GetPathArgs($ENV{PATH_INFO});
```

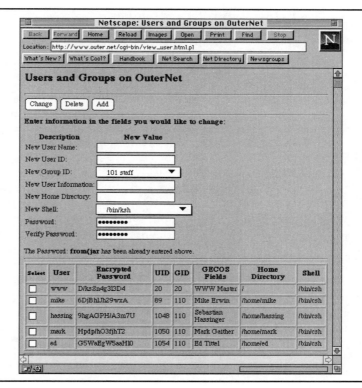

Figure 16-1
The view_user.pl account management interface.

Putting Variables and Constants in Their Places

We'll then take the data from the %in array and assign them to variables for ease of use later in the script. We'll do the same for the values of the submission buttons. The $selection variable is a pound(#)-delimited list of user ID numbers selected by the checkboxes on the HTML form:

```
$new_user    = $in{new_user};
$new_uid     = $in{new_uid};
$new_gid     = $in{new_gid};
$new_gcos    = $in{new_gcos};
$new_home    = $in{new_home};
$new_shell   = $in{new_shell};
```

```
$password     = $in{password};
$password2    = $in{password2};
$Change       = $in{Change};
$Delete       = $in{Delete};
$Add          = $in{Add};
#
# The selection variable is a "#"-delimited list of UIDs that the
# user has passed by selecting with checkboxes. See the main
# section for where we do some pre-processing of this variable
# into a list called: "user_offsets".
#
$selection    = $in{selection};
```

Here's the section where you're going to have to make the changes for your system. You'll need to input the location of your password file, the place where you want to put the password file changes, the name of your site, and the location of your *grep* program.

```
################################################################
#
# Setup and configuration.  Some common places to find things and
# some global constants.
#
################################################################

#! Password file location
$PASSWD_FILE     = "/etc/passwd";

#! Full path to the new file
$NEW_PASSWD_FILE = "/www/cgi-bin/new.passwd.clone";

#! A string for display
$SITENAME        = "OuterNet";

#! location of grep
$GREP_APP        = "/usr/local/bin/grep";
```

If the $new_shell we selected on the form was "None," then we need to make that variable null because there's no "None" shell. In this section we also set a "blank" $new_uid and variable to zero (0). If the $new_gid is set to "None" then we make it zero as well.

Otherwise, we split the group name from the group ID number and only store the group ID number in the $new_gid variable. Why are we defaulting $new_uid and $new_gid to the *root* UID and GID? We're not really. In this script we use zero as a cue not to make changes to the current UID and GID.

```
############################################################
#
# Doctor up the variables. Here we check the consistency of the
# various variables that we have loaded into this script. We set
# the user and group ID variables to zero (0) as our tests for
# no-changes rely on this. Using zero as the "stay the same"
# decision also prevents users from trying to modify the root
# account or root group by default.
#
############################################################

if ($new_shell =~ "None") {
  $new_shell = "";
}
if (!$new_uid) {
  $new_uid = "0";
}
#
# The else part of this if statement separates off the group IDs
# from the group names, since we are only interested in the value.
#
if ($new_gid =~ "None") {
  $new_gid = "0";
}
else {
  @new_gid_parts    = split(" ",$new_gid);
  $new_gid          = $new_gid_parts[0] + 0;
}
```

There Can't Be Two of You!

Our first subroutine checks to see if the username we're working with
already exists in the password file. This is important when creating a new
user or changing a username so that you don't have two users with the same
name. It does this by *grep*ping the username field in the password file for
the name you're seeking to define. If the user returned by *grep* is the same as
the user it's looking for, then it returns true, otherwise it returns false.
(Remember, for this to work, the *grep* must be on an exact match.)

```
############################################################
#
# does_entry_exist
# This function looks through the password file as defined by
# "PASSWD_FILE" for a given user, passed into this function as
# $user_to_find. This procedure is used to determine if a new
```

```
# account can be created or if an existing account can be changed
# to another username. The function returns true if the entry
# exists already and false if it does not.
#
################################################################
sub does_entry_exist {
  local($user_to_find)= @_;
  #
  # If the argument is blank or does not exist, fail immediately.
  #
  if (! $user_to_find) {
    return (0);
  }
  # Run a grep and poke the result into a variable (pass_lines).
  #
  $pass_lines = `${GREP_APP} "${user_to_find}\:" ${PASSWD_FILE}`;
  chop ($pass_lines);
  local ($user,$crypt_passwd,$uid,$gid,$gcos,$home,$shell) =
  split(":",$pass_lines);
  # This is used for displaying the results to the user later on.
  #
  $user_tag = $user;
  return( $user eq $user_to_find );
}
```

I've Got Your Number

The next function, does_uid_entry_exist(), operates the same way and for the same reason as does_entry_exist(). But it's concerned with checking out the user ID number rather than the username.

```
################################################################
#
# This function looks through the password file as defined by
# "PASSWD_FILE" for a given UID, passed into this function as
# $user_to_find. This procedure is used to determine if a new
# account can be created or if an existing account can be changed
# to another username. The function returns true if the entry
# exists already and false if it does not.
#
# There is no difference between this function and the previous
# one except for the difference in the field being checked.
#
################################################################
```

```
sub does_uid_entry_exist {
  local($user_to_find)= @_;
  #
  # If the argument is blank or does not exist, fail immediately.
  #
  if (! $user_to_find) {
    return (0);
  }
  # Run a grep and poke the result into a variable (pass_lines).
  #
  $pass_lines = `${GREP_APP} "\:${user_to_find}\:"
    ${PASSWD_FILE}`;
  chop ($pass_lines);
  local ($user,$crypt_passwd,$uid,$gid,$gcos,$home,$shell) =
    split(":",$pass_lines);
  # This is used for displaying the results to the user later on.
  #
  $user_tag = $uid;
  return( $uid == $user_to_find );
}
```

Making the Changes

The set_passwd_entries subroutine does most of the work of this script. Its functions are:

- Take a user ID number as an argument.
- Create a clone password file.
- Make desired changes to the clone password file.
- Copy the clone file over the original.

Scary, eh? Giving a script that's run by a Web user the ability to copy a modified password file *over* the original opens your server up to an incredible security hole. We'll discuss these concerns further later on and give recommendations for avoiding some of the risks. You'll also see in the script that the code that performs the copy has been disabled. ▲

Opening and Reading the Password File

This portion of the code copies the original password file to the new password file. It then starts to read in each line of the new password file, splitting off the fields into corresponding variables as it goes along.

```
###################################################################
#
# set_passwd_entries
# This function takes a user ID as an argument, reads in the
# password file, creates a new password file, makes the changes
# as needed, then copies the new file over the old one. As you can
# see, this could be a huge security risk and it is not
# recommended that you fully enable this script to modify your
# password file on-the-fly. It is better to tweak this script to
# modify a stale version, then have a system administrator copy the
# new file over the old one as needed.
#
###################################################################
  #
sub set_passwd_entries {
  local($user_to_change)= @_;

  # Open the files to operate on (both old and new).
  #
  open(PASSWD_FILE,"$PASSWD_FILE");
  open(NEW_PASSWD_FILE,"> $NEW_PASSWD_FILE");

  while (<PASSWD_FILE>) {
    $passwd_line = $_;
    /^([^:]+)/;
    #
    # Split off the field into separate variables.
    #
    ($user,$crypt_passwd,$uid,$gid,$gcos,$home,$shell) = split(/:/);
```

Processing Changes

Next we check to see if the user ID we wish to change is equal to the UID on the line we're on. If so, then we systematically replace all values with the valid changes we've made:

```
        if ($user_to_change == $uid) {
        #
        # If we match the right user id, replace all the values with
        # valid changes
        #
          if ($new_user) {
            $user = $new_user;
          }
          if ($new_uid) {
            $uid = $new_uid;
          }
```

```
if ($new_gid) {
  $gid = $new_gid;
}
if ($new_gcos) {
  $gcos = $new_gcos;
}
if ($new_home) {
  $home = $new_home;
}
if ($new_shell) {
  $shell = $new_shell;
}
```

For the password, we use the text password entered in our $password field and run the Perl crypt() call to get our encrypted password. The salt method we've chosen here simplifies things to where we don't have to include error-checking for salt characters that crypt() may not like. We use a randomized two-character salt of one uppercase ASCII character and one lowercase character:

```
if ($password) {
#
# This crypt call could be much better, but it makes
# a good example.
#
srand;
$salt = sprintf("%c%c", rand(25)+65, rand(25)+97);
$crypt_passwd = crypt(${password}, $salt);
}
```

Modifying the Lines

Now that we've got all of our values loaded into the variables, we can construct a new password line by concatenating them together. Once we have this line, we'll check to see if the Delete button was clicked. If not, then we'll replace the line in the password file with our new line. If we did want to delete the user, then we'll make the line null. Once it's all tidy, we close both files.

```
# Construct the new output line.
#
$new_line =
$user.":".$crypt_passwd.":".$uid.":".$gid.":".$gcos.":".$home.":".$shell;

  if (! $Delete) {
```

```
        print NEW_PASSWD_FILE $new_line;
    }
  }
  else {
    print NEW_PASSWD_FILE;
    }
  }
  close (PASSWD_FILE);
  close (NEW_PASSWD_FILE);
```

Making the Changes Stick

Here's the part that we told you not to do! If you're feeling brave, uncomment the system() calls below. Otherwise, leave them be, and we'll discuss how to get around this later.

```
  #
  # Here we write back the new password file over the real password
  # file.
  # Notice that these line are commented out.
  #
  #  system("cp $NEW_PASSWD_FILE $PASSWD_FILE");
  #  system("rm $NEW_PASSWD_FILE");
  }
```

HIGH RISK PROGRAMMING

If you do allow this script to copy the new password file over the original, then you'll have to make your Web server's user ID (generally *www*) the owner of the file, or put that user in whatever group has write privileges to the password file. **WARNING:** Neither of these options is a good idea! We'll describe security concerns more in the installation portion of the chapter. In most system implementations, NO ONE has write permission to the "passwd" file, including *root*. To modify it, *root* must first change permissions on the file, then open it for writing, then change permissions back. You'll have to check your environment to understand how it works, but we deliberately left this code as an "exercise to the reader" because we don't think this practice is a good idea. ▲

Putting Our Subroutines to Task

In the main portion of the script, we call the subroutines described previously and give the administrator feedback on the execution of their action.

The first section of code sends the browser the HTML MIME type and the tags to set up the basic HTML page, such as <TITLE> and <BODY>. We'll also print a header letting them know where the modifications will take place (as indicated by $SITENAME).

```
################################################################
#
# main
# Here's where the main execution tree is started.  First off,
# some HTML output is dumped to the screen, then a security check
# is made to see if the user requested some action against the
# root account. Following that, the main action selection area
# does various if statements on the status of the buttons. Since
# only one button can be pressed at a time, only one of the ifs
# will be true, and only one action can result.
#
################################################################
{
  #
  # Output some basic HTML header information— more will come as
  # actions occur.
  #
  print STDOUT "Content-Type:\ttext/html\n\n\n";
  print STDOUT "<HTML><HEAD><TITLE>Modify Users and Groups on
${SITENAME}</TITLE>";
  print STDOUT "</HEAD><BODY>\n";
  print STDOUT "<H2>Modify Users and Groups on ${SITENAME}
</H2><HR>\n";
```

A Modicum of Security

In several places throughout our scripts, we have rules that prevent us from making changes to the *root* account. Here we have another one, which makes sure that *root* wasn't entered into the 'New User' field. If it was, it displays a warning message:

```
#
# Fail if "root" was selected or typed in.
#
if ($new_user eq "root") {
print STDOUT "<STRONG>You may not change the root user or the root
group.</STRONG><BR>";
}
```

Processing the Selections When Not Adding a User

If there wasn't a problem trying to change the *root* user, then we process the user depending on which button was clicked. Before we do that, we need to split off the UIDs selected by checkboxes into a list:

```
else {
#
# Split the checkbox selections into a list of UIDs.
#
 @user_offsets = split("\#",$selection);
```

We then test to see if the Delete or Change buttons were clicked. If so, then we run the &get_passwd_entries() subroutine on each of the user IDs selected. To let the administrator know what's going on, we send a message to the browser that the entry was deleted or changed:

```
#
# If the Delete button was pressed, loop through the users
# selected, and modify the password file accordingly.
#
if ($Delete) {
for ($ct=0; $ct <= $#user_offsets; $ct++) {
  print STDOUT "User Number: <STRONG> $user_offsets[$ct] </STRONG> was
deleted successfully<BR>";
  &set_passwd_entries ( $user_offsets[$ct] );
  }
 }
```

The "Change" option does a little error-checking using the subroutines, &does_entry_exist() and &does_uid_entry_exist(), to make sure there isn't already a user with the name or UID entered. We also check to make sure that the two new password entries are equal to each other. If any of these are true, we report back an appropriate message.

```
#
# Again loop through the selected users and change where
# appropriate. First, check to see that user doesn't already
# exist, and the password entered by the user is correct.
#
if ($Change) {
  if ( &does_entry_exist ($new_user) || &does_uid_entry_exist ($new_uid) )
  {
  print STDOUT "<STRONG>User: $user_tag already exists in the password
file.</STRONG><BR>";
  }
```

```
else {
  if ( $password ne $password2 ) {
    print STDOUT "<STRONG>The two password entries do not match.
 Please re-enter them.</STRONG><BR>";
  }
else {
  for ($ct=0; $ct <= $#user_offsets; $ct++) {
    print STDOUT "User Number: <STRONG> $user_offsets[$ct]
</STRONG> was changed successfully<BR>";
    &set_passwd_entries ( $user_offsets[$ct] );
      }
    }
  }
}
```

Processing the Selections When Adding a User

If we plan to add a user, things are done a little differently. Since only one user can be added at a time, we don't use the $selection variable or the $user_offsets listing of UIDs.

The first part of the conditional starts with another conditional that checks to make sure that the user is not creating a user with the name *root*, with the user ID of 0, or as part of the group *root* (GID of 0). If so, a message is sent to the user that it can't be done.

```
#
# Since only one user can be added at a time, the $selection
# variable and the list used for the other two buttons,
# $user_offsets, is ignored. We check that the user isn't trying
# to create a root account, or another account with root priv's.
# We also check the consistency of the passwords, and that every
# field was properly filled out before creating the account.
#
if ($Add) {
  if (($new_user eq "root") || ($new_uid == 0) || ($new_gid == 0))
{
    print STDOUT "<STRONG>You may not change the root user or
 the root group.</STRONG><BR>";
  }
  else {
```

The next conditional checks to see if any of the required fields for creating a new user are blank. If so, we display an error message to that effect:

```
if (!$new_user || !$password || !$password2 || !$new_uid ||
```

```
       !$new_gid || !$new_gcos || !$new_home || !$new_shell ) {

       print STDOUT "<STRONG>Please fill out all of the fields to add a new
user.</STRONG><BR>";
       }
```

We then run `&does_entry_exist` and `&does_uid_entry_exist` again to check that the selected username or user ID isn't already in the password file. The final check makes sure that both of the new passwords entered are the same:

```
else {
  if ( &does_entry_exist ($new_user) || &does_uid_entry_exist
  ($new_uid) ) {
  print STDOUT "<STRONG>User: $user_tag already exists in the
password file.</STRONG><BR>";
  }
else {
  if ( $password ne $password2 ) {
  print STDOUT "<STRONG>The two password entries do not match.
Please re-enter them.</STRONG><BR>";
  }
```

The last section is what actually creates the new user. It's similar to what happens when a user gets information changed. First, the original password file is copied to a new password file. We then encrypt the password using `crypt()`, with the same salt technique described earlier.

HIGH RISK PROGRAMMING

Our new user line is then constructed by concatenating the fields we've entered and the encrypted password. This line is then appended to the end of the new password file, and then the new password file is closed. Again, the disabled system calls—that copy the new password file over the old one and then delete the new one—are here. We advise that you don't allow this script to modify the actual password file. The administrator is also sent a message that the new user was added. ▲

```
else {
  system("cp $PASSWD_FILE $NEW_PASSWD_FILE");

  open(NEW_PASSWD_FILE,">>$NEW_PASSWD_FILE");

  srand;
  $salt = sprintf("%c%c", rand(25)+65, rand(25)+97);
  $new_password = crypt(${password}, $salt);
```

```
$new_line=$new_user.":".$new_password.":".$new_uid.":".$new_gid.":".$new_gcos.":
".$new_home.":".$new_shell;

    print NEW_PASSWD_FILE $new_line;
    close (NEW_PASSWD_FILE);
#
# Here we write back the new password file over the real password
# file. Notice that these lines are commented out.
#
#  system("cp $NEW_PASSWD_FILE $PASSWD_FILE");
#  system("rm $NEW_PASSWD_FILE");

    print STDOUT "User: <STRONG> $new_user </STRONG> was added
successfully<BR>$new_uid";
                }
              }
            }
          }
        }
      }
    }
```

That's it! We're out of code. These two CGIs provide you with a modifiable skeleton for a user account manager on UNIX systems. Now that you're familiar with how the code works, let's discuss installation.

INSTALLING THE ACCOUNT MANAGER

Because there are only two major pieces to this application, it's rather easy to install. We'll go over what should be changed in the scripts, where the files should be placed, and what permissions they need.

Tuning the Manager to Your System

For both *view_user.html.pl* and *change_user.pl* you'll need to modify the values that have the #! comments next to them. Most of these values set up the location of the "passwd", "group", and "shells" files, as well as other machine-specific information.

For instance, in *view_user.html.pl*, the following lines of code need to be modified:

```
$PASSWD_FILE    = "/etc/passwd"; #! Full path to the passwd file
$GROUPS_FILE    = "/etc/group"; #! Full path to the group file
$SHELLS_FILE    = "/etc/shells"; #! Full path to the shells file
$SITENAME       = "OuterNet";    #! A description of this site

$clear_text     = `/www/cgi-bin/mk.passwd.pl`; #! Replace this
```

Another item that should be changed in this script is the URL specified in the <FORM> tag. It is currently set to *http://www.outer.net/cgi-bin/change_user.pl*, but this should be changed to the URL location of *change_user.pl*.

In *change_user.pl* these values should be changed to reflect your system:

```
#! Password file location
$PASSWD_FILE     = "/etc/passwd";

#! Full path to the new file
$NEW_PASSWD_FILE = "/www/cgi-bin/new.passwd.clone";

#! A string for display
$SITENAME    = "OuterNet";

#! location of grep
$GREP_APP    = "/usr/local/bin/grep";
```

Once changed, we can start putting all components in the right places, with permissions set correctly.

Location and Permissions for Account Manager Files

Table 16-2 describes each Account Manager file, its name, location, owner and group, and permissions.

As for the scripts *view_user.html.pl*, *change_user.pl*, and *mk.passwd.pl*, we've set the permissions so that the Web user can run them, but only *root* is allowed to write over them. Allowing someone besides the superuser to modify these scripts could be dangerous. For instance, they could intentionally break all of the safeguards we've included to prevent the *root* account from being edited.

This brings us to security issues for this package, of which there are many. We'll try to cover as many ways to prevent unauthorized usage of this application as possible.

Table 16-2

Location and permission for Account Manager files

Description	Name	Location	Owner & Group	Permissions
Dynamic GUI	view_user. html.pl	/www/cgi-bin	root.httpd	750
Back-End Manager	change_user .pl	/www/cgi-bin	root.httpd	750
Random Password Generator	mk.passwd .pl	/www/cgi-bin	root.httpd	750
Cloned Password File	new.passwd clone	/www/cgi-bin	www.httpd	640
Original Password File* (NOT recommended!)	passwd	/etc	root.httpd	664

HIGH RISK PROGRAMMING

* **WARNING:** Even though permission changes are shown above for the "passwd" file, we recommend you NOT make those changes. They apply only if you are allowing your CGI to copy the clone password file directly over the original. If you are allowing this, you should *understand the security risks involved!* The changes shown allow anyone who's part of the *httpd* group to write over the "passwd" file. This is necessary to allow the CGI to perform the copy, but opens you up to more people being able to alter the file. ▲

SECURITY CONCERNS WITH THE ACCOUNT MANAGER

"Concerns" is an understatement: With a package as powerful and potentially destructive as this one, you should be downright paranoid. Listing all of the risks that this application poses would take up a chapter in itself. Instead we'll discuss ways to protect yourself—focusing on permissions, network security, secure protocols, and secure sockets.

Copying the New Password File Over the Original

We've already warned you several times that you shouldn't allow the script to copy the cloned password file over the original. By doing this, you're giving your Web server's user ID (typically *www*) the ability to modify accounts—you might as well give them the superuser password or run the server as *root*. There are a few alternative methods for doing this, which we'll list below.

Make the Sysadmin Copy the File by Hand

This makes the process slightly more tedious, but it means that only the superuser can copy the new password file over the old. It also gives the sysadmin a chance to see if the changes are acceptable. To make things a little easier we could change a few things on the script.

1. Add a subroutine to *change_user.pl* that lets the sysadmin know what changes were made. It could mail the changes to the sysadmin and then the sysadmin could decide whether to copy the file. To verify that all changes were made correctly, you could send the subroutine two things: the process *change_user.pl* went through to change the file and a diff of "passwd" and "new.passswd.clone."

2. Write a script that the sysadmin could run to do the copy after accepting the changes that were sent in the mail. It could be very simple, like the one below, or you could embellish it to report back or log the actions taken:

```
#!/usr/local/bin/perl
system("cp new.passwd.clone passwd");
system("rm new.passwd.clone");
```

Copy the File in a cron Job

This method is not quite as safe as the one above, but nonetheless effective. Early in the code for *change_user.pl* you would want to check for the existence of the "new.passwd.clone" file. If it exists, then the "passwd" file shouldn't be copied over it, and all subsequent modifications should be made to "new.passwd.clone". Otherwise, the code will go on as it's currently listed.

As in the first item of the previous subsection, the script will e-mail the sysadmin with all modifications made. The sysadmin can look at these alterations throughout the day to make sure they're okay. Then, sometime in the evening, a *cron* will run the script we created to perform the actual copy and delete "new.passwd.clone". There's a window where the sysadmin may not see the changes made, but it frees him or her from having to run the job each time a modification is made.

Log Everything

As long as you keep your logs well organized, you can never have too many of them. For example, it's a good idea to store all alterations made to the password file in a log so that you'll have a history of them. This, in conjunction with the e-mail feature, should keep you abreast of what's going on. Security aside, the log will also help you correct any mistakes you might make.

Create Backups

Although it wasn't done in our version of the script, it would be easy to modify *change_user.pl* to create a backup of the original password file. You could call this file "passwd.old" and use it as an escape vehicle if something goes wrong. Better yet, you can create an entire archive of original password files, making their extension the date and time they were backed up (e.g., "passwd.121595.152346"). That way, you can always go back to an older version if successive problems occur.

Password Protect the CGIs

By placing an ".htaccess" file in the CGI directory that houses *view_user.html.pl* and *change_user.pl*, you can prevent the CGIs from being run without a password. It's also a good idea to put them in a directory separate from your other CGIs.

For instance, instead of just putting them in *./cgi-bin*, you should put them in *./cgi-bin/usradm* and add the ".htaccess" file and an encrypted password file. Now, when someone tries to access the CGI at the URL:

```
http://www.outer.net/cgi-bin/usradm/view_user.html.pl
```

a dialog box will pop up asking for their username and password.

NIS and Password Shadowing Caveats

Our Account Manager will work almost as-is on many UNIX systems. If you're running any special database services on your system, however, it may have problems. Two of these database services are the NIS and *Password Shadowing*.

NIS, also known as *yp* services, provides a means for you to share the same administration files across networked systems by turning them into databases called *NIS* maps. These maps are stored on a central system, and other hosts on the network can query the central system when they need information from the files.

Two of these files are "passwd" and "group". If you're running NIS, you may need to make your script that copies the new password file over the original also run a make in your *yp* directory so that the latest "passwd" file will get converted into a map.

Password Shadowing is a security measure that helps prevent someone from finding, reading, and decrypting your password file. It comes standard on most distributions of FreeBSD and BSDI UNIX, and it can also be found for almost all other UNIX flavors.

Here's how it works: A program called pwd_mkdb takes a master password file (called something other than "passwd" and readable only by superuser), converts it into a password database (usually "pwd.db") and into a "fake" "passwd" file, that replaces the encrypted passwords with an asterisk (*) or an **x**.

As you can see, you'll have to change both *view_user.html.pl* and *change_user.pl* to read and copy the master password file rather than "passwd". You may also have to change the number and names of fields, as the master password file may not be in the standard UNIX format. You'll also need to add the *pwd_mkdb* step after the new master password file is copied over. Check the *man* pages on *pwd_mkdbs*, and on the subject of Trusted Computing Base (TCB systems) which work similarly, for more information on what else may need to be changed.

Don't Put the Account Manager on a Publicly Accessible Web Server

For any administration CGI, it's a good idea to put them only on Web servers you've set up specifically for administration. By doing so, you can deny access to all but a few IP addresses from which you'll be performing your management. This can be done either at the network level with a firewall or at the server level by using the "allow" and "deny" lists in the "access.conf" file for your *httpd* server.

You can also run your administration Web server at a TCP/IP socket higher than 1024, rather than at the default of 80. This means you can have a publicly available Web server running on 80, and a second one running on 8080 for administration, both on the same machine. It would be accessed in the following manner:

```
http://www.outer.net:8080/cgi-bin/usradm/view_user.html.pl
```

By doing this, you can firewall the second server's socket or use its "access.conf" file to control access.

Use a Secure Web Server

In Chapter 15, we discussed how Web technologies such as Secure HTTP (S-HTTP) and TCP/IP technologies like Secure Socket Layer (SSL) can be used to ensure secure financial transactions over the Net. If you have a Web server that can use either of these security features, then it would be ideal for an administration server.

You'll recall from the code that when a password is entered on the Account Manger's form, it isn't automatically encrypted: i.e., it's in clear text. The same applies to the random password generated by *mk.passwd.pl*. Someone packet-sniffing on your network, the network you're accessing your server from, or any of the networks in the path between the two can pick this unencoded information up in transit. S-HTTP and SSL both help prevent packet-sniffers from understanding what they're seeing.

Keep Up with What's Going on in Security

Just because there may not be a way to get around security measures today, doesn't mean there won't be tomorrow. It's important for you to keep up with the latest developments in security and the latest information on compromised systems.

Often, the best place to find the latest on security are the USENIX newsgroups. For the latest Computer Emergency Response Team Coordination Center (CERT-CC) advisories and the other security updates, try the following newsgroup:

```
comp.security.announce
```

For WWW-specific security issues, there's the WWW-Security mailing list. Send an e-mail to *majordomo@nsmx.rutgers.edu* with "subscribe www-security" in the body of the message.

In newsgroups and mailing lists, look for alerts on *httpd*, SSL, S-HTTP, or any hole that allows a user to run something as *root*. When these issues pop up, see how they might affect your Account Manager.

ENHANCEMENTS TO THE ACCOUNT MANAGER

We've already gone over several possible enhancements to the Account Manager in the section on security. In fact, those are probably the ones you'll want to implement first. But there are a few other things that can ease the burden of UNIX user administration even further.

Make the Account Manager More Like adduser

Why would we want to make our Account Manager more like *adduser*? Mostly for one feature that *adduser* has that ours does not: the ability to automatically create a home directory, populate it with "dot" files (e.g., ".kshrc", ".cshrc", ".login", and ".logout"), and grant the user ownership of the directory and files. The code for this could be added to the "Add" portion of *change_user.pl*. Another nice thing that *adduser* does is let you know the next available UID number.

Add the Ability to Modify Groups

Although it's less frequent that the "group" file needs to be modified, you can add this feature to the Account Manager to save time. You could create an administration page that gives you the option to "Manage Users" or "Manage Groups." The group manager would operate basically the same way the Account Manager does, but it requires fewer fields. You could also have it let you know the next available GID number when creating a new group.

Send "New User" Information to Someone Whose Account Was Just Created

You can also have *change_user.pl* send standard e-mail to a username that was just created. These could include new user information, system rules and regulations, how to change their password, and frequently asked questions (FAQ). This doesn't directly affect the account information, but could save you hours in user support later!

These are just some of the enhancements that can be made. The Account Manager is very open-ended, and you probably have several additions that are specific to your environment and users.

SUMMARY

In this chapter, we've made a case for our Account Manager by discussing some of the things that make user management a problem. We've described the tools that are already available and discussed their pros and cons. We compared these tools to an Account Manager that's Web-based, and outlined what the Account Manger should do.

We've also taken you through the code we've written for our Account Manager and described what needs to be done to run it on your system. We've addressed several security concerns with making user management so accessible, and given examples of how to protect yourself. Finally, we've described a few enhancements that can be made to the Web-based Account Manager.

Those of you who aren't UNIX system administrators may think that this isn't fair: Most of the tools we've created so far in this book are designed to aid sysadmins. As sysadmins ourselves, what can we say? "Necessity is the mother of invention." We didn't leave end users out completely. We realize that many users who never *wanted* a UNIX account suddenly find themselves with one when they get Internet access. The next chapter sketches out some forms that help those of us who aren't gurus perform some common UNIX tasks!

FROM A PROGRAM USAGE STATEMENT TO AN HTML FORM

17

*I*n this chapter, we present a simple, effective method for creating an HTML form interface to an executable typically run from the command line. Both UNIX and MS DOS use a command-line interface to the operating system shell. On UNIX, such command-line programs include Perl scripts; Bourne, C, or K shell scripts; an executable program of just about any kind; or a system command. Another example is a Perl script named *sub.pl* that accepts a list of files as input and substitutes one string for another in each file.

The general form of a typical program usage statement, sometimes called a syntax statement, for an executable command can be expressed as:

```
command expression[s]...
```

where command is the name of the program, script, or command and expression is a list of expressions. Typically an expression contains required and optional switches, flags, and fields. Table 17-1 summarizes a typical usage statement.

Table 17-1

Summary of the general form of a usage statement

Component	Description	Function
command	name of command, program, or script	identifies program
{-abc}	optional switches; any combination of a, b, and c	instruction used by command for processing; no associated data field
[-abc]	required switches; any combination of a, b, and c	instruction used by command for processing; no associated data field
{-[a|b|c]}	optional switch; only one of the set allowed	instruction used by command for processing; no associated data field
[-[a|b|c]]	required switch; only one of the set allowed	instruction used by command for processing; no associated data field
{-a data}	optional flag with accompanying data field	instruction used by command for processing; associated data field
[-a data]	required flag with accompanying data field	instruction used by command for processing; associated data field
{[-a data]|[-b data]}	optional flag with data; one or the other	instruction used by command for processing associated data field
[[-a data]|[-b data]]	required flag with data; one or the other	instruction used by command for processing; associated data field
{-a data...}	optional flag with repeatable data	instruction used by command for processing; one or more associated data fields
[-a data...]	required flag with repeatable data	instruction used by command for processing; one or more associated data fields

Here's an example of the usage statement for the *sub.pl* script:

```
sub.pl {-h} [-o old_string] [-n new_string] [-f file_names...]
```

This usage statement says that the *sub.pl* script has one optional switch { -h } which is the help flag, and three required flag/data pairs. The last flag/data pair states that the data can list one or more file_names. Here are some valid uses of the *sub.pl* script:

```
sub.pl -h
sub.pl -o "Elvis Presly" -n "Elvis Presley" -f one.html two.html
sub.pl -n "NFL" -o "FNL" -f *.html
```

The first invocation simply prints the help information for the program; the second replaces all instances of the string "Elvis Presly" with "Elvis Presley" in the files named "one.html" and "two.html". The third invocation replaces all instances of the string "NFL" with "FNL" in all files that end with a ".html" extension in the current directory.

PROGRAM USAGE STATEMENT MARKUP LANGUAGE (PUML)

PUML (pronounced "pummel") is a new language created by Mark Gaither, one of the authors of this book. This new language is built following the SGML (ISO-8879-1) philosophy, and it's an actual application of SGML. (Note: PUML's design was also heavily influenced by the Davenport Group's DocBook DTD.)

PUML's purpose is to describe the valid structure of a program's usage statement. Why do this? To facilitate the automagic generation of an HTML forms interface to a command-line-oriented program. This lets you run commands directly from your Web browser, without requiring the opening of a separate Telnet session in another window to execute the command line.

Figure 17-1 shows what the HTML 2.0 form interface to *sub.pl* looks like.

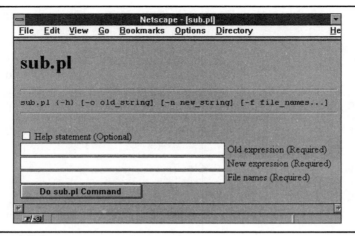

Figure 17-1
HTML form interface to sub.pl command.

The HTML 2.0 compliant document shown in Figure 17-1 was generated by a Perl script called *puml2html.pl*. This script handles part of the process of transforming a typical program usage statement into an HTML form and its corresponding CGI script. Figure 17-2 describes the process of transforming the UNIX program usage statement into the necessary Web equivalent components.

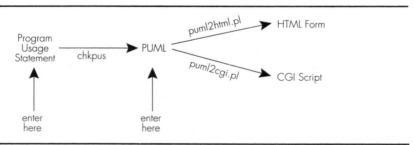

Figure 17-2
Transforming a program usage statement into its Web equivalent.

In this process a program usage statement is first converted to its PUML representation; this is an intermediate representation. From the PUML specification, you can create either an HTML form or a CGI script.

In this chapter, we will investigate only the HTML form creation. What's needed to complete this process is a *yacc* program—let's call it *pus2puml*—that checks the syntax of the program usage statement. Once the usage statement is deemed syntactically correct by *pus2puml*, it generates a valid intermediate PUML file. Notice that you can enter the process in two places, either at the beginning with the original program usage statement, or by creating a PUML representation of your program's usage statement. We will investigate the PUML representation process in this chapter.

PUML DTD

The PUML document type definition (DTD) describes PUML's structure and content. Here's the DTD specification:

```
<!—    puml.dtd
Description: Document Type Definition for the Program Usage
Statement Markup Language(PUML DTD)
Date: 18 Oct 1995 (about tea time)
Author: Mark Gaither (markg@webtechs.com)
—>

<!ENTITY % PUML.Version
  "-//WebTechs//DTD PUML 1.0//EN"

 —Typical usage:
  <!DOCTYPE PUML PUBLIC "-//WebTechs//DTD PUML 1.0//EN">
  <PUML>
       ...
  </PUML>
  —
>

<!—========Document Elements====================—>
<!ELEMENT body - - (command,(arg|group)+)>
<!ELEMENT command - - (name&type&lang&usage)>
<!ELEMENT (choice,descr,lang,name,flag,type,usage) - - CDATA>
<!ELEMENT repeat - O EMPTY>
<!ELEMENT arg - - (name&choice&flag?&repeat?&descr&value?)>
<!ELEMENT value - - (type&descr?)>
```

```
<!ELEMENT group - - (name&choice&descr&repeat?&(arg|group)+)>

<!-======= Document Structure =================->
<!ENTITY % version.attr "VERSION CDATA #FIXED '%PUML.Version;'">
<!ELEMENT puml - - (head,body)>
<!ATTLIST puml
        %version.attr;
        >
<!ELEMENT head - - (title,base*)>
<!ELEMENT title - - (#PCDATA)*>
<!ELEMENT base - O EMPTY>
<!ATTLIST base
        href          CDATA          #REQUIRED
        >
<!- <PUML>            PUML Document    ->
```

PUML

This required element must contain a <HEAD> element followed by a
<BODY> element. Its purpose is to act as a container element for other
subelements. Typical usage is:

```
<PUML>
...
</PUML>
```

HEAD

This required element contains a <TITLE> element followed by an optional
<BASE> element. It is a container element found at the beginning of a
PUML document. Typical usage is:

```
<PUML>
  <HEAD>
  ...
  </HEAD>
</PUML>
```

BASE

This optional singleton element contains no content. It does have a required
attribute, HREF, which is the URL for the current PUML document. Just
like the HTML <BASE> element, it requires an absolute, fully qualified
URL to contextualize later relative references. Typical usage is:

```
<HEAD>
  <BASE HREF="http://www.webtechs.com/index.html">
  <TITLE>...</TITLE>
</HEAD>
```

TITLE

This required element is the title of the current PUML document. Typical usage is:

```
<HEAD>
  <TITLE>Foundations of WWW Programming</TITLE>
  <BASE HREF="foo">
</HEAD>
```

BODY

This required element contains the structure of the PUML document. The structure is a <COMMAND> element followed by one or more combinations of <ARG> and <GROUP> elements. The <BODY> element follows the <HEAD> element. Typical usage is:

```
<PUML>
  <HEAD>
  . . .
  </HEAD>
  <BODY>
  . . .
  </BODY>
</PUML>
```

COMMAND

This is the required first element in the context of the <BODY> element. Its purpose is to describe the command-line oriented program. It must have NAME, TYPE, LANG, and USAGE elements, in any order. Typical usage is:

```
<BODY>
  <COMMAND>
    <LANG>Perl</LANG>
    <TYPE>script</TYPE>
    <NAME>foo.pl</NAME>
    <USAGE>foo.pl {-agfu} [-f file_specs...]</USAGE>
  </COMMAND>
  . . .
</BODY>
```

NAME

This is a required element that can be found in the context of <BODY>, <ARG>, or <GROUP> elements. It provides a handle that identifies individual document element objects with a unique name that can be referenced elsewhere in a PUML document.

TYPE

This is a required element found in the context of <COMMAND> or <VALUE> elements. It describes the type of document object.

LANG

This is a required element found in the context of a <COMMAND> element. It describes the programming language used to define or execute a command.

USAGE

This is a required element found in the context of a <COMMAND> element. It provides the usage statement for the command in a typical format.

ARG

This required element is found in the context of <BODY> or <GROUP> elements. Its purpose is to describe each argument available for the command-line program. It must contain the element's NAME, CHOICE, and DESCR, in any order. It can also contain the optional elements FLAG, REPEAT, and VALUE. Typical usage is:

```
<ARG>
  <NAME>file_specs</NAME>
  <REPEAT>
  <VALUE>
    <TYPE>string</TYPE>
  </VALUE>
  <CHOICE>Required</CHOICE>
  <FLAG>-f</FLAG>
  <DESCR>File Name Specifications</DESCR>
</ARG>
```

CHOICE

This is a required element found in the context of <ARG> or <GROUP> elements. It describes whether an argument is required or optional. Its content is user-supplied. Its two values may be 'Required' or 'Optional'. These are expected by *esis2html* (this script handles output from an SGML parsing program and turns it into an HTML representation; it's described later in this chapter). Typical usage is:

```
<CHOICE>Required</CHOICE>
<CHOICE>Optional</CHOICE>
```

FLAG

This optional element is found in the context of <ARG> or <GROUP> elements. Its content is the associated flag part of a flag/data pair (such as `-d destination_printer`), or a switch with no associated data field (such as `ls -l`). Typical usage is:

```
<FLAG>-f</FLAG>
```

REPEAT

This is an optional element found in the context of <ARG> or <GROUP> elements. It has no content. It's a singleton tag that indicates that the ARG or GROUP is repeatable (i.e., that it may occur more than once in the context defined by the PUML statement).

DESCR

This is a required element found in the context of <ARG> or <GROUP> elements, or an optional element in the context of a <VALUE> element. Its content is a description of the element to which it refers. This description is used to label HTML form input widgets.

VALUE

This is an optional element found in the context of the <ARG> element. It signifies that the current <ARG> element requires the user to provide a value for the current argument. This is typical when creating a flag/data pair. For instance, the usage statement:

```
foo [-f file_spec]
```

specifies a flag/data pair where the flag is `-f` and the data is `file_spec`. Typical usage is:

```
<VALUE>
  <TYPE>string</TYPE>
</VALUE>
<FLAG>-f</FLAG>
```

TYPE

This is a required element in the context of a VALUE element. It identifies the type of the value for the current argument or group of arguments. At present PUML will accept any string as a TYPE name, but should you want to build data- or type-checking into CGIs based on PUML, you'd want to restrict the names to a defined set for which checks could be enabled. Some typical TYPEs would be 'string', 'filename', 'URL', 'date', and 'number'.

GROUP

This element can be found in the context of the <BODY> element. Its purpose is to group command arguments. For instance, the usage statement:

```
foo {-f [one|two|three]} [-[A|B|C]]
```

specifies two groups of arguments, one for the optional `-f` flag and its associated data field, and another for the set of switches A, B, or C. Typical usage is:

```
<GROUP>
  <NAME>foo</NAME>
  <DESCR>This is a foo widget</DESCR>
  <CHOICE>Required</CHOICE>
  <ARG>
    . . .
  </ARG>
  <ARG>
    . . .
  </ARG>
</GROUP>
```

At this point, you may ask: Why are attributes not used for the document elements? The answer is: because PUML is intended as an intermediate form. Typically, it is much easier to write lexical scanners and parsers for languages without attribution. For instance, a <COMMAND> element of PUML for the *sub.pl* script would look like this:

```
<COMMAND>
    <TYPE>script</TYPE>
    <LANG>Perl</LANG>
    <NAME>sub.pl</NAME>
    <USAGE>sub.pl {-h} [-o old_string] [-n new_string][-f
file_names...]</USAGE>
</COMMAND>
```

Compare this to a specification of the <COMMAND> element of an attributed PUML DTD:

```
<COMMAND lang="perl" type="script" usage="sub.pl {-h} [-o
old_string] [-n new_string] [-f file_names...]">sub.pl</COMMAND>
```

Granted, this <COMMAND> element specification is more compact, but you must remember that the PUML representation is an intermediate form. Normally, you wouldn't sit down at your favorite SGML editor and begin creating a PUML instance of your usage statement. Intermediate forms without attribution are still human- as well as computer-readable; they just look a little more cumbersome.

Finally, using elements rather than attributes was a deliberate design choice because the downstream tools in the transformation process (see Figure 17-2) use the output of an SGML-compliant parser as their input. This parser outputs a normalized form of the PUML instance, called the "Element Structure Information Set (ESIS)." This is a simple ASCII text representation of the PUML document instance. The ESIS could be used to construct a tree of document elements present. Here, we'll use this data to construct an HTML 2.0 form.

Here's a PUML instance for the *sub.pl* command:

```
<!DOCTYPE PUML PUBLIC "-//WebTechs//DTD PUML 1.0//EN">
<PUML>
<HEAD>
<TITLE>sub.pl</TITLE>
</HEAD>
<BODY>
<COMMAND>
    <TYPE>script</TYPE>
    <LANG>Perl</LANG>
    <NAME>sub.pl</NAME>
```

```
      <USAGE>sub.pl {-h} [-o old_string] [-n new_string] [-f
file_names...]</USAGE>
</COMMAND>
<ARG>
  <NAME>help</NAME>
  <CHOICE>Optional</CHOICE>
  <FLAG>-h</FLAG>
  <DESCR>Help statement</DESCR>
</ARG>
<ARG>
  <NAME>old</NAME>
  <CHOICE>Required</CHOICE>
  <FLAG>-o</FLAG>
  <VALUE>
   <TYPE>string</TYPE>
  </VALUE>
  <DESCR>Old expression</DESCR>
</ARG>
<ARG>
  <NAME>new</NAME>
  <CHOICE>Required</CHOICE>
  <FLAG>-n</FLAG>
  <VALUE>
    <TYPE>string</TYPE>
  </VALUE>
  <DESCR>New expression</DESCR>
</ARG>
<ARG>
  <NAME>filenames</NAME>
  <CHOICE>Required</CHOICE>
  <REPEAT>
  <FLAG>-f</FLAG>
  <VALUE>
    <TYPE>string</TYPE>
  </VALUE>
  <DESCR>File names</DESCR>
</ARG>
</BODY>
</PUML>
```

puml2html.pl

This tool is a Perl script that takes a PUML instance as input and generates
a valid HTML 2.0 form. *puml2hmtl.pl*'s data flow description is presented
in Figure 17-3.

The SGML parser we used in our transformation process is *sgmls*, written by James Clark. It is an SGML ISO-8879 compliant parser. You can find his new and improved SGML parser, named *sp* (the successor to *sgmls*), at the following URL. ▲

```
http://www.jclark.com/sp.html
```

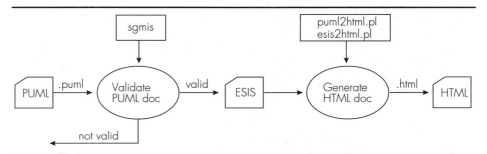

Figure 17-3
Data flow for puml2html.pl.

Typical usage of *puml2html.pl* is:

```
puml2html.pl {-h} [[-s script_file_name] | [-p PUML_spec]]
[-f form_file_name]
```

and some valid examples are:

```
puml2html.pl -h
puml2html.pl -s /usr/local/bin/sub.pl -f /www/sub.pl-form.html
puml2html.pl -p /usr/local/puml/sub.pl.puml -f /www/sub.pl-form.html
```

The difference between the last two examples is that the first looks in the actual script file for a variable named '$pumlfile'. If it finds the variable, it uses that value as a reference to the script's associated PUML instance. The second invocation provides the PUML instance explicitly.

Here's the source for *puml2html.pl*:

```
#!/usr/tools/bin/perl
# Location of the Perl directory may vary, depending on your
# site's directory structure; if so, the Perl shell line must
# change to match local conditions.

print "\npuml2html Utility by Mark Gaither (WebTechs)\n\n";
```

```perl
# PUML specification related to this script; adjust directory
# spec to match local conditions
$pumlfile = "/u/markg/secrets/puml/puml2html.pl.puml";

$usage = 'Usage: puml2html.pl {-h} [[-s script_file_name] |
    [-p PUML_spec]] [-f form_file_name]';

# get the command line options
require 'getopts.pl';
&Getopts('hs:f:p:');

if(defined($opt_h)) { print $usage; exit; }
if(!defined($opt_f)) { print $usage; exit; }
else { $form_file_name = $opt_f; }
if(defined($opt_s)) { $script_file_name = $opt_s; }

if(!defined($opt_s) && !defined($opt_p)) {
    print $usage; exit;
}

if(defined($opt_s) && defined($opt_p)) {
    print $usage; exit;
}

# define my own trap for interrupts
$SIG{'INT'} = 'exit_gracefully';
$SIG{'PIPE'} = 'exit_gracefully';

# set up environment
$ENV{'PATH'} = "/bin:/usr/tools/bin:/cgi-bin:" . $ENV{'PATH'};
&which('sgmls');
&which('date');
&which('esis2html');

# identify already installed sgmls repository; these
# directories will need to be adjusted for local conditions.
# Logfile for puml2html transformations
$LogFile = "/u/markg/secrets/puml2html.$$.log";
# location of sgmls library files
$SGMLLib = "/am/www/users/markg/HaLSoft/html-check/src/lib";
# locaiton of sgmls html DTD declaration to be used in parsing
$SGMLdecl = "$SGMLLib/html.decl";
# location of sgmls internal declarations to be used in parsing
$Catalog = "$SGMLLib/catalog";

# see if a PUML file is associated with the script. If so,
# use it to generate the HTML
if($opt_s) {
```

```perl
open(SCRIPT,"< $script_file_name") || die "Can't open script
    $script_file_name: $!\n";
undef $cmdfilename;

# look through the script for the PUML specification
while(<SCRIPT>) {
  if(/\$pumlfile\s*=\s*[\"|\'](.+)[\"|\']\;$/) {
    $pumlfilename = $1;
  }
}

if(!defined($pumlfilename)) {
  print "*** ERROR: Program Usage Mark Language (PUML)
specification not found\n";
  print "             in file $script_file_name. Exiting ...\n";
  exit;
  }
}
# PUML spec is listed on the command line
else { $pumlfilename = $opt_p; }

# validate the PUML instance before transforming to HTML
$cmd = "cat $pumlfilename";
open(DATA, "$cmd |") || die "Can't list $pumlfilename: $!\n";
$data = join('', <DATA>);
close(DATA);

# set up external files to hold the errors and ESIS output
# from the SGML parser
$ESIS = "/tmp/ESIS";
$ERRORS = "/tmp/ERRORS";

# create the parser command; Note: if you're using the earlier
# version of this program, sp, please change the command line that
# follows:
$command = "sgmls -m $Catalog $SGMLdecl - >$ESIS 2>$ERRORS";
die "$0: $Catalog: $!\n" unless -r $Catalog;
open(OUT,"| $command") || die "Pipe problem $cmd: $!\n";
print OUT $data;
close(OUT);

# a successful parse results in an ERRORS file of zero length.
if(-z "$ERRORS") {
  print "\tValid PUML spec\n";
}
else {
  print "\t*** Invalid PUML spec ***\n\n";
  &print_file($ERRORS);
```

```perl
    unlink("$ESIS");
    unlink("$ERRORS");
    exit;
  }
  unlink("$ERRORS");

  # if valid PUML, create an HTML form
  print "\tCreating HTML form ...\n";

  # use the ESIS output from the SGML parser as input
  # to the esis2html tool which generates 2.0 HTML
  open(PIPE,"esis2html $ESIS |") || die "Can't open pipe: $!\n";
  $html = join('',<PIPE>);

  unlink("$ESIS");

  # set up the command to validate the resulting HTML
  $command = "sgmls -m $Catalog $SGMLdecl - >$ESIS 2>$ERRORS";
  die "$0: $Catalog: $!\n" unless -r $Catalog;
  open(OUT,"| $command") || die "Pipe problem $cmd: $!\n";
  print OUT $data;
  close(OUT);

  # a successful parser results in an ERRORS file of length zero
  if(-z "$ERRORS") {
    print "\tValid HTML spec\n";
  }
  else {
    print "\t*** Invalid HTML spec ***\n\n";
    &print_file($ERRORS);
    unlink("$ESIS");
    unlink("$ERRORS");
    exit;
  }

  print "\tCreating HTML form file: $form_file_name\n\n";

  # finally, create the HTML form
  open(FORM,"> $form_file_name") || die "Can't open HTML form file
$form_file_name: $!\n";
  print FORM $html;
  close(FORM);

  exit;

  # print the content of a file to STDOUT
  sub print_file{
    local($f) = @_;
```

```
    open(IN,"< $f") || die "Can't open errors file $f: $!";
    while(<IN>){ print; }
    close(IN);
}

# which executable?
sub which{
  local($name) = @_;
  local(@dirs) = split(':', $ENV{'PATH'});

  # look for the executable in the given path variable
  foreach (@dirs){
    if(-e "$_/$name"){
      print STDERR "$name ==> $_/$name\n" if $Verbose;
      return;
    }
  }

  die "$0: $name not found\n";
}

# my interrupt handler
sub exit_gracefully {
  local($sig) = @_;

  print "\tCaught trap. Exiting gracefully ...\n\n";
  kill 9, $pid if $pid;
  exit 2;
}
```

esis2html

Figure 17-3 also shows the use of a program called *esis2html*, a lexical
scanner written using *lex*. This program takes the ESIS output of the *sgmls*
parser (or *sp*, if you're using the earlier version) as its input and generates
valid HTML 2.0. *puml2html.pl* provides validation of the PUML instance
as well as the generated HTML. An upgrade to *puml2html.pl* would result
in the generation of a user-defined DTD such as HTML 3.0 or Netscape's
Mozilla. As it stands, the program generates valid HTML 2.0.

Typical usage of *esis2html* is:

```
esis2html ESIS_file_name
```

Usually this tool is not run standalone, although it can be. Typically,
however, you'll want to capture the ESIS output from the SGML parser and
use a pipe to pass it on to *puml2html.pl*. If you'll examine the *puml2html.pl*

source code, you'll see how it works, and how you might run it in standalone mode. Nevertheless, *esis2html* is usually executed from within *puml2html.pl*.

Here's the *lex* source for *esis2html.l*:

```
%{
#include <stdio.h>
#include <string.h>
#include <malloc.h>
#include <ctype.h>
#include <varargs.h>

/* GLOBALS */
int REPEAT = 0;
int VALUE = 0;
int GROUP = 0;
int REQUIRED = 0;
char *cmd;
char *fieldname;
char *valuestr;
char *descrstr;
char *argchoicestr;
char *grpchoicestr;
char *grpnamestr;
char *flagstr;
char *repeatstr;
char *usagestr;
%}

%START command arg group cmdname argname grpdescr argchoice flag
repeat descr value valuetype grpchoicename grpchoice grpname usage

%%

^"(COMMAND" { BEGIN command; }

^"(ARG" { BEGIN arg; }

^"(GROUP" { GROUP = 1; BEGIN group; }

^")PUML" {
  printf("<INPUT TYPE=\"submit\" VALUE=\"Do %s Command\">\n",cmd);
  printf("</FORM>\n");
  printf("</BODY>\n");
  printf("</HTML>\n");
}
```

```
<group>"(DESCR" { BEGIN grpdescr; }

<group>")GROUP" {
  GROUP = 0;
  REQUIRED = 0;
  VALUE = 0;
  printf("<P>\n");
  BEGIN 0;
}

<group>^"(NAME" { BEGIN grpname; }

<grpname>^[-].+ {
  grpnamestr = (char *)malloc(strlen(yytext)-1);
  stripchar(yytext);
  strcpy(grpnamestr,yytext);
  BEGIN group;
}


<group>^"(CHOICE" { BEGIN grpchoice; }

<grpchoice>^[-].+ {
  grpchoicestr = (char *)malloc(strlen(yytext)-1);
  stripchar(yytext);
  strcpy(grpchoicestr,yytext);
  if(strcmp(grpchoicestr,"Required") == 0) { REQUIRED = 1; }
  else { REQUIRED = 0; }
  BEGIN group;
}

<grpdescr>^[-].+ {
  stripchar(yytext);
  printf("<H2>%s</H2>\n",yytext);
  BEGIN group;
}

<arg>")ARG" {
  if(GROUP == 0 && VALUE == 0 && REQUIRED == 0) {
    printf("<INPUT NAME=\"%s\" TYPE=\"checkbox\"> %s
(%s)<BR>\n",fieldname,descrstr,argchoicestr);
  }
  else if(GROUP == 0 && VALUE == 0 && REQUIRED == 1) {
    printf("<INPUT NAME=\"%s\" TYPE=\"radio\"> %s
(%s)<BR>\n",fieldname,descrstr,argchoicestr);
  }
  else if(GROUP == 1 && VALUE == 0 && REQUIRED == 0) {
    printf("<INPUT NAME=\"%s\" TYPE=\"checkbox\" VALUE=\"%s\">
```

```
%s (%s)<BR>\n",grpnamestr,fieldname,descrstr,argchoicestr);
  }
  else if(GROUP == 1 && VALUE == 0 && REQUIRED == 1) {
    printf("<INPUT NAME=\"%s\" TYPE=\"radio\" VALUE=\"%s\">
%s (%s)<BR>\n",grpnamestr,fieldname,descrstr,argchoicestr);
  }
  else if(VALUE == 1) {
    printf("<INPUT NAME=\"%s\" TYPE=\"text\" SIZE=\"40\"
MAXLENGTH=\"80\"> %s (%s)<BR>\n",fieldname,descrstr,argchoicestr);
  }
  else if(REPEAT == 1) {
    printf("<P>%s (%s)<BR>\n",descrstr,argchoicestr);
    printf("<TEXTAREA NAME=\"%s\" ROWS=\"5\"
COLS=\"40\"></TEXTAREA>\n",fieldname);
  }

  if(GROUP == 1) { BEGIN group; }
  else {
    REQUIRED = 0;
    VALUE = 0;
    REPEAT = 0;
    BEGIN 0;
  }
}

<arg>"(NAME" { BEGIN argname; }

<arg>"(CHOICE" { BEGIN argchoice; }

<arg>"(FLAG" { BEGIN flag; }

<arg>"(REPEAT" { REPEAT = 1; }

<arg>"(DESCR" { BEGIN descr; }

<arg>"(VALUE" { VALUE = 1; BEGIN value; }

<value>")VALUE" { VALUE = 0; BEGIN arg; }

<value>"(TYPE" { BEGIN valuetype; }

<value>")TYPE" { BEGIN arg; }

<valuetype>^[-].+ {
  valuestr = (char *)malloc(strlen(yytext)-1);
  stripchar(yytext);
  strcpy(valuestr,yytext);
  BEGIN value;
}
```

```
<descr>^[-].+ {
  descrstr = (char *)malloc(strlen(yytext)-1);
  stripchar(yytext);
  strcpy(descrstr,yytext);
  BEGIN arg;
}

<flag>^[-].+ {
  flagstr = (char *)malloc(strlen(yytext)-1);
  stripchar(yytext);
  strcpy(flagstr,yytext);
  BEGIN arg;
}

<argchoice>^[-].+ {
  argchoicestr = (char *)malloc(strlen(yytext)-1);
  stripchar(yytext);
  strcpy(argchoicestr,yytext);
  BEGIN arg;
}

<argname>^[-].+ {
  fieldname = (char *)malloc(strlen(yytext)-1);
  stripchar(yytext);
  strcpy(fieldname,yytext);
  BEGIN arg;
}

<command>^"(NAME" { BEGIN cmdname; }

<command>^")COMMAND" {
  printf
    ("<!DOCTYPE HTML PUBLIC \"-//IETF//DTD HTML 2.0//EN\">\n");
  printf("<HTML>\n");
  printf("<HEAD>\n<TITLE>%s</TITLE>\n",cmd);
  printf("<BASE HREF=\"%s.html\">\n",cmd);
  printf("</HEAD>\n");
  printf("<BODY>\n");
  printf("<H1>%s</H1>\n",cmd);
  printf("<HR>\n");
  printf("<CODE>%s</CODE>\n",usagestr);
  printf("<HR><P>\n");
# the following line needs the actual CGI script name to
# be supplied, when known
  printf("<FORM METHOD=\"POST\" ACTION=\"\">\n");

  BEGIN 0;
}
```

```
<cmdname>^[-].+ {
  cmd = (char *)malloc(strlen(yytext)-1);
  stripchar(yytext);
  strcpy(cmd,yytext);
  BEGIN command;
}

<command>^"(USAGE" { BEGIN usage; }

<command>^")COMMAND" { BEGIN 0; }

<usage>^[-].+ {
  usagestr = (char *)malloc(strlen(yytext)-1);
  stripchar(yytext);
  strcpy(usagestr,yytext);
  BEGIN command;
}

.|\n   ;

%%

int
stripchar(str)
char *str;
{
  char *tmp, *auxt, *auxs;

  tmp = (char *)malloc(strlen(str)-1);

  auxt = tmp;
  auxs = str+1;

  while((*auxs)) *auxt++ = *auxs++;
  *auxt= '\0';

  strcpy(str,tmp);
}

int main(argc, argv)
int argc;
char *argv[];
{
  if (argc == 2) {
    if ((yyin = fopen(argv[1], "r")) == NULL) {
      (void) fprintf(stderr, "Bad input file name: %s \n",
          argv[1]);
      exit (1);
    }
  }
```

```
        else {
          printf("Exiting...\n");
          exit;
        }

        (void) yylex();
        return(0);
      }
```

esis2html could have been written in Perl, but *lex* has the advantage of not being line-oriented. *lex* is much better suited to perform lexical scanning of the data input stream. We tried Perl and the results weren't pretty—the *lex* version is more straightforward and efficient. ▲

To compile the *lex* source file into an executable program, use this Perl wrapper script with a few modifications for your own local environment:

```
#!/usr/tools/bin/perl
# Location of the Perl directory may vary, depending on your
# site's directory structure; if so, the Perl shell line must
# change to match local conditions.

$usage = 'Usage getopts.pl {-d} [-f lex_file_name]
';

require 'getopts.pl';
&Getopts('df:');

if(defined($opt_f)) {
    $lfile = $ARGV[0];
}
else { print $usage; exit; }

($base = $lfile) =~ s/\.l(ex)?$//;
$cfile = $base . ".c";

# modify the command variables according to your site configuration
if(defined($opt_d)) {
    $command = "/usr/tools/pubs/0/ica/bin/flex -d -t8 -
S/usr/tools/pubs/0/ica/bin/flex.skel " . $lfile . " > " . $cfile;
}
else {
    $command = "/usr/tools/pubs/0/ica/bin/flex -t8 -
S/usr/tools/pubs/0/ica/bin/flex.skel " . $lfile . " > " . $cfile;
}

system($command);
```

```
if($? != 0) { exit 1; }
else {
    $command = "cc -o " . $base . " " . $cfile;
    system($command);
}
exit;
```

This script uses *flex* (fast lexical analyzer generator) as its *lex* compiler. If you don't have *flex* on your system, try the standard *lex* program. You'll also want to edit the command variables referenced in this script to reflect your local configuration.

The -d switch turns on debugging for *flex*. This reports a plethora of debugging information, so you can watch the progress of your lexical scanner.

After successfully creating an executable binary—*esis2html*—from the *lex* source, move it to a widely accessible directory at your site. We recommend */usr/local/bin*. (At the end of this chapter, you'll find a step-by-step list of tools and how to get them.)

ESIS

We mentioned earlier that the SGML parser used in this toolset—*sgmls*—outputs an ESIS representation of the PUML document to STDOUT. Here's the beginning of the ESIS output after running *sub.pl.puml* through *sgmls*:

```
#SDA
AVERSION CDATA -//WebTechs//DTD PUML 1.0//EN
(PUML
(HEAD
(TITLE
-sub.pl
)TITLE
)HEAD
(BODY
   .... rest of ESIS
```

To read ESIS, if a line starts with an A character, the string that follows the A is an attribute of the next element in the data stream. If the line starts with a (, this specifies the beginning of an element (a start tag). If a line starts with a), this designates the end of an element (an end tag).

For instance, these two lines from the ESIS:

```
AVERSION CDATA -//WebTechs//DTD PUML 1.0//EN
(PUML
```

specify that the string `VERSION CDATA -//WebTechs//DTD PUML 1.0//EN` is the attribute of the PUML element that follows the attribute specification in the ESIS output. If an element has more than one attribute, each attribute is listed prior to the beginning of the element. Here's an example of an element ARG with three attributes: NAME, CHOICE, and REPEAT:

```
ANAME CDATA argname
ACHOICE TOKEN opt
AREPEAT TOKEN norepeat
(ARG
  ...
)ARG
```

The SGML used to generate this ESIS chunk is:

```
<ARG name="argname" choice="opt" repeat="norepeat">...</ARG>
```

Let's look at the ESIS chunk for the COMMAND element:

```
(COMMAND
(TYPE
-script
)TYPE
(LANG
-Perl
)LANG
(NAME
-sub.pl
)NAME
(USAGE
-sub.pl {-h} [-o old_string] [-n new_string] [-f file_names...]
)USAGE
)COMMAND
```

The COMMAND element includes four subelements: TYPE, LANG, NAME, and USAGE. Notice that text items are identified in the ESIS data stream by the - first character on the line. For instance, for the NAME element:

```
(NAME
-sub.pl
)NAME
```

The content of this element is specified as -sub.pl. In the *esis2html* program, we strip off the preceding - character.

Now that you have a good feel for what ESIS output can do, we'll turn to HTML generation from the PUML specification. For a real taste of the power of PUML, here's the *puml2html.pl.puml* specification:

```
<!DOCTYPE PUML PUBLIC "-//WebTechs//DTD PUML 1.0//EN">
<PUML>
<HEAD>
<TITLE>puml2html.pl</TITLE>
</HEAD>
<BODY>
<COMMAND>
    <TYPE>script</TYPE>
    <LANG>Perl</LANG>
    <NAME>puml2html.pl</NAME>
    <USAGE>puml2html.pl {-h} [[-s script_file_name] | [-p
PUML_spec]] [-f form_file_name]</USAGE>
</COMMAND>
<ARG>
  <NAME>help</NAME>
  <CHOICE>Optional</CHOICE>
  <FLAG>-h</FLAG>
  <DESCR>Help statement</DESCR>
</ARG>
<GROUP>
  <NAME>pumlsource</NAME>
  <CHOICE>Required</CHOICE>
  <DESCR>PUML Source</DESCR>
  <ARG>
    <NAME>scriptname</NAME>
    <CHOICE>Optional</CHOICE>
    <FLAG>-s</FLAG>
    <VALUE>
     <TYPE>string</TYPE>
    </VALUE>
    <DESCR>Script File Name</DESCR>
  </ARG>
  <ARG>
    <NAME>pumlname</NAME>
    <CHOICE>Optional</CHOICE>
    <FLAG>-p</FLAG>
    <VALUE>
      <TYPE>string</TYPE>
    </VALUE>
    <DESCR>PUML File Name</DESCR>
  </ARG>
</GROUP>
<ARG>
  <NAME>formname</NAME>
```

```
<CHOICE>Required</CHOICE>
<FLAG>-f</FLAG>
<DESCR>HTML Form Name</DESCR>
<VALUE>
  <TYPE>string</TYPE>
</VALUE>
</ARG>
</BODY>
</PUML>
```

Notice that the <VALUE> element has a <TYPE> subelement. This element is not used in building the HTML form, but will be valuable when building a CGI application to support the HTML form derived from this PUML specification. Your CGI application could check the type of data the user might enter into the text widget. The content of the <TYPE> element could be a string, digits, or a file depending on your particular application and its requirements.

HTML Generation

puml2html.pl calls the SGML parser, *sgmls*, and then generates the ESIS and saves it to a local file. Next, it feeds this file to the lexical scanner *esis2html*. The lexical scanner then takes each token from the data stream—the ESIS—and finally generates individual HTML form widgets: checkbox, radio, text, and textarea widgets.

Here's the HTML that results from transforming the *sub.pl* command written in PUML using *puml2html.pl*:

```
<!DOCTYPE HTML PUBLIC "-//IETF//DTD HTML 2.0//EN">
<HTML>
<HEAD>
<TITLE>sub.pl</TITLE>
<BASE HREF="sub.pl.html">
</HEAD>
<BODY>
<H1>sub.pl</H1>
<HR>
<CODE>sub.pl {-h} [-o old_string] [-n new_string] [-f
file_names...]</CODE>
<HR><P>
# Please insert the name of the CGI script to which you wish
# to associate this program's activity in the next line, after
# the ACTION keyword (between the empty double-quotes).
<FORM METHOD="POST" ACTION="">
```

```
<INPUT NAME="help" TYPE="checkbox"> Help statement (Optional)<BR>
<INPUT NAME="old" TYPE="text" SIZE="40" MAXLENGTH="40"> Old
expression (Required)<BR>
<INPUT NAME="new" TYPE="text" SIZE="40" MAXLENGTH="40"> New
expression (Required)<BR>
<INPUT NAME="filenames" TYPE="text" SIZE="40" MAXLENGTH="40"> File
names (Required)<BR>
<INPUT TYPE="submit" VALUE="Do sub.pl Command">
</FORM>
</BODY>
</HTML>
```

Checkbox

An HTML checkbox widget is used when a switch is optional for the command. For instance, *sub.pl* has an optional switch -h. This is represented in the HTML form interface as a checkbox widget, as shown here:

```
<INPUT TYPE="checkbox" NAME="help"> Help statement
```

When this checkbox is chosen, the widget takes a value of 'on', which is used as input to the underlying CGI program invoked to process the HTML form. By default, a checkbox has the value 'undefined'.

An HTML checkbox widget is of the general form:

```
Choice 1: <INPUT TYPE="checkbox" NAME="c1" VALUE="1">
Choice 2: <INPUT TYPE="checkbox" NAME="c2" Value="2">
Choice A: <INPUT TYPE="checkbox" NAME="cA" Value="A">
```

Notice that each widget has a different NAME.

If a command has an argument that is defined to include one or more optional switches, the whole group of switches can be specified in a typical usage statement as:

```
foo [-ABCD]
```

The foo command would expect one or more of these four switches in order to execute.

This group of options could be represented in HTML as:

```
<H2>Options</H2>
A: <INPUT TYPE="checkbox" NAME="opt_A" VALUE="A">
B: <INPUT TYPE="checkbox" NAME="opt_B" VALUE="B">
C: <INPUT TYPE="checkbox" NAME="opt_C" VALUE="C">
D: <INPUT TYPE="checkbox" NAME="opt_D" VALUE="D">
```

Notice that each widget has its own unique identity and value, which will ultimately be used as input data to the form's underlying CGI application. A browser's-eye view of this HTML is shown in Figure 17-4.

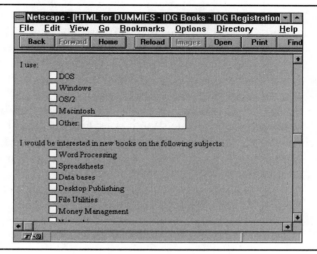

Figure 17-4
HTML checkboxes provide a handy way to select multiple options on a form.

Radio

An HTML radio widget is used when a maximum of one switch in a group of switches may be selected; if a selection is required, it's typical to find the button for the default already selected when the bank of choices is displayed. For instance, 'foo' might have a group of options where one is required. This is represented in the HTML form interface as a group of radio widgets as shown here:

```
Choice 1: <INPUT TYPE="radio" NAME="option" VALUE="A">
Choice 2: <INPUT TYPE="radio" NAME="option" Value="2">
Choice A: <INPUT TYPE="radio" NAME="option" Value="A">
```

When one of the radio widgets is chosen, that widget is assigned the value 'on' which is used as input to the underlying CGI program. By default, a radio button takes the value 'undefined'. If no radio button is chosen, the value of the widget named radio remains undefined (if no default is supplied, as is the case in our previous HTML fragment).

In the example that follows, we've chosen to add the keyword CHECKED to Option A's definition to indicate it as our default selection, because a value is required for this set of radio buttons.

Notice that each widget has the same NAME (in this case `option`).

If a command takes an argument that is defined to require one member of a group of switches, this group of switches could be specified in a typical usage statement as:

```
foo [-[A|B|C|D]]
```

The foo command expects one and only one of these four switches. Specifying more than one switch is invalid, as would be specifying no switch (which is why selecting a default, using the CHECKED keyword, is strongly recommended), and the command would exit without performing any action at all.

This group of options could be represented in HTML as:

```
<H2>Options</H2>
A: <INPUT TYPE="radio" NAME="opt" VALUE="A" CHECKED>
B: <INPUT TYPE="radio" NAME="opt" VALUE="B">
C: <INPUT TYPE="radio" NAME="opt" VALUE="C">
D: <INPUT TYPE="radio" NAME="opt" VALUE="D">
```

Notice again that each widget has the same identity (NAME) but each selection produces unique values to be used as input data to the form's CGI application.

Text

An HTML text input widget is used when the user is requested to enter a text string. For commands, such strings will usually, but not always, be associated with flag/data pairs that take the form:

```
foo [-f file_name]
```

The -f flag requires a filename. This string is input by the user into a text input widget.

An HTML text input widget takes the general form:

```
Filename: <INPUT TYPE="text" NAME="filename" SIZE="40"
MAXLENGTH="256">
```

When text is entered into this widget, it's associated with the appropriate flag by the CGI application. For example, if the user enters the string 'text.txt' into the text input widget named `filename`, the CGI application would build the command as:

```
foo -f text.txt
```

By default, the text input widget takes the value 'undefined'. You should strip away any excess leading or trailing whitespace like tabs, spaces, or carriage returns when assigning this value to a variable.

Textarea

An HTML textarea widget is used by a user to enter multiple lines of text strings. For instance, if 'foo' requires a list of repeatable filenames such as:

```
foo [-f file_names...]
```

the user would be presented in the HTML form with a textarea input widget that is scrollable. For instance, the HTML specification for 'foo' would look like:

```
<TEXTAREA NAME="text" ROWS="5" COLS="40"></TEXTAREA>
```

This is rendered as a textarea widget with 5 rows and 40 columns. The user would enter each filename specification on a line to itself. This could also be done with a plain text input widget that expects a blank delimiter between each filename specification. This is not as intuitive, so we opted for the textarea.

Select

An HTML select widget was not addressed in this tool because it is an alternative to a group of checkboxes. The *esis2html* tool could easily be altered to generate either a group of checkboxes or a <SELECT> element. This, again, was a deliberate design choice on our part, motivated in part by near-universal support for checkboxes in most browsers, but less support for <SELECT> lists in many browsers, especially older ones. Feel free, however, to make any changes you deem necessary.

SETTING UP YOUR OWN TRANSFORMATION ENVIRONMENT

In this section, we present you with a step-by-step method to install your own *puml2html* environment.

Step 1: Download a WebTechs HTML Check Toolkit

In this step, you instruct a Web server to build a customized HTML Check Toolkit. If you complete the series of forms found at:

```
http://www.webtechs.com/html-tk/
```

you'll be guided through every step you need to take. The resulting toolkit includes the specific binaries for the SGML parser, the SGML declaration, the HTML DTDs, and the PUML DTD. The Web server builds either a UNIX compressed *tar* file or a pkzipped distribution, depending on your computing platform. To our knowledge, there isn't a Macintosh SGML parser that's freely available.

If the *www.webtechs.com* site doesn't support your computing platform, try this one:

```
http://www.jclark.com/sp.html
```

and retrieve the *sp* source code. You can then compile it for your native machine. If this is the case, you still need to build a custom HTML Check Toolkit to get all the other parts—choose any operating system—of the HTML Check Toolkit. You can then substitute your newly compiled *sp* binary in the distribution's *bin* directory. The *www.webtechs.com* site intends to support all reasonable computing platforms. You're welcome to donate *sp* and *sgmls* binaries that aren't already available.

The following platforms are currently supported at WebTechs:

sp

- MS DOS 3.1 and higher
- SPARC running Solaris 2.3 and higher
- Intel architecture running Windows NT 3.5 and higher
- Linux

sgmls

- SPARC running SUNOS 4.1.3 and higher
- Alpha running OSF 1.3 and higher
- OS/2 version 2.1 and higher

Note that *sgmls* is antiquated and is no longer supported by its author; we include it here because of the large body of code (including our own) that still requires this environment. If you're still using it, we hope you're in the process of migrating to *sp* (as we are).

Step 2: Install the WebTechs HTML Check Toolkit

In this step, follow the instructions to install the HTML Check Toolkit on your local machine. After you install your custom distribution, you'll be able to validate HTML and PUML documents locally using your new SGML parser environment. You'll be required to append an SGML prolog to each document. For more information about the supported SGML prologs for HTML and PUML, see:

```
http://www.webtechs.com/html/
```

Step 3: Download, Install, and Test the puml2html Distribution

In this step, you'll download the source code *puml2html* distribution. To download the distribution, start an anonymous FTP session and FTP to this site:

```
ftp.webtechs.com /pub/html/tools/puml2html/
```

In the *puml2html* directory you'll find each individual script as well as numerous archived and compressed distributions. Choose the one that's appropriate for your local computing platform. You will need Perl 4.*, either *lex* or *flex*, and a C compiler.

Once you have the distribution, unarchive it and uncompress it. Along with the distribution, you'll also find installation and testing instructions. Follow these carefully. Install all executables such as *puml2html.pl* and *esis2html* in a publicly accessible directory such as */usr/local/bin*. In fact, it's a good idea to install it in the same place as the HTML Check Toolkit distribution.

THE MISSING PIECES

In this chapter, we presented a transformation process that takes a program usage statement and creates either an HTML form or a CGI application. The missing tools are:

- *pus2puml*—a *yacc* application to check the syntax of the program usage statement and generate a PUML equivalent. For example, *pus2puml* would take the usage statement for *sub.pl* written as:

```
 pus2html -u 'sub.pl {-h} [-o old_string] [-n new_string] [-f
     file_names...]' -o sub.pl.puml
```

The result would be a skeleton PUML file. You would have to edit the "sub.pl.puml" file and add content to the DESCR elements. These elements supply descriptions about each argument of the command. This information could not possibly be derived from the plain vanilla usage statement.

- *puml2cgi*—this tool could easily be written in Perl. It would take the ESIS output from the SGML parser as input and generate a skeleton CGI script. The most basic implementation would generate a Perl script. Additional functionality, like saving the form input to a local file or mailing the form data to some e-mail address, would need to be hand-coded. A typical invocation of the standalone tool might look like:

```
puml2cgi.pl -p /usr/local/puml/sub.pl.puml -c /www/cgi-bin/sub.pl
```

A more advanced tool would allow the user to specify the language of the CGI application, specify how to save the form data to a log directory, and indicate who should receive a copy of the form data via e-mail.

Finally, this tool would be quite efficient for building CGI scripts for commands usually run on the command line. It would build one big command string that is then either handed to the system or directed to a named pipe as in the *puml2html.pl* script. It is not very efficient for other automagic CGI script generation, though. It's like a jack used as a hammer: It wasn't designed for the job, but it's doable if you're really careful!

With the completion of the full-blown PUML transformation environment, if you're a Web tool creator like we are, you can immediately begin creating Web interfaces to your tools and utilities. A next step could be to create Web interfaces for system calls, but this might be dangerous. It's not beyond the capabilities of HTML to create a simple text input widget that would let a user input a system-level command (like our favorite */bin/rm -rf ** which deletes everything in the file system), but it's definitely not a good idea! If you want to venture into this area, please password-protect such capability (using ".htaccess" or other, more stringent means) to protect users (and yourself) from the possible side effects of unauthorized stupidity!

SUMMARY

Creating HTML forms by hand for your command-line applications is very time consuming and tedious. Tie that to the time it takes to generate a CGI application for each HTML form interface and you're left with little time to create new and inventive command-line tools. The PUML environment may add one more step and some intellectual overhead, but the payoff will be the efficient generation of HTML form interfaces and associated CGI applications.

WEB-ASSISTED UNIX FOR END USERS

18

*I*n this chapter, we present several HTML form interfaces to common UNIX system commands. These forms are intended for ordinary users who may not be very UNIX-savvy. As presented here, the common UNIX system commands for end users fall into three categories:

1. *account management*—UNIX commands for users to manage their own accounts, including passwords and file permissions
2. *file management*—UNIX commands for users to manage files, including *cp*, *ls*, *rm*, *mv*, etc.
3. *miscellaneous*—a grab-bag of UNIX system commands, including *ps*, *grep*, and *kill*

UNIX SYSTEM COMMANDS

UNIX supports a plethora of commands that can be executed in a shell interpreter, or from within a shell script. Commands executed on the command line can be quite complex, and may have numerous command-line options to control their execution. For that reason, such commands may be misused by novice UNIX users.

The forms interfaces introduced in this chapter should help alleviate confusion, and provide adequate information about every option and argument required by all the commands delivered through this interface. The usual alternative is to invoke the corresponding UNIX *man* page—an electronic online manual or help document—and read about each option for a command. Alternatively, X11 Windows users would normally invoke the *man* page in one window and attempt to run the command in another window, resulting in increased use of system resources.

The forms interfaces we introduce in this chapter present substantial verbiage about each command's options. They also provide clues to users about required versus optional switches, fields, arguments, and other command elements.

One problem with this approach to forms-assisted UNIX commands is that it takes no advantage of the real power of UNIX, which relies on chaining individual UNIX system commands to create more powerful tools. For example, should a user want to view all the currently executing processes on a particular UNIX machine, he or she could request a report on all currently executing processes. The Solaris 2.4 command string to request this information is entered as follows:

```
ps -aef
```

This reports the process status (ps) for all currently executing processes (-e), prints all process information (-a), and generates a full listing (-f). But should the user wish to know what processes are associated with a particular owner, he or she needs to chain another system command to this one to obtain the desired process status information.

To do this, the user must first request a report of all currently executing processes (just as in the preceding example), and then display only the processes associated with a particular User ID, discarding all others. The Solaris 2.4 command sequence for this task is as follows:

```
ps -aef | grep markg
```

This takes the output of the process status command and passes it to another command through a special system buffer called a pipe, represented by the | (vertical bar) character in the previous command example. Finally, the grep command parses the data in the buffer and searches for the string markg. In essence, this looks for all currently executing processes owned by markg. Among other things, this will return the *grep* process itself, so don't be surprised when it shows up recursively!

This ability to pipe commands is a real boon to those who seek to harness the power of UNIX, despite its somewhat arcane commands and syntax. This power will not be accessible through our forms-based front end to these commands because it is incapable of concatenating the individual forms for particular commands, as the pipe operator can do at the command line.

To overcome this deficiency would be difficult because it would require us to write a Web interface to a shell interpreter. A compromise would be to create HTML forms interfaces for the most commonly chained command sequences like the *ps|grep* example discussed earlier.

One possible drawback to this solution is that in this chapter we provide a PUML instance for several UNIX system commands. None of these was built to facilitate chaining, but rather to be used separately. We therefore leave this chaining exercise to our readers, especially those who want to automate more complex commands for their users. For most purposes, what we've supplied here should provide examples for other individual UNIX commands that you might want to automate.

The specific implementation we're showing here is reliable ONLY for Solaris 2.4—each flavor of UNIX has its own flavor for many system commands. Even something as popular as *ps -aef* is actually *ps -aux* on other systems, and *ps -auxww* on still others, and something else entirely on still other UNIX implementations. This implementation is a good example of what our readers should customize for their particular flavors of UNIX.

GENERATING A PUML INSTANCE FOR A SYSTEM COMMAND

Here, we continue the concept of creating a PUML instance for a system command, introduced in Chapter 17. Remember, PUML stands for "Program Usage Modeling Language" and is a way of representing the "Program Usage Statement" that formally describes the syntax for UNIX commands and related programs in *man* (online manual) pages. Creating a PUML instance for a commands allows you to generate a valid HTML 2.0 form and a CGI script from the same data. To make sure you understand this process completely, we'll present several PUML instances for a handful of common UNIX commands.

Each PUML instance contains information needed to create an HTML form, as well as the data required to generate a CGI script to support that form. For example, in each PUML instance, each COMMAND has a TYPE, LANG, NAME, DESCR, and USAGE tag. Here's an excerpt from a PUML instance for the ps command:

```
<COMMAND>
<TYPE>Solaris 2.4 command</TYPE>
<LANG>system</LANG>
<NAME>ps</NAME>
<DESCR>Report Process Status</DESCR>
<USAGE>ps {-acdefjl} {-g grplist} {-p proclist} {-s sidlist}
       {-t term} {-u uidlist}</USAGE>
</COMMAND>
```

This states that the *ps* command is a Solaris 2.4 system command, that it is part of the operating system, and that it reports on the system's process status. It also states usage for this command. Most of this information isn't critical for machine processing and generating the HTML form—it is typically read by humans to decide the nature, source, and context of the PUML instance.

If you are a Web or system administrator with a heterogeneous computing environment, you might need to create a PUML instance for the *ps* command for each different version of UNIX in use. For example, the options for *ps* are different for a SunOS 4.1.3 UNIX machine and a Solaris 2.4 machine, resulting in two different PUML instances, two different forms interfaces, and two different CGI scripts. Whew!

SGML does offer one solution to the multiple PUML instances problem, however, and that is to use marked sections. Each marked section encapsulates a section written for a particular context or condition. These sections can then be conditionally compiled into a particular PUML instance based on the particular context.

We generated a PUML instance for common commands in each of these three areas:

- Account management—*chown, chmod*
- File management—*find, ls, cp, mv, rm, rmdir, compress, uncompress, gunzip, gzip*
- Miscellaneous—*ps, grep, kill*

We built each PUML instance using GNU *emacs* 19.12 running in PUML mode (defined by Mark Gaither, one of the authors of this book). The Lisp code for PUML mode is part of the PUML distribution presented in the previous chapter.

Basically, PUML mode is sensitive to particular keystrokes and aids the author in creating a series of tags. For instance, a Control-C-c key sequence creates a <COMMAND> tag and its corresponding tags (<NAME>, <TYPE>, <DESCR>, <USAGE>, and <LANG>). *emacs* prompts the user for content for each tag contained by <COMMAND>; once all the tags and their contents have been defined, it then writes the entire tag set into the current PUML instance.

PUML instances can also be created within an SGML authoring environment like Author/Editor from SoftQuad or ArborText Publisher from ArborText. To use these SGML authoring tools, you'll need the PUML DTD (Document Type Definition), which is included in the PUML distribution.

All the PUML instances created in this chapter were validated using James Clark's SGML parser called *sp*. The validation process requires several other pieces. For most UNIX operating systems, you can find a WebTechs HTML Check Toolkit distribution that contains the PUML DTD, the SGML parser binary for your particular UNIX operating system, and other assorted files required to validate any SGML document. This includes HTML and PUML documents. You can find the WebTechs HTML Check Toolkit distribution at:

```
http://www.webtechs.com/html-tk/
```

UNIX kill Command

In this section, we present a fairly simple UNIX command named *kill*, which is used to terminate a running UNIX process. Its usage statement reads as follows:

```
kill {-(HUP|INT|KILL|TERM)} [pid]
```

This means that the `kill` command takes one of a set of optional arguments (`HUP`, `INT`, `KILL`, or `TERM`) and a required process ID (`pid`). Remember, curly braces around a group of arguments indicate they are optional, while square brackets indicate a required argument. Here are some valid examples of the `kill` command:

```
kill 144
kill -TERM 144
kill -9 144
kill -HUP 144
```

The first two examples are actually the same because the TERM option is the default signal. This is important when creating the PUML representation for this command.

kill.puml

The following listing shows the PUML instance we created for the kill command. Notice that it is a Solaris 2.4 command as indicated by the content of the \<TYPE\> element in the \<COMMAND\> element.

```
<!DOCTYPE PUML PUBLIC "-//WebTechs//DTD PUML 1.0//EN">
<PUML>
<HEAD>
<TITLE>kill - Terminate a Process</TITLE>
<BASE HREF="http://www.webtechs.com/tools/sysadmin/kill.puml">
</HEAD>
<BODY>
<COMMAND>
<TYPE>Solaris 2.4 command</TYPE>
<LANG>system</LANG>
<NAME>kill</NAME>
<DESCR>Terminate a Process</DESCR>
<USAGE>kill {-(HUP|INT|KILL|TERM)} [pid]</USAGE>
</COMMAND>
<GROUP>
<CHOICE>Optional</CHOICE>
<NAME>signals</NAME>
<DESCR>Signals</DESCR>
<ARG>
<CHOICE>Required</CHOICE>
<FLAG>-HUP</FLAG>
<NAME>HUP</NAME>
<DESCR>Hang up and restart the process</DESCR>
</ARG>
<ARG>
<CHOICE>Required</CHOICE>
<FLAG>-INT</FLAG>
<NAME>interrupt</NAME>
<DESCR>Interrupt (rubout) process</DESCR>
</ARG>
<ARG>
<CHOICE>Required</CHOICE>
<FLAG>-KILL</FLAG>
<NAME>kill</NAME>
<DESCR>Kill (cannot be caught or ignored) process</DESCR>
```

```
</ARG>
<ARG>
<CHOICE>Required</CHOICE>
<FLAG>-TERM</FLAG>
<NAME>term</NAME>
<DEFAULT>
<DESCR>Software termination signal from kill</DESCR>
</ARG>
</GROUP>
<ARG>
<CHOICE>Required</CHOICE>
<FLAG></FLAG>
<NAME>pids</NAME>
<DESCR>Process ID numbers</DESCR>
<REPEAT>
<VALUE>
<TYPE>string</TYPE>
</VALUE>
</ARG>
</BODY>
</PUML>
```

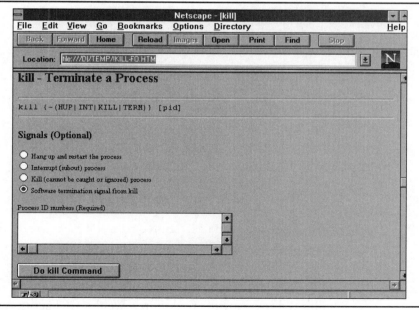

Figure 18-1

Screen capture of the kill HTML form.

kill-form.html

In this section, we will present the generated HTML form for the *kill* command. This form was created with the following invocation:

```
puml2html.pl -f kill-form.html -p kill.puml
```

This results in the transformation of the PUML instance to an HTML instance for the *kill* command. Figure 18-1 shows a screen capture of the initial *kill* HTML form.

Let's look closer at the HTML source. The HTML statement:

```
<H1>kill - Terminate a Process</H1>
```

is generated from two PUML elements, command <NAME> and command <DESCR>:

```
<COMMAND>
<TYPE>Solaris 2.4 command</TYPE>
<LANG>system</LANG>
<NAME>kill</NAME>
<DESCR>Terminate a Process</DESCR>
<USAGE>kill {-(HUP|INT|KILL|TERM)} [pid]</USAGE>
</COMMAND>
```

This is rendered as a level 1 heading in the HTML form as shown in Figure 18-1.

Next, the HTML statement:

```
<CODE>kill {-(HUP|INT|KILL|TERM)} [pid]</CODE>
```

is generated from the PUML <USAGE> element for the kill command:

```
<USAGE>kill {-(HUP|INT|KILL|TERM)} [pid]</USAGE>
```

Third, notice in the HTML source that you need to add the required ACTION attribute for the FORM element:

```
<FORM METHOD="POST" ACTION="">
```

You'll need to create (or find on the Web) a CGI script to support this HTML form for the *kill* command. You can find all the CGI Perl scripts to support each of the forms found in this chapter at:

```
http://www.webtechs.com/IDG/
```

We encourage you to take the Form Generator Tool introduced in Chapter 3 to create your own CGI script. This should give you practice at using the Form Generator, as well as understanding better the relationship between input widgets in an HTML form and the corresponding CGI code.

Next, notice that the first group named `signals` corresponds to an optional group of arguments from the *kill* PUML instance, as the value of the `<USAGE>` element. Notice also that for each argument in this optional set, each one takes the value `Required` for the `<CHOICE>` element. What this means is that only one argument in the set is required when executing the *kill* command. This results in a series of HTML `INPUT` elements of `TYPE` `radio`.

Fifth, notice the `<DEFAULT>` element in the `<ARG>` element named `term`. What this does is to initially check the corresponding radio button that will be rendered to the user in the HTML form as a checked radio button labeled `Software termination from kill`.

Sixth, in the HTML source, there is a `TEXTAREA` element named `term`. This is generated as a result of the PUML `<REPEAT>` element in the `<ARG>` named `term`. This is where the user inputs multiple process IDs, one per line.

```
<!DOCTYPE HTML PUBLIC "-//IETF//DTD HTML 2.0//EN">
<HTML>
<HEAD>
<TITLE>kill</TITLE>
<BASE HREF="kill.html">
</HEAD>
<BODY>
<H1>kill - Terminate a Process</H1>
<HR>
<CODE>kill {-(HUP|INT|KILL|TERM)} [pid]</CODE>
<HR><P>
<FORM METHOD="POST" ACTION="">
<H2>Signals (Optional)</H2>
<INPUT NAME="signals" TYPE="radio" VALUE="HUP"> Hang up and restart the
process<BR>
<INPUT NAME="signals" TYPE="radio" VALUE="interrupt"> Interrupt (rubout)
process<BR>
<INPUT NAME="signals" TYPE="radio" VALUE="kill"> Kill (cannot be caught or
ignored) process<BR>
<INPUT NAME="signals" TYPE="radio" VALUE="term" CHECKED> Software
termination signal from kill<BR>
<P>
<P>Process ID numbers (Required)<BR>
<TEXTAREA NAME="term" ROWS="5" COLS="40"></TEXTAREA>
<P><INPUT TYPE="submit" VALUE="Do kill Command">
</FORM>
</BODY>
</HTML>
```

UNIX chmod Command

In this section, we'll look closely at the *chmod* command, its PUML instance, and its automatically generated HTML form. This command is used to change permissions on a file or a set of files in UNIX. Its Solaris 2.4 UNIX usage statement is taken from chmod's *man* page:

```
chmod {ugoa}[+|-|=]{rwxlsStTugo} [filename ...]
```

This usage statement is typical. It has optional and required options and fields. In our notation, optional switches, fields, and options are enclosed in curly braces. For example, {ugoa} are optional switches used to control the execution of the chmod command. Required fields are enclosed in square brackets. For example, [+|-|=] denotes that one of the three characters is required. Finally, the ellipsis following a field indicates that the field is repeatable. For example, [filename ...] indicates that the filename field is required and repeatable. Here's a typical invocation:

```
chmod a + one.html two.html three.html
```

Notice the three files listed at the end of the command line.

chmod.puml

Here's the PUML instance for the *chmod* command:

```
<!DOCTYPE PUML PUBLIC "-//WebTechs//DTD PUML 1.0//EN">
<PUML>
<HEAD>
<TITLE>Solaris 2.4 chmod</TITLE>
</HEAD>
<BODY>
<!- Define the command attributes ->
<COMMAND>
<TYPE>Solaris 2.4 system command</TYPE>
<LANG>system</LANG>
<NAME>chmod</NAME>
<DESCR>Change Permissions Mode</DESCR>
<USAGE>chmod {ugoa}[+|-|=]{rwxlsStTugo} [filename ...]</USAGE>
</COMMAND>
<!- Define an optional group of attributes defining -
 -whose persmissions to change ->
<GROUP>
<NAME>who</NAME>
<!- Define this group of arguments is optional ->
<CHOICE>Optional</CHOICE>
```

```
<DESCR>Specify whose permissions are changed or assigned</DESCR>
<!- Define an optional switch designating -
-to change user permissions only ->
<ARG>
<NAME>userpermissions</NAME>
<CHOICE>Optional</CHOICE>
<!- Define the 'u' option. This will be used when -
-creating the CGI script from this PUML instance ->
<FLAG>u</FLAG>
<DESCR>User's permissions</DESCR>
</ARG>
<ARG>
<NAME>grouppermissions</NAME>
<CHOICE>Optional</CHOICE>
<FLAG>g</FLAG>
<DESCR>Group's permissions</DESCR>
</ARG>
<ARG>
<NAME>otherpermissions</NAME>
<CHOICE>Optional</CHOICE>
<FLAG>o</FLAG>
<DESCR>Other's permissions</DESCR>
</ARG>
<ARG>
<NAME>allpermissions</NAME>
<CHOICE>Optional</CHOICE>
<FLAG>a</FLAG>
<!- This argument is the default choice in the current -
-group of arguments. This causes the input widget -
-to be CHECKED for the user. ->
<DEFAULT>
<DESCR>All permissions</DESCR>
</ARG>
</GROUP>
<GROUP>
<NAME>operator</NAME>
<!- One argument in this group is required -
-for successful execution of chmod ->
<CHOICE>Required</CHOICE>
<DESCR>Specify how to change permissions</DESCR>
<ARG>
<NAME>addpermission</NAME>
<CHOICE>Required</CHOICE>
<FLAG>+</FLAG>
<DESCR>Add permissions</DESCR>
</ARG>
<ARG>
```

```
<NAME>removepermission</NAME>
<CHOICE>Required</CHOICE>
<FLAG>-</FLAG>
<DESCR>Remove permissions</DESCR>
</ARG>
<ARG>
<NAME>absolutepermission</NAME>
<CHOICE>Required</CHOICE>
<FLAG>=</FLAG>
<DESCR>Assign permissions absolutely</DESCR>
</ARG>
</GROUP>
<GROUP>
<NAME>permissions</NAME>
<CHOICE>Required</CHOICE>
<DESCR>Specify permissions</DESCR>
<ARG>
<NAME>readpermission</NAME>
<CHOICE>Optional</CHOICE>
<FLAG>r</FLAG>
<DESCR>Read permission</DESCR>
</ARG>
<ARG>
<NAME>writepermission</NAME>
<CHOICE>Optional</CHOICE>
<FLAG>w</FLAG>
<DESCR>Write permission</DESCR>
</ARG>
<ARG>
<NAME>executepermission</NAME>
<CHOICE>Optional</CHOICE>
<FLAG>x</FLAG>
<DESCR>Execute permission</DESCR>
</ARG>
<ARG>
<NAME>lockingpermission</NAME>
<CHOICE>Optional</CHOICE>
<FLAG>l</FLAG>
<DESCR>Mandatory locking permission</DESCR>
</ARG>
<ARG>
<NAME>setid</NAME>
<CHOICE>Optional</CHOICE>
<FLAG>s</FLAG>
<DESCR>User or group set-ID</DESCR>
</ARG>
<ARG>
```

```
<NAME>bitstate</NAME>
<CHOICE>Optional</CHOICE>
<FLAG>S</FLAG>
<DESCR>Undefined bit-state</DESCR>
</ARG>
<ARG>
<NAME>stickybit</NAME>
<CHOICE>Optional</CHOICE>
<FLAG>t</FLAG>
<DESCR>Sticky bit</DESCR>
</ARG>
<ARG>
<NAME>1000biton</NAME>
<CHOICE>Optional</CHOICE>
<FLAG>T</FLAG>
<DESCR>The 1000 bit is on and execution is off</DESCR>
</ARG>
<ARG>
<NAME>assumeuserperm</NAME>
<CHOICE>Optional</CHOICE>
<FLAG>u</FLAG>
<DESCR>Assume current user permission</DESCR>
</ARG>
<ARG>
<NAME>assumegroupperm</NAME>
<CHOICE>Optional</CHOICE>
<FLAG>g</FLAG>
<DESCR>Assume current group permission</DESCR>
</ARG>
<ARG>
<NAME>assumeotherperm</NAME>
<CHOICE>Optional</CHOICE>
<FLAG>o</FLAG>
<DESCR>Assume current other permission</DESCR>
</ARG>
</GROUP>
<ARG>
<NAME>filename</NAME>
<CHOICE>Required</CHOICE>
<!- This designates that this argument is repeatable. -
-This generates an HTML TEXTAREA element ->
<REPEAT>
<VALUE>
<!- Indicate the user-defined type of data required from -
-the user. This is useful in error checking by the CGI -
-script. ->
<TYPE>string</TYPE>
```

```
</VALUE>
<DESCR>File names</DESCR>
</ARG>
</BODY>
</PUML>
```

The PUML instance for *chmod* includes three GROUPs of attributes:

1. who—a group of options that defines what permissions are to be changed. The last option—all—is the default. All of these are optional.

2. operator—a group of choices that defines how to change permissions. One of these options is required.

3. permissions—a group of permission choices. At least one of these is also required.

The PUML instance also includes a singleton <DEFAULT> element for an <ARG> element. This causes the generated input widget to be checked for the user.

For example, in the PUML instance for the *chmod* command, the <ARG> named allpermissions is designated as the <DEFAULT> argument. Running *puml2html.pl*—the transformation tool introduced in Chapter 17—on the PUML instance for the *chmod* command generates an HTML INPUT element of TYPE checkbox which is then CHECKED.

When the HTML INPUT element is displayed to the user, the corresponding checkbox input widget will be initially checked or selected for the user. Deciding whether to insert a <DEFAULT> element is usually influenced by the command. In *chmod*'s case, the *man* page asserts that the a option is the default. In the case of the *mv* command, on the other hand, we have chosen to set the option to ask the user before moving any files. The rule of thumb to follow when making this decision should be: "If the command takes a default, use that default; if not, try to decide what will best protect the (possibly unwary) user."

The PUML instance also includes a <VALUE> element for an argument. This specifies that the <ARG> element requires data input into a text widget from the user. By default, this is a single-line HTML INPUT element of size 40. If a <REPEAT> element is specified for this argument, instead of an INPUT element, an HTML TEXTAREA element will be generated. This is a scrollable text input widget that accepts multiple-line data input from the user.

If the user is to input multiple entries, each entry should occur on a line by itself. For the <VALUE> element, a <TYPE> is required. This is a user-defined type such as 'string', 'integer', or 'filename'. These are not used when generating the HTML form but they could be used when building error checks into the CGI script supporting the form. For example, if an INPUT element is meant to accept an integer, the CGI script could check the user-supplied data in this input widget and report on errors, depending on how the programmer elects to implement that program.

Once we have defined the PUML instance for the *chmod* command, we can then run *puml2html.pl,* which outputs a valid HTML 2.0 form. Figure 18-2 shows a screen capture of this automatically generated form. Here's the invocation necessary to create "chmod-form.html":

```
puml2html.pl -f chmod-form.html -p chmod.puml
```

This takes as input the PUML instance and generates an HTML form.

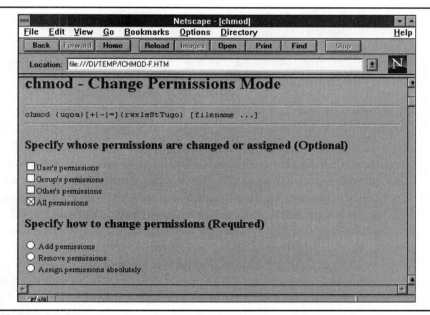

Figure 18-2

Screen capture of chmod-form.html.

chmod-form.html

The following HTML source results from submitting the "chmod.puml" PUML source to the *puml2html.pl* transforming script. In the HTML source, the HTML statement:

```
<H1>chmod - Change Permissions Mode</H1>
```

is generated from two PUML elements, command NAME and command DESCR. The HTML statement:

```
<CODE>chmod {ugoa}[+|-|=]{rwxlsStTugo} [filename ...]</CODE>
```

is generated from the PUML USAGE element for the *chmod* command. In the *chmod* HTML source, the HTML statement:

```
<H2>Specify whose permissions are changed or assigned (Optional)</H2>
```

is generated from the PUML GROUP element. The text of the level 2 head is copied from the content of the PUML DESCR element found in the GROUP named who.

The Optional string enclosed in the parentheses is copied from the content of the PUML CHOICE element found in the group named who. The who group of options is rendered as HTML checkbox INPUT elements, because the CHOICE element for the group as well as its ARG elements are designated as optional. These checkboxes indicate that zero or more of the options in the group can be passed as arguments to the *chmod* command.

In contrast, the arguments in the operator group are rendered as radio buttons. The value of each argument's CHOICE element in the operator group has the value Required. This indicates that only one of the set of options is required as an argument for *chmod*.

The HTML TEXTAREA element—a multiple-line text widget—is generated from a couple of PUML elements. The first is the ARG element named filename. This becomes the NAME attribute for the TEXTAREA element. The PUML element REPEAT creates a TEXTAREA element rather than the single-line text widget created by its counterpart named INPUT.

Finally, the last INPUT element is the submit button rendered for the HTML form. The VALUE attribute's content is assembled from its PUML command NAME content. Here's what the results look like:

```
<!DOCTYPE HTML PUBLIC "-//IETF//DTD HTML 2.0//EN">
<HTML>
<HEAD>
<TITLE>chmod</TITLE>
<BASE HREF="chmod.html">
</HEAD>
<BODY>
<H1>chmod - Change Permissions Mode</H1>
<HR>
<CODE>chmod {ugoa}[+|-|=]{rwxlsStTugo} [filename ...]</CODE>
<HR><P>
<FORM METHOD="POST" ACTION="">
<H2>Specify whose permissions are changed or assigned (Optional)</H2>
<INPUT NAME="userpermissions" TYPE="checkbox"
VALUE="userpermissions">User's permissions<BR>
<INPUT NAME="grouppermissions" TYPE="checkbox"
VALUE="grouppermissions">Group's permissions<BR>
<INPUT NAME="otherpermissions" TYPE="checkbox"
VALUE="otherpermissions">Other's permissions<BR>
<INPUT NAME="allpermissions" TYPE="checkbox" VALUE="allpermissions"
CHECKED>All permissions<BR>
<P>
<H2>Specify how to change permissions (Required)</H2>
<INPUT NAME="operator" TYPE="radio" VALUE="addpermission"> Add
permissions<BR>
<INPUT NAME="operator" TYPE="radio" VALUE="removepermission"> Remove
permissions<BR>
<INPUT NAME="operator" TYPE="radio" VALUE="absolutepermission"> Assign
permissions absolutely<BR>
<P>
<H2>Specify permissions (Required)</H2>
<INPUT NAME="readpermission" TYPE="checkbox" VALUE="readpermission">Read
perission<BR>
<INPUT NAME="writepermission" TYPE="checkbox" VALUE="writepermission">Write
permission<BR>
<INPUT NAME="executepermission" TYPE="checkbox"
VALUE="executepermission">Execute permission<BR>
<INPUT NAME="lockingpermission" TYPE="checkbox"
VALUE="lockingpermission">Mandatory locking permission<BR>
<INPUT NAME="setid" TYPE="checkbox" VALUE="setid">User or group
 set-ID<BR>
<INPUT NAME="bitstate" TYPE="checkbox" VALUE="bitstate">Undefined
 bit-state<BR>
<INPUT NAME="stickybit" TYPE="checkbox" VALUE="stickybit">Sticky
 bit<BR>
<INPUT NAME="1000biton" TYPE="checkbox" VALUE="1000biton">The
 1000 bit is on and execution is off<BR>
```

```
<INPUT NAME="assumeuserperm" TYPE="checkbox" VALUE="assumeuserperm">Assume
current user permission<BR>
<INPUT NAME="assumegroupperm" TYPE="checkbox"
VALUE="assumegroupperm">Assume current group permission<BR>
<INPUT NAME="assumeotherperm" TYPE="checkbox"
VALUE="assumeotherperm">Assume current other permission<BR>
<P>
<P>File names (Required)<BR>
<TEXTAREA NAME="filename" ROWS="5" COLS="40"></TEXTAREA>
<P><INPUT TYPE="submit" VALUE="Do chmod Command">
</FORM>
</BODY>
</HTML>
```

UNIX cp Command

In this section, we will investigate the UNIX *cp* command, its PUML
instance, and its automatically generated HTML form. This command is
used to copy a file or set of files to another location on the file system. The
Solaris 2.4 UNIX usage statement is taken from its *man* page:

```
cp {-ipr} [filename] [target]
```

This indicates that cp has one optional group of arguments and two
required arguments. The optional group {-ipr} states that one or more of
these options may be used. The argument [filename] is a required
argument. Finally, the last argument is the required target or destination for
the copied file or files.

Here are some typical invocations:

```
cp one.html ../one.html
cp *.html /www/html
cp ../two.html .
```

cp.puml

In this section, we will look at the PUML instance for the *cp* command. In
this instance, you can see that this command is a Solaris 2.4 command by
viewing the contents of the <TYPE> element of the <COMMAND> element. This
instance has one group of optional arguments named options. Also notice

the <DEFAULT> element of the <ARG> named interactive. This dictates that this particular option will be initially checked in the HTML form for the *cp* command generated by the *puml2html.pl* transformer.

This PUML instance also has a required argument named filename. This <ARG> element is required, designated by the value of the <CHOICE> element's value as Required. The <ARG> element also contains a <REPEAT> element indicating that multiple inputs from the user can be accepted by its corresponding TEXTAREA input widget. Finally, the last argument named target is a required argument, as indicated by the value of its <CHOICE> element. This argument is rendered to the user as a single-line HTML INPUT element named target.

```
<!DOCTYPE PUML PUBLIC "-//WebTechs//DTD PUML 1.0//EN">
<PUML>
<HEAD>
<TITLE>cp - Copy Files</TITLE>
<BASE HREF="http://www.webtechs.com/tools/sysadmin/cp.puml">
</HEAD>
<BODY>
<COMMAND>
<TYPE>Solaris 2.4 command</TYPE>
<LANG>system</LANG>
<NAME>cp</NAME>
<DESCR>Copy Files</DESCR>
<USAGE>cp {-ipr} [filename ...] [target]</USAGE>
</COMMAND>
<GROUP>
<CHOICE>Optional</CHOICE>
<NAME>options</NAME>
<DESCR>Options</DESCR>
<ARG>
<CHOICE>Optional</CHOICE>
<FLAG>-i</FLAG>
<NAME>interactive</NAME>
<DEFAULT>
<DESCR>Ask before overwriting an existing target</DESCR>
</ARG>
<ARG>
<CHOICE>Optional</CHOICE>
<FLAG>-p</FLAG>
<NAME>preserve</NAME>
<DESCR>Preserve modification time and permission modes</DESCR>
</ARG>
<ARG>
<CHOICE>Optional</CHOICE> ·
<FLAG>-r</FLAG>
<NAME>recursive</NAME>
<DESCR>Recursively copy all subdirectories</DESCR>
```

```
</ARG>
</GROUP>
<ARG>
<CHOICE>Required</CHOICE>
<NAME>filename</NAME>
<DESCR>File names</DESCR>
<REPEAT>
<VALUE>
<TYPE>string</TYPE>
</VALUE>
</ARG>
<ARG>
<CHOICE>Required</CHOICE>
<FLAG></FLAG>
<NAME>target</NAME>
<VALUE>
<TYPE>string</TYPE>
</VALUE>
<DESCR>Target file or directory of copy</DESCR>
</ARG>
</BODY>
</PUML>
```

Once we've defined the PUML instance for the *cp* command, we can then run the *puml2html.pl* transformation script. It outputs a valid 2.0 HTML form. Figure 18-3 shows a screen capture of this automatically generated form. Here's the invocation used to create "cp-form.html":

```
puml2html.pl -f cp-form.html -p cp.puml
```

This takes as input the PUML instance and generates an HTML form.

cp-form.html

The following HTML source is the result of submitting the "cp.puml" PUML source to the *puml2html.pl* transforming script. In the HTML source, the HTML statement:

```
<H1>cp - Copy Files</H1>
```

is generated from two PUML elements, command NAME and command DESCR. The HTML statement:

```
<CODE>cp {-ipr} [filename] [target]</CODE>
```

is generated from the PUML USAGE element for the *cp* command.

In the *cp* HTML source, the HTML statement:

```
<H2>Options (Optional)</H2>
```

is generated from the PUML GROUP element named `options`. The text of the level 2 head is copied from the content of the PUML DESCR element found in `options`. The `Optional` string enclosed in the parentheses is copied from the content of the PUML CHOICE element found in the group named `options`. The `options` group of options is rendered as HTML checkbox INPUT elements because the CHOICE element for the group as well as the ARG elements of the group are designated optional.

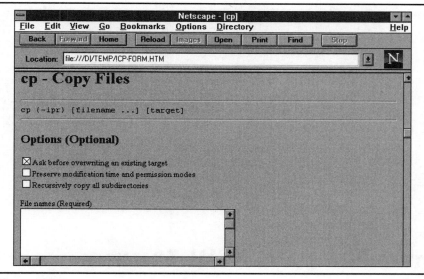

Figure 18-3
Screen capture of cp-form.html.

The HTML TEXTAREA element is created from two PUML elements. The first is the ARG element named `filename`. This becomes the NAME attribute of the TEXTAREA element. The PUML element REPEAT creates a TEXTAREA element rather than its single-line HTML text widget counterpart INPUT. Each filename is entered on its own line.

The last INPUT element is the required target of the copy. It is created as a result of the PUML element ARG named `target`. It is rendered in the form as a single-line text input widget.

```
<!DOCTYPE HTML PUBLIC "-//IETF//DTD HTML 2.0//EN">
<HTML>
<HEAD>
<TITLE>cp</TITLE>
<BASE HREF="cp.html">
</HEAD>
<BODY>
<H1>cp - Copy Files</H1>
<HR>
<CODE>cp {-ipr} [filename ...] [target]</CODE>
<HR><P>
<FORM METHOD="POST" ACTION="">
<H2>Options (Optional)</H2>
<INPUT NAME="interactive" TYPE="checkbox" VALUE="interactive" CHECKED>Ask
before overwriting an existing target<BR>
<INPUT NAME="preserve" TYPE="checkbox" VALUE="preserve">Preserve
modification time and permission modes<BR>
<INPUT NAME="recursive" TYPE="checkbox" VALUE="recursive">Recursively copy
all subdirectories<BR>
<P>
<P>File names (Required)<BR>
<TEXTAREA NAME="filename" ROWS="5" COLS="40"></TEXTAREA>
<INPUT NAME="filename" TYPE="text" SIZE="40" MAXLENGTH="40"> Target file or
directory of copy (Required)<BR>
<P><INPUT TYPE="submit" VALUE="Do cp Command">
</FORM>
</BODY>
</HTML>
```

OTHER PUML AND HTML EXAMPLES

In this section we present some other interesting examples of UNIX commands represented as PUML and transformed into HTML with the *puml2html.pl* script.

chown

This UNIX command changes the ownership of files or directories. Use this transformation:

```
puml2html.pl -f chown-form.html -p chown.puml
```

chown.puml

```
<!DOCTYPE PUML PUBLIC "-//WebTechs//DTD PUML 1.0//EN">
<PUML>
<HEAD>
<TITLE>chown</TITLE>
<BASE HREF="http://www.webtechs.com/tools/sysadmin/chown.puml">
</HEAD>
<BODY>
<COMMAND>
<TYPE>Solaris 2.4 command</TYPE>
<LANG>system</LANG>
<NAME>chown</NAME>
<DESCR>Change Ownership</DESCR>
<USAGE>chown {-fhR} owner filename ...</USAGE>
</COMMAND>
<GROUP>
<CHOICE>Optional</CHOICE>
<NAME>Options</NAME>
<DESCR>Command Line Options</DESCR>
<ARG>
<CHOICE>Optional</CHOICE>
<FLAG>-f</FLAG>
<NAME>no-errors</NAME>
<DESCR>Do not report errors</DESCR>
</ARG>
<ARG>
<CHOICE>Optional</CHOICE>
<FLAG>-h</FLAG>
<NAME>sym-link</NAME>
<DESCR>Change owner of symbolic link, if owner</DESCR>
</ARG>
<ARG>
<CHOICE>Optional</CHOICE>
<FLAG>-R</FLAG>
<NAME>recursive</NAME>
<DESCR>Recursively change all directory and subdirectories contents</DESCR>
</ARG>
</GROUP>
<ARG>
<CHOICE>Required</CHOICE>
<NAME>owner</NAME>
<DESCR>New owner</DESCR>
<VALUE>
<TYPE>string</TYPE>
</VALUE>
</ARG>
```

```
<ARG>
<CHOICE>Required</CHOICE>
<NAME>filename</NAME>
<DESCR>File names</DESCR>
<REPEAT>
<VALUE>
<TYPE>string</TYPE>
</VALUE>
</ARG>
</BODY>
</PUML>
```

chown-form.html

```
<!DOCTYPE HTML PUBLIC "-//IETF//DTD HTML 2.0//EN">
<HTML>
<HEAD>
<TITLE>chown</TITLE>
<BASE HREF="chown.html">
</HEAD>
<BODY>
<H1>chown - Change Ownership</H1>
<HR>
<CODE>chown {-fhR} owner filename ...</CODE>
<HR><P>
<FORM METHOD="POST" ACTION="">
<H2>Command Line Options (Optional)</H2>
<INPUT NAME="no-errors" TYPE="checkbox" VALUE="no-errors">Do not report
errors<BR>
<INPUT NAME="sym-link" TYPE="checkbox" VALUE="sym-link">Change owner of
symbolic link, if owner<BR>
<INPUT NAME="recursive" TYPE="checkbox" VALUE="recursive">Recursively
change all directory and subdirectories contents<BR>
<P>
<INPUT NAME="owner" TYPE="text" SIZE="40" MAXLENGTH="40"> New owner
(Required)<BR>
<P>File names (Required)<BR>
<TEXTAREA NAME="filename" ROWS="5" COLS="40"></TEXTAREA>
<P><INPUT TYPE="submit" VALUE="Do chown Command">
</FORM>
</BODY>
</HTML>
```

find

This UNIX command finds a file or set of files in the file system. Use this transformation:

```
puml2html.pl -f find-form.html -p find.puml
```

find.puml

```
<!DOCTYPE PUML PUBLIC "-//WebTechs//DTD PUML 1.0//EN">
<PUML>
<HEAD>
<TITLE>find</TITLE>
<BASE HREF="http://www.webtechs.com/tools/sysadmin/find.puml">
</HEAD>
<BODY>
<COMMAND>
<TYPE>Solaris 2.4 command</TYPE>
<LANG>system</LANG>
<NAME>find</NAME>
<DESCR>Find File</DESCR>
<USAGE>find root-directory [-name pattern]</USAGE>
</COMMAND>
<ARG>
<CHOICE>Required</CHOICE>
<NAME>root-dir</NAME>
<DESCR>Root directory of search</DESCR>
<VALUE>
<TYPE>string</TYPE>
</VALUE>
</ARG>
<ARG>
<CHOICE>Required</CHOICE>
<FLAG>-name</FLAG>
<NAME>pattern</NAME>
<DESCR>Search for pattern</DESCR>
<VALUE>
<TYPE>string</TYPE>
</VALUE>
</ARG>
</BODY>
</PUML>
```

find-form.html

```
<!DOCTYPE HTML PUBLIC "-//IETF//DTD HTML 2.0//EN">
<HTML>
<HEAD>
<TITLE>find</TITLE>
<BASE HREF="find.html">
</HEAD>
<BODY>
<H1>find - Find File</H1>
<HR>
<CODE>find root-directory [-name pattern]</CODE>
<HR><P>
<FORM METHOD="POST" ACTION="">
<INPUT NAME="root-dir" TYPE="text" SIZE="40" MAXLENGTH="40">
 Root directory of search (Required)<BR>
<INPUT NAME="pattern" TYPE="text" SIZE="40" MAXLENGTH="40">
 Search for pattern (Required)<BR>
<P><INPUT TYPE="submit" VALUE="Do find Command">
</FORM>
</BODY>
</HTML>
```

ls

This UNIX command lists the contents of a directory. Use this transformation:

```
puml2html.pl -f ls-form.html -p ls.puml
```

ls.puml

```
<!DOCTYPE PUML PUBLIC "-//WebTechs//DTD PUML 1.0//EN">
<PUML>
<HEAD>
<TITLE>ls</TITLE>
<BASE HREF="http://www.webtechs.com/tools/sysadmin/ls.puml">
</HEAD>
<BODY>
<COMMAND>
<TYPE>Solaris 2.4 command</TYPE>
<LANG>system</LANG>
```

```
<NAME>ls</NAME>
<DESCR>List Directory Contents</DESCR>
<USAGE>ls {-abcCdfFgilLmnopqrRstux1} filename ...</USAGE>
</COMMAND>
<GROUP>
<CHOICE>Optional</CHOICE>
<NAME>Options</NAME>
<DESCR>Command Line Options</DESCR>
<ARG>
<CHOICE>Optional</CHOICE>
<FLAG>-a</FLAG>
<NAME>all</NAME>
<DESCR>List all entries</DESCR>
</ARG>
<ARG>
<CHOICE>Optional</CHOICE>
<FLAG>-b</FLAG>
<NAME>force-print</NAME>
<DESCR>Force printing of non-printable characters in octal
 (\ddd)</DESCR>
</ARG>
<ARG>
<CHOICE>Optional</CHOICE>
<FLAG>-c</FLAG>
<NAME>last-mod-time</NAME>
<DESCR>Use time of last modification of the i-node for sorting
 or printing</DESCR>
</ARG>
<ARG>
<CHOICE>Optional</CHOICE>
<FLAG>-C</FLAG>
<NAME>multi-column</NAME>
<DESCR>Multi-column output with entries sorted down the
 columns</DESCR>
</ARG>
<ARG>
<CHOICE>Optional</CHOICE>
<FLAG>-d</FLAG>
<NAME>dir-only</NAME>
<DESCR>If an argument is a directory, list only its name (not
 its contents)</DESCR>
</ARG>
<ARG>
<CHOICE>Optional</CHOICE>
<FLAG>-f</FLAG>
<NAME>force</NAME>
<DESCR>Force each argument to be interpreted as a directory
```

```
 and list the name found</DESCR>
</ARG>
<ARG>
<CHOICE>Optional</CHOICE>
<FLAG>-F</FLAG>
<NAME>add-slash</NAME>
<DESCR>Add / after each directory, an * if file is executable,
 and @ if file is a symbolic link</DESCR>
</ARG>
<ARG>
<CHOICE>Optional</CHOICE>
<FLAG>-i</FLAG>
<NAME>i-node-num</NAME>
<DESCR>Print i-node number for each file in first column
 of listing</DESCR>
</ARG>
<ARG>
<CHOICE>Optional</CHOICE>
<FLAG>-L</FLAG>
<NAME>link-ref</NAME>
<DESCR>List the file or directory a symbolic link references
</DESCR>
</ARG>
<ARG>
<CHOICE>Optional</CHOICE>
<FLAG>-m</FLAG>
<NAME>stream-output</NAME>
<DESCR>List output across page delimited by commas</DESCR>
</ARG>
<ARG>
<CHOICE>Optional</CHOICE>
<FLAG>-p</FLAG>
<NAME>add-dir-slash</NAME>
<DESCR>Add / after each directory</DESCR>
</ARG>
<ARG>
<CHOICE>Optional</CHOICE>
<FLAG>-q</FLAG>
<NAME>replace-question-mark</NAME>
<DESCR>Print non-printable characters in file names as ?</DESCR>
</ARG>
<ARG>
<CHOICE>Optional</CHOICE>
<FLAG>-r</FLAG>
<NAME>reverse-order</NAME>
<DESCR>Reverse order of sort to get reverse alphabetic or oldest
 first</DESCR>
```

```
</ARG>
<ARG>
<CHOICE>Optional</CHOICE>
<FLAG>-R</FLAG>
<NAME>recursive</NAME>
<DESCR>Recursively list subdirectories encountered</DESCR>
</ARG>
<ARG>
<CHOICE>Optional</CHOICE>
<FLAG>-s</FLAG>
<NAME>block-size</NAME>
<DESCR>Print size in blocks</DESCR>
</ARG>
<ARG>
<CHOICE>Optional</CHOICE>
<FLAG>-t</FLAG>
<NAME>time-stamp</NAME>
<DESCR>Sort by time stamp with latest first rather by name</DESCR>
</ARG>
<ARG>
<CHOICE>Optional</CHOICE>
<FLAG>-u</FLAG>
<NAME>last-access</NAME>
<DESCR>Sort or print using time of last access</DESCR>
</ARG>
<ARG>
<CHOICE>Optional</CHOICE>
<FLAG>-x</FLAG>
<NAME>multi-col-output</NAME>
<DESCR>Multi-column output with entries sorted across page</DESCR>
</ARG>
<ARG>
<CHOICE>Optional</CHOICE>
<FLAG>-1</FLAG>
<NAME>one-per-line</NAME>
<DESCR>Print one entry per line of output</DESCR>
</ARG>
<GROUP>
<CHOICE>Optional</CHOICE>
<NAME>long-list-options</NAME>
<DESCR>Long Listing Options</DESCR>
<ARG>
<CHOICE>Optional</CHOICE>
<FLAG>-l</FLAG>
<NAME>long-list</NAME>
<DEFAULT>
<DESCR>Long listing (mode, # of links, owner, group, size in
```

```
 bytes, time of last mod)</DESCR>
</ARG>
<ARG>
<CHOICE>Optional</CHOICE>
<FLAG>-g</FLAG>
<NAME>long-fmt-exclude-owner</NAME>
<DESCR>Same as long listing excluding owner information</DESCR>
</ARG>
<ARG>
<CHOICE>Optional</CHOICE>
<FLAG>-n</FLAG>
<NAME>long-list-gids</NAME>
<DESCR>Same as long listing, except owner's UID and group's GID
 numbers are printed</DESCR>
</ARG>
<ARG>
<CHOICE>Optional</CHOICE>
<FLAG>-o</FLAG>
<NAME>long-list-exclude-grp</NAME>
<DESCR>Same as long listing, except that the group is not
 printed</DESCR>
</ARG>
</GROUP>
</GROUP>
<ARG>
<CHOICE>Required</CHOICE>
<NAME>filename</NAME>
<DESCR>File names</DESCR>
<REPEAT>
<VALUE>
<TYPE>string</TYPE>
</VALUE>
</ARG>
</BODY>
</PUML>
```

ls-form.html

```
<!DOCTYPE HTML PUBLIC "-//IETF//DTD HTML 2.0//EN">
<HTML>
<HEAD>
<TITLE>ls</TITLE>
<BASE HREF="ls.html">
</HEAD>
<BODY>
```

```
<H1>ls - List Directory Contents</H1>
<HR>
<CODE>ls {-abcCdfFgilLmnopqrRstux1} filename ...</CODE>
<HR><P>
<FORM METHOD="POST" ACTION="">
<H2>Command Line Options (Optional)</H2>
<INPUT NAME="all" TYPE="checkbox" VALUE="all">List all entries<BR>
<INPUT NAME="force-print" TYPE="checkbox" VALUE="force-print">Force
 printing of non-printable characters in octal (\\ddd)<BR>
<INPUT NAME="last-mode-time" TYPE="checkbox" VALUE="last-mode-time">Use
time of last modification of the i-node for sorting or
 printing<BR>
<INPUT NAME="multi-column" TYPE="checkbox" VALUE="multi-column">Multi-
column output with entries sorted down the columns
<BR>
<INPUT NAME="dir-only" TYPE="checkbox" VALUE="dir-only">If an argument is a
directory, list only its name (not its contents)<BR>
<INPUT NAME="force" TYPE="checkbox" VALUE="force">Force each argument to be
interpreted as a directory and list the name found<BR>
<INPUT NAME="add-slash" TYPE="checkbox" VALUE="add-slash">Add / after each
directory, an * if file is executable, and @ if file is
 a symbolic link<BR>
<INPUT NAME="i-node-num" TYPE="checkbox" VALUE="i-node-num">Print
 i-node number for each file in first column of listing<BR>
<INPUT NAME="link-ref" TYPE="checkbox" VALUE="link-ref">List the
 file or directory a symbolic link references<BR>
<INPUT NAME="stream-output" TYPE="checkbox" VALUE="stream-
output">List output across page delimeted by commas<BR>
<INPUT NAME="add-dir-slash" TYPE="checkbox" VALUE="add-dir-
slash">Add / after each directory<BR>
<INPUT NAME="replace-question-mark" TYPE="checkbox"
 VALUE="replace-question-mark">Print non-printable characters in
 file names as ?<BR>
<INPUT NAME="reverse-order" TYPE="checkbox" VALUE="reverse-order">Reverse
order of sort to get reverse alphabetic or oldest first<BR>
<INPUT NAME="recursive" TYPE="checkbox" VALUE="recursive">Recursively list
subdirectories encountered<BR>
<INPUT NAME="block-size" TYPE="checkbox" VALUE="block-size">Print
 size in blocks<BR>
<INPUT NAME="time-stamp" TYPE="checkbox" VALUE="time-stamp">Sort
 by time stamp with latest first rather by name<BR>
<INPUT NAME="last-access" TYPE="checkbox" VALUE="last-access">Sort
 or print using time of last access<BR>
<INPUT NAME="multi-col-output" TYPE="checkbox" VALUE="multi-col-
output">Multi-column output with entries sorted across page<BR>
<INPUT NAME="one-per-line" TYPE="checkbox" VALUE="one-per-line">Print one
entry per line of output<BR>
```

```
<H2>Long Listing Options (Optional)</H2>
<INPUT NAME="long-list" TYPE="checkbox" VALUE="long-list" CHECKED>Long
listing (mode, # of links, owner, group, size in
 bytes, time of last mod)<BR>
<INPUT NAME="long-fmt-exclude-owner" TYPE="checkbox" VALUE="long-
fmt-exclude-owner">Same as long listing excluding owner information<BR>
<INPUT NAME="long-list-gids" TYPE="checkbox" VALUE="long-list-gids">Same as
long listing, except owner's UID and group's GID numbers are printed<BR>
<INPUT NAME="long-list-exclude-grp" TYPE="checkbox" VALUE="long-list-
exclude-grp">Same as long listing, except that the group is
 not printed<BR>
<P>
<P>File names (Required)<BR>
<TEXTAREA NAME="filename" ROWS="5" COLS="40"></TEXTAREA>
<P><INPUT TYPE="submit" VALUE="Do ls Command">
</FORM>
</BODY>
</HTML>
```

mv

This UNIX command moves or renames a file. Use this transformation:

```
puml2html.pl -f mv-form.html -p mv.puml
```

mv.puml

```
<!DOCTYPE PUML PUBLIC "-//WebTechs//DTD PUML 1.0//EN">
<PUML>
<HEAD>
<TITLE>mv - Move Files</TITLE>
<BASE HREF="http://www.webtechs.com/tools/sysadmin/mv.puml">
</HEAD>
<BODY>
<COMMAND>
<TYPE>Solaris 2.4 command</TYPE>
<LANG>system</LANG>
<NAME>mv</NAME>
<DESCR>Move Files</DESCR>
<USAGE>mv {-fi} [filename] [target]</USAGE>
</COMMAND>
<GROUP>
<CHOICE>Optional</CHOICE>
```

```
<NAME>options</NAME>
<DESCR>Options</DESCR>
<ARG>
<CHOICE>Optional</CHOICE>
<FLAG>-f</FLAG>
<NAME>force</NAME>
<DESCR>Force the move</DESCR>
</ARG>
<ARG>
<CHOICE>Optional</CHOICE>
<FLAG>-i</FLAG>
<NAME>interactive</NAME>
<DEFAULT>
<DESCR>Ask before moving</DESCR>
</ARG>
</GROUP>
<ARG>
<CHOICE>Required</CHOICE>
<NAME>filename</NAME>
<REPEAT>
<VALUE>
<TYPE>string</TYPE>
</VALUE>
<DESCR>Filenames</DESCR>
</ARG>
</BODY>
</PUML>
```

mv-form.html

```
<!DOCTYPE HTML PUBLIC "-//IETF//DTD HTML 2.0//EN">
<HTML>
<HEAD>
<TITLE>mv</TITLE>
<BASE HREF="mv.html">
</HEAD>
<BODY>
<H1>mv - Move Files</H1>
<HR>
<CODE>mv {-fi} [filename] [target]</CODE>
<HR><P>
<FORM METHOD="POST" ACTION="">
<H2>Options (Optional)</H2>
<INPUT NAME="force" TYPE="checkbox" VALUE="force">Force the
 move<BR>
```

```
<INPUT NAME="interactive" TYPE="checkbox" VALUE="interactive"
 CHECKED>Ask before moving<BR>
<P>
<P>Filenames (Required)<BR>
<TEXTAREA NAME="filename" ROWS="5" COLS="40"></TEXTAREA>
<P><INPUT TYPE="submit" VALUE="Do mv Command">
</FORM>
</BODY>
</HTML>
```

rm

This UNIX command removes a file from a file system. Use this transformation:

```
puml2html.pl -f rm-form.html -p rm.puml
```

rm.puml

```
<!DOCTYPE PUML PUBLIC "-//WebTechs//DTD PUML 1.0//EN">
<PUML>
<HEAD>
<TITLE>rm - Remove Files from a Directory</TITLE>
<BASE HREF="http://www.webtechs.com/tools/sysadmin/rm.puml">
</HEAD>
<BODY>
<COMMAND>
<TYPE>Solaris 2.4 command</TYPE>
<LANG>system</LANG>
<NAME>rm</NAME>
<DESCR>Remove Files from a Directory</DESCR>
<USAGE>rm {-fir} [filename ...]</USAGE>
</COMMAND>
<GROUP>
<CHOICE>Optional</CHOICE>
<NAME>options</NAME>
<DESCR>Options</DESCR>
<ARG>
<CHOICE>Optional</CHOICE>
<FLAG>-f</FLAG>
<NAME>force</NAME>
<DESCR>Force removal of all files in a directory</DESCR>
```

```
</ARG>
<ARG>
<CHOICE>Optional</CHOICE>
<FLAG>-i</FLAG>
<NAME>interactive</NAME>
<DEFAULT>
<DESCR>Ask before removing file</DESCR>
</ARG>
<ARG>
<CHOICE>Optional</CHOICE>
<FLAG>-r</FLAG>
<NAME>recursive</NAME>
<DESCR>Recursively remove files and subdirectories</DESCR>
</ARG>
</GROUP>
<ARG>
<CHOICE>Required</CHOICE>
<FLAG></FLAG>
<NAME>filename</NAME>
<REPEAT>
<VALUE>
<TYPE>string</TYPE>
</VALUE>
<DESCR>File names</DESCR>
</ARG>
</BODY>
</PUML>
```

rm-form.html

```
<!DOCTYPE HTML PUBLIC "-//IETF//DTD HTML 2.0//EN">
<HTML>
<HEAD>
<TITLE>rm</TITLE>
<BASE HREF="rm.html">
</HEAD>
<BODY>
<H1>rm - Remove Files from a Directory</H1>
<HR>
<CODE>rm {-fir} [filename ...]</CODE>
<HR><P>
<FORM METHOD="POST" ACTION="">
<H2>Options (Optional)</H2>
<INPUT NAME="force" TYPE="checkbox" VALUE="force">Force removal of all
files in a directory<BR>
<INPUT NAME="interactive" TYPE="checkbox" VALUE="interactive" CHECKED>Ask
before removing file<BR>
```

```
<INPUT NAME="recursive" TYPE="checkbox" VALUE="recursive">Recursively
remove files and subdirectories<BR>
<P>
<P>File names (At least one required)<BR>
<TEXTAREA NAME="recursive" ROWS="5" COLS="40"></TEXTAREA>
<P><INPUT TYPE="submit" VALUE="Do rm Command">
</FORM>
</BODY>
</HTML>
```

rmdir

This UNIX command removes an empty directory. Use this transformation:

```
puml2html.pl -f rmdir-form.html -p rmdir.puml
```

rmdir.puml

```
<!DOCTYPE PUML PUBLIC "-//WebTechs//DTD PUML 1.0//EN">
<PUML>
<HEAD>
<TITLE>rmdir - Remove Directories</TITLE>
<BASE HREF="http://www.webtechs.com/tools/sysadmin/rmdir.puml">
</HEAD>
<BODY>
<COMMAND>
<TYPE>Solaris 2.4 command</TYPE>
<LANG>system</LANG>
<NAME>rmdir</NAME>
<DESCR>Remove Directories</DESCR>
<USAGE>rmdir [dirname ...]</USAGE>
</COMMAND>
<ARG>
<CHOICE>Required</CHOICE>
<NAME>dirnames</NAME>
<DESCR>Directory names</DESCR>
<REPEAT>
<VALUE>
<TYPE>string</TYPE>
</VALUE>
</ARG>
</BODY>
</PUML>
```

rmdir-form.html

```
<!DOCTYPE HTML PUBLIC "-//IETF//DTD HTML 2.0//EN">
<HTML>
<HEAD>
<TITLE>rmdir</TITLE>
<BASE HREF="rmdir.html">
</HEAD>
<BODY>
<H1>rmdir - Remove Directories</H1>
<HR>
<CODE>rmdir [dirname ...]</CODE>
<HR><P>
<FORM METHOD="POST" ACTION="">
<P>Directory names (At least one required)<BR>
<TEXTAREA NAME="dirnames" ROWS="5" COLS="40"></TEXTAREA>
<P><INPUT TYPE="submit" VALUE="Do rmdir Command">
</FORM>
</BODY>
</HTML>
```

compress

This UNIX command compresses a file or set of files. Use this transformation:

```
puml2html.pl -f compress-form.html -p compress.puml
```

compress.puml

```
<!DOCTYPE PUML PUBLIC "-//WebTechs//DTD PUML 1.0//EN">
<PUML>
<HEAD>
<TITLE>compress - UNIX Compress Files</TITLE>
<BASE HREF="http://www.webtechs.com/tools/sysadin/compress.puml">
</HEAD>
<BODY>
<COMMAND>
<TYPE>Solaris 2.4 command</TYPE>
<LANG>system</LANG>
<NAME>compress</NAME>
<DESCR>UNIX Compress Files</DESCR>
<USAGE>compress {-cvf} {-b bits} [filename ...]</USAGE>
```

```
</COMMAND>
<GROUP>
<CHOICE>Optional</CHOICE>
<NAME>options</NAME>
<DESCR>Options</DESCR>
<ARG>
<CHOICE>Optional</CHOICE>
<FLAG>-c</FLAG>
<NAME>stdout</NAME>
<DESCR>Echo compressed data to STDOUT; no files are changed</DESCR>
</ARG>
<ARG>
<CHOICE>Optional</CHOICE>
<FLAG>-f</FLAG>
<NAME>force</NAME>
<DESCR>Force compression and overwrite existing file</DESCR>
</ARG>
<ARG>
<CHOICE>Optional</CHOICE>
<FLAG>-v</FLAG>
<NAME>verbose</NAME>
<DESCR>Display verbose messages as uncompress works</DESCR>
</ARG>
</GROUP>
<GROUP>
<CHOICE>Optional</CHOICE>
<NAME>substring-codes</NAME>
<DESCR>Upper Limit of Substring Codes</DESCR>
<ARG>
<CHOICE>Required</CHOICE>
<NAME>code-9</NAME>
<DESCR>9</DESCR>
</ARG>
<ARG>
<CHOICE>Required</CHOICE>
<NAME>code-10</NAME>
<DESCR>10</DESCR>
</ARG>
<ARG>
<CHOICE>Required</CHOICE>
<NAME>code-11</NAME>
<DESCR>11</DESCR>
</ARG>
<ARG>
<CHOICE>Required</CHOICE>
<NAME>code-12</NAME>
<DESCR>12</DESCR>
```

```
</ARG>
<ARG>
<CHOICE>Required</CHOICE>
<NAME>code-13</NAME>
<DESCR>13</DESCR>
</ARG>
<ARG>
<CHOICE>Required</CHOICE>
<NAME>code-14</NAME>
<DESCR>14</DESCR>
</ARG>
<ARG>
<CHOICE>Required</CHOICE>
<NAME>code-15</NAME>
<DESCR>15</DESCR>
</ARG>
<ARG>
<CHOICE>Required</CHOICE>
<NAME>code-16</NAME>
<DEFAULT>
<DESCR>16</DESCR>
</ARG>
</GROUP>
<ARG>
<CHOICE>Required</CHOICE>
<NAME>filename</NAME>
<DESCR>File names</DESCR>
<REPEAT>
<VALUE>
<TYPE>string</TYPE>
</VALUE>
</ARG>
</BODY>
</PUML>
```

compress-form.html

```
<!DOCTYPE HTML PUBLIC "-//IETF//DTD HTML 2.0//EN">
<HTML>
<HEAD>
<TITLE>compress</TITLE>
<BASE HREF="compress.html">
</HEAD>
<BODY>
<H1>compress - UNIX Compress Files</H1>
```

```
<HR>
<CODE>compress {-cvf} {-b bits} [filename ...]</CODE>
<HR><P>
<FORM METHOD="POST" ACTION="">
<H2>Options (Optional)</H2>
<INPUT NAME="stdout" TYPE="checkbox" VALUE="stdout">Echo
 compressed data to STDOUT; no files are changed<BR>
<INPUT NAME="force" TYPE="checkbox" VALUE="force">Force
 compression and overwrite existing file<BR>
<INPUT NAME="verbose" TYPE="checkbox" VALUE="verbose">Display
 verbose messages as uncompress works<BR>
<P>
<H2>Upper Limit of Substring Codes (Optional)</H2>
<INPUT NAME="substring-codes" TYPE="radio" VALUE="code-9">
 9<BR>
<INPUT NAME="substring-codes" TYPE="radio" VALUE="code-10">
 10<BR>
<INPUT NAME="substring-codes" TYPE="radio" VALUE="code-11">
 11<BR>
<INPUT NAME="substring-codes" TYPE="radio" VALUE="code-12">
 12<BR>
<INPUT NAME="substring-codes" TYPE="radio" VALUE="code-13">
 13<BR>
<INPUT NAME="substring-codes" TYPE="radio" VALUE="code-14">
 14<BR>
<INPUT NAME="substring-codes" TYPE="radio" VALUE="code-15">
 15<BR>
<INPUT NAME="substring-codes" TYPE="radio" VALUE="code-16"
 CHECKED> 16<BR>
<P>
<P>File names (Required)<BR>
<TEXTAREA NAME="filename" ROWS="5" COLS="40"></TEXTAREA>
<P><INPUT TYPE="submit" VALUE="Do compress Command">
</FORM>
</BODY>
</HTML>
```

uncompress

This UNIX command uncompresses a compressed file. Use this transformation:

```
puml2html.pl -f uncompress-form.html -p uncompress.puml
```

uncompress.puml

```
<!DOCTYPE PUML PUBLIC "-//WebTechs//DTD PUML 1.0//EN">
<PUML>
<HEAD>
<TITLE>uncompress - UNIX Uncompress Files</TITLE>
<BASE HREF="http://www.webtechs.com/tools/sysadmin/uncompress.puml">
</HEAD>
<BODY>
<COMMAND>
<TYPE>Solaris 2.4 command</TYPE>
<LANG>system</LANG>
<NAME>uncompress</NAME>
<DESCR>UNIX Uncompress Files</DESCR>
<USAGE>uncompress {-cfv} [filename ...]</USAGE>
</COMMAND>
<GROUP>
<CHOICE>Optional</CHOICE>
<NAME>options</NAME>
<DESCR>Options</DESCR>
<ARG>
<CHOICE>Optional</CHOICE>
<FLAG>-c</FLAG>
<NAME>stdout</NAME>
<DESCR>Echo uncompressed data to STDOUT; no files are changed</DESCR>
</ARG>
<ARG>
<CHOICE>Optional</CHOICE>
<FLAG>-f</FLAG>
<NAME>force</NAME>
<DESCR>Force uncompression and overwrite existing file</DESCR>
</ARG>
<ARG>
<CHOICE>Optional</CHOICE>
<FLAG>-v</FLAG>
<NAME>verbose</NAME>
<DESCR>Display verbose messages as uncompress works</DESCR>
</ARG>
</GROUP>
<ARG>
<CHOICE>Required</CHOICE>
<NAME>filename</NAME>
<DESCR>File names</DESCR>
<REPEAT>
<VALUE>
<TYPE>string</TYPE>
</VALUE>
</ARG>
</BODY>
</PUML>
```

uncompress-form.html

```
<!DOCTYPE HTML PUBLIC "-//IETF//DTD HTML 2.0//EN">
<HTML>
<HEAD>
<TITLE>uncompress</TITLE>
<BASE HREF="uncompress.html">
</HEAD>
<BODY>
<H1>uncompress - UNIX Uncompress Files</H1>
<HR>
<CODE>uncompress {-cfv} [filename ...]</CODE>
<HR><P>
<FORM METHOD="POST" ACTION="">
<H2>Options (Optional)</H2>
<INPUT NAME="stdout" TYPE="checkbox" VALUE="stdout">Echo uncompressed data
to STDOUT; no files are changed<BR>
<INPUT NAME="force" TYPE="checkbox" VALUE="force">Force uncompression and
overwrite existing file<BR>
<INPUT NAME="verbose" TYPE="checkbox" VALUE="verbose">Display
 verbose messages as uncompress works<BR>
<P>
<P>File names (Required)<BR>
<TEXTAREA NAME="filename" ROWS="5" COLS="40"></TEXTAREA>
<P><INPUT TYPE="submit" VALUE="Do uncompress Command">
</FORM>
</BODY>
</HTML>
```

gunzip

This GNU command uncompresses a file compressed with the GNU gzip.
Use this transformation:

```
puml2html.pl -f gunzip-form.html -p gunzip.puml
```

gunzip.puml

```
<!DOCTYPE PUML PUBLIC "-//WebTechs//DTD PUML 1.0//EN">
<PUML>
<HEAD>
<TITLE>gunzip - GNU Uncompress Files</TITLE>
<BASE HREF="http://www.webtechs.com/tools/sysadmin/gunzip.puml">
</HEAD>
```

```
<BODY>
<COMMAND>
<TYPE>Solaris 2.4 GNU command</TYPE>
<LANG>ANSI C binary</LANG>
<NAME>gunzip</NAME>
<DESCR>GNU Uncompress Files</DESCR>
<USAGE>gunzip {-acfhlLnNrtvV} {-S suffix} [filename ...]</USAGE>
</COMMAND>
<GROUP>
<CHOICE>Optional</CHOICE>
<NAME>options</NAME>
<DESCR>Options</DESCR>
<ARG>
<CHOICE>Optional</CHOICE>
<FLAG>-a</FLAG>
<NAME>ascii</NAME>
<DESCR>ASCII text mode</DESCR>
</ARG>
<ARG>
<CHOICE>Optional</CHOICE>
<FLAG>-c</FLAG>
<NAME>stdout</NAME>
<DESCR>Write output to STDOUT; retain original files</DESCR>
</ARG>
<ARG>
<CHOICE>Optional</CHOICE>
<FLAG>-f</FLAG>
<NAME>force</NAME>
<DESCR>Force uncompression and overwrite existing file</DESCR>
</ARG>
<ARG>
<CHOICE>Optional</CHOICE>
<FLAG>-h</FLAG>
<NAME>help</NAME>
<DESCR>Help message</DESCR>
</ARG>
<ARG>
<CHOICE>Optional</CHOICE>
<FLAG>-l</FLAG>
<NAME>list</NAME>
<DESCR>List compression/uncompression statistics</DESCR>
</ARG>
<ARG>
<CHOICE>Optional</CHOICE>
<FLAG>-L</FLAG>
<NAME>license</NAME>
<DESCR>Display license information</DESCR>
```

```
</ARG>
<ARG>
<CHOICE>Optional</CHOICE>
<FLAG>-q</FLAG>
<NAME>quiet</NAME>
<DESCR>Suppress all warnings</DESCR>
</ARG>
<ARG>
<CHOICE>Optional</CHOICE>
<FLAG>-r</FLAG>
<NAME>recursive</NAME>
<DESCR>Recursively uncompress all files and subdirectories</DESCR>
</ARG>
<ARG>
<CHOICE>Optional</CHOICE>
<FLAG>-t</FLAG>
<NAME>test</NAME>
<DESCR>Test the integrity of the compressed file</DESCR>
</ARG>
<ARG>
<CHOICE>Optional</CHOICE>
<FLAG>-v</FLAG>
<NAME>verbose</NAME>
<DESCR>Display verbose messages as gunzip works</DESCR>
</ARG>
<ARG>
<CHOICE>Optional</CHOICE>
<FLAG>-V</FLAG>
<NAME>version</NAME>
<DESCR>Display gunzip version number</DESCR>
</ARG>
<GROUP>
<CHOICE>Optional</CHOICE>
<NAME>name_time_stamp</NAME>
<DESCR>File Name and Time Stamp Options</DESCR>
<ARG>
<CHOICE>Required</CHOICE>
<FLAG>-n</FLAG>
<NAME>noname</NAME>
<DESCR>Don't use original file name and time stamp</DESCR>
</ARG>
<ARG>
<CHOICE>Required</CHOICE>
<FLAG>-N</FLAG>
<NAME>name</NAME>
<DEFAULT>
<DESCR>Use original file name and time stamp</DESCR>
```

```
</ARG>
</GROUP>
</GROUP>
<ARG>
<CHOICE>Optional</CHOICE>
<FLAG>-S</FLAG>
<NAME>suffix</NAME>
<DESCR>Use this suffix instead of '.gz'</DESCR>
<VALUE>
<TYPE>string</TYPE>
</VALUE>
</ARG>
<ARG>
<CHOICE>Required</CHOICE>
<NAME>filename</NAME>
<DESCR>File names</DESCR>
<REPEAT>
<VALUE>
<TYPE>string</TYPE>
</VALUE>
</ARG>
</BODY>
</PUML>
```

gunzip-form.html

```
<!DOCTYPE HTML PUBLIC "-//IETF//DTD HTML 2.0//EN">
<HTML>
<HEAD>
<TITLE>gunzip</TITLE>
<BASE HREF="gunzip.html">
</HEAD>
<BODY>
<H1>gunzip - GNU Uncompress Files</H1>
<HR>
<CODE>gunzip {-acfhlLnNrtvV} {-S suffix} [filename ...]</CODE>
<HR><P>
<FORM METHOD="POST" ACTION="">
<H2>Options (Optional)</H2>
<INPUT NAME="ascii" TYPE="checkbox" VALUE="ascii">ASCII text mode<BR>
<INPUT NAME="stdout" TYPE="checkbox" VALUE="stdout">Write output
 to STDOUT; retain original files<BR>
<INPUT NAME="force" TYPE="checkbox" VALUE="force">Force uncompression and
overwrite existing file<BR>
<INPUT NAME="help" TYPE="checkbox" VALUE="help">Get help message<BR>
<INPUT NAME="list" TYPE="checkbox" VALUE="list">List
compression/uncompression statistics<BR>
```

```
<INPUT NAME="license" TYPE="checkbox" VALUE="license">Display
 license information<BR>
<INPUT NAME="quiet" TYPE="checkbox" VALUE="quiet">Suppress all
 warnings<BR>
<INPUT NAME="recursive" TYPE="checkbox" VALUE="recursive">Recursively
uncompress all files and subdirectories<BR>
<INPUT NAME="test" TYPE="checkbox" VALUE="test">Test the integrity
 of the compressed file<BR>
<INPUT NAME="verbose" TYPE="checkbox" VALUE="verbose">Display
 verbose messages as gunzip works<BR>
<INPUT NAME="version" TYPE="checkbox" VALUE="version">Display
 gunzip version number<BR>
<H2>File Name and Time Stamp Options (Optional)</H2>
<INPUT NAME="name_time_stamp" TYPE="radio" VALUE="noname"> Don't
 use original file name and time stamp<BR>
<INPUT NAME="name_time_stamp" TYPE="radio" VALUE="name" CHECKED>
 Use original file name and time stamp<BR>
<P>
<INPUT NAME="suffix" TYPE="text" SIZE="40" MAXLENGTH="40"> Use
 this suffix instead of '.gz' (Optional)<BR>
<P>File names (Required)<BR>
<TEXTAREA NAME="filename" ROWS="5" COLS="40"></TEXTAREA>
<P><INPUT TYPE="submit" VALUE="Do gunzip Command">
</FORM>
</BODY>
</HTML>
```

gzip

This GNU command compresses a file. Use this transformation:

```
puml2html.pl -f gzip-form.html -p gzip.puml
```

gzip.puml

```
<!DOCTYPE PUML PUBLIC "-//WebTechs//DTD PUML 1.0//EN">
<PUML>
<HEAD>
<TITLE>gzip - GNU Compress Files</TITLE>
<BASE HREF="http://www.webtechs.com/tools/sysadmin/gzip.puml">
</HEAD>
<BODY>
<COMMAND>
<TYPE>Solaris 2.4 GNU command</TYPE>
<LANG>ANSI C binary</LANG>
```

```
<NAME>gzip</NAME>
<DESCR>GNU Compress Files</DESCR>
<USAGE>gzip {-acdfhlLnNrtvV19} {-S suffix} [filename ...]</USAGE>
</COMMAND>
<GROUP>
<CHOICE>Optional</CHOICE>
<NAME>options</NAME>
<DESCR>Options</DESCR>
<ARG>
<CHOICE>Optional</CHOICE>
<FLAG>-a</FLAG>
<NAME>ascii</NAME>
<DESCR>ASCII text mode</DESCR>
</ARG>
<ARG>
<CHOICE>Optional</CHOICE>
<FLAG>-c</FLAG>
<NAME>stdout</NAME>
<DESCR>Write output to STDOUT; retain original files</DESCR>
</ARG>
<ARG>
<CHOICE>Optional</CHOICE>
<FLAG>-d</FLAG>
<NAME>decompress</NAME>
<DESCR>Decompress/uncompress file</DESCR>
</ARG>
<ARG>
<CHOICE>Optional</CHOICE>
<FLAG>-f</FLAG>
<NAME>force</NAME>
<DESCR>Force compression and overwrite existing file</DESCR>
</ARG>
<ARG>
<CHOICE>Optional</CHOICE>
<FLAG>-h</FLAG>
<NAME>help</NAME>
<DESCR>Get help message</DESCR>
</ARG>
<ARG>
<CHOICE>Optional</CHOICE>
<FLAG>-l</FLAG>
<NAME>list</NAME>
<DESCR>List compression/uncompression statistics</DESCR>
</ARG>
<ARG>
<CHOICE>Optional</CHOICE>
<FLAG>-L</FLAG>
```

```
<NAME>license</NAME>
<DESCR>Display license information</DESCR>
</ARG>
<ARG>
<CHOICE>Optional</CHOICE>
<FLAG>-q</FLAG>
<NAME>quiet</NAME>
<DESCR>Suppress all warnings</DESCR>
</ARG>
<ARG>
<CHOICE>Optional</CHOICE>
<FLAG>-r</FLAG>
<NAME>recursive</NAME>
<DESCR>Recursively compress all files and subdirectories</DESCR>
</ARG>
<ARG>
<CHOICE>Optional</CHOICE>
<FLAG>-t</FLAG>
<NAME>test</NAME>
<DESCR>Test the integrity of the compressed file</DESCR>
</ARG>
<ARG>
<CHOICE>Optional</CHOICE>
<FLAG>-v</FLAG>
<NAME>verbose</NAME>
<DESCR>Display verbose messages as gzip works</DESCR>
</ARG>
<ARG>
<CHOICE>Optional</CHOICE>
<FLAG>-V</FLAG>
<NAME>version</NAME>
<DESCR>Display gzip version number</DESCR>
</ARG>
<GROUP>
<CHOICE>Optional</CHOICE>
<NAME>speed</NAME>
<DESCR>Speed of compression</DESCR>
<ARG>
<CHOICE>Required</CHOICE>
<FLAG>-1</FLAG>
<NAME>speed-1</NAME>
<DESCR>1 - Fastest speed, worst compression</DESCR>
</ARG>
<ARG>
<CHOICE>Required</CHOICE>
<FLAG>-2</FLAG>
<NAME>speed-2</NAME>
```

```
<DESCR>2</DESCR>
</ARG>
<ARG>
<CHOICE>Required</CHOICE>
<FLAG>-3</FLAG>
<NAME>speed-3</NAME>
<DESCR>3</DESCR>
</ARG>
<ARG>
<CHOICE>Required</CHOICE>
<FLAG>-4</FLAG>
<NAME>speed-4</NAME>
<DESCR>4</DESCR>
</ARG>
<ARG>
<CHOICE>Required</CHOICE>
<FLAG>-5</FLAG>
<NAME>speed-5</NAME>
<DESCR>5</DESCR>
</ARG>
<ARG>
<CHOICE>Required</CHOICE>
<FLAG>-6</FLAG>
<NAME>speed-6</NAME>
<DEFAULT>
<DESCR>6</DESCR>
</ARG>
<ARG>
<CHOICE>Required</CHOICE>
<FLAG>-7</FLAG>
<NAME>speed-7</NAME>
<DESCR>7</DESCR>
</ARG>
<ARG>
<CHOICE>Required</CHOICE>
<FLAG>-8</FLAG>
<NAME>speed-8</NAME>
<DESCR>8</DESCR>
</ARG>
<ARG>
<CHOICE>Required</CHOICE>
<FLAG>-9</FLAG>
<NAME>speed-9</NAME>
<DESCR>9 - Slowest speed, best compression</DESCR>
</ARG>
</GROUP>
<GROUP>
```

```
<CHOICE>Optional</CHOICE>
<NAME>name_time_stamp</NAME>
<DESCR>File Name and Time Stamp Options</DESCR>
<ARG>
<CHOICE>Required</CHOICE>
<FLAG>-n</FLAG>
<NAME>noname</NAME>
<DESCR>Don't use original file name and time stamp</DESCR>
</ARG>
<ARG>
<CHOICE>Required</CHOICE>
<FLAG>-N</FLAG>
<NAME>name</NAME>
<DEFAULT>
<DESCR>Use original file name and time stamp</DESCR>
</ARG>
</GROUP>
</GROUP>
<ARG>
<CHOICE>Optional</CHOICE>
<FLAG>-S</FLAG>
<NAME>suffix</NAME>
<DESCR>Use this suffix instead of '.gz'</DESCR>
<VALUE>
<TYPE>string</TYPE>
</VALUE>
</ARG>
<ARG>
<CHOICE>Required</CHOICE>
<NAME>filename</NAME>
<DESCR>File names</DESCR>
<REPEAT>
<VALUE>
<TYPE>string</TYPE>
</VALUE>
</ARG>
</BODY>
</PUML>
```

gzip-form.html

```
<!DOCTYPE HTML PUBLIC "-//IETF//DTD HTML 2.0//EN">
<HTML>
<HEAD>
<TITLE>gzip</TITLE>
<BASE HREF="gzip.html">
</HEAD>
```

```
<BODY>
<H1>gzip - GNU Compress Files</H1>
<HR>
<CODE>gzip {-acdfhlLnNrtvV19} {-S suffix} [filename ...]</CODE>
<HR><P>
<FORM METHOD="POST" ACTION="">
<H2>Options (Optional)</H2>
<INPUT NAME="ascii" TYPE="checkbox" VALUE="ascii">ASCII text mode<BR>
<INPUT NAME="stdout" TYPE="checkbox" VALUE="stdout">Write output
 to STDOUT; retain original files<BR>
<INPUT NAME="decompress" TYPE="checkbox"
VALUE="decompress">Decompress/uncompress file<BR>
<INPUT NAME="force" TYPE="checkbox" VALUE="force">Force
 compression and overwrite existing file<BR>
<INPUT NAME="help" TYPE="checkbox" VALUE="help">Help message<BR>
<INPUT NAME="list" TYPE="checkbox" VALUE="list">List
compression/uncompression statistics<BR>
<INPUT NAME="license" TYPE="checkbox" VALUE="license">Display
 license information<BR>
<INPUT NAME="quiet" TYPE="checkbox" VALUE="quiet">Suppress all
 warnings<BR>
<INPUT NAME="recursive" TYPE="checkbox" VALUE="recursive">Recursively
compress all files and subdirectories<BR>
<INPUT NAME="test" TYPE="checkbox" VALUE="test">Test the integrity
 of the compressed file<BR>
<INPUT NAME="verbose" TYPE="checkbox" VALUE="verbose">Display
 verbose messages as gzip works<BR>
<INPUT NAME="version" TYPE="checkbox" VALUE="version">Display gzip
 version number<BR>
<H2>Speed of compression (Optional)</H2>
<INPUT NAME="speed" TYPE="radio" VALUE="speed-1"> 1 - Fastest
 speed, worst compression<BR>
<INPUT NAME="speed" TYPE="radio" VALUE="speed-2"> 2<BR>
<INPUT NAME="speed" TYPE="radio" VALUE="speed-3"> 3<BR>
<INPUT NAME="speed" TYPE="radio" VALUE="speed-4"> 4<BR>
<INPUT NAME="speed" TYPE="radio" VALUE="speed-5"> 5<BR>
<INPUT NAME="speed" TYPE="radio" VALUE="speed-6" CHECKED> 6<BR>
<INPUT NAME="speed" TYPE="radio" VALUE="speed-7"> 7<BR>
<INPUT NAME="speed" TYPE="radio" VALUE="speed-8"> 8<BR>
<INPUT NAME="speed" TYPE="radio" VALUE="speed-9"> 9 - Slowest
 speed, best compression<BR>
<P>
<H2>File Name and Time Stamp Options (Optional)</H2>
<INPUT NAME="name_time_stamp" TYPE="radio" VALUE="noname"> Don't
 use original file name and time stamp<BR>
<INPUT NAME="name_time_stamp" TYPE="radio" VALUE="name" CHECKED>
 Use original file name and time stamp<BR>
```

```
<P>
<INPUT NAME="suffix" TYPE="text" SIZE="40" MAXLENGTH="40"> Use
 this suffix instead of '.gz' (Optional)<BR>
<P>File names (Required)<BR>
<TEXTAREA NAME="filename" ROWS="5" COLS="40"></TEXTAREA>
<P><INPUT TYPE="submit" VALUE="Do gzip Command">
</FORM>
</BODY>
</HTML>
```

ps

This UNIX command reports process status. Use this transformation:

```
puml2html.pl -f ps-form.html -p ps.puml
```

ps.puml

```
<!DOCTYPE PUML PUBLIC "-//WebTechs//DTD PUML 1.0//EN">
<PUML>
<HEAD>
<TITLE>ps - Report Process Status</TITLE>
<BASE HREF="http://www.webtechs.com/tools/sysadmin/ps.puml">
</HEAD>
<BODY>
<COMMAND>
<TYPE>Solaris 2.4 command</TYPE>
<LANG>system</LANG>
<NAME>ps</NAME>
<DESCR>Report Process Status</DESCR>
<USAGE>ps {-acdefjl} {-g grplist} {-p proclist} {-s sidlist}
 {-t term} {-u uidlist}</USAGE>
</COMMAND>
<GROUP>
<CHOICE>Optional</CHOICE>
<NAME>options</NAME>
<DESCR>Options</DESCR>
<ARG>
<CHOICE>Optional</CHOICE>
<FLAG>-a</FLAG>
<NAME>all</NAME>
<DESCR>Print all process information</DESCR>
</ARG>
<ARG>
<CHOICE>Optional</CHOICE>
```

```
<FLAG>-c</FLAG>
<NAME>sch_prop_format</NAME>
<DESCR>Scheduler properties output format</DESCR>
</ARG>
<ARG>
<CHOICE>Optional</CHOICE>
<FLAG>-d</FLAG>
<NAME>except_sess_lead</NAME>
<DESCR>Print all information excluding session leaders</DESCR>
</ARG>
<ARG>
<CHOICE>Optional</CHOICE>
<FLAG>-e</FLAG>
<NAME>running</NAME>
<DESCR>Print information about running processes</DESCR>
</ARG>
<ARG>
<CHOICE>Optional</CHOICE>
<FLAG>-f</FLAG>
<NAME>full</NAME>
<DESCR>Print full listing</DESCR>
</ARG>
<ARG>
<CHOICE>Optional</CHOICE>
<FLAG>-j</FLAG>
<NAME>sess_proc_id</NAME>
<DESCR>Print session ID and process group ID</DESCR>
</ARG>
<ARG>
<CHOICE>Optional</CHOICE>
<FLAG>-l</FLAG>
<NAME>long</NAME>
<DESCR>Generate a long listing</DESCR>
</ARG>
</GROUP>
<ARG>
<CHOICE>Optional</CHOICE>
<FLAG>-g</FLAG>
<NAME>grplist</NAME>
<DESCR>List only data for these group IDs</DESCR>
<VALUE>
<TYPE>string</TYPE>
</VALUE>
</ARG>
<ARG>
<CHOICE>Optional</CHOICE>
<FLAG>-p</FLAG>
```

```
<NAME>proclist</NAME>
<DESCR>List only data for these process IDs</DESCR>
<VALUE>
<TYPE>string</TYPE>
</VALUE>
</ARG>
<ARG>
<CHOICE>Optional</CHOICE>
<FLAG>-s</FLAG>
<NAME>sidlist</NAME>
<DESCR>List only data for these session IDs</DESCR>
<VALUE>
<TYPE>string</TYPE>
</VALUE>
</ARG>
<ARG>
<CHOICE>Optional</CHOICE>
<FLAG>-t</FLAG>
<NAME>term</NAME>
<DESCR>List only data with this terminal ID (device/ID)</DESCR>
<VALUE>
<TYPE>string</TYPE>
</VALUE>
</ARG>
<ARG>
<CHOICE>Optional</CHOICE>
<FLAG>-u</FLAG>
<NAME>uidlist</NAME>
<DESCR>List only data for this user ID or user login name</DESCR>
<VALUE>
<TYPE>string</TYPE>
</VALUE>
</ARG>
</BODY>
</PUML>
```

ps-form.html

```
<!DOCTYPE HTML PUBLIC "-//IETF//DTD HTML 2.0//EN">
<HTML>
<HEAD>
<TITLE>ps</TITLE>
<BASE HREF="ps.html">
</HEAD>
<BODY>
<H1>ps - Report Process Status</H1>
<HR>
```

```
<CODE>ps {-acdefjl} {-g grplist} {-p proclist} {-s sidlist}
 {-t term} {-u uidlist}</CODE>
<HR><P>
<FORM METHOD="POST" ACTION="">
<H2>Options (Optional)</H2>
<INPUT NAME="all" TYPE="checkbox" VALUE="all">Print all process
 information<BR>
<INPUT NAME="sch_prop_format" TYPE="checkbox"
VALUE="sch_prop_format">Scheduler properties output format<BR>
<INPUT NAME="except_sess_lead" TYPE="checkbox"
VALUE="except_sess_lead">Print all information excluding session
 leaders<BR>
<INPUT NAME="running" TYPE="checkbox" VALUE="running">Print information
about running processes<BR>
<INPUT NAME="full" TYPE="checkbox" VALUE="full">Print full listing<BR>
<INPUT NAME="sess_proc_id" TYPE="checkbox" VALUE="sess_proc_id">Print
session ID and process group ID<BR>
<INPUT NAME="long" TYPE="checkbox" VALUE="long">Generate a long
 listing<BR>
<P>
<INPUT NAME="grplist" TYPE="text" SIZE="40" MAXLENGTH="40"> List
 only data for these group IDs (Optional)<BR>
<INPUT NAME="proclist" TYPE="text" SIZE="40" MAXLENGTH="40"> List
 only data for these process IDs (Optional)<BR>
<INPUT NAME="sidlist" TYPE="text" SIZE="40" MAXLENGTH="40"> List
 only data for these session IDs (Optional)<BR>
<INPUT NAME="term" TYPE="text" SIZE="40" MAXLENGTH="40"> List only
 data with this terminal ID (device/ID) (Optional)<BR>
<INPUT NAME="uidlist" TYPE="text" SIZE="40" MAXLENGTH="40"> List
 only data for this user ID or user login name (Optional)<BR>
<P><INPUT TYPE="submit" VALUE="Do ps Command">
</FORM>
</BODY>
</HTML>
```

grep

This UNIX command searches a file for a pattern or regular expression. Use this transformation:

```
puml2html.pl -f grep-form.html -p grep.puml
```

grep.puml

```
<!DOCTYPE PUML PUBLIC "-//WebTechs//DTD PUML 1.0//EN">
<PUML>
<HEAD>
<TITLE>grep - Search a File for a Pattern</TITLE>
</HEAD>
<BODY>
<COMMAND>
<TYPE>Solaris 2.4 command</TYPE>
<LANG>system</LANG>
<NAME>grep</NAME>
<DESCR>Search a File for a Pattern</DESCR>
<USAGE>grep {-bchilnsvw} [regular_expression] [filename ...]
</USAGE>
</COMMAND>
<GROUP>
<NAME>options</NAME>
<CHOICE>Optional</CHOICE>
<DESCR>Options</DESCR>
<ARG>
<NAME>blocknumber</NAME>
<CHOICE>Optional</CHOICE>
<FLAG>-b</FLAG>
<DESCR>Precede each line by the block number</DESCR>
</ARG>
<ARG>
<NAME>count</NAME>
<CHOICE>Optional</CHOICE>
<FLAG>-c</FLAG>
<DESCR>Print a count of lines containing the pattern</DESCR>
</ARG>
<ARG>
<NAME>suppressfilename</NAME>
<CHOICE>Optional</CHOICE>
<FLAG>-h</FLAG>
<DESCR>Suppress reporting the filename containing the
 pattern</DESCR>
</ARG>
<ARG>
<NAME>ignore</NAME>
<CHOICE>Optional</CHOICE>
<FLAG>-i</FLAG>
<DESCR>Ignore upper and lower case distinction</DESCR>
</ARG>
<ARG>
<NAME>printfilename</NAME>
<CHOICE>Optional</CHOICE>
```

```
<FLAG>-l</FLAG>
<DESCR>Print only the file names with matching lines</DESCR>
</ARG>
<ARG>
<NAME>linenumber</NAME>
<CHOICE>Optional</CHOICE>
<FLAG>-n</FLAG>
<DESCR>Precede each line by its file line number</DESCR>
</ARG>
<ARG>
<NAME>suppresserrors</NAME>
<CHOICE>Optional</CHOICE>
<FLAG>-s</FLAG>
<DESCR>Suppress error messages about nonexistent or unreadable
 files</DESCR>
</ARG>
<ARG>
<NAME>nonmatchinglines</NAME>
<CHOICE>Optional</CHOICE>
<FLAG>-v</FLAG>
<DESCR>Print all lines except those matching the pattern</DESCR>
</ARG>
<ARG>
<NAME>wordsearch</NAME>
<CHOICE>Optional</CHOICE>
<FLAG>-w</FLAG>
<DESCR>Search for the expression as a word</DESCR>
</ARG>
</GROUP>
<ARG>
<NAME>regularexpression</NAME>
<CHOICE>Required</CHOICE>
<DESCR>Regular expression</DESCR>
<VALUE>
<TYPE>string</TYPE>
</VALUE>
</ARG>
<ARG>
<NAME>filename</NAME>
<CHOICE>Required</CHOICE>
<REPEAT>
<VALUE>
<TYPE>string</TYPE>
</VALUE>
<DESCR>File names</DESCR>
</ARG>
</BODY>
</PUML>
```

grep-form.html

```
<!DOCTYPE HTML PUBLIC "-//IETF//DTD HTML 2.0//EN">
<HTML>
<HEAD>
<TITLE>grep</TITLE>
<BASE HREF="grep.html">
</HEAD>
<BODY>
<H1>grep - Search a File for a Pattern</H1>
<HR>
<CODE>grep {-bchilnsvw} [regular_expression] [filename ...]</CODE>
<HR><P>
<FORM METHOD="POST" ACTION="">
<H2>Options (Optional)</H2>
<INPUT NAME="blocknumber" TYPE="checkbox" VALUE="blocknumber">Precede each
line by the block number<BR>
<INPUT NAME="count" TYPE="checkbox" VALUE="count">Print a count of
 lines containing the pattern<BR>
<INPUT NAME="suppressfilename" TYPE="checkbox"
VALUE="suppressfilename">Suppress reporting the filename
 containing the pattern<BR>
<INPUT NAME="ignore" TYPE="checkbox" VALUE="ignore">Ignore upper
 and lower case distinction<BR>
<INPUT NAME="printfilename" TYPE="checkbox" VALUE="printfilename">Print
only the file names with matching lines<BR>
<INPUT NAME="linenumber" TYPE="checkbox" VALUE="linenumber">
Precede each line by its file line number<BR>
<INPUT NAME="suppresserrors" TYPE="checkbox"
VALUE="suppresserrors">Suppress error messages about nonexistent
 or unreadable files<BR>
<INPUT NAME="nonmatchinglines" TYPE="checkbox"
VALUE="nonmatchinglines">Print all lines except those matching the
pattern<BR>
<INPUT NAME="wordsearch" TYPE="checkbox" VALUE="wordsearch">Search
 for the expression as a word<BR>
<P>
<INPUT NAME="regularexpression" TYPE="text" SIZE="40" MAXLENGTH="40">
Regular expression (Required)<BR>
<P>File names (Required)<BR>
<TEXTAREA NAME="filename" ROWS="5" COLS="40"></TEXTAREA>
<P><INPUT TYPE="submit" VALUE="Do grep Command">
</FORM>
</BODY>
</HTML>
```

Summary

In this chapter, we've presented numerous examples of UNIX commands represented as PUML and transformed into HTML with the *puml2html.pl* script. The corresponding CGIs will represent the most interesting aspects of implementation, especially if you use the Perl system statement: In many cases, all this work will lead to only one- or two-line programs!

A CUSTOMER QUOTE GENERATOR

*E*ver since the business community got wind of the World Wide Web, its potential for electronic commerce has been one of the hottest Internet topics. As we mentioned in Chapter 15, "Web Commerce Options," every company with a stake in the Web, from IBM to Netscape, is developing its own "commerce servers" to provide secure financial transactions. You'll also notice that "electronic commerce companies," like First Virtual Holdings and Visa International, are busy developing ways to link their electronic payment systems to the Web.

Much of this technology remains untested in the real world. Why? You'll find articles in everything from *Internet World* to *The Wall Street Journal* harping on "security problems" and "technological hurdles." But the truth is that Web commerce is being approached with cautious optimism by its potential vendors—namely, those businesses with products and services to sell.

Selling on the Web

Many businesses are just beginning to establish a Web presence; they're quickly finding that they need to devote extra staff and resources to its maintenance. Soon, many of them will have to decide whether the profits from online sales will be worth an even larger outlay.

In other words, don't rip up your checkbook just yet! Web payment systems may someday become the norm, but it will be a slow change compared to other Internet phenomena. Businesses get into things for the long term, and that can take a long time!

A First Step to Web Commerce: The Online Catalog

It may be another year or more before payment transactions become commonplace on the Web, but online catalogs are already a standard way of providing product and service information to the connected public. After creating their initial Web site to advertise themselves on the Net, the next step most companies take is to list their product offerings. For most businesses, this is their first foray into Internet commerce!

A Few Problems

Unfortunately, such catalogs are often glorified, poorly formatted price lists slapped onto a Web server with little thought or effort. What users see is page after page of letters and numbers: this material is both harder to understand, and infinitely more boring than the old *Sears & Roebuck Catalog*!

Indices and query engines make online catalogs easier to follow. With them, a user can follow a product track or type in a keyword to search for a specific service. But what if a customer is interested in multiple products? Then he or she must search for and write the price down for each individual product, one at a time, unless the site's implementer has taken advantage of Netscape's "cookies" to permit creation of a virtual "shopping basket" along the way.

It's well known that the attention span of the average Web user is short. Users don't like to see the same thing twice, and they definitely don't want to wade through a huge listing of products or services just to find a few items! Making your Web interface interactive is a good way to make sure people get something out of your site when they visit. On the Web, interest in your products may not come from how nice your catalog looks, but what it *does*.

A final problem with catalogs is that prices change constantly. In some businesses, customers want to get an official quote for a range of services, and expect that quote to remain stable for a period of time. A catalog can provide them with prices, but you still need a sales staff to provide them with a quote—or do you?

A Simple Solution

Why not use some of the CGI skills you've developed to build an interactive quote engine? With that kind of approach, you can extend the manageability and functionality of your Web product catalogs.

THE QUOTE GENERATOR

A Web-based Quote Generator can resolve some of these online sales issues. A customer or an internal user could select services, let the program calculate the total costs involved, and return an estimate in a choice of formats.

Here's a wish list of what we would expect from such a program:

- An easy way to group and select products and services
- Quick, automatic calculation of total product or service costs
- A centralized price database, to ensure that quotes are consistent and official
- Web-based, for easy access from any Internet link
- Customer access limiting the need for outside sales staff
- Controlled access so that only certain internal users and external customers can generate quotes

- Estimates delivered to requesters in one of several formats: HTML, e-mail, or even fax

- An ability to interface with Web commerce systems in the future (including the framework we set up in Chapter 16, "A Web-Based UNIX Account Manager")

A Quote Generator's abilities can be more complex or simpler than those listed above, depending on what your company needs. The ones we've chosen provide a foundation for a versatile and powerful quote generation system.

Who Needs It?

We've already said that companies will have to decide individually whether Web commerce is their cup of tea. Likewise, they'll need to decide if the Quote Generator is a tool they can use. Nevertheless, we see two classes of potential users for this package:

- *External users*—Businesses that want customers to generate their own official quotes on the Internet. This reduces sales staff and provides the user with an interactive online catalog.

- *Internal users*—Businesses that want their sales staff to generate official quotes from a Web interface. Because it's available on the Net, this lets salespeople generate quotes anywhere, any time.

Sample Case: The Internet Service Provider

The perfect way to illustrate a Web-based Quote Generator is to return to our Internet Service Provider (ISP) example. As you know, ISPs offer a multitude of services, such as Dial-Up PPP, Dedicated ISDN, and Domain Name Services. They are also notorious for offering cryptic price lists, where you may or may not know what's included and what's an added option. The Quote Generator helps organize these services and provides a line-item listing. Here are some other reasons why the Quote Generator could be beneficial to an ISP:

- ISPs generally have a small staff. Letting the public generate its own service quotes frees up salespeople for higher-stakes, on-site pitches.

- Many ISPs are managed remotely as well as from an office. A Web-based quote interface on the Internet allows the sales force to view, e-mail, or fax quotes from any location.

- Most ISPs already have the infrastructure in place needed to run the Quote Generator. Such a service is a natural extension to their existing setup.

It's logical for a company that sells Internet services to make a quotation system available on the Internet. Now that we've determined what we'd like the Quote Generator to do, we need to design it.

Designing Our Quote Generator

From our functional description of the Quote Generator, we can extrapolate its required elements. These include a user interface, the Quote Processor itself, and a program to send the processor's output to the designated recipient. We'll look at each of these, and remember, we're not talking about specific programs yet, just "subsystems."

The User Interface

We've already decided that the UI will be Internet-based to support easy access, and the obvious choice is a Web browser with a quote entry front-end written in HTML. Since most browsers support the niceties required from a quote entry form, such as radio buttons, checkboxes, and lists, we can keep programming time to a minimum.

Second, graphical Web browsers are accessible from most users' Internet connections, and the HTML form looks much better than a command-line interface!

The Quote Processor

The Quote Processor is the part of the package that takes input from the Web and creates an estimate. It can be written in the language of your choice, depending on the size of your database and how frequently it's updated. For a small database Perl should be fine, but for a larger one you may want to consider C so as to benefit from its faster execution time. We won't discuss this program much in this chapter. As you'll see, it's situation-dependent and can even be a third-party package (like an SQL Server database on a Windows NT Server, or an Oracle or Informix database on a UNIX host). We're more concerned about the interface to the database, and how to best deliver its contents to the user.

The Quote Delivery System

The Quote Delivery System takes the output of the Quote Generator and makes it available to a user in various forms. It can deliver a quote via e-mail, via fax, or on the Web in an understandable format. It's the coolest part of the package!

This code is a prime candidate for C or Perl. We chose Perl because speed isn't really important for this subsystem. As you'll soon see, much of this part of the code is UNIX system calls and file manipulation—something that Perl handles with ease. Because it's easy to present and directly portable to a variety of UNIX systems, Perl is an ideal choice for this example.

We'll look at a Quote Generator built at OuterNet Connection Strategies, an ISP in Austin, Texas. It was built from scratch, with additions made as the company's business (and Web presence) expanded. We've left the comments in the code and expanded upon them in the text with historical notes and new ideas. That way, you'll get to follow the programmer's thought process during the implementation of the Quote Generator as we proceed.

THE FRONT PAGE: QUOTE_PAGE.HTML

The user interface in this package is an HTML form. Any UI should be functional and easy to use, so that's what we'll focus on here. We'll assume that you already have a working knowledge of the HTML forms tags and won't explain each in detail. For more information on this subject, please consult one of our other books: *HTML For Dummies* by Ed Tittel and Steve James (IDG Books, 1995) or *Foundations of World Wide Web Programming with HTML and CGI* by Ed Tittel, Mark Gaither, Sebastian Hassinger, and Mike Erwin (IDG Books, 1995).

Ready for Action?

The first part of the HTML form puts up a title. This is good, but not as important as what comes next. On a form, we need to know what type of form it is (whether it POSTs or GETs data), and what action should be performed once it's been submitted.

```
<!- quote_page.html created by mikee@outer.net (version 1.2) ->
<HTML>
<HEAD>
<TITLE>OuterNet Quote Generator</TITLE>
</HEAD>
<BODY>
<FORM METHOD="POST" ACTION="/cgi-bin/web_quote.pl">
<CENTER><H1>OuterNet Connection Strategies, Inc.<BR>
QuoteGenerator</H1></CENTER>
<HR>
```

The action of this form is to POST what users supply to the CGI program *web_quote.pl*. We'll discuss *web_quote.pl*'s job later.

Goods and Services

The next portion of "quote_page.html" gathers the data from user input on which specific services they want quoted. It's accomplished through an assortment of input text boxes, checkboxes, and selection lists. If you're familiar with HTML forms, none of this should be shocking. Notice also that the first part of the form captures a customer number to enable quote tracking.

```
<STRONG>Customer Information</STRONG><P>
Customer Number:
<INPUT SIZE=5 INPUT TYPE="text" NAME="c_customer_num" VALUE="17">
<HR>
```

The next entry field allows you to specify multiple account types for a single user. The rest are specific services that may be chosen.

```
<STRONG>Account Type (Connection Method)</STRONG><P>
Number of Accounts:
<INPUT SIZE=5 INPUT TYPE="text" NAME="accountnumbers" VALUE="1">
<P>
<SELECT MULTIPLE NAME="account_type">
<OPTION SELECTED>No Account
<OPTION>Dynamic SLIP/PPP
<OPTION>Dedicated SLIP/PPP
<OPTION>Dynamic 64K ISDN
<OPTION>Dynamic 128K ISDN
```

```
<OPTION>Network On-Demand 64K ISDN
<OPTION>Network On-Demand 128K ISDN
<OPTION>Dedicated 64K ISDN- Single Machine
<OPTION>Dedicated 64K ISDN- Multiple Machines
<OPTION>Dedicated 64K ISDN- Managed Multiple Machines
<OPTION>Dedicated 128K ISDN- Single Machine
<OPTION>Dedicated 128K ISDN- Multiple Machines
<OPTION>Dedicated 128K ISDN- Managed Multiple Machines
<OPTION>Dedicated 128K ISDN- Customer Managed
<OPTION>UUCP Dial-up Account- news/mail
</SELECT><P>
# of Nodes for a Customer Managed Net:
<SELECT NAME="custman_num">
<OPTION>1
<OPTION>16
<OPTION>32
<OPTION>64
<OPTION>96
<OPTION>256
</SELECT><BR>
<INPUT TYPE="checkbox" NAME="dialburst">
ISDN Dial Burst
<INPUT SIZE=5 INPUT TYPE="text" NAME="dialburst_num" VALUE="1"><BR>
<INPUT TYPE="checkbox" NAME="dedburst">
ISDN Demand/Dedicated Burst
<INPUT SIZE=5 INPUT TYPE="text" NAME="dedburst_num" VALUE="1"><BR>
<INPUT TYPE="checkbox" NAME="upgrade">
ISDN Network Upgrade (64k - 128k) or most ANY change of ISDN account
<INPUT SIZE=5 INPUT TYPE="text" NAME="upgrade_num" VALUE="1"><BR>
<HR>
<STRONG>Bundled Connection / Administration / Hosting
Services</STRONG><P>
<INPUT TYPE="checkbox" NAME="vsldy">
Virtual SLIP/PPP Web-Host Bundle
<INPUT SIZE=5 INPUT TYPE="text" NAME="vsldy_num" VALUE="1"><BR>
<INPUT TYPE="checkbox" NAME="vis64dy">
Virtual 64k ISDN Web-Host Bundle
<INPUT SIZE=5 INPUT TYPE="text" NAME="vis64dy_num" VALUE="1"><BR>
<INPUT TYPE="checkbox" NAME="vis128dy">
Virtual 128k ISDN Web-Host Bundle
<INPUT SIZE=5 INPUT TYPE="text" NAME="vis128dy_num" VALUE="1"><BR>
<HR>
<STRONG>Internet Administration Services</STRONG><P>
<INPUT TYPE="checkbox" NAME="dnsps">
Primary or Secondary DNS  *  Number of Domains:
<INPUT SIZE=5 INPUT TYPE="text" NAME="dnsps_num" VALUE="1"><BR>
<INPUT TYPE="checkbox" NAME="domreg">
```

```
Domain Name Registration
<INPUT SIZE=5 INPUT TYPE="text" NAME="domreg_num" VALUE="1"><BR>
<INPUT TYPE="checkbox" NAME="ftp">
FTP Site Administration
<INPUT SIZE=5 INPUT TYPE="text" NAME="ftp_num" VALUE="1"><BR>
<INPUT TYPE="checkbox" NAME="gopher">
Gopher Site Administration
<INPUT SIZE=5 INPUT TYPE="text" NAME="gopher_num" VALUE="1"><BR>
<INPUT TYPE="checkbox" NAME="wais">
WAIS Site Administration
<INPUT SIZE=5 INPUT TYPE="text" NAME="wais_num" VALUE="1"><BR>
<INPUT TYPE="checkbox" NAME="list">
Mailing List Site Administration
<INPUT SIZE=5 INPUT TYPE="text" NAME="list_num" VALUE="1"><BR>
<INPUT TYPE="checkbox" NAME="www">
World Wide Web Host Service
<INPUT SIZE=5 INPUT TYPE="text" NAME="www_num" VALUE="1"><BR>
<INPUT TYPE="checkbox" NAME="webman">
Managed World Wide Web Host Service
<INPUT SIZE=5 INPUT TYPE="text" NAME="webman_num" VALUE="1"><BR>
<INPUT TYPE="checkbox" NAME="webstat">
World Wide Web Reporting Service
<INPUT SIZE=5 INPUT TYPE="text" NAME="webstat_num" VALUE="1"><BR>
<INPUT TYPE="checkbox" NAME="sysadmin">
System Administration
<INPUT SIZE=5 INPUT TYPE="text" NAME="sysadmin_num" VALUE="1"><BR>
<HR>
<STRONG>Ancillary Services</STRONG><P>
<INPUT TYPE="checkbox" NAME="mail">
POP Mail Account
<INPUT SIZE=5 INPUT TYPE="text" NAME="mail_num" VALUE="1"><BR>
<INPUT TYPE="checkbox" NAME="shell">
Unix Shell Access
<INPUT SIZE=5 INPUT TYPE="text" NAME="shell_num" VALUE="1"><BR>
<INPUT TYPE="checkbox" NAME="fix">
Fixed IP Address
<INPUT SIZE=5 INPUT TYPE="text" NAME="fix_num" VALUE="1"><P>
Hardware Purchases (Dollar Amount):
<INPUT SIZE=15 INPUT TYPE="text" NAME="hardware" VALUE=""><BR>
Description:
<INPUT SIZE=45 INPUT TYPE="text" NAME="hardware_desc" VALUE=""><BR>
<HR>
<STRONG>Advanced Hosting and Outsourcing Services</STRONG><P>
<INPUT TYPE="checkbox" NAME="host">
OuterNOC Backbone Host Connection
<INPUT SIZE=5 INPUT TYPE="text" NAME="host_num" VALUE="1">
Amount:
```

```
<INPUT SIZE=10 INPUT TYPE="text" NAME="host_amount" VALUE=""><BR>
<INPUT TYPE="checkbox" NAME="source">
OuterNet's OuterSource
<INPUT SIZE=5 INPUT TYPE="text" NAME="source_num" VALUE="1">
Amount:
<INPUT SIZE=10 INPUT TYPE="text" NAME="source_amount" VALUE=""><BR>
<INPUT TYPE="checkbox" NAME="router_mgmt">
T1/Router Management Service
<HR>
<STRONG>Consultation Services</STRONG><P>
Network Consultation Hours:
<INPUT SIZE=4 TYPE="text" INPUT NAME="consult_hours"><BR>
Network Setup & Configuration Hours:
<INPUT SIZE=4 TYPE="text" INPUT NAME="config_hours"><BR>
Post-processing Hours:
<INPUT SIZE=4 TYPE="text" INPUT NAME="postprocess_hours"><BR>
Programming Hours:
<INPUT SIZE=4 TYPE="text" INPUT NAME="program_hours"><P>
<INPUT TYPE="checkbox" NAME="hourly_contract">
Check to use the reduced hourly rates for monthly recurring contract
with &gt; 10 hours.<BR>
<INPUT TYPE="checkbox" NAME="sysadmin_contract">
OuterNet's System Administration Anywhere contract.
<HR>
```

You'll notice that each of these fields is specific to OuterNet's business and includes items such as ISDN accounts, DNS services, Web services, and consulting hours. These are the primary things you'll want to change for your form, unless you also happen to be an ISP.

Some Useful Extensions

The next part of the form contains items useful to any business, and which add some nice extras to the form itself. We'll go through these piece-by-piece.

```
<STRONG>Other Details</STRONG><P>
Fax Number:
<INPUT SIZE=15 TYPE="text" INPUT NAME="fax_number"><BR>
E-Mail Address:
<INPUT SIZE =45 TYPE="text" INPUT NAME="mail_address"><BR>
```

The E-Mail Address and Fax Number fields are required if you wish to e-mail or fax quotes. The data from these fields is used by the Quote Delivery program.

```
Billing Option:
<SELECT NAME="billing_cycle">
<OPTION>Monthly
<OPTION>Half-Year
<OPTION>Annual
</SELECT>
<HR>
```

If your product or service has recurring charges, the Billing Option selection list allows you to decide how to bill your customers. This information can therefore also drive the Quote Generator. It's especially useful if you offer a discount for payment in advance.

```
<STRONG>Information to include with this quote:</STRONG><BR>
Note that only the 'mail' and 'fax' options use the following.<P>
<INPUT TYPE="checkbox" NAME="extra_info">
Information Page
<INPUT TYPE="checkbox" NAME="extra_price">
Price List
<INPUT TYPE="checkbox" NAME="extra_dis">
Disclaimer<BR>
<INPUT TYPE="checkbox" NAME="extra_cust">
Customer Data Sheet
<INPUT TYPE="checkbox" NAME="extra_dns">
NIC Domain Registration<BR>
<INPUT TYPE="checkbox" NAME="extra_noc">
OuterNOC Slick
<INPUT TYPE="checkbox" NAME="extra_src">
OuterSource Slick<HR>
```

If the checkboxes are selected, it tells the Quote Delivery System that the customer wants some extra information to be e-mailed or faxed. This can include any preformatted information, such as price lists, product information sheets, and warranties. It's a nice feature that extends your capabilities beyond simply faxing or e-mailing quotes.

```
<STRONG>Message:</STRONG><P>
<INPUT SIZE=70 TYPE="text" INPUT NAME="fax_message_1"><BR>
<INPUT SIZE=70 TYPE="text" INPUT NAME="fax_message_2"><BR>
<INPUT SIZE=70 TYPE="text" INPUT NAME="fax_message_3"><BR>
<INPUT SIZE=70 TYPE="text" INPUT NAME="fax_message_4"><P>
```

The Message lines let you include some text in the quote. In OuterNet's setup, a message is included with either a faxed or an e-mailed quote. This allows you to personalize a quote for a particular customer, or to notify them about pertinent information.

```
<SELECT NAME="who">
<OPTION>mikee
<OPTION>charlie
<OPTION>paul
<OPTION>singe
</SELECT>
```

This code helps keep track of its requester. OuterNet only permits a few people to generate quotes, so a selection menu is used here. It could just as easily be a text entry field, though, if you're opening it up to widespread use.

```
<SELECT NAME="Delivery_Method">
<OPTION>View Quote as Text
<OPTION>Fax Quote
<OPTION>Mail Quote as PostScript
<OPTION>Mail Quote as Text
<OPTION>Print Quote
<!—Next option is primarily for debugging purposes —>
<OPTION>View Quote as PostScript
</SELECT>
<INPUT TYPE="submit" VALUE="SUBMIT">
<HR>
<ADDRESS>staff@outer.net</ADDRESS>
<H5>web_quote.pl (v 2.1 Tue Oct 17 23:32:19 CDT 1995) created by:
<A HREF=mailto:mikee@outer.net>mikee@outer.net</A></H5>
</BODY>
</HTML>
```

The final selection menu covers the Delivery_Method for the quote. The options that OuterNet allows include: View Quote as PostScript (mostly for debugging, unless you speak PostScript), View Quote as Text, Fax Quote, Mail Quote as PostScript, Mail Quote as Text, and Print Quote. These are the functions that the current Quote Generator supports. As you add more features to your server, you can add more delivery options. Perhaps computer-generated voice quotes aren't too far off?

There's nothing more to the user interface. It's the easiest portion of this package to modify when you've made changes to the Quote Processor or Quote Delivery System. A view of OuterNet's Quote Generator Form appears in Figure 19-1.

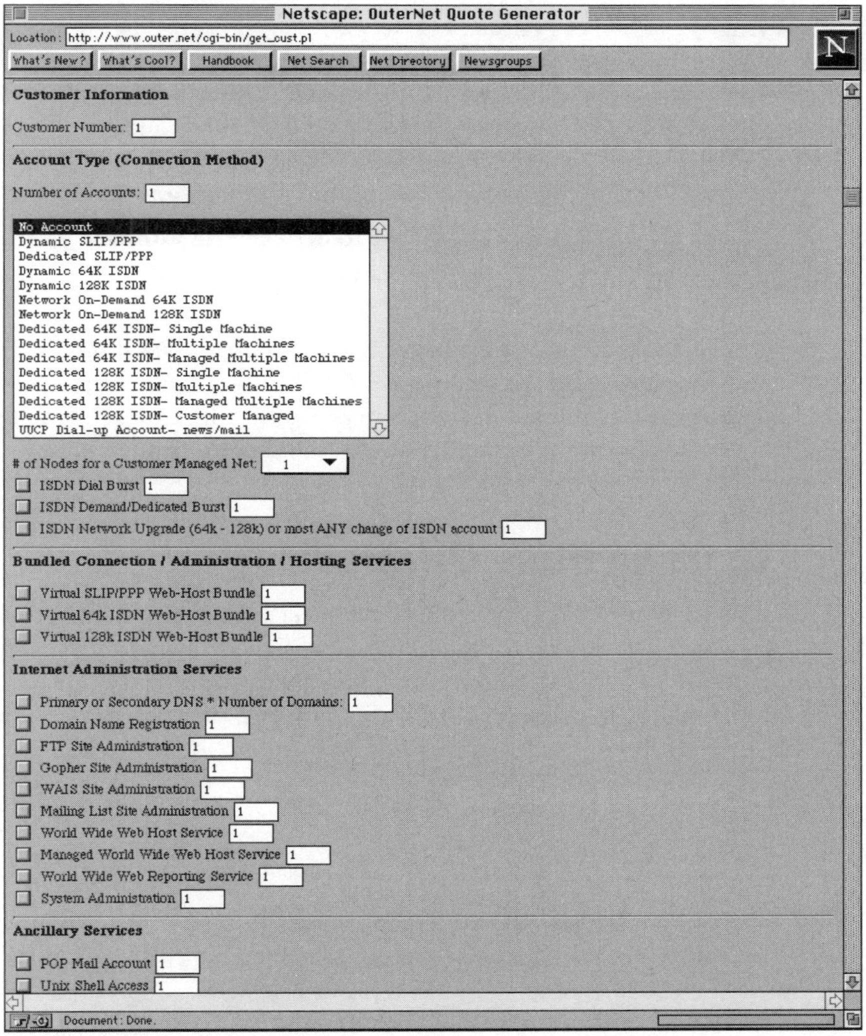

Figure 19-1
OuterNet's Customer Quote Generator Form.

Now that you have an idea of the data you'll need quotes for, you can send that data along to another program for processing. But first, let's discuss how OuterNet has set up its Quote Processor. You might find it a little peculiar, but you'll need to understand how it operates before we can move on.

Our Silent Partner: quote

To construct the estimates for the quotes, OuterNet uses a little program called, appropriately enough, *quote*. It does three things:

- Takes in the information on the products and services to be quoted
- Uses prices in its database to arrive at an estimate
- Creates text or PostScript output for the resulting estimate

This is the number-cruncher that we named the Quote Processor. It's also the subsystem we said we wouldn't fully discuss! Sorry to tease you: It's true that we won't get into the nitty-gritty of the code. But it's important to know this program's place in the overall picture of the Quote Generator.

Command-Line Oriented

Let's look at the history behind OuterNet's *quote* program. The *quote* program still retains its original basic design—it's a command-line program that takes a series of arguments. From these arguments it creates and prints an estimate, in either text or PostScript form, to a file or a printer.

To help you understand what input *quote* looks for, here's a list of its arguments:

```
Usage:  quote [-d] [-p]
        -c <customer#> -a <base account type:{}>
        [-x] [-h] [-H] [-s] [-f] [-r] [-o] [-t] [-q] [-w] [-e]
        [-b] [-z]

 -d debug mode
 -p output to printer
 -c <customer #>
 -a <base account type>
 -x <extra services>
 -h <"Hardware Description">
 -H <hardware cost in $>
 -s <consulting hours>
 -f <configuration hours>
 -r <programming hours>
 -o <postprocess_hours>
 -t Output as Text
```

```
-q <Customer Managed Network size>
-w <Number of domains to serve>
-e Hourly Contract Discounts
-b <billing period>
-z <Backbone Host cost in $>
Note: all items followed by text in "< >" require additional
input, if they appear in a quote invocation.
```

As you can probably guess, *quote* wasn't originally designed for Web use—that was an extension that came later. It was originally intended to be used from the UNIX command line. The benefit of its command-line form is that it can be interfaced to other front-ends such as Perl, Korn Shell, or X Windows.

Other Hidden Goodies

Something else *quote* does behind the scenes is to use the Customer Number (c_customer_num) field entered in "quote_form.html" to pull information out of OuterNet's Customer Quote Database. Before a quote is generated, all the user's contact information is entered into this database. The *quote* script, when generating the quote file, grabs this information to make a "Quote generated for:" section on the final output. That's how they know who the information's destined for.

Don't Quote Us!

The reason we're not delving into the *quote* program's code is that the Quote Processor can be *any* quote application! It can be a third-party package or something you write yourself. Its entire structure will be specific to your business and its focus. You can see from *quote* some basic functions that you may want, but it doesn't have to be implemented the same way. Instead of command-line options, you could read quote data from a file, or directly from an HTML form. For completeness' sake, we'll include the entire OuterNet implementation on the diskette that comes with this book.

For the record, OuterNet's *quote* program was originally written in C *and* has since been reprogrammed in Perl for manageability. If it ever becomes so large that waiting for a quote is unbearable, we'll probably port it back to C.

For our purposes, we're only concerned with how to interface the Quote Processor with the Web. The data that's posted in an HTML form doesn't automatically fit itself neatly into a format our Quote Processor can use. For that, we'll have to massage the data a bit. You'll remember that "quote_page.html" calls *web_quote.pl* when you submit the form, and that's where we're headed next.

MAKING IT ALL FIT: WEB_QUOTE.PL

The Perl script *web_quote.pl* is the first program that's actually invoked when a quote is requested. It's charged with taking the HTML form submission from "quote_page.html" and translating it into something our Quote Processor can understand. For instance, if your Quote Processor reads a certain file format to generate a quote from, you should program your version of *web_quote.pl* to write the form data into that file format. In our case, we'll convert the data into the parameter-line options that *quote* accepts.

web_quote.pl's Startup Items

web_quote.pl needs to set up a variety of items before it gets started. Essential to it is *formlib.pl*, a common Perl library that is handy for parsing HTML forms (it's so handy, in fact, that we've included a copy on the disk that ships with this book).

```
####################################################################
#
# INCLUDE THE FORMS PROCESSING PERL LIBRARY
#
####################################################################

#! Insert the location of your formlib.pl below.
require "/www/cgi-bin/formlib.pl";
```

Next are items that you shouldn't need to change; e.g., variables such as the processing of the date and time strings for quote logging.

```
####################################################################
#
#  VARIOUS STARTUP VARIABLES AND CONSTANT DEFINITIONS
#
####################################################################
```

```
$| = 1;  # Unbuffer STDOUT
# Various date formats to be used with logging and reporting
# functions.
$datestr = `date '+%m/%d/%y %H:%M:%S'`;
#! Since the millenium approaches, be prepared to change 19 to 20!
$logdate = `date '+%h %d %T 19%y'`;
$timedate = `date '+%H%M%S';  # Get a time string as well
chop ($logdate);       # Three lines of chopping
chop ($datestr);       # to remove superfluous
chop ($timedate);      # carriage returns.
```

You should change the next five constants to reflect your system. They hold the locations of various files used by *web_quote.pl*. The most important of these are $QUOTER, which is your Quote Processor, and $QUOTE_GENERATOR, which is your Quote Delivery System.

```
#! Here's the location of your Quote Generator.
$QUOTER = "/www/cgi-bin/quote";
#! The location of your log file.
$LOGFILE = "/usr/logs/quote.log";
#! Our quoter uses this file to number quotes.
$QUOTEFILE = "/www/cgi-bin/quote.num";
#! Where to put PostScript file to be made into ".g3" files.
$FAXDIR = "/home/transfer";
#! The intermediate Quote Generator.
$QUOTE_GENERATOR = "/www/cgi-bin/gen_quote.pl"
```

This next section uses the UNIX system call *cat* to view a file called "quote.num". This file contains the number of quotes generated so far. We then increment this by one for our current quote!

```
###############################################################
#
#  Get the number of the quote to be generated. We
#  use another script to produce the quote, called from
#  this script with the appropriate arguments. This lets us
#  make the correct log entries at the bottom of this form.
#
###############################################################
$quote_number = `cat "$QUOTEFILE"`;
$quote_number++;
#! Customize quote_filename to match your system settings.
$quote_filename = "\www\cgi-bin\quote_print.${quote_number}";
```

Working with the Form Data

Our first step in working with the data sent from the HTML form's POST is to separate the arguments, using *formlib.pl*'s GetFormArgs() command. This passes each piece of form data from "quote_page.html" into an '$in()' variable. We then re-assign each of these array values into a local variable of the same name, but without the '$in()', to be used in the code. This makes using the variables easier throughout the rest of the script. It also makes for a heck of a long list!

```
##########################################################################
#
# This section parses the POST arguments found in various
# environment variables from the "quote_page.html" form. You
# will notice that every environment value is assigned to a local
# variable of the same name. We could have used an associated
# '$in{}' variable wherever we use the local variable throughout the
# code, but for ease of use and readability we use reassignments.
#
##########################################################################
&GetFormArgs(); # parse arguments passed from FORM (now in %in)
$ENV{PATH_INFO} ne '' && &GetPathArgs($ENV{PATH_INFO});

# This is the popup with the delivery options.
$delivery = $in{Delivery_Method};

# This information is specific to our quoting engine. These two
# items are used to pull address and contact information.
$c_customer_num   = $in{c_customer_num};
$account_type     = $in{account_type};

# The telephone number of the fax machine to send to.
$fax_number       = $in{fax_number};

# Most of the following are specific options
# that the user has selected via the Web form:
# items relevant to OuterNet's business, such as
# hourly consulting, administration, and connection.
$config_hours       = $in{config_hours};
$program_hours      = $in{program_hours};
$consult_hours      = $in{consult_hours};
$postprocess_hours  = $in{postprocess_hours};

# Services are passed to this script in the following variables.
$hourly_contract    = $in{hourly_contract};
$sysadmin_contract  = $in{sysadmin_contract};

# Please note that since our quoter is a living
```

```
# script, it has some fields that are no longer in
# use, as well as some variables with no fields
# found on the form.
$dnsps              = $in{dnsps};
$shell              = $in{shell};
$mail_opt           = $in{mail};
$fix                = $in{fix};
$route              = $in{route};
$dialburst          = $in{dialburst};
$dedburst           = $in{dedburst};
$host               = $in{host};
$host_amount        = $in{host_amount};
$domreg             = $in{domreg};
$upgrade            = $in{upgrade};
$ftp                = $in{ftp};
$gopher             = $in{gopher};
$wais               = $in{wais};
$list               = $in{list};
$sysadmin           = $in{sysadmin};
$www                = $in{www};
$webman             = $in{webman};
$webstat            = $in{webstat};
$vsldy              = $in{vsldy};
$vis64dy            = $in{vis64dy};
$vis128dy           = $in{vis128dy};
$source             = $in{source};
$source_amount      = $in{source_amount};
$router_mgmt        = $in{router_mgmt};

$custman_num        = $in{custman_num};
$hardware           = $in{hardware};
$hardware_price     = $in{hardware_price};

$shell_num           = $in{shell_num};
$mail_num           = $in{mail_num};
$fix_num            = $in{fix_num};
$route_num          = $in{route_num};
$dialburst_num      = $in{dialburst_num};
$dedburst_num       = $in{dedburst_num};
$host_num           = $in{host_num};
$domreg_num         = $in{domreg_num};
$upgrade_num        = $in{upgrade_num};
$www_num            = $in{www_num};
$webman_num         = $in{webman_num};
$webstat_num        = $in{webstat_num};
$dnsps_num          = $in{dnsps_num};
$ftp_num            = $in{ftp_num};
```

```
$gopher_num        = $in{gopher_num};
$wais_num          = $in{wais_num};
$list_num          = $in{list_num};
$sysadmin_num      = $in{sysadmin_num};
$vsldy_num         = $in{vsldy_num};
$vis64dy_num       = $in{vis64dy_num};
$vis128dy_num      = $in{vis128dy_num};
$source_num        = $in{source_num};

$mail_address      = $in{mail_address};
$accountnumbers    = $in{accountnumbers};
$billing_cycle     = $in{billing_cycle};
$extra_info        = $in{extra_info};
$extra_price       = $in{extra_price};
$extra_dis         = $in{extra_dis};
$extra_cust        = $in{extra_cust};
$extra_dns         = $in{extra_dns};
$extra_noc         = $in{extra_noc};
$extra_src         = $in{extra_src};

$fax_message_1     = $in{fax_message_1};
$fax_message_2     = $in{fax_message_2};
$fax_message_3     = $in{fax_message_3};
$fax_message_4     = $in{fax_message_4};

$who               = $in{who};
```

The next part of the code tells all errors to report to a `null` device. We also have the obligatory `content-type`—when we send an HTML response from this program, we have to tell the browser we're sending it as HTML.

```
###############################################################
#
# Here we redirect the standard error to the trash. For debugging
# purposes we generally send the output to a file with a statement
# like:
# print STDERR "Here's where we think the error is: $some $data\n";
#
###############################################################
open (STDERR,"> /dev/null");


###############################################################
#
# APPROPRITE WEB HEADER INFORMATION
#
###############################################################
print "Content-Type: text/html\n\n\n";
```

By now all of our data should be in the proper places, and we need to translate that data into something our Quote Processor can comprehend.

Speaking to the Quote Processor

Most of *web_quote.pl*'s work is in converting the quote data we've received into a usable form for the Quote Processor. Since the input your Quote Processor needs is entirely dependent on what program you use, this is the section you'll need to change for your specific engine.

 OuterNet's *quote* script derives its quotes from command-line arguments, so our *web_quote.pl* needs to generate the parameters for it. We do this by checking for the existence of form data in each placeholder variable, such as '$wais' or '$gopher'. If it exists, then the script appends the appropriate flag (such as wais: or gopher:) to its parameter-line variable. In this case, we use the Perl string concatenation operator "dot" (.) to add the new commands to the variable '$PARAM_LINE'. This code handles everything from a POP mail account to delivering the output in text or PostScript! ▲

If your Quote Processor reads its input from a file, then this is the part of the script that you'll want to write to make that file. Again, this part of the program will be specific to your Quote Processor's needs.

Reading through the next section of code will give you the best idea of the types of things that should go on here.

```
###############################################################
#
# MAIN
#
# Here's where most of the work gets done in this script. The bulk
# of the processing requires building a parameter configuration
# line, which is then passed to the gen_quote.pl script. This
# script passes those arguments directly to the quoting engine
# (in our case a C program called:"quote"). The parameter line is
# stored in the variable '$PARAM_LINE' logically enough, with each
# service scrutinized, then appended to the running line as the
# script progresses.
#
# To create your own script, this is where
# you will need to test for the existence of services, data, or
# options. Most everything that follows is specific to our setup, but can
# easily be modified for other uses.
#
###############################################################
```

```perl
{
$PARAM_LINE = "";   # Initialize the parameter line.

@accounts = split("#", $account_type);
$PARAM_LINE .= " -c${c_customer_num}";

if ($host_amount) {
    $PARAM_LINE .= " -z${host_amount}";
}

if ($custman_num) {
    $PARAM_LINE .= " -q${custman_num}";
}

$PARAM_LINE = $PARAM_LINE." -a";
# The main popup that declares the exact service options
# is parsed within this big "for" loop.
for ($ct=0; $ct<=$#accounts; $ct++) {
if ($accounts[$ct] =~ "No Account") {
    $account_type = "nacct";
}
if ($accounts[$ct] =~ "Dynamic SLIP/PPP") {
    $account_type = "sldy";
}
if ($accounts[$ct] =~ "Dedicated SLIP/PPP") {
    $account_type = "slde";
}
if ($accounts[$ct] =~ "Dynamic 64K ISDN") {
    $account_type = "is64dy";
}
if ($accounts[$ct] =~ "Dynamic 128K ISDN") {
    $account_type = "is128dy";
}
if ($accounts[$ct] =~ "Network On-Demand 64K ISDN") {
    $account_type = "is64nod";
}
if ($accounts[$ct] =~ "Network On-Demand 128K ISDN") {
    $account_type = "is128nod";
}
if ($accounts[$ct] =~ "Dedicated 64K ISDN- Single Machine") {
    $account_type = "is64de";
}
if ($accounts[$ct] =~ "Dedicated 128K ISDN- Single Machine") {
    $account_type = "is128de";
}
if ($accounts[$ct] =~ "Dedicated 64K ISDN- Multiple Machines") {
    $account_type = "is64dem";
}
```

```
if ($accounts[$ct] =~ "Dedicated 128K ISDN- Multiple Machines") {
    $account_type = "is128dem";
}
if ($accounts[$ct] =~ "Dedicated 64K ISDN- Managed Multiple
Machines") {
    $account_type = "is64man";
}
if ($accounts[$ct] =~ "Dedicated 128K ISDN- Managed Multiple
Machines"){
    $account_type = "is128man";
}
if ($accounts[$ct] =~ "Dedicated 128K ISDN- Customer Managed") {
    $account_type = "is128cust";
}
if ($accounts[$ct] =~ "UUCP Dial-up Account- news/mail") {
    $account_type = "uucp";
}
for ($counter=1; $counter <= $accountnumbers; $counter++) {
    $PARAM_LINE .= "$account_type:";
    }
}
#
# As you can see, the script appends a string as each service is
# tested. We use the $bundle variable as a boolean placeholder
# to prevent accidently passing an incorrect string to the quoter.
#

if ($vsldy) {
    for ($ct = 1; $ct <= $vsldy_num; $ct++) {
        $PARAM_LINE .= "vsldy:";
    }
    $bundle = 1;
}
if ($vis64dy) {
    for ($ct = 1; $ct <= $vis64dy_num; $ct++) {
        $PARAM_LINE .= "vis64dy:";
    }
    $bundle = 1;
}
if ($vis128dy) {
    for ($ct = 1; $ct <= $vis128dy_num; $ct++) {
        $PARAM_LINE .= "vis128dy:";
    }
    $bundle = 1;
}
if (($bundle) && ($PARAM_LINE =~ "nacct")) {
    $PARAM_LINE =~ s/nacct\://;
}
```

```
chop ($PARAM_LINE); # Get's rid of the extra ":"

#
# These services are considered "ancillary" by our quoting engine
# and are referenced by the "-x" option followed by a string of
# service options. The section between the "if {}" builds up that
# part of the command line.
#
if ( $mail_opt || $shell || $fix || $dnsps || $domreg ||
 $upgrade || $dns || $route || $dialburst || $dedburst || $host ||
 $sysadmin || $www || $webman || $webstat || $ftp || $gopher ||
 $wais || $list || $router_mgmt ) {

$PARAM_LINE .= " -x";
if ($mail_opt) {
    for ($innerct=0; $innerct < $mail_num; $innerct++) {
        $PARAM_LINE .= "mail:";
    }
}
if ($shell) {
    for ($innerct=0; $innerct < $shell_num; $innerct++) {
        $PARAM_LINE .= "shell:";
    }
}
if ($fix) {
    for ($innerct=0; $innerct < $fix_num; $innerct++) {
        $PARAM_LINE .= "fix:";
    }
}
if ($dnsps) {
    $PARAM_LINE .= "dnsps:";
}
if ($domreg) {
    for ($innerct=0; $innerct < $domreg_num; $innerct++) {
        $PARAM_LINE .= "domreg:";
    }
}
if ($upgrade) {
    for ($innerct=0; $innerct < $upgrade_num; $innerct++) {
        $PARAM_LINE .= "upgrade:";
    }
}
if ($dns) {
    for ($innerct=0; $innerct < $dns_num; $innerct++) {
        $PARAM_LINE .= "dns:";
    }
}
```

```
        if ($route) {
            for ($innerct=0; $innerct < $route_num; $innerct++) {
                $PARAM_LINE .= "route:";
            }
        }
        if ($dialburst) {
            for ($innerct=0; $innerct < $dialburst_num; $innerct++) {
                $PARAM_LINE .= "dialburst:";
            }
        }
        if ($dedburst) {
            for ($innerct=0; $innerct < $dedburst_num; $innerct++) {
                $PARAM_LINE .= "dedburst:";
            }
        }
        if ($host) {
            for ($innerct=0; $innerct < $host_num; $innerct++) {
                $PARAM_LINE .= "host:";
            }
        }
        if ($sysadmin) {
            for ($innerct=0; $innerct < $sysadmin_num; $innerct++) {
                $PARAM_LINE .= "sysadmin:";
            }
        }
        if ($www) {
            for ($innerct=0; $innerct < $www_num; $innerct++) {
                $PARAM_LINE .= "www:";
            }
        }
        if ($webman) {
            for ($innerct=0; $innerct < $webman_num; $innerct++) {
                $PARAM_LINE .= "webman:";
            }
        }
        if ($webstat) {
            for ($innerct=0; $innerct < $webstat_num; $innerct++) {
                $PARAM_LINE .= "webstat:";
            }
        }
        if ($ftp) {
            for ($innerct=0; $innerct < $ftp_num; $innerct++) {
                $PARAM_LINE .= "ftp:";
            }
        }
        if ($gopher) {
            for ($innerct=0; $innerct < $gopher_num; $innerct++) {
                $PARAM_LINE .= "gopher:";
            }
        }
```

```
if ($wais) {
    for ($innerct=0; $innerct < $wais_num; $innerct++) {
        $PARAM_LINE .= "wais:";
    }
}
if ($list) {
    for ($innerct=0; $innerct < $list_num; $innerct++) {
        $PARAM_LINE .= "list:lstart:";
    }
}
if ($router_mgmt) {
    $PARAM_LINE .= "rtr:";
}
chop ($PARAM_LINE);
}

#
# Calculates the periodic rate to use as a multiplier (and
# discounter) for services purchased in monthly, semi-annual, or
# yearly packages.
#
if ($billing_cycle eq "Monthly") {
    $periodic = 1;
}
if ($billing_cycle eq "Half-Year") {
    $periodic = 6;
}
if ($billing_cycle eq "Annual") {
    $periodic = 12;
}

$PARAM_LINE =$PARAM_LINE." -b${periodic}";

if ($dnsps) {
    $PARAM_LINE =$PARAM_LINE." -w${dnsps_num}";
}

if ($hourly_contract) {
    $PARAM_LINE =$PARAM_LINE." -e";
}

if ($config_hours) {
    $PARAM_LINE =$PARAM_LINE." -f${config_hours}";
}

if ($consult_hours) {
    $PARAM_LINE =$PARAM_LINE." -s${consult_hours}";
}
```

```
    if ($program_hours) {
        $PARAM_LINE =$PARAM_LINE." -r${program_hours}";
    }

    if ($postprocess_hours) {
        $PARAM_LINE =$PARAM_LINE." -o${postprocess_hours}";
    }

    if ($hardware && $hardware_price) {
        $PARAM_LINE =$PARAM_LINE." -h\'${hardware}\' -
H${hardware_price}";
    }

    if ($delivery =~ "View Quote as PostScript") {
        $PARAM_LINE = $PARAM_LINE." ";
    }

    if ($delivery =~ "View Quote as Text") {
        $PARAM_LINE = $PARAM_LINE." -t ";
    }

    if ($delivery =~ "Fax Quote") {
        # $PARAM_LINE = $PARAM_LINE." -t ";
        $fax =1;
    }

    if ($delivery =~ "Mail Quote as PostScript") {
        $mail = 1;
    }

    if ($delivery =~ "Mail Quote as Text") {
        $PARAM_LINE = $PARAM_LINE." -t ";
        $mail = 1;
    }

    if ($delivery =~ "Print Quote") {
        $PARAM_LINE = $PARAM_LINE." -p ";
    }
```

As you can see, what this script actually does is pretty basic. It's just monotonous due to the number of services that may need an associated parameter. Is there any way to make this shorter? Probably—you could aggregate services, reducing the number of variables. For instance, have a selection menu for PPP or ISDN and then a checkbox for dial-up or dedicated. But this would limit the number of accounts you could quote for and require a restructuring of the HTML form itself.

Is Anyone Home?

Turning the form data into input for the Quote Processor doesn't take too long, but it's nice to let users know that something's happening before doing anything else. That's why we have the next portion of the script go ahead and send some HTML data to the Web client. It just lets them know that something's still going on!

```
# Here's where some output is given back to the Web client.  The
# document's title and a header is displayed.  Further processing
# is required to actually report that other actions have been
# performed.
#
print STDOUT "<TITLE>OuterNet Automated Quote</TITLE>\n";
print STDOUT "<H2>OuterNet Automated Quote</H2><P>\n";
print STDOUT "<B>Please wait while your quote is prepared.  This
normally takes about 1 minute.</B><P>\n";
```

Reach Out and Quote Someone

The last major section of *web_quote.pl* deals with sending the content of the quote to the Quote Delivery System. As you may remember, the Quote Delivery System is actually a subsystem rather than a specific program. If all the delivery code was removed from *web_quote.pl*, however, it would be easier to integrate with other quote engines and delivery programs. At least you'll get to learn from OuterNet's experience when you build your own version.

Back to the Command Line

Remember our parameter line? We need to store its arguments so we can use them with the Quote Delivery System, '$QUOTE_GENERATOR', when that script is called. In OuterNet's case, that is handled by *gen_quote.pl*.

```
# The first thing to do is to stash away the arguments that we
# toiled for so long to create. These are dumped into a file
# called "/tmp/quote.args". This file is read by $QUOTE_GENERATOR
# and handled from there. On a busy system, you may want to append
# the user's PID or a timestamp to this filename to ensure
# uniqueness.
#
```

```
open(PARAMS,">/tmp/quote.args");
print PARAMS "$PARAM_LINE";
close(PARAMS);
```

Calling the Quote Delivery System

Before we actually send the quote to the Quote Delivery System, we need to
decide how it's going to be sent. The script checks our form-input variables
'$mail' and '$fax' and if they're empty, it defaults to the "View as Text"
selection.

```
# Here we determine what delivery is needed for the end product.
# Note that a "View Text" selection will fall through to the
# "else" below.
#
if ($mail || $fax) {
  if ($mail) {
    ...
  }
  if ($fax) {
    ...
  }
# This is the fall through condition, which usually means that the
# user requested a view by text or similar mode. Simply put, the
# "quote" program is called directly rather than through the
# $QUOTE_GENERATOR above. (Yes, this is another prime candidate
# for housecleaning.) The following code calls the quoter, then
# opens up the file created, sending the text back at the Web
# user as <PREFORMATTED>.
#
  else {
    open(QUOTESTREAM,"/www/cgi-bin/quote ${PARAM_LINE} |");
    while (<QUOTESTREAM>) {
      $filename = $_;
    }
    close (QUOTESTREAM);
    chop ($filename);

    print STDOUT "<pre>";
    open (FILEHANDLE,$filename);
    while (<FILEHANDLE>) {
      print STDOUT;
    }
    close (FILEHANDLE);
    unlink($filename);
    print STDOUT "</pre>";
  }
```

The Mail Condition

If we've elected to mail the quote to someone, the first thing we need to do is save the Message data from the HTML form into something we can send as mail. Since it will ultimately be used by our Quote Delivery System, we need a way to pass it to that program. One method would be to pass the message as a command-line argument, but the quickest way is to generate a temporary message file that includes the data, so the quote deliverer can use it later.

```
if ($mail) {

#
# Creates the messages file for temporary storage. The data for
# these messages could be passed any number of ways, but this
# was quickest. Again on busy systems, you'd want to concatenate
# the user's PID or a timestamp for uniqueness.
#
    open (MESSAGEFILE, "> /tmp/messages");
print MESSAGEFILE "$fax_message_1\n$fax_message_2\n",
                  $fax_message_3\n$fax_message_4\n\n";
    close (MESSAGEFILE);
```

Next we call the quote deliverer, $QUOTE_GENERATOR. OuterNet named theirs *gen_quote.pl*, and it's the one we'll examine later. Notice that the script is backgrounded with the UNIX ampersand (&) operator, so the Web user doesn't have to wait for it to complete. This keeps your Web server or browser from timing out your connection. A quick return also keeps users from becoming bored or worried.

```
# Here's the call to the $QUOTE_GENERATOR. Notice we backgrounded
# the call to the script since it provides no output, and was
# designed so we don't have to wait for it to complete.
#
system("$QUOTE_GENERATOR -m -a${mail_address} &");
```

Make note of the options you're sending to the deliverer. It includes *quote*'s -m for e-mail and -a for the address.

Sending Extras

The next chunk of Perl continues its mail-handling but sends out "Extra Information," such as price lists and disclaimers, that we chose on our HTML form.

As the comments note, this might be better placed in the Quote Delivery System, *gen_quote.pl*. It's just one of those things you realize after you're already done, and you have too much to do to go back to it. Why take the extra time to fix an internal product that isn't really broken?

These items are mailed through system calls to *mailx*, a standard UNIX mailer. It's told to mail a specific, preformatted text file to whatever addresses are specified in $mail_address. That's what's wonderful about Perl; it makes passing variables to system calls so easy.

```
# Basically this just checks for the request of other information,
# then mails it out to the recipient(s).
#
if ($extra_info) {
    system ("/usr/bin/mailx -s \"Automated Information: OuterNet
            Connection Strategies, Inc.\" $mail_address <
            /usr/local/bin/information.outer.net");
}
if ($extra_price) {
    system ("/usr/bin/mailx -s \"Automated Prices: OuterNet
            Connection Strategies, Inc.\" $mail_address <
            /usr/local/bin/prices.outer.net");
}
if ($extra_dis) {
    system ("/usr/bin/mailx -s \"Automated Information: OuterNet
            Connection Strategies, Inc.: Service Agreement\"
            $mail_address < /usr/local/bin/disclaimer.outer.net");
}
if ($extra_dns) {
    system ("/usr/bin/mailx -s \"Automated Information: OuterNet
            Connections DNS Registration\" $mail_address <
            /www/cgi-bin/dns/domreg.form");
}
#
# A little feedback is always good.  That way, the Web user isn't
# scratching his or her head for too long.
#
print STDOUT "Mail has been successfully sent to: $mail_address\n";
}
```

Faxing a Quote

Unlike its mail counterpart, the fax condition doesn't do any extraneous delivery. It merely does its job of passing along information to the Quote Delivery System.

First, it makes sure that a fax number was entered (this is its only error checking). Next, like the mail portion, it concatenates the entered Message into a temporary file for later use by the '$QUOTE_GENERATOR'.

```
# Here's where the fax delivery option is realized. This script
# was designed to do minimal error checking, the least of which
# is that we check for the existence of a $fax_number before
# we try anything.
#
if ($fax) {
    if (! $fax_number) {
        print STDOUT "<H2>There was no fax number specified</H2>\n";
    }
    else {
        print STDOUT "<H2>The fax has been spooled and will be sent
                        within 1 hour</H2>";

        open(FAXMESSAGES, "> /tmp/faxmsgs");
        print FAXMESSAGES  "${fax_message_1}\n${fax_message_2}\n
                            ${fax_message_3}\n${fax_message_4}\n\n";
        close (FAXMESSAGES);
```

This final portion of the fax condition creates the argument line to send to the '$QUOTE_GENERATOR'. The important arguments are -f for Fax, -w for the fax's recipient, and -x for the fax number. The remaining arguments are specific to whatever $extra_... values you elect to send.

```
$argline = "-f -w${who} -x${fax_number} ";
if ($extra_info) {
    $argline .= "-i ";
}
if ($extra_price) {
    $argline .= "-p ";
}
if ($extra_dis) {
    $argline .= "-d ";
}
if ($extra_noc) {
    $argline .= "-y ";
}
if ($extra_src) {
    $argline .= "-z ";
}

system("$QUOTE_GENERATOR ${argline} &");
    }
  }
}
```

Once again, to keep our Web users from guessing, we run the quote deliverer in the background. That way, they don't have to wait until *gen_quote.pl* completes. ▲

Printing or Viewing Quotes

If neither mail nor fax was selected, then the default condition is to view the quote as text or print the quote. This is another portion of the code that should be in the Quote Delivery System, but isn't! Here *web_quote.pl* calls the Quote Processor directly, rather than using the '$QUOTE_GENERATOR'.

The output of the *quote* script is presented to the user as preformatted text using the HTML <PRE>...</PRE> tags. We know it's not beautiful, but it *is* easy, as shown in Figure 19-2. You could spruce it up by making the script look for certain output phrases and format them accordingly. In fact, the HTML table tags lend themselves nicely to quote output.

If the user chooses to "Print Quote," however, the -p option is set in the '$PARAM_LINE' variable, and the Quote Processor prints the quote in PostScript to your default printer. This print facility relies on your default system printer, so you'll want to check (and change) that assignment in advance if you have special printing needs for this information.

Another difference occurs between the text/print view and the mail and fax gateways: Because *web_quote.pl* uses *quote*'s output here, we can't run it in the background. The user will just have to wait!

```
# This is the default condition, which usually means that the
# user requested a view by text or similar mode. Simply put, the
# "quote" program is called directly rather than through the
# $QUOTE_GENERATOR above. Yes, this is another prime candidate for
# housecleaning. The following code calls the quoter, opens up
# the file created, and sends the text back to the Web user as
# preformatted text.
#
else {
#! Change to match the location of your cgi-bin directory:
    open(QUOTESTREAM,"/www/cgi-bin/quote ${PARAM_LINE} |");
    while (<QUOTESTREAM>) {
        $filename = $_;
    }
    close (QUOTESTREAM);
    chop ($filename);

    print STDOUT "<PRE>";
```

```
open (FILEHANDLE,$filename);
while (<FILEHANDLE>) {
    print STDOUT;
}
close (FILEHANDLE);
unlink($filename);
print STDOUT "</PRE>";
}
```

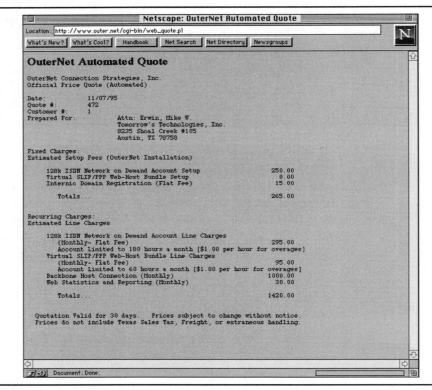

Figure 19-2
A quote from OuterNet viewed as text.

Keeping Track of Our Quotes

Since we may allow external users to access our Quote Generator, we need to keep track of what's going on. A log file allows you to build a history of quotes to track demand and activity. It also allows you to validate your quotes. You'll notice that we save command-line arguments so we can use these parameters to regenerate a quote at any time.

```
# Finally, we make a log of what's happening. Since our quote
# generator is open to public abuse in the future, we want to keep
# tabs on what's going on (by whom and when).
#
$quote_number = `cat "$QUOTEFILE"`;
open (LOG,">>$LOGFILE");
print LOG "$datestr: $quote_number: $c_customer_num: $delivery:
$PARAM_LINE\n";
close (LOG);
}
```

We now know that the primary purpose of *web_quote.pl* is to format information for the Quote Processor. We've also seen that, when coded as designed, it shouldn't actually call the quote engine itself. It's intended to call the Quote Delivery mechanism, defined as '$QUOTE_GENERATOR', which is *gen_quote.pl* in our example. Now, let's see how OuterNet sends quotes to its customers.

THE WORLD'S FASTEST QUOTES: GEN_QUOTE.PL

Our Quote Delivery System, *gen_quote.pl*, actually calls the Quote Processor and passes the parameter line generated by *web_quote.pl*. From there, it takes the Quote Processor's output and sends it to its final destination.

This script is called directly from *web_quote.pl*. If it has no output to send to the user's Web interface (as when you're mailing or faxing a quote), it can run as a background task.

In its current implementation, *gen_quote.pl* can send quotes as faxes or e-mail. It is open enough that other gateways could be added in the future. That's because this script uses a conglomeration of UNIX utilities and third-party applications to perform its gateway functions. Among these programs are: *mailx*, *enscript*, *Ghostscript*, and *mgetty+sendfax*. We'll delve into the role each of these tools plays in quote delivery.

You'll also begin to realize that you don't *have* to use some of these utilities: You may prefer others out there that provide even more functionality. Or, you might have your own applications gateway to use.

Some External Program Definitions

First we'll define the locations of a couple of programs we'll be using repeatedly. The first is the location of your mailer, *mailx*. The second is a utility that converts text into PostScript, defined at '$POSTSCRIPT_CVRTR'. For its converter, OuterNet chose *enscript* because it ships with the A/UX UNIX implementation they use. If *enscript* doesn't ship with your UNIX system, a shareware converter like *Ghostscript* will work.

```
# Defines the location of your mailer.
$MAILER            = "/usr/bin/mailx";
# A program that converts text->postscript
$POSTSCRIPT_CVRTR  = "/usr/bin/enscript -p- ";
#
# We use a program called "enscript" that comes with A/UX to
# convert our files to PostScript. However, we do have ghostscript
# installed, which would be a perfectly acceptable solution.
# You could also just produce a ".ps" file directly.
```

Ghostscript is a versatile utility that converts PostScript to and from many other file formats. We'll also be using *Ghostscript* later in *gen_qoute.pl* to convert PostScript to a Group 3 fax format. It's available for UNIX, Windows, Mac, OS/2, and other platforms. To locate a copy of *Ghostscript*, please visit:

```
http://www.cs.wisc.edu/~ghost/ghostscript/obtaina.html
```

The only way around using a converter would be to have the data in "Extra Information" sheets already in PostScript format. The only problem is that this would force you to use some type of word processor to update them!

Chewing Through Our Options

To process the command-line arguments sent to *gen_quote.pl* from *web_quote.pl*, you'll need to include the standard Perl 4 library *getopts.pl* (this library is also available with Perl5, so this shouldn't be a problem for those who wish to run it in a Perl5 environment). This library contains the 'Getopts()' procedure, which parses for the options it's given. The data from these options is then passed into variables that are easier to use.

```
################################################################
#
# PROCESS COMMAND-LINE OPTIONS
#
################################################################
require "getopts.pl";
&Getopts('mfia:psw:x:yz');

$mail = $opt_m;              # User wants to mail results to recipient.
$fax = $opt_f;              # User wants to fax the results.
$extra_info = $opt_i;       # Send along Extra Information Sheet.
$extra_price = $opt_p;      # Send along a price list.
$extra_dis = $opt_d;        # Send along a disclaimer.
$who = $opt_w;              # The name of the sender.
$fax_number = $opt_x;       # The fax telephone number.
$mail_address = $opt_a;     # The mail address of the recipient.
$noc = $opt_y;              # Send along a product slick.
$source = $opt_z;           # Send along a different product slick.
```

More Constants and Variables

There are several more items commonly used in the script. The '$FAXDIR' constant names the directory where intermediate fax work, such as format conversions, should take place. It can be anywhere, but since you'll be moving, converting, and deleting many files there, make it a dedicated directory. You'll also want to make sure that your Web server's user ID (such as www) has read and write permissions to that directory.

Quote arguments that *web_quote.pl* placed in the "quote.args" file will be moved into the '$arguments' variable. We'll be using those next.

```
################################################################
#
# SET UP SOME CONSTANTS AND SOME VARIABLES
#
################################################################

$FAXDIR = "/home/transfer";
#! If you've concatenated PID or timestamp info to make sure this
#! filename is unique, update this value here, too!
$arguments = `cat "/tmp/quote.args"`;
chop($arguments);
```

Getting Our Quote with quote

It's finally time to run the Quote Processor! The *quote* script, now complete with its arguments, is opened within a datastream. Behind the scenes, the *quote* program creates a file containing the quote in either text or PostScript form. The name of the resulting file is piped to standard output (STDOUT) and stored in a variable called '$filename'.

```
# The quoter returns the filename on standard output. This
# filename is used for processing below.
open(QUOTESTREAM,"/www/cgi-bin/quote $arguments |");
while (<QUOTESTREAM>) {
  $filename = $_;
}
close (QUOTESTREAM);
chop ($filename);
```

E-Mailing the Quote

This section of the script is quite simple. First it checks to see if the '$mail' option was selected. If so, it appends the quote file "$filename" to the "messages" file, writes the combined contents back into "$filename", and finally deletes the "messages" file. It takes the new "$filename" package and sends it to the person specified in '$mail_address' using the mailer we defined earlier.

```
########################################################################
#
# MAIL
#
# The quote engine that is engaged above will produce a text or
# PostScript file which is then mailed to the user specified below.
# Since there are 4 lines of messages that can be echoed to the
# user, these are handled by appending the text quote to the
# "/tmp/messages" file, produced by "web_quote.pl".
#
########################################################################
if ($mail) {
  system("cat $filename >> /tmp/messages");
  system("cp /tmp/messages $filename");
  system ("rm -f /tmp/messages");
  system ("${MAILER} -s \"Automated Quote Generation: OuterNet
Connection Strategies, Inc.\" $mail_address < $filename");
}
```

What gets sent looks like the e-mail message shown next. Of course, real appearances will depend on the output your version of *quote* produces.

```
Date: Thu, 9 Nov 1995 11:29:13 -0600
From: WWW Master (Outernet) <www>
To: charlie@outer.net
Subject: Automated Quote Generation: OuterNet Connection Strategies,
Inc.


Thanks for your interest in OuterNet!
Sincerely,
OuterNet Sales



OuterNet Connection Strategies, Inc.
Official Price Quote (Automated)

Date:          11/09/95
Quote #:       476
Customer #:    1
Prepared For:          Attn: Erwin, Mike W.
                       Tomorrow's Technologies, Inc.
                       8235 Shoal Creek #105
                       Austin, TX 78758

Fixed Charges:
Estimated Setup Fees (OuterNet Installation)

    Dedicated 128K ISDN- Customer Managed [32] Setup     100.00
    Internic Domain Registration (Flat Fee)               15.00


        Totals...                                         115.00



Recurring Charges:
Estimated Line Charges

    Dedicated 128K ISDN- Customer Managed [32] Line Charges
        (Monthly- Flat Fee)                               200.00
    DNS Primary or Secondary Service (Monthly)             20.00
    Backbone Host Connection (Monthly)                     95.00
    Managed Web Host Service (Monthly)                    125.00


        Totals...                                         440.00
Quotation Valid for 30 days.   Prices subject to change without
notice.
```

Faxing the Quote

Faxing a quote is a little more complex than mailing one. That's because there's some preprocessing involved to get the quote into the correct format. OuterNet uses a fax gateway shareware package called *mgetty+sendfax*. This suite of programs contains a *getty* replacement to receive faxes (*mgetty*) and a program that sends fax files (*sendfax*). You'll find documentation and archives for *mgetty+sendfax* at the following location:

```
http://www.leo.org/~doering/mgetty/
```

The *sendfax* program requires its files be in Group 3 fax format. These files typically take the extension ".g3". Any text files we need to fax must be converted into PostScript first. Then all PostScript files must be converted into ".g3" format. Don't worry, we have plenty of third-party tools at our disposal. The comments below provide a good summary of what happens.

```
################################################################
#
# FAX
#
# The quote can also be faxed to a user. Some preprocessing is
# required, since we need g3 format fax files for the transfer and
# most of our files are raw text to begin with (some may be
# PostScript). The first section converts the extra information
# pages into PostScript and places them in the middle-man fax
# directory "$FAXDIR". The $noc and $source files are
# precooked ".g3" files for some of our product slicks, made up
# with Ghostscript. We then calculate the total page count (to
# be supplied on the fax cover sheet) and process the messages
# that need to go there as well. The last part of this script
# queues the fax, which is then picked up by mgetty at the
# next fax run (faxrunq) which is every 15 minutes on our fax
# UNIX box.
#
################################################################
```

The First Step: A Conversion to PostScript

As we said, we must convert any text files into PostScript files before we can process them further. To do this we use the PostScript converter defined in '$POSTSCRIPT_CVRTR'. These text files include various "Extra Information" files selected in "quote_form.html". These files could have been in PostScript already, but storing them as text lets you create a single file for both fax and e-mail. That's one less file you'll have to update when making changes!

It would, however, be much more efficient from a processing standpoint to have a setup where a batch conversion process is automatically kicked off to generate the g3 conversion each time a change is made to the ASCII files—this wouldn't be too difficult and would prevent the need to convert each time a user requests a quote (which could be frequently on a busy quoting system). For our needs this approach was adequate, but you'll want to consider your own situation when implementing such a utility for your site.

This section of the script also contains the variables for the number of pages for each document:

```
if ($fax) {
    if ($extra_info) {
        $info_pgs = `${POSTSCRIPT_CVRTR}
                    /usr/local/bin/information.outer.net >
                    ${FAXDIR}/info.ps`;
    $info_pgs = 1;
}
if ($extra_price) {
    $price_pgs = `${POSTSCRIPT_CVRTR}
                  /usr/local/bin/prices.outer.net >
                  ${FAXDIR}/prices.ps`;
    $price_pgs = 3;
}
if ($extra_dis) {
    $dis_pgs = `${POSTSCRIPT_CVRTR}
                /usr/local/bin/disclaimer.outer.net >
                ${FAXDIR}/disclaimer.ps`;
    $dis_pgs = 1;
}
```

OuterNet does have a couple of product information sheets already in ".g3" format because they're too fancy to handle using plain text. In these cases, we simply define the number of pages for each document.

```
# We don't PostScriptize these because they're ".g3" already.
if ($noc) {
    $noc_pgs = 2;
}
if ($source) {
    $source_pgs = 2;
}
```

At the end we just add up the total number of pages for the documents selected so we can tell *sendfax* how many pages to send.

```
#
# Calculate the total number of pages in the fax.
#
$total_page_faxed = $info_pgs + $price_pgs + $dis_pgs + $noc_pgs +
                    $source_pgs + 2;
```

Looking Official: Generating a Fax Cover Page

To give your fax system a well-rounded feel, you can add a piece of code to generate a cover sheet from information you already have.

One thing you might like to include on your cover sheet is the "Message" entered on "quote_form.html". Those message lines were saved by *web_quote.pl* into a file for later use. Before you use them again, you'll need to extract them from the file and put them into a variable array. That's what the following code does:

```
#
# Get the messages from the message file and replace where
# appropriate on the cover sheet. The calling script produced a file
# in the /tmp directory, which is read into an array called
# "fax_message".
#
open(FAXMESSAGES, "/tmp/faxmsgs");
while (<FAXMESSAGES>) {
        $fax_message[$ct++] = $_;
}
close (FAXMESSAGES);
```

OuterNet's *quote* program already generates a cover sheet based on the customer information read from OuterNet's quote database. This sheet is a PostScript file that we'll continue to change on-the-fly!

All we really need to do is find certain tags within the PostScript file and replace them with our variables; i.e., number of pages to fax and the messages. The find/replace expressions in Perl make this a snap!

```
#
# The quote engine is nice enough to create a cover sheet if the
# fax option # is specified on its command line. Here we open up
# the cover sheet (which turns out to be a PostScript file) in
# need of marking up. The remainder is merely a find/replace on
# some keywords found embedded in the PostScript.
#
  open (COVERSTREAM, "cat $filename.cover |");
  open (NEWCOVER, "> $filename.cover.1");
  while (<COVERSTREAM>) {
    $line = $_;
    if ($line =~ '\<\<pages\>\>') {
      $line =~ s/\<\<pages\>\>/$total_page_faxed/;
    }
    if ($line =~ '\<\<noteline1\>\>') {
      $line =~ s/\<\<noteline1\>\>/$fax_message[0]/;
    }
    if ($line =~ '\<\<noteline2\>\>') {
      $line =~ s/\<\<noteline2\>\>/$fax_message[1]/;
    }
    if ($line =~ '\<\<noteline3\>\>') {
      $line =~ s/\<\<noteline3\>\>/$fax_message[2]/;
    }
    if ($line =~ '\<\<noteline4\>\>') {
      $line =~ s/\<\<noteline4\>\>/$fax_message[3]/;
    }
    print NEWCOVER $line;
  }
  close ( COVERSTREAM );
  close ( NEWCOVER );
```

Making PostScript Faxable

Now, we have all the PostScript files we need: a cover sheet, a quote, and any extra information to be sent. Before we can fax these files, they must be converted into the Group 3 fax format. That's where *Ghostscript* comes back into the picture.

The first step is to rename the quote and cover files to something specific to the recipient, using fax number and contact name. At the same time, we copy them into '$FAXDIR', where our fax conversions take place.

For OuterNet, '$FAXDIR' is an NFS-mounted directory available on several machines, so that different systems have access to it. This technique is used because OuterNet's fax gateway runs on a different system than their Web server.

Once the PostScript files are in the '$FAXDIR', we can begin to use them. OuterNet's fax gateway is called *goanna*, so we must spawn a remote shell on that machine for further fax processing.

In the first instance, the remote shell runs a short script called *faxout.pl*. This script simply calls *Ghostscript* to convert the ".ps" files into ".g3". Then a utility called *faxspool* runs against the ".g3" files. It's the part of the *mgetty+sendfax* package that loads ".g3" files into the fax queue.

```
# Here's where most of the fax work is done. Once the files
# have been made, the few that don't exist in $FAXDIR are copied
# there, and a script is run to feed them to the fax gateway
# (/usr/local/bin/faxout.pl).
#
# In short, the "/usr/local/bin/faxout.pl" script runs Ghostscript
# against the .ps files in the $FAXDIR directory then runs
# "/usr/local/bin/faxspool" to insert them into the fax queue.
#
system ("cp $filename $FAXDIR/${fax_number}-${who}-quote.ps");
system ("cp $filename.cover.1 $FAXDIR/${fax_number}-cover.ps");
system ("rm -f ${filename}.cover.1 ${filename}");
system ("/usr/bin/remsh goanna '/usr/local/bin/faxout.pl >
        /tmp/output.1' &");
```

The Final Pages

The last documents to be faxed are the "fancy" ones we mentioned earlier that are already in ".g3" format. Shells are spawned to the fax gateway and *faxspool* is run directly on these files. The following code gives you an idea of the arguments that *faxspool* can take:

```
# Since these packages are stored in g3 format already, all that's
# needed is to initiate the spooling process.
#
#
if ($noc) {
    system ("/usr/bin/remsh goanna '/usr/local/bin/faxspool -f
```

```
                    ${who} ${fax_number} /usr/spool/fax/templates/on1.g3
                    /usr/spool/fax/templates/on2.g3' &");
    }
    if ($source) {
        system ("/usr/bin/remsh goanna '/usr/local/bin/faxspool -f
                    ${who} ${fax_number} /usr/spool/fax/templates/src1.g3
                    /usr/spool/fax/templates/src2.g3' &");
    }
    }
```

That's it! Given the code and third-party utilities used, you should be able to generate a quote and view it on the Web, send it via e-mail, or as a fax. As with all CGI programs, placement and permissions are important to proper working. So now let's go over how to install and use the Quote Generator.

INSTALLING THE QUOTE GENERATOR

Before installing the Quote Generator itself, make sure you have these third-party applications:

- *Ghostscript* for PostScript file processing. Some Linux distributions come with it installed.

- *enscript* for text-to-PostScript processing. This may come with your UNIX distribution. If you don't have it, use *Ghostscript*.

- *mgetty+sendfax* for spooling and sending ".g3" fax files. This doesn't come with any OS distributions that we know of, though there are probably similar packages that do.

If these aren't available on your particular system, check the URLs mentioned earlier. If you can't port these tools to your system, you'll have to hunt down equivalents.

Each application has its own installation instructions; please follow them carefully. You shouldn't need to modify any of the third-party code to get it to interface with the Quote Generator.

Once you have these utilities installed, you can move on to the Quote Generator itself.

Editing the Variables

You'll recall that in the code we referenced various variables with a #! in their comments. These are the variables you'll need to tailor for your specific system. Go through the code carefully and find them!

The entire Quote Generator code is designed to be a framework. Ultimately, you should be able to change any part of it to fit your needs.

Placing the CGI

Probably the best way to describe where to put the files, who should own them, and what their permissions should be, is to use a table. Table 19-1 supplies this information for "quote_page.html", *web_quote.pl*, *quote*, and *gen_quote.pl*.

Table 19-1

Location, ownership, and permissions for Quote Generator files

File	Location	Owner	Permissions
quote_page.html	Directory containing your HTML documents.	www.httpd	644
web_quote.pl	/www/cgi-bin*	www.httpd	750
quote	$QUOTER	www.httpd	750
gen_quote.pl	$QUOTE_GENERATOR	www.httpd	750

/www/cgi-bin should be the path of the standard HTTP *cgi-bin* on your system.

Limiting Access

The Quote Generator was designed to be used inside or outside your organization. You may not necessarily want external users to be able to access every feature. Imagine anyone on the Web being able to send a fax from your gateway anywhere in the world!

For such cases, use a scaled-down "quote_form.html" that allows users only to view or e-mail quotes. The fax function is included in the full "quote_form.html", which resides in a directory protected by an ".htaccess" file (like that available in NCSA's *httpd)*. This approach allows you to limit fax ability to internal or a few external users who have a valid username and password. ▲

USING THE QUOTE GENERATOR

This program is quite easy to use—there's really only one user interface involved. It's the Web-based form generated by "quote_form.html", seen in Figure 19-1, and should be quite simple for you to update on your own.

In fact, most of the work involved in the Quote Generator is getting it to interface with your quote database and Quote Processor. Hopefully, we've given you enough information in this and other chapters to help you handle the assignment.

FUTURE ADDITIONS TO THE CGI

The Quote Generator isn't designed to be an all-in-one program. Rather, it's meant to be a CGI for whatever Quote Processor you intend to use. We're not concerned so much with how a quote's generated, as with how to gather and present quotes using the Web.

Since this package is just an extension to your quote system, it's completely open-ended about what it can do. Whenever you feel like updating the abilities of the package, go ahead and do it! Or, if you add new functionality to your Quote Processor, you can edit the scripts to facilitate those changes.

Here are a few ideas for further extensions to the Quote Generator:

- *An e-mail quote parser:* Using methods similar to those employed by *parse.in.www.mail* from our DNS Admin CGI, we can create an e-mail quote parser. Incoming mail *to quote* can be redirected to a parser that grabs quote information from a standard e-mail form. If you want to make it more complex, you can forgo the form and make it search for certain keywords, like "Dedicated" and "ISDN." However, it may take a while to iron the bugs out of parsing a free-form e-mail message. The benefit of an e-mail quote system is that any customer can use it with minimal security risk to the fax or other gateways. It could automatically reply to a sender's e-mail with its quote.

- *View quote as HTML:* This seems like a good next step for your generator. It would make the Web-based quote output look better than preformatted text. You could even include graphics of your products or services! There are several ways to go about implementing the necessary HTML:

— Have *gen_quote.pl* add HTML tags to text generated by quote. It would look for certain keywords and know what tags should be associated with those keywords.

— Make HTML another option for quote, just as it takes text as an option now. It can add HTML tags the same way it handles PostScript formatting. This would be a faster and more reliable option than Option 1.

— Create an HTML template document for output, with predefined variable entries, and have the contents of those variables filled in by quote.

The e-mail parser and the HTML translator shouldn't be hard for you to add. Both will illustrate how simple it is to add new gateways to your Quote Generator as they come along. The HTML and CGI-generating tools we've described in earlier chapters should make integrating them even easier.

For external users, the Quote Generator brings life to your online catalog through its interactivity. For internal users, it's a powerful sales tool that lets them supply customers with information in a variety of formats from anywhere there's a Net connection!

Other than sprucing up your catalog, the Quote Generator also provides the foundation for a full-fledged Web commerce system. All you need now is an electronic payment method. Once you open an online store, you'll want to find out which product areas customers find most interesting—that is, the pages they actually spend time reading, and the ones they just click straight past. That information is available in a variety of logs, but you need a way to manage it. That's where the User-Session Tracking Tool comes in handy.

Summary

As you investigate the code for the Quote Generator, remember that it represents one particular ISP's solution to the problem of managing customers online. You'll probably be able to reuse much of the code and many of the ideas that you see expressed in this collection of programs. Just make sure that you tailor its behavior to match your own peculiar circumstances—and the prices—so you don't end up quoting somebody else's services instead of your own. Now, onward to Chapter 20.

AUTOMATIC CREATION OF A MOMSPIDER INSTRUCTION FILE

*I*n this chapter we will present a series of CGI scripts designed to automatically create a Multi-Owner Maintenance spider (MOMspider) instruction file.

WALKING A WEB WITH MOMSPIDER

MOMspider is a Web-walking robot written by Roy Fielding at the Department of Information and Computer Science at the University of California, Irvine; the URL for this robot is:

```
http://www.w3.org/pub/WWW/People/
```

In 1993, Mr. Fielding joined the staff of the WWW Consortium (W3C) to develop Web maintenance tools. He is also the author of *libwww-perl*, a WWW protocol Perl library for Web clients; it can be found at:

```
http://www.ics.uci.edu/pub/websoft/libwww-perl/
```

MOMspider's specialty involves the maintenance of distributed Webs—also known as *wide-area infostructures* or just plainly *infostructures*. MOMspider is implemented in Perl 4.036 for any UNIX-based system and is freely available. Visit this URL for more information:

```
http://www.ics.uci.edu/WebSoft/MOMspider/
```

MOMspider produces a variety of reports, but its primary purpose is to produce a report that contains hypertext linking information found in each HTML document included in the search domain. Think of this report as a metamap—a map of maps, where each map is a list of any individual HTML document's links. A traversal can include three kinds of links: links inside the same document, links to other documents on the same server, and documents on multiple servers.

MOMspider is typically run on a UNIX command line by a WebMaster. It's an aid to help snoop out and fix bad links in your Web, before you get a deluge of e-mail messages complaining about a broken link. Humans have difficulty processing all that information; MOMspider, on the other hand, handles it with grace and panache.

For each Web trek, MOMspider requires an instruction file as its input. These instructions dictate where the robot goes, and what it sees (in other words, the instructions govern MOMspider's Web-walking behavior). The instruction file has two parts that must occur in this order:

1. Optional global directives
2. Required traversal tasks

The MOMspider instruction file uses a rigid syntax and organization consisting of a series of optional global directives, followed by a series of traversal tasks. Global directives are used by MOMspider to set its configuration options; it then performs each traversal task in the order found in the instruction file. Once MOMspider has completed the last traversal task, it outputs a summary of the entire process before terminating. Lines beginning with # and any blank lines are ignored. Instruction directives must be on a single line regardless of their length (effectively limiting them to 256 characters or less, on most systems).

Here's a sample MOMspider instruction file:

```
# MOMspider instruction file
#
# Global directives
```

```
AvoidFile   /www/admin/.momspider-avoid
SitesFile   /www/admin/.momspider-sites

# Traversal task
<Tree
    Name            Tree-Test
    TopURL          http://www.foo.com/docs/test/index.html
    IndexURL        http://www.foo.com/admin/MOM/Tree-Test.html
    IndexFile       /www/admin/MOM/Tree-Test.html
    IndexTitle      MOMspider Index for Tree-Test
    EmailAddress    webmaster@foo.com
    EmailBroken
    EmailRedirected
    EmailChanged    7
    Exclude         http://www.foo.com/docs/test/index.html
>
# Traversal task
<Site
    Name            Foo-Web
    TopURL          http://www.foo.com/
    IndexURL        http://www.foo.com/admin/MOM/Foo-Web.html
    IndexFile       /www/admin/MOM/Foo-Web.html
    IndexTitle      MOMspider Index for Foo-Web
    EmailAddress    webmaster@foo.com
    EmailBroken
    EmailRedirected
    Exclude         http://www.foo.com/2167A/
    Exclude         http://www.foo.com/Games/
    Exclude         http://www.foo.com/~juliosteen/
>
```

This instruction file contains two optional global directives, namely AvoidFile and SitesFile. Following the global directives are two traversal tasks—one each of types Tree and Site. MOMspider performs each task traversal in the order in which they appear in the instruction file. It is recommended that you list these from the bottom up, that is, from the farthest branch of the tree back toward the root.

For a more detailed discussion of the MOMspider instruction file, see:

```
http://www.ics.uci.edu/WebSoft/MOMspider/docs/instruct.html
```

Global Directives

Global directives are optional. They are used by MOMspider to alter its default configuration for a specific Web trek. Each directive has a keyword/value pair. Each pair is listed one per line regardless of its length and is flush with the left margin of the instruction file. Table 20-1 lists the global directive keywords, their values, and their descriptions.

Table 20-1
MOMspider global directives

Directive Keyword	Value	Description
SystemAvoid	file pathname	specify system-wide file containing URLs to avoid
SystemSites	file pathname	specify system-wide file containing sites to avoid
AvoidFile	file pathname	specify user's writable file containing URLs to avoid
SitesFile	file pathname	specify user's writable file containing sites to avoid
SitesCheck	number	number of days between checks of a site's "robots.txt" file
ReplyTo	email address	e-mail address of person receiving messages from MOMspider
MaxDepth	number	maximum depth of any MOMspider traversal

Traversal Tasks

Traversal tasks are required for the successful operation of MOMspider. Think of them as MOMspider's marching orders; instructing MOMspider what to visit, test, and traverse.

Traversal tasks are considered compound instructions consisting of a set of task directives. Here's the general form they take:

```
<type
  ... set of directives ...
>
```

Traversal Types

Each traversal task has a type, a set of required directives, and a set of optional directives. Table 20-2 summarizes the traversal task directive types.

Table 20-2

MOMspider traversal task directive types

Directive Type Keyword	Description
Site	specifies that the boundary of the infostructure traversal is the entire site
Tree	specifies that the boundary of the infostructure traversal is a specific directory in the Web
Owner	specifies that the boundary of the infostructure traversal is limited to HTML documents containing 'Owner:' META information, explained later

When specifying a traversal type in the instruction file, an accompanying < is prepended to the traversal type keyword. For example,

```
<Tree
  ...
>
<Site
  ...
>
<Owner
  ...
>
```

shows how to specify a `Tree`, `Site`, and `Owner` task directive in an instruction file. The > ends the current task directive.

For each traversal task, MOMspider walks a Web in a breadth-first fashion—it traverses all hypertext links on the same level before descending to the next level. This means that MOMspider traverses each link in the current HTML document before traversing any links found at the end of these links (this is true if the current HTML document is not a leaf node). By contrast, a depth-first traversal continues following hypertext links until a leaf is found.

It's important to understand that for each traversal type, a leaf node has a different definition. A leaf node is any information entity that isn't a

MIME Content-Type equal to HTML, or one that doesn't contain any hypertext links, or is outside of the infostructure boundary. That is, there are actually three things that make a leaf node:

1. A document that links only to other documents that are not HTML MIME-type documents.

2. An HTML document with no hypertext links outside the document.

3. A document that links only to documents that are outside the infostructure boundary.

A leaf node stops any further recursive downward traversal, so it's considered a terminator of the current traversal.

For a `Site` traversal, a leaf node is defined to be any URL that references only another remote site that is outside the infostructure boundary. For example, if a link in an HTML document references another site, MOMspider reports that link but wouldn't traverse it or start walking the other guy's site.

For a `Tree` traversal, any HTML document that is above the level of the top of the tree—specified by `TopURL`—is considered a leaf node. Any node at the same level of the top of the tree is not considered a leaf node; that is, siblings are traversed. Level is deciphered from the path name in the URL. Figure 20-1 depicts an example directory structure.

In Figure 20-1, if */www/docs/test/file1.html* contains a link that references an HTML document in either the */www/admin* or */www/protocols* directories of the structure, then the link is traversed. If the link references an HTML document in the */devel* tree, then the link is reported by MOMspider but isn't traversed because the link extends past the defined infostructure's boundary.

Finally, for an `Owner` traversal, any HTML document beyond the top URL that does not contain `"Owner:"` META information equal to the infostructure name—specified by `Name`—is considered a leaf node. For example, this HTML fragment:

```
<HEAD>
  <META http-equiv="Owner" content="MAG">
  <META http-equiv="Reply-To" content="webmaster@foo.com">
  <TITLE>...</TITLE>
</HEAD>
```

asserts that the current HTML document is owned by `MAG`. If this matches the name of the infostructure defined in the current task directive, then the HTML document is processed and all links are tested and traversed. Everything else is ignored.

For those who aren't HTML fanatics, META information is contained in the HEAD element. META is an extensible container used to identify, catalog, and index specialized document metainformation, or "information about information." It provides a mechanism for a Web robot to discover the existence of the HTML document and how it can be accessed or retrieved. It also identifies the content and features of a document which can help clarify its intended audience.

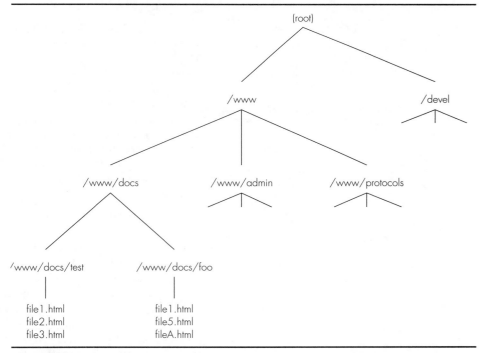

Figure 20 -1
Example directory structure showing leaf nodes for a tree MOMspider traversal.

Task Directives

Task directives are compound instructions containing a keyword/value pair. Each keyword and its associated value are case sensitive. Table 20-3 summarizes required and optional task directives.

Table 20-3

MOMspider task directives

Directive Keyword	Value	Description
Name	infostructure name	single word (no whitespace) identifying the infostructure traversed
TopURL	URL	top URL to start traversal; relative URL defaults to *file://localhost/*
IndexURL	URL	URL of the HTML index file created by MOMspider
IndexFile	filename.html	pathname to an HTML index file created by MOMspider (corresponds to IndexURL)
IndexTitle*	string	HTML index title; defaults to "MOMspider Index for Name"
ChangeWindow*	number	window (in days) prior to Last-modified date of URL; 0 means don't consider any 'Last-modified' dates; default is 7 days
ExpireWindow*	number	window (in days) after the 'Expires' date of URL; 0 means don't consider any 'Expires' dates; default is 0; rarely used
EmailAddress*	email address	specifies e-mail address of person to receive either broken or redirected link messages, or both; required if either EmailBroken, EmailRedirected, EmailChanged, or EmailExpired is specified
EmailBroken*	none	signals to e-mail broken link messages to EmailAdress
EmailRedirected*	none	signals to e-mail redirected link messages to EmailAddress
EmailChanged*	number	signals to e-mail EmailAddress if any tested links have changed within EmailChanged past number of days
EmailExpired*	number	signals to e-mail EmailAddress if any tested links will expire within EmailExpired number of days
Exclude*	URL prefix	specifies to identify any URL matching the Exclude URL prefix as a leaf node; each URL matching is tested but not traversed; the IndexURL is automatically excluded; you can specify more than one URL to exclude

*optional task directive

Notice that each instruction requires four task directives: Name, TopURL, IndexURL, and IndexFile. One notable mention is EmailAddress. It is required if any of the Email* directives are specified in the current instruction; otherwise, EmailAddress is optional.

Finally, an instruction—a set of valid task directives—is terminated by a >. This character closes the current open <traversal_type instruction. The > is on a line by itself.

USING HTML FORMS TO CREATE MOMSPIDER INSTRUCTION FILE

In this section, we introduce an HTML form and a series of CGI Perl scripts. These CGI scripts are required to build a valid MOMspider instruction file and are arranged as a finite-state machine.

For you non-computer scientists, a finite-state machine is like a soda machine. You give the soda machine its inputs, namely your shiny coins. The machine keeps track of its state by keeping a cumulative total of coins deposited so far. When the machine reaches a wait state—a state where the machine decides it now has gathered an amount equal to or greater than the price of one soda—it then prompts the user for one more input, your soda choice. Once the machine accepts your choice, it proceeds to dispense your soda and makes whatever change is necessary. It then rests, anxiously awaiting its next customer.

The series of CGI scripts needed to create a valid MOMspider instruction file comprises the pieces of a finite-state machine. Each CGI has a defined purpose, uses particular data, and has its own associated transition(s). It's our own deliberate mechanism to help our program overcome the stateless nature of the Web itself. Figure 20-2 depicts this machine.

Figure 20-2 shows that the start state is an HTML form (*MOM-inst-form.html*), where the user starts a new MOMspider instruction file. At present, this machine is designed solely for creation of new MOMspider instruction files.

If desired, you could extend this machine and its CGI scripts to allow a user either to create a new instruction file, or to add new tasks to an existing one. This adds more complexity to the machine and to the suite of CGI scripts and is beyond the scope of this book.

Arrows between objects in the figure indicate a finite-state machine's transitions to its next state(s). Such transitions are initiated by the state gathering the dependent input data. Once valid data is gathered from the user via an HTML form, the machine transitions to its next state, governed by the combination of current state and current input. The CGI scripts and the single HTML form comprise the collection of states for this machine.

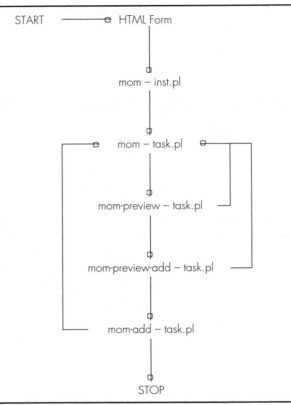

Figure 20-2
Automatic creation of MOMspider instruction file finite state machine.

At any time during the machine's execution, if you think any input to the machine is incorrect—for example, if you notice a value in a text input widget is incorrect—you may traverse backward in your Web client's history to return to the correct form.

Consequently, we must dispense an important warning: Some older Web clients won't repost form data. Why is this important? Because we take advantage of the HTML INPUT 'hidden' element TYPE. This allows us to maintain state information for each state of the machine. We pass pertinent form data to other forms so it can be incorporated into decisions made by other CGI scripts in the machine. This is how we make the stateless Web mimic a finite-state machine.

For example, the name of the MOMspider instruction file —a CGI variable named 'inst-filename' —is carried from its originating HTML form to each CGI script where it can be used to open the new MOMspider instruction filename to write new task directives. This lets us build a data set from state to state incrementally and is handled by this innocuous-seeming HTML fragment:

```
<INPUT TYPE="hidden"
       NAME="inst-filename"
       VALUE="$in{'inst-filename'}">
```

Notice the TYPE attribute: The `hidden` value instructs your WWW client not to render the value as something visible to the browser, but rather to send this data to the CGI script in the background along with any other data collected within this HTML form.

Older WWW clients may show an unlabeled input text widget for hidden data, which is incorrect, not just as an implementation, but philosophically speaking as well. You could conceivably edit the data in that widget, which could compromise its integrity. Thus, if your WWW client renders hidden INPUT elements, you probably should upgrade.

The Cogs of the Machine

The required pieces of the MOMspider finite-state machine are as follows:

- *MOM-inst-form.html*—an HTML form that gathers initial data to create a new MOMspider instruction file.

- *MOM-inst.pl*—a Perl CGI script that previews the optional global directives input by the user.

- *MOM-task.pl*—a Perl CGI script that adds the global directives to the new MOMspider instruction file and also provides a new form for the user to enter an instruction—a set of task directives.

- *MOM-preview-task.pl*—a Perl CGI script that previews the task directives entered by the user.

- *MOM-preview-add-task.pl*—a Perl CGI script that previews the current instruction in its natural form (as it will appear in the MOMspider instruction file).

- *MOM-add-task.pl*—a Perl CGI script that adds the current instruction to the open MOMspider instruction file.

MOM-inst-form.html

This is an HTML 2.0 form—an HTML document containing FORM and associated elements such as INPUT, TEXTAREA, and SELECT. This form asks you to supply a name for the new MOMspider instruction file, which is required, and any optional global task directives. Figure 20 -3 shows a screen capture of this form.

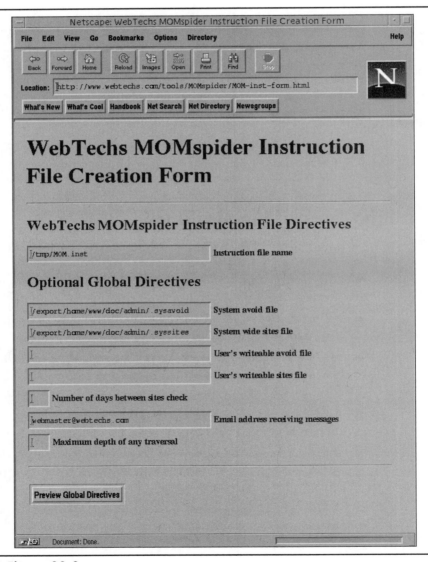

Figure 20-3

Screen capture of the HTML form MOM-inst-form.html.

After supplying the required form data, select the Preview Global Directives button. This transitions the machine to its next state, namely the CGI script indicated by the ACTION attribute for the FORM element.

In this case, the next state is labeled *MOM-inst.pl*. Table 20-4 lists the data collected by this form and how each CGI script variable relates to the MOMspider global directives. Notice that '$in{'*string*'}' is a Perl associative array, where each array entry is indexed by a string value. This associated array, '%in', is built from the input buffer when a form POSTs data to a Web server.

Table 20-4

Form data collected by MOM-inst-form.html

CGI Variable	Value	Global Directive Keyword
$in{'inst-filename'}	filename	
$in{'gd-sysavoid'}	filename	SystemAvoid
$in{'gd-syssites'}	filename	SystemSites
$in{'gd-avoidfile'}	filename	AvoidFile
$in{'gd-sitesfile'}	filename	SitesFile
$in{'gd-sitescheck'}	number	SitesCheck
$in{'gd-replyto'}	e-mail address	ReplyTo
$in{'gd-maxdepth'}	number	MaxDepth

MOM-inst.pl

This Perl CGI script represents another state for our finite-state machine, whose primary purpose is to check the validity of the data entered by the user into the prior state named *MOM-inst-form.html*. If everything checks out, *MOM-inst.pl* echoes the form data to the user. If the user agrees that the data is correct, the machine transitions to the next state when the user selects the Add Global Directives and Proceed to Next Step button.

This results in adding global directives to the new MOMspider instruction file according to its specifications. If the user isn't satisfied with the current data, he or she must traverse backward one step and re-enter the data or correct any errant fields. Figure 20-4 shows a screen capture of what a user would see during a typical session.

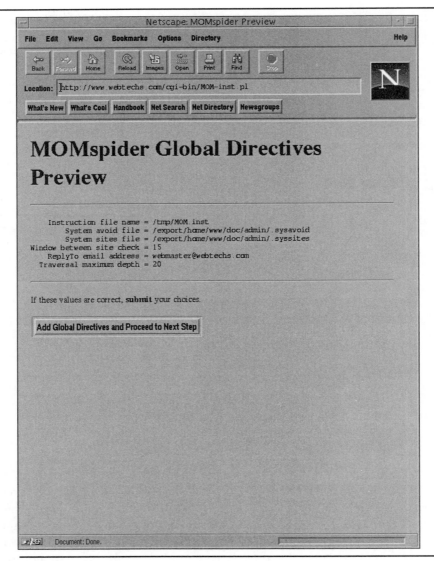

Figure 20-4
The results of posting form data to MOM-inst.pl.

MOM-task.pl

This Perl CGI script represents another state whose primary purposes are to accept any valid form data from the previous state—*MOM-inst.pl* passes these as 'hidden' input widgets to this new state—and to gather task directive form data (see Figure 20-5).

If you view the source of the URL generated by this script, you'll notice that many INPUT elements occur. Each has a VALUE resulting from form input in previous states. Notice that global directives aren't carried forward because they have already been written to the new MOMspider instruction file. They're no longer needed for proper machine function.

Table 20-5 lists the CGI variables used by *MOM-task.pl* and how they relate to the MOMspider task directives.

Table 20-5
MOM-task.pl CGI variables and their relation to MOMspider task directives

CGI Variable	Value	Task Directive
$in{'boundary'}	(Site|Tree|Owner)	<Traversal_type
$in{'info-struct-name'}	string with no whitespace	Name
$in{'topURL'}	URL	TopURL
$in{'indexURL'}	URL	IndexURL
$in{'indexfile'}	filename	IndexFile
$in{'indextitle'}	string with optional whitespace	IndexTitle
$in{'changewindow'}	number	ChangeWindow
$in{'expirewindow'}	number	ExpireWindow
$in{'emailaddress'}	e-mail address	EmailAddress
$in{'emailbroken'}	(no|yes)	EmailBroken
$in{'emailredirected'}	(no|yes)	EmailRedirected
$in{'emailchanged'}	number	EmailChanged
$in{'emailexpired'}	number	EmailExpired
$in{'exclude'}	string with fields delimited by carriage returns	Exclude

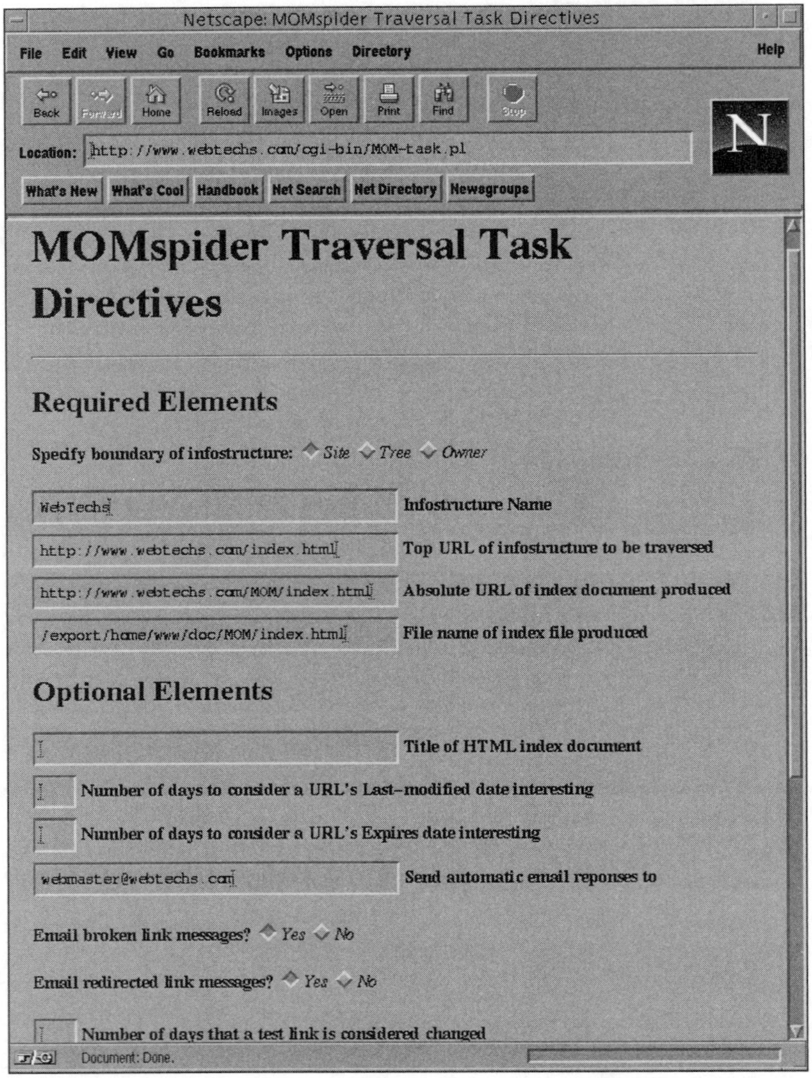

Figure 20-5
The HTML form for MOM-task.pl results from reaching the next state in the finite-state machine.

MOM-preview-task.pl

This state in the machine is a Perl CGI script that echoes output data from the previous state. This data consists of the task directive form data entered by the user and posted to the server by the *MOM-task.pl*-generated HTML form. If the data is correct, the machine transitions to the next state when the Submit and Proceed to Next Step button is selected.

If the data is incorrect, the user must back up one step to the previous state to re-enter the form data or correct any errant fields. For this reason, we'd like to suggest that an exercise for you, our gentle and talented reader, would be to create a "go back" button explicitly on the form that DOES repost the data for them. This would make the inevitability of errors much easier to swallow!

Figure 20-6 shows a screen capture while the machine is in its *MOM-preview-task.pl* state.

MOM-preview-add-task.pl

This state in the machine is a CGI Perl script whose primary purpose is to preview the current instruction—a set of task directives—entered by the user in previous states. The data is rendered to the user as a valid MOMspider instruction (as it will be written to the MOMspider instruction file). This gives the user the chance to view the results of the instructions. Some might argue that this step isn't needed, but we feel it's important to relay information about the machine's work in progress to its users and to give them a final chance to object to any instructions.

If the user accepts the current instruction by selecting the Add Task Directives and Proceed to Next Step button, the machine transitions to the next step. If the data is incorrect, the user must back up one step in the hypertext history to correct this data.

Figure 20-7 shows the rendered data from *MOM-preview-add-task.pl*, a typical MOMspider instruction built by the machine for its user.

MOM-add-task.pl

This is the machine's final state, in which the Perl CGI script appends the current instruction to the current MOMspider instruction file. Remember, any global directives input by the user have already been deposited in the MOMspider instruction file. If no global directives are specified, a couple of comments are written to the instruction file—namely, a statement about how the file was generated, followed by that day's date.

This script also utilizes 'hidden' input data from previous states to add the proper task directive keywords and their valid values. Figure 20-7 shows what the user sees once the machine reaches the *MOM-add-task.pl* state.

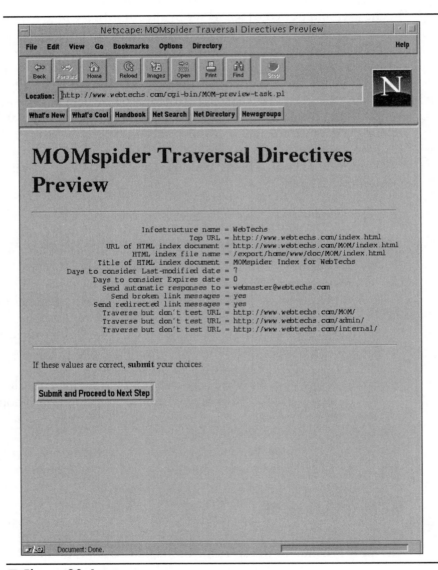

Figure 20-6

Screen capture of rendering of MOM-preview-task.pl data.

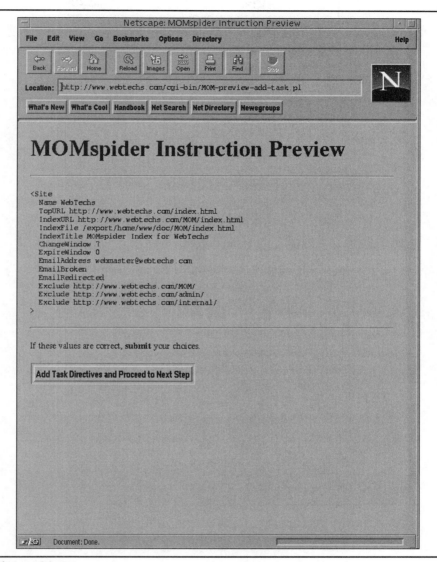

Figure 20-7
Rendered data from MOM-preview-add-task.pl.

The user is then presented with the Add Another Instruction button. If this button is selected, the machine is transitioned back to the *MOM-task.pl* state. It also sends the instruction filename—the value of the hidden CGI script variable '$in{'inst-filename'}' —to the *MOM-task.pl* state.

All other form data gathered from previous states is cleared to make way for new values whenever the user adds another instruction (see Figure 20-8). The user can also view the current MOMspider instruction file via a link provided to a local URL.

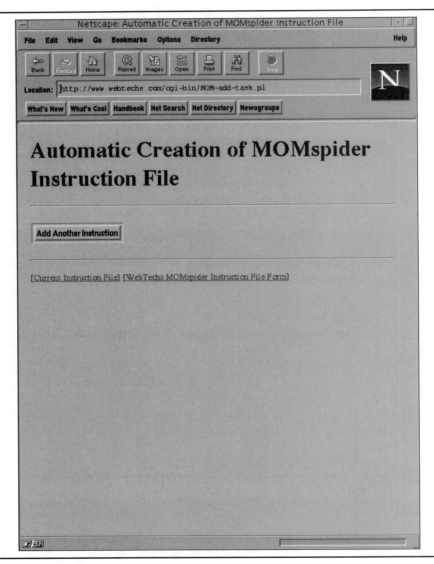

Figure 20-8
Data rendered by MOM-add-task.pl.

HTML AND CGI SCRIPT SOURCES

This section lists the source code for the initial HTML form *MOM-inst-form.html* and the sources for the CGI scripts that comprise the pieces of this machine. The first CGI script was created with *wondertwin.pl*, the CGI generating tool presented in Chapters 3 through 8. You can also find the source code on the disk that comes with this book or at the following URL:

```
http://www.webtechs.com/IDG/Secrets/MOMspider/
```

MOM-inst-form.html

This is an HTML 2.0 document that contains a FORM element and its associated INPUT elements. It's the start state of the finite-state machine which accepts user-supplied global and task directives and outputs a valid MOMspider instruction file.

```
<!DOCTYPE HTML PUBLIC "-//IETF//DTD HTML 2.0//EN">
<HTML>
<HEAD>
<TITLE>WebTechs MOMspider Instruction File Creation Form</TITLE>
</HEAD>
<BODY>
<H1>WebTechs MOMspider Instruction File Creation Form</H1>
<HR>
<H2>WebTechs MOMspider Instruction File Directives</H2>
<P>
<!- Post form data to the MOM-inst.pl CGI script ->
<FORM ACTION="/cgi-bin/MOM-inst.pl" METHOD="POST">
<INPUT NAME="inst-filename" SIZE="40"> <STRONG>Instruction
filename</STRONG>
<P>
<H2>Optional Global Directives</H2>
<P><INPUT NAME="gd-sysavoid" SIZE="40"> <STRONG>System avoid
file</STRONG><BR>
<INPUT NAME="gd-syssites" SIZE="40"> <STRONG>System wide sites
file</STRONG><BR>
<INPUT NAME="gd-avoidfile" SIZE="40"> <STRONG>User's writeable avoid
file</STRONG><BR>
<INPUT NAME="gd-sitesfile" SIZE="40"> <STRONG>User's writeable sites
file</STRONG><BR>
```

```
<INPUT NAME="gd-sitescheck" SIZE="3"> <STRONG>Number of days between sites
check</STRONG><BR>
<INPUT NAME="gd-replyto" SIZE="40"> <STRONG>Email address receiving
messages</STRONG><BR>
<INPUT NAME="gd-maxdepth" SIZE="3"> <STRONG>Maximum depth of any
traversal</STRONG></P>
<BR>
<HR>
<BR>
<P><INPUT TYPE="submit" VALUE="Preview Global Directives"></P>
</FORM>
</BODY>
</HTML>
```

MOM-inst.pl

This Perl CGI script handles the form data posted by the HTML form
MOM-inst-form.html:

```
#!/usr/bin/perl
#! Customize this line to match local Perl directory location
#          PROGRAM   :  MOM-inst.pl
#          CREATOR   :  Mark Gaither
#     CREATION DATE  :  Fri 17 Nov 1995
#       DESCRIPTION  :  Preview data to create a MOMspider
#                       instruction file.
#

# flush stdout buffer
$| = 1;

# Print this out no matter what.
print "Content-type: text/html\n\n";

# Build the %in associative array containing all form data.
if ($ENV{'REQUEST_METHOD'} eq 'POST')
{
  # How many bytes are we supposed to receive?
  read(STDIN, $buffer, $ENV{'CONTENT_LENGTH'});

  @pairs = split(/&/, $buffer);

  foreach $pair (@pairs) {
   ($name, $value) = split(/=/, $pair);
   $value =~ tr/+/ /;
```

```perl
      $value =~ s/%([a-fA-F0-9][a-fA-F0-9])/pack("C", hex($1))/eg;
      $in{$name} = $value; # Store the form data into the array.
    }
  }

# Print to STDOUT, a beginning of an HTML document.
print <<"HTML";
<!DOCTYPE HTML PUBLIC "-//IETF//DTD HTML 2.0//EN">
<HEAD>
<TITLE>MOMspider Preview</TITLE>
</HEAD>
<BODY>
<H1>MOMspider Global Directives Preview</H1>
<HR>
<P>
HTML

# If any errors are found, tell the user but don't post any data.
$ERRORS = 'false';

# An instruction filename is required.
if($in{'inst-filename'} eq '' ||
   $in{'inst-filename'} =~ /^\s*$/) {
  &error("You must provide a local instruction filename.");
  $ERRORS = 'true';
}
# A number is required for CheckSites.
if($in{'gd-sitescheck'} ne '' &&
   $in{'gd-sitescheck'} !~ /[0-9]+/) {
    &error("You must use an integer when specifying the number of days
between checking sites.");
$ERRORS = 'true';
}
# A number is required for MaxDepth.
if($in{'gd-maxdepth'} ne '' &&
   $in{'gd-maxdepth'} !~ /[0-9]+/) {
    &error("You must use an integer when specifying the maximum depth to be
checked.");
$ERRORS = 'true';
}

# If any errors, print error messages and exit.
if($ERRORS eq 'true') {
  print <<"HTML";

<P> Please go back and correct the errors.</P>
</BODY>
</HTML>
HTML
```

```perl
    exit;
}

# Echo form data provided by the user.
print "<PRE>\n";

if($in{'inst-filename'} ne '' &&
   $in{'inst-filename'} !~ /^\s*$/) {
  print "    Instruction filename = $in{'inst-filename'}\n";
}
if($in{'gd-sysavoid'} ne '' &&
   $in{'gd-sysavoid'} !~ /^\s*$/) {
  print "        System avoid file = $in{'gd-sysavoid'}\n";
}
if($in{'gd-syssites'} ne '' &&
   $in{'gd-syssites'} !~ /^\s*$/) {
  print "        System sites file = $in{'gd-syssites'}\n";
}
if($in{'gd-avoidfile'} ne '' &&
   $in{'gd-avoidfile'} !~ /^\s*$/) {
  print "          User avoid file = $in{'gd-avoidfile'}\n";
}
if($in{'gd-sitesfile'} ne '' &&
   $in{'gd-sitesfile'} !~ /^\s*$/) {
  print "          User sites file = $in{'gd-sitesfile'}\n";
}
# if not defined, set its default value
if($in{'gd-sitescheck'} eq '') { $in{'gd-sitescheck'} = 15; }
if($in{'gd-sitescheck'} ne '' &&
   $in{'gd-sitescheck'} !~ /^\s*$/) {
  print "Window between site check = $in{'gd-sitescheck'}\n";
}
if($in{'gd-replyto'} ne '' &&
   $in{'gd-replyto'} !~ /^\s*$/) {
  print "    ReplyTo email address = $in{'gd-replyto'}\n";
}
# If not defined, set its default value.
if($in{'gd-maxdepth'} eq '') { $in{'gd-maxdepth'} = 20; }
if($in{'gd-maxdepth'} ne '' &&
   $in{'gd-maxdepth'} !~ /^\s*$/) {
  print "  Traversal maximum depth = $in{'gd-maxdepth'}\n";
}

# Complete printing HTML object to STDOUT.
print <<"HTML";
</PRE>
```

```
<P>
<HR>
<P>If these values are correct, please <STRONG>submit</STRONG> your
choices.
<P>
<FORM ACTION="/cgi-bin/MOM-task.pl" METHOD="POST">
<!- Carry forward previous posted form data ->
<INPUT NAME="inst-filename" TYPE="hidden" VALUE="$in{'inst-filename'}">
<INPUT NAME="gd-sysavoid" TYPE="hidden"
  VALUE="$in{'gd-sysavoid'}">
<INPUT NAME="gd-syssites" TYPE="hidden"
  VALUE="$in{'gd-syssites'}">
<INPUT NAME="gd-avoidfile" TYPE="hidden"
  VALUE="$in{'gd-avoidfile'}">
<INPUT NAME="gd-sitesfile" TYPE="hidden"
  VALUE="$in{'gd-sitesfile'}">
<INPUT NAME="gd-sitescheck" TYPE="hidden"
  VALUE="$in{'gd-sitescheck'}">
<INPUT NAME="gd-replyto" TYPE="hidden"
  VALUE="$in{'gd-replyto'}">
<INPUT NAME="gd-maxdepth" TYPE="hidden"
  VALUE="$in{'gd-maxdepth'}">
<INPUT TYPE="submit" VALUE="Add Global Directives and Proceed to Next
Step">
</FORM>
</BODY>
</HTML>
HTML

chop($date = `date`); # get current date

# Open new MOMspider instruction file for writing.
open(INST,"> $in{'inst-filename'}") || die "Can't open $in{'inst-
filename'}: $!\n";
# This changes the output stream from STDOUT to INST.
select(INST);

# Print comments to new MOMspider instruction file.
print <<"INSTRUCTION";
# Instruction File created by WebTechs MOMspider Form.
# $date
#
# Global Directives
#
INSTRUCTION

# If global directives defined, add them to the instruction file.
```

```perl
if(defined($in{'gd-sysavoid'}) &&
   $in{'gd-sysavoid'} !~ /^\s*$/) {
  print "SystemAvoid $in{'gd-sysavoid'}\n";
}
if(defined($in{'gd-syssites'}) &&
   $in{'gd-syssites'} !~ /^\s*$/) {
  print "SystemSites $in{'gd-syssites'}\n";
}
if(defined($in{'gd-avoidfile'}) &&
   $in{'gd-avoidfile'} !~ /^\s*$/) {
  print "AvoidFile $in{'gd-avoidfile'}\n";
}
if(defined($in{'gd-sitesfile'}) &&
   $in{'gd-sitesfile'} !~ /^\s*$/) {
  print "SitesFile $in{'gd-sitesfile'}\n";
}
if(defined($in{'gd-sitescheck'}) &&
   $in{'gd-sitescheck'} !~ /^\s*$/) {
  print "SitesCheck $in{'gd-sitescheck'}\n";
}
if(defined($in{'gd-replyto'}) &&
   $in{'gd-replyto'} !~ /^\s*$/) {
  print "ReplyTo $in{'gd-replyto'}\n";
}
if(defined($in{'gd-maxdepth'}) &&
   $in{'gd-maxdepth'} !~ /^\s*$/) {
  print "MaxDepth $in{'gd-maxdepth'}\n";
}

close(INST);

exit;

# Subroutine to print error messages to STDOUT.
sub error {
  local($str) = @_;

  print "<STRONG>ERROR:</STRONG> $str<BR>\n";
}
```

MOM-task.pl

This Perl CGI script generates an HTML 2.0 form designed to query the user for a new instruction that specifies a set of required and optional task directives:

```perl
#!/usr/bin/perl
#! Please change directory specification to match your Perl
#! location.
#              PROGRAM  :  MOM-inst.pl
#              CREATOR  :  Mark Gaither
#        CREATION DATE  :  Fri 17 Nov 1995
#          DESCRIPTION  :  Create a MOMspider Instruction file.
#

# Flush stdout buffer.
$| = 1;

# Print this out no matter what.
print "Content-type: text/html\n\n";

# Build the %in associative array from the posted form data.
if ($ENV{'REQUEST_METHOD'} eq 'POST')
{
  # How many bytes are we supposed to receive?
  read(STDIN, $buffer, $ENV{'CONTENT_LENGTH'});

  @pairs = split(/&/, $buffer);

  foreach $pair (@pairs) {
    ($name, $value) = split(/=/, $pair);
    $value =~ tr/+/ /;
    $value =~ s/%([a-fA-F0-9][a-fA-F0-9])/pack("C", hex($1))/eg;
    $in{$name} = $value;
  }
}

# Print the 2.0 HTML form to STDOUT.
print <<"HTML";
<!DOCTYPE HTML PUBLIC "-//IETF//DTD HTML 2.0//EN">
<HEAD>
<TITLE>MOMspider Traversal Task Directives</TITLE>
</HEAD>
<BODY>
<H1>MOMspider Traversal Task Directives</H1>
<HR>
```

```
<FORM ACTION="/cgi-bin/MOM-preview-task.pl" METHOD="POST">
<H2>Required Elements</H2>
<P><STRONG>Specify boundary of infostructure:</STRONG>
<INPUT NAME="boundary" TYPE="radio" VALUE="Site"> <EM>Site</EM>
<INPUT NAME="boundary" TYPE="radio" VALUE="Tree"> <EM>Tree</EM>
<INPUT NAME="boundary" TYPE="radio" VALUE="Owner"> <EM>Owner</EM></P>
<P></P>
<P><INPUT NAME="info-struct-name" SIZE="40"> <STRONG>Infostructure
Name</STRONG><BR>
<INPUT NAME="topURL" SIZE="40"> <STRONG>Top URL of infostructure
 to be traversed</STRONG><BR>
<INPUT NAME="indexURL" SIZE="40"> <STRONG>Absolute URL of index
 document produced</STRONG><BR>
<INPUT NAME="indexfile" SIZE="40"> <STRONG>File name of index
 file produced</STRONG></P>

<H2>Optional Elements</H2>
<P><INPUT NAME="indextitle" SIZE="40"> <STRONG>Title of HTML index
document</STRONG><BR>
<INPUT NAME="changewindow" SIZE="3"> <STRONG>Number of days to consider a
URL's Last-modified date interesting</STRONG><BR>
<INPUT NAME="expirewindow" SIZE="3"> <STRONG>Number of days to consider a
URL's Expires date interesting</STRONG><BR>
<INPUT NAME="emailaddress" SIZE="40"> <STRONG>Send automatic email reponses
to</STRONG></P>
<P></P>
<P><STRONG>Email broken link messages?</STRONG>
<INPUT TYPE="radio" NAME="emailbroken" VALUE="yes"> <EM>Yes</EM>
<INPUT TYPE="radio" NAME="emailbroken" VALUE="no" CHECKED> <EM>No</EM></P>
<P></P>
<P><STRONG>Email redirected link messages?</STRONG>
<INPUT TYPE="radio" NAME="emailredirected" VALUE="yes"> <EM>Yes</EM>
<INPUT TYPE="radio" NAME="emailredirected" VALUE="no" CHECKED>
<EM>No</EM></P>
<P></P>
<P><INPUT NAME="emailchanged" SIZE="3"> <STRONG>Number of days that
 a test link is considered changed</STRONG><BR>
<INPUT NAME="emailexpired" SIZE="3"> <STRONG>Number of days that
 a traversed document will expire</STRONG></P>
<P></P>
<P><STRONG>URL prefix(es) to test but not traverse (one per
line)</STRONG></P>
<TEXTAREA ROWS="5" COLS="40" NAME="exclude"></TEXTAREA>
<BR>
<HR>
<BR>
<P><INPUT TYPE="submit" VALUE="Preview Task Directives"></P>
```

```
<!- Carry forward the name of the instruction -
-to the next state via a hidden INPUT element. ->
<INPUT NAME="inst-filename" TYPE="hidden" VALUE="$in{'inst-filename'}">
</FORM>
</BODY>
</HTML>
HTML

exit;
```

MOM-preview-task.pl

This is a Perl CGI script that previews any task directives entered into the task directives form:

```perl
#!/usr/bin/perl
#! Please change directory specification to match your Perl
#! location.
#               PROGRAM  :  MOM-preview-task.pl
#               CREATOR  :  Mark Gaither
#         CREATION DATE  :  Fri 17 Nov 1995
#           DESCRIPTION  :  Preview data to create a MOMspider
#                           instruction file.
#

# Flush stdout buffer.
$| = 1;

# Print this out no matter what.
print "Content-type: text/html\n\n";

# Build the %in associate array posted from a form.
if ($ENV{'REQUEST_METHOD'} eq 'POST')
{
  # How many bytes are we supposed to receive?
  read(STDIN, $buffer, $ENV{'CONTENT_LENGTH'});

  @pairs = split(/&/, $buffer);

  foreach $pair (@pairs) {
   ($name, $value) = split(/=/, $pair);
   $value =~ tr/+/ /;
   $value =~ s/%([a-fA-F0-9][a-fA-F0-9])/pack("C", hex($1))/eg;
   $in{$name} = $value;
   }
}
```

```perl
# Print a new HTML document to STDOUT.
print <<"HTML";
<!DOCTYPE HTML PUBLIC "-//IETF//DTD HTML 2.0//EN">
<HEAD>
<TITLE>MOMspider Traversal Directives Preview</TITLE>
</HEAD>
<BODY>
<H1>MOMspider Traversal Directives Preview</H1>
<HR>
<P>
HTML

# If any errors, print error messages and exit.
$ERRORS = 'false';

if($in{'boundary'} eq '' ||
   $in{'boundary'} =~ /^\s*$/) {
  &error("You must specify the boundary of the infostructure
(Site,Tree,Owner).");
  $ERRORS = 'true';
}
if($in{'info-struct-name'} eq '' ||
   $in{'info-struct-name'} =~ /^\s*$/) {
  &error("You must specify a name for the infostructure to be traversed and
tested.");
  $ERRORS = 'true';
}
if($in{'info-struct-name'} ne '' &&
   $in{'info-struct-name'} =~ /\s+/) {
  &error("The infostructure name can contain no whitespace.");
  $ERRORS = 'true';
}
if($in{'topURL'} eq '' ||
   $in{'topURL'} =~ /^\s*$/) {
  &error("You must specify either an absolute or relative top URL.");
  $ERRORS = 'true';
}
if($in{'indexURL'} eq '' ||
   $in{'indexURL'} =~ /^\s*$/) {
  &error("You must specify an absolute URL for the produced index file.");
 $ERRORS = 'true';
}
# Check to make sure its an absolute URL.
if($in{'indexURL'} ne '' && $in{'indexURL'} !~ /^(http|file|ftp)/)
{
    &error("You must specify an absolute URL (http|file|ftp) for
```

```
  the produced index file.");
   $ERRORS = 'true';
}
if($in{'indexfile'} eq '' ||
   $in{'indexfile'} =~ /^\s*$/) {
  &error("You must specify a filename for the index produced.");
   $ERRORS = 'true';
}
# Make sure input is a number.
if($in{'changewindow'} ne '' &&
   $in{'changewindow'} !~ /^[0-9]+$/) {
  &error("You must specify an integer >= 0 for number of days since the URL
was last modified.");
   $ERRORS = 'true';
}
if($in{'expirewindow'} ne '' &&
   $in{'expirewindow'} !~ /^[0-9]+$/) {
  &error("You must specify an integer >= 0 for number of days since the
expiration date of the URL.");
 $ERRORS = 'true';
}
if($in{'emailchanged'} ne '' &&
   ($in{'emailchanged'} !~ /^[0-9]+$/ ||
    scalar($in{'emailchanged'}) < 1)) {
  &error("You must specify an integer > 0 for number of days to pass before
sending e-mail that tested links have changed.");
 $ERRORS = 'true';
}
# If EmailChanged defined, the EmailAddress must also be defined.
if($in{'emailchanged'} ne '' &&
   $in{'emailchanged'} =~ /^[0-9]+$/ &&
   ($in{'emailaddress'} eq '' ||
    $in{'emailaddress'} =~ /^\s*$/)) {
  &error("If you want to receive e-mail about changed links, you
 must specify an e-mail address to receive messages.");
 $ERRORS = 'true';
}
if($in{'emailexpired'} ne '' &&
   $in{'emailexpired'} !~ /^[0-9]+$/) {
  &error("You must specify an integer > 0 for number of days notice you
want before the URL expires.");
   $ERRORS = 'true';
}
# If EmailExpired defined, the EmailAddress must also be defined.
if($in{'emailexpired'} ne '' &&
   $in{'emailexpired'} =~ /^[0-9]+$/ &&
   ($in{'emailaddress'} eq '' ||
```

```perl
       $in{'emailaddress'} =~ /^\s*$/)) {
    &error("If you want to receive e-mail about expired links, you must
    specify an e-mail address to receive messages.");
    $ERRORS = 'true';
}
# If EmailBroken defined, the EmailAddress must also be defined.
if(($in{'emailbroken'} eq 'yes') &&
     ($in{'emailaddress'} eq '' ||
      $in{'emailaddress'} =~ /^\s*$/)) {
    &error("If you want to receive e-mail about broken links, you must
    specify an e-mail address to receive messages.");
    $ERRORS = 'true';
}
# If EmailRedirected defined, EmailAddress must also be defined.
if(($in{'emailredirected'} eq 'yes') &&
     ($in{'emailaddress'} eq '' ||
      $in{'emailaddress'} =~ /^\s*$/)) {
    &error("If you want to receive e-mail about redirected links, you must
    specify an e-mail address to receive messages.");
    $ERRORS = 'true';
}
# Split, on a carriage return, the URLs to exclude into an array.
if($in{'exclude'} ne '' && $in{'exclude'} !~ /^\s*$/) {
    @URLs = split(/\n/,$in{'exclude'});
    foreach $URL (@URLs) {
       # Make sure it's a URL.
       if($URL !~ /^(http|ftp|file)/) {
          &error("When specifying a URL to be excluded, you must
 specify an absolute URL.\n");
$ERRORS = 'true';
       }
    }
}


# If any errors found, print error messages and exit.
if($ERRORS eq 'true') {
    print <<"HTML";

<P> Please go back and correct the errors.</P>
</BODY>
</HTML>
HTML

    exit;
}
```

```
# Echo form data back to user.
print "<PRE>\n";

if($in{'boundary'} ne '' &&
   $in{'gd-sysavoid'} !~ /^\s*$/) {
  print "Infostructure boundary = $in{'gd-sysavoid'}\n";
}
if($in{'info-struct-name'} ne '' &&
   $in{'info-struct-name'} !~ /^\s*$/) {
  print "Infostructure name = $in{'info-struct-name'}\n";
}
if($in{'topURL'} ne '' &&
   $in{'topURL'} !~ /^\s*$/) {
  print "Top URL = $in{'topURL'}\n";
}
if($in{'indexURL'} ne '' &&
   $in{'indexURL'} !~ /^\s*$/) {
  print "URL of HTML index document = $in{'indexURL'}\n";
}
if($in{'indexfile'} ne '' &&
   $in{'indexfile'} !~ /^\s*$/) {
  print "HTML index filename = $in{'indexfile'}\n";
}
if($in{'indextitle'} eq '') {
  $in{'indextitle'} =
      "MOMspider Index for " . $in{'info-struct-name'};
}
if($in{'indextitle'} ne '' &&
   $in{'indextitle'} !~ /^\s*$/) {
  print "Title of HTML index document = $in{'indextitle'}\n";
}
# Set default value.
if($in{'changewindow'} eq '') { $in{'changewindow'} = 7; }
if($in{'changewindow'} ne '' &&
   $in{'changewindow'} !~ /^\s*$/) {
  print "Window of Last-modified date = $in{'changewindow'}\n";
}
# Set default value.
if($in{'expirewindow'} eq '') { $in{'expirewindow'} = 0; }
if($in{'expirewindow'} ne '' &&
   $in{'expirewindow'} !~ /^\s*$/) {
  print "Days to consider Expires date = $in{'expirewindow'}\n";
}
if($in{'emailaddress'} ne '' &&
   $in{'emailaddress'} !~ /^\s*$/) {
  print "Send automatic responses to = $in{'emailaddress'}\n";
}
```

```perl
   if($in{'emailbroken'} ne '' &&
      $in{'emailbroken'} !~ /^\s*$/) {
     print "Send broken link messages = $in{'emailbroken'}\n";
   }
   if($in{'emailredirected'} ne '' &&
      $in{'emailredirected'} !~ /^\s*$/) {
     print "Send redirected link messages =
    $in{'emailredirected'}\n";
   }
   if($in{'emailchanged'} ne '' &&
      $in{'emailchanged'} !~ /^\s*$/) {
     print "Window of a tested link changed
    = $in{'emailchanged'}\n";
   }
   if($in{'emailexpired'} ne '' &&
      $in{'emailexpired'} !~ /^\s*$/) {
     print "Window traversed document expires =
    $in{'emailexpired'}\n";
   }
   if($in{'exclude'} ne '' &&
      $in{'exclude'} !~ /^\s*$/) {
     # Split into an array of URLs.
     @URLs = split(/\n/,$in{'exclude'});
     foreach $URL (@URLs) {
       print "Excluded URL = $URL\n";
     }
   }

   # Finish printing the HTML document.
   print <<"HTML";
   </PRE>
   <P>
   <HR>
   <P>If these values are correct, <STRONG>submit</STRONG> your choices.</P>
   <P></P>
   <FORM ACTION="/cgi-bin/MOM-preview-add-task.pl" METHOD="POST">
   <!- Carry forward previously posted form data ->
   <INPUT NAME="inst-filename" TYPE="hidden" VALUE="$in{'inst-filename'}">
   <INPUT NAME="boundary" VALUE="$in{'boundary'}" TYPE="hidden">
   <INPUT NAME="info-struct-name" VALUE="$in{'info-struct-name'}"
   TYPE="hidden">
   <INPUT NAME="topURL" VALUE="$in{'topURL'}" TYPE="hidden">
   <INPUT NAME="indexURL" VALUE="$in{'indexURL'}" TYPE="hidden">
   <INPUT NAME="indexfile" VALUE="$in{'indexfile'}" TYPE="hidden">
   <INPUT NAME="indextitle" VALUE="$in{'indextitle'}" TYPE="hidden">
   <INPUT NAME="changewindow" VALUE="$in{'changewindow'}" TYPE="hidden">
   <INPUT NAME="expirewindow" VALUE="$in{'expirewindow'}" TYPE="hidden">
```

```
<INPUT NAME="emailaddress" VALUE="$in{'emailaddress'}" TYPE="hidden">
<INPUT NAME="emailbroken" VALUE="$in{'emailbroken'}"
 TYPE="hidden">
<INPUT NAME="emailredirected" VALUE="$in{'emailredirected'}" TYPE="hidden">
<INPUT NAME="emailchanged" VALUE="$in{'emailchanged'}" TYPE="hidden">
<INPUT NAME="emailexpired" VALUE="$in{'emailexpired'}" TYPE="hidden">
<INPUT NAME="exclude" VALUE="$in{'exclude'}" TYPE="hidden">
<P><INPUT TYPE="submit" VALUE="Submit and Proceed to Next Step"></P>
</FORM>
</BODY>
</HTML>
HTML

exit;

# Print error messages.
sub error {
  local($str) = @_;

  print "<STRONG>ERROR:</STRONG> $str<BR>\n";
}
```

MOM-preview-add-task.pl

This Perl CGI script builds a MOMspider instruction from the user-defined
task directives. The data is presented as it will be written to the MOMspider
instruction file.

```
#!/usr/bin/perl
#! Please replace with your own Perl location.
#            PROGRAM  :  MOM-preview-add-task.pl
#            CREATOR  :  Mark Gaither
#      CREATION DATE  :  Fri 17 Nov 1995
#        DESCRIPTION  :  Preview data to create a MOMspider
#                        instruction file.
#

# Flush stdout buffer.
$| = 1;

# Print this out no matter what.
print "Content-type: text/html\n\n";

# Build the %in associative array posted from a form.
```

```perl
if ($ENV{'REQUEST_METHOD'} eq 'POST')
{
  # How many bytes are we supposed to receive?
  read(STDIN, $buffer, $ENV{'CONTENT_LENGTH'});

  @pairs = split(/&/, $buffer);

  foreach $pair (@pairs) {
    ($name, $value) = split(/=/, $pair);
    $value =~ tr/+/ /;
    $value =~ s/%([a-fA-F0-9][a-fA-F0-9])/pack("C", hex($1))/eg;
    $in{$name} = $value;
  }
}

# Print the HTML document to STDOUT.
print <<"HTML";
<!DOCTYPE HTML PUBLIC "-//IETF//DTD HTML 2.0//EN">
<HEAD>
<TITLE>MOMspider Intruction Preview</TITLE>
</HEAD>
<BODY>
<H1>MOMspider Instruction Preview</H1>
<HR>
<!- Print the required four task directives to STDOUT. ->
<PRE>
&lt;$in{'boundary'}
  Name $in{'info-struct-name'}
  TopURL $in{'topURL'}
  IndexURL $in{'indexURL'}
  IndexFile $in{'indexfile'}
HTML

# Echo the data to the user.
if($in{'indextitle'} ne '' &&
   $in{'indextitle'} !~ /^\s*$/) {
  print "  IndexTitle $in{'indextitle'}\n";
}
if($in{'changewindow'} ne '' &&
   $in{'changewindow'} !~ /^\s*$/) {
  print "  ChangeWindow $in{'changewindow'}\n";
}
if($in{'expirewindow'} ne '' &&
   $in{'expirewindow'} !~ /^\s*$/) {
  print "  ExpireWindow $in{'expirewindow'}\n";
}
if($in{'emailaddress'} ne '' &&
```

```
    $in{'emailaddress'} !~ /^\s*$/) {
  print "  EmailAddress $in{'emailaddress'}\n";
}
if($in{'emailbroken'} eq 'yes') {
  print "  EmailBroken\n";
}
if($in{'emailredirected'} eq 'yes') {
  print "  EmailRedirected\n";
}
if($in{'emailchanged'} ne '' &&
    $in{'emailchanged'} !~ /^\s*$/) {
  print "  EmailChanged $in{'emailchanged'}\n";
}
if($in{'emailexpired'} ne '' &&
    $in{'emailexpired'} !~ /^\s*$/) {
  print "  EmailExpired $in{'emailexpired'}\n";
}
if($in{'exclude'} ne '' &&
    $in{'exclude'} !~ /^\s*$/) {
  @URLs = split(/\n/,$in{'exclude'});
  foreach $URL (@URLs) {
    print "  Exclude $URL\n";
  }
}


# Finish printing the HTML document.
print <<"HTML";
&gt;
</PRE>
<P>
<HR>
<P>If these values are correct, <STRONG>submit</STRONG> your choices.</P>
<P></P>
<FORM ACTION="/cgi-bin/MOM-add-task.pl" METHOD="POST">
<!- Carry forward previously posted form data ->
<INPUT NAME="inst-filename" TYPE="hidden" VALUE="$in{'inst-filename'}">
<INPUT NAME="boundary" TYPE="hidden" VALUE="$in{'boundary'}">
<INPUT NAME="info-struct-name" TYPE="hidden" VALUE="$in{'info-struct-
name'}">
<INPUT NAME="topURL" TYPE="hidden" VALUE="$in{'topURL'}">
<INPUT NAME="indexURL" TYPE="hidden" VALUE="$in{'indexURL'}">
<INPUT NAME="indexfile" TYPE="hidden" VALUE="$in{'indexfile'}">
<INPUT NAME="indextitle" TYPE="hidden" VALUE="$in{'indextitle'}">
<INPUT NAME="changewindow" TYPE="hidden" VALUE="$in{'changewindow'}">
<INPUT NAME="expirewindow" TYPE="hidden" VALUE="$in{'expirewindow'}">
<INPUT NAME="emailaddress" TYPE="hidden" VALUE="$in{'emailaddress'}">
<INPUT NAME="emailbroken" TYPE="hidden"
```

```
 VALUE="$in{'emailbroken'}">
<INPUT NAME="emailredirected" TYPE="hidden" VALUE="$in{'emailredirected'}">
<INPUT NAME="emailchanged" TYPE="hidden" VALUE="$in{'emailchanged'}">
<INPUT NAME="emailexpired" TYPE="hidden" VALUE="$in{'emailexpired'}">
<INPUT NAME="exclude" TYPE="hidden" VALUE="$in{'exclude'}">
<INPUT TYPE="submit" VALUE="Add Task Directives and Proceed to
 Next Step">
</FORM>
</BODY>
</HTML>
HTML

exit;
```

MOM-add-task.pl

Finally, this Perl CGI script adds the new instruction to the current
MOMspider instruction file and offers the user navigational aids to proceed
further in defining new instructions:

```
#!/usr/bin/perl
#! Please replace with your own Perl location.
#            PROGRAM  :  MOM-add-task.pl
#            CREATOR  :  Mark Gaither
#      CREATION DATE  :  Fri 17 Nov 1995
#        DESCRIPTION  :  Add a task to a MOMspider instruction
#                        file.
#

# Flush stdout buffer.
$| = 1;

# Print this out no matter what.
print "Content-type: text/html\n\n";

# Build the %in associate array from posted form data.
if ($ENV{'REQUEST_METHOD'} eq 'POST')
{
  # How many bytes are we supposed to receive?
  read(STDIN, $buffer, $ENV{'CONTENT_LENGTH'});

  @pairs = split(/&/, $buffer);

  foreach $pair (@pairs) {
   ($name, $value) = split(/=/, $pair);
```

```perl
        $value =~ tr/+/ /;
        $value =~ s/%([a-fA-F0-9][a-fA-F0-9])/pack("C", hex($1))/eg;
        $in{$name} = $value;
    }
}

# Open the current instruction file for appending.
open(INST,">> $in{'inst-filename'}") ||
        die "Can't open file $in{'inst-filename'}: $!\n";
# Write to a new opened data stream.
select(INST);

# Print the new instruction to the instruction file.
print <<"INSTRUCTION";
# Instruction
<$in{'boundary'}
  Name $in{'info-struct-name'}
  TopURL $in{'topURL'}
  IndexURL $in{'indexURL'}
  IndexFile $in{'indexfile'}
INSTRUCTION

# Continuing printing defined task directives.
# to the instruction file.
if($in{'indextitle'} ne '' &&
   $in{'indextitle'} !~ /^\s*$/) {
  print "  IndexTitle $in{'indextitle'}\n";
}
if($in{'changewindow'} ne '' &&
   $in{'changewindow'} !~ /^\s*$/) {
  print "  ChangeWindow $in{'changewindow'}\n";
}
if($in{'expirewindow'} ne '' &&
   $in{'expirewindow'} !~ /^\s*$/) {
  print "  ExpireWindow $in{'expirewindow'}\n";
}
if($in{'emailaddress'} ne '' &&
   $in{'emailaddress'} !~ /^\s*$/) {
  print "  EmailAddress $in{'emailaddress'}\n";
}
if($in{'emailbroken'} eq 'yes') {
  print "  EmailBroken\n";
}
if($in{'emailredirected'} eq 'yes') {
  print "  EmailRedirected\n";
}
if($in{'emailchanged'} ne '' &&
   $in{'emailchanged'} !~ /^\s*$/) {
  print "  EmailChanged $in{'emailchanged'}\n";
}
```

```perl
if($in{'emailexpired'} ne '' &&
   $in{'emailexpired'} !~ /^\s*$/) {
  print "  EmailExpired $in{'emailexpired'}\n";
}
if($in{'exclude'} ne '' &&
   $in{'exclude'} !~ /^\s*$/) {
  @URLs = split(/\n/,$in{'exclude'});
  foreach $URL (@URLs) {
    print "  Exclude $URL\n";
  }
}
print ">\n";

close(INST);

# Switch to a new data stream.
select(STDOUT);

# Print HTML document which user will see.
print <<"HTML";
<!DOCTYPE HTML PUBLIC "-//IETF//DTD HTML 2.0//EN">
<HEAD>
<TITLE>Automatic Creation of MOMspider Instruction File</TITLE>
</HEAD>
<BODY>
<H1>Automatic Creation of MOMspider Instruction File</H1>
<HR>
<FORM METHOD="POST" ACTION="/cgi-bin/MOM-task.pl">
<INPUT TYPE="submit" VALUE="Add Another Instruction">
<!- Carry name of instruction filename to next state ->
<INPUT NAME="inst-filename" TYPE="hidden" VALUE="$in{'inst-filename'}">
</FORM>
<BR>
<HR>
<BR>
<!- Provide a link to the current instruction file. ->
[<A HREF="file://localhost/$in{'inst-filename'}">Current
 Instruction File</A>]
<!- Provide a link back to the starting HTML form ->
[<A HREF="/tools/MOMspider/MOM-inst-form.html">WebTechs MOMspider
Instruction File Form</A>]
</BODY>
</HTML>
HTML

exit;
```

And that's it—we're done!

SUMMARY

MOMspider—a busy WebMaster's best friend—collects information about vast seas of HTML documents and their hypertext links. This Web-walking robot gets its orders from an instruction file that we created using HTML forms. By using hidden INPUT elements, we were able to pass information between a series of scripts that mimic changes in state—in other words, we got the stateless Web to act like a finite-state machine!

Vendor List

AMERICA ONLINE, INC.
8619 Westwood Center Dr.
Vienna, VA 22182-2285
800-827-6364; 703-448-8700
Fax: 800-827-4595
http://www.aol.com

APPLE COMPUTER, INC.
1 Infinite Loop
Cupertino, CA 95014
800-776-2333; 408-996-1010
Direct sales: 800-538-9696
Fax: 408-996-0275
Tech support: 800-767-2775
http://www.apple.com

ARBORTEXT, INC.
1000 Victors Way, Ste. 400
Ann Arbor, MI 48108-2700
313-996-3566
Fax: 313-996-3573
Tech support: 313-996-3566
http://www.arbortext.com

COMMERCENET
800 El Camino Real
Menlo Park, CA 94025
415-617-8790
Fax: 415-617-1516
http: //www.commerce.net

COMMUNITY CONNEXION
3038-A Mabel St.
Berkeley, CA 94702
http://www.c2.org

COMPUSERVE, INC. (INTERNET DIVISION)
316 Occidental Ave., S, Ste. 200
Seattle, WA 98104
800-SPRY-NET; 206-447-0300
Fax: 206-447-9008
Tech support: 206-447-0958
Tech support BBS: 206-447-9060
http://www.compuserve.com

CONVEX COMPUTER CORP.
3000 Waterview Pkwy.
PO Box 833851
Richardson, TX 75083-3851
800-297-6381; 214-497-4000
Fax: 214-497-4848
Tech support: 800-426-8979
http://www.convex.com

DAVENPORT GROUP
http://www.ora.com/davenport/README.html
davenport@online.ora.com
For address and phone numbers, see O'Reilly & Associates.

ENTERPRISE INTEGRATION TECHNOLOGIES (EIT)
800 El Camino Real, Fourth Floor
Menlo Park, CA 94025
415-617-8000
Fax: 415-617-8019
info@eit.com
http://www.eit.com

EXCITE NETSEARCH C/O ARCHITEXT SOFTWARE
2700 Garcia, Ste. 300
Mountain View, CA 94043
415-934-3611
Fax: 415-934-3610
http://www.excite.com

FIRST VIRTUAL HOLDING CORP.
11975 El Camino Real, Ste. 300
San Diego, CA 92130-2543
http://www.fv.com/tech/www.html

GNU PROJECT C/O FREE SOFTWARE FOUNDATION
59 Temple Place, Ste. 330
Boston, MA 02111-1307
617-542-5942
Fax: 617-542-2652
gnu@prep.ai.mit.edu
http://www.delorie.com/gnu/

HAL SOFTWARE SYSTEMS, INC.
c/o Fujitsu America
3006 Longhorn Boulevard
Austin, TX 78758
512-834-9962
http://www.halsoft.com/
ftp://ftp.halsoft.com/ (*/info* directory)

HEWLETT-PACKARD
3000 Hanover St.
Palo Alto, CA 94304
800-752-0900; 800 387-3867 (CD); 415-857-1501
Direct sales: 800-637-7740 (HP Direct)
Tech support: 800-858-8867
Tech support BBS: 415-852-0256
http://www.hp.com; http://www.dmo.hp.com/nsmd/ov/main.html

HYPERMALL C/O INTERLINK CORP.
P.O. Box 7506
Everett, WA 98201-7506
206-252-4005
http://www.hypermall.com

IDG BOOKS
IDG Books Worldwide, Inc.
Corporate Support Center
919 E. Hillsdale Blvd., Suite 400
Foster City, CA 94404
800-762-2974
salesinfo@idgbooks.com
http://www.idgbooks.com

IMALL
http://www.imall.com

INFOHAUS
http://infohaus.com/
For mailing information, see First Virtual Holdings Inc.

INFORMIX SOFTWARE, INC.
4100 Bohannon Dr.
Menlo Park, CA 94025
800-331-1763; 415-926-6300
Direct sales: 800-688-INFX
Fax: 415-926-6593
Tech support: 415-926-6626
http://www.informix.com

IANA (INTERNET ASSIGNED NUMBERS AUTHORITY)
C/O USC/INFORMATION SCIENCES INSTITUTE
4676 Admiralty Way
Marina del Rey, CA 90292-6695 USA
310-822-1511
Fax: 310-823-6714
iana@isi.edu
http://www.isi.edu/iana/overview.html

InterNIC Directory and Database Services

admin@ds.internic.net
800-862-0677 or 908-668-6587
http://www.internic.net/

Microsoft Corp.

One Microsoft Way
Redmond, WA 98052-6399
800-426-9400; 206-882-8080
Direct sales: 800-MSPRESS
Fax: 206-93-MSFax
Tech support: 206-454-2030; 206-637-7098 (Windows)
Tech support BBS: 206-936-6735
http://www.microsoft.com

net.Genesis

68 Rogers St.
Cambridge, MA 02142-1119
617-577-9800
Fax: 617-577-9850
mkgray@netgen.com
http://www.netgen.com/cgi/wandex

Netscape Communications Corp.

501 E. Middlefield Rd.
Mountain View, CA 94043
800-NETSITE; 415-528-2600
Fax: 415-528-4120
http://home.netscape.com

Open Market, Inc.

215 First St.
Cambridge, MA 02142
617-621-9500
Fax: 617-621-1703
http://www.openmarket.com

ORACLE CORP.
500 Oracle Pkwy.
Redwood Shores, CA 94065
800-633-0596; 415-506-7000
Direct sales: 800-ORACLE-7
Fax: 415-506-7200
Tech support: 415-341-4333 (PC); 415-341-3003 (Mini/Mainframe)
http://www.oracle.com

O'REILLY & ASSOCIATES, INC.
103A Morris St.
Sebastopol, CA 95472
800-998-9938
Fax: 707-829-0104
mailto:nuts@ora.com (books); website@ora.com (WebSite)
http://www.ora.com (books); http://www.website.com (WebSite)

OUTERNET
info@outer.net
8235 Shoal Creek, #105
Austin, Texas 78758
512-345-3573
http://www.outer.net/

PROCESS SOFTWARE CORP.
959 Concord St.
Framingham, MA 01701-9572
800-722-7770; 508-879-6994
Fax: 508-879-0042
Tech support: 800-722-7770
http://www.process.com

RSA DATA SECURITY, INC.
100 Marine Pkwy., Ste. 500
Redwood City, CA 94065
800-782-5453; 415-595-8782
Fax: 415-595-1873
Tech support: 415-595-7705
http://www.rsa.com

SAUSAGE SOFTWARE
Suite 1
660 Doncaster Rd.
Doncaster Vic 3108
Australia
http://www.sausage.com

SOFTQUAD, INC.
(SUBSIDIARY OF SOFTQUAD INTERNATIONAL)
56 Aberfoyle Crescent
Toronto, ON, CD M8X 2W4
800-387-2777; 416-239-4801
Fax: 416-239-7105
Tech support: 800-387-2777
http://www.sq.com

SUN MICROSYSTEMS COMPUTER CO.
2550 Garcia Ave.
Mountain View, CA 94043-1100
800-821-4643; 800-821-4642 (CA); 415-960-1300;
Fax: 415-969-9131
Tech support: 800-USA-4SUN
http://www.sun.com

VERISIGN
2593 Coast Ave.
Mountain View CA 94043
415-961-7500
Fax: 415-961-7300
http://www.verisign.com

YAHOO! CORPORATION
110 Pioneer Way, Suite F
Mountain View, CA 94041
415-934-3230
Fax: 415-934-3248
http://www.yahoo.com/

GLOSSARY

#PCDATA. An SGML term that stands for "parsed character data," it refers to zero or more characters that occur in a context in which text is parsed and markup is recognized.

.gz. An abbreviation for GNU zip compression, a primarily UNIX-based data compression program. This abbreviation is found as a file extension (e.g., "filename.gz").

.hqx. A format designator associated with the (primarily Macintosh) BinHex program. To compress a file with this utility, you'd go from binary to hexadecimal; to decompress, from hexadecimal to binary.

.tar. An abbreviation for tape archival, *tar* is the eponymous UNIX compression command that creates ".tar"-formatted files. *untar* is the term used to name the operation of decompressing a *tar*red file, even though you'd use the command *tar -xvf junk.tar* to decompress the file named "junk.tar".

.Z. A format designator associated with the UNIX *compress* program. Use the UNIX *uncompress* or *zcat* programs to decompress ".Z" files.

.zip. A format designator associated with PKWare's PKZIP utilities. In a DOS environment, you'd use *PKZIP* to compress a file, and *PKUNZIP* to decompress it; in Windows, we recommend Niko Mak's outstanding WinZIP utility. On UNIX, gunzip decompresses PKZIPped files and zips files so they can be unzipped using PKZIP. (See also *gunzip*.)

abstract. A brief restatement of the contents of a file or document.

ACTION. An HTML attribute that specifies a URL that indicates a specific CGI script or program that collects the form data that a user entered.

AFS (Andrew File System). Named after Andrew Carnegie by its inventors at Carnegie-Mellon University, AFS is a distributed file system available for many flavors of UNIX and a handful of other operating systems.

algorithm. A step-by-step, programmatic "recipe" for producing a specific set of results in a computer program.

alias. A computer system name that points at another name, instead of to an underlying object. Most Web URLs are either wholly or partly aliases (to protect the underlying file system on the Web server to which they point).

America Online. An online information provider, usually known by its initials (AOL), that got its start as a non-Internet dial-up service and that's now moved onto the Internet in a big way.

anchor. An HTML term for the destination end of a link; it may sometimes be used as a synonym for hypertext links of all kinds.

ANSI (American National Standards Institute). One of the primary standards-setting bodies for computer technology in the United States.

API (Application Programming Interface). A set of interface subroutines or library calls that define the methods for programs to access external services (i.e., to somebody else's system or program).

AppleScript. Apple Computer's scripting language for the Macintosh OS, AppleScript is commonly used to program CGIs for Macintosh-based Web servers (among other uses).

AppleSearch. A WAIS-like search engine developed for use under the Macintosh operating system.

applets. An application, such as a utility program or a limited-function spreadsheet or word processor.

application-independent. A format or facility is said to be application-independent when it works in multiple environments and doesn't depend on a specific application to understand or use its contents.

archie. A program that catalogs files on over a thousand *anonymous ftp* servers worldwide and lets users search against this database using interactive queries, e-mail, or through other programs like *gopher* or a Web browser.

architecture neutral. A buzzword applied to Sun's Java programming language that is meant to imply its ability to execute under a number of computer architectures without requiring recompilation or code changes.

<ARG> (argument). In programming, a value that is passed between programs, subroutines, or functions. Arguments are independent items, or variables, that contain data or codes. When an argument is used to customize a program for a user, it is generally called a parameter.

argc. In UNIX, a counter of the number of arguments in the *argv* input argument array variable.

argv. In UNIX, *argv* is an array of variables used to pass input between programs or processes on a given machine.

associative array. A programming construct where individual elements are associated with specific names, rather than array positions or locations. Perl offers an especially good implementation of such arrays.

asynchronous. Literally, "not at the same time," the term refers to computer communications where sender and receiver do not communicate directly with one another, but rather through accessing a common pick-up/drop-off point for information.

attribute. In SGML, HTML, and most object-oriented programming languages, an attribute is a named component of an object or term, with specific value typing, element definitions, and requirements and default status.

AUTH_SCHEME. An environment variable that names the kind of authorization scheme in use, if any.

AUTH_TYPE. An environment variable that provides various levels of server access security.

authentication. A method for identifying a user prior to granting permission to access, change, or delete a system or network resource. It usually depends on a password, or some other method of proving that "User A" really is "User A."

autoresponder. An e-mail program that sends a predefined response back to anyone who sends a message to a particular e-mail address.

awk. An input-processing and pattern-matching language, *awk* scans each of its input filenames for lines that match any of a set of patterns specified in a program. All input filenames are read in order; the standard input is read if there are no filenames.

back end. The program or processes that run "behind the scenes" to make the application work as the user expects, and that is usually driven by the user interface, query facility, or some other method of submitting requests for action to the system.

backbone. A high-speed connection designed to interconnect multiple networks to facilitate rapid movement of data from one network to another.

bandwidth. The range of electrical frequencies a device can handle; more often, it's used as a measure of a communications technology's carrying capability.

Basic (Beginners All-purpose Symbolic Instruction Code). A computer language invented by John Kemeny at Dartmouth College in the late 1960s. It's popular because it's easy to learn and use.

BBS (Bulletin Board System). A synonym for electronic bulletin board, a BBS usually consists of a PC, modem(s), and communications software attached to the end of one or more phone lines. Callers call up the BBS where they can send and receive messages and download software.

binary executables. Files created by compiling (and/or linking) source code modules to create executable files.

binary. Literally, this means that a file is formatted as a collection of ones and zeros; actually, this means that a file is formatted to be intelligible only to a certain application or that it is itself an executable file.

BIND (Berkeley Internet Name Domain). BIND is the most popular implementation of the Internet Domain Name Service in use today. Written by Kevin Dunlap for 4.3BSD UNIX, BIND supplies a distributed database capability that lets multiple DNS

servers cooperate to resolve Internet names into correct IP addresses.

BITNET (Because It's Time NETwork). A network that communicates via the Remote Job Entry (RJE) protocols that work over serial lines as well as TCP/IP. BITNET mail is sent through a gateway to the Internet.

black box. A computer-speak euphemism for a program or service whose internal workings are unknown, but which produces a predictable set of outputs for a particular set of inputs.

boilerplate. One of the few computer terms to originate in the legal profession, boilerplate refers to elements of text or documents that appear consistently in many or all documents (e.g., a copyright notice).

boot. Used in computer-speak as a verb, to boot means to start up a computer from its turned-off state. As an adjective (e.g., boot-time) it refers to the computer while it's in the startup phase.

bottleneck. A point in a computer or a network where things become congested and slow down.

boundary errors. In programming, errors can occur within the range of the expected data, outside that range, or right on the edges of the expected range. When errors occur at the edges, they're called boundary errors (e.g., if a number between 1 and 100 is acceptable, what happens with 1 or 100?).

Bourne shell. UNIX machines typically have one native command interpreter or shell. On many machines, this is the Bourne shell, named after S.R. Bourne in 1975. The Bourne shell is part of the standard configuration for every flavor of UNIX.

breakpoints. A marked location in a program, usually set with a debugger or an equivalent tool, where the program will halt execution so that the programmer can examine the values of its variables, parameters, settings, etc.

bridge. A piece of internetworking equipment that operates at Layer 2 of the ISO model, and forwards packets from one network segment to another without checking address information (see also *router*).

browser. An Internet application that lets users access WWW servers and surf the Net.

BSDI (Berkeley Software Distribution, Inc.). BSDI remains one of the major flavors of UNIX available today, except that now it's distributed by a spin-off business and not the University of California at Berkeley (see Vendor List for contact info).

bug. Programmer-speak for an error, glitch, gotcha, problem, or "unsolved mystery" in a computer program.

C. A programming language developed by some of the founders of UNIX, Brian Kernighan and Dennis Ritchie, still very much in vogue among UNIX-heads.

C++. A programming language developed by Bjarne Stroustrup, C++ is a successor to the C language mentioned above. It is an object-oriented (OO) implementation of C.

case sensitive. Means that upper- and lowercase letters are not equivalent (e.g., UNIX filenames are case sensitive; "TEXT.TXT" is not the same as "text.txt").

cc (C compiler). The name of the standard C compiler program on a UNIX system.

cd (change directory). The change directory UNIX command (also used in DOS).

CD-ROM (Compact Disk–Read-Only Memory). A read-only computer medium that looks just like a music compact disk, but contains computer data instead of music.

Centre European Researche Nucleare (CERN). The Center for High-Energy Physics in Geneva, Switzerland; the birthplace of the World Wide Web.

CGI (Common Gateway Interface). The parameter passing and invocation technique used to let Web clients pass input to Web servers (and on to specific programs written to the CGI specification).

cgi-parse. A CGI for parsing standard input variables in CGI programs, available from the NCSA CGI library (see Chapter 2 or the CD-ROM for the URL).

character entities. Named SGML or HTML variables that stand for otherwise unusuable characters, in HTML entities are preceded by a & and end with a ; (e.g., < stands for <).

charset (character set). A defined set of characters used to define legal character values and appearance in HTML or SGML documents.

checkbox. An HTML term for a graphical form widget that may be either checked (to indicate the presence of an associated value) or unchecked (to indicate its absence).

chmod. A UNIX command to change the mode of operation (commonly known as permissions) for a given account.

chown. A UNIX command to change the ownership (and in BSD, the group) of files in the UNIX file system.

CIDR (Classless Inter-Domain Routing). A way of subdividing large collections of IP addresses into smaller groups (defined by subnet masks) and routing to them individually (allowing more people to share the same address blocks).

class. An object-oriented programming term, class refers to a method for defining a set of related objects that can inherit or share certain characteristics.

clickable image. A graphic (commonly known as an image map) in an HTML document that has been associated to a pixel-mapping CGI on the server; users can click on locations within the graphic and thereby retrieve specific URLs.

client pull. A Netscape method where a Web client can instruct a server to send it a particular set of data periodically (e.g., client-initiated data transfer).

client. Used as (a) a synonym for Web browser (i.e., Web client), or (b) as a requesting, front-end member for a client/server applications (like WWW).

client/server. A computing paradigm wherein processing is divided between a graphical front-end application running on a user's desktop machine, and a back-end server that performs data- or storage-intensive processing tasks in response to client service requests.

close. A formal communications term that refers to session teardown and termination, usually at the end of a networked information transaction.

CNIDR (Clearinghouse for Networked Information Discovery and Retrieval). The industry group responsible for maintenance and distribution of the *freeWAIS* program.

COBOL (Common Business Oriented Language). An old-fashioned programming language invented by Rear Admiral Grace Hopper, still in use for many legacy business applications today.

collaterals. Marketing-speak for product promotional materials, like brochures, spec sheets, white papers, etc.

command-line interface. A character mode computer interface that relies on parsing for and recognizing specific terms, called commands, and related information (parameters and arguments) to initiate system activity.

common log format. A data format agreed upon between NCSA and CERN for creating HTTP logs, used by most *httpd* implementers and vendors today.

compiler. A software program that reads the source code for a programming language and creates a binary executable version of that code.

compliant. Conforms to a defined standard of some kind.

compress. The action of compacting data to save disk space.

CompuServe. An information service provider based in Columbus, OH that hosts a large online user community and is regarded as a prime source for technical support information.

connection. A link opened between two computers for the purposes of some specific communication.

content. The hard, usable information contained in a document. Users surf the Web looking for content.

CONTENT_LENGTH. An environment variable that specifies the size in decimal number of octets of any attached entity.

Content-Privacy-Domain. A header that sets which type of encryption protocol will be used. It can be either PKCS-7 or PEM.

Content-Type. The MIME designation for file types to be transported by electronic mail and HTTP.

conversion. The process of changing from one form to another. For example, conversion may occur between a hard-copy document and its soft-copy equivalent.

cookie. The name of a proposed Netscape extension that allows contextualized information to be accessed from within an HTML document (this might be used, for instance, to include information from an environmental variable in an HTML document).

cp. The UNIX file copy command.

crawlers. A class of programs designed to ceaselessly search the Web, looking for specific content or simply following links to see where they go.

CrLf (Carriage return/Line feed). One common combination of ASCII characters used to end one line of text and start a new one.

cron. A UNIX system utility that allows tasks to be executed at regularly scheduled intervals (e.g., indexing a large data collection for use by a search engine).

CSU/DSU (Channel Service Unit/Data Service Unit). A device to terminate a digital telephone channel on a customer's premises (commonly used to terminate T1 or higher bandwidth connections).

CVS (Concurrent Version System). A document management or version control system widely used for larger-scale software development projects to track progress and status of code modules. Such systems are widespread in most UNIX-based document and program production operations.

daemon. A UNIX term for a program that runs constantly and without human intervention, listening for requests for a particular connection or service (which it will answer and then spawn off a child process to fulfill).

DARPA (Defense Advanced Research Projects Agency, originally known as ARPA). The branch of the Dept. of Defense that funds advanced research, including the initial work that led to the development and deployment of the Internet.

data content model. SGML-speak for the occurrence notation that describes what other markup is legal within the context of a specific markup element.

Data Encryption Standard (DES). A shared secret-key encryption system originally developed by IBM.

data validation. The process of performing data integrity checks on input data, or other data delivered from an uncertain source, before permitting that data to take up permanent residence within a database or other application.

datagram. The smallest independent data unit within the IP layer of the TCP/IP protocol stack.

data-type negotiation. The process of requesting information about and agreeing on the format that will be used to exchange data between two networked computers.

DBMS (DataBase Management System). A complex system of programs and utilities used to define, maintain, and manage access to large collections of online data.

de facto. A set of common practices that attains the value of standards through widespread and repeated usage.

debugger. A programming tool used to control the execution of programs under development so that they can be halted and queried at any point during execution.

decompress. The action of expanding a compressed file to its original format.

delimiter. A special text character that indicates a record or field boundary within a text stream, rather than being interpreted as an actual part of the text itself (e.g., the characters < and > act as delimiters for HTML tags).

deprecated. Within the context of the HTML DTDs, a deprecated term is one whose use is no longer recommended, but which is still supported for backward compatibility.

descriptive markup. A descriptive markup system uses embedded codes to describe or annotate document elements, like paragraphs or quotations. These codes or tags simply supply names for a document's structural elements.

development environment. The collection of tools, compilers, debuggers, and source code management resources used as part of the software development process.

digital ID. A person's public key that has been "digitally signed" by someone trusted to do so.

directory structure. The hierarchical organization of files in a directory tree.

DNS (Domain Name Service). An Internet service that maps symbolic names to IP addresses, by distributing queries among the available pool of DNS servers.

document annotation. The process of attaching comments, instructions, or additional information to a document (usually with annotation software for electronic copy).

document root. The base of a Web server's document tree, the root defines the scope of all the documents that Web users may access (i.e., access is allowed to the root and all its children, but not to any of the root's peers or parents).

document tree. A description of the collection of all directories underneath the document root, with all the documents that each such directory contains.

DoD (Department of Defense). The people who brought you the Internet, among other things (see *DARPA*).

Dr. Web. A group of dedicated individuals who answer Web-related questions through a Web screen form available at *http://www.stars.com/Dr.Web/*.

DTD (Document Type Definition). An SGML specification that defines the markup elements, their content-models, and other aspects of a markup language.

DVI (DeVice Independent file). An intermediate output format created by TeX and related programs when printing from those markup environments.

editor. A program used to edit a file; editors for specific programming languages, markup languages, and text formats are all available.

electronic commerce. The exchange of money for goods or services via an electronic medium; many companies expect electronic commerce to do away with mail order and telephone order shopping by the end of the century.

element type. The kind of value that an element can take (text, number, tag, etc.).

element. A basic unit of text or markup within a descriptive markup language.

emacs. A powerful, programmable text editor common on many UNIX systems, *emacs* can be configured as an HTML or SGML editor.

e-mail (electronic mail). The service that lets users replace software with service exchange messages across a network; the major e-mail technology in use on the Internet is based on SMTP (Simple Mail Transfer Protocol).

encoding. A technique for expressing values according to a particular notation (binary, ASCII, EBCDIC, etc.).

ENCTYPE. A variable that specifies the MIME encoding type used to deliver data by e-mail or HTTP.

end tag. In HTML an end tag closes the section of text to which a particular markup operation will be applied when that text is rendered.

Enterprise Integration Technologies (EIT). A Stanford spinoff that provides tools for installing and maintaining Web services.

entity. In HTML and SGML an entity is a named or numbered reference to a particular character value, which may not be otherwise expressible (because it will be interpreted if it's simply dropped into the text stream).

environment variables. Like other UNIX programs CGIs obtain and store their input rather than reading it in every time it's needed. This stored information — in the form of environment variables — is passed to the program by the HTTP server (from the submitting client). An environment variable, therefore, is a value passed into a program or script by the runtime environment on the system where it's running.

error checking. The process of examining input data to make sure it is both appropriate (within specified value or scalar ranges) and accurate (correctly reflects the input).

Ethernet. A network access method developed by Digital Equipment Corporation, Intel, and Xerox in the early 1970s, Ethernet is the most widely used local area network technology available today.

exception handling. If a program behaves abnormally, encounters an unexpected input, or detects an anomaly in its operation, it must react to such an event. This is called exception handling.

extensibility. A measure of how easy it is to write applications that build upon core mechanisms while adding functionality; new methods or subclasses (depending on the paradigm).

extension language. A programming language, like Python, that can be used to extend the functionality of other programmable languages or interfaces.

external entities. Data elements or entities defined outside the context of a formal definition environment (like SGML).

FAQ (Frequently Asked Questions). A list of common questions with their answers, maintained by most special interest groups on the Internet, as a way of lowering the frequency of basic questions and archiving the collective knowledge base.

field. In a database, a named component of a record and its associated values; in an HTML form, a named input widget or text area and its associated value.

file mapping. A method of supplying a filename to the outside world that does not reveal the complete internal file structures involved (see also *alias*).

filehandle. A pointer to a filename or some other way of identifying a file.

filtering. The process of removing certain objects from a document. For example, removing processing instructions important to a specific scheme not used in a general markup scheme eliminates unintelligible materials.

finger. A UNIX command that provides identification information about Internet servers and user names.

First Virtual Internet Payment System (FVIPS). First Virtual is an Internet commerce company that has defined a secure payment system that requires no potentially damaging information to be transmitted across the Internet; FVIPS is the name of that system.

flex (fast lexical analyzer generator). The name of a program that can be used to generate a token-generator for a specific set of terms (usually used as a more modern replacement for *lex*, the prototypical UNIX lexical analyzer program).

foo. A name for a temporary file, function, or variable, in computer programming.

fork. A UNIX command that's become synonymous with an execution style where one process splits off another to perform a particular subtask.

Form Generator. The name of the program covered in Chapters 3-9 of this book, also known as the "Tool."

forms library. A Perl or other source code library that contains routines, functions, or other software tools useful in handling HTML forms input within the context of a CGI program.

FORTRAN (FORmula TRANslation language). An old-fashioned computer language originally developed for calculation-intensive applications, still widely used in the engineering community today.

front end. The user interface side of a client/server application, the front end is what users see and interact with.

FTP (File Transfer Protocol). An Internet protocol and service that provides network file transfer between any two network nodes for which a user has file access rights (especially a remote host and your local host or desktop machine).

FTP daemon. A process that runs continuously in the background on a network host that is ready to handle connection requests for FTP services.

functional. A type of programming language for which all operations are defined through the evaluation of functions (e.g., LISP).

gateway. A program or service that knows how to convert input from one type of system to another type of system. The word is central to CGI because it handles input from Web clients as an extension of the Web server and supplies output to those same clients.

GATEWAY_INTERFACE. The name of a variable used to identify the Web server where a CGI program will execute.

gcc (GNU C Compiler). A version of the C compiler implemented as part of the GNU Tools that is highly regarded in the UNIX development community.

general-to-specific. A component of a formal translation scheme that converts data from a generic, canonical format to the specific requirements of a particular system. Such a component is therefore the final element in a text or document conversion system like ICA or Rainbow.

GET. An HTTP method for moving input from the client to the server, GET delivers all of the input parameters inside the command-line parameter's value.

gif (also GIF, Graphics Interchange Format). A compressed graphics file format patented by Unisys and widely used in HTML documents for inline graphical elements.

GNU. An association of people and organizations devoted to bringing high-quality freeware and shareware computing tools to the public.

Gopher. A program/protocol developed at the University of Minnesota, Gopher provides for unified, menu-driven presentation of a variety of Internet services, including WAIS, Telnet, and FTP.

graphical dividers. Visual elements in an HTML document used to divide text regions. For example, <HR> is a built-in graphical divider, but very often, HTML authors use special graphical elements for the same purpose for more visual impact.

grep (General Regular Expression Parser). A standard UNIX program that looks for patterns found in files and reports on their occurrences. *grep* handles a wide variety of patterns, including so-called "regular expressions" which can use all kinds of substitutions and wildcards to provide powerful search-and-retrieve operations with files.

guestbook. A listing of all the people who have registered their visits to a particular Web site; guestbook registration is usually a conscious act, like signing the guestbook when you visit a museum.

GUI (Graphical User Interface). A generic name for any computer interface that uses graphics, windows, and a pointing device (like a mouse or trackball) instead of a purely character-mode interface. Windows, MacOS, and X11 are all examples of GUI interfaces.

gunzip. The name of the program that decompresses ".gz" compressed file formats, primarily used in the UNIX world.

gzip (GNU zip). The name of the program that produces ".gz" compressed file formats, primarily used in the UNIX world.

hash table. A computer data structure that performs a mathematical calculation on a field identifier (called a hash) to determine where a data element in a large table or index is located.

HEAD. HTML code for marking a document head.

helper applications. Applications invoked outside a Web browser to render, display, or play back data that the browser itself cannot handle (e.g., multimedia files).

hexadecimal. A form of computer data format where all values are expressed as a sequence of Base 16 digits (0-9, A-F).

hierarchical. A form of document or file structure, also known as a tree structure, where all elements except the root have parents, and all elements may or may not have children.

hostname. The name of the Web server being accessed.

HREF. An HTML reserved word that indicates the "Hypertext REFerence" for a specific anchor (<A>), <BASE>, or other locational tag, within an HTML document.

HTML+. An early successor to HTML 2.0 developed by Dave Raggett and since abandoned by the IETF, HTML+ prefigured many of the elements now under consideration for HTML 3.0.

HTML-on-the-fly. The method of creating HTML documents on demand, whenever the output from a CGI program or a request for information from a client, requires delivery of such a document.

HTTP (HyperText Transfer Protocol). The TCP/IP-based communications protocol developed for use by WWW, HTTP defines how clients and servers communicate over the Web.

httpd (HTTP daemon). The daemon (or listener) program that runs on a Web server, listening for and ready to respond to requests for Web documents or CGI-based services.

hyperlink. A shorthand term for hypertext link.

hypermedia. Any of the methods of computer-based information delivery, including text, graphics, video, animation, sound, etc. that can be interlinked and treated as a single collection of information.

hypertext link. In HTML, a hypertext link is defined by special markup that creates a user-selectable document element that can change the user's focus from one document (or part of a document) to another.

hypertext. A method of organizing text, graphics, and other kinds of data for computer use that lets individual data elements point to one another; a nonlinear method of organizing information, especially text.

IAB (Internet Architecture Board, formerly Internet Activities Board). The governing body for the Internet, which manages standards, contracts certain aspects of the network's operation, and handles what little administration there is over the Internet.

IANA (Internet Assigned Numbers Authority). The arm of the IAB that assigns new IP address ranges to those who request them (and meet other necessary criteria).

IETF (Internet Engineering Task Force). The technical arm of the IAB responsible for meeting current engineering needs on the Internet, the IETF also has custody of RFC content and related standards status.

imagemap. An HTML construct identified by the <ISMAP> tag, an imagemap is a graphical image that has an associated map file of coordinates that lets users select links by clicking on certain portions of the image.

instance. A particular incarnation of an object, class, or record, an instance includes the data for one single specific item in a data collection.

integrity. Verifies that the contents of a message arrives at its destination in the same form as it was sent.

inter-document. Used as a modifier for a document link, this refers to a link that points from one document to a different document.

interface. The particular subroutines, parameter passing mechanisms, and data that define the way in which two systems (which may be on the same or different machines) communicate with one another.

international standard. In generic terms, an international standard is one that is honored by more than one country; in practice, this usually refers to a standard controlled or honored by the International Standards Organization (ISO).

Internet. The worldwide, TCP/IP-based networked computing community with millions of users worldwide that links government, business, research, industry, education, and private citizens together.

InterNIC. The quasi-governmental agency responsible for maintaining a registry of existing IP addresses and domain names on the Internet, and which also handles requests for new addresses and domain names.

interpreter. A software program that reads source code from a programming language every time it is run, to interpret the instruction it contains. The alternative is to use a compiler, which translates source code into a binary form only once and which is executed thereafter instead.

intra-document. A hypertext link that points from one location inside a document, to another location inside the same document. This capability lets hypertext provide good navigation within documents, as well as between them.

Intranet. A restricted collection of networks, typically within a single company or organization. Intranets are designed to service a particular user community and only those invited or included can use it.

IP (Internet Protocol). The primary network layer protocol for the TCP/IP protocol suite, IP is probably the most widely used network protocol in the world.

ISDN (Integrated Services Digital Network). A high-bandwidth communications service, ISDN combines voice and digital services over a single medium, enabling telephone lines to handle both on a single wire. ISDN is a subset of the CCITT broadband ISDN (B-ISDN) standard.

ISO Latin-1. An ISO-standard character set used as the default character set within HTML.

ISO-8879. The ISO standard that governs SGML.

ISP (Internet Service Provider). Any organization that will provide Internet access to a consumer, usually for a fee.

I-way. A synonym for "information superhighway," it usually refers to the Internet as the only example of the highway that's working today.

Java. A new object-oriented programming language and environment from Sun Microsystems. Along with C and C++, Java is compiled into an architecture-neutral binary object and then interpreted (like Perl or Tcl) for a specific computer architecture.

jpeg (also JPEG, Joint Photographic Experts Group). A highly compressible graphics format, designed to handle computer images of high-resolution photographs as efficiently as possible.

kerberos. In Greek mythology, Kerberos was the three-headed dog who guarded the gates of hell against escapees. On the Internet, kerberos is one of a number of security servers that guard access to network resources.

keyword. An essential or definitive term that can be used for indexing data, for later search and retrieval.

kill. The UNIX command used to terminate an executing process (for example, to terminate a print job, you'd instruct the system to *kill* the process with the PID for that print job).

kludge. A programming term for a workaround or an inelegant solution to a problem.

Korn shell. A shell that supports processes, pipes, directories, filters, and other standard UNIX functions.

LAN (Local Area Network). A network linked together by physical cables or short-haul connections, with a span that is generally less than one mile.

latency. The time interval between when a network node seeks access to a transmission channel and when access is granted or received.

leaf node. In graph theory, a leaf node is any node in the graph that has no subsidiary nodes. When using the MOMspider program, a leaf node identifies any Web URL that defines the search boundary, beyond which recursive URL searches will not extend.

lex. A lexical analyzer program commonly used in the UNIX environment, *lex* usually helps programmers build the front ends of parsers (which recognize individual terms or lexical units).

library. A collection of programs or code modules that programmers can link to their own code to provide standard, predefined functionality.

linear structure. A way of organizing text or information flow, so that one element follows after another, in linear fashion.

link. A basic element of hypertext, a link provides a method for jumping from one point in a document to another point in the same document, or another document altogether.

Linux. A shareware version of UNIX that runs on a personal computer rather than a workstation.

Lisp (LISt Processing language). A functional, self-modifying programming language commonly used for artificial intelligence applications and other complex programming tasks.

load balancing. The process of involving multiple computers in serving a common processing task to divide the work, and therefore, to balance the load between or among them.

logic. A type of computer language that implements some type of logical notation (e.g., predicate calculus) as its processing paradigm.

lower bound. The lowest value in the range of acceptable data for a particular attribute or variable.

ls. The UNIX directory list command, which displays the files and directories relative to the current file system context.

Lynx. A character-mode (non-graphical) Web browser.

Mac/OS. An abbreviation for the Macintosh Operating System, currently version 7.5.

macro. A series of special instructions for a program or a metalanguage (like SGML) that allows a name to be substituted for a repeated sequence of operations or text within a document or a program.

mail server. Any member of a class of Internet programs (e.g., *majordomo*, *listserv*, and *mailserv*) that allows users to participate in ongoing data exchanges or file retrieval via electronic mail.

mailing list. The list of participants who exchange electronic mail messages regularly, usually focused on a particular topic or concern.

mailx. A UNIX e-mail handling program, commonly used as an alternative to *sendmail*.

man. The UNIX command used to display manual pages (a.k.a. help files) for system commands, utilities, etc.

map files. The boundary definitions for a clickable image, stored in a file specifically formatted for a particular HTTP server implementation (usually NCSA or CERN), used to assign URLs to regions on an image for user navigation.

markup. A special form of text embedded in a document that describes elements of document structure, layout, presentation, or delivery.

MAXLENGTH. The maximum number of characters that a value in a TEXT element can contain.

message traffic. The amount of information that circulates on a mailing list or newsgroup on a regular basis. A mailing list with one or two messages a day has light message traffic; a list with 100 or more a day has heavy traffic.

METHOD. The HTML approach to passing input data from a browser to the server (and possibly, on to a CGI program).

middleware. Software that hides the underlying network and its communications protocols from applications.

MIME (Multipurpose Internet Mail Extensions). Extensions to the RFC822 mail message format to permit more complex data and file types than plain text. Today, MIME types include sound, video, graphics, PostScript, and HTML, among others.

minimization. When a markup element is defined without a closing tag, it is said to be minimized. While this makes parsing the resulting markup language more difficult, it makes coding markup tags a lot easier for authors.

mirrored servers. Heavily used file archives, Web servers, or other network servers may be copied *in toto* and located around a network, to lower the demand on any one such server and to reduce long distance network traffic. Whenever one server acts as a full and exact copy of another, the second server is said to be a *mirror* of the first server.

mnemonic. Programmer-speak for a name that's easy to remember.

modularity. The concept that a program should be broken into components, each of which supplies a particular function or capability.

MOMspider. The name of a program written by Roy Fielding, covered in Chapter 20 of this book.

Motif. A GUI-based front-end for UNIX.

mount. A specialized file-handling command, usually associated with the Network File System (NFS), used to attach a remote file system access point (called a mount point) to a local file system, using NFS protocols and services.

Mozilla (A cross between Mosaic and Godzilla). The name of the DTD and the language description for the Netscape extensions to HTML 2.0.

multithreaded. A computer runtime environment that uses a lightweight process control mechanism, called *threading*, to switch contexts among multiple tasks. Whereas a full-context switch may require 150 or more instructions in some operating systems, a thread switch can occur in as little as 30 instructions on some operating systems.

mv. The UNIX "move file" command. That is, *mv* copies the file from one location to another, then deletes the original.

named pipes. A high-level interface for passing data between processes that are running on separate computers that are connected by a network.

navigation bar. A graphical or lexical set of controls on a Web page, intended to assist the process of Web navigation.

navigation. The act of finding one's way around the WWW.

NCSA (National Center for Supercomputing Applications). An arm of the University of Illinois where Mosaic, the first high-end graphical Web browser, was originally developed.

Netizens. Citizens or denizens of the Internet.

net-pointers. URLs, *ftp* addresses, or other locations on the Internet where you can go to get the "good stuff."

Network Information Services (NIS).
Provides a means for you to share the same administration files across networked systems by turning them into databases called *NIS maps*.

Network News Transport Protocol (NNTP). A protocol by which articles from USENET newsgroups are transferred.

network services. Access to shared files, printers, data, or other applications (e-mail, scheduling, etc.) across a network.

network utilization. The amount of network usage, usually expressed as the percentage of bandwidth consumed on the medium, for a specific period of time. (Peak utilization of 80% is no big deal; sustained utilization of 80% usually means it's time to divide and grow your network.)

newsgroups. On USENET, individual topic areas are called *newsgroups*. Such groups exchange regular message traffic, and are a great source of information for technical topics of all kinds.

NFS (Network File System). A distributed file system originated by Sun Microsystems that's in wide use in TCP/IP networking environments today. NFS lets users access remote file systems as if they were an extension of their local hard drives.

NIC (Network Interface Card). The hardware that lets your computer talk to a network and vice versa.

NULL. In programming (and UNIX) terms, the representation for a missing or empty value.

numeric entities. In SGML or HTML, a way of referring to characters using a numeric notation (e.g., in HTML the string © is the numeric entity for the copyright symbol ©).

Nutshell Handbook. A series of books from O'Reilly and Associates, the *Nutshell Handbooks* provide excellent learning tools about UNIX programs and facilities.

object-oriented. A programming paradigm that concentrates on defining data objects and the methods that may be applied to them.

obsoleted. In the context of the HTML DTD, a markup element, tag, etc., is said to be obsoleted when it is no longer supported by the current official DTD.

OCR (Optical Character Recognition).
Software that can recognize characters as they occur in bitmapped data (faxes or scanned documents) and convert them into ASCII or other character codes.

octet-stream. An HTML Content-Type, octet-stream is the basic type for binary data, since it's nothing but a stream of 8-character bytes.

OO (abbreviation for object-oriented; see *object-oriented*).

OpenLook. A UNIX-based graphical user interface (GUI) toolkit.

parameter. A value passed into or out of a program, subroutine, or across an interface, whenever code components communicate with one another.

parse tree. A graphical representation of the designation of, and relationships between, tokens or lexical elements in an input stream after that stream has been parsed.

Pascal. A programming language designed for general information processing.

Password Shadowing. A security measure that helps prevent someone from finding, reading, and decrypting your password file.

path. The fully qualified directory specification for any particular file, or a search list of directory specifications to be traversed when seeking to resolve an otherwise unclear reference to a command, program, or other file.

PATH_INFO. The environment variable that provides the path to be interpreted by the CGI application.

PATH_TRANSLATED. An environment variable signifying the virtual–to–physical mapping of the file in the system.

pattern-matching. A computerized search operation whereby input values are treated as patterns, and matches are sought in a search database. Whenever exact matches occur, this is called a *hit*; the results of a search produce a list of hits for further investigation.

PEM/PGP Encapsulation (Privacy Enhanced Mail and Pretty Good Privacy). These two techniques use private/public key encryption to protect e-mail and networked communications, respectively.

Encapsulation means that these techniques are applied to fully formed messages on the sending end, and removed on the receiving end, acting as an extra "security envelope" around information.

Perl (Practical Extraction and Reporting Language). An interpreted programming language developed by Larry Wall, Perl offers superb string-handling and pattern-matching capabilities and is a favorite among CGI programmers.

Personal Digital Assistant (PDA). A palmtop computer that performs specific tasks, such as a journal, personal database, calculations, etc.

pid (process ID). The unique number that identifies any process in execution on a UNIX host.

pixel (PICture Element). A single addressable location on a computer display, a pixel is the most primitive individual element for controlling graphics. (It's also how image maps are measured and specified.)

placeholder. A parameter is an ideal example of a placeholder, because it is a symbolic representation that will be manipulated by a program, but only when it's running and an initial input value is defined. While the code is being written, all parameters are merely placeholders.

platform independent. Indicates that a program or device will work on any operating system or computer, irrespective of make, model, or type.

POP mail. POP is an abbreviation for Post Office Protocol, the protocol that PPP or SLIP-based e-mail programs use to transfer outbound messages from the workstation to the Internet, through a POP mail server on some Internet host.

port (short for transport, usually used as a verb). In computer jargon, "porting code" refers to the effort involved in taking a program written for one system and altering it to run on another system.

port address. In TCP/IP-speak, a port address refers to the socket identifier that a program or a service seeks to address for a specific type of communications. Most TCP/IP protocols have "well-known port addresses" associated to them (e.g., HTTP's is 80), but system configurations allow other port addresses to be used (which can sometimes be a good idea for security reasons).

Portable Bitmap (PBM). A UNIX graphics file format for black and white images developed by Jef Poskanzer that lists pixels in the picture (either binary or ASCII) with no compression or other special encoding.

POSIX (Portable Operating System Interface for UNIX). A set of standards by the IEEE and ANSI to promote common interface standards for UNIX.

POST. An HTTP method whereby an array of associated names and values is passed to the server (and on to a CGI program) for further analysis and handling. POST permits arbitrarily long and complex collections of parameters, unlike GET which is limited to a maximum of 255 characters for most versions of UNIX.

PostScript. A page description language defined by Adobe Systems, PostScript files usually carry the extension ".ps" in the UNIX world, and are a common format for exchanging nicely-formatted print files.

PPP (Point-to-Point Protocol). A newer, more efficient asynchronous TCP/IP protocol, designed specifically for users who wish to make the most of a dial-in connection to the Internet.

principle of locality. The notion that it's a good idea to stay in your own data neighborhood whenever possible. It's a way of designing data retrieval programs to access the hard disk or other, slower forms of storage as seldom as possible, by grabbing larger chunks of information and dealing with them as completely as possible before asking the operating system to deliver more.

problem domain. A topic or area of interest or concern that a particular application covers (e.g., the problem domain for a statistics program might be "the analysis and interpretation of correlations in specific populations").

procedural markup. A way of describing document contents and layout that emphasizes the *how* of display, rather than the structural elements embodied in the document. Procedural markup is common in proprietary document formats, since they are concerned with telling a single program how to display (or print) a file.

processor-intensive. An application that consumes lots of CPU cycles (i.e., runs for a long time) is said to be processor-intensive. Good examples include heavy graphics rendering like ray-tracing, animation, CAD, and other programs that combine lots of number-crunching with intensive display requirements.

production Web. A Web server, or collection of Web documents used for everyday production work or access.

Program Usage Markup Language (PUML). A new language created by Mark Gaither, one of the authors of this book. This new language is built following the SGML (ISO-8879-1) philosophy and it's an actual application of SGML. PUML's purpose is to describe the valid structure of a program's usage statement.

Prolog. An object-oriented logic programming language.

propeller-heads. A synonym for nerd, a propeller-head is someone who delights in figuring out the optimal algorithm for the traveling salesman problem. If you don't know what we mean, you ain't one!

proprietary. Technology that's owned or controlled by a company or organization, and that may or may not be widely used.

protocol suite. A collection of networking protocols that together define a complete set of tools and communications facilities for network access and use (e.g., TCI/IP, OSI, or IPX/SPX).

ps. A common file extension for PostScript files, used as a method to supply print images all over the Internet.

Public Key Cryptosystem (PKC). The algorithm used in RSA's patented public key cryptosystem. PKC uses a pair of matched keys instead of just one shared key. A user will have both an RSA Public Key and an RSA Private Key for accessing PKC encrypted data.

public-key encryption. A method of encrypting information for delivery across a public medium that relies on the combination of a widely available decryption key (the "public key" that must be combined with a unique "private key") in order for decryption to occur. This is regarded as a highly reliable security technique.

Python. Python is an interpreted, interactive, object-oriented programming language that combines an understandable and readable syntax with noteworthy power.

query decomposition. The process of analyzing a database query for delivery to multiple underlying database servers or data collections for data access and retrieval.

query string. The parameters passed to a Web-based search engine, usually using the GET method (because search strings are nearly always short, this is quite safe).

QuickTime. Apple Computer, Inc.'s format for multimedia data files.

Quote Generator. The name of the program discussed in Chapter 19, which generates quotes for Internet services based on the contents of an order form for such services.

radio button. An HTML input widget used in forms where only a single choice may be made among a predefined set of choices (i.e., only a single button may be pushed at any one time in a set).

RCS (Revision Control System). A source code control system used in some UNIX environments to manage the software development process.

regex (REGular EXpression). A formal notation for pattern specification for input to a search engine or language, regular expressions make use of wildcard characters and placeholders to let patterns match a variety of strings, as well as specific strings.

remote location. A site or machine elsewhere on the network, remote location can also refer to a machine that is only intermittently connected to a network (usually via a dial-up connection).

REMOTE_ADDR. An environment variable that represents the IP address of the agent making a request.

REMOTE_HOST. An environment variable that represents the fully qualified domain name of the requesting agent.

REMOTE_IDENT. An environment variable that signifies the identity data reported about the agent connection to a server.

REMOTE_USER. An environment variable that signifies the user identification sent by a client.

remsh. Synonym for the TCP/IP-based *rsh* (remote shell) command used to execute single system commands on remote systems over the Internet, or other IP-based networks.

render. To interpret the contents of a document, image, or other file so that it can be displayed or played back on a computer.

replication. The process of duplicating information on multiple servers, usually according to some strict synchronization protocol or scheme, so that a copy can be said to be an exact replica (or mirror) of the original.

repository. A place where data is kept, like a file archive, database server, document management system, etc.

request header. The preamble to a request, the header must identify the requester and provide authentication and formatting information where applicable. This lets the server know where to send a response, whether or not that request should be honored, and what formats it may be allowed to take.

request. A network message from a client to a server that states the need for a particular item of information or service.

REQUEST_METHOD. A CGI environment variable that represents the method with which a client request was made.

response header. The preamble to a response, the header identifies the sender and the application to which the response should be supplied.

response time. The amount of time that elapses between the transmission of a request for service and the arrival of the corresponding response.

response. A network message from a server to a client that contains a reply to a request for service.

retagger. An application used in document conversion, a retagger replaces implicit markup from a (usually procedural) markup language with explicit markup for a (usually descriptive) markup language.

reusability. The degree to which programs, modules, or subroutines have been designed and implemented for multi-function use. The easier it is to take the same code and employ it in a number of applications, the higher that code's degree of reusability.

rm (remove). The UNIX file deletion command.

rmdir. The UNIX remove directory command, which deletes empty directories from the UNIX file system.

robot (synonyms: spider, crawler, wanderer, WebCrawler). An autonomous Web-traversing program that seeks out and records information about Web documents that it encounters and examines during its travels.

root access. The root is the root of the UNIX hierarchical file system; normally, only administrators are permitted access to this level of the file system because it allows access to any and all aspects of the system.

router. An internetwork device or program that reads the addresses of incoming packets and forwards them to their destination, or to other routers that can bring them closer to that destination.

RSA (Rivest Shamir Adelman, an encryption algorithm named for its inventors at MIT). RSA encryption uses a public/private key approach, and is regarded as one of the secure methods for protecting data on the Internet. Many companies have adopted RSA (e.g., IBM, Novell, and Microsoft) for their encryption needs, and it is widely used around the Internet.

RTF (Rich Text Format). An export file format supported by many word processors and desktop publishing programs.

runtime variables. Program input or output values that cannot be assigned until the program is running.

scaleable. Able to accommodate arbitrarily large or small processing loads. Also, a program or tool that is designed for expansion to cover additional tasks or situations.

script. A synonym for *program* or *application*; programmers usually refer to their work as a script when it is written in an interpreted language (because it's like a script telling actors what to do and say).

SCRIPT_NAME. A CGI environment variable that provides the URI path that identifies a CGI application.

search string. The input passed for keyword search and pattern matching in an index to a search engine or database management system.

secure communications. This term is used to refer generically to networked information exchanges that are protected, whether by encryption or some other means, from access by unauthorized persons.

Secure HyperText Transfer Protocol (S-HTTP). A new form of the HTTP protocol that includes built-in encryption to provide more secure communications on the Web.

Secure Sockets Layer (SSL). A protocol providing a secure layer underneath an application protocol.

sed. A UNIX program, *sed* is a powerful stream editor for UNIX systems that includes a variety of pattern-matching and substitution capabilities.

sendmail. The name of the most common UNIX mail delivery program, used to transmit and receive mail messages to and from other sendmail hosts. Sendmail routes mail for users to the proper delivery program based on the e-mail address.

server push. A Netscape-designed technique to let a server initiate data transfer, especially useful for time-sensitive data like voice or video, where rapid delivery is crucial for continuity and intelligibility.

server. A network machine.

SERVER_NAME. An environment variable that represents the server's hostname, DNS alias, or IP address as it would appear in URLs.

SERVER_PORT. An environment variable that represents the port in which a client request was received.

SERVER_PROTOCOL. An environment variable that represents the name and revision of the information protocol that the requesting client utilizes.

SERVER_SOFTWARE. An environment variable that represents the name and version of the information server software.

setuid. A UNIX command that allows an application to run at a different privilege or file permissions level from its owner for the duration of execution (this permits certain kinds of operations that would otherwise be impossible for some programs). It's a dangerous thing to do and should only be used with great care in Web programs.

SGML (Standard Generalized Markup Language). A metalanguage suitable for describing all kinds of markup languages, including HTML.

sgmls. An application developed by James Clark that provides powerful SGML parsing and validation capabilities. Now superseded by his *sp* program.

shell. A UNIX user interface language, a shell provides the basic command environment for the UNIX operating system.

Shockwave. A technology for delivering animated Macromedia Director files across the Internet into a Web page.

S-HTTP (See *Secure HyperText Transfer Protocol*.)

signal to noise. The ratio of good information to irrelevant junk in a newsgroup or mailing list.

Simple Mail Transfer Protocol (SMTP). The underlying protocol and service for Internet-based electronic mail.

sleep. A technique for momentarily pausing an application, by suspending execution (usually for a specified period of time).

Smalltalk. An object-oriented programming language widely used for system prototyping and rapid applications development.

snail mail. The antithesis of e-mail, snail mail requires envelopes and stamps, and takes a whole lot longer to get there (at least, when the network's up).

source code. The original text files containing instructions in a particular programming language that programmers write when creating software. If you can see the source code, you have a good shot at understanding what a program is and how it works.

sp. James Clark's replacement for *sgmls*, a powerful SGML parsing and validation program.

specification. A document that describes the requirements, inputs and outputs, and capabilities of a protocol, service, language, or software program (a kind of "blueprint" for a computer system or service of some kind).

specific-to-general. A software program used in the document conversion process that converts documents from a specific — and usually proprietary — form to a standard, generic intermediate form.

spider (synonyms: robot, wanderer, crawler). A class of programs designed to ceaselessly search the Web, looking for specific content or simply following links to see where they go.

spoof. To instruct a router or bridge to act as if certain kinds of network traffic were being received; in general, a technique for instructing software to act as if certain conditions that may not prevail are true.

SQL (Structured Query Language). A database query language developed at IBM in broad use in database management systems worldwide.

SSLeay. A full-featured SSL protocol that supports the most popular encryption algorithms.

standard. A program, system, protocol, or other computer component that may be the subject of an official published standard from some standards-setting body, or may simply have acquired that status through widespread or long-term use. When talking about standards, it's always important to find out if the designation is official or otherwise.

standards aware. Describes software that understands standards and can work within their constraints.

standards compliant. Describes software that rigorously implements all of a standard's requirements and capabilities; it's a lot more work than standards aware.

start tag. A markup element that marks the beginning of a block of text to which a specific operation is to be applied.

stateless. A stateless protocol needs no information about what has happened in the past (or is expected to happen in the future) about communications between sender and receiver. It's the easiest and most efficient kind of network communication to implement.

static content. Document elements that remain consistent and don't have to change, even for on-the-fly information.

STDIN. The UNIX standard input device, *stdin* is the default input source for programs and facilities, including Web servers and clients.

STDOUT. The UNIX standard output device, *stdout* is the default output source for programs and facilities, including Web servers and clients.

step-by-step execution. When debugging a program, locating the exact line of code where an error occurs can be essential to detecting and fixing the problem. Debuggers let developers *step through* their code for this very reason.

stepwise refinement. A phrase coined by Edsger Dijkstra to indicate the repeated respecification and analysis of program elements needed to create elegant designs and implementations.

string. In programmer-speak, a string consists of character data like 'Mark' or 'Sebastian'.

style guide. A set of guidelines for document layouts, structures, and presentations.

style sheet. A set of named formats, suitable for inclusion in documents that make it easy to distinguish among an individual document's elements (and easy to use such definitions when authoring such documents). At present, this is hotly debated item for inclusion in a future HTML specification.

su. The UNIX command used to let an administrator take complete control over a system (*su* is an abbreviation for "superuser").

sub-elements. Component parts of a document element (a single item in a list of attribute values, individual attributes, etc.).

SUBMIT. A type attribute that creates a button labeled "submit" in an HTML FORM.

symbolic link. A mechanism whereby one name points to another name in a system, rather than directly to an object. Symbolic names are common for Web servers, document roots, and other system objects.

synchronous. A method of communications wherein all communicating parties interact with one another at the same time.

syntax. The rules for placing and ordering terms, punctuation, and values, when writing statements in a particular language (including programming languages, where the rules tend to be pretty exact).

system administrator. The individual responsible for maintaining a computer system, managing the network, setting up accounts, installing applications, etc.

system clock. A built-in time counter available in most computer systems that keeps track of what time it is, in addition to other responsibilities.

T1. A digital transmission link with a capacity of 1.544 Mbps. T1 (also written T-1) is a standard for digital transmission in the US, Canada, Hong Kong, and Japan.

tar (Tape ARchival program). A UNIX utility used to compress and uncompress files. (Files compressed with this program normally have the extension ".tar".)

Tcl (Tool Command Language, pronounced "tickle"). A simple scripting language for extending and controlling applications. Tcl can be embedded into C applications because its interpreter is implemented as a C library of procedures. Each application can extend the basic Tcl functions by creating new Tcl commands that are specific to a particular programming task.

TCP/IP (Transmission Control Protocol/Internet Protocol). The basic suite of protocols upon which the Internet runs.

telnet. A TCP/IP protocol and service that lets a user on one computer emulate a terminal attached to another computer.

template. An example or pattern for a program or document, that acts as a predefined skeleton that only needs to be filled in to be complete.

test plan. A formal document that describes the steps required to test a software application, the data values to be tested, and the actions to be taken when bugs are discovered.

test Web. A separate implementation of a Web document collection where new HTML documents and CGI programs can be tested and debugged before exposure to the public at large.

text widget. In HTML-speak a text widget is any <FORM> input element that permits text entry (e.g., <TEXTAREA> and <INPUT TYPE="TEXT"...>).

text/html. The MIME Content-Type for HTML documents (most commonly used by HTTP and CGI programs for output, Web browsers for input).

text/plain. The MIME Content-Type for plain text (will be displayed as-is as preformatted text by most Web browsers).

tiff (Tagged Image File Format). A popular graphics file format, most often seen as a file extension (on PCs, ".tif").

title. In HTML, the <TITLE> is inside the <HEAD> ... </HEAD> elements, and is the name that identifies an HTML document. It's important, not only for displaying the document, but as a data element for spiders or robots seeking to identify information on the Web. Therefore, titles should be descriptive but not too long.

toolset. A collection of software tools useful for performing certain tasks (e.g., CGI input handling or image map creation).

traffic reports. Information on the number of visits to a Web site or to specific documents.

transformation. The process of changing one structure to another. For example, transformation of a document from one governing DTD to another DTD can involve significant changes in structure.

trap command. A particular technique for handling program errors that relies on capturing information about such errors or exceptions and reporting them through a hierarchical error-handling subsystem within a program.

tree. A hierarchical structure for organizing data or documents, common examples of which include file system directories and family trees.

unbuffering. The process of unpacking data from a storage area in a program, usually as it's being parsed or otherwise digested.

unescape. To restore character codes from hexadecimal format into whatever format is normal for the processing environment. Special care must be taken to avoid introducing spurious instructions or unintended behavior during this process.

UNIX. The powerful operating system developed by Brian Kernighan and Dennis Ritchie as a form of recreation at Bell Labs in the late 60s, still running strong today.

upper bound. The highest value in the range of acceptable data for a particular attribute or variable.

URI (Uniform Resource Identifier). Any of a class of objects that identify resources available to the Web; both URLs and URNs are instances of a URI.

URL (Uniform Resource Locator). The primary naming scheme used to identify Web resources, URLs define the protocols to be used, the domain name of the Web server where a resource resides, the port address to be used for communication, and the directory path to access a named Web document or resource.

URL encoding. A method for passing information requests and URL specifications to Web servers from browsers, URL encoding replaces spaces with plus signs, and substitutes hex codes for a range of otherwise irreproducible characters. This method is used to pass document queries (via the GET method) from browser to servers (and on to CGIs).

URN (Uniform Resource Name). A permanent, unchanging numeric-based address for a Web resource (seldom used in today's Web environment).

USENET hierarchy. The way in which newsgroups are organized is hierarchical. The most interesting collection of newsgroups, from the standpoint of this book is the *comp.infosystems.www* hierarchy.

USENET. An Internet protocol and service that provides access to a vast array of named *newsgroups*, where users congregate to exchange information and materials related to specific topics or concerns.

USPS (United States Postal Service). (See *snail mail*.)

valid HTML. An HTML document that's survived the rigors of validation; i.e., has successfully passed through HTMLchek or an equivalent program.

version control. An important aspect of a source code or document management system, version control refers to the ability to associate particular versions of documents or programs together (which may be necessary to maintain a production version and a development version for a program).

vi. A powerful and popular UNIX text editor.

Virtual Reality Modeling Language (VRML). A special-purpose programming language designed specifically for the creation of three-dimensional spaces, and for managing light sources, points of view, and display of such spaces from one or more individual perspectives.

virtual Web mirror. A collection of Web documents and related CGIs that completely reflects the contents of some other Web server.

W3 (World Wide Web).

W3C (World Wide Web Consortium). The consortium that includes CERN, MIT, and other organizations that currently have custody over HTTP, HTML, and other Web-related software and standards.

WAIS (Wide Area Information Service). A collection of programs that implement a specific protocol for information retrieval, able to index large-scale collections of data around the Internet. WAIS provides content-oriented query services to WAIS clients and is one of the most powerful Internet search tools available.

wanderer (synonyms: robot, spider, crawler). A class of programs designed to ceaselessly search the Web, looking for specific content or simply following links to see where they go.

Web sites. Individual Web document collections named by home pages or other unique URLs.

WebCrawler (synonyms: robot, spider, crawler). A class of programs designed to ceaselessly search the Web, looking for specific content or simply following links to see where they go.

Webification. The act of turning complex electronic documents in some other format into HTML, usually programmatically rather than by hand.

Webify. (The verb form of Webification; see preceding definition.)

WebMaster. The individual responsible for managing a specific Web site.

whitespace. The all-important, unoccupied space on a page or electronic document that provides the "breathing room" for the reader.

whoami. A UNIX command that delivers information about the process from which this command is invoked (owner, PID, permissions, etc.).

widget. In HTML-speak, any of the <FORM INPUT> types, which may be TEXT, CHECKBOX, RADIO BUTTON, etc.

WRAP. A Netscape extension to the TEXTAREA form widget that allows text entered into a multi-line text entry area to wrap at a certain number of characters (which may be hard-coded into the data thereafter, or simply entered to help manage the display of that data).

WYSIWYG (What You See Is What You Get). A term used to describe text editors or other layout tools (like HTML authoring tools) that attempt to show their users on-screen what final, finished documents will look like.

X Windows. The GUI of choice for UNIX systems, X Windows offers a graphical window, icon, and mouse metaphor similar to, but much more powerful and robust than, Microsoft Windows.

X11. A GUI standard controlled by the X/Open Corporation (also the owner of the UNIX trademark and design).

Xview. A GUI toolkit.

Yahoo! (Yet Another Hierarchical Officious Oracle). A database written and maintained by David Filo and Jerry Yang, who style themselves "self-proclaimed Yahoos." This is an inauspicious introduction to one of the best search engines for the World Wide Web. When we go surfing, we often start from Yahoo!

Z39.50. The name of the data transfer protocol used for WAIS requests and responses.

zero-length value. An empty Perl string has zero length; thus a zero-length value generally indicates a null string. An empty Perl array has zero cells filled; a zero-length array has no entries.

ABOUT THE DISK

Web Programming Secrets includes a PC-formatted 3.5" disk. As long as the machine you're using can read this kind of medium, you should be able to get at the disk's contents. We've tested it successfully on the following platforms:

- PC's running DOS/Windows 3.x, Windows 95, Windows NT Workstation and Server
- Macintoshes running System 7.x, with PC File Exchange used to read the files from the disk.
- A variety of UNIX platforms, including Linux (use the *mdir* and *mcopy* commands), Solaris and SunOS (requires the use of WABI or a DOS disk-reading utility), and BSDI (requires a DOS disk-reading utility).

In general, as long as the machine has a 3.5" floppy drive and you have access to a DOS disk-reading utility, you should be able to access the disk's contents. Otherwise, you might just want to read the disk on a PC running DOS or Windows, and then FTP the single archive file on the disk, ("wps.tar") to a server that you can access from your UNIX workstation.

UNPACKING THE DISK

You'll find two files on the disk. One is a text file named "readme.txt": It contains a brief set of instructions that explain what to do with the other file on the disk, "wps.tar". Inside this archive, you'll find all of the code mentioned in the book, ready for your perusal and use. To gain access to the various code files within this archive, please follow these steps:

1. Move "wps.tar" onto a platform that supports long filenames; because most of the programs do not adhere to the DOS 8.3 filename syntax, you won't be able to use this material successfully in a DOS/Windows 3.x environment without systematically renamed all the files and changing the file includes and external file references within the code to match your new filenames.

2. To decompress the "wps.tar" archive, you must obtain a tar utility. If you don't already have one, you can find a version that's appropriate for your platform at:

   ```
   http://www.matisse.net/files/formats.html
   ```

3. Extract the *Web Programming Secrets* archive from "wps.tar" with the following syntax:

   ```
   tar -xvf wps.tar
   ```

4. Repeat the procedure for the "formgen.tar" archive in the *wps/formgen* directory and the "calendar.tar" archive in the wps/calendar directory with the following syntax:

   ```
   tar -xvf formgen.tar
   tar -xvf calendar.tar
   ```

THE DISK'S CONTENTS

As we've already indicated, there are only two files on the disk as we include it with the book. These are:

- "readme.txt": a brief explanation of unpacking the disk
- "wps.tar": the archive that contains all the code examples

The Disk's Directory Structure

If you follow the instructions in the preceding section, the file named "wps.tar" unpacks to the following directory structure:

```
wps
    /calendar : Subdirectories containing code and example data
                structures from Chapter 13 "An Interactive
                Calendar"
    /commerce : Code from Chapter 15 "Handling Web Commerce"
    /dns_admin: Code from Chapter 10: "DNS Administration"
    /esis_puml: Code from Chapter 17 "From a Program Usage State-
                ment to an HTML Form" and Chapter 18 "Web-assisted
                UNIX for End Users"
    /faxgw    : Code from Chapter 11 "A Web-based Fax Gateway"
    /formgen  : Code from Part I "The Form Generation Tool"
    /maitre-d : Code from Chapter 12 "A MailServer Front End"
    /MOMspider: Code from Chaper 20 "Automatic Creation of a
                MOMspider Instruction File"
    /quote    : Code from Chapter 19 "A Quote Generator"
    /renovator: Code from Chapter 14 "Web-based HTML Document
                Editing"
    /user     : Code from Chapter 16 "UNIX User Management"
```

The Uncompressed Directory Contents

After uncompressing the master archive "wps.tar", and two subsidiary archives "calendar.tar" (from *wps/calendar*) and "formgen.tar" (from *wps/formgen*), the following list of files results. (Note that if you are working on a Windows 3.x platform, you must be using either WinZip version 6.0 or higher or a real Windows-based *tar* utility to open the "calendar.tar" file.) To preserve the organization, these listings are organized by directories and subdirectories, where appropriate.

wps/calendar

As delivered, this directory contains a single file named "calendar.tar", which contains all of the code and related data elements from Chapter 13. When unpacked, however, the following directory structure results.

wps/calendar/calendar

cal.pl: end-user calendar access program, main entry point for calendar program

request_event.pl: end-user program used to request the calendar administrator to schedule or modify an event

/admin: sub-directory for calendar administration programs

/data: root sub-directory for calendar data directories & files

wps/calendar/calendar/admin

cal2.pl: administrative calendar display and management program

caladmin.pl: top-level calendar administration program

create_event.pl: used to define new event types and schedule new event instances

notify.pl: sends e-mail notifications of scheduled or modified events

wps/calendar/calendar/data

notifylist: the list of recipients for event notification

notify.message: the text for the current notification message

/events: the directory that contains event type descriptions

/95: the 1995 calendar of events, organized by month and day

wps/calendar/calendar/data/95

/November : November, 1995 events

/September: September, 1995 events

wps/calendar/calendar/data/95/November

1   : current list of 11/1/95 events

1.bak: previous version of 11/1/95 events (indicates original list has been modified)

29   : current list of 11/29/95 events

2   : current list of 11/2/95 events

3   : current list of 11/3/95 events

5   : current list of 11/5/95 events

5.bak: previous version of 11/5/95 events

wps/calendar/calendar/data/95/September

```
1    : current list of 9/1/95 events
1.bak: previous version of 9/1//95 events
9    : current list of 9/9/95 events
9.bak: previous version of 9/9/95 events
9.new: indicates new set of events defined for 9/9/95
```

wps/calendar/calendar/data/events

```
eventslist: the master list of defined events
eventslist.bak: previous version of master list
detail.n: within the events list, events are identified by
          number, therefore detail.1 is the first event, .2
          is the second event, etc. The number corresponds to
          the order in which events are listed in the master
          events list file.
```

wps/commerce

This is the directory associated with Chapter 15, "Handling Internet Commerce."

```
perl_hack_tshirt.pl: the Perl script for the First Virtual order form for
"The Perl Hacker's T-Shirt"
```

wps/dns_admin

This is the directory associated with Chapter 10, "DNS Administration." It includes a number of programs and related data elements used to create forms.

```
dns_action.pl: handles reassigning DNS definitions
dns_edit.pl  : used to edit contents of DNS database
dns_lines.pl : presents DNS information to the administrator via a Web
  interface
domreg.form  : DNS Domain request form data, massaged for user viewing and
  input
new.dns.form : DNS Domain request form, massaged for delivery to  the
  InterNIC
parse.in.www.mail.pl: parses incoming mail to the Web server ID (usually
  www) to look for domain registration or status requests or reports
```

wps/esispuml

This is the directory that contains the code samples from Chapters 17 and 18, which provide a method for creating HTML forms from UNIX command program usage statements, for easy user access via the Web.

```
esis2html.l: the lex source file for output from an SGML parsing program,
  that turns it into and HTML representation
puml2html.pl: the Perl program that handles output from an SGML lex parsing
  program, and turns it into and HTML representation
<command>.<suffix>: any of a number of UNIX commands, that have both .HTML
  and .PUML files, where the PUML file is the formal SGML-based statement of
  the command's program usage statement,and the -"...form.html" file is its
  HTML equivalent (for display to end users)
```

The commands for which such files are defined are:

chmod	find	kill	rm
chown	grep	ls	rmdir
compress	gunzip	mv	uncompress
cp	gzip	ps	

Other files include the following:

```
passwd.puml: an equivalent to the ps command in Solaris, this handles a
  more common version of the "set password" command
puml2html.pl.puml: the PUML source for the PUML to HTML translator
sub.pl.puml: the PUML source for the translation subsystem
sysadmin.tar.Z: a compressed archive of useful PUML-related utilities
```

wps/faxgw

```
g3togif.pl : translation file to turn native fax image formats into .gif
  equivalents
get_fax.pl: polling program that obtains incoming fax files from a fax
  server
view_fax.pl: viewing program that permits fax images to be viewed on a Web
  page
```

wps/formgen

As delivered, this directory contains a single file named "formgen.tar", which contains all of the code and related data elements from Part 1 of this book (particularly, Chapters 4 through 8). When unpacked, however, the following directory structure results.

wps/formgen

```
formgen.pl    : the Perl script for the forms generator
formlib.pl    : Brigitte Jellinek's forms-handling Perl library
debugforms.pl: turns on debug mode when testing the forms
                generator
```

wps/formgen/formgen

```
form_install.pl: program to aid installation of forms generator
formgen.end    : HTML page footer information
formgen.perl   : information about Perl version and system calls
                  used in program
formgen.pl.log : captures output of generator's logging facility
validate.html  : pointers to HTML validation services for use with
                  on-the-fly generated Web pages from the forms generator
```

wps/maitre-d

This is the directory associated with Chapter 12, "A MailServer Front End," which helps to automate Majordomo-based mailing list servers.

```
maitre-d.pl: the program that handles the mail server interface
```

wps/momspider

This is the directory associated with Chapter 20, "Automatic Creation of a MOMSpider Instruction File," which provides a friendly, Web-based front end to Roy Fielding's excellent link-checking program, instead of a dreary and somewhat intimidating command line interface.

```
addtask.pl    : adds a task to MOMspider's task list
inst-form.html: gathers initial data to create new MOMspider
                instruction file
inst.pl       : previews optional global directives input by user
p-addtsk.pl   : previews current instruction in its natural form
                (as it will appear in MOMspider instruction file)
p-task.pl     : previews task directives entered by user
task.pl       : adds global directives to new MOMspider
                instruction file and provides new form for user
                to enter an instruction (set of task directives)
```

wps/quote

This is the directory associated with Chapter 19, "A Quote Generator," which demonstrates how to build a forms-based front end to request services from an ISP.

```
gen_quote.pl: the quote generator program
quote_page.html: the HTML source for introductory, static pages
web_quote.pl: the quote delivery program that permits quotes to be
delivered by fax, e-mail, or Web documents
```

wps/renovator

This directory is associated with Chapter 14 "Web-based HTML Document Editing," which supplies a home (or other single) page editing utility through a pre-loaded TEXTAREA on a simple Web form.

```
renovator.pl: The Web-based page edit utility
```

wps/user:

This directory contains two UNIX user management utilities available through a Web interface, that include the ability to set up and administer user accounts, including file and directory permissions, and passwords.

```
change_user.pl: the modification utility for changing or adding user
accounts, privileges, and other information.
view_user.html.pl: the interface utility, that generates HTML pages on the
fly to display fill-out forms for adding and changing user information
```

USING THE DISK'S CONTENTS

Once you've unpacked and investigated the disk's contents, another series of moves may be required. Although it's okay to test Perl scripts and other Web utilities from whatever working directories make sense, if you plan to put any of these programs into production use, you'll probably need to install them into a common CGI directory. On our system, that's *www/cgi-bin*; consult your system administrator for the details appropriate for your server.

We strongly recommend that you attack our code with your own version of Perl and whatever debugging tools you have at your disposal before trying to turn the world loose on the programs and utilities you'll find on the disk. For one thing, you'll need to change the system variables and references to local files to match your own system's setup, rather than ours. For another, you should thoroughly test and become familiar with these programs before allowing other people to depend on them for system services. If you don't know and understand this code, it'll be a lot harder for you to support your users when they start having problems!

But even if you only use these materials for your own edification, we hope you find them instructional and illuminating. We've designed them to help you learn how to write CGI programs, and use system facilities by example. If you're not using UNIX, you'll have to learn more about your native system to figure out how to do what we did with UNIX system calls using whatever's appropriate to your chosen environment. If your version of UNIX differs from ours, you'll have to figure out how to translate our Linux and Solaris based efforts into your own particular idiom. Either way, you should learn a lot about your own environment in the process: in the long run, that kind of learning will probably be the most valuable information you'll take away from this book!

Enjoy!

INDEX

& (ampersand), 19, 692
* (asterisk), 13, 537, 539
@ (at sign), 252, 364
\ (backslash), 157
: (colon), 537
, (comma), 308
{} (curly brackets), 192
" (double quotes), 157
$ (equal sign), 19
< (left-arrow sign), 145, 167, 715
() (parentheses), 155
% (percent sign), 482
+ (plus sign), 15, 25, 537
# (pound sign), 280, 288, 315,
    537–538, 545, 712
? (question mark), 25
> (right-arrow sign), 145, 167, 719
; (semicolon), 134
_ (underscore character), 13
| (vertical bar), 604

%contents associative array, 38–39
&does_entry_exist() function,
    554, 556
&does_uid_entry_exist() function,
    554, 556
&GetFormsArgs() function, 230,
    345, 544
&get_groups() function, 540
&get_passwd_entries() function,
    543, 554
&get_shells() function, 540

A

<A> tag, 115, 122
access.conf, 231
ACTION attribute, 37, 610
ACTION option, 211
<ADDRESS> tag, 469, 485
adduser, 528–531, 534, 564
Adelman, Len, 498
admin_menu, 404
Adobe PageMill, 90–91
afn_survey.html, 223–225
AIX, 504
aliases, 380–382
ALIGN option, 241
Alpha, 599
Alternative Software Solutions,
    34–39
alternative subtype, 10, 11
America Online, 491–492, 503,
    753, 762
ampersand (&), 19, 692
ampersand operator, 692
animation, 242
ANSI (American National Standards
    Institute), 63
Ant HTML Tools for Word 6.0,
    87–88
Apache-SLL, 508–509
APIs (application programming
    interfaces), 6, 513, 762
APNIC (Asia Pacific NIC), 272

C

C (programming language), 43, 46–49, 102
    basic description of, 49, 765
    compilers, 599
    development environments and, 252
    the Quote Generator and, 667–668, 677
    Tcl/Tk and, 55
C++ (programming language), 43, 47–50, 54–55, 765
cal2.pl, 418, 420, 438–443, 454, 464
caladmin.pl, 418, 420, 442–454, 461, 464
cal command, 442
CalendarMaker, 413
calendars, 409–466, 528
    design of, 413–418
    installing, 464–465
    modeling data flows for, 420
    organizing data for, 415–418
    situating end-user/administrative
    elements for,418–420
    suggestions for improving, 465–466
cal.pl, 418–432, 437, 440, 442, 464
capitalization. See case sensitivity
Carnegie-Mellon search engine, 79
carriage return/line feed (CrLf) character,
    29, 767
carriage returns, 29, 237, 767
CASE (Computer Added Software
    Engineering), 97
case sensitivity, 23, 717, 765
cat (UNIX system call), 679
catalogs, online, 663–710
    designing, 667–668
    front page of, 668–675
    further extensions for, 709–710
    installing, 707–709
    keeping track of quotes with, 696–697
    limiting access to, 708–709
    log files, 696–697
    printing/viewing quotes with, 695–696
    Quote Delivery Systems and, 668,
      673–674, 679, 690–695, 697
    Quote Processors and, 667, 676–697,
      709
    useful extensions for, 672–675
    the user interface and, 667, 668
    working with form data and, 680–683
CD-ROMs, 46, 765

CERN (European Particle Physics
    Laboratory), 4, 253, 262–263, 765
CERT-CC (Computer Emergency Response
    Team Coordination Center), 563
CE Software, 413
CGI (Common Gateway Interface)
    data input, 21–31
    data output, 21–23, 39–42
    definition of, 4–6, 765
    development tools, third-party, 95–96
    overview of, 3–42
    resources, 67–80, 258–265
    sites, tour of selected, 258–265
    specification, 6–22
    variables, accessing, 7–8
cgi-bin directory, 223, 231–233, 322, 419,
    421, 464, 561, 708
cgi-lib.pl, 230, 262
cgi-parse, 263, 765
CGI.pm, 259–260, 262
cgi-pm@webstorm.com mailing list, 73–74
ch8cgi.pl, 234, 236, 238
Change button, checking, 554
change command, 456
change_user.pl, 535, 542, 544–562,
    564–565
ChangeWindow keyword, 717
Chapman, Brent, 359
characters. *See also* symbols
    carriage return/line feed (CrLf) character,
      29, 767
    newline character (\n), 158, 179, 528
    wildcard characters, 339–340
checkboxes, 32, 111, 124, 531, 594–595,
    597. *See also* forms
chmod command (UNIX), 606, 612–620
chmod-form.html, 617–620
chmod.puml, 612–617
<CHOICE> tag, 574, 575, 611, 621, 623
chown command (UNIX), 129, 234, 606,
    624–626
chown.puml, 625–626
chown-form.html, 626
Citibank, 503
CITY field, 140–141
Clark, James, 579, 607
class libraries, 64–65
cleanup.pl, 247
client/server systems, 221, 766
COBOL, 50

I

U

V

VALID keyword, 216
VALIGN option, 241
Value field, 139, 224
<VALUE> tag, 574, 575–576, 593
variables. *See also* variables, environment (listed by name)
    MOMspider and, 725
    the Quote Generator and, 699–700, 708
    the UNIX Account Manager and, 545–552
variables, environment (listed by name)
    AUTH_TYPE environment variable, 8, 17, 107, 763
    CONTENT_LENGTH environment variable, 8–9, 21, 38, 107, 767
    CONTENT_TYPE environment variable, 8, 9–13, 107
    GATEWAY_INTERFACE environment variable, 8, 13, 107, 772
    PATH_INFO environment variable, 8, 14, 15, 107, 780
    PATH_TRANSLATED environment variable, 8, 15, 107, 780
    QUERY_STRING environment variable, 8, 15–16, 20, 26–28, 107
    REMOTE_ADDR environment variable, 8, 16, 107, 783
    REMOTE_HOST environment variable, 8, 16, 107, 783
    REMOTE_IDENT environment variable, 8, 16–17, 107, 783
    REMOTE_USER environment variable, 8, 17, 107, 469, 474, 783
    REQUEST_METHOD environment variable, 8, 17, 26, 27, 107, 784
    SCRIPT_NAME environment variable, 8, 17, 107, 130, 154, 785
    SERVER_NAME environment variable, 8, 18, 107, 130, 785
    SERVER_PORT environment variable, 8, 18, 107, 785
    SERVER_PROTOCOL environment variable, 8, 18, 107
    server_root, 14, 785
    SERVER_SOFTWARE environment variable, 8, 18, 107, 785
VAXen, 359
VeriSign, 500, 508, 759
vertical bar (|), 604

vid editor, 527
video MIME Content-Type, 10, 13
viewfax, 334
view_fax.pl, 343–354
View Source feature, 138, 145–146, 166, 182–184, 213–214, 219
view_user.html.pl, 535–543, 545, 557–559, 561–562
virus-checking, 45
VisualAge, 96
Visual BASIC, 96
VRML (Virtual Reality Modeling Language), 56–59, 242, 790

W

Wall, Larry, 51, 105, 251
Wandex search engine, 80
Web Crawler search engine, 80, 791
Web Developer's Virtual Library, 257, 262
Web Developer's Web Page, 263–264
webedge-talk@webedge.com mailing list, 74
WebEdge Technology Conference, 74
web_quote.pl, 669, 678–699, 704, 708
WebSTAR, 253
WebTech, 598–600, 607
welcome forms, 110, 123, 134, 137, 155–158
whereis command, 46
which command, 46, 188
while constructs, 51
whoami command, 234
wildcard characters, 339–340
Windows (Microsoft)
    choosing a programming language and, 56, 60
    development environments and, 250
    fax systems and, 337
    newsgroup for, 72
    Python and, 56
    the Quote Generator and, 698
    the UNIX Account Manager, 532
Windows 95, 60
Windows NT, 56, 60, 221, 252–253
    online commerce and, 504, 514
    S-HTTP and, 504
    the Quote Generator and, 668
    usage statements and, 598
WinSock, 99
Wintel platforms, 333

IDG BOOKS WORLDWIDE LICENSE AGREEMENT

Important — read carefully before opening the software packet. This is a legal agreement between you (either an individual or an entity) and IDG Books Worldwide, Inc. (IDG). By opening the accompanying sealed packet containing the software disk, you acknowledge that you have read and accept the following IDG License Agreement. If you do not agree and do not want to be bound by the terms of this Agreement, promptly return the book and the unopened software packet to the place you obtained them for a full refund.

1. <u>License</u>. This License Agreement (Agreement) permits you to use one copy of the enclosed Software program(s) on a single computer. The Software is in "use" on a computer when it is loaded into temporary memory (i.e., RAM) or installed into permanent memory (e.g., hard disk, CD ROM, or other storage device) of that computer.

2. <u>Copyright</u>. The entire contents of this disk and the compilation of the Software are copyrighted and protected by both United States copyright laws and international treaty provisions. The individual programs on the disk are copyrighted by the authors of each program respectively. Each program has its own use permissions and limitations. You may only (a) make one copy of the Software for backup or archival purposes, or (b) transfer the Software to a single hard disk, provided that you keep the original for backup or archival purposes. To use each program, you must follow the individual requirements and restrictions detailed for each in the "About the Disk" section of this Book. Do not use a program if you do not want to follow its Licensing Agreement. None of the material on this disk or listed in this Book may ever be distributed, in original or modified form, for commercial purposes.

3. <u>Other Restrictions</u>. You may not rent or lease the Software. You may transfer the Software and user documentation on a permanent basis provided you retain no copies and the recipient agrees to the terms of this Agreement. You

may not reverse engineer, decompile, or disassemble the Software except to the extent that the foregoing restriction is expressly prohibited by applicable law. If the Software is an update or has been updated, any transfer must include the most recent update and all prior versions. Each shareware program has its own use permissions and limitations. These limitations are contained in the individual license agreements that are on the software disks. The restrictions include a requirement that after using the program for a period of time specified in its text, the user must pay a registration fee or discontinue use. By opening the package which contains the software disk, you will be agreeing to abide by the licenses and restrictions for these programs. Do not open the software package unless you agree to be bound by the license agreements.

4. <u>Limited Warranty</u>. IDG Warrants that the Software and disk are free from defects in materials and workmanship for a period of sixty (60) days from the date of purchase of this Book. If IDG receives notification within the warranty period of defects in material or workmanship, IDG will replace the defective disk. IDG's entire liability and your exclusive remedy shall be limited to replacement of the Software, which is returned to IDG with a copy of your receipt. This Limited Warranty is void if failure of the Software has resulted from accident, abuse, or misapplication. Any replacement Software will be warranted for the remainder of the original warranty period or thirty (30) days, whichever is longer.

5. <u>No Other Warranties</u>. To the maximum extent permitted by applicable law, IDG and the author disclaim all other warranties, express or implied, including but not limited to implied warranties of merchantability and fitness for a particular purpose, with respect to the Software, the programs, the source code contained therein and/or the techniques described in this Book. This limited warranty gives you specific legal rights. You may have others which vary from state/jurisdiction to state/jurisdiction.

6. <u>No Liability For Consequential Damages</u>. To the extent permitted by applicable law, in no event shall IDG or the author be liable for any damages whatsoever (including without limitation, damages for loss of business profits, business interruption, loss of business information, or any other pecuniary loss) arising out of the use of or inability to use the Book or the Software, even if IDG has been advised of the possibility of such damages. Because some states/jurisdictions do not allow the exclusion or limitation of liability for consequential or incidental damages, the above limitation may not apply to you.

7. <u>U.S.Government Restricted Rights.</u> Use, duplication, or disclosure of the Software by the U.S. Government is subject to restrictions stated in paragraph (c) (1) (ii) of the Rights in Technical Data and Computer Software clause of DFARS 252.227-7013, and in subparagraphs (a) through (d) of the Commercial Computer—Restricted Rights clause at FAR 52.227-19, and in similar clauses in the NASA FAR supplement, when applicable.

Alternate Disk Format Available.

The enclosed disk is in 3 1/2" 1.44MB, high-density format. If you have a different size drive, or a low-density drive, and you cannot arrange to transfer the data to the disk size you need, please contact IDG Books Disk Fulfillment Department, Attn: *Web Programming SECRETS with HTML, CGI, and Perl* IDG Books Worldwide, 7260 Shadeland Station, Indianapolis, IN 46256, or call 800-762-2974. Please specify the size of disk you need, and please allow 3 to 4 weeks for delivery.

Introducing the Foundations™ Series
For Working Programmers...

IDG BOOKS WORLDWIDE™

Order Center: **(800) 762-2974** *(8 a.m.–6 p.m., EST, weekdays)*

Quantity	ISBN	Title	Price	Total

Shipping & Handling Charges

	Description	First book	Each additional book	Total
Domestic	Normal	$4.50	$1.50	$
	Two Day Air	$8.50	$2.50	$
	Overnight	$18.00	$3.00	$
International	Surface	$8.00	$8.00	$
	Airmail	$16.00	$16.00	$
	DHL Air	$17.00	$17.00	$

*For large quantities call for shipping & handling charges.
**Prices are subject to change without notice.

Ship to:

Name _____

Company _____

Address _____

City/State/Zip _____

Daytime Phone _____

Payment: ☐ Check to IDG Books (US Funds Only)

☐ VISA ☐ MasterCard ☐ American Express

Card # _____ Expires _____

Signature _____

Subtotal _____

CA residents add applicable sales tax _____

IN, MA, and MD residents add 5% sales tax _____

IL residents add 6.25% sales tax _____

RI residents add 7% sales tax _____

TX residents add 8.25% sales tax _____

Shipping _____

Total _____

Please send this order form to:

**IDG Books Worldwide
7260 Shadeland Station, Suite 100
Indianapolis, IN 46256**

*Allow up to 3 weeks for delivery.
Thank you!*